The Forgotten

First Holy Communion class, 1921, Holy Mother of God Cathedral, Vladivostok, Russian Far Eastern Republic.

The Forgotten

Catholics of the Soviet Empire from Lenin through Stalin

Rev. Christopher Lawrence Zugger

For the
Germans from Russia Heritage
Collection
North Dakota State University
Libraries
Fargo

Rev. Christopher Lawrence Zugger
January 25, 2002

 SYRACUSE UNIVERSITY PRESS

First Edition 2001
01 02 03 04 05 06 07   7 6 5 4 3 2 1

Frontispiece: First Holy Communion class, 1921, Holy Mother of God Cathedral, Vladivostok, Russian Far Eastern Republic. Seated *(left to right):* Father Yezhi Yurkevich (arrested in 1931); Monsignor Karol Sliwowski (later first Bishop of Vladivostok). The child seated to the monsignor's right is Stanislaus Francevich, shot on August 15, 1935. Immediately behind the monsignor is Sophia Michaelovna Berzhinskaya (born in 1911 and sister to Stanislaus), whose family hid the photo for seventy-four years. The flags in the back are of the Holy See, and possibly the independent Far Eastern Republic, of which Vladivostok was the capital. Many of the children in this photo died with their parents in the Great Terror. The crucifix, buried after the cathedral was closed, was discovered during utility excavations. It was put in the Vladivostok city museum, where it was held for a "ransom" demanded from the Catholic parish in the form of foreign goods. This photograph was found in the false bottom of a trunk in 1998. Courtesy of Father Myron Effing, CJD, Vladivostok Mission.

The paper used in this publication meets the minimum requirements of American National Standard for Information Sciences—Permanence of Paper for Printed Library Materials, ANSI Z39.48–1984.∞™

Library of Congress Cataloging-in-Publication Data
Zugger, Christopher Lawrence.
    The forgotten : Catholics of the Soviet empire from Lennin through Stalin / Christopher Lawrence Zugger.—1st ed.
        p. cm.
    Includes bibliographical references and index.
    ISBN 0-8156-0679-6 (alk. paper)
    1. Catholic Church—Soviet Union—History—20th century. 2. Church and state—Soviet Union—History—20th century. 3. Soviet Union—Church history—20th century. I. Title.
    BX1558.3.Z84 2001
    282'.47'0904—dc21   00-058333

GFR

Manufactured in the United States of America

To the memory of not only the Catholics

but of all of the forgotten victims

of religious persecution in the Soviet Union

and to my parents, Henry and Margaret,

for teaching me the importance of both faith and justice

Father Christopher Zugger, a native of Buffalo, New York, received his secondary teaching certification from Saint Bonaventure University in 1977, a master of divinity from the Washington Theological Union in 1981, and was ordained to the priesthood for the Byzantine Catholic Eparchy of Passaic in the same year. He has served in parishes in Beltsville, Maryland, Rahway, New Jersey, Phoenix, Arizona, and founded the parish in Gilbert, Arizona. Since 1985, he has served as pastor of the Byzantine Catholic parish in Albuquerque, New Mexico. Father Zugger is a member of numerous historical and religious societies and lectures on Eastern Christianity, Byzantine Catholic history, Carmelite mysticism, Catholic-Jewish relations, and Holocaust history.

It is a terrible thing to be forgotten by one's own brothers

—Russian Orthodox priest, speaking to a Roman Catholic
delegation to the Patriarch of Moscow that refused to
attend Mass in the last open church in Moscow, 1980.

Contents

PART ONE | 1914–1922

Maps

Illustrations

Tables

Embroidered Gospel Book pillow. Used in secret celebrations of the Greek Catholic Liturgy from 1955 to 1978. Gift from Maria Tar to author. Courtesy of the author.

Preface

In 1981, I was honored with a presentation from Maria Tar, an elderly Byzantine Catholic woman who had emigrated from the Zakarpatska oblast of Ukraine, in the Soviet Union. Living in a village outside Mukachevo, Maria had maintained a "house chapel" in her garden shed from 1954 to 1969. When she was allowed to leave to join her husband in America—after forty years of separation—the young priest who secretly served her community gave her an embroidered Gospel Book pillow to take along. With this gift, he told her, a part of their congregation would always know freedom, and perhaps freedom would come to them someday.

Maria gave this pillow to me after my ordination because I reminded her of that anonymous young priest of the underground Greek Catholic Church, and because I was the first priest in America to take interest in the life of the Church for which she had suffered harassment, fines, and abandonment. She asked me never to forget the parish of that village and to keep my interest in the Soviet Catholic Church alive. I have sought to be faithful to her charge.

Since my early years, I have been drawn to learning about and understanding the situation of believers in Communist countries. In particular, I have had a long-standing interest in Soviet Catholics, devoting more than three-quarters of my life to reading, praying, and studying on this topic.

I am continually amazed at how little is known in the West about these believers. That appalling lack of knowledge has impelled me to learn more and to share what I have learned.

Another curious fact. Although literature about the atrocities of the Nazis and other right-wing totalitarian dictatorships between 1933 and 1945 abounds, the Soviet atrocities, which lasted from 1917 to 1991, have garnered nowhere near as much interest. Indeed, many in the West seem determined to excuse or minimize the enormous waste of humanity in the former Soviet Union and Eastern Europe, from the beginning of Bolshevism down to our day. Although I do not subscribe to the "Evil Empire" school of the last days of the Cold War, I find this dismissive attitude dismaying.

My goal has been to record the legacy of Soviet Catholics so that their past, their uncertain future, and what they now teach us will not be forgotten—and because their stories have moved me to the depths of my soul. My hope in presenting the Soviet Catholics as fully as possible is to provide directions for further research and reading. God willing, that goal and that hope will be realized.

The idea of this book germinated in correspondence with Felix Corley, then of Keston College in England in 1988, and I was encouraged by him as my subject started to take shape. What was originally to be a "nice little pamphlet" grew as I began digging, writing, searching, and collecting. This work is the result of not only my own labors but also the help of many individuals and institutions. Despite my rechecking the list, I will probably forget to list someone, and so my apologies are offered in advance.

My sincere thanks to the staff of many libraries who helped me on visits and sift through correspondence: Hulija Kuuk and staff of the Hoover Institute Library, University of Stanford; Keston College of England for invaluable materials so willingly sent to me; Sister Judy Connolly, SSND, at Mundelein Seminary; John Vital and the staff of the interlibrary loan department of the Albuquerque Public Library; Clara Watral, Assistant Dean, and the research staff of the University of New Mexico Library; Brother David Carroll, FSC, and Michael LaCivita for permitting research done in the archives of Catholic Near East Welfare Association, of the Slavic Department of the New York City Public Library and their faithful encouragement; Sarkis Boghjalian and Robert Lulley of Aid to the Church in Need, New York office, and the staff of the international headquarters in Königstein, Germany; those who hosted me on my research trips—Monsignor Robert Stern and Chorbishop John Faris of Catholic Near East Welfare Association; the Sisters of Saint Agnes at Leo House, New York City; and Lieutenant Colonel Gary Henry, USAF.

There are many correspondents around the globe who have helped me. It is a sign of the effects of Communist rule and the fears that it has left behind that several correspondents from Ukraine, Armenia, and elsewhere wish no identification to be given at all, and they are referred to in the endnotes with simple initials, which do not necessarily correspond to the their names. May God bless and strengthen them in their continued work. Thanks go to His Eminence, Kazimir Cardinal Swiatek, Bishop of Pinsk and Archbishop of Minsk-Moghilev, for the inspiring story of his life and his prayers for me; Bishop Josef Werth, SJ, and Father Alexander Kahn, SJ, of the Apostolic Administration of Novosibirsk; Father Vello Salo of Estonia; Athanasius Pekar, OSBM of Rome; Very Reverend Father Myron Effing, Administrator of the Vladivostok Mission in the Russian Far East; Father Sergius Golavanov of the Russian Orthodox in Communion with the Holy See in Omsk, Siberia; Father Norbert Gaschler, originally from Czernowitz/Chernovtsy; Father Daniel Bendas and Father Taras Lovska of the Eparchy of Mukachevo for access to the carefully preserved archives and oral stories; Father Edmund Idranyi of the Eparchy of Van Nuys; Reader Methodios Stadnik of Saint Michael Russian Catholic Church, New York City; the staff of Saint Anne's Armenian Catholic Cathedral, New York City; Sister Arousiag, SIC, of the Armenian Catholic Administration at Gumri, Armenia; Anita Kalninis of the Curia of the Archdiocese of Riga, Latvia; Orsolya Molnar of the Latin Catholic Apostolic Administration of Zakarpattia, Ukraine; Sophie Senyk of the Pontifical Oriental Institute, Rome; Boris Mirkin of the Association of Jews from China for information on Harbin; Felix Corley, formerly of Keston College, England; Oren Windholz, Irma Bornemann, Tim Kloberdanz, Rick Rye, the late Joann Kuhrr and several members of the Bukovina German Association, American Historical Society of Germans from Russia, Germans from Russia Heritage Society (all in the United States) and the Carpatho-German, Bessarabian, and Bukovina German societies in Germany for books, family letters, and information freely given; Peter Anderson, a great supporter of Saint Catherine's parish in Saint Petersburg; Brian Lenius of the Eastern European Genealogical Society; Len Latkovski for information on Catholic Latvia, especially Latgalia; the Sisters of Saint Agnes in Chelyabinsk; Ruthven Ryan of Keston College and RCDA; Maria Tar and her son Ivan, formerly of Mukachevo, members of Saint Thomas the Apostle Church in Rahway, New Jersey; the pastor of Saint Thomas the Apostle, Father John Zeyack, who introduced me to priests and faithful of the Mukachevo Greek Catholic Eparchy in Europe and America. Jeffrey Lockridge did an exceptionally detailed editing of this work; any remaining errors are definitely mine!

My special thanks go to John Robert Greene, of Cazenovia College, who "went to bat" for me so well, and to the parishioners of Our Lady of Perpetual Help Byzantine Catholic parish in Albuquerque who encouraged me, their pastor, for the ten years it took to produce this work. In particular, I want to acknowledge their help in translating (Katrina Anderson, Amy Anduaga-Arias, Ricardo Cambesi, Helga Dzek, Stanislaus and Iwona Matejczuk, Ingeborg Pommer, David Watral), their assistance with constantly changing computer software (Debra Hratko and Brent Anduaga-Arias), their persistence with the final editing (Christopher Fuqua, Steve Horner, Debra Hratko,

Gary and Jane Plisga), and their stamina to keep everything rolling in the parish office (Agnes Adamsko). May God grant that this endeavor turns out well.

Albuquerque, New Mexico   Rev. Christopher Zugger
January 6, 2000
Feast of the Baptism of the Lord

Introduction

> In the next century, there will be left only one form of government, the soviet, and one religion, the Catholic—it's a pity that we won't live to see it.
>
> —Lenin, conversing with Fr. Viktor Bede in Moscow in 1923

Most citizens of the West now know that religion not only survived seventy-four years of Communist rule in the Soviet Union but also that it has begun to flourish in Russia and the successor states. Western Christian religious interest in Orthodox belief grew steadily during the last three decades of the Soviet Union, and the rise thereof of such Protestant groups as Baptists and Pentecostals became a familiar story in the Western media.

Yet what of the Soviet Catholics? Apart from occasional references in the press to "Soviet Cardinals" or to the "80 percent of Lithuanians who are estimated to be Catholic," most people in the West knew little about them. Indeed, many had no idea where Lithuania or Latvia (the homes of the Soviet-era cardinals) were or what their status was in the USSR. The Eastern Catholics in Soviet Ukraine often did not get accurate coverage, and the Armenian Catholics were totally unknown.

Soviet Catholicism was incredibly diverse, including faithful drawn from more than a dozen of the country's 104 nationalities. They might participate in Eucharist in a splendid baroque church that had survived the persecutions—or in a living room because no church was available. Some belonged to Eastern Catholic Churches that were completely illegal in the USSR; they were persecuted by heavy fines and repeatedly arrested until December 1989—after which they still faced the challenge of integration into society and public life.

However small, the Soviet Catholic Church has produced more than its share of martyrs and confessors. Although some believers compromised their faith by cooperation with the police, and others abandoned it under the pressures of both persecution and secularization, far more were sent to jail, labor camps, and psychiatric hospitals and suffered hardships at work, school, and in their daily lives because of their adherence to Catholicism. All have tasted the bitterness of discrimination—and many, of personal suffering.

This work seeks to bring an awareness of the complexities and marvels of the Soviet Catholic Church, which comprised barely 1 million souls in 1925. By 1991, Soviet Catholics numbered perhaps 12 million, scattered from Kaliningrad on the Baltic Sea near Poland to the lonely ex-prison port of Magadan near Alaska. Their history is a record of martyrdom, betrayal, victory, and the triumphs of ordinary people facing extraordinary times.

Guide to Acronyms

AA   Assumptionists

ASSR   Autonomous Soviet Socialist Republic, within Russian Soviet Federated or other Soviet Socialist Republic; named after particular national minority

BSSR   Belorussian Soviet Socialist Republic

Cheka   Extraordinary Commission (ChK) to Combat Counterrevolution, Sabotage, and Speculation, first formal secret police organ in soon-to-be-founded Soviet Union; formed in December 1917; dissolved in February 1922

CIS   Commonwealth of Independent States; includes most of former Soviet Union except Baltic States

CJD   Canons of Jesus the Lord

CPSU   Communist Party of the Soviet Union

CSFN   Sisters of Holy Family of Nazareth

CSP   Paulist Fathers

CSSR   Congregation of Most Holy Redeemer, Redemptorists

FSB   Federal Security Service, post-Soviet secret police organ; successor to Committee of State Security (KGB); formed in October 1991

FSU   Former Soviet Union

GCC   Greek Catholic Church

GPU   State Political Administration, Soviet secret police organ, under People's Commissariat of Internal Affairs (NKVD); replaced Cheka in February 1922; as United State Political Administration (OGPU), ran terror for Stalin; founded and administered Gulag and Soviet spy system; dissolved in March 1954

KGB   Committee of State Security, Soviet secret police organ, under Council of Ministers; formed in March 1954 to gain control of secret police; purged of worst elements in 1956; under Director Yuri Andropov, gained control over Soviet Union's political, eco-

nomic, social, and cultural life; created Fifth Directorate to persecute dissidents; KGB and Fifth Directorate dissolved in October
1991 after Director Vladimir Kryuchkov took part in August
1991 putsch against Gorbachev

LiSSR	Lithuanian Soviet Socialist Republic
MIC	Marian Fathers
MP	Moscow Patriarchate of Russian Orthodox Church
NKVD	People's Commissariat of Internal Affairs; formed in 1922; over-saw State Political Administration (GPU) and other Soviet secret police organs; dissolved in 1954
OGPU	United State Political Administration, Soviet secret police organ; successor to State Political Administration (GPU); formed in 1923; dissolved in July 1934
OFM	Order of Friars Minor, Franciscans
OP	Order of Preachers, Dominicans
OSA	Order of Saint Augustine, Augustinians
OSBM	Order of Saint Basil the Great, Basilians
OSU	Order of Saint Ursula, Ursulines
RC	Roman Catholic Church
RSFSR	Russian Soviet Federated Socialist Republic, largest of all Soviet republics
ROC	Russian Orthodox Church (generally, MP)
ROCA	Russian Orthodox Church outside Russia; founded in exile
SAC	Society of the Catholic Apostolate, Pallottines
SCIM	Sisters of the Immaculate Heart of Mary
SD	Social Democrat
SJ	Society of Jesus, Jesuits
SR	Social Revolutionary
SSMI	Sisters Servants of Mary Immaculate
SSR	Soviet Socialist Republic, constituent republic of Soviet Union, whose fifteen SSRs were each named after particular national minority
SVR	Foreign Intelligence Service, post-Soviet secret police organ, under president of Russian Republic; successor to Committee of State Security (KGB); formed in October 1991
UAOC	Ukrainian Autocephalous Orthodox Church
UGCC	Ukrainian Greek Catholic Church
UkSSR	Ukrainian Soviet Socialist Republic
UOC-KP	Ukrainian Orthodox Church, Kyiv Patriarchate

UOC-MP   Ukrainian Orthodox Church, Moscow Patriarchate

USSR   Union of Soviet Socialist Republics; founded in 1922; dissolved in 1991

VRK   Military-Revolutionary Committee; precursor to Cheka; formed in October 1917; dissolved in November 1917

Guide to Names for States, Churches, Peoples, Factions, and Places

When dealing with the Soviet Union and with Catholicism, to avoid confusion, it is best to sort out the sometimes bewildering variety of names from the beginning, especially those for nationality and religion. The USSR was home to over 100 nationalities, and specific nationalities are referred to by their name or by "Soviet" where appropriate. Catholicism is made up of nearly two dozen autonomous Churches, often referred to by more than one name. This section is designed to give the reader a helping hand with these and other names appearing in the chapters to follow.

Russian versus Soviet

It is common still in Western writing to find "Soviet Union" interchanged with "Russia," and "Soviet" with "Russian." In this work, however, "Russian" is used to refer only to the Russian language, the Great Russian nationality, the Russian Empire, Federation, or Republic, or the Russian Church, both Catholic and Orthodox. "Soviet" is used for all references to the Union of Soviet Socialist Republics and the citizens and institutions of that state, from its founding in 1922 to its collapse in August 1991, and the creation of the Commonwealth of Independent States in December 1991—and to Soviet Russia (RSFSR) and the citizens and institutions of that state, from its founding in 1917 to the dissolution of the Soviet Union in 1991. Proper national names are used throughout for the members of the different nationalities that inhabit the USSR.

"Russian Catholic" means only those Catholics who adhere to the pure Byzantine-Russian Rite as was followed in the Byzantine-Russian Exarchate and as is found in a few émigré parishes in the West. There have been and are

Catholics of Russian nationality who adhere to the Latin Catholic Church, and they will be identified as "Russian Roman" or "Latin Catholics."

"Soviet Catholic" means a citizen of the Soviet Union (or of Soviet Russia from 1917 to 1922) who was a member of the Catholic Church. It does not imply legitimization of the annexation of the Baltic States, eastern Poland, or parts of Romania but is used as term of convenience, particularly when dealing with all-Union issues.

Church Names

A majority of both Roman Catholics and non-Catholics still do not know that there are many ways to be Catholic. The Catholic Church is composed of twenty-two autonomous Churches, which differ in spirituality, style of worship, and interior government, while all being equally part of one Catholic Faith and united with the Holy See at Rome. The pope serves as both head of the entire Universal Church, and patriarch of the largest Church, the Roman Church, also referred to as the "Latin Church" or "Latin Rite."

"Catholic," by itself, refers to a person or institution of the Catholic Church, centered at Rome.

"Roman Catholic" and "Latin Catholic" are used interchangeably for all Catholics who belong to the Western Church of Catholicism, that is, to the Patriarchate of Rome.

The non-Roman Catholic Churches are collectively known as the "Eastern Catholic Churches" (formerly called the "Eastern" or "Oriental Rites" before Vatican II). With the exception of the Italo-Albanian and Maronite Churches, they were formed by faithful and clergy from Orthodox, Oriental Orthodox, or Nestorian Churches. They are also known as "Uniate Churches" or the "Uniate Rite." The name derives from the Latin word *unia* for "union." Because it was and still is used pejoratively by some Eastern Orthodox to denote Eastern Catholics who have abandoned their heritage through attachment to the West, and because it carries connotations of betrayal, "Uniate" is not used in this work, except when quoting from or paraphrasing sources.

In the Soviet Union, most Eastern Catholics were from one of the Byzantine-Slavic Churches, which share much in common with Russian, Ukrainian, and Belorussian Orthodoxy and the Byzantine-Georgian tradition. A minority were from the Armenian tradition, which is sister to the larger Armenian Apostolic (Gregorian) Church centered at Echtmiadzin, Soviet Armenia. An even smaller minority were from the Chaldean Church, formed out of the Ancient Church of the East, or the Nestorian Church.

"Greek Catholic" was the accepted name for all Byzantine-Slavic Catholics in the Russian and Austro-Hungarian Empires until modern times. The name was coined to find a brief way in which to describe those faithful who were once Slavic Orthodox but were now in full union with Rome. Although no longer used in much of Ukraine, it is still a current name in official documents of both Church and State, in popular use in Belorussia and is still preferred by part of the leadership and most of the clergy of the eparchy of Mukachevo in the Transcarpathian oblast of Ukraine.

"Ukrainian Catholic" was introduced in the days of the late Metropolitan Sheptytsky (d. 1944) into the Greek Catholic Church of Galicia in western Ukraine, and that Church is referred to by that name during the appropriate time period. This is also the name favored in the postwar diaspora to emphasize the Ukrainian heritage, although, in the 1990s, the name was changed to "Ukrainian Greco-Catholic" in some circles.

"Belorussian Greek Catholic" refers to Byzantine Catholics who adhere to the Byzantine-Belorussian Catholic Church, whereas "Belorussian Catholic" generally refers to ethnic Belorussians who belong to the Latin Catholic Church. The same holds true for similar Georgian Church names.

"Ruthenian Catholic" was the official Vatican name for all Byzantine Catholics of the Austro-Hungarian Empire and Polish-Lithuanian Commonwealth who inhabited modern Poland, Czech Republic, Slovakia, Ukraine, Belorussia, and Hungary. In this work, it is used exclusively to designate the one Church that retained it in modern times: the Church of the Mukachevo Eparchy in the Transcarpathian oblast of Ukraine, and for a time, adjacent territory in Czechoslovakia and Hungary. This is also the original name for the Byzantine Catholic Metropolia of Pittsburgh in the United States.

"Armenian Catholics" refers to ethnic Armenians who belong to the Armenian Catholic Church. Although, by default, some former Soviet Armenian Catholics must now attend Latin Catholic churches, there remains a distinct Armenian Catholic consciousness outside Armenia and Georgia.

"Latinization" was an ill-fated policy whereby the spirituality, liturgy, and government style of the Latin Catholic Church was intruded into Eastern Catholic religious life. Latinization came about because of the perception that the qualities of the Latin Catholic Church were superior to all other Christian Churches. It was sometimes forced on an Eastern Catholic Church by Latin Catholic missionary orders, or by Latin Catholic clergy working in an Eastern Church. Often it was brought about by Eastern Catholic clergy who felt inferior to the larger Latin Catholic Church or who wanted to make their

Churches appear more "Catholic." Latinization cripples the development of an Eastern Church, and provides support for Orthodox fears of what would result after a full union of the two Churches. Though condemned by popes and by Vatican II, the spirit of Latinization is still alive. Its problems figure prominently in the history of Soviet Eastern Catholics.

"Uniatism" is the now-abandoned policy whereby a portion of the faithful and clergy of an Eastern Church united with Rome, and became an Eastern Catholic Church. Since Vatican II, it has been replaced by efforts toward corporate reunion of the Catholic, Byzantine, and Oriental Orthodox Churches and the (Assyrian) Church of the East.

"Russian Orthodox" refers only to the faithful and structures of the Moscow Patriarchate. "Belorussian Autocephalous Orthodox" and "Ukrainian Autocephalous Orthodox" refer to the Churches founded among those peoples after the October Revolution of 1917 and revived during World War II, and in the Orthodox diaspora after 1945. The Belorussian Orthodox Church and the Ukrainian Orthodox Church were established in 1990 by the Moscow Patriarchate inside those two Soviet republics and are canonical members of the Russian Orthodox Patriarchate.

"True Orthodox" or "Free Orthodox" are those Russian Orthodox hierarchs, clergy, monastics, and faithful inside the USSR who rejected Patriarch Sergius' Letter of 1923 as being pro-Communist and formed a catacomb Church, which survived the Soviet era, and is linked with the émigré "Russian Orthodox Church Outside of Russia" or "Synodal Church."

"Old Believers" are the faithful of the Moscow Church who rejected liturgical reforms in the seventeenth century. There are Old Believers who are in union with the Moscow Patriarchate.

Ethnic Names

"Pole" refers to members of the Polish nationality who are or were citizens of the Republic of Poland, Soviet Union, or former Soviet Union. Those in the former Soviet Union do not necessarily speak Polish, but are aware of their Polish heritage. Some are descended from people of other nationalities who became Polonized over the centuries, and carry non-Polish surnames, but consider themselves Poles.

Polish citizens of 1939 who were not ethnic Poles are described according to their national origin as well as Polish citizenship in the sections dealing with the annexation of eastern Poland.

"German" in this work usually refers to Russian or Soviet citizens of Ger-

Table 1

Changes in Place-Names—General

Tsarist	*Communist*	*Independent*
Armenia		
Alexandropol	Leninakan	Gyumri
Georgia		
Tiflis	Tbilisi	*
Russia		
Mariupol'	Zhdanov	Mariupol'
Nizhni Novgorod	Gorki	Nizhnii Novgorod
Novonikolaevsk	Novosibirsk	*
Saint Petersburg, Petrograd	Leningrad	Saint Petersburg
Samara	Kuybyshev	Samara
Tsaritsyn	Stalingrad, Volgograd	Volgograd
Vladikavkaz	Ordzhonokidze, Dzaudzhikau	Vladikavkaz
Yekaterinburg	Sverdlovsk	Yekaterinburg
Yekaterinodar	Krasnodar	*

* Indicates no change from nearest entry on left.

man descent, whose forbears were settlers of the Baltic region in the Middle Ages or settlers invited by Catherine the Great and her successors into the Volga valley and southern Ukraine. These original German colonies persisted, and descendants of the colonists spread across the empire. The various communities of Germans are collectively known as "Russia Germans." Most of the original western colonies were destroyed by collectivization or by forced relocation of their inhabitants in World War II.

Ethnic Germans inside the Russian Empire or Soviet Union are also referred to as *"Volksdeutsche,"* or by regional title: "Black Sea Germans," "Carpathian Germans," "Galician Germans," and so on. Germans from the German state are identified as "Reich Germans" in the 1933–1945 era.

"Romania" spelled with an "o" designates a Western orientation (originally with Rome), with a "u" an Eastern orientation (originally with Byzantium). The Romanians themselves prefer the Western spelling, whereas the Soviets insisted on the Eastern, for political reasons. In this work, the Romanians' preference is followed, for the country, nationality, and those living inside the USSR. "Moldavians" refers to people of Romanian nationality who were brought under Soviet rule and were given the name of the old Romanian

Table 2

Changes in Place-Names—By Republic

1914	1919–1939	1940–1991	Independence
The Baltic States			
Estonia			
Dorpat	Tartu	*	*
Revel	Tallinn	*	*
Walk	Valga	*	*
Latvia (Courland, Latgale)			
Dvinsk	Daugavapils	*	*
Lithuania (Samogitia)			
Kovno	Kaunas	*	*
Vilna	Wilno	Vilnius	*
Memel	Klaipeda[a]	*	*
The Western Republics			
Belarus (White Russia, Belorussia)			
Gomel	*	*	Homyel'
Grodno	*	*	Hrodna
Mogilev	*	*	Mahilyow
Ukraine (Little Russia)			
Lemberg	Lwów	Lvov	L'viv
Stanislav	Stanislaviv	Ivano-Frankovsk	Ivano-Frankivs'k
Czernowitz	Cernausti	Chernovtsy	Chernivtsi
Kieff	Kiev	*	Kyiv
Kharkov	*	*	Kharkiv

(continued on next page)

province. In 1990, they adopted the form "Moldovan," corresponding to contemporary Romanian usage—and the form used in this work. Moldovan history is complicated by its repeated transfer from Russia to Romania and back again as Bessarabia and internal changes.

Political Names

Most of Russian public opinion in 1917 was pro-socialist; the conservatives were very weak after the tragedy of the war and the collapse of the dynasty.

Table 2 *(continued)*

1914	1919–1939	1940–1991	*Independence*
Transcarpathian Oblast			
(Zakarpatska Rus', Transcarpathian Ukraine, Zakarpatia)			
Ungvar	Uzhgorod	*	Uzhorod
Munkacs	Mukachevo	*	Mukacheve
Kaliningrad Oblast (East Prussia), est. 1945			
Cranz	*	*	Zelenogradsk
Frisches Haff	*	*	Kaliningrad Lagoon
Insterburg	*	*	Chernyakhovsk
Königsberg	*	*	Kaliningrad
Pillau	*	*	Baltysk
Tilsit	*	*	Sovetsk
Moldova (Bessarabia, Moldavian ASSR, Moldavian SSR)			
Kishinev	Chișinău	Kishinev	Chișinău
Central Asian States			
Kazakhstan			
Alma Ata	Vernyi	*	Almaty
Tselinograd	*	*	Aqmolak
Kyrgyzstan (Kirghiz SSR)			
Frunze	*	*	Bishkek

* Indicates no change from nearest entry on left.

ᵃ When Klaipeda was reannexed by Nazi Germany, the name "Memel" was restored (1938–1945).

The majority of the populace supported the Socialist Revolutionary Party in the 1917 elections.

The Communist Party of the Soviet Union was descended directly from the radical wing of the old Social Democratic Party, called the "Bolsheviks" (from Russian for "majority," which they most certainly were not). The Bolsheviks eventually established a separate party, and led the October Revolution of 1917. Members of the other wing of the Social Democratic Party were known as the "Mensheviks" ("minority"), and they were eventually destroyed, despite initial successes. In 1990, Social Democrats were again presenting themselves to the Soviet public.

The delegates of the Constituent Assembly were elected by the population of the Russian Empire in 1917 to determine the future development of the nation. A majority were from the Social Revolutionary and other parties: only 24 percent were Bolsheviks. The Constituent Assembly was disbanded by Bolshevik troops on its only day in existence, January 5, 1918.

In the civil war of 1918–1922, two principal factions were the "Reds," who supported Lenin and the Bolsheviks, and the "Whites," a broad range of anti-Bolsheviks, including Russian nationalists and supporters of the monarchy or the Constituent Assembly, who were organized in various governments and movements but were never united under a single administration.

Place-Names

Because Eastern European history is complex and there are many nationalities living in one region, one soon finds out that there have been many name changes, and that the use of a name in a text can often define a writer's ethnic or political orientation. For example, the capital of Lithuania has been known as "Vilna" by the Russians, "Wilno" by the Poles, and "Vilnius" by the Lithuanians, and the name of the city has been changed according to who was in power. The cultural heart of eastern Galicia/western Ukraine has had even more names: "Lemberg" to the Austro-Germans, "Lwów" to the Poles, "Lvov" to Russians, and "L'viv" to Ukrainians. Naturally, people are deeply tied to using their own names for cities they claim historically as their own.

Within the Soviet Union, many cities and towns lost their historic names. Tsarist and religious names were abandoned after the Communist victory. Other names were changed to memorialize the heroes of the Party.

For the sake of clarity and historical accuracy, this work uses the official name in the time period being written about. Tsarist names are given in the early chapters along with the newer Soviet names, to help orient the reader using a pre-1918 map. In addition, maps of the Russian Empire are provided with the tsarist names.

PART ONE

1914–1922

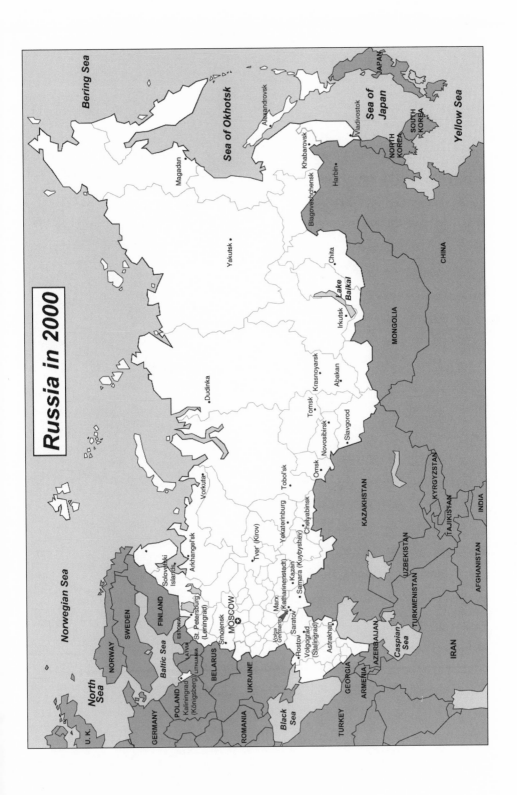

Russia in 2000

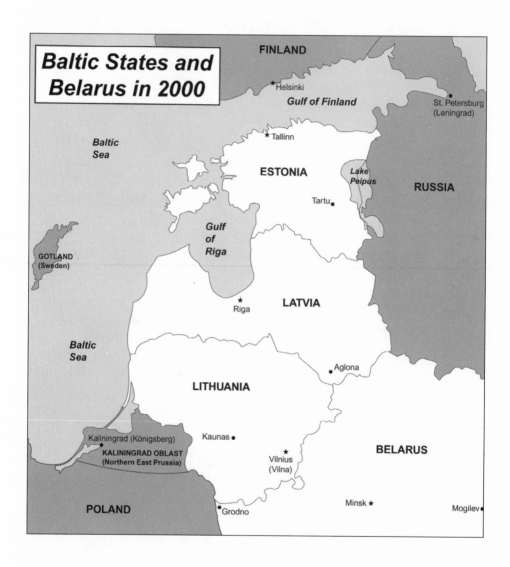

Baltic States and Belarus in 2000

FINLAND

★Helsinki

Gulf of Finland

St. Petersburg
(Leningrad)

*Baltic
Sea*

★ Tallinn

ESTONIA

*Lake
Peipus*

RUSSIA

Tartu

*Gulf
of
Riga*

GOTLAND
(Sweden)

★
Riga

LATVIA

*Baltic
Sea*

Aglona

LITHUANIA

Kaunas

Kaliningrad (Königsberg)
KALININGRAD OBLAST
(Northern East Prussia)

★
Vilnius
(Vilna)

BELARUS

POLAND

Grodno

Minsk ★

Mogilev

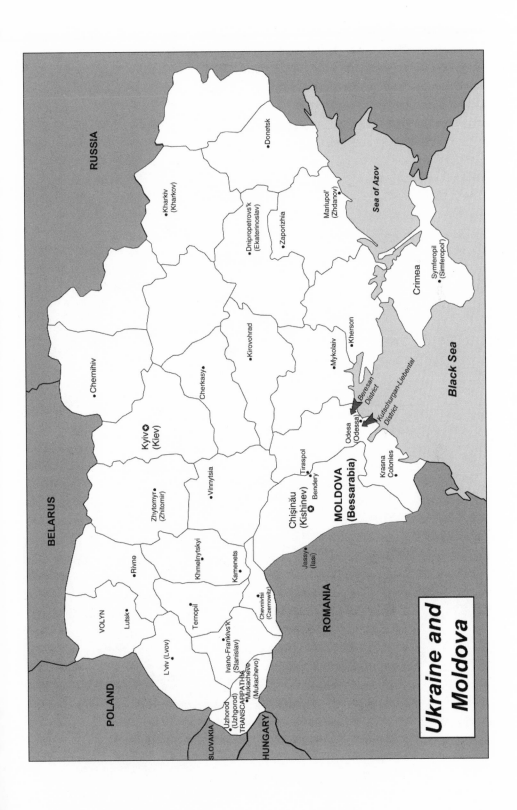

Ukraine and Moldova

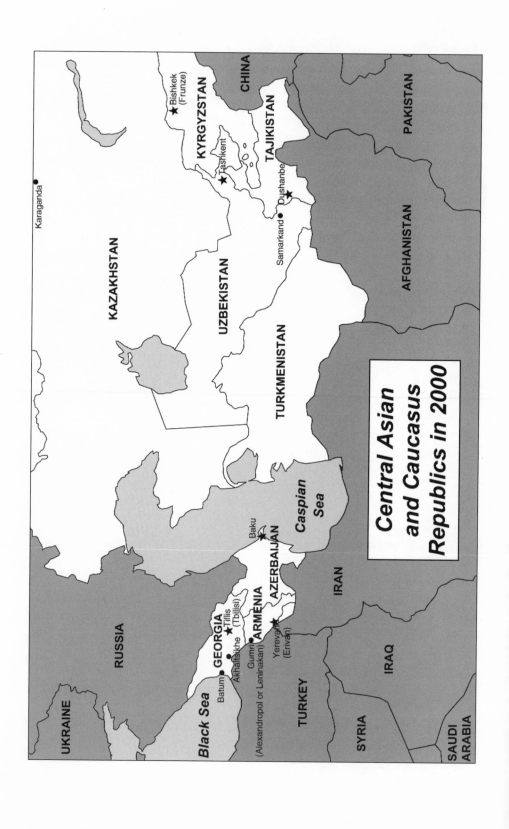

Central Asian and Caucasus Republics in 2000

CHAPTER 1

The Inheritance

> The Bolshevik *coup d'état* ... did not sever all ties to the past. ... [The
> Bolsheviks] were the heirs of the tsars, and in regard to the Catholic
> Church, received an inheritance that was distinct and long-standing.
> —Dennis Dunn, *The Catholic Church and the Soviet Government*

In 1913, with all the pageantry it could muster, the Russian Empire celebrated three hundred years of rule by the Romanov dynasty. Within a few years, however, the Romanovs would either be slaughtered or scattered abroad, and the structures of the empire shattered.

The rapid collapse of the autocratic empire in February 1917 and the establishment of the Provisional Government seemed to herald a new spring for Russia, one in which democratic hopes would finally find fulfillment. But then the Provisionals were overthrown in the October Revolution, and the Bolsheviks gradually took over most of the old Russian Empire. As Dennis Dunn points out in *The Catholic Church and the Soviet Government,* the victory of Communism did not mean a complete change. Rather, in time, the Bolsheviks assumed many of the traditional Russian practices and viewpoints.

Where the Catholic Church was concerned, the Bolsheviks inherited a relationship based on misunderstandings and a lack of trust. Catholicism was barely tolerated during the last years of Imperial Russia and would be poorly tolerated throughout the Soviet era. The intolerance arose primarily from policies fundamental to the tsarist and Soviet empires[1] and from a distortion of Christian history, a distortion maintained by tsars, commissars, and Orthodox bishops alike—an unlikely combination but one that occurs repeatedly when discussing Soviet Catholics.

Government Policies of the Tsarist Era

Since the reign of Nicholas I (1825–1855), the empire was based on three pillars: Orthodoxy, Autocracy, and Nationality (better translated as "national

7

spirit"). These led to Russification and became sources of conflict with the Catholic Church and the Holy See of Rome (antipathy to Catholicism pre-dates Nicholas I's reign, however; relations between Muscovy/Russia and Catholics had long been difficult).

"Orthodoxy" referred to the Orthodox Patriarchate of Moscow, which had been subjected to the State by Peter the Great (ruled 1689–1725). The Russian Orthodox faith served as a protection against outside enemies and as a means of converting non-Russians into loyal subjects. The Russian Ortho-dox continually conducted missionary work among national minorities and against the united Greek Catholic Church.

"Autocracy" dated from the sixteenth century, when the tsar was an ab-solute monarch over both Russian and non-Russian lands. Western ideas of government were spurned. Direct rule by Moscow eventually replaced the Western European systems that operated in Finland, Poland, and the Baltic.

"Nationality" was, of course, Great Russian. The other East Slavs were considered "White Russians" (Belorussians) and "Little Russians" (Ukraini-ans). The appellations were a legacy from the old Byzantine Empire. "Little Rus' " referred to the territory known by Greek cartographers, whereas "Big" or "Great Rus' " referred to an area whose boundaries were unknown. The names endured, although their meanings shifted with Russian nationalism. The preferred language was Great Russian; subjects were to identify with the ancient state centered at Moscow, under the code of Russian imperial admin-istration. Although Russification policies varied across the empire, all were driven by belief in the Great Russian language and culture as superior, fear about the loyalty of non-Russians in the borderlands, zeal for Orthodoxy as the True Faith, and bureaucratic enthusiasm for the universal administration of Russian law.

This environment directly affected Catholics. Both Orthodoxy and Catholicism saw themselves as being the only True Church of Christ on earth. Each considered the other a dissident, not a sister Church. The Catholics in-cluded millions who followed Eastern ritual and practices while being united to Rome. Catholicism was definitely the faith of national minorities, who were concentrated in sensitive frontier areas, or "Russian" Slavs who were becom-ing more conscious of their uniqueness and separateness from the Great Rus-sians. Those Russians who became Catholic did so after serious searching and generally came from the upper classes.

Although the Catholic Church of the early 1900s hardly opposed monar-chist rule, it was based in the West and so defended values that protected the rights of the Church, the individual person, and non-Russian nations. A clash between the policies of the empire and the goals of the Catholic Church was inevitable. Furthermore, the Russian state was accustomed to regulating religious affairs. Its Ministry of Public Worship dealt with the religious life of all the faiths within the empire. The Orthodox Patriarchate of Moscow had long been suppressed, replaced by a Holy Synod led by a layman. The independent Georgian Orthodox Church had been absorbed into the Russian Orthodox Church by state decree and was led by ethnic Russians. The entire Greek Catholic Church had been driven underground by 1875. A Roman Catholic College based in Saint Petersburg governed the Latin Catholic Church. It regulated the relations between the dioceses and the Ministry of Public Worship and administered Church property, although the Latin Catholics were never completely subordinated to state control.

Government Policies of the Soviet Era

During the Soviet era, the three pillars became Ideology, Dictatorship, and Nationalism.

Soviet ideology, which lasted from the winter of 1917 until the summer of 1991, declared that the nations of the tsarist empire—and ultimately of the world—would find true equality and fulfillment of their hopes inside the new socialist empire and under the Communist Party's leadership. "Ideology" also included the goal of scientific atheism: the radical denial of the existence, importance, and influence of the divine in human life and a concerted effort to eliminate all awareness of and reference to God. Marxism-Leninism ultimately pushed for creation of truly totalitarian states. The classic Communist governments of the twentieth century claimed a complete monopoly over all aspects of society, including truth itself, thus setting themselves up in opposition to anyone who would present truth from science, art, literature, or religion. In 1864, in his *Syllabus of Errors,* Pius IX condemned the claims of the State to be the source of all rights and to have no limits. The conflict between Church and State would only deepen in the Soviet era.

The Soviet dictatorship, theoretically based on the power of industrial workers (proletariat) and peasants, dates from 1917 and reached its peak under the tyranny of Joseph Stalin (ruled 1929–1953). In reality, the dictatorship was maintained by a small elite group that favored industry and looked down upon the peasants; the importance of the State and the victory of the Communist revolution both in the USSR and throughout the world superseded all human values. In other words, nothing could stand in the way of the Revolution and the power of the Party. Under Communism, all rural and traditional life came second. Indeed, the changes introduced by the Communists, such as the collectivization of farming and the closing of the churches totally devastated rural life.

Under Stalin, "Nationalism" focused again on the Great Russians, at the expense of all other nationalities (although, as Boris Yeltsin and Alexander Solzhenitsyn have noted, Great Russians also suffered terribly under Communism). Great Russians dominated most parts of the USSR, regardless of the locals' feelings. "Nationalism" also encompassed the idea of the Soviet Man, *Homo sovieticus,* according to which the different peoples of the Soviet Union would merge into one Communist-oriented, atheistic, scientific people, based on—but surpassing—the Russian identity. Here, too, is the groundwork for Catholic-Soviet difficulties. Catholic national minorities remained attached to the Church. In many parts of the western Soviet Union especially, Catholicism became the only vehicle for the defense of human rights. Because the Church demands that people be allowed to find their own spiritual home, and that the natural rights of religion and moral law cannot be subjugated to the requirements of any state, the Church and the USSR engaged in a bitter struggle.

Lenin and Religion

Vladimir Ilyich Ulyanov, known as "Lenin" (1870–1924), the driving force behind the small band of Bolsheviks who succeeded in imposing an alien ideology upon Russia and its territories, aimed for the Party's complete control of the State and its citizens. Cold, calculating, and ruthless to all opponents, he allowed cooperation with believers only to achieve the ends of the Soviet system.

At the age of 16, Lenin tore off his crucifix, spat on it, and trampled it into the dirt. (Interestingly, his wife, Krupskaya, reported that Lenin's father died as a devout Orthodox believer.) Although Marx had dismissed religion as "the opium of the people," Lenin went much further, condemning it as "tasteless idealistic nonsense," poisonous, and the source of man's moral and mental degeneration. To flirt with God "is unspeakably hateful," he wrote; indeed, "a Catholic priest who rapes girls . . . is less dangerous to democracy than a priest without vestments or the crude trappings of religion who is yet possessed by an idea, who is democratic, who preaches the creation of a god."[2]

Lenin believed that, whereas the State had to regard religion as a private affair, the Party was committed to freeing the workers and peasants from "religious bamboozling." Even though Lenin knew that persecution usually gives religion impetus, his negative views and the supremacy of the Party in all things guaranteed that such persecution would occur. Again and again, he launched full-scale attacks against belief in God.[3]

Lenin was not sure that religion would wither away with the State, as claimed by classical Marxist theory. Scientific atheism had to free the masses from the "gendarmes in cassocks," and the Party had to lead the way in exposing the foolishness of religious belief. At the same time, the war on religion had to yield to pragmatic concerns that would render antireligious work less important than other parts of the Party's program. This happened during World War II and at various times in the history of the USSR, giving mixed and inconsistent signals to the Soviet Union's believers.

Russia and Catholicism: Two Interpretations

Soviet history is thus partly a continuation of Russian history and attitudes. Especially after Stalin's Russification drive in the 1930s, Russian elements strongly colored Soviet life and profoundly affected the fate of Soviet Catholics. The USSR adopted the traditional imperial Russian history regarding State and Church, then adapted it to the Marxist-Leninist view.

That "created history" teaches the following:

1. There was one ancient Russian state, centered at Kiev, that embraced all East Slavs (that is, all Slavs east of Poland), in one great family and country called "Rus'."

2. This great state also experienced full unity under one Church, headed by the metropolitan of Kiev, founded by Vladimir the Great in 988, and known as "Kiev-Rus'."

3. The Church—the Russian Orthodox Church—has been the Church of the Russian people ever since, with no changes other than residence of the head bishop.

4. The Mongol invasion of 1240 and the rise of feudal Poland-Lithuania on the western ruins of Kiev-Rus' shattered this great union of Orthodox Slavs. This led to

    a. the rise of three separate nationalities: Great Russian, Ukrainian (Little Russian), and Belorussian (White Russian); feudal and anti-Russian nobles and an equally anti-Russian Latin Catholic Church encouraged the existence of these separate groups;

    b. the formation of a separate Church (the Greek Catholic Church created by the Union of Brest in 1596); the result of the machinations of Jesuit missionaries and Polish nobles, the Greek Catholic Church was designed to absorb the East Slavs into Polish culture and Roman religion.

5. Moscow was the new Kiev, the principality to which all Russian cultural and religious life willingly and consciously moved.

6. According to the "Third Rome" theory, Moscow fulfilled its messianic destiny by driving out the Mongols, ending foreign rule over the western territories, and reuniting many East Slavs again into a state with one tsar and one Church. This theory, introduced by a Muscovite monk, teaches that the First Rome had fallen into heresy and that the Second Rome—Constantinople (now known as Istanbul)—had fallen under infidel rule. As the third (and final) Rome, Moscow was entrusted with spreading salvation to the world.

7. After the Worker and Peasant Revolution of 1917, the struggle for full unity entered its true historic phase. The victories of the Red Army in 1945 united the East Slav peoples and restored the full unity of Kiev-Rus' by

a. breaking the power of the Polish aristocracy and introducing socialism beyond the borders of old Russia;

b. Destroying the false Union of 1596 and restoring the original Orthodox Church;

c. enabling the East Slavs to walk the path of unity that would lead to the fusion of one Soviet people, based on science, atheism, and socialist progress.

According to this history, the East Slavs could live out their authentic destiny in full harmony, under the guidance of the Great Russian people and the centrality of Moscow. They could introduce the real messianic message of Communism to the world.

Many Westerners accept this view. Popular textbooks still copy both the Romanov and Stalinist versions of Russian history and the formation of the Russian state, omitting only the florid phrases. Yet what actually took place is quite different. Just as people's lives are rarely neat and orderly, neither are those of entire nations.

To serve as a reference point for succeeding chapters, here is a more accurate overview of the formation of the states and churches:

1. A single Kievan empire never existed—Kiev Rus' was a loose communion of principalities. Although the Mother of Cities and a great commercial and political power, Kiev never served as the capital of a united state. Nor were there three distinct nationalities. Nationalism was not to develop in Eastern Europe until much later.

2. Despite Soviet and Russian Orthodox proclamations during the Millennium of 1988, there was no foundation of Orthodoxy in 988. Vladimir (Volodomyr), Prince of Kiev, converted to Byzantine Christianity in 988 and subsequently introduced it as the state religion in Kiev, which determined the

permanent orientation of Russia, Ukraine, and Belarussia toward Eastern Christianity. In 988, Byzantine Christianity was part of an unbroken and universal Catholic Church, in which Rome and Constantinople remained partners.

Christianity had long existed in Ukraine, having been brought by missionaries and merchants from the Greek colonies on the Crimea, where numerous Latin Catholic saints had been martyred in the first three centuries, including Saint Clement (Pope Clement I), who was slain and whose body was thrown into the Black Sea. But what really enabled Christianity to spread was the baptism of Kiev in 988; Vladimir's sincere conversion to a devout Christianity; his importation of Byzantine clergy, religious art, and writings; and Kiev's new spiritual relationship with Constantinople.

3. The Russian Orthodox Church did not exist in 988 in Kiev-Rus', although Kiev and its sister states did turn most of their attention to the Christian East. In 1054, when Rome and Constantinople split over liturgical differences and theological misinterpretations, the result was not the immediate formation of two Churches. Rather, the two Patriarchates began to drift apart, a process that would lead to the formation of separate Orthodox and Catholic Churches.

Kievan contacts with the Latin West and the Catholic Church continued, from royal marriages to trade. Latin Christianity remained known to the people of the states of Rus' because the neighboring and local Poles, Lithuanians, and Germans adhered to it. At the same time, Kiev-Rus' maintained close contacts with Constantinople. As a result, the East Slavs inherited Byzantine antipathy toward the Latin Catholics—an antipathy that greatly increased after the Fourth Crusade shattered the Byzantine Empire in 1204. Memories of this tragedy, combined with later events in the East Slavic lands, perpetuated the fear of Roman Catholicism.

Some unity did exist, as demonstrated by the Orthodox and Catholic calendars. Thirty Russians are venerated as Catholic saints; of the twenty-one who lived after 1054, most came after the time of the Fourth Crusade and the brutal rupture of Latin-Byzantine communion in 1204. The group includes some of the most venerated and popular Russian saints: Abraham of Rostov and Abraham of Smolensk, Anthony and Theodosius of the Caves, Boris and Gleb, German and Sergius of Valaam, Isaiah of Rostov, Michael of Chernigov, Sergius of Radonezh and Theodore of Pechersky Lavra.

Other saints dating from the time of full unity include Theodore the Varangian and his son John (d. 984), Olga (d. 969), and Vladimir (d. 1015)—all Varangians, the Rus' term for the Scandinavian invaders and settlers who founded the first ruling house of Kiev-Rus'. The list also includes Moses the

Hungarian (d. 1043) and his brother Ephraim of Novotorzhok (d. 1053), Anne of Novgorod (d. 1051)—a Swedish princess baptized by the English Latin Catholic bishop Saint Sigfrid—and Ingvar (Igor; d. 1147), another Swede.

It is not possible to precisely date the separation of the Churches of Moscow, Kiev, and Rome. As was true in the Middle East, intercommunion continued on a local level for many years after the supposed "split" of 1054, and even after 1204. The drift was gradual, though anti-Latin Catholic feelings continued to deepen and intensify in the fourteenth century as the Russian Church (Byzantine Rite) strengthened its alignment with Constantinople.

As early as 1207, Pope Innocent III asked the Kievan government to unite with the Roman Church. Dominican friars who came to minister to Latin Catholics in Kiev-Rus' brought about enmity because of their attempts to Latinize the local Church and proclaim Roman supremacy. On the other hand, Archbishop Petro Akerovych of Rus' took part in the Council of Lyons in 1247. Bishop candidates of the southwestern eparchies often went to the local Latin Catholic archbishop to be ordained as bishops. The Latin Catholic residents—both clergy and laity—of Novgorod principality considered themselves and the Rus' to be in full communion with one another until the Council of Florence in 1439.

In 1441, Metropolitan Isidore of Kiev attempted to reunite the two Churches at Moscow; he was forced to flee for his life. From then on, the Moscow Church was definitely non-Catholic, splitting from the Church of Kiev in 1461. The Mother Church of Kiev retained specifically Catholic leadership from 1458 until 1481, when Symon was installed as metropolitan of Kiev and Rus' with the approbation of the patriarch of Constantinople.[4]

In 1588, Constantinople yielded to Russian pressures and elevated Moscow to a Patriarchate, which confirmed the city's sense of being the "Third Rome." Moscow became the first new Patriarchate since ancient times, surely a fulfillment of its destiny. By that time, the schism between Rus' and Rome was complete. Indeed, many on both sides considered the other side to be heretical.

4. Because three separate nationalities did not exist in the medieval era, local loyalties dominated. The Western states of Poland and Lithuania and the local Catholic Church had no interest in promoting "national divisions."

As for the formation of the Greek Catholic Church, in 1596, several Orthodox bishops in the lands of Poland-Lithuania declared a union of the ancient Slavic Church with the Roman Church. Prompting this move was

a. the Orthodox Church's serious need of reform, which many leaders felt that only union with the Roman Catholics could provide; the priests were poorly educated because of a lack of theological schools and the church had fragile links with Constantinople;

b. the extensive discrimination experienced by Orthodox living in Poland-Lithuania; it was believed that a Church union would give full equality as well as peace and justice.

The union did not produce the results desired by the theologians. Many leading Slavic noble families opted to join the Latin Catholic Church and embrace Polish culture, and full equality was never achieved either within Church or State. In the long run, however, the union endured among the ordinary people and fostered the development of the Carpathian, Ukrainian, and Belorussian nationalities.

5. The Grand Duchy of Muscovy evolved slowly into the central Rus' state. In particular, Muscovy was viewed as the successor to Constantinople after that city had been conquered. The duchy incorporated the Byzantine Eagle into its coat of arms and aggressively worked for Church autonomy. Its claims to be Constantinople's successor escalated during and after the rise of Ivan the Great (ruled 1462–1505), when Muscovy began to call itself "Rossiya," (which we translate as "Russia"), engaged in wars against Polish-Lithuanian territory, and began to actively expand against its western neighbors.

6. In the course of Muscovy's rise, the duchy came into direct conflict with Poland, Lithuania, and the Catholic religious and military orders of the Livonian and Teutonic Knights. Because all these states and orders adhered to the Latin Catholic Church, they became Russia's civil enemies. The messianism of the "Third Rome" dictated that the Latin Catholics were heretics, that the Greek Catholics were partners to heresy and national destruction, and that the Catholic states were blocking Russia's natural destiny.

Compounding the problem, Poland and the Livonian and Teutonic Knights used secular military invasions to impose Church union or to convert Baltic peoples to Latin Catholicism. The memory of the Latin Mass being celebrated by victorious Poles in Moscow during the Time of Troubles (1603–1613), when no central government existed, remained a vivid one, along with the Latin Catholic attitude that Kiev-Rus' was missionary territory despite its long Christian heritage.

For centuries, the standard Russian view of Western powers was that they sought to break up the lands of Mother Russia. According to this view, foreigners were to be feared as potential enemies. Moreover, the Latin Mass and the Polish White Eagle operated hand in hand, always to the detriment of Mother Russia. The fear went beyond Poland to include Germany, and to this day includes the United States of America and a host of other nations.

7. Soviet power definitely expanded Moscow's rule not only over the lands of Kiev-Rus' but also over territory the tsars had never even considered. After 1945, Moscow expanded its influence and indirect control well into Central Europe, and Communism spread through a significant part of the world. It did not, however, provide economic or social salvation to those under its rule, as was demonstrated by the crumbling of the Eastern Bloc in the late 1980s.

Moreover, the "false Union" (as the Orthodox called the Union of Brest) has survived Orthodox and Communist cooperation; forty-four years after its supposed destruction in 1945, it was revealed as a living Church. In the 1990s, helped by Gorbachev's glasnost and the final collapse of Communism, the East Slavs began to reassert their ethnic identity and heritage.

The fusion of nationalities into one Soviet Man never occurred. Rather, national identity has blossomed, raising concerns among a host of different peoples. How this will turn out remains to be seen.

Soviet Definition of Religious Freedom

All Soviet governments promised some religious freedom, but the exact definition of that freedom remained narrow. Ultimately, the Soviets restricted religious freedom to the actual ceremony of worship inside a church, mosque, or synagogue rented to the believers for that specific purpose. Nothing more was allowed.

These conditions characterized the worst eras, when virtually no churches remained in the entire USSR or when bans on other activities—such as printing new religious books or producing new religious items—were enforced. Repair of old and construction of new churches became a bureaucratic nightmare; building churches in new urban areas became an impossibility. In the early days of the USSR, there were even attempts at institutional child raising to eliminate religious influences from the family.[5]

Because congregants jammed the few surviving churches, naïve foreign travelers would report that obviously the Soviet Union had religious freedom. They ignored the presence of the NKVD or KGB—the Soviet secret police—monitoring sermons or writing down names of attendees. They also ignored the reality that the Church claims the right to provide as many churches and priests as necessary; the right to religious education without restriction;

and for organized, independent parishes and religious communities of men and women to exist.[6]

In its quest to destroy organized belief, Communism eventually became a pseudo-religion. The Old Bolsheviks—many of whom, like Lenin and Stalin, came from Orthodox families—created school curricula to replace religion. The Orthodox icon corners and Catholic "dear Lord's corners" in schoolrooms were replaced with busts of Lenin and Stalin, where the children would place bouquets of flowers. "Our dear Father Comrade Stalin" replaced "Our Father in heaven." The depth of indoctrination was such that, when Stalin died, even the prisoners in his forced labor camps wept.

One difficulty for believers was that Communist theory addressed basic economic and social issues that the Churches and other religions had not resolved in Russia or anywhere else. In short, the Christian ideal and Christian justice did not prevail in the modern world. Christians allowed the rhythm of that world to take a greater place in their lives than the rhythm of the Church year. Communion with one another, of true fraternity under God the Father, was not achieved.

The Bolsheviks thus usurped the Christian ideal of humanity. They created a new society by force, as opposed to Christianity's voluntary organization and preservation of free will. The Communists rejected the value of the human person, approached all aspects of human life with materialist answers, ridiculed capitalism and the bourgeoisie as cruel and unfair, and denied the values of the Christian religion in favor of the new Communist religion. To explain the world, they developed a new catechism based on the beliefs of Karl Marx and later Communists and on the historical destiny of the industrial workers to create paradise on earth. In effect, they promised to achieve the Kingdom of God—but without God.

Many young people in the USSR sincerely became attached to this messianic vision. Inspired by it, youngsters destroyed churches and religious objects, scorned their parents and teachers, and denounced their relatives, while enthusiastically supporting Father Stalin.

The Soviets gradually invented ceremonies to replace religious rites such as baptism, marriage, confirmation, and funerals. Russian Orthodoxy emphasized that a sign of holiness was incorruption; the bodies of the incorrupt saints were great objects of pilgrimage. That is why Lenin's body was repeatedly treated to remain incorrupt and why it was exposed under glass for the veneration of the faithful who came on pilgrimage to Moscow. Lenin's tomb was set up in the shadow of the Kremlin cathedrals and Saint Basil's, which had been built in honor of the Virgin Mary in thanksgiving for her intercession in saving Moscow (all these buildings had been stripped of their religious significance and converted into museums). In processions to the tomb, pilgrims carried banners much like those used in Orthodox and Catholic religious processions. Instead of striving for heaven, the goal of life became building the Revolution and the socialist paradise on earth. Religious language permeated the culture: economic prosperity was a "sin," and Stalin's political opponents were referred to as "heretics" and "Judases." The Communists often referred to their attack on religion as a "struggle for the human soul." Communism became the new gospel that brought true salvation, and Communist martyrs replaced Jesus.

Religion became a "pernicious influence" on the minds of children. In later years in the USSR, one pretext for closing a church was to build a school near it, then order the church closed or destroyed because its bells, domes, or crosses had a bad effect on children. Trends such as wearing neck crosses—popular in the 1980s—were condemned because of the "harmful religious emotions" that would be aroused in those who wore or saw them.[7] To replace the moral code for building the Kingdom of Heaven, atheism had to produce a moral code for the building of Communism. It failed. Even atheists mourned the fact that, where religion declined, alcoholism, theft, sexual immorality, and laziness arose. Religion and Communism remained locked in a battle for the human mind, human freedoms, and the human soul until the demise of the Soviet Union.

The Treatment of Eastern Catholics

Orthodox leaders from the sixteenth to the twentieth century generally feared Catholicism as a danger to both the Orthodox Church and the Russian state. In 1914, both Catholics and Orthodox found the concept of interchurch meetings, prayer, and dialogue absolutely foreign. Soviet literature denied that the Byzantine-Slavic Catholic Church (or Greek Catholic Church) actually fostered Belorussian, Rusyn,[8] Russian, and Ukrainian national identity. It ignored the illegality of the methods used to suppress the Catholic Church, the questionable character of many of the leaders of the pro-Orthodox reunion movements, and the faithful's widespread resistance to the destruction of Church union with Rome.

In addition, some Catholic leaders and faithful exhibited chauvinism by equating Catholicism with national identity and with the Latin Rite or by promoting the superiority of the Latin Rite. Such people mistreated the Eastern Catholic faithful and often their fellow Latin Catholics who were of the "wrong" ethnic group. For example, Eastern Catholics were encouraged and even pressured to be "truly Catholic" by introducing purely Latin Catholic elements into their churches, liturgical and prayer life, and Church discipline, while being denied equal rights in their own Church. Many Eastern Catholics perpetuated these "Latinizations" in their Churches. As another example, Polish Roman Catholic clerics resisted Lithuanian nationalism and the introduction of Lithuanian into catechesis and prayer life into the early twentieth century. They continued to do so in Soviet Belorussia regarding the demands of Belorussian Roman Catholics.

The Latin Catholic mistreatment of Eastern Catholics who were completely loyal Catholics following a different spiritual path fed difficulties between the two Churches, gave impetus to anti-Church union sentiments within the Eastern Churches, provided ammunition for the Soviet enemies of Church unions, and discredited believers who were all facing equally dangerous times. Thus Poles from Poland might visit Soviet Ukraine and be upset that Ukrainian Greek Catholics were worshiping in "their" Latin Rite churches, rather than rejoice at the Ukrainians' fidelity to the Holy See.

Furthermore, many Catholic leaders failed to approach Orthodoxy with a spirit of religious understanding, even though they now faced a common enemy in Bolshevism. Obviously, tensions existed between the two Churches that had once been one. Even in the twentieth century, Catholics dismissed the Orthodox as "dissidents" (Pope Benedict XV was the first pontiff to call the Orthodox by their own name in 1919, and his example was not followed immediately within the Church). In turn, the Orthodox condemned Catholics as "heretics" and "foreigners."

Genuine ecumenism began in the Soviet prisons and forced labor camps of the 1930s and 1940s, when everyone faced the same enemies: atheism, starvation, hard labor, and death. But this warming of relations chilled after 1945, when the Patriarchate's cooperation with the State led to the suppression of the Greek Catholics, denunciations of the Vatican as an enemy of peace, and the denial of religious persecution.

Centuries of Misunderstandings

Thus both the Russian tsars and the Soviet commissars distorted history, with the distortion becoming particularly acute during Stalin's dictatorship. As a result, Soviet Catholics were—and often still are—seen either as hostile foreign minorities or as East Slavs who have made a serious error in allegiance. That so many of the Latin or Roman Catholics are of Polish, Baltic, or German ancestry has only confirmed this perspective for average Russian citizens, given their country's past history of foreign invasions.

The Catholic foundation of the conversion of Saint Vladimir was totally lost in Soviet and Russian consciousness. Indeed, 1988 was celebrated as the millennium of Russian Orthodoxy, even though neither Russia nor the Orthodox Church existed in 988.

As early as 1925, Pope Pius XI condemned totalitarianism in *Quas primas,* a document that put the Holy See at odds with the Fascists in Italy. In establishing the Feast of Christ the King, he pointedly stated that although Christ, "whose Kingdom is not of this world," did not wish His Church to interfere with governments, that same Church, in obedience to Her Lord, was obliged to remind the states of "the spiritual and moral principles to which their labor should conform, and declare repeatedly that they too are bound to promote the Kingdom of God."[9] Such a declaration, which remains a Catholic tenet, meant that confrontation between the Church and the USSR was inevitable.

Centuries of misunderstandings and confused perceptions have resulted in a sad legacy among the peoples of the western borderlands of the USSR and for Soviet Catholics as a whole. The distorted images of the past remain alive and can be used to raise fears or tensions, as was done successfully throughout the Soviet era. Correcting those distortions and overcoming those misunderstandings remain principal challenges of the new era.

In the following chapters, you are invited into Soviet Catholic life, into its sad yet brilliant history, to experience the foundations of its uncertain—but promising—future in the successor states.

CHAPTER 2

The Silver Mosaic
of the Church in Russia

> Whatever disasters or whatever successes were in store for it, the Catholic
> Church in Russia had become too large to be easily wiped out, even
> though its hierarchy should disappear.
>
> —James Zatko, *Descent into Darkness*

Early in the summer of 1914, twenty-two Greek Catholic peasants were mowing hay in the fields near a Greek Catholic chapel dedicated to the Blessed Trinity outside the village of Hrushiv, in Galicia, Austria-Hungary (now located in western Ukraine). The chapel surrounded a water well blessed with healing powers and commemorating several appearances of the Virgin Mary and a revelation of the Trinity at the site. Suddenly, the Mother of God appeared to the farm workers. She announced that there would be a terrible war and that Russia would become godless, bringing suffering for the next eighty years to believers and bringing all humanity to the edge of destruction—unless Russia would turn to Christ.

This message bewildered the peasants. The Russian Empire was officially Eastern Orthodox in religion, and no one in rural Galicia had ever heard of a nation becoming godless. Yet the Virgin's predictions would come true and dramatically change the lives of Catholics in the Russian Empire. Eventually the village of Hrushiv would be affected as well (while under Soviet rule, the village would be the scene of another series of apparitions of the Mother of God in 1987—long after the Greek Catholic Church had been officially extinguished).

Catholicism's Many Facets

As with just about everything related to the Russian Empire or the Soviet Union, it is not possible to make generalizations about its large Catholic population. In 1913, the empire's Catholics, who numbered some 5 million excluding Russian Poland, presented a fascinating mosaic. Denounced as "the Polish religion" and the "faith of the Polish lords," Catholicism encompassed a wide range of nationalities and all the social classes: Polish peasants whose families worshiped in Roman Catholic churches dating back to the 1300s; the descendants of German colonist-farmers; Italian and French immigrants in cosmopolitan Odessa; the tiny movement of Russian converts that appeared in the two capitals; Armenian villagers in the Caucasus; and workers and domestics in the urban slums. Their churches could stand in a prominent part of Siberian towns, amid the crowded tenements of factory workers, in the heart of prosperous villages, or as lonely beacons in the vast grasslands of the Russian steppe.

The structures of normal Catholic life were often lacking. The imperial government dissolved dioceses at will, moving borders and imposing restrictions. It enacted laws that could cripple religious congregations or instantly close parish churches. Both papal letters and internal diocesan letters were subject to censorship, further reminding Catholics that the tsar's government did not favor them. Many parishes had no connection with one another through the deanery system, relying instead on communication with a distant office for any link with the greater Church.

Catholic Roots in the Empire

The Russian Orthodox Patriarchate generally characterizes Catholicism as a "foreign religion" with no place in Russia or its "near abroad" where Slavs form a majority. Certainly, Catholic ethnic Russians have been few since the two Churches drifted apart in the eleventh century. There is, however, a long history of Catholics among the national minorities under Russian rule, of Catholic-Orthodox contacts, and of hopes for restoring unity between Rome and Moscow.

Politics, tragic military episodes, and rival ethnocentrisms have frustrated these hopes. Metropolitan Nicephorus I (1103–1121) considered the two Churches to be in schism (and even considered the Latin Catholics heretical, a view that still prevails in some Russian Orthodox circles). Saint Hyacinth brought the Dominicans to Kiev in the early thirteenth century, but their mission was short-lived. Although many Catholic Germans, Poles, Bohemians, and Hungarians needed their services, the Dominicans' attempts to convert the local Rus' population to the Latin Catholic Church and to Latinize church services led to their expulsion in 1233.[1] Latin Catholicism would nevertheless be established in the empire's Ukrainian lands, with Franciscan (and later Dominican) parishes and monasteries serving Polish and other Latin Catholic settlers. The descendants of these medieval colonists now live in modern-day Ukraine.

Catholicism eventually took hold in the pagan Grand Duchy of Lithuania (modern Ukraine, Belarus, and Lithuania), where rival Orthodox and Latin missionaries worked. The country became officially Catholic when Poland and the Grand Duchy were united through marriage in 1386. Lithuania eventually became a fervently Catholic country, but its distinction as a Catholic holdout in Europe resulted in much suffering under both tsarist and Communist rule. In 1323, Kiev became the seat of a Latin Catholic bishop. For a time, the Benedictines undertook a Slavonic-language Latin mission to the Ukrainians.[2] The members of the two Churches continued to live separately, although Rome often expressed hope that union could be restored. Metropolitan Isidore of Kiev's Orthodox Church declared himself in favor of union at the Council of Ferrara-Florence in 1439. At this council, union was restored between Rome and the Churches of Constantinople and Kiev and portions of the Syrian Jacobite and Armenian Churches (though hopes were high, the affected Eastern Christian populations never fully accepted the unions. Rome's union with Constantinople ended with the latter city's fall to the Turks in 1453). Metropolitan Isidore's announcement was not well received at home: on his return in 1441, he was imprisoned and declared a heretic. Any talk of union ceased among the Rus' Orthodox in Poland-Lithuania and Muscovy.

Shortly thereafter, conditions for Latin Catholics under Muscovite/Russian rule deteriorated. They were not permitted to build churches and were denied citizenship. With the conquest of Novgorod in 1475, they came under direct Russian rule. The tsar closed the Novgorod parish in 1494; there would not be another for more than 200 years. Ivan the Terrible (ruled 1533–1584) expanded Russia's borders and exiled the first Catholics (Baltic Germans and Estonians) to Siberia. Hoping to achieve a Church union with Ivan, the Jesuit missionary Antonio Possevino held a disputation—a public religious debate—with the tsar in 1582, but made no headway.

In 1596, the Rus' bishops in Poland-Lithuania declared union with Rome at a synod in Brest-Litovsk, giving birth to what became known as the "Greek Catholic Church," sometimes referred to as the "Uniate Church." (The Orthodox invented the name "Unia" to imply that those who accepted union with Rome ultimately became Latin Catholics; "Uniate" was used as a derogatory and derisive name throughout tsarist and Soviet Communist history.) At its height, the Greek Catholic Church embraced the ancient Metropolia of Kiev, from southern Ukraine to Lithuania, although a strong Orthodox minority remained outside of Galicia. At the same time, many Latin Catholics in the Polish Kingdom never accepted the Greek Catholics as being "fully" Catholic, a situation that endures to this day.

Catholic Poland and Protestant Sweden took advantage of Muscovy's lack of a government during the Time of Troubles (1604–1613) to intervene in its affairs. The "False Dmitri," allegedly a prince of the old dynasty whose claims were supported by Poland, converted to Roman Catholicism in 1604. That act, along with the behavior of Polish occupiers during that period, hardened Russian hearts against Rome and its supposed intrigues.

A Succession of Persecutions

When Russia opened its "window to the West" under Peter the Great by importing foreign technology and trade goods and by expanding its borders, Catholicism was allowed to reenter the country, albeit under restrictions. Catholic diplomats and foreign specialists still had great difficulty practicing their religion. They were granted imperial tolerance long after the Protestants, with a chaplain settling at the Austrian Embassy in Moscow in 1684. Orthodox fears of Catholic proselytizing led to the expulsion of the Jesuits five years later.

In 1691, Saints Peter and Paul was established as the first Catholic parish in Moscow; in 1705, permission was granted to build a church in Saint Petersburg. But this did not mean the Catholics faced a peaceful future. Tsar Peter himself tore open a monastery church's tabernacle in Polotsk and dumped the Sacred Host onto the floor, then murdered the Basilian Greek Catholic monk Theophane when he tried to retrieve it. Enraged that the relics of Blessed Josaphat had been successfully evacuated from the church, Peter ordered the destruction of icons of the saint, the Greek Catholic Bishop of Polotsk and a martyr for the cause of union. The Basilian monasteries of Polotsk were looted; three monks were brutally murdered and their bodies burned to prevent their relics from being venerated.[3] Having been readmitted to Moscow in 1684 and to Saint Petersburg in 1691, the Jesuits were expelled again in 1719. Laws on mixed marriages were strictly enforced in favor of the Orthodox, and monstrous parodies of papal conclaves were held in 1722 and 1725 at the imperial court for Peter's amusement.

Empress Anna (ruled 1730–1740) persecuted Catholics, forbidding missionary work among Orthodox. Orthodox converts to Catholicism were exiled or imprisoned and deprived of all their property. The Capuchins were expelled in 1747 from Astrakhan because of their successful work for Church union among the Armenians. Catherine the Great (ruled 1762–1796) restricted the Catholic parishes to only nine for the entire country and again forbade missionary work, although she admitted the Capuchins and Reformed Franciscans into the country to care for believers.

The gradual annexations of eastern and central Poland-Lithuania brought more Catholics under Russian rule, as did the policy of immigration promoted by Catherine in the German states, starting in 1763. Catherine persecuted the Greek Catholic Church of Kiev by closing monasteries, naming Orthodox pastors, and eventually ordering 9,000 parishes and more than 8 million faithful into Russian Orthodoxy. The Metropolia of Kiev was suppressed in 1795, along with the eparchies in Pinsk, Brest, and Lutsk. Only the archeparchy of Polotsk survived, but its archbishop was jailed.

A disloyal Catholic, Stanislaus Siestrzencewicz, cooperated with the empress in persecuting the Greek Catholics, crippling the autonomy of the orders, and isolating Catholics from Rome. He became the first bishop of Mogilev, later archbishop, and served as an independent Latin Catholic metropolitan in Russia. At the same time, in an act meant to contradict the Western powers, Catherine gave refuge to the Jesuits being persecuted by their own Church. She also ordered that Catholic churches be built of stone, an important privilege in a country of wooden buildings that burned easily.

Under Catherine's son, Paul I (ruled 1796–1801), who hated his mother and who worked to counteract much of her reign, Catholicism regained some ground. The Latin Catholic dioceses of Lutsk, Vilna, Kamenets, Minsk, and Samogitia were established, exiles came home from Siberia, the Jesuits continued to prosper, and the Roman Catholic population rose to more than 1.6 million. The Greek Catholics restored the eparchies of Brest and Lutsk and retained Polotsk.

With Alexander I (ruled 1801–1826), a curious mix of liberalism and persecution developed. The Latin Catholic dioceses achieved a basic structure that would survive until 1917. Nearly 400 monasteries and convents continued to function. In 1817, the Greek Catholics installed a new metropolitan archbishop, and their membership rose to more than 1.4 million. But conditions worsened. Metropolitan Siestrzencewicz created a type of a Catholic Holy Synod under the title "Catholic Ecclesiastical College" to run the Russian Church and to give the tsar greater influence in the Church's affairs, from communication with the Vatican to monastic elections and parish life. He also tried to force the Greek Catholic Church into the Latin Catholic Church, thus alienating many.

The Jesuits were expelled once again from the capital in 1815 and finally from Belorussia in 1820. Young Catholics were banned from studying abroad. Yet at the same time, a Catholic chapel was built near the imperial residence in Tsarskoe Selo; it endured until after the Bolshevik Revolution.

The Renewal of Persecution

It was under Nicholas I (ruled 1825–1855) that Catholicism experienced its greatest difficulties before the Bolsheviks. Nicholas promoted the policy of "one Tsar, one Church, and one Nation," all of which meant trouble for the Catholics.

Catholicism of both rites was associated with Polish nationalism. After each of the Polish uprisings against the tsar and Russia in general, Catholic monasteries, convents, and churches had invariably been closed. For example, the persecution that followed the Uprising of 1830 saw 202 religious houses closed on Russian territory. Repeated Russification drives resulted in the abolition of different religious orders in the provinces. The Catholic schools based at the monasteries became secular Russian schools. The teaching of the Polish language was banned in 1836 in Vitebsk and Mogilev provinces, and by 1843, throughout Belorussia. In 1840, the names of "Belorussia" (White Russia) and "Lithuania" were taken off the maps and replaced by "Northwestern Russia."[4]

Nicholas I also began suppression of the Greek Catholic Church. A traitorous Greek Catholic priest, Josef Siemaszko, was promoted to create a fifth column of pro-Orthodox clergy and sentiments by building both on tsarist support and on the disaffection created by Siestrzencewicz's interference. Greek Catholic monks and laity had participated in the Uprising of 1830, which further aggravated the tsar, who gave the great Catholic shrine at Pochaev to the Orthodox in 1831. Even so, Catholics continued to pray to Our Lady of Pochaev, where the Virgin Mary had appeared during the thirteenth century Mongol invasions and left her footprint in stone.

On the death of Greek Catholic Metropolitan Bulhak, the tsar saw his opportunity. In June of 1839, Nicholas convened the fake Synod in Polotsk, where the Church (except for one eparchy in Russian Poland) was declared reunited with its supposed Mother Church (never mind that the Greek Catholic Church traced its origins to Kiev and Constantinople, not to Moscow). Much of the laity and the bulk of the clergy bitterly resented this imposed union. (History would repeat itself in 1947–1949, when Stalin followed the same policies.)

The Concordat of 1847 was never fulfilled. Twenty more convents were closed in 1850; sermons were censored, the restoration of old churches and the construction of new ones banned, and the right to refute anti-Catholic propaganda revoked. When the bishops appealed for relaxation of the laws in 1861, Alexander II (ruled 1855–1881) met their efforts with accusations of treachery, and a severe persecution engulfed Russian Poland.

In the Uprising of 1863, the violent acts suffered by Catholic Poles contributed to the rebellion. Both priests who supported the Uprising and those who did not were arrested; several were executed, and others deported. The archbishops of Warsaw and Vilna were imprisoned. Again, attempts were made to create a new national Catholic Church under a college, an imperial government institute. Polish was banned from all official locations, and fines levied on the Catholics were used to build Orthodox churches and import Orthodox priests.[5]

Alexander III (ruled 1881–1894) opened negotiations for a new concordat and a treaty was signed in 1882. Once again, however, new laws nullified the concordat with Rome and oppression continued in each diocese. In 1875, the last Greek Catholic stronghold, the eparchy of Chelm, was destroyed and ordered united to the Orthodox. The imperial government tried to impose Russian as the language of worship in Catholic churches and, in the 1880s, even took over the admission of seminarians and novices for the dioceses and remaining monasteries (yet another practice later imitated by the Communists).

The End of the Tsarist Era

In 1897, Nicholas II (ruled 1894–1917) finally allowed the archbishop of Mogilev to fill Church offices that had long been vacant. Only with the Revolution of 1905 did the tsar grant some freedom to Russia's Catholics, though without restoring the old Greek Catholic Church. A Catholic press was established, religious revivals took place, and 500,000 people joined the Church. A new Greek Catholic Church, following the Russian ritual, also took shape.

By 1907, restrictions were back in place against the former Greek Catholics. The government closed church schools, required that children of mixed marriages be baptized and raised Orthodox, restricted the press, and dissolved social activist organizations. Russification resumed.

In 1911, the archbishop of Mogilev was deposed and the bishop of Vilna forced to resign and move to the interior. The two Russian Greek Catholic chapels were forcibly closed, and a Polish Jesuit who had converted more than 1,000 Russians was exiled from Moscow.

According to the concordat with the Holy See, the Russian Empire should have had twenty-two auxiliary bishops. It had four. The few dioceses that survived often went years without leadership. Russian Poland, a solid bastion of Polish Roman Catholic identity, had seven dioceses and 8 million faithful. Russia and its borderlands had five very different dioceses, of widely varying sizes, with more than 5 million believers in 1911. In Russia, impediments to Catholic life varied. For example, in the united dioceses of Lutsk, Zhitomir, and Kamenets, only native-born Russian subjects could be ordained and serve as priests; such restrictions did not exist elsewhere.[6]

Other impediments were universal; permissions were needed for the most basic elements of Catholic life. Civil law or bureaucratic practices interfered with the sacraments of marriage, baptism, extreme unction, the raising of children in mixed marriages, preaching, holding "missions" in parishes, and what language was to be used outside of the celebration of Mass. There was even a "Russian Ritual," composed by the government and imposed by the State on parishes.

In general, religious orders were banned, priestly ministry was subject to police impediments, and the work of the Church was "trammeled by a thousand obstacles in the exercise of its apostolic ministry."[7] Thus Bishop Cieplak needed government authorization in 1909 to undertake his historic tour of the empire,[8] and Bishop Denisowicz's confirmation tour of Belorussia in the same year was cut short because the crowds were deemed too large and enthusiastic.[9] In 1913, the Russian Greek Catholic parish in Saint Petersburg was forcibly closed down.[10]

Few nuns could be found outside of the Polish provinces, and surviving orders of both men and women faced extinction because of the ban on new members. Only foreign-based orders, such as the French Assumptionists, the Dominicans and Franciscans (men), and the French Sisters of Saint Joseph of Chambery had the right to have new members. A large number of French religious came into Russia following the secularization laws in France in 1902. Orders from Russian Poland also had some members in the Empire beyond Poland, and there were a handful of religious from Austria-Hungary.

Parishes throughout the empire were usually large in area and membership and had too few priests. A great many imperial Catholics had no access to daily or Sunday Mass; the people relied on lay leadership for the Faith to endure.

Catholic and Polish?

Although rooted in traditional rural strongholds of the Baltic and in old German and Polish farming settlements, the Church was also part of Russia's industrial expansion. Many Catholics labored in urban factories and sweatshops, part of the urban masses Bolshevism was aiming to convert. Large numbers of Catholics took part in the opening up of Siberia, both in agricultural colonies and in the rapidly growing settlements that sprang up along the rail lines.

One issue that recurs throughout the history of Soviet Catholicism is that of identifying Catholics as Poles and of the anger felt by some nationalities regarding real and imagined Polonization by Polish Roman Catholic priests. Catholicism was specifically seen as the Polish Faith. To this day, in ordinary Russian usage, a Roman Catholic church is never called by the Russian word for church, *"tserkov',"* but rather is known as a *"kostel"* (a Polish church).

Defining a Pole was difficult. Because Polish culture appealed to the local upper classes of Belorussia, Lithuania, and Ukraine in the time of the Polish-Lithuanian Commonwealth, large numbers became Polonized despite their non-Polish names. On the other hand, many people who identify themselves as "non-Polish" today have Polish surnames, showing that the process of acculturation and assimilation worked both ways. Russifying policies and trends both "converted" Poles into Russians and dispersed ethnic Poles as far away as the shores of the Pacific Ocean, where they retained their identity even when the Polish language died out. Finally, neither imperial, Polish Republic nor Soviet censuses are accurate indicators of nationality; they tend to be biased toward particular opinions.

What is certain is that, in the early 1900s, local nationalism was on the rise in Russia's western provinces and feared by the Russian state. Polish nationalism was also ascendant and persecuted. To this day, many Catholic priests and believers in the western reaches of the former Soviet Union remain mired in the debates and behaviors of the past.

The Church in Russia: 1914

Russian Catholicism before World War I is often seen as restricted to national minorities, to the fringes of society, almost to a ghetto-like existence. True, the Church was restricted, and in some areas nearly crippled. Eastern Catholicism had been banned except for the Armenian Rite, and countless barriers to Catholic growth enshrined in the legal code. Yet Russian Catholicism was undergoing dramatic growth and facing many internal challenges and changes. The old Latin Catholic Church was expanding into the ethnic Russian population, and nationalism was affecting the traditionally Catholic minorities. Eastern Catholicism was also coming into its own in the universal Church, as heralded by the Byzantine Divine Liturgy celebrated in Saint Peter's Basilica in 1908 in the presence of Pope Pius X. That liturgy became the hallmark of the movement to reject Latinization of the Eastern Catholics, who were reemerging in the Russian Empire with both problems and promise.[11] For example, although the State did not recognize the Eastern Catholics, many of them remained loyal to the union. Russia's upper classes were attracted to both forms of Catholicism, and some Orthodox clergy were becoming more favorable to the idea of union with Rome.

From the 1890s through 1914, the Russian Empire experienced its "Silver Age"—an "extraordinary flowering" in art, literature (especially poetry), architecture, economics, theology, and philosophy. A growing interest in religion and religious thought, a reaction to the atheism and religious indifference of the alienated nobility,[12] also characterized the period, which has been overshadowed by the Revolutions of 1905 and 1917. Society was in a creative ferment.

In religion, Russian Orthodoxy had begun to awaken from its slumber of empty ritual and acceptance of state control. Thanks to careful restoration and new study, believers rediscovered the power of the sacred icons. In their fervent search for holiness, they explored the rich Orthodox tradition for new answers. The 1905–1906 *sobor* (the Eastern Orthodox term for a church council) for Church renewal—cruelly frustrated by secular politics—symbolized this revival. The same Orthodox *sobor* faced an uncomfortable reality; namely that non-Orthodox religious propaganda was gaining ground in the empire. Islam had reemerged in areas thought firmly Orthodox, such as around Kazan'. Baptists and Stundists (followers of a Protestant German offshoot of Lutheranism), once restricted to the ethnic Germans, were attracting Russian and Ukrainian converts, especially in areas where the Orthodox Church's presence was weak for lack of priests or education. Old Belief, or Old Ritual, was enjoying a revival; this movement dated back to the rejection of the Nikonian Reform of the Russian Church's rituals in the seventeenth century. Sectarian movements that had broken away from Old Belief and Orthodoxy, some marked by bizarre rituals such as bathing in animal blood, were also becoming more common.[13]

Some Russians, both seekers and practicing Orthodox, converted to the Catholic Church. Catholics themselves, drawn ever more strongly to inner renewal, undertook missionary efforts, an activity severely limited by the government. Both Latin Catholics and Greek Catholics proselytized among the Orthodox at all levels. The spiritual vacuum of the state Church, rigid state controls of that Church, and powerful memories of Church union in the western provinces helped their work. Between 1869 and 1872, for example, the government closed many small and poor Russian Orthodox parishes that could not pay their own way; some remained closed until 1905. At the *sobor*, it was pointed that the closings buttressed Catholic (and Stundist-Baptist) claims of Orthodoxy's failures.[14] The archpriest of the Orthodox cathedral in Lida—a town that still has a strong Catholic presence—warned that allowing Latin Catholics to succeed would inevitably bring people under Latin and Polish influence because the Greek Catholics were still banned.[15]

Catholic Spirituality in 1914

Silver Age Catholicism reflected themes common in the pre-Vatican II Church familiar to older Catholics of the Western world, as well as unique practices and devotions.

For the average Catholic in late imperial Russia, prayer focused heavily on devotion to Christ, particularly His Sacred Heart and the Passion and Death, and to the Blessed Virgin Mary, especially in the Rosary. This focus was well demonstrated at home, where families would meet for prayers in the vernacular. Most Catholics had decorated prayer corners; the Germans had the "Dear Lord God's Corner" and Ukrainians and Belorussians had "the beautiful corner," where holy pictures, candles, prayer books, and sacramentals were displayed. All Catholics used crucifixes, holy pictures of Christ and the saints, the Rosary, novenas, and statues to help them focus their prayers. The Rosary, with the lives of Jesus and Mary as the source of meditation and comfort, became a mainstay of Catholic life in the years when there were no churches. Even in the 1990s, many Catholics still confessed not saying the Rosary as a mortal sin.

The different ethnic groups enriched the Church year with a broad variety of customs. Thus, although all believers fasted on Christmas Eve, there were various menus to be followed for the holy supper. Different populations cherished particular titles of Mary and favored certain saints, such as Our Lady of Czestochowa and Saint Casimir for Poles, Our Lady of the Gate of the Dawn for Lithuanians, and Saint Francis for Germans. Vernacular religious songs of the seasons taught the basics of the Faith. Choirs were a major teaching tool, especially in regions where preaching was curtailed by police edict or confined to a language other than that spoken by most of the parishioners. Music would survive the October Revolution and provide a way to pass on the Faith when catechesis became illegal.

In the cities and large towns, parish life was a rich mix of regularly scheduled masses, popular devotions, and church leagues and sodalities (organizations of laypeople dedicated to specific saints, devotions, or intentions). Despite anti-Catholic persecution and rules, public processions of the faithful were allowed, and Corpus Christi was publicly celebrated, at least on church property, until the October Revolution. Far more impressive pageants of faith took place in the pilgrimages of the Baltic, Volga, and Black Sea provinces.

Village Catholics experienced their faith as occasional celebration of the Mass, strict fast days and fasting seasons, administration of the sacraments of baptism, confession at Easter, and anointing for the severely ill and pregnant (childbirth was difficult and risky). Seasonal rituals, such as blessing crops and animals, blessing willows and palms during Holy Week, and blessing homes helped reinforce teachings. Frequent communion, recommended by Pope Pius X in 1910, was an unknown innovation and, for many people without priests or parishes, simply an impossibility. Most Catholics never received Confirmation: government opposition to the bishops rendered that sacrament inaccessible.

Religious education was generally well organized in the two capitals and major cities. German villages provided basic religious instruction in their schools, as did the Poles. These lay teachers, though they had no specialized Catholic training, were marked for persecution under the Bolsheviks. The laws denied any Catholic education for the children of Catholic-Orthodox marriages.

Journeys of Faith

Pilgrimages were very important to Baltic Catholics. The unique pilgrimages of the region, known as *"atlaidai,"* occurred in the territory inhabited by Lithuanians and in the adjacent areas inhabited by Belorussians, Latgalians, Latvians, and Poles. They were occasions for the granting of plenary and partial indulgences for the remission of temporal punishment due to sins *(atlaidai* translates directly to "indulgences"). The pilgrimages were also times

1. to celebrate the Catholic faith; in addition to the celebration of Solemn High Mass, recitation of the Rosary, celebration of the canonical Hours, and special sermons preached by notable guest priests, complicated processions of portable altars honored the Sacred Heart, the Virgin Mary, and particular saints; choral vespers and Benediction of the Blessed Sacrament followed all;

2. to celebrate folk culture; the pilgrimages featured the singing of medieval music, sales of ethnic and religious art, and the presence of the beggars'

class with its own subculture of preserving the oral heritage of the people with songs and stories; and

3. to renew old acquaintances and make new ones as believers arrived from all over the Baltic, Polish, and Belorussian countryside.[16]

Under oppressive tsarist rule, these *atlaidai* served as continual sources of spiritual renewal, national encouragement, and emotional release. (They would do so again under Soviet rule.)

The Kalvarija pilgrimage, which lasted from July 1 to 12, typified the traditional *atlaidai*. As the believers walked and reflected on the sufferings of Jesus, they had an opportunity to enter into the mystery of His Passion and death. Crowds would lie prostrate on the ground, their arms extended, or kneel with arms upraised, in front of particular chapels. A sacred spring at the site provided holy water for the faithful to take home.[17]

In the southern portion of the empire, public processions also provided a focal point for Catholic renewal. In the Volga region, processions of petitioners were held on Sundays or certain holy days with the Way of the Cross (Stations of the Cross) or focusing on special chapels. Where there were no chapels, crosses were raised in the fields. Either cross or chapel would serve as the site of Masses of petition. In the Black Sea region, cemetery chapels took the place of field crosses.

Although the south did not have large shrines such as those in the Baltic, local pilgrimages took place there as well. The German colonists had particular devotions to Mary, Saint Joseph, Saint Mark, Saint Anthony of Padua, and the Holy Cross. Pilgrims always visited churches with those titles on the patron feast days. For example, several thousand people and all the priests would observe the Finding of the Cross on May 3 in Kamenka deanery, on the upper Volga.

The church at Köhler contained a small chapel dedicated to the Cross. According to a popular legend, the crucifix in the chapel had been found by a farmer while plowing. Because it was of the size usually found in Catholic homes, he took the crucifix home and hung it on the wall. The crucifix vanished, only to be found on the altar of the church. After this happened several times, the villagers finally built a separate chapel for venerating the cross. The pilgrimage to this chapel was so popular that special steamships were chartered to carry people up the Volga, and confessions would be heard throughout the night.

Many people also came to pray in Franzfeld, in the Black Sea region, where a renowned statue of the Mother of God stood in a chapel built in

1819. Confraternities of the Sacred Heart, Immaculate Conception, and the Third Order of Saint Francis could be found in all the villages. These pious evangelizing groups brought the fallen-away back to the Church and assisted the poor and destitute.

Great numbers of believers would converge in German villages to celebrate the anniversary of the consecration of a church *(Kirchweihfest)*. This event was always observed with Vespers, recitation of the Rosary, High Mass, Benediction, and solemn processions accompanied by the ringing of the church bells. Special sermons were given based on Luke 19:1–10, with particular emphasis on the Real Presence in the Blessed Sacrament and the effect that this should have on the faithful. These anniversaries provided opportunities for reconciling with enemies, for renewing family ties, and for feasting.[18] In the 1920s and early 1930s, such practices would offer strength to those who remained faithful to the Church.

CHAPTER 3

The Catholic Communities
of Imperial Russia, Part One

In 1914, the Roman Catholic Church of the Russian Empire was operating with the remnants of the structure of the Latin Catholic Church that had survived various tsarist suppressions. There were no eparchies (dioceses) left of the Greek Catholic Church.

The majority of imperial Catholic subjects came under the ecclesiastical province of Warsaw, which embraced the heart of the old Polish-Lithuanian Commonwealth with seven dioceses, where the Church was persecuted but strong, forming the majority religion of the majority (Polish) nationality. This territory became the Republic of Poland after World War I, with additions from the German and Austro-Hungarian Empires and from some of the western provinces of the Russian Empire. The ecclesiastical province of Mogilev covered the rest of the empire and was divided into a few dioceses, which struggled to serve the five million faithful under strict limitations. Most of this province came under Soviet rule in 1918—1920 or after 1939, and the rest of it, by 1945.

The Samogitia Diocese and the Baltic Region

The Baltic region of the archdiocese of Mogilev consisted of Samogitia diocese, which covered Kovno and Courland provinces, with its seat at Kovno (Kaunas); the provinces of Estonia, Livonia, and (part of) Vitebsk; and the Grand Duchy of Finland. The last named became the republic of Finland (independent in 1918; most of whose territory escaped Communist control); the other regions became the republics of Estonia, Latvia, and Lithuania (the Baltic States, independent until World War II).

Lutheranism was the principal faith of the Finns as well as of the Estonians, most of the Latvians, and the German nobility who dominated them.[1] Catholicism was the faith of only a tiny minority in Estonia and the Grand

Duchy of Finland; adult Estonian or Finnish Catholics were usually converts to the Faith. The farther south one went in the Baltic region, however, the larger the Church's following became, until it grew to a majority. As in 1991, this region accounted for a significant portion of Roman Catholics under Muscovite rule. Most of the faithful were Lithuanians, Poles, Latvians, Latgalians, and, in the urban centers, immigrants of other nationalities. In Samogitia diocese counted 1.25 million faithful in the territory that became independent Lithuania and the southern part of Latvia, with 225 parishes that included 115 filial churches.[2]

The Northern Baltic

Finland is known as the "most Lutheran country in Europe." It attained that status as a result of the Swedish imposition of the Reformation in the 1520s. A number of Finnish Catholics were martyred for the Faith, and the Dominican and Franciscan monks and the Bridgettine nuns were expelled. Extinct in Finland by the 1590s, Catholicism was legally banned there in 1595.[3] The Swedish Empire expanded eastward into Karelia, a predominantly Orthodox region, in 1617, but eventually gave way to the Russian Empire, with all of Finland coming under Russian rule in 1809. There would be no Finnish Catholic priests again until 1903, when one was ordained in Paris.[4]

The Catholic Faith returned to Finnish territory by way of Polish and Lithuanian Dominican missionaries, who reestablished the presence of their order in 1799 at the important garrison city of Viborg, in order to minister to Polish soldiers in the Russian army there. These monks were not allowed to receive novices, and so the order died out a second time; secular clergy from Saint Petersburg replaced them. The parish of Saint Henrik, patron of Finland, was founded in the capital, Helsingfors (Helsinki), in 1860, through the auspices of a Polish military chaplain, Father Gorbacki. The church was consecrated in 1904 by a bishop of the archdiocese of Mogilev. There was another tiny parish at Abo (Turku). In eastern Karelia and Saint Petersburg, a future beata of the Catholic Church, Blessed Julia Urszula Ledochowska, and her Grey Ursuline nuns were working in a Catholic boarding school they had established there, an important venture for the scattered believers.[5]

Across from Finland lay the land of Estonia, divided between the two provinces of Estonia and Livonia. In 1911, the province of Estonia's population was predominantly Lutheran (96 percent) with an Eastern Orthodox minority. About 20 percent of the population in Estonian-populated areas in the two northern provinces was Eastern Orthodox (both Russian and Estonian).

Even so, there were Catholic churches and chapels in Revel (Tallinn), Dorpat (Tartu; the university center), Walk (Valga), on the southern edge of Estonia, and elsewhere. The Revel parish, Saints Peter and Paul (Saint Ann), still stands inside the ruins of the former Dominican cloister.[6]

Adjacent to Estonia lay the territory of the Latvians, in Livonia, Courland, and Vitebsk provinces. Two separate deaneries based at Dünaburg (Daugavapils) counted 142,000 faithful in the villages of Livonia and Vitebsk provinces; a third deanery connected the urban parishes of Riga (three parishes) and the Estonian towns with another 42,000 faithful.[7] In Livonia, Catholics formed less than 3 percent of the population in 1906.[8] The bulk of these deaneries became independent Latvia and Estonia, with the eastern part of Vitebsk province coming under Soviet rule in 1919.

The Southern Baltic

Samogitia, the heartland of Lithuania and Lithuanian national identity, was a region in turmoil. The area was (and is) heavily Catholic: in 1911, nearly 77 percent of the people were Roman Catholic in Kovno province, and there was a small but staunch Catholic population in Courland, home to Latvians, Latgalians, and Poles.[9] Although Courland had become Lutheran in the Reformation, Samogitia experienced a Catholic revival in the 1600s, partly because of the region's proximity to Polish territory, and thus to priests and Polish state favoritism toward Catholics; partly because of the Church's tolerance of pagan-based traditions in the countryside; and also because of the impressive way it celebrated its services there. These last two factors combined to make Catholicism more attractive than the austere Lutheran Church to the Latvian peasants, and it remained strong in the south and east.[10]

As a rule, Poles in western Russia were Roman Catholics. The same was true of the Lithuanians, with the notable exceptions of the Memel Lithuanians in German East Prussia, who were Lutheran, and several strong pockets of Calvinists in the interior from the Reformation days. The provinces and diocese were both being torn by nationalist and religious tensions. These were fed by the imperial government's mandating (1864–1904) that all publications in Lithuanian be in Cyrillic script (which Lithuanians saw as a blatant attempt at Russification), its closing of churches and suppression of the religious orders, its attempts to introduce a Russian-language ritual into services, and its arbitrary decisions on which churches should remain open, as well as by regional concern over the continued use of the Polish language in religious life.

The imperial ban on publishing in Latin script led Bishop Valancius (d.

1875) to engage the Church in creating an underground literature and smuggling books from abroad. The diocese actually founded Lithuanian printing houses in the adjacent German province of East Prussia, and priests, lay idealists, and professional smugglers engaged in steady trafficking as "book carriers." This nurtured the growing Lithuanian nationalist movement. Although the Samogitian hierarchy withdrew its support for the national movement in 1875, the local clergy did not.[11]

Suppression of the religious orders crippled pastoral work in the provinces. To the growing anger of believers, popular shrines were closed down, monasteries abandoned, and cloisters left to a few aging monks and nuns. After a two-year struggle, the governor of Kovno (Kaunas) province ordered the Benedictine monastery and church at Kraziai shut down. When, however, he came to close it in person, his way was barred by a defiant crowd carrying a portrait of the emperor. In the ensuing Kraziai Massacre of 1893, Cossacks killed Lithuanian Catholics and swept through the town, raping, burning, looting, and flogging. The massacre inflamed both Lithuanian and foreign public opinion against the Romanovs.

Tension Between Catholic Nationalities

Rising Lithuanian national awareness led parishioners and younger priests to resist both the imperial government's efforts at Russification and the continued Polonization of their Church by so many of their older pastors. Russification had introduced the Russian language into popular devotions and sermons and the "Russian Ritual" into Catholic parishes. It had banned the use of minority languages in schools and government. It had even gone so far as to force cab drivers to wear Russian-style coats and drive teams of horses yoked in the Russian manner. Polonization, for its part, was the continued effort by the Polish clergy to use Polish in sermons and services and to promote specifically Polish devotions and saints; and by Polish clergy and nobility alike to encourage or force parishioners and peasants to see themselves as Poles and to reject any other ethnic identity. It was motivated by fear of Russian ethnic and religious absorption and by Polish chauvinism which automatically held Polish culture to be superior to that of the Balts and non-Polish Slavs.

Polonization in Lithuanian territory was especially resented because Poles were a distinct minority (only 9 percent in Kovno province in 1910), yet they still had a strong influence on Church life.[12] The Lithuanian-Polish rivalry was intense, though not public, in the seminaries, rectories, and chanceries. In the parishes, however, it was very public: the issue of using Polish or Lithuanian for prayers and sermons degenerated into actual fights, which gave the government the opportunity to order more church closings.[13] Dividing the Catholic minority along national lines would be favored by the Soviets, as would Russification.

Some churches and monastic complexes were closed outright, remaining silent and empty monuments to tsarist oppression. Others were given over to the Orthodox for use. Both practices only increased Catholic anger (and would be followed in the Soviet era, with similar consequences). Thus the Camaldolese monastery and church at Kovno (Kaunas), described as the "center of the Catholic life of Kaunas and the surrounding area" was converted to use as a monastery of the Russian Orthodox diocese of Kovno. Only the church's Pozhaiskaya Icon of the Mother of God—venerated by the Catholics, Orthodox, and Old Believers—remained in Catholic hands, being transferred to their cathedral.[14]

Erection of new Catholic churches was impeded at every step (again, a practice that would be imitated by the Soviets). At coastal Libau, Canon Edward von der Ropp, future archbishop of Mogilev, had to pay for the construction of the new church out of his own pocket.[15]

Shrines of Consolation:
The Catholic Landscape in the Baltic

The Catholic regions of the Baltic were permeated with symbols of the Faith; from roadside shrines of the Crucifixion, the Suffering Christ, and the Madonna or simple shrines at crossroads and in peasant yards, to small chapels crowning hillsides, to elaborate basilicas. Travelers were continually presented with reminders of the basic dogmas of Catholicism and the consolations of the Faith for suffering people.

In the territory of Samogitia, which had held the title "Land of Mary" before the Reformation, there were still a number of Catholic Marian shrines. Among these were the church at Skaistkalne (1658); the church at Sarkani (1897), which had a miraculous image; and the Dominican church at Pasiene, which held a copy of the miraculous icon from Saint Mary Major's in Rome and which was attributed as the source of many graces under the title of Our Lady of the Rosary. At Izvalta, a church dating to 1625 (and rebuilt in the nineteenth century) held another miraculous image brought by the Jesuits in the late 1600s.[16] All of these shrines were sites of pilgrimage.

At the premier Latvian pilgrimage shrine, Our Lady of Aglona, founded as a Dominican chapel in 1699, the icon was a faithful reproduction of Our

Lady of Troki from Lithuania and was credited with many miracles. The pilgrimages to Aglona were well attended, and the shrine, rebuilt as a splendid center in 1768, was visited by tens of thousands of faithful.[17] (Aglona would provide great solace under the Soviet occupations during and after World War II, and remains a center of Latvian Catholic life to this day.)

In the Lithuanian territory of Samogitia, the principal shrines were Kalvarija (the "Samogitian Calvary"), nineteen chapels built in 1637–1639 at Z'emaac'iu on hilly terrain and arrayed to approximate the distances between the Stations of the Cross; the famed Hill of Crosses at S'iauliai; and the miraculous image of the Virgin at S'iluva.

The interweaving of religion and national identity is well demonstrated at S'iauliai, where originally a small chapel was used by Lithuanian revolutionaries during the Uprising of 1861–1864. Cossacks covered the chapel with earth, suffocating the patriots inside. Eventually, the roof of the chapel collapsed, creating a hollow in the hill, which can still be seen today. A cross was raised in memory of those entombed inside, and a custom arose of bringing crosses to the hill for both petition and thanksgiving, with prayers inscribed on or attached to the crosses.[18] Reverend Michael Bourdeaux described it thus: "In its original state it was a remarkable sight—a hummock rising from a flat cornfield, the top of which bristled with a burgeoning of crosses in their thousands, wedged thicker than the trees of a forest."[19]

The S'iluva shrine commemorated the appearance of the weeping Virgin in 1608 to a Calvinist catechist and shepherds on the spot where Protestant worship had replaced Catholic. The original Catholic deed to the property was miraculously recovered, and Catholic worship and veneration of the Madonna restored.[20] Both the S'iauliai and the S'iluva shrines survived Soviet persecution and attempts at destruction, and both, along with Aglona, were sites of triumphant masses during Pope John Paul II's historic visit in 1993.

S'iluva received many pilgrims on September 8, the feast of the Nativity of the Virgin and the titular feast of the parish. A notable feature of this *atlaidai* was the presence of Protestant Lithuanians from East Prussia.[21] Another popular destination was the miracle-working picture of Saint Anthony of Padua at the Franciscan church in Kretinga. After the fashion of the Russian icons, the picture was hidden from view by a silver cover, with only the faces and hands of the saint and Jesus exposed.[22] All these shrines served as sources of spiritual renewal in the face of tsarist oppression (and would do so again under Communism).

Many of Samogitia's Catholics had emigrated abroad or to other parts of the empire. In 1908, Lithuanian Catholics formed large colonies in Saint Petersburg (40,000), Riga (35,000), and Odessa (7,000),[23] as well as on the Siberian frontier.

The Vilna-Grodno Diocese

Also a result of government-forced unions, this diocese counted over 1.4 million faithful in 1911, who were organized into 23 deaneries of 266 parishes,[24] covering the former Greek Catholic archeparchy of Vilna and the once-separate Latin dioceses of Vilna and Grodno. Catholic strength ranged from a high of more than 58 percent in the northwest (Vilna) to some 30 percent in the east (Grodno).[25] Bishop Edward von der Ropp was transferred to the diocese from Tiraspol. It was hoped that, owing to his connections with members of the imperial court, on the one hand, and to his spiritual successes in the Tiraspol diocese and in his priesthood at the persecuted parish of Libau, on the other, he could protect the Church without coming into open conflict with the anti-Catholic authorities.[26]

This diocese was composed of Belorussian, Polish, and Lithuanian faithful, the Vilna-Grodno diocese was also in turmoil over what language should be used for vernacular devotions, for sermons, and in catechesis.[27] At the same time, the Vilna (Vilnius or Wilno) diocese was a main target of Russification by the government. Indeed, Bishop von der Ropp, considered a "vigorous prelate" who would work hard among the suppressed Greek Catholics and other Russian Orthodox,[28] was sentenced to jail in 1907 because he opposed the Russification of his flock.[29] (Here again, Russification would be repeated by the Soviets.)

Only the far western deaneries, as part of Poland, escaped Bolshevik rule; the eastern deaneries became part of the Soviet Union after 1921, and the central ones, in 1939. The diocese was also a stronghold of the "stubborn ones"(see "The Great Return of the Stubborn Ones" in chapter 4), believers who continued to secretly adhere to the old Greek Catholic Church.

The Church and National Identities

Here, too, there was a tragic tension growing between the predominantly Polish (or pro-Polish) clergy and their Lithuanian and Belorussian faithful. Despite a history of Polish political rule in the past, Poles in the 1897 census showed as a small minority of 10 percent or less in 40 of the 41 districts (the exception being Vilna district, and even there Polish speakers accounted for only one-fifth the population). On the other hand, in 35 of the 41 districts, Belorussians represented more than 66 percent of the population.[30] In ethnically Belorussian territory, there were over 2.2 million Roman Catholics in 1911.[31] Of the 5.4 million people who spoke Belorussian in the 1897 census; more than 18 percent were still Catholics.[32]

Still, most priests insisted on counting all Catholics as Poles and using Polish for vernacular devotions, sermons, and conversation. This collided with a rising sense among the Belorussian peasants of being "non-Polish." As it was, the Belorussian language was forbidden by the State until the Revolution of 1905. The chauvinistic attitude of the Poles against the Lithuanian and newly restored Belorussian languages was to have serious negative consequences in the space of just five years, and continues to reverberate today in the newly restored dioceses of independent Belarus.

Belorussian Roman Catholicism was concentrated in Grodno and Vilna provinces. In the eastern provinces of Minsk, Mogilev, and Vitebsk—once heavily Greek Catholic—Russian Orthodoxy claimed the loyalty of almost all Belorussians (though they were still cognizant of their Catholic background, as will be seen in the early 1920s, and again in the 1990s).[33]

Catholicism had been important to Belorussian national consciousness. The suppressed Greek Catholic Church had been a particularly important source for national identity. Whereas the Greek Catholic Church had used Belorussian, the Russian Orthodox hierarchy permitted only Great Russian and Old Church Slavonic in sermons and devotions, rendering worship unintelligible to the ordinary peasant. Three leading poets in Belorussian were Catholic priests: Fathers Frantsishak Bahushevich, Yanka Kupals, and Vintsent Dunin-Martsinkevich. Father Kastus Kalinouski had been an important figure in the 1863 uprising against tsarist rule.[34] The Church had also published three religious books in Belorussian: a catechism, *Karotki katechizm* (1907); *Slova ab pakucie* (1913); and a prayer book, *Boh z nami* by B. Pac'obka (1915)—all at Vilna, where Belorussian Catholic publishing continued under the Polish Republic into the late 1920s. A Belorussian Catholic paper, *Bielarus,* began publication in 1913, but was forced to close in 1915 with the German occupation.[35] After the failed Uprisings of 1830 and 1863, however, education in Belorussia had been Russified, with mass dismissals of Catholic teachers and a ban on the use of either Polish or Belorussian in teaching. And after 1864, all the schools in the territory had come under the control of the Russian Orthodox Church, and all classes had been taught in Russian.[36]

Suffering for the Faith

Catholicism suffered serious blows in the Vilna-Grodno diocese. The Greek Catholic Church was destroyed, and a number of Latin Catholic parishes suppressed as a result of the battle with the government over the language issue. All monastic communities were banned, and their monasteries given over to Orthodox or secular use or left in the hands of a few aging religious. Many of the Marian shrines—Belorussia counted 26 "major" and 50 "minor" sanctuaries dedicated to the Mother of God—were taken over by the Russian Orthodox following the forced church union.

Belorussian Catholic peasants could only own small farms of 60 dessiatines (about 160 acres), which had to be worked only by hand and the family. Upper-class Catholics were denied employment by the State and forbidden to own agricultural land. The imperial government exploited any possible antagonism between the peasants and Polonized nobles.[37]

Practice of the Faith

On the other hand, the religious life of the laity was fortified by the presence of strong lay organizations, especially the Living Rosary societies for men and women, and confraternities of the Scapular and Marian Sodalities. Devotion to the Virgin remained strong, and the different Marian societies provided the laity with inspiration and loyalty to the Catholic religion. In particular, recitation of the Rosary was a common practice in Belorussia, as was the wearing of the rosary around one's neck. (This strong reverence for Mary would serve well in the years ahead under Bolshevik rule.) Devotion to Our Lady of Zhyrovitsi was a special Belorussian piety. In 1480, in the branches of a pear tree a small icon had appeared to shepherds in a brilliant light. When the light had faded, the shepherds discovered that the icon bore the inscription, "More honorable than the Cherubim, and beyond compare more glorious than the Seraphim, who a virgin gave birth to God the Word; you, truly the Mother of God, we magnify"—a common verse in Byzantine-Slavic liturgical services. The icon became the focal point of pilgrimages, and has remained so. In 1613, Saint Josaphat founded a Basilian Greek Catholic monastery at the shrine, which encouraged the growth of pilgrimages. Though the Basilian Fathers were suppressed with the Greek Catholic Church in 1839, the icon remained, though in Orthodox hands, and the pilgrimages continued.[38] (The devotion would be used by the Jesuits in interwar Poland in their missionary work to re-

Former Greek Catholic church, Belarus. Used as a museum.

store the Greek Catholics in northeast Poland, and has been a constant in Belorussian religious practice.)

The Cities of Vilna and Grodno

Monastic churches remaining in Catholic hands were used as parish churches.
This was the case in Grodno, where the former Bernardine monastery
church, noted for its modern Stations of the Cross, carved of stone, continued to be used for worship as the last functioning Catholic center.[39] This
church was destined to be one of the few to survive in Catholic use, thanks to
Polish rule (1918–1939) and to local tenacity thereafter, and to emerge in 1990
as a focal point of Catholic revival. The secularized monastery also gained a
place in Belorussian Catholic history, becoming the first legal seminary in the
Soviet Belorussian republic and the foundation of the Church in independent
Belarus.

Vilna proper had a number of magnificent Catholic parishes, but was especially famous for the miraculous icon at the Ostrabama/Aus'ros Vartai
(Gates of Dawn/Gates of the East) Chapel. The icon of the Madonna is enshrined in a chapel above an old gateway, and windows are opened to reveal it

during services. During the day, the street below was "continually filled with kneeling worshippers," its icon being "highly revered by Greek [Orthodox] and Latin alike."[40] The city also had a magnificent set of Stations of the Cross, a network of 36 chapels that received as many as 150,000 pilgrims, especially around feasts of the Holy Cross, from throughout the northwest.[41] (Vilna will feature prominently in our story: although, at that time, its inhabitants were mostly Jewish and Polish, it was still emotionally important to patriotic Lithuanians as their former capital.)

The Lutsk-Zhitomir-Kamenets Diocese

Created by the Russian imperial government in 1866, this diocese had its seat in Zhitomir and covered the provinces of Volhynia (Lutsk), Podolia (Kamenets), and Kiev (Zhitomir). It embraced the former Greek and Latin Catholic dioceses of Chelm, Lutsk, Kamenets, and Kiev.[42] The former Latin Catholic dioceses, dating back to the Middle Ages, had become extinct due to repression and government violations of the concordats. Although all of the Greek Catholic sees had been violently suppressed by 1875,[43] the title of the Greek Catholic eparchy of Kamenets was still held by the Greek Catholic metropolitan in Lemberg, Austria-Hungary (which would later prove important).

By 1866, the former Latin Catholic dioceses, restored in 1798, were merged into the Lutsk-Zhitomir-Kamenets diocese. According to treaties with the Holy See, there was to be a bishop at Zhitomir (transferred from Kiev), with auxiliaries residing in the other two cities and Kiev itself. This never took place. In 1914, these southwestern territories bore the brunt of intensified Russification efforts by both government and Orthodox Church directed against the Polish Roman Catholics and the Greek Catholics who had returned to public profession of Catholicism.[44] The eastern and central areas became part of the Soviet Union after 1920, as did most of the remainder in 1939.

Covering much of what is called "Right Bank Ukraine," this diocese counted over 817,000 faithful in 1911. These were predominantly Polish, with German, Armenian, and Czech minorities. Interestingly, the German Catholics around Chernigov were steadily assimilated into the Ukrainian nationality, while retaining their Latin Rite. (In the Soviet era, this phenomenon would affect Poles in Ukraine.) A few of the Poles still formed a noble elite; others were either farmers or were part of the bureaucracy. The other three Catholic groups were mostly urban merchants and workers; in rural Volhynia Germans were Protestant and the Czechs were Orthodox. Catholic strength

Miracle-working icon of Our Lady of Ostrabama, Vilnius (Vilna). Courtesy of the author.

was in Volhynia and in Podolia, where Poles formed more than 5 and 3 percent of the population, respectively. In Kiev province, Poles numbered only 92,000 out of 4.2 million people.[45]

Conditions for the Church were especially hard here. Only men born in these provinces who were also imperial subjects could enter the seminary or serve in the parishes, which prevented the easy movement of priests (elsewhere in Russia, the Church depended heavily on foreign clergy or on priests from the Warsaw Metropolitan Province). Moreover, religious orders were banned from admitting new members. These restrictions kept the Church chronically under-staffed. By 1911, in the entire diocese, there were only fourteen priests of or-ders: ten who had survived from days long past and four at a tiny Franciscan friary in Zaslav.[46] There were no Catholic schools or charitable institutions whatsoever. As the Orthodox bishops were quick to point out, unless public education was kept under strict Orthodox control in these provinces, the lo-cals, with their enduring pro-Greek Catholic and pro-Polish sympathies, would quickly revert to their Polish and Ruthenian nationalities and thus also to Catholicism.[47]

On the other hand, Catholic leadership here was outstanding. Archbishop Stanislaus Niedzaglkowski, resident in Zhitomir, was vigorous and worked at uniting his faithful, assisted by the acquiescence of Zhitomir's governor, who was also Polish. Indeed, because the region had been Greek and Latin Catholic for most of its history, even its supposedly Russian Orthodox believers strongly opposed the anti-Catholic efforts of both government and Ortho-dox Church.[48]

Catholics in the Mother of Rus'

Evidence of the ancient presence of the Latin and Greek Catholic Churches was long gone, and in the fading years of empire, Kiev had only two modern Latin Catholic churches—Saint Nicholas's and Saint Alexander's. It also had one new Greek Catholic community, at the village of Nizhnaya Bogdanovka, where the large Orthodox parish was to be led into Catholicism through the reading of its pastor, Father Potapii Emilianov, who later became one of the great confessors of the Byzantine-Russian Exarchate.

The Latin Catholic churches held a prestigious position, being built near either end of the famous Kreshchatyk, Kiev's commercial and social hub. Saint Nicholas's a great Gothic church, rising up at the south end off the Bog-dan Khmelnitsky Square near the bustling market, was finished in 1909 and named in honor of the last tsar. It was noted for its great organ. Saint Alexan-der's was built between 1817 and 1849 as part of the newly created Kreshchatyk Avenue.[49] Their locations and styles destined them for sad fates under the Bolsheviks.

A second Greek Catholic community would later focus on a nineteenth-

Республіканський будинок органної і камерної музики.
Концертний зал. Інтер'єр.

КИЕВ
КИЇВ

Saint Nicholas's Church, Kyiv (Kiev). Used as a concert hall. Note the pipe organ installed in place of the high altar. Courtesy of the author.

century wooden Greek Catholic church, removed from the Carpathian region during World War I and reassembled, established on Pavlivska Street, west of Lvivska Square. This was popular with immigrants from western Ukraine and converts, and was the focal point of a long-lived Greek Catholic parish from 1918 to 1937.[50]

Other Catholic Centers

The other diocesan centers held churches that better symbolized the long Catholic presence in the borderlands. Zhitomir, for example, was home to Saint Sophia's, built in 1225, and Kamenets, to the Cathedral of Saints Peter and Paul, built in 1386.[51] As witness to the region's incredibly diverse history, this church served as a mosque for over two centuries under Ottoman rule. Lutsk diocese dates back to 1358 (at Vladimir), making it the oldest Latin Catholic diocese in the empire. The seminary for the region was at Zhitomir, and the ten survivors of the orders of men worked alongside 300 diocesan clergy. There were 267 parish churches open in 1911.[52]

In addition, this area had been home to the last Greek Catholic diocese on Russian soil. When the eparchy of Chelm had been suppressed in 1875, there had been a strong underground movement of its faithful in Volhynia and farther north, in the area of the Vilna-Grodno diocese (see "The Great Return of the Stubborn Ones" in chapter 4). After the Edict of Tolerance of 1905, Chelm district was witness to a Catholic revival that resulted in the overcrowding of the surviving Latin churches, and to a Greek Catholic revival when it was under German military rule during World War II. The title of the Greek Catholic eparchy of Kamenets was transferred to the metropolitan of Lemberg (Lwów), which became important during the legalization of the Greek Catholics during the revolutionary years.

The Tiraspol Diocese

Stretched across the lower half of the Ukraine (in a region then called "South Russia"), the homeland of the Crimean Tatars and the legendary Don Cossacks, across the polyglot Caucasus, and into Russia proper, the Tiraspol diocese covered all or part of ten provinces, making it the second largest diocese in the empire. Many non-Russians, including Catholics, had been brought here to colonize the region when it was conquered, and others were descended from ancient colonies such as the Greeks. In Kherson province, nearly one-third of the population was neither Russian nor Ukrainian.

Catholic roots in the territory dated back to legendary imprisonment of Saint Clement (Pope Clement I) in Crimea. Said to have been exiled there by Emperor Trajan, Clement was martyred by being thrown into the sea tied to an anchor because he continued to minister to Christian and pagan alike (some of his relics were removed by Saint Cyril, Apostle of the Slavs, to Rome in the ninth century, and some from Kherson in 989 to Kiev's Church of the Tithes before its destruction by the Mongols).

Christianity endured in Crimea, among both Greek colonists and Slav converts (eventually becoming part of Russian Orthodoxy), and later among Italian Catholic settlers. Although Roman Catholic churches staffed by Dominicans and Franciscans had dotted the peninsula until the Tatar Khans destroyed them in the 1450s,[53] Eastern and Roman Catholics continued to worship in both Crimea and the Caucasus region. Roman Catholicism expanded across the entire south, rejuvenated by later European settlers who mixed with the imperial colonists of what was once known as "New Russia" or "South Russia": German and Swiss Protestants; Greek, Bulgarian, and Gagauz Orthodox; Cossacks; Ukrainians; Russians; Romanians; and various peoples from the polyglot southern mountains and steppes.

In Tiraspol diocese, "churches" were defined as buildings of stone, properly speaking, with a bell tower. Churches without a bell tower were specially noted in the diocesan register; many of these, though serving small rural communities, were decorated with ornate altars and a host of statues. "Prayer houses," by contrast, were almost always made of mud brick or wood and generally smaller, sometimes sharing space with the local school. Their ornamentation was simpler, though they were liturgically complete.

The Tiraspol diocese published its own newspaper, *Klemensblatt,* and a bimonthly magazine, *Deutsche Rundschau.*

The primary centers of Catholic life in this vast and complex diocese were
1. among the Latins

    a. German rural colonies on the Volga River, founded in the 1700s under Catherine the Great, and along the Black Sea, founded in the early 1800s under Alexander I;

    b. Polish rural colonies in the Volga Basin, founded by Polish and Belorussian exiles from the Uprisings of 1831[54] and 1863;

    c. German and mixed parishes in the Kuban' and Stavropol' provinces;

    d. mixed parishes of Armenians, Germans, Georgians, and Poles in the Caucasus provinces;

    e. mixed parishes of Germans, Swiss, Czechs, and other nationalities in Crimea;

    f. urban groups of all these peoples plus new Italian, French, Spanish, and Portuguese settlers, ranging from a large group in Odessa to smaller ones in a host of nearby towns;

    g. Cherkassians in the Caucasus provinces;

2. among the Armenians

 a. the apostolic administration of Artvin, joined to the Tiraspol diocese in 1870, while remaining immediately subject to the Holy See, and whose administrator continued to administer parishes in southern Armenia;

 b. Armenian parishes in northern Armenia and southern and coastal Georgia;

 c. the Armenian parish of Crimea, which consisted of two churches in the Tiraspol diocese's Simferopol' deanery, at Feodosia;

3. among the Assyrians

 a. one Chaldean Rite parish in the Caucasus, with one priest, subject to the bishop of Tiraspol;

4. among the Russians

 a. a tiny Greek Catholic community, initiated at Saratov.

The Latin Catholics

In 1911, there were over 400,000 Latin Catholics in the Tiraspol diocese, of which an estimated 195,000 were Black Sea and Crimean Germans; 155,000 were Volga Germans; 40,000 were Poles and Lithuanians; 5,000 were French, Spaniards, Italians, and Portuguese; 32,000 were Georgians; 5,000 were Russian converts; and 261 were Cherkassians. There were about 114 Latin parishes in the entire region with more than 100 filial churches and chapels, organized into 12 deaneries, extending all the way to the Ottoman frontier, on the southwest, and to a missionary outreach in the Turgai region of Siberia, on the east.

A particular legacy in the Volga region was left by the first religious order missionary priests who had come in the 1700s, especially the Jesuits. So devoted were these priests to their widely scattered parishioners on the steppes, that all priests in the Volga basin are still known as "Pater" (Father) instead of the traditional "Pfarrer" (Pastor).[55] This emotional closeness would come to be important in the 1920s and 1930s, and later in exile.[56]

At the same time, imperial regulations forbade the priests of the German colony parishes from any priestly activity outside the sacraments, at the risk of losing their salary and posts. Taking a Lutheran position, imperial ordinances also made the Bible the sole basis for regulating Catholic Church life and gave Russian officials the power to decide what was sacred and what was secular. Not surprisingly, these restrictions weakened Catholic life in the Tiraspol diocese.[57]

It was common among both the Latin and Armenian Catholic for a parish to have several filial churches and only one priest. This was especially true, in the 38 Volga and 1,077 Black Sea German colonies with Catholic residents, but was also true in Crimea and the Caucasus.[58] Some 85 percent of the priests were ethnic Germans serving the Latin parishes, with the remainder being Czechs, Georgians, and Poles for the Latin Rite. The Chaldean Rite parish and the Armenian parishes at Feodosia were both part of Tiraspol's structure, and had priests from the respective ethnic and ritual populations.

For the Germans, the diocesan seminary at Saratov was an important link with their ancestral homeland. Originally graduating Poles and Lithuanians, the seminary had a German faculty, including teachers from the German Empire, and in the latter half of the 1800s produced Volga and Black Sea German clergy who became leaders of their ethnic groups.[59] On the other hand, the seminary also trained Georgians, Czechs, Poles, and Latvians for the Latin Church and Armenians for the Armenian Church.[60] Armenian clergy included both married parish priests and celibate Mekhitarist Fathers from the Austrian and Italian provinces of the order. At Karlsruhe the sisters of Saint Francis had their motherhouse.

The Strengths of Catholics in the Steppes and Hills

Rural Catholicism in Tiraspol diocese reflected the common elements listed above. In particular, devotion to the saints was strong: their intercession was frequently implored for health and protection of the crops, with processions and special Masses. There was, however, a great zeal for the Mass and the Blessed Sacrament, a result of the work of the Jesuit missionaries. Jesuits had also strengthened the rural Germans against being tempted by Protestantism.[61]

Finally, there was a strong attachment to the Passion of Our Lord. In the Volga valley, Stations of the Cross would be erected in a long passage to outlying chapels. Villagers would go out to the first Station saying the Sorrowful Mysteries of the Rosary. The people made the actual Way of the Cross on their knees, from Station to Station.[62] There were several popular sites along the Volga and in the Black Sea colonies for pilgrimages in honor of the Cross and the Virgin Mary; in addition, the anniversaries of church dedications *(Kirchweihfeste)* were significant gatherings. All of these were similar in purpose to the Lithuanian *atlaidai* seen in the north, and will be detailed below.

Rural churches could be as ornate as the large town churches. Catholic and Protestant steeples dotted the landscape of southern Ukraine and Russia, soaring above the fields. Villagers went to great expense to beautify God's house in their midst, importing statues, windows, and altars from central Europe.

Ruins of Kamenka church in the Volga valley. Site of annual pilgrimage in honor of the Finding of the Cross. Courtesy of Edward Gerk.

Most of the rural priests spent weeks traveling from village to village. Many Catholics here had Mass only once a month or so; on the other Sundays and feasts, the laity held prayer services. (This tradition of lay spiritual and liturgical leadership would soon prove important.)

Catholics in the Towns

Besides a strong rural presence, Tiraspol diocese had a number of urban parishes, many of which were substantial, and a few military parishes in the Caucasus and Crimea. New churches were built in the cities throughout the Silver Age.

The parishes of Odessa were home to a dozen or more imperial nationalities and to many foreign citizens: there were designated preachers and confessors for French, German, Italian, Lithuanian, and Polish parishioners, as well as nuns, the French Sisters of Saint Joseph of Chambery. The French church of Saint-Pierre, located near the famous Richelieu Steps (named after the first mayor of Odessa, the Catholic Duc de Richelieu), would be the only Odessa parish to survive all the persecutions, though without a priest for many years.[63] The German church of the Assumption of the Blessed Virgin Mary, with its distinctive front tower, rear dome, and long nave, was in the heart of the city, on Ykaterinskaya (later Karl-Marx) Street. It was destined to become the cathedral of the diocese during and after the Civil War, until its closure under the Soviets, and again in World War II.

Other notable "foreign" parishes were the "Italian Catholic Church" in Mariupol' (founded 1860; with 3,500 souls in 1919, of whom few were still Italians) and Saint Joseph's (1914–1915) at Makeyevka, serving the French and Belgian mining engineers and local Germans. Many Poles had migrated into the southern cities, finding work in the new industries.[64] In addition (and important in the Stalinist years), there were foreign diplomats in these industrial areas, staffing consulates of Germany, France, Italy, and, later Poland, who would later try to aid local Catholics.

The center of the diocese was in Saratov, the principal city in the lower Volga region and home to the diocese's seminary as well as to the region's German press, at Saint Clement's Cathedral, a massive brick church dedicated in 1881 to Pope Clement I, who had been exiled to Crimea by the Roman emperors. (Appropriately enough, given the ethnic composition of the diocese, the cathedral stood on Nemetskaya (German) Street).[65] Completed in 1880 in the New Renaissance style, the cathedral dominated its surroundings, with two great towers. (Its original design—a Gothic church with one tall spire—had to be changed because it would have made the cathedral taller than Saratov's Orthodox churches.) Its interior was filled with imported statues and altars, and its choir was famous. Pontifical ceremonies according to the Roman Rite were "strictly carried out" in full glory.[66] Chapels adorned the seminary, the bishop's palace, and the churchyard. (Of all this, only the rear wall of the cathedral remains today.) Dating to 1803, the parish had German, Polish, Italian, and French members. In 1914, Saint Clement's served nine filial churches in the Volga colonies, and the Parish had a Catholic population of 8,150 at the end of the World War I.[67] Within the cathedral parish were the first beginnings of a Russian Catholic community, worshiping secretly according to the Byzantine Rite.

Because, in 1803, the priests in Saratov were responsible for Catholics living as far away as Simbirsk, many Catholics had gone without the sacraments for years. A century later, every major southern city had a Roman Catholic church; one could attend Mass in Rostov-on-Don or Novocherkassk or Novorossiisk (where the Catholics had to celebrate Mass in private homes until just after 1898, when they finally were able to build a church for their 3,500 parishioners). Even where city parishes were very small, as in Tsaritsyn, with only 600 Catholic parishioners in 1911, they sponsored at least schools of religion, and often day schools. Although all these parishes were eventually closed, many of their churches have survived to this day.

In 1911, Latin parishes were scattered about the Kuban' and Stavropol provinces, above the Caucasus: in Pyatigorsk (stone church: 1,738 souls), Ykaterinodar (stone church: 2,500 souls), Grozny (stone prayer house: 5,800 souls), Nikolaevka (stone church: 500 souls), and in a few German farm colonies.[68] At the eastern end of Stavropol province lay the city of Astrakhan, with a very old Polish-German Catholic parish founded by Capuchins in 1715 (with 1,350 souls in 1919). The parish church, south of the bazaar, was built in 1762. (Even after it was closed, its chapels in the rectory and cemetery continued to serve Catholics well into the Stalinist persecution.)[69]

Georgia and the Caucasus

South of Crimea, in the Caucasus, lay the formerly independent kingdom of Georgia. An ancient Christian country, evangelized in the fourth century by a woman apostle, Saint Nino, Georgia has been autonomous under its own catholicos since the year 467.[70] The Georgian Orthodox Church followed the Byzantine tradition, celebrating services in Georgian, and was known for its vigorous monastic life and unique music; it was in communion with Rome until after the Fourth Crusade: a definitive split seems to have taken place by 1250. Even so, Catholic religious work continued, and Catholic sympathies could be found in the royal family and the hierarchy.[71]

When Tsar Alexander I annexed Georgia in 1801, deposing the Bagratian royal family and various noble families who had divided the country between themselves, there were about 50,000 Latin Catholics in the kingdom.[72] The Russian Holy Synod took over the Georgian Orthodox Church in 1811; it was led by Russian exarchs from 1817 until 1917. The Church leadership was replaced with Russians; the services were celebrated only in Old Church Slavonic; and preaching and teaching were done only in Russian; and sixteen of the twenty dioceses were suppressed, along with many monasteries and parish churches.[73] In short, Georgian Orthodoxy was treated almost as brutally as Roman Catholicism in the same era.

A Roman Catholic diocese existed on and off from 1328 at the capital, Tiflis (Tbilisi), with a parish dating from 1663, although there were never many native Catholics. Although Georgian Catholics remained faithful to the Church, the tsarist government required that they worship only in the Latin or Armenian Rites, and forbade all use of Georgian in church. More numerous were Polish Catholics, German Catholics (most Caucasus Germans were Evangelicals, Mennonites, or Baptists), and Armenian Catholics, who worshiped in both their own and Latin churches. There were about 32,000 Latin Catholics and 8,000 Armenian Catholics in the Georgian provinces in 1914.

Theatine (from 1624) and Capuchin (from 1661) missionaries carried on energetic work, converting Georgian Orthodox bishops, princes, and nobles, and maintaining an atmosphere sympathetic to union with Rome among several Georgian catholicoi (especially Nicholas VII and Anthony I from 1742 to 1788). Dominican missionaries worked among the Armenian Catholics there.

Driven out by war and political intrigue, the Capuchins returned in 1802, following Georgia's annexation. They restored Tbilisi church and founded a parish at Gori. Anti-Catholic legislation, trumped-up charges, and their refusal to form an "independent" Catholic Church having no connection with Rome led once more to their expulsion in 1845.

By the time the Capuchins were expelled, the churches of the Immaculate Conception had been built in Batum and Kutaisi.[74] The priests and sisters of the Immaculate Conception, founded in 1861 at Constantinople by Father Peter Karischiaranti, ministered to all Catholic Georgians of both rites: they would return to their homeland only after 1918[75] for an ill-fated mission.

Tiflis (Tbilisi) was the seat of a Latin dean; in 1911, its principal churches were Assumption of the Virgin (3,302 souls; founded 1866), and Saints Peter and Paul (7,000 souls; founded 1897), with two chapels affiliated to that parish. The military parish at Menglis had a stone church and 13,600 parishioners; Holy Family in Gori, with 495 souls, had a stone parish church and a chapel to serve a farm village; Kutaisi, with more than 2,000 souls, had a stone parish church; and Batum completed a splendid church to serve its 1,300 faithful in 1898. The venerable parish of Akhaltsike counted 173 hardy souls in 1914.[76] Finally, there was Baku, a busy oil port jutting into the Caspian Sea above Persia and the southernmost parish of Tiraspol. Although Catholics there were originally served by one of the rare military chaplains, after 1902 the parish came under regular diocesan control and a new church was finished just before World War I. Father Stefan Demurov, who served in this parish from 1904 on, was destined to become both the head of the Church after the Communist conquest and, like so many of his confreres, a martyr for the Faith.[77]

Beyond the Diocese

From the easternmost boundary of Tiraspol diocese, the Kirghiz Steppe (also known as the "Kulunda Steppe") rolled eastward across the Samara province and the land of the Ural Cossacks. Here, in the Turgai province, at the south-western edge of Siberia, lay a network of small and widely scattered Catholic settlements. Missionary priests from Tiraspol traveled from settlement to settlement in a continual series of pastoral visits. At the time of the October Revolution, Father Josef Wolf, a scholar and former seminary rector from Odessa, was the administrator for these missions and priests, a post he would hold throughout the coming years of chaos.[78]

Germans had settled here since the time of Catherine the Great, but especially in the nineteenth century and last years of tsarism: German colonies were founded through 1914.[79] Of South German and Bavarian origin, from the Volga and Black Sea colonies, Catholics were a minority in the Turgai province (Lutherans and Mennonites formed the majority): out of 27,000 Germans in Slavgorod district in 1918, only 3,660 were Roman Catholic, with just over 400 German Catholics in Slavgorod proper, and over 3,200 in three colonies around the city.[80] Other German Catholics lived beyond the Slavgorod district: two known Catholic settlements were at Hochheim and Schönfeld, and many colonies were mixed in religion.

The Great Renewal

Tiraspol diocese entered World War I under the leadership of Bishop Joseph Kessler, ordained in 1904 at the age of 42, a native Russia German from the village of Louis in the Volga Region. His predecessor had been Edward von der Ropp, bishop of Vilna and archbishop of Mogilev. Within the diocese was another bishop, Anton Zerr, a Black Sea German, who had resigned in 1902 due to serious health problems, and who would be the last bishop to remain in the western Soviet Union. In the years before the war, Bishop Kessler emphasized the institution of popular missions. Austrian Redemptorists from Vienna conducted a ten-week series in the Odessa deanery in which 17,000 believers made their confessions and 190 sermons were preached in German, French, and Italian.

Polish-speaking Franciscans from Lwów (Lemberg) and Redemptorists from Krakow (both in Austria-Hungary) visited the different urban parishes from Odessa to Astrakhan and to the German-Polish parishes in the Caucasus to preach missions. Such events, marked by dramatic sermons on the lives of Jesus and Mary, calls to interior renewal and the opportunity for that renewal to be confirmed in Confession and the reception of Holy Communion, led to a strong religious revival among the Tiraspol Catholics. Bishop Kessler accompanied the religious, administering Confirmation and blessing new churches. When the imperial government forbade the Caucasus tour, and news of the ban did not reach the bishop until the tour was nearly complete, he simply waited until the mission was over to pass the news on.[81]

The Rosary was a popular devotion, especially after the dedication of the month of October to Our Lady of the Holy Rosary by Pope Leo XIII, and May devotions to Mary were also popular. Stations of the Cross were held in the chapels all through Lent. The visitation of a bishop was a rare event, and the occasion for great numbers to be presented for Confirmation and for special masses to be celebrated. Only Bishop Kessler was able to tour the entire diocese, and after the October Revolution such visitations became rare indeed. Moreover, religious education had been assigned to priests in 1906, when they replaced laypeople as religion teachers in the schools,[82] a development that would seriously weaken the role of the laity in Church life.

Tensions in Tiraspol

In the years before World War I, Roman Catholicism was experiencing a revival of Gregorian plainchant as the proper music for the Mass. In the Black Sea German parishes, this caused a serious conflict between priests and parishioners: the Latin chant and Masses by composers such as Palestrina were pushing aside traditional German-language hymns that once accompanied the prayers of the Mass. (The official Latin hymnal came from Polish dioceses and had no German hymns.) Teachers were brought from the Catholic Music Academy in Regensburg, Germany, to assist in the introduction of the new music. In the countryside, the innovations were bitterly resisted; in the southern towns, youth choirs sang German hymns before and after Mass as a compromise. Feelings ran very high over the music issue, requiring the transfer of some pastors.[83] In World War I, the government banned the use of German in preaching, singing, and religious education (Polish had already been banned by imperial law), a crippling move in this diocese. There was also the serious problem of growing emigration from the entire area. Overcrowding in the colonies and a lack of land for young families, conscription of men into the imperial army, and animosity among the Russian right-wing nationalists toward the Germans was causing many to leave for Siberia or the Americas. Other tensions had come into play during the Revolution in 1905, when many priests supported the autocracy against their parishioners.

The Armenian Catholics

The Apostolic Administration of the Armenian Catholic Church of the Russian Empire had its headquarters at Artvin in the empire's deep south, but embraced faithful across the diocese of Tiraspol and up into Mogilev-Minsk. There were at one time 172 Armenian Catholic houses of worship in the empire and 71 priests. Although concordats with the Holy See called for three Armenian Catholic dioceses to cover the western half of the empire, the government had permitted only this apostolic administration, headed by a priest, Sarkis Der Abrahamian.[84] Der (Father) Abrahamian was born in 1868, and ordained in 1894. He was named apostolic administrator by the Holy See in 1909[85] and would have a tumultuous life under both tsars and commissars. Although in charge of all imperial Armenian Catholics, he was subject to the Latin bishop of Tiraspol for all-important decisions.[86] Priests from the administration served on the Tiraspol diocesan canons' council, and all had received imperial awards.[87] The administration had its last bishop in 1870; the government did not allow the installation of a new one. No Tiraspol bishop could undertake a visitation of these parishes until 1902, when Bishop von der Ropp became the first, devoting himself to encouraging the Armenian priests and laity in their faith.[88] Stretching from Crimea to the southernmost border of the empire in Kars province, with more than 61,000 believers in 1915, the administration had seven vicariates and two separate missions, as well as two separately administered entities—the parish of the Assumption at Tiflis (Tbilisi) and the Armenian Catholics living immediately around the city along the Baku Railroad.

Historical Background

The Armenian Catholics were heirs to a movement for Church union dating back to the 1600s and even earlier. Those in the Crimea were descended from Church unions that had their origins in the Crusades and had remained Catholic with a remarkable tenacity. When Bishop Pietro Cedulini visited Kaffa, Crimea, in 1581, he discovered that the local Armenian bishop still considered his diocese to be Catholic, even though Crimea had been cut off from all contact with Catholicism for more than 100 years.[89] The stone church of the Holy Cross in Ivlidi, Akhaltsike vicariate, dated from 1691, and the prayer house in Grimsgiy hamlet, outside Ykaterinodar, was the oldest one in the entire Caucasus.[90] Akhaltsike in southern Georgia had counted 4,000 Armenian faithful in 1749,[91] and has remained a Catholic center until our own times.

Artvin Vicariate

Once a separate diocese of the Armenian Catholic Church, founded in 1850, the Artvin vicariate had its seat at the frontier town of Artvin, on the border of the Ottoman Empire. It spread from Batum in the north down to the border of Kars province. Here the Russian imperial government actively encouraged Armenian Catholics to abandon their Church for the national Armenian Gregorian Church, and tried to eliminate the separate Armenian Catholic jurisdiction. After the death of Anton Halajean in 1870, there would never be an Armenian Catholic bishop in the empire again. The Artvin cathedral was Saints Peter and Paul, built in 1837, its large parish served by three priests. There were two other churches in the city, built in 1865 and 1881, and six parishes inland, with one at the port of Batum. The vicariate counted 7,173 believers in 1915.[92]

Kars Vicariate

In the southernmost province of the Russian Empire, with stone churches built from 1876 to 1902 and a number of missions in private houses, the Kars vicariate had more than 4,200 faithful in 1908. Nearly all the churches in the Artvin and Kars vicariates were built in the nineteenth century, as were indeed most churches serving imperial Armenians outside of the Alkhalek-Akhaltsike and Crimea regions. In the 1850s, the Mekhitarist priest Father Yeprem Setian had led an exodus of thousands of Armenian Catholics from around the city of Erzerum, on the Anatolian plateau of the Ottoman Em-

pire, to safety inside the Russian Empire's boundaries.[93] (The Ottomans subjected the Armenians and other Christians to repeated pogroms, culminating
in the great genocide of 1915–1917.) The colonists spread across the southern provinces of the Caucasus, creating a belt of Catholic settlement that re-
inforced the more ancient parishes. Tragically, most of this territory (except
immediately south of Batum) fell to the Turks in 1918–1921, and the survivors were forced to flee into Soviet territory or abroad. The following vicariates and missions eventually became part of the USSR after 1920.

Other Vicariates and Missions

To the north of the Kars vicariate lay the Akhaltsike vicariate, now in modern
Georgia and home to large numbers of ethnic Armenians. There were seventeen parishes with over 10,000 faithful in 1914. Despite the old roots of
Catholicism here, there were still communities worshiping in private houses or
wooden churches; probably this was a result of the immigration from Turkey.
Farther east lay the Alkhalek vicariate, also in modern Georgia, whose thirteen
parishes had over 13,000 Catholics in 1914, and most of whose stone
churches were built between 1856 and 1900. The Alexandropol Vicariate,
which covered Erevan province, the ancient homeland of the Armenian people, and which was to form the northwest counties of modern Armenia, had
fourteen parishes and missions, with 11,348 faithful worshiping in churches
built from 1843 to 1903. The Lori vicariate, whose churches were built from
1852 to 1869, covered much of the Tiflis region and had almost 8,000 parishioners in 1914.

Outside the "traditional" Armenian lands, Crimea reflects the Armenian
diaspora that spread across eastern and central Europe in flight from the
Turks. Covering Tauride province (Crimea and part of independent Ukraine),
Simferopol' vicariate counted 2,920 believers in 1915. On the peninsula, it
had four parishes, which included two former mosques. The Sudagh chapel of
the Protection of the Virgin became an Italian Catholic church in 1112, and
was given to the Armenians in a state of ruin in 1885; the Feodosia Church of
the Assumption was given to the Armenian Catholics by Empress Catherine
II in 1787. The 1915 Armenian almanac notes that Bishop Kessler consecrated the Church of the Savior at Simferopol' in 1909—with the approval of
the administrator.[94]

Besides the seven vicariates, there were two missions: one administered
from Feodosia, with more than 1,300 Armenian Catholics, as of 1915, in a
host of southern and western Russian cities, most notably Saint Petersburg

Saint Catherine's Church, Rashkovo, Moldova (Bessarabia). Courtesy of Aid to the Church in Need.

(Leningrad), Kharkov, Kiev, and Odessa; and the second administered from Ykaterinodar, with over 400 parishioners, as of 1914 in the city proper (Kuban' region) and 146 at "the oldest Armenian Catholic prayer house" in Grimsgiy. The missions' priests were responsible for another 1,600 people living across the Kuban' and Stavropol' provinces, and up the Volga to Tsaritsyn. Finally, there were the Armenian Catholics of Bessarabia, registered with the Latin churches there.

The Chaldean Catholics

The Chaldeans had one parish, in Erevan province in Armenia, in the village of Syagut, which counted only 319 souls in 1912.[95] Ethnically considered to be Assyrians, they came as part of the wave of Assyrian immigration in the nineteenth century from the Nestorian, Jacobite, and Catholic settlements of Lake Urmia in Persia to safer havens in Transcaucasia.[96] Isolated and bereft of con-

Krasna church in Moldova (Bessarabia). Courtesy of the author.

tact with the Chaldean Church in their Persian homeland, these sturdy mountaineers continue to maintain their Catholic identity in the present day.

The Russian Greek Catholics

The Russian Greek Catholic movement, concentrated at Saratov, dated to 1899. Father Ivan Deubner, who came to Saratov in 1914, had been ordained by Archbishop Andrew Sheptytsky in Austria-Hungary and had served here as priest secretly while employed by the government. Saratov remained a center of the Russian Catholic movement, with the faithful dependent upon its Cathedral. This community remained small: in 1922, when Exarch Leonid Feodorov finally assigned a parish priest, there were only fifteen families. Priest and community were all destined for martyrdom.

Only two parts of Tiraspol diocese would avoid Soviet rule: the province of Bessarabia (present-day Moldova), until 1940; and the territory of Kars, altogether. In Bessarabia, half the population was Romanian (defined for political reasons as "Moldavians"), but there were German colonies in the steppe west of the coastal town of Akkerman, and Germans, Poles, and Catholic Armenians lived elsewhere in the province. Reannexed by Romania in 1920, Bessarabia, with its 250 Catholic communities, came under Soviet rule in 1940.

The Kars region, annexed by Turkey in 1918, remains Turkish to this day. During the Turkish massacres of Armenians and other Christians in 1915–1917, local Catholics fled north into modern-day Armenia, losing everything they had so painfully built up over many years.

CHAPTER 4

The Catholic Communities
of Imperial Russia, Part Two

Archdiocese of Mogilev

In 1914, Mogilev was geographically the largest archdiocese in the entire world, covering 5,450,400 square miles and serving (or trying to serve) 1,023,000 Roman Catholics in 28 deaneries composed of 245 parishes with 399 priests. Besides the diocese of Minsk, administered by Mogilev since the death of the last bishop in 1869, with 51 parishes, 77 priests, and 262,000 faithful, the archdiocese was responsible for 34 parishes of Siberia and Central Asia, which were in especially difficult situations, and where deaneries could not be organized until after the February Revolution.[1]

The territory organized into deaneries before World War I embraced the former Greek Catholic archdiocese of Polotsk and its suffragan sees of Pinsk, Chernigov, and Turov (Belorussia and Ukraine), and the former Latin Catholic dioceses of Pinsk, Polotsk, Turov (Belorussia), Briansk, Smolensk (European Russia), Chernigov, Belgorod, and Kharkov (Ukraine). Catholic strength lay in the west, in the dioceses of Pinsk, Minsk, and Polotsk, and in the cities.

Though Mogilev was in Belorussia, the seat of the archdiocese had been moved by government order to the imperial capital itself, Saint Petersburg. Bishops could visit sections of the diocese, but only with government permission, and no one bishop was ever able to go to all of the parishes. In 1909, Bishop John Cieplak was finally granted permission to undertake the first ever tour of the vast eastern region. He journeyed the length of the empire, and found Catholics everywhere he went, as far as Russian Sakhalin (above Japan), which boasted colonies of Polish exiles and workers who had retained their faith despite the lack of priests and sacraments. Nearly the entire archdiocese was to come under Bolshevik rule by 1925 (the far western corner at Pinsk was spared as part of Poland until 1939; the northwestern corner at Vi-

borg was part of Finland, until 1940). Its diversity can be seen by the following examples.[2]

Saint Petersburg

Home of nearly two million people, the imperial capital and Peter the Great's
famous "window to the West" reflected the empire's diversity. Before the October Revolution, the capital was less than 82 percent Russian Orthodox, with
Protestants forming more than 7 percent and Catholics nearly 5 percent of
the city's population (both forming a higher percentage in the capital than in
the empire as a whole). More than 3 percent of the population was Polish, and
more than 3 percent German.

Saint Catherine's stood on fashionable Nevsky Prospekt, nicknamed the
"Street of Toleration" because of the number of non-Orthodox churches
that graced it. This handsome Renaissance-style "international church" was
the heart of the first Catholic parish in the city, founded by Lithuanian and
German workers in 1710, and serving as a German parish until the summer of
1914. The present church was built in 1763–1783 and was famous for its mu-
rals, magnificent organ, and converts from among the aristocracy (all to the
Latin Catholic Church, none to the Byzantine).

Saint Catherine's was a church of the Silver Age—numerous Russians
came here seeking answers to their questions about faith and ultimate destiny.
These included members of the aristocracy and intelligentsia in search of rea-
sons for life in a decadent society. Illustrious names such as Volkonsky,
Gagarin, Ushakov, and Shuvalov appeared on Catholic registers. Indeed, the
Orthodox theologian Alexi Khomiakov was reported to have said that, if
there were freedom of conscience, the upper classes would all convert to the
Catholic Faith.[3] An important spiritual father for these people was Monsignor
Constantine Budkiewicz, who would be one of the first martyrs of the Church
under Communism. The stream of converts would increase after 1918.

Confessions were heard and sermons preached not only in Russian but
also in French, German, Spanish, English, and Italian; diplomats, servants,
and foreign tourists alike attended Mass there regularly. Saint Catherine's
carved angels still hold the Latin Cross high above the principal street of the
former capital, very close to the massive Orthodox Our Lady of Kazan'
Cathedral. The faithful of its parish included Western Europeans, Poles, and
Russians of all classes. Another distinguished church, that of Saint Boniface,
named for the apostle of the Germans, occupied a handsome new building in
1905. Its Austrian friars served Germans from the German Empire, and Aus-

Saint Catherine's Church on Nevsky Prospekt, Saint Petersburg. Interior destroyed in 1985. Courtesy of Mark Sevachko.

trians out of Austria-Hungary. Its congregation of diplomats, merchants, and specialists left Russia or were interned as enemy aliens in the Great War, when Saint Boniface's became part of the archdiocesan structure for a short time, serving all of the Catholics in the capital without distinction. Notre Dame on Kovensky Lane, just off Nevsky Prospekt, served as the French national parish. A modest church in a "good" neighborhood, this was destined to be the sole survivor of Catholic Petersburg.

To focus on a parish such as Saint Catherine's or on the foreign churches, however, would be to miss the fact that the most of Saint Petersburg's Catholics attended Mass far from the museums and palaces of the "Inner Town." Concentrated mostly to the south, in churches described as "poor and shabby" with decorations of tin and wood,[4] these were poor factory workers, who went to Confession in Polish or Lithuanian. Catholicism in Saint Petersburg was very much the religion of the oppressed and those on the margin of Russian society.

In the Nevsky Quarter, far to the south of the city's center, in the shadow of the Orthodox Ismailovsky Cathedral, close to the Warsaw and Baltic rail stations, and serving railway workers, domestics, and the like, a large procathedral, the Assumption of the Virgin, had been opened in 1873 and re-modeled in 1896–1902 (appropriately enough in Byzantine style). Other churches in the southern districts, such as Saint Stanislaus's (1823), the second oldest in the city, and Saint Casimir's (1903), served working-class Lithuanians and Poles. These churches were in the midst of the slums, and their parishioners were involved in series of strikes that were firmly repressed by the police and Cossacks. Their ornamentation reflected the poverty of the workers: they had only "a crucifix over the altar, a cheap set of Stations of the Cross, and a few, brightly-painted statues, as fragile and inartistic as a child's wax doll."[5]

Baedeker describes Saint Stanislaus's, on the corner of Torgovaya and Malankaya Masterskaya Streets, as being in the "unattractive" Kolomenskaya Quarter of the capital.[6] The polyglot nature of this Russian church could be seen in its pastor: Count Edward O'Rourke, a descendant of Irish Catholic exiles.[7] Under the pastoral care of French Assumptionists, it also was destined to see a stream of Russian converts after 1917.

Saint Casimir's served a Polish-Lithuanian congregation who lived next to—and who were often employed in—the Putilov ironworks, made famous in the Revolution of 1905. In other words, many of Saint Petersburg workers for whom the Bolsheviks were supposedly fighting turned out to be practicing Catholics. Saint Casimir's parish had several schools, a radical innovation for slum dwellers, and also received into the Faith a number of Russians, breaking free from ethnic prejudices.

Above the Inner Town of the Nevsky Prospekt and across the Neva from the palaces was the Church of the Visitation of the Blessed Virgin (1850) in Viborg Cemetery, whose parish had its own school, with Franciscan Tertiary Sisters.[8] This was the site of the electrifying public liturgy in the Byzantine-Russian Rite celebrated after the February Revolution. It would also be one of the first Catholic church buildings marked for elimination after the Bolshevik victory.

The city also boasted fourteen chapels. Some were private; some were in public institutions or belonged to Catholic organizations. A convent of Polish Franciscan Sisters was at the chapel of the Immaculate Conception. Another chapel served the French Ursuline nuns and their hospital. A principal chapel was at the Theological Academy, distinguished by a set of historic frescoes. The Russian Greek Catholics and their several priests had their own chapel, Descent of the Holy Spirit or Church of the Pentecost, on Barmalayeva Street. They also had a side chapel in Saint Catherine's, as well as partial use of the chapel of the Knights of Malta in the Church of Saint John the Baptist at the building of the imperial pages.[9]

As can be seen, Saint Petersburg also happened to be one of the few places in Russia proper that had active religious orders. In addition to the orders of women noted above, there were eight Missionaries of Mary as well as a handful of French and Polish Sisters of Charity and Sisters of Saint Joseph of Chambery in 1911, who conducted schools and asylums for orphans and the elderly. There were also priests of several orders, namely, Capuchins (who returned in 1910 after having been expelled in 1845 for refusing to break with Rome), Franciscans, Dominicans, Oblates, and French Assumptionists; the last assumed an important role in saving a vestige of Catholic sacramental life under Stalin. Occasionally, too, Jesuits were able to circumvent the laws against their presence. Rare in Russia, Saint Petersburg's Catholics sponsored special homes for children and a hospital.[10]

Unique, as well, were the two military chaplains exclusively serving its garrisons: relatively few forts and naval bases in Russia had Catholic priests attached to military service (the Catholic presence among the sailors of the naval base at Kronshtadt would be important when the Red Terror first moved against the clergy). Too often Catholic soldiers had to rely on nearby parish priests (as at Sebastopol in the Crimea), or else were bereft of sacraments and spiritual guidance by their own priests in an army which had paid Orthodox clergy.

In addition, the Catholic Church of Petersburg sponsored the Theological Academy,[11] home to an important collection of *Polonica* literature and 70,000 volumes;[12] a preparatory seminary; a number of schools, and religious education in sixty-nine public schools and military academies.

Moscow

The ancient capital of Russia was never as diverse as Saint Petersburg, nor as friendly to non-Russian elements, despite the long history of foreigners being in the city. Catholic services had been held in Moscow since the arrival of the Jesuits in 1648, and there had been a Catholic church since 1691. Assumptionists, Capuchins, Dominicans and Jesuits all served Moscow Catholics, although their number remained small: in 1911, only 27,700[13] in a population of 1.6 million. Appropriately enough, Moscow was a center of the Russian Catholic movement and home to the beginnings of a Russian Catholic order

Immaculate Conception Church, Moscow. Closed in
1937; used as a metalworking factory. Courtesy of Aid
to the Church in Need.

of Dominican nuns; in the years before World War I, its Russian Roman
Catholic population was both energetic and well formed.

In 1914, there were three churches in Moscow: Saint Louis des Français,
the Polish church of Saints Peter and Paul, and its suburban filial church of
the Immaculate Conception.[14] Not having its own separate parish, the nascent
Russian Rite community worshiped at Saints Peter and Paul and in private.

Founded in 1791, the parish of Saint Louis des Français survives to this
day; the present church, built in the mid-1800s to serve French residents, also

served the city's non-Polish Catholics, in particular, foreign diplomats and merchants. The church is colored soft yellow and ivory; it is set back from the street, just off Malaya Lubyanka, with a tiny park in front, surrounded by the presbytery and school (of Saint Philip Neri). Right beside it stands an ocher-colored nine-story building with an ornate entrance, once the Russian Insurance Company but now Communist secret police headquarters. Thus the agency that would labor for the destruction of Soviet Catholicism would be at the very gates of one of only two Catholic parishes to survive in all of Russia.

The French residents of Moscow were noted for their loyalty to the dynasty: indeed, when Napoleon's army occupied the city, they remained loyal to the tsar. The French character of their church was obvious: it was decorated with statues of Saint Louis of France, Blessed Joan of Arc, and Blessed Bernadette, and with a large painting of Blessed Therese of the Child Jesus [15] at the altar of the Virgin; French hymns were sung and French customs observed throughout its existence.[16] Spared closure because of its status as a foreign parish, Saint Louis des Français would become the site of one of the Vatican's most daring and desperate initiatives, carried out by the pope's own secret envoy under the nose of the Soviet secret police.

Saints Peter and Paul was Moscow's oldest Catholic parish, established even before the 1705 decree granting permission to Roman Catholics to build churches,[17] and having a grammar school as part of the complex that surrounded its paved courtyard. It stood at the end of the same street as Saint Louis des Français, a few blocks to the northeast. Serving Moscow's Poles, who were mostly members of the urban working class, the church had a large banner with Jesus' words to Peter: "On this rock I shall build my church," an affirmation of the papal primacy in Orthodoxy's Third Rome.[18] Immaculate Conception was the newest parish, established to serve Catholics in the growing suburbs.

The leaders of the fledgling Russian Catholic movement were Vladimir and Anna Abrikosov, who had joined the Church in Paris. Under the inspiration of Father Felix Werczynski, a Polish priest responsible for many conversions, the Russian Roman Catholics were being encouraged to return to their ancestral rite. A chapel in the Abrikosov house served as Moscow's newest Catholic church, in the Byzantine-Russian Rite, with Father Werczynski celebrating until his arrest and deportation in 1911.[19] Father Ignatius Czajewski, who became pastor of Saints Peter and Paul in 1912, became a good friend of the Russian Catholic movement—a brave stance for a Polish priest to take in a Polish parish. A new religious community, the Russian Catholic Dominicans, was founded in 1911 under the guidance of the French Dominican pastor of

Saint Louis des Français, Father Albert Lerbecier. The Abrikosovs took their vows in the new community, and lived as monk and nun thereafter.[20]

In 1911, the two Latin Catholic parishes served 22,700 believers. Most lived in Moscow, although the church in Grusiny (now part of Moscow) was listed as having 5,000 faithful.[21] The Sisters of Saint Joseph of Chambery were active in Moscow as well.

European Russia

The bulk of the archdiocese's faithful lived in cities, small towns, and rural communities between the Baltic and the Urals. Major centers like Arkhangel'sk, Minsk, Smolensk, Vitebsk, Vladimir, Kazan', Kaluga, and Kharkov all had parishes. Some of these town churches were old, dating back to the days of Polish rule in the west, such as the stone church (completed 1762) of Astrakhan parish (founded in 1715 by the Capuchins), the venerable Saint Mary's Cathedral (completed in 1798) in Minsk and Saint Anthony's (1731) in Vitebsk. Others were more recent, built to serve expanding communities in old Catholic centers (thus in Minsk Saints Simon and Helen's Church was opened in 1910 to augment the older parishes).

In the western rural areas, the parishioners were Belorussian and Polish peasants. In towns, parishes counted Poles, Lithuanians, Germans, and Western European immigrants. Urban Catholics belonged to the working class generally (domestics and factory workers), with very few in the middle class.

Many Catholics lived in rural districts in parishes that had several churches and chapels. Priests thus traveled constantly, and, as in Tiraspol, when there was no Mass, lay-led prayer services had to be held. In Belorussian territory in 1911, Gomel deanery (southern Minsk province) counted 24 villages with chapels, the Lepel deanery (southern Vitebsk province) 7 parish churches, and 25 chapels; and one of the Dünaburg deaneries counted 10 chapels and filial churches.[22]

With rising national awareness and with assimilation to larger groups, the ethnic composition of Catholics in European Russia was changing. Thus in Chernigov province there were several German Catholic villages southeast of the city, some of which were partly Ukrainianized, while remaining Roman Catholic.[23] In Astrakhan, in the first months of the Great War, the Polish parishioners actually reported their pastor for continuing to use German, and he was removed within the day by the imperial authorities.[24] Catholic Belorussians were shedding their Polish identity, even as Catholic Lithuanians (in Minsk province), under pressure from Polish priests, were retaining theirs.

Saints Simon and Helen's Church in Minsk. Used as a garage and a film studio. Reopened from 1941 to 1948. Courtesy of the author.

During the bitter Russification campaign waged by the imperial government in the latter part of the nineteenth century, parishes were forced to accept the Russian language in devotions and sacraments. Fearing that the next step would be Orthodoxy, and fearing for the loss of their own culture and heritage, they resisted, and many churches were shut down. Despite the Edict of Toleration in 1905, not all of these churches were reopened. Instead, they stood as silent sentinels of a stubborn faith in the midst of their villages.[25] An example of that stubbornness can be found in Vilna-Grodno diocese at Miadzviedzici, where the local Catholics kept the church Catholic by meeting daily to recite the Rosary from 1888 to 1907. Their presence and vigilance thwarted the government's plan to introduce Orthodoxy into the parish.[26] (Similar courage would save several parishes deprived of pastors in Soviet Belorussia.)

In Minsk diocese, Auxiliary Bishop Francis Simon arranged for the reopening of 30 churches that had been forced to accept the "Russian Ritual," restoring the use of Polish. In 1910, the area had 285,000 Catholic believers with 85 working churches, and only 80 priests. In June 1910, Bishop John Cieplak was able to visit these parishes. Large crowds attended the services, and Confirmation was administered to thousands. At Wiazyn, the bishop introduced radical practices: he concelebrated the Mass with twenty priests in the open air. One thousand were confirmed. At Kojdanow, 1,500 people were confirmed and a public Corpus Christi procession held. Indeed, Catholics held similar processions in all of the villages and towns, despite local laws that forbade outdoor preaching and celebrations. The bishop's tour peaked in August at Pinsk, where he was approached by oppressed Greek Catholics and lapsed Roman Catholics, and where he impressed the Russian Orthodox favorably. When, however, the local authorities protested, the bishop was deprived of his government pension and five priests were fined.[27]

Siberia, the Pacific East, and Central Asia

Infamous as the land of frozen exile and desolate forced labor camps, Siberia in the early twentieth century was a flourishing frontier region experiencing major immigration from the rest of the empire. The first European settlers had been adventurers, soldiers, missionaries, and intrepid trappers and farmers. Catholics were found among all these populations, and Catholicism dated to the first days of European colonization. In addition, Siberia had a proud cultural history of its own: Irkutsk was known as the "Paris of the East"; Tomsk was home to a well-known university, engineering school, and teachers' college. By 1900, electricity had been introduced into the major cities; movie theaters were already established; there was a Siberian stock exchange. Up to 70 percent of the population in the towns belonged to the middle class, with middle-class values, and there was an active political life.

Due to the construction of the Trans-Siberian Railroad (1891–1916) and the agrarian reforms of 1904–1914 and accompanying colonization plans, much larger tracts were opened for settlement. German Siberians numbered only 5,424 in 1897, but had grown to 44,838 by 1914.[28] Retired soldiers, railroad men, convicts, merchants, industrial workers, farmers: all included Catholics who needed the services of the Church.

German Catholic Teutonic Knights, their servants and Latvian believers had been sent to Siberia during the Livonian Wars under Ivan the Terrible in the late 1550s.[29] Poles were continually being exiled to the east throughout the Russian-Polish struggles. Later, Catholic Poles, Balts, and Germans freely joined the exodus to the "land beyond the sun."

Bishop Cieplak's 1909 tour found a diverse Church. The foundation of Catholicism had been laid by Polish exiles since the 1650s, whose descendants were joined by Belorussian and Ukrainian Greek Catholics after 1839. Most of the Poles remained devoutly Catholic.[30] Waves of Poles and Lithuanians were sent east after the partitions of Poland in the late 1700s (100,000 exiles), as well as after the Uprising of 1830–1831 (80,000 exiles), and the Uprising of 1863 (150,000 exiles). In the malaria-infested town of Tunka, southwest of Irkutsk, a colony of 200 exiled priests and monks was established. At Kuznetsk, Polish families built several small churches after they were sent there following the 1863 uprising.

These exiles and their descendants worshiped in Latin Catholic churches side by side with the settlers lured to Siberia by the prospects of land and economic opportunity. The steady expansion of the Trans-Siberian Railroad created centers of metallurgy and mining, and also gave access to rich agricultural zones. The Catholics included the new settlers, exiles, and retired Polish soldiers who married local Siberian women and established new homes.[31] The priests often cared for several communities, traveling enormous distances and living in poverty. Early missionaries included Jesuits and Bernardine Fathers.

Whereas Siberia and the Pacific Far East had only 5 churches in the 1870s, the archdiocese reported 15 churches and 21 chapels for 7 parishes there in 1909, to serve nearly 74,000 faithful, with 25 traveling priests who usually spent the entire year riding the railroad or sleighs. Centers of the Catholic Church in these eastern reaches of the empire were at Omsk, home of the Church of the Immaculate Conception (completed 1867); at Slavgorod, the nucleus of a large German colony that boasted several Catholic churches; and at Irkutsk (completed 1884), Tomsk (completed 1806), Novonikolaevsk (later Novosibirsk, whose church was begun in 1906 and which also had a cemetery chapel), Tambov, Krasnoyarsk, and Chita (at the eastern end of Siberia); and in the Far East, at Blagoveshchensk, Nikolaevsk-on-the-Amur, Khabarovsk, and the coastal port of Vladivostok. A priestless parish existed at Alexandrovsk on Sakhalin.[32] As a result of Bishop Cieplak's tour, these statistics were revised in 1909 to register a Catholic population of 200,000, with 31 parishes of 14 churches and 21 prayer houses, 40 parish priests and 1 military chaplain, with another 50,000 Catholics needing to be brought into contact with the institutions of the Church.[33]

The Siberian Roman Catholic churches were usually prominently located, reflecting Catholic self-confidence and pride in this exciting region: at Omsk, the church stood near Nicholas Square and the Cadet School, close to the rail station; at Novonikolaevsk (Novosibirsk), the parish had "a magnificent church" atop a ridge dominating the city; in Tobol'sk (completed 1907), it was in the lower town near the Modern School; in Tomsk, the Church of the Intercession of the Mother of God was on Resurrection Mountain, just four blocks from the river and open bazaar; at Irkutsk, across from the Orthodox

Cathedral and on Speransky Square; in strategic Vladivostok, on the steep slopes rising above the Golden Horn of the harbor. Gothic steeples soared above the Siberian skylines, marking churches built at great sacrifice by workers and farmers.[34]

Catholics formed a significant presence in some of the towns: in 1911, Vladivostok's parish of the Holy Mother of God had nearly 11,000 faithful,[35] which accounted for 10 percent of the city's population (120,000 in 1897, including Asians). Krasnoyarsk had 80,000 residents, of whom 13,000 were Catholics. In 1910, the university city of Tomsk had 112,000 inhabitants, with the Catholic parish counting 10,000 as members. Other parishes were quite small: a 1910 survey listed only 59 parishioners in Barnaul, 140 in Kansk; 640 in Tyumen; and 775 in Mariinsk.

As in European Russia, Catholic construction continued up to and through the October Revolution: Saint Ignatius Church in Blagoveshchensk was built in the late 1890s, Transfiguration Church at Khabarovsk in 1911. The Vladivostok church was not finished until after the close of the civil war.[36]

Bishop Cieplak's Great Tour

The auxiliary bishop of Mogilev, John Cieplak (ordained as bishop in 1908), was granted government permission to undertake the first (and thus far the only) episcopal visitation of the entire Russian East in 1909. Bishop Cieplak visited settlements from the Urals to the island of Sakhalin, including forced labor camps.[37]

The bishop's tour began in the cultural and industrial center of Ykaterinburg, future site of the Romanov massacre in 1918. From there, he followed the Trans-Siberian Railroad and its branch lines, visiting all the important cities, with a host of stops in between, including visits to the Asian kingdoms being incorporated into Russia and the colony of Harbin in Manchuria, for a total of sixty-five visitations. On the tour, he took with him Father Zygmunt Lozinski, a future beatus of the Church and also future bishop of Minsk,[38] and Latvian, Lithuanian, and Polish priests. At Tashkent, his traveling party was joined by Father Justin Pranajtis, pastor to a congregation of 10,000 Poles and Germans following Russia's expansion into the south.[39]

Every visitation became an occasion for spiritual renewal and recommitment to the Catholic religion. Some adults would receive five sacraments at one Mass: baptism, confession, communion, confirmation, and marriage. Bishop Cieplak administered Confirmation to 21,408 faithful during the tour:

Assumption of Our Lady Church, Irkutsk, Siberia, 1920. Used as a concert hall and a movie theater. Courtesy of the Vladivostok Mission.

to 3,173 in Omsk; to 2,355 in Tomsk; to 1,738 in Spasskoye; and to 800 in Irkutsk. The bishop impressed the Siberian Catholics by his humility (among other things, he made breakfast for his traveling companions) and by his willingness to share their hardships. He slept on floors and atop the clay stoves that heated Siberian huts, and even slept in the prison camps, accepting the presence of vermin in the barracks so as to minister to prisoners. At Irkutsk, the church was consecrated and a public Corpus Christi procession was held. The bishop preached a four-day mission, and everyone present received the

Transfiguration Church, Blagoveshchensk, Russian Far East.

sacraments of confession and communion. (The Far East and Sakhalin held some 11,000 Polish Catholics by 1914.) At Vladivostok, he blessed the foundation of Most Holy Mother of God Church (completed in 1922).[40]

One of the most poignant visits of the bishop's tour was to Sakhalin. Taking the ferry to Alexandrovsk as so many others had since the island became a place of exile in 1875, the clerics discovered a handsome little church erected by Polish political prisoners in 1879, and faithfully attended by them and by their descendants since that time. (Bishop Cieplak was able to send a priest to this lonely outpost of faith in 1910.) As in Tiraspol diocese, these scattered parishes had experienced a powerful revival as a result of a 1908 mission preached by Redemptorist Fathers.[41] Thus they unknowingly prepared themselves to face the storm of destruction lurking down the road of history.

The Nestorian Church, which had once counted a host of dioceses in Central Asia, where Bishop Cieplak also visited, was extinguished in the atrocities of Timur the Lame in the late 1300s, to be replaced by Islam. A mix of Turkic Muslim kingdoms and khanates had been incorporated into the empire as a result of campaigns and treaties from 1865 to 1885. European settlement had been confined to the cities, although the agrarian reforms brought colonists to establish new outposts there. Thus the German population grew from 8,874 in 1897 to 50,160 in 1914.[42] Settlers brought Orthodoxy, Catholicism, and Protestantism with them into the European quarters of the towns and the new agricultural colonies.

Central Asia

Russian rule was completely extended over the various states until just a generation before the Revolution (the Pamir Plateau was annexed only in 1895). What are now Kazakhstan, Turkmenistan, Uzbekistan, Tajikistan, and Kyrgyzstan were in those times a collection of various emirates and kingdoms annexed either directly or indirectly as protectorates under the tsar, with Turkic and Persian subjects who followed various forms of Islam.

Thanks to the missionary labors of the Nestorians (with small colonies of Latin Catholics and Greek Orthodox), Christianity had been very strong throughout Central Asia until Timur Leng (Tamerlane; d. 1405) devastated Asia and swept those communities away. Archaeological digs have proven their long existence, through rediscovered cemeteries and churches and Christian artifacts.[43] Although it is generally believed that Christianity became extinct, Catholics from the territory are firm in stating that the Latin Catholic missionaries, merchants, and captives who transversed the Silk Road left behind tiny communities of Christians who intermarried with the Nestorian remnant and other natives. These families continued to hold to their Catholic identity, and joined the new settlers who came with the Russians in the nineteenth century to establish Catholic parishes. German and Polish soldiers, tradesmen, and farmers followed Russian rule and established parishes in Tashkent, Samarkand, and a few other locations in a mostly Muslim world.[44] Imperial-era statistics counted 74,000 Catholics living in Siberia (before Bishop Cieplak's tour), with 112,000 living in all of Russia's Asian possessions. Thus the Catholic population of the Central Asian provinces and states may have been as high as 38,000, entirely possible given the size of the Tashkent parish alone. This parish counted about 15,000 Catholics in the region after the tour (but because it was just putting up a church, Baedeker does not even list it). It had four filial churches to the east, and another seven stretching to the Caspian Sea divided between Tashkent and Baku parishes.[45]

Punishment of Cieplak

Bishop Cieplak did visit at Tashkent and, with the permission of Premier Stolypin, went to central Russia, where he journeyed for two months, starting at Rybinsk. He was able to consecrate a few churches and chapels, dedicated to Our Lady of Czestochowa or of Ostrabama, indicating the strong Polish and Lithuanian influence. At Kazan', his sermon was reported to the government, and he lost his salary as auxiliary bishop.[46] If one of the most important Catholic bishops in Russia could lose all his income simply for performing his pastoral duties, what more could happen to local priests who might be considered to have "strayed" beyond what was acceptable to the Orthodox authorities? How difficult it must have been for isolated parish priests to function under such circumstances. Evangelization was totally out of the question in these territories, where the Catholic Church was definitely known as "the Polish church," and where mixed marriages with Orthodox almost inevitably led to the Church's losing the whole family.

Isolated Parishes Outside the Deaneries

Though Siberia had no deaneries until the February Revolution, the parishes there had some contact with each other through the circuit-riding priests. This was not so in northern European Russia at places such as Yaroslavl', Murmansk, and Arkhangel'sk, in the Russian heartland south of Moscow and west of the Urals, and in the newly annexed or "protected" Muslim states of Central Asia.

These places accounted for thirty-four Catholic parishes in 1909, including most of Siberia, Russian Asia, and the north of Russia. Though many were quite large, and had a respectable history, they were all directly dependent on the archbishop for administration. Because the government forbade the organization of deaneries,[47] the priests had no structure to provide guidance or moral support, and there was no legal way to bring parishioners together and unite the priests for discussions or retreats.

A dean in the Catholic world of that time could convoke the clergy, supervise ecclesiastical life, ensure that parishes were cared for properly, arrange for both leave and sick care for parish priests, and generally provide a central reference point, arbiter, and counselor for laity and clergy alike.[48] Thus the presence of deaneries elsewhere in the empire offered substance to the Church, at least in the first 10–15 years of state persecution, and the lack of deaneries in so many other areas emphasized the isolation of the Catholic believers.

As a result of Bishop Cieplak's tour and working knowledge of the east, deaneries were instituted in Siberia (Omsk, Vladivostok) and Central Asia (Tashkent) after the February Revolution, through 1920. Parishes elsewhere remained unconnected to the larger Church, save for the curia in Petrograd.

Imperial Russian Catholicism in Manchuria

The Russian Empire had important holdings in China's northern province of Manchuria, homeland of the Ching dynasty, deposed in 1911. The province, described by a Russian émigré as a "vast nature preserve with few towns"[49] was crossed by the (Russian-owned) Chinese Eastern Railway, which branched off the Trans-Siberian at Blagoveshchensk (see map 1), and provided Russia with routes to the south and warm water. The center for the railroad was in the colony of Harbin.

Harbin was founded as a railroad town, with separate European and Chinese sections. Settled by veterans of the Russo-Japanese War (1904–1905), attracted to the rich farmland in the river valleys, it grew into a handsome, well-planned Russian city with parks, schools, churches, theaters, and tree-lined boulevards. Indeed, with buildings designed by noted Russian and Western European architects, Harbin rivaled any great Russian center.[50] It also reflected imperial Russian diversity: in 1913, barely 50 percent of Harbin's 66,000 people were Russian. More than 34 percent of its residents were Chinese; more than 7 percent were Jews; nearly 4 percent were Poles; and there were large communities of Germans, Armenians, Estonians, Tatars, Georgians, Latvians, and Japanese.[51]

Harbin had churches, synagogues, temples, and mosques supported by all these groups. European Roman Catholics (mostly Poles) worshiped in Saint Stanislaus's Cathedral, built in the Gothic style in 1907, and Saint Josaphat's Church; Chinese Catholics worshiped in a third parish.[52]

Because it and the whole region around it would fall within the boundaries of the Republic of China, Harbin was spared Bolshevik excesses. Its presence as a thriving reminder of Russia's prerevolutionary past and its proximity to the Far Eastern provinces proved providential for tens of thousands of people in the years ahead. Both Roman and Eastern Catholics would have an important place in Harbin's turbulent future.

The Russian Greek Catholics

Reference has been made to the Russian Greek (Byzantine) Catholics. Their existence, loyalty to traditional Russian liturgical usage, and steady growth defied the traditional view of the Church as a Polish institution.

In 1896, Father Alexis Zerchaninov had left the Russian Orthodox Church and become a Catholic. Denied jurisdiction by the Roman Catholic metropolitan despite four years in prison away from his family, he continued to serve in an Orthodox parish while suffering persecution as a Catholic. In 1905, he visited Metropolitan Andrew Sheptytsky in Lemberg (later, Lwów, Lvov, L'viv), Austria-Hungary, the head of the Ukrainian Greek Catholic Church, and in 1907 sought the establishment, through the metropolitan, of a separate Russian Catholic eparchy that would follow the pure Russian liturgical tradition. By that time, there were "several priests and . . . one thousand faithful" who were either Greek or Latin Catholic, mostly of the Russian aristocracy and intelligentsia.[53]

Bishop Cieplak had encouraged the nascent movement. He was a close friend of the philosopher Vladimir Soloviev, and he received Soloviev into the Church secretly. In 1899, Father Nikolai Tolstoy, a chaplain of the imperial court, also converted. Secret meetings of Russian Greek Catholics were held at Tver' and Nizhni Novgorod, both venerable sites of Russian history. Another convert was Father Ivan Deubner, an official of the Saratov government, who secretly converted in 1899 and who was ordained in 1902 by Metropolitan Sheptytsky.[54] After the Edict of Toleration in 1905, the Russian converts were hopeful for recognition of their community by the State.

As noted above, the Greek Catholic eparchy of Kamenets was still legally alive and part of the Lemberg metropolia. As a result, Sheptytsky had jurisdiction in that little southwest corner of the Russian Empire, and in February 1907, replying to a request of the metropolitan to extend that jurisdiction Pope Pius X directed him: "Make use of your rights." Thus when Father Zerchaninov's request came to him two months later, Sheptytsky named Zerchaninov his representative for Kamenets and all Russia under the title "Vicar-General of the Eparchy of Kamenets-Podolsk." Papal documents confirming the metropolitan's jurisdiction were signed in 1908, and confirmed in 1909, 1910, and 1914. In 1908, Sheptytsky toured Russia in disguise, visiting the Russian Greek Catholics and sympathizers in Saint Petersburg,

Moscow, and Kiev.[55] From 1910 until World War I, he was linked with the community through Father Leonid Feodorov, who made brief visits annually to Lemberg.[56]

In 1908, Father Zerchaninov opened the first Greek Catholic chapel, in Saint Petersburg, where an apartment was converted over into one room for his residence and two rooms into one liturgically complete chapel on Polozovaya Street. There were by then several other public Russian Catholic priests, all converts from Orthodoxy or Old Belief, with the exception of Father Deubner, who was the only priest ordained for the movement.[57] At Easter in 1909, in response to an Easter telegram to the tsar from Father Susalev, who had united from Old Believers to Russian Catholics, the community received a telegram from the imperial court granting tenuous recognition under the curious title "Old Believers in communion with the Apostolic See of Rome." This telegram from the imperial household was prominently posted for protection against the police.[58] In 1912, the chapel was able to post a sign reading "Orthodox Catholic Church of the Eastern Rite." Though small, this new Church offered a new horizon at a time of increased interest among Russian citizens in "things Catholic."

The tiny community of faith was torn by internal struggles over retaining the pure Russian tradition and introducing Latin Catholic customs, anxiety over their legal status, ill will from the Latin Catholic metropolitan and some of his priests, and harassment by the police and Orthodox authorities.[59] There was also the perennial problem of whether Russian converts to the Church should be prevented from entering the Latin Rite and restricted to the new Russian community, as had been decreed by Pope Leo XIII in *Orientalium dignitas* back in 1894.[60]

The Austro-Hungarian missionary priest Father Jan Urban, who had great influence among Russian Roman Catholics, influenced the introduction of specifically Latin Catholics devotions and the Latinization of the ritual among some of the Greek Catholics.[61] There were thus two separate chapels, Polozovaya with Latinized services held by Father Deubner, and the new chapel on Barmalayeva Street, with "pure" ones. In this time of trial, Princess Maria Volkonskaya and Natalia Ushakovna (a cousin of Prime Minister Stolypin) stand out as eminent lay apostles. They fought for legalization of the new Russian Catholic Church by the government, support from the Vatican for removing the Latinizations, and promotion of their cause by the archdiocese of Mogilev, a cause of Russian Catholicism that was constantly obstructed by Archbishop Kluczinsky.

Eventually they gained intercessions from Rome and encouragement from friendly Latin Catholic clergy, especially Bishop Cieplak and the Dominicans and Assumptionists. Their work bore fruit: the Russian Catholics expanded their horizons into charitable work with the poor of the slums and the foundation of a journal, *Slovo Istiny* (Word of Truth). Despite their efforts, the two chapels were finally sealed in February 1913. Because Roman Catholic Archbishop Kluczinsky did not protest the closures, the Russian Greek Catholics' supporters in the imperial Duma were unable to act in their favor.[62]

At this time, the saintly Father Leonid Feodorov (ordained by the Bulgarian Byzantine Catholic archbishop in 1911) arrived in Saint Petersburg, and revived the flagging hopes of the faithful and the fortunes of their journal *Slovo Istiny*. He was the second Russian ordained to the Catholic priesthood for the Byzantine Russian Catholics, who numbered 743 in 1911, including those outside the capital itself. A side door to the Barmalayeva chapel had not been sealed, and in 1914 Father Feodorov offered the Holy Week services in great secrecy. He was forced to leave the city, however, and went on to Moscow to visit the devout Abrikosovs and their little community, as well as to several other cities where there were faithful. Finally, he left Russia, heading to Constantinople in the summer, planning to go to the Orthodox monastic center at Mount Athos. At the same time, two new Russian Catholic priests entered the country: Father Gleb Verkhovsky, a noted artist and confrere of Diaghilev, and Father Trofim Semiatsky, a "colorful figure" from the Petersburg community. Both had studied abroad, under the influence of the soon-to-be famous Jesuit priest Michel d'Herbigny, and had been likewise ordained in Bulgaria.[63]

In Moscow, the Russian Catholic community continued to pray and grow, committed to interior sanctification and the pure Russian services, and ministered to at Saints Peter and Paul. The Abrikosovs continued to provide leadership. In Saint Petersburg, discreet services continued on Barmalayeva Street and public services at a side chapel in Saint Catherine's (Father Zerchaninov) and the church of the Knights of Malta (Father Verkovsky) in the Imperial Pages Building.

The Great Return of the Stubborn Ones

A mass movement emerged in the Russian Empire's western and southwestern provinces after April 1905, with the emergence of the Greek Catholics (disparagingly known as Uniates by the Orthodox) from their twilight existence. From Lithuania down along the Austro-Hungarian frontier, tens of thousands of people abandoned the state Church for their ancestral faith. They represented one of the truly heroic and sadly unknown epics of the

Catholic Church that took place in Belorussia and southern Lithuania from 1839 to 1905, and in the region of Chelm from 1875 to 1905. The fate of this people and their Church is important to our story, both in 1914 and to understand the bitter persecution of the tiny community inside the USSR before 1937 and the tragedies spread by Stalin's forces after World War II to other Greek Catholic Churches across Europe.

The Church Destroyed?
The "Uniate Metropolia of Russia" and Its Fate

In the suppressions of 1773 and 1792 under Catherine the Great, millions were ordered to become Orthodox and subjected to Russification (many Greek Catholics escaped forcible conversion by changing over to the Latin Catholic Church, especially after 1792). Although numerous priests and lay believers of eastern Ukraine died bitterly opposed to the Russian Church, the Greek Catholic Church died there with them. This was the hope of later tsars for the whole empire, and it motivated the suppressions by Nicholas I (1839) and by Alexander II (1875), suppressions that failed in their goals of Russification and eradication.

The first suppression, under Nicholas I, took place after the (Polish) Uprising of 1830–1831, in which the Catholics were seen as enemies of the empire. The ability of the Russian state to obtain the cooperation of the Orthodox Church, influence the choice of leadership, and the acquiescence of some Greek and Latin Catholic hierarchs in the destruction of Catholicism, is a sorrowful testimony to the effect of state domination of Church affairs and the weakness of the human spirit.

The apostate Bishop Joseph Siemaszko (recruited by the tsar in 1828)[64] organized the suppression of his own Greek Catholic Church, the Church in which he had been born, and in which his priest-father and his entire family continued to live and worship until their dying days. The depth of popular opposition in many provinces can be seen by the fact that Siemaszko had to arrange for the relocation of his parents from their home to his diocese, and his father was forbidden to celebrate the Divine Liturgy. The bishop's brother, John, openly proclaimed that Joseph had damned his soul and lost the people; at John's death, Orthodox priests who forcibly buried the body in Orthodox rites received personal commendations from Joseph. John's widow publicly changed to the Latin Catholic Church so as to avoid that fate.[65] At least 200 Greek Catholic priests who refused to convert to the state Church were imprisoned in Orthodox monasteries.[66]

The bishop arranged for the forcible union of the Greek Catholic Church with the Russian Orthodox Church, thus also for the Russification of both the religious worship and daily life of the faithful (and for his personal glorification as well).[67] The process took nine years of closures, forcible installation of Orthodox bishops and priests, introducing Russian rituals and service books, shutting down the Basilian monasteries, and gradual subordination to the Holy Synod. Many priests and their families were exiled to Siberia; in the famine of 1833–1834, food was withheld from Greek Catholic peasants in Belorussia unless they agreed to convert.[68]

Although many Greek Catholic priests and lay believers were confused by the machinations of the State,[69] outraged by betrayal on the part of their leaders, or simply weary of unrelenting persecution, the final destruction of the Church was achieved only with violence and the intrusion of Russian Orthodox priests at the bayonet points of the Cossacks. In many villages, entire populations were exiled along with their priests to Siberia and the villages repopulated with ethnic Russians. Loyal Catholic priests were sent to forced labor, and monks were imprisoned in a special monastery-prison camp in Kursk. Priests were beaten with chains and staves and thrown into filthy cells. Greek Catholic priests were explicitly told in their prisons that if they did not convert they would be "liquidated" and indeed many did die from their sufferings. Lay believers in villages were literally dragged to church to receive Holy Communion from Orthodox priests. Children were taken from their parents to be raised by the State.[70] (All of these horrors would be repeated on the Greek Catholics who came under Soviet control after 1939.)

At the same time, the Greek Catholic population resisted. Secret societies were founded. Some Latin Catholic priests continued to baptize the Greek Catholics' children and to bury their dead by night. Secret Greek Catholic priests came secretly from Austria to minister to networks of families. Russian subjects in turn went secretly into Austria to receive the sacraments and keep up connections with their Church and the Ruthenian people, and many permanently emigrated.[71] (This pattern of repression, resistance, and underground activity would be duplicated under the Soviets in 1946–1950 in western Ukraine and Belorussia, as well as in the Soviet-occupied countries of Eastern Europe.)

Some Latin Catholic bishops betrayed their fellow Catholics as well. The Catholic College forbade Latin priests to hear the confessions of secret Greek Catholics in the churches or during the *atlaidai*. The bishop of Minsk turned over to the Russian Church the names of all Catholics whose families had been Greek Catholic before 1790, and he received the Orthodox bishop with full Catholic honors in Saint Mary's Cathedral. All Latin Catholic priests in the empire were ordered to turn in lists to the local Orthodox pastors of parishioners whose families had been Greek Catholic before 1798.

The Last Greek Catholic Holdout

Chelm had survived the destruction of 1839 because it was part of the Russian-ruled Kingdom of Poland. The eparchy, however, faced internal struggles following the Uprising of 1830–1831: many priests participated in Polonization and Latinization out of loyalty to the Polish cause. Polish sermons, bibles, and even missals and devotions became common. A new bishop tried to clean things up liturgically, but did so by importing Russian books. Rome suspended him, and a second bishop was brought in from Austria-Hungary. His efforts foundered on the opposition of pro-Moscow clergy and government officials.

In 1871, the apostate priest Popel became the willing tool of the Russian Church. He was named by the tsar, while still officially Catholic, and worked to establish union with Orthodoxy. Popel ordered the elimination of prayers for the pope, an end to both Latinizations and traditional West Slavic practices, and the new offering of prayers for the Orthodox synod. Although some members converted to Orthodoxy, and some to the Latin Catholic Church, the rest decided to hold out. In 1875, an official union of the Orthodox and "Uniate" Churches took place. A population of 246,100 believers in 330 parishes was formally lost to the Church.[72]

The union resulted in open conflict. As in 1839, the army was called in, and massacres took place at Pratulyn and Dreliv.[73] In addition, these atrocities were combined with the mass suicides of Greek Catholics dying inside their burning churches singing Catholic hymns, possibly imitating the past practices of their Old Believer neighbors.[74] Polish sympathizers assisted the secret Catholics, and the now-Orthodox churches often stood empty.

The stalwart resistance in Chelm inspired descendants of the Greek Catholics in the 1839 territories to remember their Church and to hope for its restoration. In 1895, it was rumored that Nicholas II would grant the restoration of the Greek Catholic Church after his coronation. There were occasions in which (formerly Catholic) Russian Orthodox parishes turned out their state-appointed priests to await the return of their legitimate pastors.[75]

Yet the Church did not die out: among those exiled to Siberia, the survivors and their descendants merged into Roman Catholic parishes, refusing to attend Orthodox ones. Of those who were left in their traditional villages, many fled to Austria-Hungary and found refuge in Galicia. Inside the Russian Empire, some few were able to join Latin Catholic parishes, eventually becoming Polonized and Latinized. Still others formed an underground network, dependent on Jesuit missionaries from Austria-Hungary, who were disguised as peddlers. These believers people worshiped in secret and kept the Catholic faith alive.

In 1877, two Galician Jesuits began a mission to the Greek Catholics in Polesie region. Disguised as laborers, blacksmiths, and pig traders, priests ministered to these believers for twenty-six years. They had to defend themselves against the imperial police and customs officers, and against an apostate Greek Catholic who became a hunter of his former co-believers. The more noted of the two was Father Jan Urban, SJ, who served until 1903, and who wrote of baptizing babies in Dubnica while his sweat collected in a pool around his feet. Urban later became involved in the Neo-Uniate movement.[76]

Many became known as the *"Uporstvuyushchie,* (the stubborn ones), who lived in areas not tended to by the Jesuits. They numbered some 100,000 people in 1905, and had not received any sacraments at all except baptism for some thirty years because of their refusal to even set foot in an Orthodox church.[77] (The same pattern of forcible destruction and conversion, Catholic resistance, and occasional self-serving apostasy, was to be repeated under Soviet rule in 1945–1949, with similar results.)

As a result of the Revolution of 1905, Nicholas II was forced to grant some religious liberties. Among these was permission to abandon the Orthodox Church and to join another Church. After 1905, there were 500,000 who joined the Catholic Church, and at least 230,000 to 300,000 of these were the descendants of the Greek Catholics, of whom 100,000 were from the territory of Chelm.[78] Because they still could not restore their Greek Catholic Church, they packed the surviving Latin Rite churches of southern Lithuania, Belorussia, and western Volhynia. At the same time, this substantial return was only a small portion of believers previously lost to the Church.

The Uniate question was a major topic at the 1905–1906 *sobor* of the Russian Orthodox Church. Strong Catholic sympathies, pro-union ideas, attractions to the Latin Catholic Church, and the presence of Catholic theology in worship were reported throughout the borderlands. The Orthodox reacted by placing the Chelm district directly under Saint Petersburg's diocesan control. An "energetic renewal" of Russification was undertaken to recruit Catholics back into Orthodoxy; at the same time, attacks on the Old Believers were renewed, which impelled some into sympathy with the Russian Greek Catholic movement.[79] (Smaller "returns" would take place in the interwar Republic of Poland and in the Chelm territory during World War II.)

August 1914: Status on Eve of War

The 300th anniversary of the founding of the Romanov Dynasty in 1913 had been remarkable for its tense atmosphere. At the celebrations in Saint Petersburg, Nicholas II was grave and aloof; the empress was overwrought and withdrawn. At Moscow's Red Square, the crown prince, frail from hemophilia, had to be carried by his Cossack guards. The prime minister wrote that "the crowd seemed to feel some sort of deep impending tragedy in the helpless condition of the Sovereign's only son." The great wave of patriotism and loyalty to the dynasty that met Russia's declaration of war served only as a temporary balm. Russia was so sunk in gloom and repression that Lenin did not think he would even live to see a revolution.[80]

The Catholic Church of the Russian Empire entered the first years of World War I with a changed leadership: Archbishop Vincent Kluczynski had resigned from Mogilev in 1913. His auxiliary, Bishop Cieplak, was elected in July 1914 by the archdiocesan chapter as vicar capitular and administrator. Fifteen days later, on July 29, Russia and Austria-Hungary mobilized their forces along the frontier. On August 1, Germany and Russia mobilized. The Great War began, and on August 20 Pope Pius X died, shocked by the rapid spread of hostilities. Throughout the remainder of the war, and into the first horrendous years of Bolshevism, the Catholic Church would be led by Pope Benedict XV, a pontiff committed to charity and peace.

There were other changes and problems afoot in the Catholic Church of the Russian Empire as well:

1. Catholicism made a belated entry into the Silver Age's literature: a number of fine journals were published under Catholic auspices by 1917, reflecting both the drive for spiritual knowledge in the empire and growing interest in the Church.

2. The Constitutional Catholic Party was strong enough in the Vilna-Grodno diocese to send the bishop as delegate to the Duma. Catholics were also organizing politically in the Petrograd region, hoping to bring about relief in both the economic and religious spheres. A Russian Roman Catholic priest, Father Alexander Sipiagin, was elected to the first state Duma.

3. The size of the population that converted to Catholicism after 1905, when not including the returning "stubborn ones" of the borderlands, came

to 200,000 souls, indicating a whole new approach to the Church on the part of many Russian subjects. Most of the religious seekers from Saint Petersburg's upper society did not join the Russian Greek Catholic community: they wanted nothing to do with a Church that reminded them of the Orthodox Church. That caused tension between Latin and Greek Catholics.

4. In the cities, Catholic life was undergoing further changes. The industrial workers and domestics remained loyal to the Church, especially the Poles and Lithuanians. Among the working class, the parishes were the center of life, and trust in the parish priest was without limits. Workers flocked to Sunday Mass and devotions and sent their children to the parochial schools.

On the other hand, many of the Germans who moved to the towns became lax or went to German Protestant churches. Some waited years to baptize their children, and many adults abandoned the sacraments: this was especially so if there was not a German Catholic parish or priest available. Among the educated urban Catholics, many were affected by the religious formalism that afflicted Russian Orthodoxy in the last years of the empire. Although there was a spiritual ferment taking place, these lapsed Catholics tended to fall into the trap of rationalism. Educated Polish women still made their Easter duty, but this was not true for the men or most of the educated Germans. The latter were especially susceptible to the "trends" of the day when there was not a German priest in their city.[81]

5. A major problem in urban areas was one of mixed marriages: Poles would marry Orthodox Russians, and their children had to be raised in the Orthodox faith by law. Germans would marry Protestants, and there was danger of the children of those marriages also being lost to the Catholic faith.[82] Conversely, the Catholics of the southern cities that would be so afflicted in the civil war had experienced a deep renewal of their faith through the missions of 1907 and follow-up ministries of the priests through the Forty-Hour Devotions and youth seminars. The examples of Saints Aloysius Gonzaga and Agnes the Martyr were given to parish youth as models of constancy, purity and faith under difficult circumstances,[83] surely a prophetic choice.

6. A final serious problem faced the urban Catholic who was dying. If the person was in a city hospital, the priest was not allowed to visit to administer the sacraments. This held true for the dying soldiers as well, despite the increase in Catholic chaplaincies during the World War I under Archbishop Cieplak. Civil and military authorities alike would prevent a priest from coming to their aid.[84] (This tsarist prejudice would be resurrected in Communist laws.)

7. There were other worrisome events: the Revolution of 1905 had weakened the authority of many priests in the Tiraspol diocese because they

had supported the autocracy against the aspirations of their faithful. Priests who held tsarist medals and honors continued to defend the absolutist monarchy. This was resented by their faithful, who wanted changes.[85]

There was also the language issue in Vilna-Grodno diocese, and rising nationalism and anti-Polish feelings among the Belorussian, Latvian and Lithuanian laity and some non-Polish clergy in the western districts of the province.

8. No matter their location, most Catholics experienced daily discrimination because of their religion and ethnic background. Many urban Catholics were, as seen above, poor people with no prospects for economic or social improvement. Rural life was becoming difficult, and emigration was a painful and inadequate solution. A great many Catholics were living in regions where they formed a minority feared or resented by ethnic Russians.

Even Catholics faithfully serving the tsar could not escape discrimination. Although diocesan registers show priests serving as military chaplains to garrisons in Saint Petersburg, Viborg (Mogilev), Sebastopol-Simferopol', and Odessa (Tiraspol) and parish clergy providing access to sacraments to some of the troops in the Caucasus[86] (Tiraspol), many Catholic soldiers and sailors were stationed elsewhere. At those posts only Orthodox services were offered. Because Catholic military chaplaincies staffed by the Franciscans in Pinsk, Minsk, Mogilev, Arkhangel'sk, Moscow, and elsewhere had all been closed after the 1863 Uprising,[87] Catholic young men could spend years without the sacraments. This was rectified only during the war. Catholic soldiers in the imperial army increased from 100,000 to 700,000, and Bishop Cieplak was able to have graduates of the theological academy appointed as chaplains, with broad mandate for celebration of the sacraments.[88] At other posts, the Catholic chaplains served as the only source of sacraments for civilians as well, a reminder that there were not enough priests for the population as a whole.

9. Although there were new churches being erected in some cities until the outbreak of the war, there were still many churches whose doors had been locked by imperial decree. In 1914, there was absolutely no prospect of those churches being reopened; where there were working churches, there were definitely not enough priests for *any* of the Catholic believers. Government restrictions on who could be trained, ordained, and where they could be assigned did not guarantee a better future. Tens of thousands of believers were in worshiping communities that did not have weekly Mass, and not just in the scattered rural parishes. This is borne out by the priest:parishioner ratio. In Samogitia, it was 1:1,973; in Tiraspol, 1:2,400; in Lutsk-Zhitomir-Kamenets, 1:2,515, in Mogilev, 1:2,820; and in Vilna-Grodno, an astounding 1:3,944.[89]

10. Catholic numbers had jumped because of the "Great Return" and the converts of 1905–1912. For the large population of former Greek Catholics, there was no hope for the restoration of their Church. Both they and the converts put a new strain on overworked clergy and buildings. Furthermore, the repression after 1907 refused to recognize these people as being legitimately Catholic. The Polish Jesuit Father Felix Werczynski, who had converted a thousand Moscow Russians to the Faith, was expelled from the city, and Bishop Stephen Denisowicz was removed from his position and deprived of his income.[90] Father Jan Urban, another clandestine Jesuit from Austria-Hungary, had been expelled or recalled to his province under Russian pressure because of his successful propagation of Catholicism in the Russian language at Saint Petersburg.[91]

11. Catholic ranks were depleted by emigration. Although many left the countryside for the city, and the western provinces for Siberia and the Far East, many others were leaving the empire altogether. Both the Belorussian territory and the German colonies in the south and the Lithuanian provinces experienced a mass emigration in the early 1900s. Many people were leaving for the Americas, and few of those emigrants returned.

12. When war was declared between Russia and the Central Powers, German and Austro-Hungarian subjects were interned, including priests and nuns. Most of these, such as the Grey Ursulines in Finland and the Austrian friars in Saint Petersburg, were deported to their homelands. The churches that belonged to those governments were confiscated or given over to local Catholics. Plans were afoot regarding the Russia Germans as well. Rules banning the German language were passed, nationalist mobs sacked German businesses in the towns, and right-wing extremists moved against the rural Germans. German colonists were forcibly relocated from Volhynia to the interior, and the government had plans for the forced relocation of all the Russia Germans in the southern provinces.

In September 1914, the cardinals of the Catholic Church elected a new pope, Benedict XV, a man who would prove instrumental in the relief of both Russia and its Catholics after the close of the terrible war and the devastation it would bring to the empire.

CHAPTER 5

World War I

The lights are going out all over Europe. We shall never see them lit again
in our lifetime.

—Sir William Grey

Sir William's words were more prophetic than anyone knew in August of
1914. What became known as the Great War changed the face of Europe
irrevocably, and along with it Western society. When the war erupted, no one
expected it to spread as far or to last as long as it did.

Mass Destruction

The debacle on Germany's western front is a tragic tale. In France and a corner of Belgium, troops were repeatedly sent to pointless battles that resulted
in enormous casualties. Trench warfare evolved as one of the most brutal
forms of fighting, and the front stagnated, with British and French generals,
on the one side, and German generals, on the other, bearing responsibility for
the death of a generation of young men. Average death counts on the Somme
were 7,000 per day in 1916.

Russia was soon reeling on Germany's eastern front by 1915, and suffered
a series of catastrophic defeats that were compounded by severe winters. Soldiers had few weapons and less ammunition, and they died in bloody massacres as a result. Supplies could not reach them because of the collapsing
transport system and bureaucrats' corruption. In the trenches, Communist
propaganda had a ready audience. The autocracy was rotting, and the obvious
inefficiency of the State led to the February Revolution (March 8, 1917).

Spiritual Moments in Destruction

In the summer of 1916, the Angel of Peace appeared to the three future visionaries of Fatima: Lucia Abobora and her cousins Jacinta and Francisco

Marto. The Guardian Angel of Portugal also came to them, and an angel gave Jacinta and Francisco their First Holy Communion.[1] Portugal was then in its seventh year of an anticlerical dictatorship that had exiled the country's Cardinal and was working to destroy the Catholic Church. It was also under pressure to enter the war with the Entente powers.

On March 2, 1917, the villagers of Kolomansk, in Moscow region, discovered a forgotten icon of Mary, Queen of the Universe, robed in royal garments and wearing a crown, with her Divine Son clasped to her; thousands of prints were made of this icon and distributed across the empire. Following the October Revolution, scores of old icons were miraculously renewed. This pattern of miraculous restoration continued into the 1920s, providing both consolation to believers and a challenge to state atheism. One of the most dramatic incidents took place near Vladivostok, at Krolevitz, where an icon of Christ renewed itself from an old dark picture to a radiant one. Soviet police tore the paper icon up, but, as reported in European papers, it reassembled itself.[2] Such incidents would strengthen the godly against the godless.

In late 1916, Emperor Franz Josef of Austria-Hungary died, with his heir reciting the Rosary for his soul. The new emperor-king is known today as the "Servant of God Karl of Austria," and his cause for beatification in Rome is proceeding apace. He and his devout wife, Zita, were crowned in Vienna and Budapest by the end of the year.

Karl had devoted his time as crown prince to staying in touch with his people and soldiers. Appalled by the human losses and truly desiring a stable peace, as emperor, he refused to go along with the German policy of unrestricted submarine warfare announced in January 1917. Through his brother-in-law, Prince Sixtus of Bourbon-Parma, he attempted to end the war once and for all, with a bold peace plan in February. The negotiations, supported by Pope Benedict XV, unfortunately came to naught. Revolution finally erupted in Russia; Nicholas II abdicated on March 15, also renouncing the throne for his son. Nicholas's uncle refused to ascend the throne, the Provisional Government took over, and a Soviet committee dedicated to Communist expansion was formed.

On April 2, the day after Palm Sunday (new style), America's President Wilson called for entry into the war "to make the world safe for democracy" and in retaliation for a German attack on an American ship off France. On Holy Tuesday, the German imperial government decided to send the bacillus of Communist revolution into Russia in the person of Lenin. Karl refused to allow Lenin access across Austrian territory, and implored Germany to work with him to bring peace by the summer, or by early autumn at the latest. President Wilson wanted to impose democracy on the world; Lenin wanted to impose Communism. Kaiser Wilhelm and his staff were determined to win the war; Karl wanted to save Christian Europe. It was quite a Holy Week, ending with America declaring war on Germany on Good Friday. Had Karl's plan succeeded, Bolshevism would not have had the fertile soil of Russia's anguish at the lingering war and this book would not be written.

Lenin arrived in Sweden on Orthodox Good Friday, April 13, 1917. On Easter Sunday, he landed on Russian soil for the first time since his exile, and on Easter Monday, he arrived at the Finland Station in Petrograd to an enthusiastic Bolshevik crowd that ignored the pleas of the Mensheviks for democracy.[3] Russia's crucifixion would soon begin. On Easter Tuesday, the Allies lost 9,000 men in one battle on the Western Front. By April 19, Karl's peace plan was dead: Catholic Italy had demanded Austrian territory it had been fighting for since 1915 but had failed to win, territory that had been the refuge of the Habsburg imperial family for centuries and that Karl did not feel he could abandon in good conscience. On May 13, 1917, the Virgin Mary appeared to the three same children at Fatima with the words "Don't be afraid. I won't hurt you." Surely the kindest words heard on that bleeding continent that year.

The First Revolution

The collapse of the empire was hastened by the influence of the infamous Rasputin on the imperial family, by the behavior and interference of the Empress Alexandra, and by the tsar's decision to lead the imperial army at the front and thus take direct responsibility for victory or defeat. In the countryside, up to 75 percent of the labor force in some areas consisted of women, and the villages were losing their skilled workers as well as their best draft animals. In the cities, the breakdown of the transportation system led to food shortages. Police repression throughout the empire and the steady advance of the Central Powers into Russian territory added to discontent. Even the Orthodox Church refused to support the monarchy in 1917: the Holy Synod supported the abdication of both the tsar and Grand Duke Michael.

With the end of the imperial system, Grand Duke Michael left the future of the Russian state open to the decision of a nationally elected Constituent Assembly, which resulted in the Provisional Government's coming to power in the first of Russia's two revolutions, the February Revolution, so called because it started on February 23, 1917 (old style). Meanwhile, Russia—fearful of territorial losses if she entered a separate peace with the Central Powers—

remained loyal to the Allies, and continued to fight in the war, playing into the hands of the Bolshevik agitators.

Russia's Catholics in the Great War

During the war, Catholics had demonstrated their loyalty to the empire, having been active in organizing famine and refugee relief. Polish priests had led entire villages in flight in 1916 in the mass evacuations of Russian Poland when the retreating army torched the countryside. Great crowds of battered and starving Catholics descended on the cities and towns seeking refuge, traveling in tiny carts with few possessions and herding their surviving livestock. Thanks to the energetic work of Bishop Cieplak, additional Catholic chaplains had been able to serve in the army. Catholic men had served in the army and navy; Catholic farmers had produced food for the empire; Catholic nuns and lay women had served as nurses.

At the same time, Bishop Cieplak, as administrator of the archdiocese of Mogilev, had also organized support for the Austro-Hungarian clergy and seminarians of both the Latin and Greek Catholic Churches who had been exiled to the Saratov region and beyond (including Metropolitan Andrew Sheptysky of the archdiocese of Lemberg), and had provided sacraments for Catholic prisoners of war from the Central Powers. Churches in Petrograd (as Saint Petersburg was now called) that belonged to the Central Powers had been turned over to the archdiocese of Mogilev for pastoral use. The ethnic German population of the empire was at risk during the war. The Volhynia Germans were forcibly relocated en masse to the interior, and plans were drawn up for the forced relocation of the entire Russia German people.

The Russian Greek Catholics counted 743 souls at the outbreak of the war: a tiny group to be sure, but symbolically very important. Persecution of the movement had begun again, and there was a split in Petrograd between followers of two priests. Father Feodorov was exiled to Tobol'sk, Siberia, once the war broke out. Services in Petrograd continued, though, in three chapels.[4]

In 1915, Metropolitan Andrew Sheptytsky, the head of the Ukrainian Greek Catholic Church and responsible prelate for the Russian Greek Catholics, was captured when Lemberg (Lwów) fell to the Russian army. The occupiers persecuted his Church: the military governor called the Uniates "renegades, apostates." He was sent into exile, incarcerated first at Nizhni Novgorod, then at Kursk, and finally at Suzdal monastery. This was significant, as a sign that the tsarist government saw him as a religious prisoner. Only in 1916 was he allowed to attend Mass and go to Confession in Kursk's Latin

Catholic parish. When Sheptytsky was moved to Suzdal, the Orthodox archbishop, Alexis, refused to speak to him.[5] (This same archbishop would later find refuge in Sheptytsky's home when he fled the civil war.)

The February Revolution presented Catholicism, both Roman and Russian Greek, with a dramatic opportunity. Although the Orthodox Church remained the official Church of Russia, people had lost faith in the institutions of the failed autocracy. There was great interest in Roman Catholicism; in Petrograd, Masses with sermons in the Russian language were packed. It also was a time of full emergence for the Russian Greek Catholic Church.

For the Orthodox Church, on the other hand, it was a time of great ferment. Congresses were held in dioceses, at which motions were made for the election of bishops, for the opening of the episcopate to the married parish priests, and for the distribution of all Church land except that needed to actually support the priests. The Holy Synod was purged of reactionaries; in August, the All-Russian Sobor of the Church was convened to chart a new course for Russian Orthodoxy. Also in August, the Provisional Government established the Department of Religious Affairs and placed Orthodox Christians at its head.

In April 1917, Bishop Cieplak submitted a memorandum to the Provisional Government in the name of the Catholic Church, asking for religious freedom, freedom for the Church to communicate with the Holy See, freedom for the bishops to regulate life in their dioceses, freedom for the Church to own property, and freedom for Catholics to marry in their Church.[6] The Countess Julia Ursula Ledochowska,[7] the leader of the Ursulines who had been deported in 1914 to Sweden because of her Austrian citizenship, wrote to the Vatican to support this memorandum, because delay would cause more difficulties for the Church in the revolutionary period.

On May 9, Bishop von der Ropp was freed from exile, and on May 20, the interior minister asked the Holy See to name Bishop von der Ropp of Vilna to the archdiocese of Mogilev. In June, Constantine Skirmunt, an active Catholic Pole who was a member of the Council of State in Petrograd, sent a memorandum to Cardinal Gasparri on the state of the Church in Russia also recommending that Bishop von der Ropp be named archbishop for Mogilev, and that he be given two auxiliary bishops. Despite Baron von der Ropp's obviously German name, he was known for his strong Polish sympathies; he had served in the first Duma after the Revolution of 1905 and had been exiled and imprisoned under the tsar.[8] Skirmunt made several other recommendations for ordinary and auxiliary bishops throughout the former empire, several of whom were indeed named by Rome.[9]

On July 14, 1917, in a decree on religious freedom, the Provisional Government granted freedom of conscience to all citizens, a move welcomed by all the non-Orthodox. Pope Benedict XV nominated Bishop von der Ropp on July 25, and he was installed as archbishop on December 2. He promptly began to establish deaneries in Siberia and Central Russia, a practice repeated in the Tiraspol diocese. On July 25, the Provisional Government proposed Bishop Cieplak for the Vilna-Grodno diocese. On July 26, the government issued draft protocols for regularizing nominations to the Catholic hierarchy and control of Church property.[10]

Greek Catholics

Metropolitan Sheptytsky was in Yaroslavl' at the time of the February Revolution. Through the good offices of a Russian Roman Catholic priest, Father Sipiagin, the terms of Sheptytsky's exile lightened, and his case discussed in the imperial Duma. He was allowed to go to Mass at the local Latin Catholic parish and to receive visitors and correspond with the Petrograd Russian Catholics. With the collapse of tsarism, the indomitable Natalia Ushakova applied to Kerensky for the archbishop's release. Sheptytsky arrived in Petrograd shortly before the religious restrictions were abolished, on March 20. He was met by Bishop Cieplak, to whom he presented his papers demonstrating jurisdiction over the Greek Catholics of the empire, and his nomination of Father Feodorov as exarch.[11]

Ukrainians

In 1907, Pope Pius X had told Metropolitan Sheptytsky: "Make use of your rights" regarding the Russian Empire. Sheptytsky did so to help both the nascent Russian Catholic movement and those seeking to restore their ancestral Greek Catholic church in the border provinces.[12] He did so as Bishop of the Kamenets eparchy, which had never been suppressed by the Church, indeed had been confirmed by the pope in 1908. Pius X renewed and extended the authority and powers of the eparchy repeatedly, telling the metropolitan in 1910: "The time will come when [they] will be very useful to you."

In 1915, while under arrest in Kiev, Sheptytsky secretly ordained Joseph Botian,[13] naming him bishop of Lutsk (Greek Catholic) and superior for the faithful in all the former eparchies of the old Kiev Metropolia, suppressed by the tsars. (With the Treaty of Riga in 1921, however, the Polish government would frustrate Bishop Botian's work in Lutsk.)

After his release from exile and on completing his ministry in Petrograd and Moscow, Sheptytsky returned to Kiev. Large numbers of Catholic Ukrainians had been exiled there from Galicia in the war, and construction of a Greek Catholic church was begun. Friendly conversations were held with the Orthodox priests in Kiev as well. The archbishop consecrated the foundations of a Ukrainian Greek Catholic church in Kiev, the first since the tsarist suppression of Catherine II in the 1790s. Stefan Hryniuk built a church in the traditional Hutsul style of the Carpathian Mountains, and it became a popular parish. (Its priest would heroically remain through some of the worst excesses of Soviet rule.)[14]

Russians of the Byzantine Rite

On March 20, 1917, Metropolitan Sheptytsky arrived in Petrograd, just after freedom of religion had been proclaimed. He was invited to the Knights of Malta chapel to celebrate the Byzantine Liturgy, which was done with all solemnity and all the Russian Catholic clergy. Among the concelebrants was Vladimir Abrikosov of Moscow, newly ordained to the holy priesthood; his ordination had been announced by the capital's newspapers (the first such announcement in Russia), and thus the church was packed with the faithful and with curious visitors.[15]

In April, the Russian Greek Catholic community in Petrograd received Father Feodorov in the last hours of Holy Saturday, 1917, and at midnight they began the Easter service for the first time in public. The traditionally splendid ceremonies were further enhanced when Archbishop von der Ropp, the future Latin metropolitan and heroic confessor jailed for his faith, joined the exarch and his community, thus displaying Catholic unanimity and diversity.[16]

The Russian Catholics all felt that the hand of God was evident in this moment. Unknown to them, Metropolitan Sheptytsky had already used the powers given him by Pius X, and named Father Leonid Feodorov, who was then still not home from exile, as the first exarch of the Byzantine-Russian Catholic Church. It is also believed that Sheptytsky secretly ordained Feodorov as the first Russian Catholic bishop in Petrograd.[17] Father Feodorov had been professed as a Studite monk under the metropolitan's authority, and this monastic vocation complemented his leadership role in Russian eyes.

Feodorov's nomination as exarch was important because the title

1. gave the Byzantine-Russian Catholic mission a structure;
2. was purely Byzantine, which helped allay fears of Latinization;

3. gave full powers to the holder, so that an exarchate could function as a local Church; and

4. left the door open for a corporate reunion with the larger Russian Orthodox Church.[18]

Exarch Feodorov was chosen for his piety, humility, and devotion to both the authentic Russian spirit and the Holy See. He was a remarkable man, whose deep Russian spirituality can be plainly seen in photographs from that time. The announcement of his nomination was made at the Russian Greek Catholic Synod held in May 1917. The acts of that synod, organizing the exarchate's structure and mission, tell of the high hopes held by all those involved.[19]

On August 8, 1917, the Provisional Government removed all restrictions on Byzantine Russian Catholic worship and organization, and even set up plans for an endowment to be provided by the State.[20] The parish of the Nativity of the Virgin was established in Moscow under Father Abrikosov, whose wife founded a community of Dominican tertiaries following a somewhat Latinized Byzantine Russian rite.

Changes in the Latin Catholic Church

Spring of 1917 truly seemed to signify a resurrection for the Catholic Church in Russia. Although the nomination of the aristocratic von der Ropp was bitterly resented by the Petrograd workers, who favored Cieplak as one of their own, the bishop bowed to Rome's decision, and urged his flock to support the new metropolitan.[21] Petrograd Catholics established a national monthly journal, set up a social council, and formed the Christian Democratic Party, whose strength lay in the voting districts along the Neva River, and which did energetic work in Polish, Latvian, and Lithuanian among the Petrograd laborers to counteract Bolshevik propaganda. Classes on Catholic social teaching, given after Sunday Vespers in the workers' parishes, proved highly popular.[22]

Because the Poles considered Catholic religious instruction to be a normal part of a school curriculum, when they were granted permission to open schools, the way was cleared to expand Catholic education. In 1917, 500 schools were started in Volhynia, 546 in Podolia, and 194 in Ukraine, with over 73,000 children enrolled and a staff of 1,663 teachers. In the province of Vilna, there were 60 schools with 7,000 students. The city of Minsk had seven secondary schools, and the province had schools in each of the major Catholic towns; the city of Mogilev had a secondary school, and the province, 200 primary schools.[23] The pattern was repeated elsewhere in Russia: in distant Vladivostok, a *Dom Polski* (House of Polish Culture) was founded in late 1917 and a four-grade Polish school was established.[24] The Catholics in the Bashkir region around Ufa were among the most energetic in European Russia, with Germans, Poles, and many Russian converts.[25]

The law on freedom of association, drafted July 26, granted Catholics the right to organize brotherhoods, societies, and restore the monastic orders. Throughout the territory still under the control of the Russian government, restoration of Catholic Church property was sought.[26] Because so many former Catholic churches, shrines, and monasteries were in Orthodox hands, the Liquidation Commission had to tread carefully. Nevertheless, a few were restored to the Church, most notably the Capuchin monastery in Vinnitsa and the Carmelite monastery church in Berdichev.[27]

The structures of the Church were changed as well. The Minsk diocese, suppressed in 1869, was restored in 1917, with 292,000 faithful and 82 churches. Saint Mary's, a handsome brick church on the Alexander Square (now Lenin Park), was again used as a cathedral, although the new bishop, Canon Lozinski, was not installed until August 1918.[28] Minsk itself was a Catholic center: more than 23,000 of its 92,000 residents (more than 25 percent) were Catholics,[29] and they had founded seven schools for their children by 1918.[30] Saint Mary's location, its silver-covered miraculous icon of the Mother of God, and its tomb holding the relics of Saint Felix sent by the pope (both of which will figure later in our story) reflected the Catholic past in the heart of Belorussian territory. Alexander Square was also the location of the Orthodox cathedral, district courts, and governor's residence.[31]

The Kamenets-Podolsk diocese, suppressed in 1866, was restored as a separate diocese in 1919, under Bishop Peter Mankowski, with 312,000 faithful in 101 churches as of 1919. The Lutsk-Zhitomir diocese became a manageable size under Bishop Ignatius Dubowski, who had worked hard to achieve the restoration of the Kamenets diocese. The former administrator of the archdiocese of Mogilev, Bishop Cieplak, who had served throughout the war, was honored by the Provisional Government when it asked the pope to give him the personal title of archbishop. This was done, along with the official title Metropolitan of Ochrid. He was also nominated by the government to replace Bishop von der Ropp at Vilna.[32] In the Baltic, in the German zone, the Riga diocese—by then in the new republic of Latvia—long suppressed, was restored in November 1918, with a membership of some 300,000 Latvians[33] and another 300,000 Poles and Latgalians under the former Petrograd priest Count Edward O'Rourke.[34] The diocese of Tiraspol continued to exist across the south, although the diocese of Mogilev had its territory slightly reduced by the restoration of the Minsk diocese.

It is important to note that the restoration of dioceses, which may not be considered a source of excitement among Western Catholics today, was extremely important to the laity concerned. After the February Revolution, it was the laity who sent petitions to the Provisional Government requesting that their dioceses, suppressed for so long, be restored, and public meetings were held, which sent petitions to both Bishop Cieplak and the government.[35] (It was precisely such lay involvement that would enable something to survive of the interwar Soviet Catholic Church.)

On October 30, 1917, the Russian ambassador to the Holy See accepted the restoration of Minsk diocese. The Holy See named Bishop Cieplak's coworker Father Zygmunt Lozynski, a canon in Mogilev, the new bishop of Minsk on November 2, 1917,[36] by which time the Provisional Government had been swept from power by the Bolsheviks who had risen in Petrograd and Moscow.

Events at Fatima

Our Lady of Fatima has become inextricably intertwined with Communism.[37] This tie would become so strong that for many years it was absolutely forbidden to mention the Fatima miracles or messages in the USSR, although images of the Immaculate Heart of Mary (revealed at Fatima) abounded in homes and churches.

In May 1917, the Virgin Mary asked Lucia, Jacinta, and Francisco of Fatima to pray the Rosary for an end to the war. The three children added prayers for Pope Benedict XV and undertook voluntary fasting in atonement for sin. On May 13, Eugenio Pacelli was ordained archbishop in Rome, and sent to the autonomous Kingdom of Bavaria in Germany with a peace proposal from the pope. In May, Karl's attempt to cede the Italian-speaking Tyrol to Italy was rejected, with the French preferring to keep Italy and Austria at war. On June 13, the Virgin revealed her suffering Immaculate Heart to the children and confided a secret. In France, the horrible offensives continued. Also in June, the German emperor rejected the pope's peace plan in an interview with Archbishop Pacelli, even as Emperor Karl pursued peace with Italy through the same Pacelli. The war would continue.

On July 13, before a throng of two thousand at Fatima, the Virgin appealed for peace, prayer, sacrifice, and the consecration of Russia (still ruled by the Provisional Government). This was the day she gave her famous warning, that if she were not heeded, Russia would "spread her errors throughout the world, provoking wars and persecutions of the Church," which is exactly what happened. A failed uprising in Petrograd led to the revelation of Lenin's German connection, and his forced flight to a cabin in Finland until October.

On August 12, Pope Benedict XV sent a letter to all of the governments at war, with seven principles for peace. Emperor Karl and Tsar Ferdinand of Bulgaria welcomed the proposal joyfully—all the other warring states rejected it. On August 13, the Portuguese government procurator kidnapped the three visionaries, and six thousand pilgrims heard thunder at the Cova da Iria and saw a light from the sky. The children were released and consoled with a vision, on August 19, in which Mary asked for a chapel.

September saw General Lavr Kornilov, Russia's ablest general seek to end the anarchy destroying the nation. Kornilov prayed to Our Lady at the venerable shrine of the Iberian Virgin at the Kremlin Gates in Moscow to bless his efforts. He was defeated, though he would lead the White Army until his untimely death. Still, Kornilov's call was not to warfare, but for Russia's citizens to go to their churches and pray to God for relief. On August 13,

1. Germany refused to restore Belgium, and thus also to accept the pope's peace plan;

2. the Bolsheviks achieved a majority in the Petrograd soviet;

3. Our Lady appeared again, with the promise of a miracle in October and the blessing of Jesus.

The Overthrow of the Provisional Government and the Constituent Assembly

The Bolsheviks formed one wing of the Social Democratic Workers' Party (the Mensheviks forming the other wing) and supported their own soviets, which existed side by side with the soviets loyal to the Provisional Government and staffed by people from the parties of the former imperial Duma. At first, many supporters of the Bolshevik soviets believed that the February Revolution was the first step in Marx's classic prediction (a bourgeois revolution) and that because Russia was still a predominantly rural society and industrialization just beginning, Communism lay far in the future. Lenin disagreed. He saw dramatic changes sweeping Mother Russia, changes he interpreted as the harbingers of the Communist revolution, first in Russia, and then worldwide. Like many Russian thinkers before him, Lenin was influenced by the messianism of the Third Rome theory. He also found encouragement in the radicalization taking place in the cities, military, and society at large. Lenin's

"April Theses" proclaimed that the true revolution was now at hand. Even though, in June 1917, the Bolsheviks counted only 105 out of more than 800 delegates at the All-Russian Congress of Soviets, Lenin declared that the Bolsheviks were ready to rule. When, in July, the Provisional Government banned the Bolsheviks, Lenin fled to the autonomous Grand Duchy of Finland, from where he continued to urge revolution in Russia. By then, Germany had advanced to the Gulf of Finland and was threatening the capital. Social and economic conditions in Russia continued to deteriorate, with revolutionaries calling strikes, questioning the government's military authority, and challenging traditional mores. By October, the Bolsheviks formed a majority in the soviets of Petrograd and Moscow. On October 10, the Central Committee of the Bolsheviks voted for armed revolt against the government; on October 12, Lenin announced that "the crisis is ripe."

On October 13, commemorated today as the Feast of Our Lady of Fatima, seventy thousand people gathered at the Cova da Iria for the promised miracle. They stood in a pouring rain. The globe of light appeared, the sun broke through the thunderstorm, and the Virgin came to the children as Our Lady of Sorrows, with the Christ Child and Saint Joseph, converting skeptics and confirming believers in their faith. The miracle was seen at a distance of twenty-five miles. But Russia was already falling into the prophesied deadly errors.

Contrary to Soviet legend of a mass uprising of soldiers and workers, the October Revolution took place in stages, with relatively few participants, given the immense size of Russia. At first, the ministers of the government did not even know they had lost control of the capital. On October 30 old style—November 13 (new style)—the Kremlin of Moscow, and its cathedrals and palaces, fell to the Bolsheviks. A new workers' and peasants' government began to issue decrees on land and peace, while avoiding all use of the word "Communism" and still pledging that the Constituent Assembly would decide the fate of Russia. Resistance was prolonged only in Moscow,[38] and Bolshevik control spread slowly over those parts of Russia unoccupied by the Central Powers.

At the same time, the map was changing. Russia's subject nations had been clamoring for independence under the Provisional Government; after its fall, declarations were issued in the winter of 1917–18 restoring ancient states and creating new ones, including Poland, Lithuania, Latvia, Estonia, Finland, Georgia, and Armenia. Meanwhile the German-Austrian armies continued to advance, occupying ever larger areas.

CHAPTER 6

"And the Flood Swept Them All Away,"

November 1917–Winter 1918

Catholics, like most Russians, were not sure what to expect from the Bolsheviks. Bolshevism came out of the Social Democratic Workers' Party, but was more extreme. Yet given the chaos that had engulfed European Russia's cities, and given the collapsing military and economic situations, the Bolsheviks seemed to be the only force that could bring Russia some level of stability. The founding of the Cheka in December 1917 followed by the forcible dissolution of the Constituent Assembly and the introduction of terror in January 1918, were harbingers of what was to come.

The promised elections were held on schedule, the most democratic ones held in Russia to that time. The Socialist Revolutionaries (SRs) seated 267 delegates and the Bolsheviks 161 (24 percent) with Constitutional Democrats and Mensheviks seating the balance of the Assembly's delegates. Because greater importance was assigned in the new structure to urban delegates, however, the Bolshevik seats were given more weight; because the SRs were split between right and left—the leadership losing touch with its radicalized supporters in the garrisons—they were further weakened vis-à-vis the Bolsheviks.

Lenin created the Cheka (Chk) "to defend the Revolution" and to defeat its enemies. Its first head was Feliks Dzerzhinsky, a Polish Communist and apostate Catholic, whose wife later took charge of supervising the Catholic Church in the USSR.

When, on January 5, 1918, the Constituent Assembly met and refused the Bolsheviks' bid to rule Russia, Lenin banned the Constitutional Democratic Party (Cadets) on grounds of "sabotage," and then shut down the Assembly itself by force of bayonets. When Social Democratic workers marched on the Tauride Palace to protest, the Red Guards opened fire. The Revolution had begun to consume its own.[1]

The Intrusion of Atheism and Secularization

A central tenet of the Communist system is atheism, the denial of God and the divine. This was alien to Russia and its peoples. Though the Orthodox Church's position in society had been weakened by its connection to the autocracy, religion was still strong in 1917 Russia, home to the world's largest population of Jews, to one of the largest populations of Muslims, to significant Protestant, Buddhist, and animist populations, and to the headquarters of the ancient Armenian Apostolic Church. Old photographs of the empire show that every city's skyline bristled with church steeples or minarets. Railroad stations had shrines to Saint Nicholas, patron of travelers. Schools had icon corners and crosses. Rural roadways and busy city streets alike had shrines to various saints, the Crucified Christ or the Virgin, filled with flowers and candles. A vast network of schools, hospitals, orphanages, asylums, and homes for the elderly was operated under religious (mostly Orthodox) patronage. The countryside was dotted with Orthodox monasteries and convents throughout the Slavic territories. The vast majority of the ordinary people followed both folk religion and Orthodox beliefs. Indeed, when Patriarch Tikhon was enthroned at the Kremlin on November 21, 1917, the Red soldiers who had been insolent in their behavior during the procession, removed their hats in the patriarch's presence and leaned forward to receive his blessing.[2]

Even though atheism was alien to the great masses of the Russian population, Russian liberalism was generally anticlerical. Most of the educated intelligentsia had become atheistic or religiously indifferent (though many returned to Orthodoxy in the Silver Age, and a few expressed interest in Catholicism). Indeed, contempt for all religion had permeated the upper classes since the time of Peter the Great.

The Communist state, however, intruded into religious life on a scale never before seen in Russia: all Church property was nationalized; all religious influence was banned in the schools; all Church land was confiscated; and the Churches' right to hold property and be considered legal persons was denied.[3] In 1919, the Bolsheviks boldly declared that they would "liberate the toiling masses from religious prejudices and [would] organize the broadest scientific-educational and antireligious propaganda."[4] They made elimination of religion a central goal, even as the new Bolshevik state was fighting for its survival in Russia's civil war. It would remain a central goal throughout Soviet history.

Separation of Church and State

Decrees regarding the confiscation of estates were passed immediately after the Bolshevik Revolution, affecting the property of the Churches as well as that of the nobility and gentry. These decrees were followed by the decree on the separation of Church and State, on January 24, 1918, and, six months later, by the instruction of August 24/30, 1918.

Originally seen as giving relief to the non-Russian Orthodox religions, the January decree began a process of eliminating religious values from public life—one intended ultimately to extinguish all religious belief. Although this decree was bitterly condemned by the Orthodox *sobor,* and the patriarch ex-communicated those who enacted or supported it, the Catholics did not see it as a threat. In the January 1920 issue of the archdiocesan newspaper, *The Chronicle,* published under difficult circumstances, Catholic priests expressed their belief that only "what had been united with the State could be separated from it"—thus they did not foresee the disasters that were fast approaching.[5]

Indeed, the non-Orthodox hailed the January 1918 decree: they would no longer be second-class citizens. As Exarch Feodorov stated at his trial in 1923, it was only under the Communists that the Greek Catholics found themselves on an equal footing with other Churches. The decree, and the sympathy of some Bolsheviks to the many Catholics who had been tsarist prisoners, meant that the Catholic faithful generally were favorable to the new regime. When the Bolsheviks signed the Treaty of Brest-Litovsk, surrender-ing large areas of the Russian patrimony, the recently elected Orthodox patri-arch, Tikhon, condemned the treaty; no such condemnation came from the Catholics.

With the instruction of August 24/30, 1918, which ended all religious in-struction in state, public, and private schools, the unforeseen disasters began to arrive.[6] Under the January decree, August instruction, and successive laws, Churches were no longer legal persons and lost the right to own property. The Bolshevik state extended recognition to individual Church members only, not to any Church as a whole. Before any church, synagogue, mosque, or temple could continue to be used, twenty believers from its religious community had to register with the government, thus fragmenting the various religions into thousands of tiny groups. The State was given virtually unlimited control over each religious community, its former buildings, and the inventory of religious articles.

Religious oaths were banned. Religious marriages had validity only when registered with the State, and Church registers had to be turned over to the State. Religious instruction was allowed only in private, and banned in both school and church. All seminaries and all religious academies, schools, and institutes, along with all their property, became property of the State; the churches and their sacred objects were "ceded to religious communities" by special government permission.[7] The connections between the newly created tens of thousands of isolated worshiping communities and any religious centers were simply ignored by the State. Parishioners were thus made to feel extremely vulnerable in their lonely struggles against Soviet power. With the confiscation of all Church property and funds, Catholic assets of over 11 million rubles vanished overnight, removing all support for retired priests.[8]

Protests and Conferences

In August 1918, the Catholic clergy of Petrograd resolved not to sign any agreements, launching what would become the first major struggle between Catholicism and Bolshevism. Although the Roman Catholic, Russian Greek Catholic, and Russian Orthodox Churches filed a "sharp protest"[9] with the government to protest the laws on registration, there was no retreat by the State. The future martyr, Petrograd's dean, Monsignor Constantine Budkiewicz, who had already been negotiating with the new government, was now assigned to continue the talks. Although the Soviet Catholic Church would agree to turn over the register books, all property issues had to be dealt with by the Holy See. A series of conferences for the Petrograd and Moscow priests began in December 1918, and continued throughout much of the civil war, trying to find answers to the new situation.

The Church's response was not restricted to the capitals. In outlying towns and cities, many priests wired their bishops asking for advice, and passed it along to their faithful. This was normal activity in the face of a new threat, but in the 1920s, all such work was condemned by both State and Party as "counterrevolutionary activity." In the city of Ufa, at the eastern edge of European Soviet Russia, Catholics founded the Roman Catholic Union of the Sacred Heart of Christ movement as well as, briefly, a Christian Democratic Party outpost. The union was headed by one of many local Russian converts, V. Zenkin, who was also a Russian nationalist.[10] A British observer wrote that the "iron discipline" to be found in the ranks of the Catholic clergy disturbed the Bolsheviks enormously.[11]

Corpus Christi Procession of 1918

On May 30, 1918, the Catholic hierarchy and clergy stunned the population of Petrograd with a public Corpus Christi procession through the streets. Highly popular Latin Catholic services, in which a Consecrated Host in a monstrance is carried outdoors under a canopy, Corpus Christi processions had been rare even in the Catholic districts (due to imperial government opposition), and there had never been one off church property in Petrograd, let alone down the principal street of the capital. The February Revolution, however, saw a broad expansion of this devotion to the Holy Eucharist.

Exarch Feodorov and his seven Russian priests marched with the Latin Catholic clergy, preceding Archbishop von der Ropp, who was carrying the Sacred Host in the monstrance under a canopy. In the procession was a large Byzantine banner of Saint John Chrysostom, carried by the members of the new Byzantine Catholic society of the same name. When the procession crossed the Neva over Alexandrovski Bridge (now Liteiny Bridge), Orthodox churches rang their bells in welcome, and Orthodox crowds knelt and blessed themselves. The procession stopped at the important Viborg Cemetery and the Catholic church of the Visitation of the Blessed Virgin, where Exarch Feodorov, two priests, and two deacons celebrated the Divine Liturgy according to the Byzantine-Russian Rite: that is, exactly as it was celebrated in the Orthodox Church with the exception of the prayers for the pope. The Corpus Christi procession and the outdoor Divine Liturgy were considered a great sensation in Petrograd at the time, and sparked interest in both the Roman and Byzantine Catholic Churches.[12]

Education

The losses in education were considered by the clergy to be the worst disaster of all. The Church could survive without assets, but to lose all connection with the youth and all hope of training future priests and teachers meant the loss of moral influence and the loss of the future generations. In December 1917, Lenin and Lunacharskii had ordered a complete severance of all connections between clergy and education. The instruction put education, schools, their libraries and property, and all capital and possessions directly under the People's Commissariat of Education. This was furthered with the decree of August 1918, which—together with the January 1918, decree—left no room for maneuvering whatsoever.

All parochial schools were ordered turned over to state control. This included everything from the little village schools in the steppes to the large net-works of parochial schools in the cities. In Petrograd, Saint Catherine's parish maintained 20,000 elementary and 1,500 gymnasium students in its schools. Many of the Polish schools that had flourished in the western provinces were simply closed: there were not enough Communists to staff them.[13]

In July 1918, the surviving Polish schools in Petrograd were ordered to cease teaching religion and Latin, using religious books and displaying religious pictures.[14] All the diocesan seminaries were closed, along with the Theological Academy in Petrograd, an incalculable loss to Russian Catholicism, although the academy's staff and many of its students were eventually evacuated to Lublin to create a Catholic university there. Finally, the workers' clubs and libraries as well as parish libraries and reading circles were all closed or turned over to state control.

Church land had dwindled in size since the time of Peter the Great, and Orthodox Church lands, already small in 1905, had dropped even further by 1917. Catholic land holdings in 1917 were far smaller than the Orthodox ones. Decrees in Soviet Ukraine, Belorussia, and Russia confiscated all Church land, whether urban or rural, and all income from produce or rent.[15] Though a bitter loss after the hope of growth, Catholics had been through worse and, with the 1918–1919 measures, would go through worse still.

In the July 1918 Constitution, religious clergy, along with other members of the so-called exploiting classes, criminals, and the mentally defective, were denied the right to vote and deprived of all civil rights. This also denied them food because they could not obtain ration cards. Whereas atheist propaganda was declared a right of all citizens, believers were permitted religious propaganda only until 1924. And only industrial workers were guaranteed the rights of free speech and free assembly.[16]

Continuation of Catholic Expansion

In this period of great difficulty, the Church was still able to take decisive actions. The Theological Academy staff and students were successfully evacuated to Lublin. Archbishop von der Ropp continued to establish deaneries in Siberia and Asia at Irkutsk, Omsk, Tashkent, and Vladivostok to unite the parishes and provide stability in the revolutionary era. Saint Louis des Français, which had been closed as property of an enemy power (France), was later reopened under French protection (the Anglican church in Moscow, however, was closed until 1997, and its vicarage was used as a Bolshevik machine gunners' nest during the 1917 street fighting). Founded for Mogilev and

Minsk in late 1917, the archdiocesan newspaper, *The Chronicle,* sent two copies to each parish. It was suppressed by the Bolsheviks in June 1918, revived again briefly in 1919–1920, and permanently suppressed in 1923.[17]

In August 1918, Bishop Lozinski was installed at Minsk. During the civil war, other bishops and administrators were also installed. A network of Polish organizations continued to serve the Church in Belorussia and Siberia, where a *Dom Polski* was present in every city with Polish residents, and where Polish schools did their best to incorporate religion.

Atrocities Against the Churches

Although Lenin, in March 1922, would condemn the harsh measures taken against religion in November 1918, his secret order of November 19, 1918, to the Politburo called for the mass execution of priests in the struggle over confiscating sacred vessels.[18] At first, the Catholics were not as harshly persecuted as the Orthodox. The Old Bolsheviks commonly viewed the Catholics as fellow victims of the tsars: many Catholics had been imprisoned, at least six priests had been martyred in living memory, and the Catholic population had been severely restricted (as seen in chapter 3). Moreover, there was the possibility that the Holy See might be swayed to recognize the Bolsheviks as Russia's new rulers.

The Orthodox Church, on the other hand, was viewed both as a supporter of tsarism and as a principal enemy of Bolshevism. Thus, at the very beginning of the October Revolution, in November 1917, Archpriest Ivan Kochurov had been brutally murdered in Tsarskoe Selo, outside Petrograd. In January 1918, when the Reds took Kiev, Metropolitan Vladimir was tortured and shot; that spring, the rector of the Cathedral of Our Lady of Kazan' in Petrograd was shot and his body thrown into the sea; later that year, two of the most popular Orthodox priests in Russia were also killed. On August 23, the archpriest of Saint Basil's Cathedral on Red Square was shot, along with a bishop and several important senators and cabinet members.[19]

In January 1918, the Russian Orthodox Church had issued a decree of excommunication against the Bolsheviks because of their atheism. This led to the slaughter of Russian Orthodox priests of the Moscow Patriarchate, who were arrested and shot for resistance to the Soviet state. As yet another form of persecution of the Orthodox, the Bolsheviks sponsored the schismatic Renovationist or "Living" Church.[20] Some "Living" clergy were trying to reverse stagnation in the Patriarchal Church—substituting Russian for Old Church Slavonic, bringing services closer to the people. Others, however, were all too willing to collaborate with the Bolsheviks, although neither this nor other State-sponsored Orthodox movements ever did well among the mass of believers.

By this time, conditions for the Catholics were also deteriorating. Nevertheless, as noted by foreign diplomats in Petrograd, Catholic priests holding foreign passports or identity papers that would have allowed them to leave all remained (unless forcibly expelled), whereas the Protestant foreign clergy all left. It was not until 1918 that Red soldiers would kill the first Catholic priest.

The Holy See

Pope Benedict XV appointed a Vatican diplomat to Warsaw in May 1918, with responsibility both for the emerging Republic of Poland and for all territories of the former Russian Empire. This was Achille Ratti, the future Pope Pius XI. Although Ratti was blocked from entering Soviet Russia by the Bolsheviks, he maintained contact with the government by telegram (interceding on behalf of the imperial family and Grand Duke George to urge their lives be spared); the Warsaw nunciature stayed in touch with the Church in Russia as best it could over the years ahead.[21] Unfortunately, the nunciature was in Poland, Russia's archenemy, and thus the Communists suspected all communications between it and priests in Russia of being treasonous.

Brest-Litovsk

During this revolutionary period, the Bolsheviks were by no means the sole power throughout the former Russian Empire. New countries had been proclaimed at the end of 1917 and early 1918; indeed, widespread discontent had surfaced within the old imperial borders. And in February 1918, Trotsky left the peace conference with the Central Powers, thus opening Russia up to the Eleven Days' War. By March, the Germans were at Narva, within striking distance of the revolutionary government in Petrograd. The Bolsheviks were forced to sue for peace.

On March 3, 1918, they signed the Treaty of Brest-Litovsk, which ceded to the Central Powers an enormous expanse of territory, including the supposedly independent countries of Estonia, Latvia, and Lithuania, as well as a number of regional Bolshevik states. With the Germans in Estonia, the Bolsheviks moved their capital to Moscow (something anticipated by the Provisional Government and bitterly attacked by the Bolsheviks in 1917). Moreover, the Central Powers were allowed to continue their advance in the south, and by May 8, Ukraine, all southern lands as far as Rostov and the Kuban', and all lands north to the Gulf of Finland were occupied.

This foreign occupation, which would remove a large portion of western and southern Catholics from Bolshevik rule until 1920 or 1921—combined with the Bolsheviks' persecution of the religious (especially of the Orthodox), confiscation of grain, expropriation of businesses, closing of the Constituent Assembly, shutting down of newspapers, and oppression of their political foes—fueled the discontent that would lead to civil war.

CHAPTER 7

The Civil War in the West

We have destroyed the country to defeat the Whites.

—Trotsky

At the beginning of our rule we had two formidable enemies . . . the Tsar, whom we have since rendered impotent to harm our cause; and . . . the Roman Catholic Church, headed by a Pope . . . who is the avowed enemy of all liberty.

—Communist speech, 1919

The breakup of the Russian state had been accompanied by the formation, first, of independent nation-states around the entire periphery of the old empire; and second, of disparate anti-Bolshevik governments and military forces collectively known as the "Whites," within those nation-states and the territory of Russia proper. To make matters worse, there were foreign armies from both the Allies and Central Powers, which supported or fought alongside the Whites, as well as local peasant armies, anarchist forces, and underground partisans of opposing sides.

The old empire was torn apart by a vicious civil war between Whites and Reds, by peasant uprisings, and by famine and disease. The army, demoralized by revolutionary propaganda, had been decimated by purges, and at several points in the years from 1918 to 1920, it seemed that Bolshevism was on the brink of collapse.

Effects on Catholicism

The war, Allied interventions, and civil insurrections had fateful consequences for the Catholic Church. First, the Church was deeply entrenched in the border national minorities, who were seen as blocking the advance of the Red Army into revolutionary Europe. The Poles, Latvians, Belorussians, Lithuanians, and Ukrainians had all declared national republics; Catholicism was seen as part of those nationalist movements. Second, the Church was seen as preventing the assimilation of minority populations remaining under Bolshevik rule, or brought into the Bolshevik republic during the civil war. (This would become even more the case in the years after the establishment of Soviet power.)

Third, the Bolsheviks were convinced that the Church was backing the forces of counterrevolution and foreign intervention, even though there was no proof of such support on a universal scale. The war with Poland also resulted in the forcible emigration of bishops, priests, and laity, and left a lingering suspicion in the popular mind that Catholics were Polish agents. Moreover, the Church remained attached to a foreign center at the Vatican. And finally, the Bolsheviks had also inherited the traditional anti-Catholic phobias of their tsarist predecessors.

By December 1917, although independent countries had been proclaimed all around their borders, the Bolsheviks were in control of the rest of the empire. By May 1918, however, their territory was sharply reduced to the Russian heartland; their hopes for a European revolution were dashed, as foreign enemies pressed in. General opinion was that Bolshevism would not last long.

Actual fighting within Russia began in the south, under General Mikhail Alexeev's Volunteer Army, and in the east, under the Czechoslovaks in Siberia. The Volunteers were defeated by Red forces in an 80-day campaign that saw the most able anti-Bolshevik military leader, General Kornilov, killed in action. Because, however, of Red atrocities against captured Volunteers, of the shame many Russians felt about the Brest-Litovsk Treaty and loss of territory, and of anger over persecution of the Orthodox and over the forcible requisition of grain from the peasants, neither Kornilov's death nor the defeat of the Volunteers meant an end to internal fighting. In April, the Don Cossacks rebelled against the Bolsheviks, and on May 17, angry Czechoslovak soldiers, who were prisoners of war from the Austro-Hungarian army on their way across Siberia to take ship for Western Europe and the Allied front there, rose in revolt east of the Volga River and took Chelyabinsk. A host of peasant risings erupted as well. The civil war had begun.

The Formation of Independent Republics

The Bolshevik government issued the Declaration of the Rights of the Peoples of Russia, which proclaimed the right of nations to self-determination and the formation of nation-states. This historic decision was based on

Lenin's condemnation of the Russian Empire being a "prison of nations." Scores of nationalities took the Bolsheviks at their word and declared independent governments. Many were eventually conquered under Stalin's claim of the need to expand the revolution to those who requested it (thus the smallest of Bolshevik uprisings, engineered from Moscow as in the case of Georgia, would serve as ample pretext to send in the "fraternal" Red Army).

Several independent countries in the western borderlands—Finland, Estonia, Latvia, Lithuania, and Poland—all successfully defended themselves against the Red Army and were recognized by Lenin's government in various treaties between the years 1918 and 1922. Although governments established in Belorussia and Ukraine (the situation in Ukraine became especially confused) were short-lived, the Bolsheviks granted full recognition to three new countries carved out of the Caucasus: Georgia, Armenia, and Azerbaijan. Within the southwestern lands, there were several White movements and governments, ending only with Wrangel's evacuation of the last White army from Crimea.

To the east, the situation was much more chaotic. Independent Islamic and Turkic states such as Bukhara and Khorezm were set up—or in some cases, restored—but all were destined to be absorbed by the Soviet Union, although bitter Islamic guerrilla warfare raged into the 1930s. Anglo-American forces based at Murmansk temporarily occupied the northern part of European Russia. French troops held the city of Odessa in Ukraine, and Polish forces were to crisscross the west. Siberia was the locale of the Czech Legion; of British, Japanese, American and Canadian armies; and of several White governments whose objectives ranged from restoring the monarchy to restoring the Constituent Assembly. The pro-Bolshevik but independent Far Eastern Republic and a Japanese protectorate over the Maritime Provinces were established in eastern Siberia. These were overthrown by the Bolsheviks in 1922, in a final conquest (dealt with below) that would mark the end of the civil war.

Catholic Emigrants and the Baltic States and Poland

The establishment of the new countries along the western frontier provided places of sanctuary for Catholics from Russia. Polish, Lithuanian, and Latvian faithful, tired of the constant shortages, police terror, and uncertainties of life under War Communism, moved across the borders in the tens of thousands. An estimated one million Poles abandoned their ancient homes and emigrated to the west, as did 200,000 Balts. These two emigrations removed a significant number of Roman Catholics from Soviet Russia. Catholic, Mennonite, and

Lutheran Germans from the Volga region and Volhynia also emigrated, with the aid of the Red Cross, in many cases, only to be forcibly repatriated.

Although Finland's defeat of the Reds and establishment of a republic freed about two thousand Catholics from the Bolsheviks, the success of the Baltic Republics removed a much larger resident Catholic population from Communist rule. Although few Catholics lived in Estonia, Latvia was home to more than 200,000, centered in Latgalia, the southeast part of the country, directly on the frontier with Soviet Russia; Lithuania, to some 2.6 million. Indeed, after independence was secured, Lithuania would eventually have five dioceses with over two thousand priests to serve this strong concentration of faithful.

Poland's successful conclusion of the Russo-Polish War resulted in a new border, which embraced several hundred thousand Polish, Belorussian, and Lithuanian Catholics once under Bolshevik rule. The Treaty of Riga in 1921 guaranteed religious and cultural rights to the Polish minority within Soviet Russia, which only confirmed anti-Catholic opinion that Catholicism was a Polish fifth column.

Other Catholic Refuges

Caucasus Catholics were able to reorganize during the period of independence, and these new jurisdictions survived for a time. Rome established two centers there: one for the Armenian Rite and one for the Latin Rite at Tiflis (Tbilisi), the capital of Georgia. Both centers survived the Bolshevik invasion of February 1921. Turkey annexed the Kars region during the Caucasus Wars. Given the massacres of Christians in both the Ottoman Empire and the Republic of Turkey, the Turkish annexation impelled the ethnic Armenians of the Kars region to emigrate north into Georgia and Armenia.

In the southwest, Romania's occupation of Bessarabia and the Czernowitz region of Austria-Hungary affected 250 Roman Catholic churches and guaranteed protection to northern Bukovina's Greek Catholic enclave of seventeen parishes and missions. Romania's successful expansion provided a refuge for many southern Catholics who fled the Ukraine, and a haven for Catholic development until 1940. Refugee clerics found employment in the Latin Catholic diocese of Jassy in ministry to the Romanian, Polish, and German villages of the province.

CHAPTER 8

The Russo-Polish War:
Red Star versus White Eagle

Most solemn services of thanksgiving were joyfully conducted everywhere; speeches and agitation on behalf of the Polish cause swept
Catholic circles. The word everywhere was that the Bolsheviks had gone
forever.

—James Zatko, *Descent into Darkness*

The fate of Catholics in the former Russian empire was particularly affected by the results of the Russo-Polish War. The establishment of an
independent Poland in December of 1918 had not come with laid-out borders. Poland had historically been a major power in Eastern Europe, and many
Poles—under the leadership of General Pilsudski—hoped for a restoration of
the eastern borders, and thus a revival of the multinational commonwealth of
days gone by. This became particularly important, as the nature of Bolshevism
became known to people.

As German troops withdrew after November 1918, they left a power vacuum in the east. The Poles moved eastward, while the Bolsheviks moved westward, hoping to hold both the imperial borders and spread the cause of
Communist revolution into the West, where the workers were believed to be
longing to rise up against their capitalist oppressors. A major focal point in
the eastern borders was a vast, flat stretch of giant plains broken only by the
swamps and riverlands of the Pripet Marshes in Polesie in the center and
the lakes of Mazuria in the north—what is now southern Lithuania, western
Belarus, and western Ukraine. At that time, it was inhabited by members of
all three nationalities in the country, and also by Jews, Karaites, Muslim
Tatars, Poles, Germans, Armenians, and of course Russians in the towns and
cities.

Poles were driven by romantic and patriotic sentiment to recover these
lands; the Bolsheviks by a sense of inheritance and revolutionary ardor to oc-

cupy them as the bridgehead to the West. Patrols of the two armies collided on the morning of February 14, 1919, in the muddy streets of Bereza Kartuska, and the war began.[1]

In the opening weeks of the war, it seemed at first that the commonwealth would indeed be restored. Polish troops moved steadily westward, and they were widely welcomed by people—Catholic, Jewish, and Orthodox alike—tired of Bolshevik atrocities and plundering. The Catholics especially rose up in joy: at Saint Mary's Cathedral, having been escorted there from his hiding place, Bishop Lozinski of Minsk addressed the Polish troops as liberators and crusaders when they took back the city on August 8, 1919. Indeed, the liberation of Minsk was acclaimed by the Polish army as the reunion of old provinces torn asunder, and a civilian government was promptly installed, not one of military occupation.[2]

A Polish compromise with the Ukrainian nationalist Petliura, founder of the Ukrainian Directorate, to the south enabled Polish troops to attack the Red Army on a second front, and to enter Kiev on May 7, 1920. Though it was the fifteenth government to rule in the ancient Ukrainian capital since 1914, it was the first time Poland had ruled this far east in 250 years. Moscow called on the Russian people to rise in defense of their motherland, to fight against the "Polish lords" and to expel the invaders from sacred ground. The Polish-Ukrainian alliance thus caused the strange mix of Russian nationalism and Communist internationalism that would mark Soviet policy to the end.

Troops and officers who had survived the murderous purges of the army now enlisted under the Red banner, bringing skilled strategists to the Bolshevik cause. As traditional anti-Polish emotions and loyalties to Mother Russia overcame antipathy to Bolshevism and the Red Army grew and improved, the tide of the war turned.

For the Catholics who had been under Polish rule, this was a tragedy. Catholic priests had greeted the Polish troops with ringing bells, the singing of Te Deums in parish churches and cathedrals; Catholicism had once again been acclaimed as the "Polish religion." The bishops of Kamenets, Lutsk-Zhitomir, and Minsk dioceses had all compromised themselves in their enthusiasm, and Polish priests everywhere in the borderlands became leaders of the anti-Bolshevik cause.[3] Bishops Peter Mankowski (Kamenets) and Ignatius Dubowski (Lutsk-Zhitomir) both sought refuge temporarily in Poland. Only a week after the fall of Kiev, the Bolsheviks struck back, and the shocking breakthrough of Budenny's cavalry in three places on June 5, 1920, struck fear into all who had welcomed the Polish army.[4]

Throughout the summer, the Poles were driven back, and their retreat was accompanied by thousands of refugees, among them two bishops, activist priests, and priests whose families had been condemned as being "bourgeois." Priests who had hidden Jews during the pogroms were urged now by those they had saved to flee for their own lives. Scores of parishes were left without pastors. At the same time, however, some Polish priests left the safety of Poland and returned to Bolshevik territory, including Father Anthony Liniewicz and the elderly Canon John Lewinski.[5]

On July 14, the Red Army captured Wilno (Vilnius, Vilna), breaking through a major line of defense and dealing the Poles a severe psychological blow. Moreover, in a gesture of reassurance to the nervous Baltic States, Lenin ceded the city to Lithuania (it had been the ancient capital).

The Miracle of the Vistula

Poland pleaded for arms from the Allies: none came. The Polish bishops wrote a letter in July to their fellow Catholics around the world begging for prayers to avoid the victory of Bolshevism and its horrors. "Bolshevism is the living incarnation and the manifesting on earth of the spirit of Antichrist . . . in its passionate zeal for desecration of churches, murder of priests, savage massacre of Catholic populations. . . . Prayer, winning the Divine Mercy, will awaken the conscience of the nations."[6] It was surely the soaring prayers begged for by the Poles and ordered by the pope that led to the Miracle of the Vistula.

By the middle of the summer, the Bolsheviks stood at the gates of Warsaw itself, and Europe trembled at the thought of the Red Army storming into revolution-torn Germany. Warsaw was besieged, with the soldiers of Tukhachevsky and Budenny's armies drawn up on the banks of the Vistula River, a third army pushing across northern Poland aimed directly at Germany (only a hundred miles from Danzig), and a fourth driving hard across the south, with a Soviet Polish government waiting in the wings to assume control. The fate of Poland and, it was felt, of all Europe hung in the balance. It was at this point that the diplomatic corps withdrew from Warsaw—with the sole exception of the papal nuncio, Monsignor Achille Ratti, the future Pope Pius XI. The Church, at least, would not abandon Poland. The Polish bishops had earlier commended their country to the protection of the Virgin of Czestochowa, as was the practice in times past. On August 6, the population of Warsaw began a novena to Our Lady, with litanies and processions for deliverance. On August 14, the capital's suburbs fell to the Red Army.[7]

Then the Miracle of the Vistula took place. For many peasant conscripts, it was a vision of Our Lady of Czestochowa in the fire-lit skies above the city that inspired them to fight on; for the strategists, it was the daring gamble of Poland's national hero to bring his troops around to the Reds' rear; for the Bolsheviks, it was a shocking rout that would leave one army obliterated and four severely weakened.

On the Feast of the Assumption of the Blessed Virgin Mary, August 15, General Pilsudski's maneuvers began to bear fruit, with the capture of Bolshevik codes. The link with revolutionary Europe was lost, Warsaw and Poland were saved, and the Bolshevik army and the Communist border were pushed back.[8] In a letter to the primate of Poland, Pope Benedict XV wrote of his joy at the power of prayer in saving "the rampart of Europe, all Christianity and civilization."[9]

Galicia, central Poland, and western Belorussia were all cleared of the Bolsheviks. When, however, the Poles pushed north and retook the city and province of Vilnius from the Lithuanians, they permanently prevented an anti-Bolshevik federation from ever being formed, and they dashed all hopes of restoring the commonwealth. Moreover, the Polish occupiers of Galicia failed to make good on their promise of autonomy to the Ukrainians, and a later Polish government attempted to Polonize the people of western Belorussia. The seeds for 1939 were sown.

The Plight of Soviet Catholics During the Russo-Polish War

For the Church inside Soviet Russia, the war brought immediate suspicion with it, especially in light of the behavior of the clergy in the Polish-occupied zones. The drive by the State to close churches was only aggravated by the Polish offensive; the State now demanded the surrender of all the sacramental registers, and the registration of all parishes; atrocities in town and village against the Church spread throughout the Bolshevik zone. In 1921, Father Jean Vidal of Saint Louis des Français was deported, and for three months the Moscow parish had no Mass. Typhus epidemics and starvation claimed thousands of lives, including parish priests.

Priests were at risk for forcible conscription into the Red Army. Although such an eventuality was usually thwarted by strenuous protests on the part of believers, the parish clergy were forced to do clerical work for local soviets on weekdays, being released for religious duties only on Sundays and feasts.[10] The Church countered by encouraging the parishes to begin secret religious instruction to replace what the State had banned. Classes of the Theological Academy had already been removed to Lublin, Poland, in 1918. A secret seminary was founded in Moscow, and youth groups were founded in Petrograd. Still, no one in the Church seemed to realize that the Bolsheviks were determined to eradicate all religious practice and belief.[11]

Food and the basics of life were desperately lacking in Petrograd and Moscow, yet Catholic parishioners always managed to provide for their priests. Urban residents had to forage in the countryside to feed their families, and Catholics made sure that "the Fathers were well supplied." The Latvian, Polish, and Russian branches of the Saint Vincent de Paul Society did exemplary work in the hospitals of the two cities.[12]

Despite the hardships and the Bolsheviks' obvious antireligious feelings, many university students in Petrograd and Moscow became involved in spiritual searches that led them to Orthodoxy and Catholicism. The Institute of Eastern Theology was founded in Petrograd, and students properly organized the patristic collection at the university there. To force them to abandon their "religious fallacies," students and teachers in Petrograd, Moscow, and Saratov were denied the right to vote at faculty committees and denied their monthly rations of food and money; the State suppressed the Church history degree in 1920. Nevertheless, these Christians held on until 1922, when most were arrested.[13]

Martyrdom of Priests and Parishioners

That the Bolsheviks' rule was brutal in the west should not be in doubt. Russian Orthodox works detail the suffering of that Church: over a thousand clerics and monastics were killed from 1918 to 1919. In 1919, three Orthodox bishops from the White zone of Siberia appealed to the pope to publicize the sufferings of their Church at the hands of the Bolsheviks—its many martyrs (through execution, burial alive, and massacres) and the deliberate desecrations of churches and convents. Pope Benedict XV responded with both a reply to the bishops at Omsk and an appeal to Lenin to cease persecution of believers. Foreign Commissar Chicherin rudely retorted that he could not conceive of the pope intervening for those Rome had recently called "dissidents," and he then condemned Catholic persecution of other believers abroad.[14]

Bishop Dubowski of the Lutsk-Zhitomir diocese sent a report to Warsaw in October 1919 detailing the slaughter of Poles and Ruthenians alike, who were either shot or buried alive. The Bolsheviks had tried to convert the Zhitomir cathedral into a theater. The bishop himself escaped an assassination attempt and spent five days hiding in a cemetery. Three priests in the diocese were shot during Bolshevik rule: Fathers Boleslas Lisiecki, Theophilus Szeptycki, and Adolph Kowalski.[15] Outside Petrograd, an elderly priest died from a heart attack when the church was desecrated.

Arrests and shootings spread to the Tiraspol diocese, where Bishop Kessler was subjected to increasing harassment after the Bolsheviks took over in October 1917. They made the seminary into a military hospital and the school into a commissary, and they confiscated the residences of the seminary faculty and cathedral priests.

When the bishop was threatened with a military trial, he and the canons agreed that he should leave the city and flee south, to Odessa in the German-occupied zone. On August 14, 1918, he preached his last sermon at Saint Clement's Cathedral, in German and Polish, exhorting the Catholics to fidelity. In December 1918, when the Germans withdrew from Odessa, the bishop had to be hidden. The Bolsheviks terrorized the population, killing three priests.[16] When Odessa was taken by the Whites on August 23, 1919, the city received a French garrison, and the bishop could begin to reorganize Catholic life in the liberated southern lands. The priests still in Saratov were dispersed or imprisoned, save for one who retreated to the hills and continued to offer Mass at Saint Clement's.

Father Jakob Dukert was part of a wave of refugees trying to escape from the Bolsheviks' destruction of German farm villages in the Beresan region, as the Red Army pushed over the Bug River into Poland in late 1919. Trapped between the Reds and Whites in a pitched battle, some of the refugees were killed or injured by a grenade. When Father Dukert began to administer Extreme Unction, the Red Army troops ordered him to stop. When he persisted, he was dragged away from the dying and injured, put up against a barn wall, and shot.[17] In Crimea, at about the same time, the anarchist troops of the Ukrainian Nestor Makhno executed Father Johannes Hoffmann, dismembered his body, and left it for the wild animals and birds.

When Selz, Ukraine, resisted the Reds' confiscation of grain, the Red Army seized the town on August 4, 1919. After the by-now "traditional" orgy of rape, plundering, and arson, the Red soldiers rounded up 87 men, herded them into the town hall, and then took them to the cemetery. Father Clement Weissenburger, who was recently ordained and had come to Selz to visit his mother, went to console the men. He offered himself in exchange for their lives, but was rebuffed by the Bolshevik commander. When he turned to absolve the men of their sins before they were executed, he uttered the words

"Ego vos absolvo" and raised his hands, only to have both sliced off by two Red swordsmen. After a third Red soldier plunged his bayonet into the young priest's chest and he fell to the ground, the Bolsheviks' "clattering machine guns mowed down the eighty-seven men into a horrendous hecatomb of bleeding bodies. The godless executioners then strode around the heap, firing their pistols at the victims who still showed signs of life."[18]

Infirm and elderly, Father Georg Sauer came down from his hut in the hills outside Saratov to celebrate Sunday and holy day Masses at the Cathedral in late 1918-early 1919. He was the only priest left free in a city that had once been served by a dozen. One night, he and his elderly housekeeper were brutally murdered, and their bodies burned.[19]

Imprisoned on false charges of concealing weapons in 1917, Monsignor Xavier Klimaszewski of Saratov was thrown into a cell with neither window, nor bed, nor chair. When he was released three months later, in late 1918 during the Russo-Polish War, he came to the attention of local Communists, who sought him out. Parishioners disguised Klimaszewski as a German colonist, and concealed him in Schuck. There, toward nightfall, Bolshevik soldiers tracked him down to his hiding place in a sandpit. The colonists, however, had dressed the monsignor in a yellow sheepskin coat, which served to camouflage him from the soldiers and they finally withdrew. After this near-miraculous escape, the Catholics were able to send him on to Poland.[20]

In Georgsburg, Makhno ordered that the women of the village be surrendered to his men for the night: the priest administered the sacraments to the endangered women and girls and all the people prayed fervently that they be spared this horror. Miraculously, the anarchists left before sunset.[21]

Desecrations in the Civil War

The Catholic curia in Petrograd continued to receive reports of Churches being nationalized, priests being arrested or killed, and Church property being confiscated.[22] Orthodox churches were ruined throughout Soviet Russia, and literally thousands of Orthodox bishops, priests, monks and nuns, and parishioners butchered, during the civil war.

As early as Easter 1919, Red Army soldiers had entered some of the Catholic churches of Petrograd and Moscow, dragged the priests from the altars in their vestments, and hauled them and any Catholics who resisted off to prison. Although everyone was soon released, and the Bolsheviks claimed that this had been done in a burst of Russian patriotism, it was an ugly prelude of far worse to come.[23]

In August of 1919, the Bolsheviks attempted to expose the incorrupt body of Blessed Andrew Bobola at the church in Polotsk. (They had already spent two years digging up the relics and bodies of Orthodox saints and desecrating them.) When Archbishop Cieplak and the Catholic central committee protested, however, and the Catholics from the Putilov factories in Petrograd demonstrated, the body was spared.[24]

In 1920, at Gatchina (outside Petrograd), Bolsheviks demanded that the priest give up the keys of the tabernacle, so they could gain access to "the greatest treasure of the Catholics." The elderly priest refused; he was assaulted, and a locksmith ordered to break open the tabernacle doors. The Holy Eucharist was dumped onto the floor, and the ciborium stolen. The priest died from the shock.[25] Attacked by local Bolsheviks, the German colonists of Rastatt (Beresan region) fought back valiantly. When the town finally fell, the Reds torched eighty-five farmsteads and looted the Catholic church, using the vestments and altar cloths for saddle blankets and deliberately trampling the Blessed Sacrament underfoot. At Heidelberg in South Ukraine, Makhno's troops did the same to the church there.[26]

Beginning of the Registration Struggle

Twenty adults had to represent the parish as a believer's soviet *(dvadtsatka)*. Monsignor Constantine Budkiewicz, in Petrograd, felt there should be no registration whatsoever with the Bolsheviks. Archbishop von der Ropp felt that some cooperation was necessary so as to save the Catholic Church in Russia until the Bolsheviks were overthrown. On April 2, 1919, as conditions for the Bolsheviks worsened, the archbishop published a letter in the Mogilev *Chronicle* allowing for the establishment of parish committees, by the parish priests, so as to protect the churches and property. Agreements could be signed, as long as "obnoxious" conditions were avoided. It was emphasized that the members of the committees were to work with the priests and be active believers (such was not Bolshevik intent: atheists were intruded into such church soviets so as to disrupt parish life, as would happen in the Orthodox parishes, especially in the 1960s). A Catholic central committee coordinated regional parish committees, linking them with the archdiocesan curia, the seminary, and the archbishop himself. In Petrograd, fifty adults signed up to save the Theological Academy, its church, chapel, and important library. The chapel came under the care of Father Michael Dmowski (who was to be arrested in 1925).[27]

Arrest of the Metropolitan

Such cooperation did not save Archbishop von der Ropp. After the Poles attacked Vilnius (Vilna), he was arrested on April 19, 1919, during Eastertide. Three priests of Polish ancestry—including eighty-year-old Father Ladislas Issajewicz—and one Byzantine-Russian priest were also arrested. The archbishop was placed at Grochov prison, where 170 people were crammed into two tiny rooms, then moved to Shalperna prison with jailed nobility and intellectuals. On May 25, Archbishop Cieplak celebrated a special Mass of intercession at Saint Catherine's, 13,000 Catholic demonstrators packed the streets in front of the Cheka headquarters. Cieplak offered to take von der Ropp's place in prison, despite the obvious dangers.

This resulted in a police sweep of Petrograd for Catholic priests (all of whom were successfully hidden by their parishioners until things calmed down). Pope Benedict XV, Archbishop Cieplak, and the Mogilev archdiocesan clergy made repeated interventions with the Bolshevik government even as the war raged on. When the Polish front moved away from the Soviet Russian heartland, their efforts began to bear fruit. Although on July 5 Archbishop von der Ropp was transferred to the fearful Lubyanka in Moscow and then to the Butyrka, he was finally moved to the rectory at Immaculate Conception. Released "as a subject of the Pope of Rome,"[28] the archbishop was expelled from Russia on November 17, finally reaching Warsaw ten days later.

The New Latin Catholic
Administration of Mogilev

Although Archbishop Cieplak now assumed the role the Catholic workers of Petrograd had sought for him in 1918—leadership of the Latin Catholic Church in Russia—he did not have the full support of all of his priests.[29] While the Russo-Polish War dragged on, Archbishop Cieplak was compelled to introduce new policies to help the parishes deal with pressure to sign the documents for the use of the churches. Inspired by Monsignor Budkiewicz, the Church had adopted a hard-line response, according to which no one could sign as a member of the *dvadtsatka* and remain in communion with the Church. Budkiewicz felt that von der Ropp's accommodating position had proved usless. The Bolsheviks were very much in control, there was still no guidance from the Pope on the registration question, and there were real canonical principles at stake. In September 1919, the archbishop announced that the Church could not turn over the church buildings and sacred vessels to the control of civil authorities. In January 1920, he ruled that Catholics could not belong to the Communist party. In February 1920, the Church went on the offensive: parish committees were to be kept informed as to what was really going on and protests were to be filed to reinstate religious instruction in the schools; Monsignor Budkiewicz proposed that the State's registration of the churches and its threats of closure be energetically resisted.[30]

The arrests and the flight of so many priests and parishioners weakened the position of the Church inside Soviet Russia, both in numbers and morally. Emigration of both Russians and non-Russians was reaching epic proportions, and Catholic sympathies were interpreted as being with the "Polish landlord" enemy. Communications with Poland, White-ruled areas, and even in Bolshevik-held territory collapsed. A literal flood of Catholics headed west.

Treaty of Riga

Signed on March 18, 1921, the Treaty of Riga guaranteed Soviet Russia's non-interference in Polish independence, the return of Polish cultural treasures, and religious freedom for Poles under Bolshevik rule. The Poles inside Soviet Russia now became Soviet citizens. The treaty's guarantees resulted in thousands of claims for the return of ecclesiastical property, sacred items, and churches by Poles in places as widely scattered as the new western borders and Astrakhan on the Caspian Sea.

Nevertheless, the appeals all proved useless in the end. Moscow ruled that the Catholics of Polish descent could not claim any restitution or protection. The clause was violated on the grounds that Orthodox subjects in Poland did not have full freedom of worship. Thus the treaty did not help the Catholics at all, and the Russo-Polish War only left ethnic Russians and the Communists angry with all Poles. The Catholics in the affected areas were even poorer as a result of all the fighting and under a cloud of suspicion as probable spies and saboteurs. (In the paranoiac years of Stalin, their link with "counterrevolutionary Polish lords" would prove fatal.)

The Civil War in the Caucasus

Although the Bolshevik invasion of the Caucasus region directly contravened the 1920 treaties guaranteeing the independence of the newly established nation-states, Stalin pointed out that the Communist revolution had to expand to any area where it was invited. This was the pattern in each republic: local

Bolshevik minorities would stage uprisings, then invite the "fraternal" Red Army to enter and establish Communism.

In Azerbaijan, for example, local Communists in league with Lenin planned an uprising on April 27, 1920. The country was promptly invaded on April 28, even before the Bolsheviks' ultimatum to surrender all power to the Communists had expired. Comrades Ordzhonikidze and Kirov arrived in Baku that very day, and a wave of repression against Azerbaijani leaders commenced.

At the end of the year, Stalin arrived in Baku and began operations against Armenia. Again an ultimatum was issued for surrender, and again the Red Army entered before the Armenians could even respond. An Armenian Revolutionary Committee took power on December 6, 1920, and on December 21, Russian Bolshevik laws were introduced, and non-Communist leaders repressed.

The invasion of the Menshevik-governed Republic of Georgia was the last stage of the civil war in the west, with Red troops moving swiftly to respond to a Bolshevik committee formed in a tiny border village there on February 14, 1921. A member state of the League of Nations, Georgia appealed frantically to the West for weapons, but was met with silence from the very powers that had encouraged its independence. The Georgian government fled by steamship from Batum just ahead of the Red Army, and independent Georgia surrendered on March 18.

Ordzhonikidze rapidly and brutally Sovietized the country, despite Lenin's fears of Georgian nationalist feelings and the possibility of a revolt.[31] Some 20,000 Georgians were deported, and non-Communist uprisings suppressed with executions, which spread to the Churches. Georgia became the first example of national persecution by the Soviets, and its experience from 1921 to 1930 ranks still as one of the most brutal.[32]

The Caucasus Catholics

In 1918, Georgia had some 24,000 Catholics of the Latin Rite (mostly Germans, Georgians, and Poles), and one parish of the Chaldean Rite (composed of ethnic Assyrians). Azerbaijan had one lonely Latin Catholic parish, consisting of Germans and Poles, in the capital of Baku. In between the Caucasus and the Volga delta were the parishes of the Kuban', Stavropol', and the Don Cossack provinces, part of Russia, and partially under White rule during the civil war. There were also 8,000 Armenian faithful in Georgia, and another

60,000 Armenian Rite Catholics lived in the Armenian and Azerbaijan Republics. They established a new diocese, responding to Turkey's annexation of the Kars region, which included the seat of the bishop at Artvin.

The front in Armenia-Georgia shifted often and dramatically in 1918–1922 and Turkish troops regularly engaged in organized massacres of the different Christian populations. The Christian countries of Georgia and Armenia had their own conflicts, and were ruthlessly abandoned by the Western powers, which had encouraged their independence and made repeated promises of protection on behalf of all the Christians and those non-Turkish Muslim minorities who rejected continued Ottoman rule. When the border situation was finally clarified, a broad belt of western Armenians found themselves in southern Georgia, which included the ancient Catholic centers at Alkhalek and Akhaltsike, and the remaining Armenian Catholics, inside northwestern Armenia, in the old Alexandropol province and north of Yrevan (Erivan) province. In 1920, this population in Georgia and Armenia would be reorganized into a new Armenian Catholic administration, which would embrace the bulk of Armenian Catholics in the southern part of the former Russian Empire, with parishes as far north as Ykaterinodar (Krasnodar) and including the great Armenian center at Tiflis (Tbilisi).[33] In May 1921, the Latin Catholic Church received Bishop Gabriele Moriondo, the apostolic delegate to Persia, as vicar apostolic and apostolic administrator,[34] and the Church was totally reorganized, with the Armenian administration restored in the Georgian capital as well.

For the Catholics of Transcaucasia, the events of 1920–1921 were catastrophic. No one had thought Bolshevik power would extend to the new republics, and the invasions came at a time when the Catholics were organizing vibrant new lives.

By contrast to the Bolsheviks, however, the Mensheviks, though hostile to religion, did not engage in antireligious activity. Indeed, in Menshevik Georgia, the State subsidized the Georgian Orthodox Church, which had split from the Moscow Patriarchate, though there were some tensions. The Menshevik proposal for separation of Church and State was nothing like the Bolshevik one and the last constitution of independent Georgia guaranteed the individual's right to either profess or not profess religious beliefs.[35] The Georgian Republic had diplomatic relations with the Holy See: a delegate was appointed to Tbilisi in 1919. This ancient city was home already to an ornate church, built on the style of a miniature Saint Peter's Basilica, along with parishes of both of the rites. It now became the residence for future martyrs and confessors of Soviet Catholicism.

Byzantine Catholicism in Georgia

In 1920, several Byzantine-Georgian Rite priests arrived in Georgia from Turkey. (Their congregation had been founded in 1861 by Father Peter Karischiaranti to serve all Georgians, along with a community of nuns.) The priests set about restoring a Byzantine Georgian Catholic community (illegal under the tsars) from among the Georgian Roman Catholics. After the Edict of Toleration in 1905, some 5000 Georgian Catholics had adopted the Byzantine Rite.[36] Although the mission would eventually grow to 8,000 faithful, as early as 1922, there are reports that some of these priests had been shot by the Communists.[37] One of the missionaries from Turkey, Bishop Shio Batmalashvili, would serve as the Byzantine Rite administrator until his arrest in 1928.[38]

Latin Catholicism in Georgia

The Latin Catholics had several parishes, churches, and chapels established in Georgia: as of 1914, their principal churches were in the capital, with two churchyard chapels in the vicinity; one rural chapel at Betlemi, a prayer house in Akhaltsike, which was mostly Armenian (173 souls), and stone churches in Batum (1,100 souls), Gori (Stalin's hometown; 500 souls), Kutasai (2,100 souls, which also had a chapel in the cemetery); and Manglis (13,600 souls).[39] The Batum church was new, having been consecrated only in 1903 by Bishop von der Ropp.[40] There were also rural stations. The organization of the Latin Catholic Church of Georgia, its handsome churches, and its faithful shared in the brutal religious and national oppression that swept their country after the end of the civil war.

Armenian Catholicism in Armenia and Georgia

The old Armenian Catholic administration of Artvin was reestablished at Tbilisi during independence, in 1920, under Bishop James Bagratian with the assistance of Monsignor Karapet Durlughian. The bishop had over 66,000 faithful, 45 churches, and 15 chapels under his jurisdiction, served by 47 priests in Armenia and Georgia.[41] Priests included both natives and missionaries who came from Italy. One, Father Peter Alagiagian, SJ, who had been born in Kars province but held Italian citizenship, would minister in Armenia and Georgia until 1930.[42] Notice that the number of Armenian priests had dropped since 1912: presumably this was due to losses during World War I (the Armenians in Tiraspol diocese continued under that jurisdiction).

An attempted Dashnak uprising against the Bolsheviks in 1921 was brutally put down, and Sovietization continued with terror and force as elsewhere. Although there were Communist sympathizers in both Armenia and Georgia, and the Armenians feared a Turkish invasion, union with the Soviet Russia was resisted and resented. As late as 1924, there was a major revolt in Georgia against the Reds.[43]

The End of the Civil War in the West

For a variety of political, military, and economic reasons, the Whites' struggle in the west against Bolshevism finally collapsed. Allied troops in the north and south were withdrawn, and despite several victories, the various White armies were finally broken. The last White stronghold was in Crimea, under General Wrangel, and this was lost in November 1920.

As previously discussed, Odessa, the lively cosmopolitan city on the Black Sea that was under Allied and White control, became the Tiraspol diocese's new seat with seminary and offices, and the church of the Assumption became its new cathedral. On January 20, 1920, however, Bishop Kessler was forced to leave; hidden aboard a French ship, he went to Romania, to the Catholic colony at Krasna. From there, he appealed to the Holy See to unite his suffering diocese with the Latin Catholic diocese of Jassy in Romanian Bessarabia, that is, to concede that, for southern Soviet Russia, direction of Church life could only take place from abroad.[44] Contact with the interior was slowly being lost, although there were priests serving as vicars general in different areas.

Bishops Dubowski (Lutsk-Zhitomir) and Mankowski (Kamenets) were in exile in Poland. Archbishop von der Ropp was in Warsaw. All three were trying to stay in contact with their priests in Soviet Russia. Kidnapped from Poland by the Red Army during World War I, the bishop of Kielce, Augustine Lozinski, had been interned in Mogilev. He escaped from the train repatriating him to Poland, and spent six months ministering to the local Catholics, but was finally deported on July 12, 1921.[45] Only Archbishop Cieplak and Bishop Lozinski of Minsk remained in western Soviet Russia.

When, on Holy Thursday in April 1920, Archbishop Cieplak was arrested, 800 Catholic marines of the Red Navy marched to the Cheka headquarters in his defense. He was released, but only after he agreed, in writing, that neither he nor the priests would engage in political activity. In June, the chapel of the Theological Academy was confiscated, despite strong protests; in November, the chapel was permanently lost to the Church. The only bright side in this affair was that both the Orthodox and Protestants tried to help the Catholics save the chapel and recover property stolen from both chapel and Academy.[46]

CHAPTER 9

The Golgotha of Siberia
and the Far East, 1918–1922

Sasha, my dearest, we passed through here on December 15. Mama died
of typhus before she knew about poor Kolya. You are all I have now! If
you make it to Irkutsk, leave a note for me at the church nearest the
railway station. Your Katya

—Note at Krasnoyarsk Station, 1920

The vast lands of Siberia witnessed some of the most vicious fighting of
the civil war. Refugees from European Russia, Siberian natives, and a
confusing mosaic of armies and gangs crisscrossed its steppes and taiga. Villages and families alike were wiped out, and normal life became a distant memory. To the south, independent Islamic and Turkic states such as Bukhara and
Khorezm were set up—or in some cases, restored—but all would be absorbed
by the Soviet Union, even though bitter Islamic guerrilla warfare would rage
into the 1930s.

Siberia itself became a vast battleground, where the Czechoslovak Legion and armies from Britain, Japan, America, and Canada joined with the
forces of several White governments, whose constituents ranged from
monarchists to parliamentary democrats to bandits. There were armed
groups of local peasants who just wanted their villages to be left alone, bands
of anarchists who despised everybody else, and occasional troops of adventurers. Western and central Siberia were engulfed in steady warfare from
1918–1921. Eastern Siberia was granted breathing space under the pro-
Bolshevik but independent Far Eastern Republic and the Japanese protectorate over the Maritime Provinces. This space would last until 1922 and the
end of the civil war.

Siberian Catholicism

Whether native or nonnative, exiled or free, and often no longer speaking their native languages, the faithful of Siberia remained firmly attached to their Catholic religion. Deaneries were established at Irkutsk, Omsk, Tomsk, and Tashkent by Archbishop von der Ropp only in 1917, when the change in governments allowed him to do so. The Apostolic Vicariate of Siberia, containing the first three deaneries, was founded by the Vatican in February 1921, at Omsk (a Siberian center and a White capital), for western and central Siberia. Under the French missionary Monsignor Jean de Guebriant,[1] who had been in China's Szechuan Province, and who for five years had been the bishop of Canton (now Guangzhou),[2] the vicariate had 35 churches, 75,000 Catholics, and only 12 priests living within its boundaries.[3]

Captain Francis McCullagh, traveling through Siberia in January 1920 wrote of the Catholic priests:

> I found a Catholic church functioning in every town along the Siberian Railway, the acolyte lighting the altar candles in the grey of the morning and the priest saying exactly the same Mass as is said every day . . . as calmly as if the fierce tides of revolution were not roaring and swirling around his church. . . . It was the calmness and regularity of a system which did not depend on the will of man.[4]

It was of course this spirit of confidence in a force beyond that of the Communist revolution that so enraged the Bolsheviks. This confidence, and the universality of the Catholic Church, affected the Orthodox in Siberia as well. In 1919, Archbishop Sylvester, of Omsk, in his role as president of the Supreme Administration of the Church, and Archbishop Benjamin of Simbirsk sent Pope Benedict XV a telegram detailing the atrocities suffered at the hands of the Bolsheviks and listing the bishops and priests who had been massacred. The pope responded with a telegram promising his prayers, and Cardinal Gasparri wrote to Lenin asking him to show respect to the ministers of religion "no matter of what persuasion they are," a letter that was curtly rebuffed by Chicherin.[5]

Siberian Fighting

As a major grain producer having extensive storage facilities, Siberia was important to any serious war effort. With its much enlarged population, it was obviously an important part of Russia's economy and military strength. Thus the Bolsheviks moved swiftly to secure it against their enemies. In late October 1917, the Red Army captured Yenisek; by December, the Bolsheviks ruled the region from Omsk to Irkutsk. They were firmly resisted in western Siberia, particularly when they closed down the Siberian Duma in January 1918, and the people realized there would be no sharing of power.

Wartime shortages and police repression after 1916 paled before Siberia's quick descent into the revolutionary hell of civil war. Abuse, robbery, barbaric treatment, torture all became commonplace, and once sedate cities degenerated into anarchy. Inflation ran rampant, as money lost all value. In May 1918, organized resistance began, and the new White forces and the Czechoslovak Legion defeated the Bolsheviks. Three factors would, however, overshadow these early victories. First, the White leaders had no clear program to rally the people; indeed, many simply favored a return to the autocratic past. Second, the support they received from Allied troops raised the specter of foreign control of Mother Russia. Third, and most important, these White leaders and Allied officers managed to kill off the original, educated Siberian Bolshevik leaders, whose replacements would be men described as "callous, dehumanized, and brutal." In a civil war filled with atrocities, where prisoners were thrown into locomotive furnaces and where the epaulets of White officers were burned into their naked shoulders, these replacements "became the type of men who would let a Stalin control the land."[6]

In the Golgotha that Siberia became, Catholics joined their neighbors in suffering. The gradual retreat of White forces was marked by endless streams of humanity fleeing in sleighs across the frozen taiga or packing the cattle cars of eastbound trains on the Trans-Siberian Railway. The fall of a city was accompanied by massacre of defeated opponents, and peasants and burghers alike feared to render support to Red or White for fear of later retribution. When Tomsk fell to the Reds in 1920, it was said that a caravan of 100,000 people set out in the dead of winter to flee to the east. The winters were so cold that the trains carrying refugees froze to the tracks. When sleighs had to be left by the wayside because of damage, horses and passengers struggled to keep up with the other refugees for fear of being devoured by wolves. Typhus epidemics swept towns and trains alike, killing tens of thousands. As the agony dragged on, most of the Allies withdrew; the White forces became torn by dissension, and the Reds emerged victorious. Two separate states offered sanctuary: the pro-Bolshevik but independent Far Eastern Republic, centered at Chita, and the Japanese-protected Maritime Province, with its capital of Vladivostok, which became the last White stronghold in the Russian East.

In June 1922, Japan decided to withdraw, the last Allied Power to do so. As the Japanese pulled out, the People's Revolutionary Army of the Far Eastern Republic advanced against the Whites, some of whose officers refused to believe that the Japanese were serious about evacuation. Only when the Red forces finally broke through Vladivostok's defenses in October did the White commander overrule his foolish subordinates and organize evacuation by sea. Even so, many did not escape because there were not enough ships. The fall of Vladivostok on October 26, 1922, marked the end of the civil war. The victory was accompanied by a massive wave of executions, arrests, and deportations that affected thousands of people.[7] On November 14, 1922, the Far Eastern Republic petitioned Moscow for absorption into the Russian Soviet Federated Socialist Republic, and all hopes for independence ended.

Catholic Survival

It was under these critical conditions that the new deaneries became so important, helping to preserve the basics of Catholic life, and providing local religious authorities for the parish clergy and laity to turn to in the persons of the priests appointed as deans. The deaneries survived both the civil war and the collapse of the apostolic vicariate when Bishop de Guebriant was exiled. In 1921, the exile of the French missionary was countered with the appointment of Father Gerard Piotrowski, OFM, as administrator of Siberia. The centers were kept at Omsk, Irkutsk, and Tashkent. In 1922, There were 39 churches, 15 priests, and 75,000 faithful; this administration would survive until 1932.[8]

The Diocese of Vladivostok

In 1923, even as the city was experiencing the Red Terror, the Holy See decided to establish a diocese in the battered port of Vladivostok, which was also designated as the home of a new seminary, under the care of the Franciscan Friars directed by Father Maurice Kluge, OFM. These friars were Bernardines, who had a history of missionary work among the Poles. The Holy Mother of God Church, which became the cathedral, survives today as the largest remaining church building in all Siberia, though it was confiscated during the Great Terror.

The diocese of Vladivostok was international, covering (1) the parishes of Nikolaevsk, Blagoveshchensk, Khabarovsk, and Vladivostok, which had been organized into a deanery[9] in the Primorskaya and Amurskaya oblasts of Siberia; (2) the parish of Alexandrovsk and the Polish communities on Japanese-occupied northern Sakhalin island; and (3) the Polish churches of Manchuria,[10] then part of the Republic of China. From the very start, it was clear the new diocese could not survive. Indeed, all hope had gone when the Far Eastern Republic became part, first of Soviet Russia, then of the new Union of Soviet Socialist Republics, proclaimed on December 30, 1922. This region held well over 30,000 Catholics in 1923, according to research conducted by the restored Catholic missions in 1990, although official Church statistics give a population of 20,000 with 6 churches.[11] There were only four priests inside the new Soviet boundary of 1922 to serve 20,000 Far Eastern Catholics.[12]

With its destruction during the civil war, there was no longer a base in Nikolaevsk for the Church, which had maintained a mission chapel there for over sixty years. Vladivostok and Khabarovsk had both experienced bombardments, an enormous influx of refugees, and displacement of their residents. The new Catholic bishop, Dean Charles Sliwowski, was born in Warsaw in 1848. He took office in February 1923, at the age of 75,[13] and was ordained as bishop of Vladivostok in Harbin, by the bishops of Peking and Girin and the Apostolic Delegate to China on October 28, 1923. He had charge of a far-flung population in difficult times. There were still Japanese troops occupying the northern half of the island of Sakhalin and some White troops in Kamchatka, and both places had Catholic faithful. When the Red Army occupied Kamchatka in 1922, and Japan ceded northern Sakhalin to Russia in 1925, the last of the Siberian Catholic parishes came under Communist rule.

Conditions for the Church were especially violent in the Far East. The bloody takeover of Vladivostok was a harbinger of the worse days to come. Catholics were butchered en masse, according to the few survivors and their descendants, and the last priest was arrested during the Terror. The large Polish, Korean, Chinese, and German population was apparently very vulnerable during the war scares inflamed by Stalin in later years, with reports of Catholics being executed as "Polish spies."[14] Many Catholics joined the thousands who fled across the frozen Amur River into Manchuria, settling around Harbin, where a Latin Catholic diocese was established as an administration apostolic in 1924, or trying to head down the coast to the international city of Shanghai.

The fate of Bishop Sliwowski was clouded by conflicting reports: that he escaped to Shanghai, and then returned to minister in the Harbin area, where he died among his fellow refugees in 1927—and that he disappeared in the late 1920s during a persecution.[15] However, Bishop d'Herbigny (see Chapter 18: "Secret Agent and Secret Hierarchy") reported that he remained at his post and that diocesan life continued in Vladivostok until 1932. The bishop's continued presence among his people is now an established fact. Bishop Sliwowski is known to have been working in the city in 1927, when he gave

Bishop Karol Sliwowski at ordination in Harbin, 1923. Courtesy of the author.

orders for the restoration of a monument at Blagoveshchensk,[16] and to have remained at his post, until he was prevented from doing so in 1933 by the GPU. Exiled to a cabin north of the city, the elderly bishop was attended by a Polish Sister, who cooked for him and nursed him as his health declined. A number of people made the trek out into the woods to hear his masses and receive the sacraments. Here he died, and was buried in the forest. The Sister was allowed to return to Poland before World War II broke out. Although the intention had been to return the bishop's body as well, and for this purpose he had been buried in a lead casket, permission was never granted, and the German-style wrought-iron cross above his grave is now lost in the pines.[17]

Central Asia

The war to recover the emirates and khanates of Central Asia was a brutal one. Until now, the pro-independence and anti-Bolshevik forces have been reviled in Soviet learning as bandits and counterrevolutionaries. Not only were the Turkic and other peoples rising for nationalist reasons, but the Bolsheviks' attempt to requisition grain caused serious peasant resistance.

The fighting was cruel and prolonged. When Bukhara fell to the Red Army, its entire population was slain, and the citadel reduced to ruin. Its ruins stand as a poignant reminder to the present-day inhabitants of how Bolshevik rule came. Tens of thousands of people fled over the borders into China's Sinkiang region, both Russians and Turks.

There seems to be little information on the fate of Central Asian Catholicism. I have not found any records of letters to the chancery in Petrograd or later to Saint Louis des Français in Moscow from these parishes, although there were letters from Yaroslavl' and Arkhangel'sk. What is clear, is that those forcibly relocated here in the 1930s found that Church life had been devastated. Once Soviet rule was established, the Poles of Tashkent parish were not allowed to complete their church. Mass had to be held elsewhere. All of the churches still functioning in Central Asia in 1929 were closed during collectivization.[18]

CHAPTER 10

Survival—But What Next?

1920–1922

> There were no lights in the houses, none in the streets, of course . . . the
> electric power being only for the powerful. . . . No sound, either. . . . The
> usual fear-shackled silence. Broken windows, boarded doors . . . gaping
> into the street with black, glassless holes.
>
> —Olga Ilyin, *The White Road*

Devastation seemed to be the lot of poor suffering Russia in 1920. Besides the conflict between Whites and Reds, there had been a host of peasant uprisings. These were known as the "Peasant War," and were a series of revolts and long-term struggles waged by the Greens, Makhno's anarchists, and simply groups of farmers who were fed up with seeing two minorities (the Whites and the Reds) fight it out without offering any help to the majority-the peasants, most of whom had supported the Social Revolutionary Party. Catholic farmer communities were affected by these, particularly the Poles and Germans in Belorussia and Ukraine. It was the chaos of the countryside and worsening political repression that led to the great Kronshtadt Revolt at the Petrograd naval base.

The revolt began on March 1, 1921, with demonstrators at Kronshtadt Fortress on Kotlin Island demanding political reforms including secret elections and restoration of the Constituent Assembly-a revolt that saw hundreds of revolutionary leaders quit the Communist Party. Soldiers, sailors, and workers rose up against the Bolsheviks and their new autocracy. Lenin and Trotsky ordered that the rebellion be crushed; on March 16, a force of 50,000 Red soldiers stormed Kronshtadt. The rebels' positions were overrun and hundreds killed. Those who did not escape across the ice to Finland were slaughtered or exiled to the north to die in the dreaded labor camps. Lenin and his comrades, knowing it was false, declared that the revolt had been led by White Guards, monarchists, counterrevolutionary organizations, and foreigners. It was just another step in Lenin's campaign of lies and terror.[1] (The Kronshtadt Revolt would enable Lenin to convince the Communist Party of the necessity for his New Economic Policy or NEP.) On March 18, peace was achieved in the West when the Treaty of Riga was signed with Poland.

In the years 1918–1920, according to official Soviet estimates, more than nine million died. (In addition, two million had died in World War I, and even more had fled abroad to escape the Reds.) By 1923, thousands more would be slaughtered by the Reds or by the Whites, or would die from typhus, dysentery, cholera, and starvation. Inside Soviet Russia, Lenin's Red Terror claimed victims who had survived the war and its attendant horrors.[2] Among these, the Catholic minority was not spared.

A major consequence of the civil war was that there was never again an organized national opposition to the Communist system. The last fragments of the old political parties were destroyed during these years (though Stalin would claim that his opponents had kept those parties alive). The Party and the State became synonymous. Party positions became part of the State's laws and its basic approaches: pragmatism could still require a relaxation of persecution or even ordinary restrictions, but never would the Party-State end its hostility to religious beliefs.[3]

The flight and deaths of so many Catholics made things worse for those who remained. Some were killed because of their "counterrevolutionary" social origins, or because they belonged to the wrong ethnic group or the wrong political party, and a very few because they were found to oppose the political aims of the Revolution. But many died for the sake of their religion.

It is not true that only as the civil war drew to a close did the State turn its attention to the Churches. In 1919–1920, Bolshevik "inspections" of the churches as state property rented by the Catholics became excuses for desecration: at Gatchina, in the suburbs of Petrograd and thus close to foreign eyes, the Blessed Sacrament was dumped onto the floor.[4] The same-or worse-was taking place in the countryside.

Arrest of Archbishop Cieplak, More Restrictions: 1920

Throughout World War I, Orthodox clergy were cruelly oppressed. Many of their churches were closed, and priests were massacred at Perm' and Osa in 1919. The fate of the Tiraspol diocese-to become leaderless and isolated-was the fate in store for the rest of the Catholic Church in Soviet Russia. Bishop Kessler went into exile in January 1920. In April, on Holy Thursday, Archbishop Cieplak himself was arrested and accused of counterrevolutionary activity under the cover of religion and of colluding with Polish agents. Cieplak was spared, however, when 800 Catholic marines from the Red Navy joined a crowd of Catholic civilians outside Cheka headquarters in Petrograd and demanded his release. On April 17, as the Polish armies thundered across the Ukraine, the Cheka informed the Catholic clergy that any anti-Soviet activity would be dealt with ruthlessly.[6]

The Deprivations of the Faithful and Martyrdom in the German Colonies: 1921

Reacting to grain requisitions that were "robbing them of their last piece of bread," the Volga Germans engaged in a peasant revolt in 1921. German Communists had led the plundering; the colonists murdered some and drove others out. The Red Army crushed the revolt, and a wave of atrocities followed.

At Mariental in the Volga region, on the basis of alleged anti-Bolshevik activity, Father Nikolaus Kraft was executed with 270 of his parishioners. They were thrown, living and dead, into a manure pit.[5] When the noted Volga German historian Father Gottlieb Beratz, of Herzog, was ordered freed from prison by higher tribunals, the local Bolsheviks ignored the order and shot him atop a high bluff overlooking the Volga.

Father Jakob Kayser, ordained only five years before, was brutally murdered at Marienberg in 1921 by apostate Catholics who had joined the Communists. At his death, believers saw him surrounded by a bright light, the vindication by God of his martyr. In Kamyschin, Father Joseph Baumtrog (whose brother, Augustin, would later be named an apostolic administrator by Rome), charged with accepting foreign money to be used to help local priests, was imprisoned and then killed.[7]

Growing Hardships, Famine, and Death: 1922

As we have seen, two other bishops were soon forced to flee during the Polish retreat, leaving the Lutsk-Zhitomir and Kamenets dioceses without leadership. In 1921, the White collapse in Siberia resulted in the exile of the French administrator of Omsk; the confiscation of the chapel of the Theological Academy in Petrograd broke the last connection the Church had with the seminary building.

By 1922, the Catholics were faced with a terrible situation. Along with there being no open seminary left to train priests,

1. tens of thousands of parishioners were trying to leave or had already left their parishes;

2. food and work shortages had resulted in the depopulation of urban centers (Moscow lost 45 percent of its people at one point);

3. children and adolescents were prohibited not only from receiving religious education but even from worshiping;

4. in many areas there had been massacres of believers and desecrations of churches (the incident at Gatchina was only one example);

5. the priests who remained behind and at liberty were overworked, underfed, and under constant stress;

6. government pressure against public worship was mounting: even when permits were obtained, those who held processions could be prosecuted;

7. the arrest of Archbishop Cieplak had shown that no Catholic was safe, and the removal of the foreign armies and the final defeat of the Whites in Crimea and the Far East showed that Bolshevik rule was here to stay;

8. the grain requisitions and Bolshevik reprisals against rural revolts were taking a heavy toll on Catholic peasants;

9. episcopal leadership was being lost across the different Soviet republics, and Catholics were being executed in Georgia, Ukraine, and the Volga basin.

To this depressing picture was added the horror of the Great Famine, when Death stalked one-fifth of Soviet Russia's citizens. In the course of the famine, Rome attempted to connect again with its Soviet faithful and reach an understanding with the Bolsheviks. At the same time, the famine would end with more hardship for those same faithful.

CHAPTER 11

The Surprising Interlude:
Germany, the Vatican,
and the Bolsheviks

Rapallo . . . the name of a beautiful place on the Italian Riviera, it is still
haunting Europe's chancelleries today.
—Hansjakob Stehle, *The Eastern Politics of the Vatican*

In 1922, while the papal famine relief mission was still in Soviet Russia, the World Economic Conference was held in Genoa, Italy. It was the Bolsheviks' first appearance on the world stage. Isolated from the rest of the world, Soviet Russia had no diplomatic contacts, and when the famine relief agencies left, it stood alone, a bastion of Communism against a hostile planet. The only other power so treated was Weimar Germany, broken under the weight of the unfair and foolish Versailles Treaty. At this conference, the two stepchildren of the world were present, as was the world's smallest state, Vatican City.

On April 16, 1922, Germany and Russia signed the Rapallo Treaty, establishing diplomatic, commercial, and military ties, what became known as the "Rapallo Pact." Germany's Chancellor was Joseph Wirth, a member of the Catholic Center Party. The Holy See had been contacted by Wirth, who had encouraged Vatican participation and who was delighted to see Foreign Commissar Chicherin and Archbishop Signori exchange a mutual toast. Yet, even though the Vatican continued to hope for an ongoing connection with Moscow (a connection that would be provided for a time by the good offices of the German foreign ministry), this hope did not materialize.[1]

Papal and Bolshevik Negotiations

The last days of the papal famine relief mission were guided by Father Eduard Gehrmann, a German cleric appointed at the end of 1923, whose daunting

144

task it was to administer a poverty-stricken mission and to deal with German and Soviet diplomats all at the same time.[2] In late January 1924, a delegation of Soviet Catholic priests implored Father Gehrmann to keep the mission present in Moscow, and thus provide a link with Rome. Lenin had died on January 21, and now all were wondering what was in store for their country and Church.

From February on, the papal nuncio to Bavaria,[3] Bishop Eugenio Pacelli (the future Pope Pius XII) began negotiations with the Soviet Embassy to Germany in Berlin, capital of the Weimar Republic. (In August 1925, he would be named Nuncio to the entire German state, and would settle in Berlin, allowing the talks to proceed much more easily). But in spring 1924, the Soviets arrested scores of Latin and Byzantine Catholic priests, and all the Byzantine-Russian nuns, while releasing Archbishop Cieplak to exile in the West. Cieplak acted with great discretion abroad, not wanting to worsen the situation; the Soviet ambassador to Italy told him that the priests would be freed only if the Holy See opened formal negotiations and gave Russia de facto diplomatic recognition.

The loss of the relief mission was met with tears. Although relatively little food had gone out, compared to other agencies, the mission had provided food and medicine for imprisoned Catholics, and had given accurate information about the Church and the world to many; its priests had served as a living link with Rome and the Universal Church.

Contact by bishops in Poland or other foreign exile only worsened the situations for Soviet Catholics. Priests' letters to relatives or visits to or from foreign consuls who were Catholic could result in police harassment and arrest.

Establishment of Contacts

Throughout 1925, Bishop Pacelli and Soviet Ambassador Krestinski continued to meet. The German foreign ministry continued to act as a go-between, often being asked by the Holy See—under increasingly difficult conditions—to communicate with Moscow and even to intervene on behalf of Soviet Catholic citizens of non-German origin. At the same time, because of deteriorating conditions in the Soviet Union, the Vatican looked for alternatives. The first would come in the person of a French Jesuit. To understand the growing papal concern about Soviet Russia, we must first examine what was happening to its Catholic citizens.

CHAPTER 12

As Soon as Grass Began to Grow, It Was Eaten

> According to the . . . USSR, 5,053,000 lives were lost because of the famine. . . . All the unique features of the system were displayed: cruelty, vengefulness, an obstinacy. Lenin was willing to sacrifice a substantial section of the peasantry as long as the industrial centers were kept in food.
> —Mikhail Heller and Aleksandr Nekrich, *Utopia in Power*

> There were not enough coffins . . . corpses were gathered and loaded one upon the other. . . . The deserted houses of the suburbs were burned down with corpses inside. . . . Cats and dogs were all eaten long ago. As soon as grass began to grow, it was gathered and eaten.
> —Natalia Petrova, *Twice Born in Russia*

The famine of 1921–1922 was the result of years of civil war, a drought, and, above all, the Bolshevik policy of requisitioning grain from the farmers, including all the traditional reserves against famine and for spring planting. The disaster affected millions of people, and up to 20 percent of the population died or nearly died of starvation.[1]

The policy of forcible Sovietization had failed miserably, and the industrial proletariat suffered an absolute lack of food for the first time. The transportation system had collapsed, the countryside was in revolt, and the sailors of the Red Navy, leaders of the Revolution, went into open revolt at Kronshtadt Fortress demanding free elections, free press, and relief for their suffering peasant relatives. Lenin faced the threat of total ruin, and in private conversation admitted that the Bolsheviks were just barely holding on to power.

Lenin's response to the famine was twofold. First, he allowed the All-Russian Relief Committee, composed of non-Communist intellectuals, to coordinate relief efforts from the imperialist West and to appeal to the Western powers. When, however, Herbert Hoover's American Relief Administration began to feed the starving masses in August 1921, all of the committee intellectuals, who had worked so hard, were arrested and sent to prison camps or shot. (Hoover did arrange for many of those sent to the camps to be safely expelled abroad.) Among the many relief organizations that came to Soviet Russia's aid was the Pontifical Relief Mission, whose work will be dealt with in the second part of this chapter.

Second, Lenin initiated the campaign to confiscate church valuables as a way to break the Churches' hold on the people. The Christian Churches had responded to the famine with traditional charity; in particular, the Orthodox Patriarchate ordered special collections in the parishes and organized the Orthodox Church Famine Relief Committee. The government denounced such efforts as "counterrevolutionary" because they implied—correctly, as it turned out—that the State and Party were unable to help the masses. What was worse from the Party's perspective, the enormous response by the Orthodox faithful inside and outside Soviet Russia proved the great influence of the Church despite persecution.[2] Still worse, Patriarch Tikhon and the Orthodox Church announced their decision to sell all remaining Church valuables, except those needed for Holy Communion and divine worship, to raise money for famine relief. The reaction of the State was swift and violent, and the fate of Orthodoxy presaged what was to come for the Catholics.

The Devastation of Orthodoxy

One week after the Orthodox Church's decision, in its decree of February 26, 1922, the State ordered the confiscation of *all* Church valuables. It was felt, first, that the confiscation would provide "a final blow" to religion", as was published in Moscow in 1922,[3] and second, that because the Churches were likely to resist the confiscation of Communion vessels, the Bolsheviks could then portray the Christian Churches to the peasants as being more concerned with money than with feeding the hungry. (Indeed, antireligious displays would repeat this canard throughout Soviet history.)

As an aside, although the Soviet state now owned all the crown jewels of the imperial dynasty, and had long ago begun to confiscate private jewelry and valuables from the upper classes, there is no record of its ever selling any of these treasures to feed its starving citizens. Also, it is worth noting that, because of the government's reluctance to part with confiscated property of any kind, the confiscation of all remaining Church valuables provided only meager famine relief. Paul Scheffer of the *Berliner Tageblatt* reported that, even though an enormous amount of church plate of all kinds, amounting to tens of thousands of boxes, was seized, there was little to show for it. In the provinces, many piles of items were senselessly destroyed, and there was "strict darkness" regarding the ultimate fate of much of the balance. Indeed, by mid-1923, the foreign sale of church objects had produced only 700,000 rubles,[4] a paltry sum given the extent of the famine and the devastation wrought on the Churches. Although the 1921 plundering of the Tiraspol diocese netted 7 million gold rubles, most would find its way into the pockets of antireligious agitators and party workers.[5]

Religious Endurance and Resistance

Soviet Christianity, of course, survived the loss of all the valuable material objects inside the churches. Further, the response of Orthodox peasants contradicted Bolshevik expectations: within three months of the February 1922 decree, there were 1,414 clashes between Red Army soldiers violating the churches and Orthodox believers defending their churches. Lenin seized on their violent resistance as an opportunity to break religious strength in the countryside.

In May, after the Moscow-based Shuya show trial of Orthodox peasants who had defended their church in that village, five of the believers were shot. Also in May, with the tacit approval and encouragement of the government, a pro-Soviet group of "progressive" priests took over the patriarchal chancery and initiated the Renovationist or Living Church schism. Sponsoring radical changes (as well as a few legitimate reforms), this movement never garnered much strength, although it helped the State further weaken the Orthodox Church.

Metropolitan Benjamin's Trial

Orthodox Metropolitan Benjamin of Petrograd was popular with the Orthodox working class, and was praised by the head of the city militia for his attitudes. In response to the State's confiscation of Church valuables, he proposed a compromise, whereby the faithful could make financial offerings to aid the hungry and save the Communion vessels. This was not acceptable to the Bolsheviks, for whom the issue was not money to feed the starving, but a chance to break the Church. Headed by the renegade priest Alexander Vvedensky,[6] the Living Church clergy denounced the brave metropolitan and cooperated with the GPU (successor to the Cheka) in arranging his destruction. In July, a total of 86 people were put on trial in Petrograd for their alleged counterrevolutionary activity. Metropolitan Benjamin and three of the defendants were shot, and the others given lengthy prison sentences. It was clear to all at the time that the metropolitan, one of the leading and most popular Orthodox clerics in all Russia, had been executed both for his activity in famine relief and because he opposed the clerics who promoted the Living Church schism in Orthodoxy.[7] The State continued to violate Orthodox Churches and, in the course of 1922, executed some 8,100 Orthodox priests, monks, and nuns.[8] At the same time, the Bolsheviks insisted to the West that there was no persecution of religion in Soviet Russia whatsoever—and most in the West naïvely accepted such assurances as Gospel.

If this was the fate of the majority religion inside and outside Soviet Russia, what would happen to the long-despised Catholic minority, now reduced to only 1.6 million people?

Vatican-Kremlin Contacts

In March 1922, the Vatican and Soviet Russia signed an agreement on famine relief, and the Holy See withdrew the accreditation of the imperial legation to the Vatican. Anti-Bolshevik émigrés were furious, but the Church hoped both to fulfill a humanitarian mission and to establish contacts that would help the Soviet Catholic Church. On April 16, the Bolsheviks stunned the world by signing the Rapallo Treaty with Weimar Germany. The two international pariahs agreed to cooperate, and the Vatican followed through on this dramatic development by using the good offices of the German foreign ministry to open secret negotiations with Moscow. As a result of these talks, thirteen Catholic missionaries, defined in the agreement as "workers," arrived in the Crimea to open the Pontifical Relief Mission in July.

Catholic Expropriations Begin

On March 22, 1922, the Soviet Catholic Church was ordered to sign government contracts before it could use the nationalized churches. The Church refused this order and also refused to allow the confiscation of all its precious items. Here, we will focus on the Church in the provinces during the famine period. (Details of the confiscations and resistance of the Catholic laity—especially in Petrograd—and the resultant "Cieplak Trial" are discussed in Chapter 15.)

The government moved swiftly; indeed its swiftness showed how well everything had been prepared.[9] Of Catholic churches throughout Soviet Russia, only the very poor ones were spared. In the archdiocese of Mogilev, churches and chapels in thirty-three cities were attacked, including those in Moscow, Petrograd, and Novgorod, in full view of foreigners. In Siberia, every single church was plundered. The newly appointed pastor of Tambov, Father Lavrinovich, was shot because of "zealous religious service," and he would not abandon his parishioners.[10] In the Minsk diocese, in Belorussia, the grave of Blessed Andrew Bobola was opened, and his remains hauled off to a Moscow museum. For two days, Red soldiers looted the Cathedral of Saint Mary, stripping the silver off the cover of the icon of the Mother of God and from the tomb that held the relics of Saint Felix.

The devastation was greatest, however, in the Tiraspol diocese. Of 68 churches in Ukraine, 52 were looted; the 16 that were spared were simply prayer houses, too poor to offer anything. Everything that could be removed was hauled away. In the cemeteries, metal crucifixes were confiscated, stones broken up, wooden crosses, fences, and hedges burned or torn out of the ground. Workers or farmers rallied around every single church, and had to be driven off by soldiers at bayonet point.[11] The Bolsheviks also confiscated the 202,000 rubles Bishops Zerr and von der Ropp had collected for the construction of a new seminary, as well as all funds for seminarian scholarships, Mass stipends for the priests, and memorial donations, both from Church accounts in the Saratov bank and from the assets of the Catholic Church in Petrograd.[12] Bishop Kessler noted that the persecutions suffered by Catholic villages in the Volga region were generally worse than those in Lutheran villages, even though the Lutherans outnumbered the Catholics overall.[13]

The desecration of the Blessed Bobola's relics had a special significance for all Catholics. Known as the "soul catcher" for his successful missionary work among the Orthodox in Belorussia, he had been subjected to brutal tortures and finally murdered by the Cossacks in 1657. His miraculously incorrupt body had been rescued and enshrined in the Belorussian city of Polotsk, seat of the Greek Catholic martyr Saint Josaphat. Now the Polish Catholic Jesuit (who combined in himself three traditional "enemies" of Russia) was dragged out of his resting place and put on public display. It was as a final, particularly hurtful blow against a Church that was being humiliated and torn apart, as Bobola's body had been by the Cossacks. Despite his barbarous murder, however, the body was incorrupt at the time of the martyrdom, again in 1730, and now once again in this desecration. For the Orthodox, incorruptibility is a singular sign of holiness; for suffering Christians of all denominations, his continued state of miraculous preservation served as a reminder of the possibility of divine victory over God's sworn enemies.

Hardships of Parish Life Before
the Church Closings of 1922

Famine was also taking its toll among laity and clergy alike, who died either from starvation or from disease. Many provincial priests died of typhus,[14] and those parishes were now bereft of sacraments. After the Cieplak Show trial, many priests were jailed. In addition, the famine and religious and political persecutions prompted many believers to emigrate to Poland, the Baltic States, or Germany, further weakening the Soviet Catholic Church. Because so many parishes in Ukraine and Belorussia had lost their pastors during the Polish retreat in the summer of 1920, those priests who remained behind and were still at liberty were overworked, ministering to congregations suffering in new ways. Father Adolph Lassatowicz, for example, ministered to 5,000 in Immaculate Conception parish in Smolensk itself, to another 1,000 in Mazalcew, and to still more in Vyazma. In Samara deanery, Father Ladislaus Kunda served 2,000 faithful in the city of Samara, 1,000 in Orenburg, and still others in Hoffenthal and Reinsfeld.[15]

In Lesnoy, under the direction of the parish committee, the last Catholic school remained open (with 100 students). In the factory town of Kolpino, Father Anton Niemancziewcz was able to hold the last Corpus Christi procession in the spring of 1921. Even though the priest had received official permission, he was nevertheless arrested and charged with counterrevolutionary activity; for the procession and for his effective work with local youths and factory workers, he was sentenced to one year in prison. (Permission to hold a Corpus Christi procession in Petrograd was refused outright in 1921 on the basis of the "evil influence" of religion on the population.)[16] By 1925, the archdiocese of Mogilev had lost some 200,000 faithful; by mid-1924, there were only 111 priests alive and at liberty in all of Soviet Russia.[17]

The Papal Famine Relief Mission to Russia

Pope Benedict XV inaugurated the Pontifical Relief Mission as a natural extension of his continual charity to all sides ever since the start of the Great War in 1914. In the summer of 1921, the pope wrote eloquently to Cardinal Gasparri of the spread of typhus, cholera, and starvation and of the Bolsheviks' cruelty in not allowing their citizens to flee from the famine areas; he urged the League of Nations to intervene, and he called on Catholics throughout the world to contribute what they could to famine relief. Previous appeals to the League had failed on the grounds that Soviet Russia was still in the middle of a civil war.[18]

The Vatican relief team could not bring much aid to starving Russia: the Catholic world contributed only $2 million, whereas the American Relief Association distributed $66 million worth of food. Furthermore, the Holy See had been bankrupted by Benedict's generosity throughout the Great War and by his aid to refugees after the war. (Indeed, Cardinal Gasparri had to take out a loan to pay for the conclave to elect Benedict's successor.)[19]

But the Vatican work was important. Soviet Russia was hoping it would lead to de jure recognition by the Holy See, at a time when the Western world refused to grant such diplomatic status. For its part, Rome was hoping to keep a foothold inside the country, both for contact with the Soviet Catholic Church and to be available in case of future changes in Soviet Russia.[20]

The priests, the workers who were hired inside Soviet Russia, and the unfortunates who were being helped by the papal mission were all subjected to GPU surveillance. In particular, some Bolsheviks did not want to allow people hired by the mission from the bourgeoisie or nobility to work, and thus find sustenance. The GPU moved quickly to interrogate "suspicious" persons. Because government forms always asked about the social origin of workers, there was constant fear on the part of these employees that they would not only be deprived of life-giving food, but also be arrested and taken away.[21] Some 160,000 children were fed daily by the Vatican's soup kitchens. Overall, more Orthodox than Catholics were helped by the papal workers; throughout, Pope Benedict XV insisted that the name "Orthodox" be used in place of the offensive "dissident."[22]

At the same time, the papal Secretariat of State emphasized to the priests that they could not interfere in the local situation in any way: they were in Soviet Russia to exercise pure charity, and they were forbidden to intervene in the tragic scenes of plundering and arrests that plagued the Catholic churches in the cities they served in. Nor was there any active proselytism or overt religious work among non-Catholics.[23] Even their own Soviet workers did not know that the "workers, professors, doctors" of the Pontifical Relief Mission were clerics. (Realization came slowly, even to the secretary of the mission in Crimea.)[24]

On the other hand, the Vatican's caution and consideration had its limits. Mother Catherine Abrikosovna, of the Russian Catholic nuns, was stunned to discover that the Vatican had assigned a Jesuit, Father Edward Walsh, SJ, to head the mission, despite Russians' "terrible aversion to" the order and the Communists' paranoiac fear of them.[25]

The tiny relief mission was somehow able to spread itself throughout Soviet Russia. In Crimea, two centers served at Dianko and Eupatoria, helping 25,000 children in a region heavily settled by Catholic Germans, Czechs, and Poles (but all references to Crimea make it clear that non-Catholic Russians, Ukrainians, and Estonians of the settlement region were also aided). At Rostov, in the land of the Don Cossacks, (whose Catholic church was doomed to be plundered of all its silver ornaments and vessels), two Spanish priests worked quietly but effectively among the poor. Three priests were also working in Krasnodar' (formerly, Ykaterinodar'), in the Kuban', above the Caucasus, and one in distant Orenburg at the gateway to southwestern Siberia. Five priests were assigned to Moscow, where a soup kitchen served university students, children, and invalids.[26]

In Moscow, Father Walsh held quasi-diplomatic status "in the name of the Holy Father . . . to ease the religious situation of the Catholics in Russia," as authorized by Cardinal Gasparri. He worked closely with the German Embassy and the Weimar Republic's foreign ministry so as to be in regular contact with Rome.[27] There were great hopes of establishing a permanent Vatican mission. Furthermore, intellectuals came to the relief station serving students in Moscow and expressed serious interest in conversion.

The relief mission undoubtedly saved many lives during its operation. In addition, the devoted and selfless work of the priests impressed local people, and did much to alleviate anti-Catholic bigotry. The presence of the Moscow mission, which managed to hang on until September 18, 1924, also reminded the Soviet Catholics that they were not forgotten, and served as a living link with Rome. (Indeed, as we shall see, Father Walsh was able to communicate some information to Archbishop Cieplak from the Vatican, and to get some aid to imprisoned priests, sisters, and laypeople.)

On the other hand, the Vatican was not able to increase its positions in Russia. The papal relief mission only began toward the end of the famine, and was a small effort compared to those launched by the United States and by European countries. Although the great asset of the mission was its center in Moscow, the Bolshevik capital, and although contacts had been carefully maintained in Berlin through the Nuncio, Cardinal Pacelli (the future Pope Pius XII), and Soviet Counselor Bratmann-Brodowski, with a focus on the Holy See granting full diplomatic recognition to the Soviets, such recognition would not take place until 1990. Instead, in early 1924, several Western nations, led by Italy, were the first to end the Soviets' diplomatic isolation. Furthermore, though the carrot of an apostolic delegation was held out, the Holy

See simply did not have the money to fund it; resistance was raised by conservative foreign Catholics against a rapprochement with Russia; and the Soviets tired of a process that bore so few tangible results.[28]

The relief mission did endure until the summer of 1924, feeding children and supplying aid to imprisoned Catholics (whose numbers steadily increased), but finally all the stations closed, and weeping crowds gathered to say good-bye to the Fathers at each place.[29] On August 23, Cardinal Gasparri ordered the last priests out; they left on September 18. That same day, the *Osservatore Romano* published memoirs by Father Viktor Bede of his conversations with the recently deceased Lenin, conversations in which Lenin was sympathetic to the Church. The Vatican still retained hope, then, for the future of the Church left behind in the Soviet Union.

A Miracle in the Midst of Suffering

In the summer of 1921, a powerful event took place in a village north of Petrograd, near Finland. Although the former Catholic orphanage for Lithuanians had been closed in 1917 and, with it, the church, the village was still home to Catholic families. When three boys and a girl overheard the plans of Red Army soldiers to break into the church, they resolved to "shield the dear, loving Jesus": they did not know that the Blessed Sacrament had been removed in 1917. The children entered the church through an open window and greeted the soldiers. The Red Army men ordered them out, and threatened to shoot them. When the boys replied that they "would not suffer their dear Jesus to be insulted," two of them were killed. The third boy then blocked the altar steps with his body, and was brutally beaten. That boy died a few hours later, but not before he had told the people of the miracle in the church.

Jesus had appeared on the altar steps, and blessed the two dead boys. The Red soldiers screamed that the church was haunted and fled. The third boy died "radiant, saying: 'We have shielded Jesus.' "[30] It was with such faith that the Church would survive.

PART TWO

1922–1939

CHAPTER 13

The Passion Bearers of the Russian Catholic Exarchate

> The true messianism of the Russian Church is not what the Slavophiles have imagined, but it is the example of suffering. It is in this way that she shows that she is the continuation of Christ in this world.
> —Exarch Feodorov, August 1928, at Solovetski

The first saints of Rus' were the martyred brothers Boris and Gleb, who accepted death at the hands of a renegade brother prince rather than plunge Rus' into civil war and destruction. They were hailed as "passion bearers," saints who willingly took upon themselves the sufferings of the Lord, even unto death, so as to bring redemption to others. Exarch Feodorov and the faithful of his tiny Church exemplified this spirit to the fullest. They were a tiny community; yet their witness has endured the obscurity of history and the dark of Arctic nights.

Missionary Work, 1918–1923

Established in 1918, the exarchate was not formally recognized until 1921, by Pope Benedict XV. Pope Pius XI confirmed Leonid Feodorov in his title as Exarch.[1] Although Metropolitan Sheptytsky held a grand vision of Orthodox reunion with Rome, and although the rapid secular and religious changes of the time seemed (to optimists) to favor such a reunion, the Byzantine-Russian Catholics were a very small community. Feodorov himself estimated the exarchate's population in 1922 at only 380 in three parishes (Moscow: 100, Petrograd: 70, Saratov: 10; elsewhere: 200), noting that only 2,000 other believers had emigrated or died in the first famine (1921–1922).[2] At its peak, in 1923, it is said that the Russian Catholic Exarchate counted 20 priests and deacons, and 25 nuns[3] (these estimates did not include the isolated parish of Nizhnyaya Bogdanovka, whose priest was flogged nineteen times by various govern-

157

ments for having led his Orthodox flock into Byzantine Catholicism). This was the size of a community put on its own, with only a single exarch at a time when Soviet Russia was being torn apart by forces that would destroy the much larger Latin Catholic Church. Destroy the exarch, and the structure of the newborn Church would be destroyed with him.[4]

Nevertheless, in 1918–1922, despite the ravages the war and famine, there was hope for reunion. Exarch Feodorov wrote to Pope Benedict XV in 1922 proposing standards for the mission work in Russia, by which (1) the Latin Catholic hierarchy would be confined (per *Orientalium dignitas*) to the Latin Catholic faithful; (2) ethnic Russian converts would be received only as Greek Catholics; and (3) foreign priests working in the Byzantine Rite would have to come under the jurisdiction of the exarchate.[5] These standards were never accepted by Rome and tensions between Byzantine and Latin Catholics in Soviet Russia and Poland persisted until the Byzantine missions were finally destroyed.

Moscow

In Moscow, Vladimir and Anna Abrikosov (converted in France in 1909 and 1908, respectively) were the exarchate's guiding lights. Anna became a Dominican nun under the name Sister Catherine of Siena in 1913, and Vladimir was ordained a priest shortly after the February Revolution, on May 29, 1917. The Moscow center at the Abrikosovs' apartment, a gathering place for Russian and Roman Catholics and for interested Orthodox, grew into the parish of the Nativity of the Blessed Virgin Mary, with a chapel and school.

Moscow was also the home for the second community of women in the exarchate. In 1921, the community of Russian and Polish women who had gathered around Sister Catherine, and who included also one Jewish convert, became a Dominican Order, with the permission of the Dominican master general. While retaining the traditions of the Byzantine-Russian Rite, the order added the Latin Catholic practices of the recitation of the Rosary, adoration of the Blessed Sacrament, and daily meditation and examen on the Western style to its spiritual life.[6] Father Nikolai Alexandrov, an electrical engineer ordained in 1922 by Archbishop Cieplak as a married priest, served as chaplain of the nuns and pastor of the Moscow parish (his wife joined the Dominican Sisters).[7] The timing of his ordination and appointment was fortuitous: in September, Father Vladimir was one of the many intellectuals expelled from Soviet Russia. The Sisters continued to work with children privately from 1922 to 1923 (some who taught in public kindergartens were expelled by the State) and to live in community.

The Sisters were heroic figures: one was the daughter of an Orthodox deacon, who was locked up by her furious father and deprived of food because of her conversion. Another was a Polish Roman Catholic who chose not to leave with her family when they emigrated, but rather to face an uncertain future for the sake of saving Russia. All of the Sisters consecrated their work, prayers, and entire lives for the sake of Russia. The community followed the Byzantine fasts and the full liturgical office of the Byzantine-Russian Rite (with the noted additions from the Latin Rite); all Sisters took the names of Dominican Saints from the Latin Rite.[8]

Petrograd

Slovo Istiny was closed down with other independent journals in 1918. The community of women initiated by Exarch Feodorov had evolved into the Sisters of the Order of Saint Basil, under the leadership of Sister Julia Danzas,[9] yet another heroic figure in this little Church. Father Epiphan Akulov served as vicar at Holy Spirit Church, and Father Ivan Deibner was still working in the city. Worship continued in Saratov under Father Onesimov, attached to Saint Clement's Cathedral parish, though under great difficulties: the vicar forbade the singing of the Byzantine Liturgy, calling it too "scandalous" for the faithful.[10]

Nizhnyaya Bogdanovka

The exarchate's last community was that of Nizhnyaya Bogdanovka in Ukraine, where a parish of 828 adult Russian Orthodox using the Old Rite (Edinoverie) was founded under Father Patapii Emilianov in 1918. Metropolitan Sheptytsky confirmed Emilianov as pastor in 1919. He was imprisoned by the Whites, but released—ironically—by the Red Army at the end of the Russo-Polish War.[11]

"The Union Has Returned!"

This was the cry in 1922 in Belorussian territories, where the depth of the loyalty of the "stubborn ones" was borne out. At Mogilev and Vitebsk, the appearance of the exarch was greeted with shouts of joy. The dean of Mogilev invited the exarch to come to his parish, Saint Anthony of Padua, for its patronal pilgrimage in June. The exarch's celebrations of the Divine Liturgy were well received in Mogilev and in the Catholic parish of Sophiisky, where Orthodox clergy joined the exarch in services at the church and cemetery. As a result of the visit, a delegation of Belorussian intellectuals petitioned for reunion as soon as possible. Enthusiastic crowds attended his return in November.

The growing popularity of the exarchate to Russian intellectuals in the Soviet era disturbed not only the Communists, who were paranoiac about any increase in Catholic strength, but also the schismatic Living Church. Indeed, Living Church priests who had developed a hatred of Eastern Catholicism may well have assisted in the arrests of 1923–1924.[12]

Tensions with the Latin Catholic Church

Although many priests in the Latin Catholic Church were well disposed to the Greek Catholic movement, as is seen by the fact that Latin Catholic churches and chapels were used for the Divine Liturgy, others had their misgivings. Some were simply prejudiced against the Byzantine Rite; some read much into the Holy See's not recognizing the exarchate until 1921. Many thought that reunion of the two Churches was simply impossible, and thus continued to convert the Orthodox.

At the root of tensions between the Churches were three major problems. The first problem was Exarch Feodorov's categorical refusal to subordinate his clergy to the Latin Catholic Metropolitan. Attempts to alleviate the clergy shortage of the exarchate by authorizing Latin Catholic priests to practice both the Byzantine and the Latin Rite were also rebuffed: such priests would come under the jurisdiction, not of the exarch, but of the archdiocese of Mogilev—tantamount, in Russian eyes, to being placed under Polish rule. The exarch insisted that the priests be under the jurisdiction of Russian Catholic bishops.[13] The second problem was, as noted, the continuing admission of Orthodox converts into Catholicism. The majority were received into the Latin Rite, and remained there, in violation of papal decrees ignored by most Latin Catholic priests in both imperial and Soviet Russia. The third problem was the introduction of Russian-language prayers in Petrograd and Yaroslavl' in the early 1920s. To the Orthodox, the Russian Rosary, Litanies, and devotions all smacked of proselytizing attempts to lure Orthodox Russians into Roman Catholicism and ultimately a Polish identity.[14]

At the same time, it is worth pointing out that both Archbishop von der Ropp and Archbishop Cieplak were favorably disposed to the exarchate, and several Latin Catholic priests gave financial support during the terrible inflationary periods. Indeed, many Russian Greek Catholics were saved from starvation in 1921–22 by the aid given from English Catholics and the Bishop of Kaunas in Lithuania.[15]

Relations with the Orthodox Church

In 1918, Exarch Feodorov had begun relations with the new Orthodox patriarch, Tikhon, and with the metropolitan of Petrograd, the future martyr Benjamin. In 1919, the first joint Catholic-Orthodox protest was published against Bolshevik persecution. Moreover, during the Russo-Polish War, plans were made for the Orthodox priests of Petrograd to make their retreat under the exarch's spiritual direction.[16] None of this would have been considered possible in 1914.

These promising ventures into cooperation were turned back by the success of the Monday Lectures at Saint Catherine's, through which so many Orthodox entered the Latin Catholic Church with public "abjurations of schism" (ironically, nearly 100 of these converts were ethnic Polish women returning to the Church of their ancestors). When Exarch Feodorov spoke at the lectures to explain Eastern Catholicism, the Orthodox presumed he approved of the practice of receiving Russian Catholics into the Latin Catholic rite. Metropolitan Benjamin rejected further overtures.[17]

Exarch Feodorov formed a small community of consecrated women at the Barmalyeva church. In 1922, he received a large number of priest-monks into the Church from the Orthodox Alexander Nevsky Monastery. Some of these remained officially Orthodox, and a tradition of crypto-Catholicism inside the Patriarchal Church was born, long before the massive forced absorption of Greek Catholics after 1944.

Nevertheless, Russian Catholic meetings with Patriarch Tikhon continued, and went well. When the patriarch was placed under house arrest in May 1922, Moscow Russian Catholics joined an Orthodox delegation to a special meeting in his support. The success of this meeting, and the reception of Pope Benedict XV's "Prayer for Unity" led to further meetings and discussions in Moscow—all of which would result in the inclusion of Father Vladimir Abrikosov among intellectuals deported by the Soviets.

The Destruction of the Exarchate

The Russian Catholic Exarchate was progressively crippled by Soviet persecution from 1923 on. Its members were all called upon to become passion bearers like Saints Boris and Gleb.

On November 21, 1922, Exarch Feodorov was arrested in Petrograd and released after interrogation. Sister Julia Danzas successfully removed the Blessed Sacrament before the police could desecrate it, and the church on Barmalayeva Street was sealed. Services were removed to Sister Julia's apartment, where they were celebrated in great secrecy, and with less than twenty people present, into 1923. When they were over, the exarch would kneel for hours in silence before the altar and icons. He wrote of these moments, "Not only does calm return, but my body seems to be annihilated; the only true life begins, the life of that which is intangible." It was this deep spirituality that would sustain both him and his faithful in the trials ahead.[18]

In February 1923, Exarch Feodorov was again arrested, along with the Latin Catholic leadership of Petrograd, and taken to Moscow for trial. There he made his dramatic presentations against the Sovieet prosecutor, Krylenko, and was convicted and sentenced to 10 years in prison. Although Father Walsh and others were allowed to pay frequent visits to the exarch at Sokolniki prison, bringing news, food, and writing supplies, the exarch could not receive Holy Communion. During his imprisonment there, he produced two Russian Catholic catechisms, and he renewed his ecumenical contacts, this time with Orthodox bishops and priests at the prison. From Sokolniki, Exarch Feodorov ordered his faithful to assemble in small groups and to recite the services in whispers. The priests were to teach the adults catechism, so that they could teach their children.[19] Five months later, the exarch was moved to Lefortovo.

In November 1923, the Pontifical Relief Mission left the USSR. That winter, the government moved against the exarchate's congregations, motivated by hatred of the Russian Catholics and by anger over the publication of a secret letter of Sister Julia (at the instance of naïve Western Europeans). A total of 41 members were arrested, including all the Dominicans, the Petrograd priests, Father Alexandrov, and Sister Julia. Most were tried on May 24, 1924. Father Abrikosov was sent to Solovki, Father Zerchaninov and a young priest to Siberia, Father Deibner to Vladimir prison. A total of 37 Russian Catholics were sent to prison, as were 43 Orthodox, accused of having had friendly relations with them.[20] Only Father Serge Soloviev, nephew of the great philosopher, was left at liberty; barred from using the Nativity of the Virgin chapel, he celebrated Byzantine services in the Latin Catholic parishes.

Persecution of the Nuns

In 1922, Father Abrikosov's mother was permitted to emigrate and join her son in exile. Permission was extended to Mother Catherine, but she refused to leave, stating that she wished to "accomplish *until the end* my vow of immolation for the priests and for Russia."[21]

In late 1923, according to Father Walsh of the papal famine relief mission, the nuns numbered 25, crowded into three small rooms, and subject to constant searches. On November 12, Mother Catherine's apartment was raided at 11 P.M. and the Sisters interrogated until 5:30 A.M. the next morning. On November 13, Mother Catherine and twenty-two of the nuns were incarcerated in the Lubyanka. Offered freedom if they would renounce both the Byzantine-Russian Rite and the Dominican Order, the nuns refused. Jailed together at Butyrka, they sang the Liturgy in quiet voices and made a Lenten retreat. On April 30, 1924, the feast of Catherine of Siena, they made a public renewal of their vows. In May, the Sisters were sentenced: Catherine to 10 years, a second Sister to 8 years, and others to lesser terms in prison or Siberian exile. Also sentenced were Fathers Alexandrov and Deibner and several lay believers.

The Sisters were fortunate in that they were imprisoned or exiled in pairs and almost never with criminals, something they had prayed for most fervently. The Sisters' ministry continued in prison and exile: the Armenian Catholic priest at Krasnodar wrote that the two novices exiled there were truly edifying; a Catholic priest imprisoned in Yaroslavl' and driven nearly insane by continual interrogation was saved from despair by another of the Sisters.[22] Although Sister Imelda was executed at Solovetski in 1923,[23] Sister Julia Danzas survived to complete her term there in 1933. Liberated from Soviet Russia by her brother in 1934, Sister Julia moved to France, where she wrote copiously on the Russian Catholics. She died in Rome in 1942.[24]

As was true with so many other religious prisoners, Mother Catherine affected both guards and criminals.[25] So great was her positive influence that the fearful Communists placed her in isolation from 1926 to 1932. Following her transfer from Tobol'sk to Yaroslavl', she was able to confess occasionally to Monsignor Skalski, another prisoner for the Faith. Operated on for breast cancer, she was finally released in August 1932, on the eve of the Assumption.

Although exiled to Kostroma, whose Catholic parish was long closed by then, she was permitted regular visits to Moscow for cancer treatment; there she attended services at Saint Louis des Français and received Holy Communion at last.

In 1933, Mother Catherine was arrested for speaking with Komsomol members about religion, and again exiled to Yaroslavl'. Afflicted with cancer of the face, she finally died in the Butyrka prison on June 23, 1936. She was refused the right to Extreme Unction or Communion, and her body was cremated to deny the Catholics any relics.

Release and Disaster

The depth of the animosity of the Soviets to this small Church is evident in Moscow's reaction to a 1924 attempt by Poland to obtain the release of prisoners taken in the previous winter's arrests.[26] Moscow categorically forbade the release of Mother Catherine, Sister Julia, and two non-Russian laywomen, along with that of Exarch Feodorov, and of Fathers Alexandrov, Akulov, and Deibner, even though the draft agreement stated that no prisoner could be excluded. Negotiations dragged on until 7 of the 220 candidates for freedom were shot, at which point the Poles acquiesced to Moscow's intransigence.[27] By 1924, the exarchate's priests were scattered: two had chosen to emigrate, three had been exiled, and six had been sent to prison camps.[28] Although the exarch and many of his clergy, nuns, and parishioners suffered and died in prison, Poland was able to obtain the release of a number of the other priests, who were then able to emigrate. None of them ever returned home.[29]

As a result of the intervention of Maxim Gorky's wife, Exarch Feodorov was released from prison in April 1926, in time for Holy Week. He was sent to Kaluga, where he took up residence at the Latin Catholic church, substituting three weeks of the month, for the Lithuanian pastor, Father Pavlovich, who had a total of ten parishes to care for in the north. Here he celebrated the Byzantine Divine Liturgy in the parish church for the Latin Catholics (while also celebrating traditional Latin Catholic devotions to the Virgin), and established contacts with both Old Believers and Orthodox.

In the 1926 reorganization of the Soviet Catholic Church by the Holy See, Exarch Feodorov was made vicar general for the Oriental Rite, under Bishop Neveu, the new metropolitan of Russia. In July, he had returned to Saint Anthony's in Mogilev, where he celebrated Liturgy to a great crowd. As a result, he and Father Josef Bielogolov were arrested. Father Bielogolov was shot; the Exarch was sentenced to three years at Solovetski.[30]

Solovetski

A complex of monasteries and churches on islands in the White Sea, Solovetski was a brutal prison under the Soviets. Part of the monks were jailed, part were banished to one portion of the monastery. Tens of thousands of Soviet citizens passed through Solovetski over the years, and its name became synonymous with hard labor under brutal conditions.

For a time, the "free" monks at the cemetery chapel held Orthodox services. In November 1925, the chapel of Saint Hermann, cofounder of the monastery, was given over for Byzantine Catholic use on Sundays and feasts. Thanks to the generosity of Russian Catholics in Moscow and the labor of convict Catholics in Solovetski, the chapel was fully decorated, and sacramental wine was obtained, as were four sets of Byzantine vestments. The Latin Catholic dean of Vitebsk, Father Leon Baranowski, arrived at Solovetski in 1926. Although at first reluctant to say Mass in the Byzantine (Rite) Chapel, he nevertheless obtained permission; a form to make hosts was prepared, the little store of altar wine was shared, and from then on, the camp officials permitted Latin Rite services to be held in the chapel as well.[31]

Exarch Feodorov organized the concelebration of the Liturgy with other imprisoned priests. Though they had no antimension (consecrated cloth with relics), the Orthodox monks imprisoned there showed the priests books, hidden from the Communists, in which a Syrian text stated that, in extreme need, the Eucharist could be celebrated on a page of the Holy Gospel.[32] Moreover, the pope sent permission to celebrate without an antimension, while uniting oneself to the tombs of the nearest saints: given the scale of executions, there were certainly many unknown saints' graves close at hand.

During the worst of persecutions at Solovetski, the Liturgy was celebrated with humble items: the discos was a tin box, the chalice a little glass, and the spoon for distributing Communion came from a sardine can. Eventually the chapel's store of vestments and vessels grew much larger, but the humble items are the ones preserved in Rome.[33]

Father Emilianov, the heroic confessor of Nizhnyaya Bogdanovka, was sent to Solovetski in 1927.[34] Sister Julia Danzas was transferred from the Irkutsk prison to Solovetski and ordered to give antireligious tours in the museum created out of the monastic religious objects (she used the opportunity to give religious teachings instead; her coworker, a young Russian man, was shot for his religious beliefs in 1928). Even so, the Russian Catholic movement continued to attract converts. The Orthodox priest Alex Vassiliev was received into Russian Catholicism in December 1928, at Leningrad.

The Catholic population of Solovetski grew dramatically in 1928, including the Byzantine-Georgian archimandrite of the Society of the Immaculate Conception, Father Shio Batmanashvili, twenty Latin Catholic priests, and two more Russian Catholic priests. Latin and Byzantine Catholic services alternated, and believers outside Solovetski sent four sets of Latin vestments and a Latin altar. Also in 1928, having survived the barbaric tortures of the GPU, Bishop Sloskans was sent to Solovetski, where he was rescued from near death by one of the Orthodox monks, and where he ordained another Russian Catholic priest, Father Donat Novitski, on September 5.

Madame Novitskaya, a Russian Catholic in Moscow, served as a courier between the imprisoned priests and Bishop Neveu. Among the messages she transmitted was the 1924 petition from Father Alexandrov to celebrate the Divine Liturgy without an antimension.[35] Another was a message from the exarch, proclaiming his loyalty to the Holy See, telling of conversions among the Orthodox clergy and the celebrations of the Liturgy and Hours, while lamenting the terrible physical condition of his priests and fellow sufferers.

Closing of the Chapels

On November 1, 1928, the Orthodox and Catholic chapels at Solovetski were both closed, and celebration of the Liturgies went underground. In January 1929, the guards raided the prison holding the Orthodox and Catholic priests and dispersed the clergy among the criminals. Still, the Liturgy continued to be celebrated; indeed, Bishop Sloskans held a concelebrated Mass that very night with what little remained in the former common residence. Exarch Feodorov exhorted his priests to remember that their services might be "the only ones that are celebrated in Russia and for Russia. We must do all in order that at least one Liturgy is celebrated every day."[36] This was fulfilled, and secret services continued to be held and Communion distributed among both the men and women.

In the spring of 1929, the camp administration allowed public Orthodox, Byzantine Catholic, and Jewish celebrations for Old Calendar Easter and Passover. After Easter, following an appeal for leniency by the archbishop of Canterbury,[37] the priests were removed to a smaller and stricter prison on the island of Anser, where the churches were all used as part of the prison system, and religious worship was forbidden. Yet celebration of the Eucharist continued even here.[38] The priests celebrated on the sills of dormer windows. When the wine ran out, a priest remembered that one could make altar wine with raisins. This was done, and the custom spread throughout the Gulag over the years to come.

The celebration of Holy Mass and the Divine Liturgy continued, using only seven or eight drops of wine and a drop of water, and with the priest "vested" in his prison garb. Celebration of the Eucharist continued until July 1932, when all of the priests still on the islands were taken to Leningrad and exchanged for prisoners from Poland.[39]

Last Ministry and Death of Exarch Feodorov

In August 1929, the Exarch was transferred to the little town of Pinega in Arkhangel'sk oblast, on the mainland,[40] where he resumed his teaching of adults and children, sharing his Red Cross packages with others who were impoverished and in need. The Orthodox pastor in Pinega wrote that "Father Leonid is dangerous not only to Bolsheviks but to the whole Orthodox Church. If he stays among us for a longer time, I doubt that I would be able to keep my faithful because he has shaken even my firmest convictions."

Such success could not be allowed, and Patriarch Tikhon intervened, thus focusing (perhaps unwittingly) the Soviets' attention on the exarch. He was removed from Pinega to two remote villages. When his term finally ended, in 1933, he was allowed to settle at Viatka, the tsarist "city of exiles" in the Urals, where he lived his last year in the home of a railroad worker, Andrei Kalinin, and his family. Worn down by asthma, rheumatism, and gastritis, the exarch died there without the sacraments, on March 7, 1935. As his body lay in the house, a white dove flew in through an open door, circled his corpse, and then departed: the Kalinins were so struck by this that they made a point of mentioning it in their report to the Red Cross. The family buried him at night, and they "did all that was required under such circumstances." It is presumed that this was a coded reference to the celebration of Christian burial—according to Orthodox rituals—made necessarily secret because of the Great Terror. The exarch was only 55 years old.

Dispersal

In 1931, the last members of the Moscow parish and Dominican community were either arrested or forced to end their common services.[41] Yet interest in the mission of the exarchate continued among Orthodox. Bishop Neveu received a number of Orthodox priests and parishioners into the Latin Catholic

Church well into the 1930s. Many of theses made secret professions of faith, as allowed by Rome, while remaining officially Orthodox. His close friend, Archbishop Bartholomew Remov, was among these converts. This was a practice that endured until the end of the Soviet Union.

The last community of the exarchate was organized under Father Serge Soloviev, a coworker of Bishop Neveu. For this, and for serving as a priest when there were less than twenty people present, celebrating the Liturgy in private homes, hearing confessions secretly, and baptizing three converts from Judaism, he was arrested in February 1931, along with a crypto-Catholic Orthodox priest (who was offered freedom if he would return to Orthodoxy, but who remained steadfast), and eight women of the parish.

Father Serge was subjected to relentless interrogations under constant bright light with no opportunity for sleep. When he learned he had been betrayed by one of his own parishioners—and his closest friend—he went insane. Exiled to Turkestan, he died there, alone, in March 1942.[42]

The "patriarchs" of the Russian Catholic movement all suffered: Father Alexis Zerchaninov was finally exiled to Tobol'sk, where he died in 1934; Father Ivan Deibner was brutally murdered in exile in 1936 in Tver' oblast;[43] Father Alexander Alexeev of Kiev died in prison.[44] Father Patapii Emilianov of Nizhnyaya Bogdanovka survived Solovetski and was released to do work in northern Russia; he died in 1937 at the Podvoitsa rail station on the Murmansk railroad at the age of 47.[45]

Although a titular diocese with residence outside of Moscow at Sergievo was established for the Russian Catholics under the secret Bishop Bartholomew Remov, this diocese was never formally recognized and has been vacant since the archbishop's death. An unknown number of Orthodox bishops, priests, and monks (especially at the Saint Alexander Nevsky Monastery in Leningrad) became Catholics after Metropolitan Sergei Stragorodsky's controversial declaration, issued in 1927 under extreme pressure, that the Russian Church would be loyal to the "Motherland." Many of these men were uncovered for being members of the exarchate, or were caught up in the anti-Orthodox persecutions. In 1935, Archbishop Bartholomew's secret Catholicism was discovered. Long suspected because of his friendship with Bishop Neveu, the archbishop was betrayed, interrogated, tortured, and shot. (Under torture, he had confessed to leading a "terrorist organization."[46]

Father Diodor Kolpinsky first emigrated to Poland, where he edited a journal on Orthodox-Catholic relations in Warsaw. Sickened by both Polish chauvinism and Vatican intrigues, he then emigrated to Harbin to work among the Russian Catholics there, where he died in 1932; the burial of his body was contested by both Latin and Orthodox clerics.[47] Father Nicholas Alexandrov, the pastor of the Moscow parish, survived Solovetski and was transferred to Anser, but nothing is known of the remainder of his life or place of death.[48] Father Nicholas Tolstoy, unbalanced by tsarist persecutions, regained his sanity in 1923–1924 and died in Kiev in 1926 as a Catholic.[49] During the mass relocation of "former persons" and supposed enemies of the regime, Father Nicholas Mikhailov was expelled from Leningrad in May 1935 to forced labor in Taganrog, Crimea.[50] Father Vladimir Abrikosov never returned home, and never saw his beloved Anna again. He ended his days in Paris, living as a hermit in prayer.

CHAPTER 14

"Icicles Formed Fantastic Gargoyles above the Altars," 1922–1923

> [T]he church [cathedral] of the Assumption was sealed up on December 5, 1922, in the presence of Citizen Smirnov . . . When the Government officials ordered all those present to leave the church, the faithful refused to obey and, going down on their knees, they started singing hymns. [T]he troops were marched into the church with orders to expel all those who did not go out of their own accord. The order was executed.
>
> —Statement of Accusation read at the Cieplak trial

The looting of the churches under the pretext of famine relief had devastated Soviet Catholicism. It would be accompanied by the steady elimination of the Church hierarchy and by the nationalization of virtually all church buildings.

Reduction of the Hierarchy

In 1922, Bishop Lozinski of Minsk was arrested, then expelled to Poland. Bishop DeGuebriant, vicar apostolic of Siberia, was expelled from Omsk and escaped to Harbin, Manchuria. The Tiraspol diocese had already lost Bishop Kessler to exile.[1] In 1923, the only bishops in the western Soviet Union were the archbishop himself, Exarch Feodorov, Bishop Mankowski of Kamenets (who had returned from Poland), and the frail former bishop of Tiraspol, Bishop Zerr. In Siberia, Bishop Sliwowski was just taking office in bloodied Vladivostok. Within a very short time, even this remnant of the Church hierarchy would vanish.

Archival information on the archdiocese of Mogilev, and the Zhitomir, Tiraspol dioceses and other jurisdictions in a 1923 report to the Holy See paints a clear picture of the structures of the Soviet Catholic Church on the eve of the Cieplak trial. The years 1923–1924 would see increasing anti-

170

Catholic persecution, giving rise to repeated and fruitless attempts at reshaping these structures in 1926.

In 1923, Mogilev had 145 churches, 245,000 faithful, and 130 priests in European Soviet Russia and eastern Soviet Belorussia. Archbishop von der Ropp was exiled to Warsaw, Archbishop Cieplak was arrested in 1923, and Father Stanis Law Przyembel was administrator.

The Minsk diocese covered central Soviet Belorussia with 150,000 believers, 46 churches, and 15 priests in 1923. After Bishop Lozinski's exile to Poland, he took up residence in Pinsk, near the border. The Zhitomir diocese covered part of the Soviet Ukraine (UkSSR), with 350,000 faithful, 107 churches, and 60 priests in 1923. Bishop Dubowski was in exile; Father Adolf Szelazek was the most prominent priest remaining. The Kamenets-Podolski diocese covered central Soviet Ukraine and had 300,000 faithful in 110 churches with only 40 priests left in 1923. The vicar general was Father Peter Mankowski.

The large southern diocese of Tiraspol had its headquarters in Odessa, UkSSR, and administrative centers at Saratov, RSFSR (later the Volga German ASSR) and in the Tatar ASSR. There were another 300,000 faithful, 140 churches, and 120 priests. Bishop Kessler was in exile; Bishop Zerr remained in the USSR. The Vladivostok diocese was, by 1923, restricted to the Soviet Union's Far East, with 20,000 faithful, 6 churches and 4 priests, under Bishop Sliwowski, the other remaining Latin bishop after 1923.

The Apostolic Vicariate of Siberia was arranged to form a large slice from the Arctic to the southernmost borders. In 1923, there were 75,000 faithful and 39 churches, with only 15 priests to cover the enormous territory of Siberia and the Asian Soviet republics. In 1923, the Apostolic Vicariate of Crimea and the Caucasus had 70,000 Latin Catholics, with 50 churches and only 30 priests. Monsignor Adrian Smets was the administrator, at Tbilisi. Also at Tbilisi, Administrator Sarkis Abrahamian had set up his headquarters for the Armenian Catholic Administration, with 47 priests, 45 churches, and 66,000 faithful under his jurisdiction in the Caucasus. Following its statutes from the 1917 synod, the little Russian Catholic Exarchate came under the jurisdiction of Metropolitan Sheptytsky in Poland.

The Vladivostok, Siberia, and Caucasus administrations were directly subject to the Holy See. In 1923, Mogilev was still the metropolitan see, with residence in Petrograd; the USSR as a whole had 620 working Catholic parish churches and 400 priests. Filial churches and chapels still existing in 1923 brought the total of Catholic places of worship to nearly 1,200 (for which there were not nearly enough priests). Of the faithful, Poles formed the largest group (92 percent of the priests in the Soviet Union were Polish), followed by Germans, Lithuanians (who had formed 40 percent of the Mogilev arch-diocesan clergy in 1914), Latvians, Belorussians, Armenians, Georgians, Russians, and Ukrainians (of both rites).[2]

Closed Churches and Institutions

In Petrograd, the cathedral gardens were converted into an open-air theater—to provide entertainment for the masses and to disrupt celebration of the Holy Mass. The Church of the Immaculate Conception was the first church in the city to be closed, in 1918 together with its convent of Polish Franciscan Sisters. In 1918, the Theological Academy was given over to the Estonian University of Proletarian Science. The Church of Saint Louis des Français in Moscow, although closed in 1917, was eventually able to reopen thanks to its French ownership. The suburban Kolpino church, site of the impressive Corpus Christi procession was closed. When the French Ursulines left Petrograd in the spring of 1920, their convent and chapel were closed and converted into a hospital.[3]

Bishop Kessler lamented that exorbitant taxes and rents would be assessed on the churches in his diocese, and then of course the State would close the parishes on the grounds of nonpayment. The churches became social clubs, dance halls, and Party meeting halls.[4] Other churches began to disappear entirely, even ones considered to be of historic and artistic interest, under the guise of projects like "road improvements" or subway construction. Blasphemous processions and displays became the norm in Soviet cities, especially at the religious holidays, with mockery of Orthodox, Catholic, Jewish, and Muslim symbols and clergy alike.[5]

Life in the Open Churches

As for the nationalized church buildings that were still open, the State required that believers sign contracts before using these buildings. Some Catholic parishes had cooperated, not having had any advice from diocesan centers; others tried to make amendments to the contracts, and still others refused to sign. In April 1922, Archbishop Cieplak wrote secretly to Rome that he had issued a circular on January 3 that ordered all of the priests to refuse the contracts, as violating canon law, the hard-line position advanced by Monsignor Budkiewicz. By this time, all that was left to the Catholics were the church buildings themselves: in some places, even cemeteries had been desecrated and the burial grounds rented out by the State as farmland. Some clerical and religious education continued, illegally and secretly, in Moscow, Petrograd, and the southern countryside, despite the danger.

In 1922, the struggle between Church and State in the USSR had three principal aspects. First, church buildings were now property of the people, and therefore believers had to sign contracts with the State, representing the dictatorship of the proletariat, before they could use them. Second, clergy were disenfranchised, depriving them of both their right to vote and their ration cards. And third, sermons were to be subject to censorship, and ordinary religious life to continual interference. Activities such as religious teaching, singing, and so on were increasingly restricted (and eventually banned altogether). The main objectives of the State's registration drive were to (1) break up the organic unity of the Churches, isolating them into individual communities; (2) establish an administrative form of persecution that would provide a "legal" means of removing priests and closing churches; (3) identify, for future attack, leading figures among both clergy and laity. In Petrograd, the efforts at confiscation and the struggle over the contracts led directly to the Cieplak trial.

Spiritual Revival: 1921–1923

Mass continued to be well attended, and Soviet Catholic churches were "more crowded than before the Revolution."[6] Daily Mass became much more popular with the faithful, with large numbers receiving Holy Communion. Happily, the national tensions between Latvian, Lithuanian, Polish, and Russian Catholics in the Latin Catholic Church finally began to subside.

Despite the obvious persecution, ethnic Russians continued to enter the Catholic Church. In Petrograd, there were many converts to the Latin Rite at the Assumption Cathedral, in a working-class district; at Saint Catherine's on Nevsky Prospekt; and at Saint Stanislaus's and Saint Casimir's, in the factory districts. Monday lectures at Saint Catherine's attracted hundreds of people until the spring of 1923, many of whom converted or at least learned not to fear Catholicism. (In 1920, that parish had also introduced Russian-language devotions, including the Litany of Our Lady, Sacred Heart service, and the Rosary, a practice that spread elsewhere.) Several priests became noted for their apostolate to Russians: Monsignor Budkiewicz, Father John Vasilevsky (arrested in 1921), Father Casimir Velichko, and Latvian priest Father Boleslaus Sloskans, a future bishop and confessor of the Faith who suffered horribly for his devotion to the Church. The lectures and Russian devotions, however, were deeply resented by the suffering Orthodox Church, which saw these as bold attempts to proselytize among its own believers in a time of crisis. Many of the new converts to Catholicism, however, were ethnic Russians who had been religiously indifferent, or Polish women who had been forced to abandon the Catholic faith when marrying Orthodox men in the tsarist era.

Other Soviet Russians converted to the Byzantine Rite through the Russian Greek Catholic Exarchate. The chapel in Saratov was crowded with converts and curious Orthodox until the closings in 1923. In 1921, a new theological seminary was begun in Petrograd for the Latin Catholics; the students (seven Russian converts and two Poles) held government jobs by day to protect them from conscription into the army. Two other converts studied under Exarch Feodorov for the Greek Catholics.

The Struggle Intensifies

> We Communists feel sure we can triumph over London Capitalism. But Rome will prove a harder nut to crack. . . . Without Rome, religion would die. But Rome sends out, for the service of her religion, propagandists of every nationality. They are more effective than guns. [I]t is certain that it will be a long struggle.
>
> —Foreign Commissar Chicherin to Bishop d'Herbigny

In a pastoral letter of January 3, 1922, Archbishop Cieplak had ordered the parishes that had previously signed to withdraw their contracts, and to institute secret religious education for the children in defiance of Soviet laws. The Church had taken a final, strict position, under the inspiration of Monsignor Budkiewicz. In response, the State ordered that meetings be ordered held in the churches or their halls, where comrades were to explain the laws, register committees, and have the contracts signed. The Soviets made especially strenuous efforts in Petrograd, the structural center of the Soviet Catholic Church.

In the meetings, it was clear that the parishioners had listened closely to their pastors (indeed, Soviet prosecutors would cite parishioners' knowledge of canon law as evidence of conspiracy by the Catholic leadership during the Cieplak show trial). Parishioners stood up to the comrades in the State-ordered church meetings and denounced the contracts as violations of the Treaty of Riga. They pointed out—correctly—that Catholic canon law forbade secular administration of church property. And what had happened, they asked, to the separation of Church and State proclaimed back in 1918? What right did the workers' state—their state—have now to interfere in church life?[7]

In May 1922, as famine spread through Soviet Russia, the Holy See informed Foreign Commissar Chicherin that the Vatican would gladly redeem all of the sacred objects still at risk, and pay Soviet Russia in hard currency. Throughout the spring and summer of 1922, the Polish government tried to use the Treaty of Riga's stipulations to protect the Catholic parishes. All protests and efforts failed.[8] A renewed offer by pope to redeem both Orthodox and Catholic Church valuables using hard currency,[9] was also rejected by the Soviets, whose real objective was, not to feed their starving masses, but to decimate Orthodox and Catholic parishes alike.

In August 1922, the Soviets rejected the last of the Polish protests, over the violation of the relics of Blessed Andrew Bobola. Bobola's remains were exhibited at the Museum of Hygiene (Father Walsh was able to rescue the relics a year later). At the same time, the government ordered all the parishes to sign new contracts.

Also in August, the Communists began the expulsion of the intellectuals, and more people were lost to Soviet Russia. Still, there were hopes inside the country that things would change: the "changing landmarks" theory proposed by the Party led many people to expect that the Bolsheviks would restore a strong, organized state, and then allow the transformation of that state into a democracy.[10] This added to Catholic confusion.

Emigration was continuing to weaken the Church. Sixty-eight priests of Moghilev archdiocese who had gone to Poland during the warfare were refused permission to return to their parishes. The Smolensk parish of the Immaculate Conception, which had dropped from over 6,000 members in 1904 and to 1,000 in 1921, was down to barely 100 by 1923.[11] When, in September 1922, the future confessor of the Faith, Father Michael Dmowski, who had been rector of the Theological Academy chapel, traveled to Poland, his parish, Saint Boniface (the former Austrian church in Petrograd), was promptly shut down in his absence.[12]

Resistance and the First
Church Closing: June 1922

When the parishes refused to observe the new laws regarding parish committees and registration with the State, orders were given to close the Petrograd churches. In the industrial slums of Petrograd, whose workers supposedly backed the Revolution, resistance was firm, however. At Saint Casimir's, a boy rang the tocsin bell as a warning to the neighborhood at the approach of the comrades' committee, and an angry crowd of workers quickly assembled to deter the police. At Saint Stanislaus's, Father Yunevich begged the soldiers for permission to celebrate a last mass on June 22, one that continued until the soldiers intruded at 6:30 P.M. To shut the church down, the Red Army found itself marching over the kneeling bodies of the very workers for whom the Revolution and civil war had been fought.

At Saint Catherine's on Nevsky Prospekt, the resistance was no less firm. The attempt of commissars to search the tabernacle, spurred on by an apostate Catholic, on June 24, the feast of Saint John the Baptist, was only prevented when Father Khodnevich grabbed the altar and announced that the desecration would take place only if the soldiers "pass over my dead body." Still, the soldiers looted the sacristy, stealing chalices and a monstrance.

Attempts to get new contracts signed at the procathedral, Saint Francis, at Immaculate Conception, Sacred Heart, Sacred Heart of Mary, Saint Boniface, and at the Greek Catholic chapel of the Descent of the Holy Spirit were all turned back by angry shouting crowds. At Assumption Cathedral, Fathers Francis Rutkowski and Augustine Pronckietis called on the people present to fall on their knees and pray, again presenting the Red Army with the prospect of shoving aside praying workers.[13] In Moscow, the poor Immaculate Conception church was plundered: all the commissars got for their trouble was 2.75 pounds of silver.[14]

The Great Closing: December 1922

In the end, the Catholics' resistance failed. On December 5, soldiers appeared outside most of the churches. The procathedral, Saint Stanislaus, Saint Casimir, Saint Catherine, Saint Francis, Saint Boniface, and Sacred Heart; the chapels of the Immaculate Conception, Sacred Heart of Mary, and the Knights of Malta; and the eleven private and semipublic Catholic chapels were all shut down, as well as the church in Lesnoy, which served the members of the closed Kolpino church as well.[15] By December 1922, there had been no parish north of the river since the Church of the Visitation of the Blessed Virgin, at Viborg cemetery, site of the famous public Byzantine-Russian Catholic Liturgy in 1917, had been burned to the ground in 1922.[16] The Greek Catholics lost all of their chapels, plus the use of Saint Catherine's. Exarch Feodorov's chapel on Barmalayeva Street had been officially closed on November 22;[17] before then, there had long been two Russian Greek Catholic services in Old Slavonic with sermons in Russian vernacular at Saint Catherine's.[18] In Moscow, Saints Peter and Paul, the Immaculate Conception, and the Greek Catholic chapel were also closed in December 1922. Only the French national parishes survived.

The Catholics celebrated Advent and Christmas in private apartments and warehouses. Although "home liturgies" have become common since Vatican II, in 1922, Catholics had never really experienced the divine mysteries in any setting except a properly appointed church. McCullagh eloquently describes the scene: "Masses were said surreptitiously in the huge, deserted buildings of half-empty Petrograd wherein, during winter-time, the cold was so great that the icicles formed fantastic gargoyles above the altar, and the faithful had to keep in constant motion or to wrap themselves in layer upon layer of clothing or sheepskin."[19]

Monsignor Budkiewicz wrote that "great crowds of faithful congregate" in these locations,[20] but the situation could not continue. After Exarch Feodorov's congregation dared to raise their voices above a whisper after a successfully sung Christmas service, on January 6, a neighbor denounced them to the police for holding religious worship. They avoided arrest only because there were no minors present, and there were less than twenty people present.[21] Nevertheless, even though they were running a great risk, crowds with minor children attended the Latin Catholic services.

On December 30, Soviet Russia founded the Union of Soviet Socialist Republics (USSR). The rest of the world, save Germany, still did not recognize it.

Archbishop Cieplak and his curia worked frantically to find a resolution to the crisis. Protests were drafted pointing out to the government that it was making a poor impression on world opinion by shutting down churches at a time when the Soviets wanted to obtain the world's recognition. The very procedures of Soviet law had been ignored: no warnings were published in the newspapers or posted on the doors: how could the Soviet Union then proclaim to the world that it was establishing an ordered state based on laws, when its own laws were violated by its own government? In addition, the Church pointed out again that it had no connection with the State, save for a concordat with the tsarist government, a concordat that ended with the fall of the monarchy in 1917. And resort was had again to the Treaty of Riga and the possibility of a Polish protectorate over Soviet Catholics, like that of France over Middle Eastern Catholics.[22]

Tensions in the Catholic Church

All these attempts to halt and reverse the church closings failed. Dissension broke out between Exarch Feodorov, Father Abrikosov, and many Latin Catholic clerics (the first two declaring that all ethnic Russian converts must join the Byzantine Rite; the Latin Catholics pointing out that many Russians wanted no reminders of Russian Orthodoxy in their new religious lives).[23] Archbishop von der Ropp's efforts to intervene in the dispute from exile in Poland were widely perceived as interference; and a general demoralization was setting in among priests and parishioners, as they watched their closed churches and chapels deteriorate and as the crisis dragged on.[24]

Nevertheless, no one would agree to sign the contracts. Resistance was firm: congregations of anywhere from 100 to 300 would gather for Mass in apartments, factories, and subterranean vaults. On Sundays, great crowds would also kneel in the snow outside the sealed doors of the churches to recite the Rosary and say other prayers. This became most noticeable when there were Communist processions going by, to which the Catholics' backs were pointedly turned.[25]

Archbishop Cieplak continued to write to Rome, and to confer with the pope's representative in Moscow, Father Walsh, who had come with full powers by authority of Cardinal Gasparri. New contracts were proposed that did not declare the churches to be state property, contracts that the priests might at last be able to sign in good conscience and in accord with canon law.

Finally, on February 12, 1923, Father Walsh sent a telegram to Petrograd, advising that these contracts could be signed "for the present";[26] with the pope's agreement, he traveled there to resolve the crisis. On February 16, Catholic parishioners went to the city soviet at the Smolny Institute to present the contracts. They would be sorely disappointed. Even though Father Walsh had an agreement from the pope, letters from the Bolshevik Commissariat of Justice's fifth section (dealing with religion), and the cooperation of the archdiocesan curia, he received no cooperation from the city soviet.[27] Rome's response was too late: both the Kremlin and the Petrograd city soviet were moving against the Church.

On the night of March 2–3, 1923, every priest in the city was informed that he must appear before the Supreme Revolutionary Tribunal in the capital on March 5. They had only to (1) sign the contracts, (2) submit their sermons to censorship, (3) agree not to teach religion to children, (4) agree to celebrate Mass only with state permission, and (5) issue approvals of Bolshevik religious policies, and they would be spared. In sum, what was at stake was the whole position of Catholic life in Soviet Russia.[28]

The Departure from Petrograd

The priests, two bishops, and seventeen-year-old James Sharnas boarded the train at the former Nicholas Station on the night of March 4, 1923. Practically the entire remaining Catholic population of Petrograd came to bid them a sad farewell. Thousands of people jammed the station and the platform that evening, and there were fears of a demonstration that would bring down the wrath of the soldiers.[29] As the train began to pull out of the station, this enormous crowd collectively invoked the protection of the Mother of God for their clergy. The steam of the engine mixed with the clouds of half-frozen breath as everyone sang the hymn *"Sub Tuum Praesidium."* The clergy waved farewell to the singing crowd, joining in the words: "We come to your protection, O Blessed Mother of God. Do not turn away from us in our need, but deliver us from danger, O pure and blessed Lady."[30] For some aboard the train, this would be their last sight of their parishioners and friends, and of the lovely city on the Neva where they had served. Prison or martyrdom awaited them all.

CHAPTER 15

The Cieplak Trial and
Disruption of the Church

> Prosecutor Krylenko: There is no law here but Soviet law. . . . You
> must choose which you will obey.
> Father Rutkowski: I will obey the law of God and my conscience.
> Krylenko: Your conscience does not interest me in the least.
> Rutkowski: But it is of very great importance to me.
>   —Testimony from the Cieplak trial

This dialogue reflects the basic conflict that marked the great trial, the results of which left the Latin and Byzantine Catholic Churches stunned and leaderless. The leading figures of the Church in Petrograd and thus of the Soviet Union, were all involved, and the proceedings were a painful introduction to the destiny of Catholicism in the new Soviet entity centralized in Moscow. Stalin was beginning to come into his own regarding the national minorities (of which Catholics were an important part). In the spring and summer, the Party was dealing with the issues of establishing a Constitution for the USSR.

Significantly, Lenin was incapacitated, and the Soviets torn by dissension. Lenin suffered his third and final stroke on March 9, and he never took part in governing again. In the opinion of Captain McCullagh, a British officer who attended the whole trial and kept careful notes upon leaving the "courtroom," and of others, the trial would never have taken place were Lenin well, and it was pushed through at the instigation of Zinoviev (then the head of Petrograd), Trotsky, Bukharin, Kamenev, and Dzerzhinsky. Foreign Commissar Chicherin, his deputy, Litvinov, and Ambassador Leonid Krassin were fearful of Western public opinion and were against the whole idea of the trial. Unlike the recent martyrdom of Archbishop Benjamin of Petrograd, which had not reached many Western ears, it was reasonable to expect that the trial of a

Catholic metropolitan was going to be carefully followed and reported by Poland and the Holy See.

Archbishop Cieplak had been arrested twice before by the Bolsheviks. After his arrest on Holy Thursday, 1920, the Catholics had protested by refusing to sing "Alleluia" in their churches at Easter, by stopping work, and by marching on the Cheka. Their demonstrations finally freed him. In June 1922, the archbishop was again arrested, this time when saying good-bye to Catholics emigrating to Poland, and was imprisoned in Archbishop von der Ropp's old cell. Then, too, he was released.[1] When the Polish Fathers arrived in Moscow for the archbishop's trial, they were sent to Saints Peter and Paul, where they stayed with Father Peter Zielinski. The rest stayed with other Catholics.

On March 10, an open truck carried the seventeen defendants through the streets of Moscow to the former Noblemen's Club, which now housed the Revolutionary Tribunal. These men represented a cross-section of contemporary Soviet Catholicism in age, national origin, social class, and, because Russian-Byzantine Catholics were included, also religious affiliation. Besides Archbishop John Cieplak (age 65) and Exarch Leonid Feodorov (43), they were

• Monsignor Constantine Budkiewicz (65), of Polish noble origin noted for his successful lectures at Saint Catherine's and for his effective leadership;

• Monsignor Anton Malecki (62), who had directed the secret seminary in the bishop's house in Petrograd;

• Father Edward Yunevich (25), a Belorussian priest who served in both the Latin and Byzantine Catholic Churches;

• Father Teofil Matulianis (50), a Lithuanian priest;

• Father Stanislaus Eismont (35), from Saint Casimir's;

• Father Luke Khvetzko (33), another Belorussian;

• Father Francis Rutkowski (39), who had called the people to prayer in the presence of the Red Army and had served at Yaroslavl';

• Father Paul Khodnevich (42), nicknamed "Apostle of the Russians" for his successful ministry;

• James Sharnas (17), a Lithuanian youth who had intervened to protect an elderly handicapped woman when she was being expelled from a church;

• Father Augustine Pronckietis (26), a Lithuanian priest;

• Fathers John Wasilewski (59), Dominic Ivanov (39), John Troigo, Peter Janukowicz (59), and Paul Chodniewicz (42), who were accused of having conspired to form a counterrevolutionary organization with the two bishops, the monsignors, and Father Eismont.

Archbishop Cieplak was also charged, under Article 77, with disobedience to the legal demands of the state; Father Chodniewicz, under Article 119, with having used religious superstitions of the masses to encourage resistance; Father Yunevich, under Article 62, with resisting confiscations in his parish church; Fathers Rutkowski and Pronckietis under Article 119, for their resistance activities; and James Sharnas, under Article 77, with "interference with Red Army soldiers in the performance of their duties."[2]

The Bolsheviks had already orchestrated several "show trials." The Cheka had staged the "Trial of the Petersburg Combat Organization"; its successor, the new GPU, the "Trial of the Socialist Revolutionaries." In these and other such farces, defendants were inevitably sentenced to death or exiled to long prison terms in the north. The Cieplak show trial is a prime example of Bolshevik revolutionary justice at this time. Normal judicial processes did not restrict revolutionary tribunals at all; in fact, the prosecutor, N. V. Krylenko, stated that the courts could trample on the rights of members of classes other than the proletariat. Appeals from the courts went not to a higher court, but to political committees.

Western observers found the setting—the grand ballroom of the former Noblemen's Club, with painted cherubs on the ceiling—singularly inappropriate for such a solemn event. Neither judges nor prosecutors were required to have a legal background, only a proper "revolutionary" one. That the prominent "No Smoking" signs were ignored by the judges themselves did not bode well for respect of legalities. At this time, independent defense attorneys were still available, and two fine lawyers from the tsarist era defended the Latin Catholic clergy and James Sharnas: Bobrishchev-Pushkin and M. Kommodov. Exarch Feodorov conducted his own defense, a move that led to one of the most dramatic moments in the whole trial. The judges were Galkin, an apostate priest who was hostile toward all religious expression, Nemtsov, a worker, and Chelyshev, a peasant. Nemtsov showed himself to be ignorant of religious matters and Chelyshev only spoke once, to read a document aloud.[3]

Prosecutor Krylenko, who "distinguished" himself in other show trials, was a rude and violent man. Examples of his pronouncements were recorded by Captain McCullagh. Thus Krylenko defined teaching religion as "frightening the ignorant and children . . . terrorization of the ignorant is a political act"; he described sermons as a "monopoly of propaganda in the pulpit"; he called Father Rutkowski's falling on his knees to pray when the Assumption pro-cathedral was being shut down a "counterrevolutionary act"; and, at one point, he cried out, "I spit on . . . all religions!" As one writer observed, "the crucial and central issue was . . . whether the laws of God should prevail over the laws of man."[4]

The trial opened in the last week of Lent (according to the Gregorian calendar used by the Latin Catholic Church), and closed in Holy Week. In a probably unconscious paraphrase of John 19:7—words directed against Jesus Christ—Krylenko stated, "There is no law but Soviet law, and by that law you must die." In the course of the trial, Krylenko strove to demonstrate that the actions of the Catholic leadership were political, not religious; that the Church was pro-Polish and anti-Soviet; and that it was engaged in an active conspiracy to oppose the Soviet state and the Communist revolution. All communications with Polish government or Vatican representatives in Warsaw were construed as illegal contacts with a hostile power. To further the Soviets' case, state witnesses either lied or chose not to give complete evidence.

The defendants could not call witnesses on their behalf; when not in "court," they were "crammed into one cell in Butyrka [prison] without writing material, and without any opportunity [to] consult[ ] with their lawyers."[5] Their attorneys were unable to prepare a proper defense (Kommodov was arrested when he tried to get information in Petrograd), and were continually being intimidated by the prosecution, police, and the general pressure from the state. The Communists controlled the only newspapers left in the USSR, *Pravda* and *Izvestia,* which both printed slanted commentaries designed to inflame the people. Foreign journalists, Western observers, and Soviet Catholics had a terrible time trying to get into the courtroom; diplomats from the Polish mission were absolutely forbidden entry. Father Zielinski of Saints Peter and Paul was arrested so as to deprive foreigners of a translator.

On March 21, 1923, Several state witnesses were called to testify about the confiscation of Church valuables, the registration of the Catholic churches, and their closing. The witnesses described the opposition they encountered from priests and people. When Father Rutkowski questioned witness Director Smirnov, and caught him in a contradiction, Krylenko took the opportunity to question the priest about other charges, including teaching religion to children and not submitting sermons to state censorship. From this testimony came the excerpt at the heading of this chapter, which neatly summarizes the conflict.

In addition, the priests were questioned as to whether they had continued to say Mass after the churches were closed (they all had, with attendance figures given as 150 or more), and instructed children (which all had done). All had used Mass sets given to them for their private use, so that they could not be accused of using state property (i.e., the vessels belonging to the parishes). Krylenko found himself confounded by Monsignor Malecki's description of his possessions consisting of a bed, kneeler, table, crucifix, and a portable altar, delivered with such "simplicity, frankness, and saintliness" that Krylenko barely dealt with him during the following days.

The first day ended with the interrogation of "the youngest priest," presumably Father Yunevich.

> Krylenko: Between the laws of the Soviet Republic and that other law, you must make your choice.
>
> Priest: In the conflict between these two laws, I shall forever follow the divine law and the law of the Church."[6]

On its second day, amid Krylenko's attempts to establish a political conspiracy against the Soviet Union by the clergy, came the "surprise revelation" of Exarch Feodorov. Feodorov was originally presented as the pastor of the Church of the Descent of the Holy Spirit, but Krylenko was astonished to discover that the exarch was under the direct jurisdiction of the metropolitan of Lwów, a city in Polish hands, and that he belonged to the Byzantine Rite, an entirely different rite from that of his codefendants. All the conferences of the clergy between 1918 and 1923 were characterized in the press as "political," and the prosecution declared that the different committees of the archdiocese had been founded with the intent of trying to provide a way of holding out "until the overthrow of Soviet power." Archbishop Cieplak, now 69 years old and exhausted from the tension, was not interrogated until 11 P.M. Even so, he refused to recant his pastoral letter on religious education or his condemnation of the Bolshevik laws on religion.

On the trial's third day, Krylenko strove to prove the Church's connection with Poland and the Polish "lords" opposed to the Communist revolution. He even referred to the Church as "the Polish Church," an appellation Monsignor Budkiewicz refuted in describing the Church as "international." When Krylenko presented letters sent to the to the Polish and German embassies by the monsignor as evidence for contact with foreign powers, Budkiewicz pointed out that in 1917–1920, due to the chaos of the times, the national citizenship of many people was unknown.

In a desperate move, Krylenko declared that the archdiocese had received communications from the "Polish Nunciature," but this was corrected by Archbishop Cieplak to the proper title, "Apostolic Nunciature in Warsaw." Again, here was clear proof that the traditional Russian fear of Western, Catholic Poland had been inherited by the Bolsheviks, and exaggerated by the Communist fear of the capitalist states. The prosecution then presented its most damaging "evidence": Archbishop von der Ropp had blessed the new Polish Embassy in Moscow in 1918; a telegram of congratulations had been sent by Monsignor Budkiewicz in 1918 to the Regency Council of newly independent Poland; and the possessions of Polish hostages and Russian exiles alike had been stored by Budkiewicz. Regarding the telegram, Budkiewicz pointed out on the next day of the trial that, in 1918, he could be legally considered a Polish subject, because the Treaty of Riga had not yet been officially adopted. As for storing the possessions, there were scores of people fleeing Petrograd, and no one expected it to be permanent; the Church was simply providing a charitable service. Finally, the embassy blessing had been done publicly, with the full knowledge of the Moscow authorities.

In the matter of the church committees, Archbishop Cieplak pointed out that committee members were not from the believers, that the committees served to split the unity of the Church, as had happened to the Orthodox, and that they violated canon law. The third theme of the day was religious education. The futility of discussion with the Communists was borne out in this discussion:

> Krylenko: What is it that gives the Catholic clergy so strong an influence? . . . Are not the schools your principal means?
> Cieplak: Not only the schools, but above all, our teaching of the truth, of the moral precepts of Christ, the influence of the faith and divine grace.
> Krylenko: Let us talk of things a man can understand. We see clearly that, by your teaching about torments in the other world, you frighten and mystify the ignorant and the children. Now, the terrorization of the ignorant is a political act.[7]

On March 24, the trial's fourth day, Archbishop Cieplak opened the testimony with a surprising statement, explaining that he had received the Holy See's permission to sign a modified form of contract for use of the churches, as negotiated between the Vatican and Justice Commissar Krassnikov; that the Catholic Church—like the Orthodox—was willing to surrender non-sacred valuables for famine relief; and that he had wanted to reach an agreement with the State.

Krylenko brought in Krassnikov, who said that he and his section knew nothing "officially"—even though Father Walsh of the Pontifical Relief Mission had letters from him, and had been thwarted in his efforts to have the Petrograd city soviet accept the parishes' agreements in early 1923. Because

Krassnikov denied official knowledge, the prosecution and the court ignored all of this.

Also on March 24, Exarch Feodorov was subjected to a long examination. Again, he created a sensation: he was an ethnic Russian, grandson of a serf, son of workers, a Catholic "from conviction," he conducted his own defense, and he did it well. Again, this was to no avail.

Krylenko began his closing arguments on the evening of March 24. "Your religion—I spit on it," he proclaimed, "as I do on all religions—on Orthodox, Jewish, Mohammedan, and the rest." When he demanded the death penalty, he declared that it was to show the Catholic clergy that "our law will not joke with those who trifle with it," a statement met with applause by the Communists.[8]

The defense attorneys pleaded for clemency from a court that had no intention of hearing them (indeed, Krylenko read a novel during their speeches). They pointed out that there was no conspiracy against the Soviet state, that the bishops and priests had awaited only the permission of Rome to sign the contracts, and that there was no sign of counterrevolutionary activity by any of the priests or James Sharnas. Finally, they asked for deportation and decried the application of the death penalty as totally inappropriate.

Dressed in the traditional Russian black cassock, with his long hair, beard, and gentle face, often described as "Christ-like," Feodorov was a grandson of a serf—a man of the *narod,* of the ordinary Russian people for whom the Revolution had been fought. His presence put the lie to the usual description of Catholicism as the "Polish religion." His presentation—a moving testament of Russian spirituality and the history of the Church in that country—evoked the best of Russian Christendom. He pointed out that Greek Catholics greeted the Revolution with joy, for only then did they have equality. There were no secret organizations, and they had simply followed Church law. Religious education, the celebration of Mass, and the administration of the sacraments of marriage and baptism had to be fulfilled. He pointed out that the Church, accused of having neglected the starving, was at that very moment feeding 120,000 children daily.

Following a scathing rebuttal by Krylenko, Exarch Feodorov rose for his final remarks: "Our hearts are full, not of hatred, but of sadness. You cannot understand us. We are not allowed liberty of conscience. That is the only conclusion we can draw from all we have heard here."[9]

March 25, the last day of the trial, was also the feast of Christ's Incarnation at the Annunciation, and the day of Jesus' entry into Jerusalem for His Passion and Death—Palm Sunday. Krylenko delivered his closing speech, probably better defined as a tirade. He demanded the death penalty for Archbishop Cieplak, Monsignor Budkiewicz, and Fathers Eismont and Chodniewicz, and stiff penalties for all others save James Sharnas, for whom he asked six months due to his youth. The priests' speeches that they were not against the Soviet power, that they were obliged to follow divine law in case of conflict of conscience, that the cooperation of the Vatican was needed for them to make final decisions: all their words made no difference to the prosecutor or his court. At 4 P.M., the court withdrew.

Eight hours later, at midnight, marking the beginning of Holy Monday, the sentences were handed down. Archbishop Cieplak and his chancellor, Monsignor Budkiewicz, were sentenced to death, and everyone else, to terms of imprisonment. When it was over, the handful of Catholic women who had managed to get inside burst into tears and "threw themselves down on their knees with cries of horror and anguish which pierced the stillness of that cold night."[10] The *New York Times* wrote that "other screams burst forth, to which the silence and unmoved faces of the accused clerics showed a startling contrast."[11] These women and the archbishop's elderly Polish manservant were manhandled by the soldiers present; Captain McCullagh and the others were forced out of the doors. The archbishop raised his hand to bless the struggling Catholics—such was the last sight of him before the doors were slammed shut.

The Vatican, Germany, Poland, Great Britain, and the United States undertook frantic efforts to save the archbishop and his chancellor. In Moscow, the ministers from the Polish, British, Czechoslovak, and Italian missions appealed "on the ground of humanity," and Poland offered to exchange any prisoner to save the archbishop and the monsignor.

Finally, on March 29, the archbishop's sentence was commuted to ten years in prison, in recognition of his trials under tsarist persecution of Catholics, but the monsignor was not to be spared. Again, there were appeals from foreign powers, from Western Socialists and Church leaders alike. These appeals were for naught: *Pravda* editorialized on March 30 that the tribunal was defending the rights of the workers, who had been oppressed by the bourgeois system for centuries with the aid of priests. Pro-Communist foreigners who intervened for the two men were also condemned as "compromisers with the priestly servants of the bourgeoisie."

Monsignor Budkiewicz was condemned as having conspired with an enemy of the Soviet Union and committed treason.[12] Father Rutkowski recorded later that Budkiewicz surrendered himself over to the will of God without reservation. On Easter Sunday, the world was told that the monsignor was still alive, and Pope Pius XI publicly prayed at Saint Peter's that the Soviets would spare his life. Moscow officials told foreign ministers and reporters that the monsignor's sentence was just, and that the Soviet Union was a sovereign nation that would not accept foreign interference. In reply to an appeal from the rabbis of New York City to spare Budkiewicz's life, *Pravda* wrote a blistering editorial against "Jewish bankers [who] rule the world," and bluntly warned that the Soviets would kill Jewish opponents of the Revolution as well.

Only on April 4 did the truth finally emerge: the monsignor had already been in the grave for three days. When the news came to Rome, Pope Pius fell to his knees and wept as he prayed for the priest's soul. To make matters worse, Cardinal Gasparri had just finished reading a note from the Soviets saying that "everything was proceeding satisfactorily" when he was handed the telegram announcing the execution.[13]

On March 31, 1923, Holy Saturday, at 11:30 P.M., after a week of quiet prayer and a firm declaration that he was ready to be sacrificed for his sins, Monsignor Constantine Budkiewicz had been taken from his cell and, sometime before the dawn of Easter Sunday, shot in the back of the head, on the steps of the Lubyanka prison.[14] All the other priests, Exarch Feodorov, and young James Sharnas went to prison. Exarch Feodorov and Fathers Eismont, Yunevich, Khvetzko, and Chodniewicz were all sentenced to 10 years' solitary confinement. Monsignor Malecki, and Fathers Wasilewski, Janukowicz, Matulianis, Troigo, Ivanov, Rutkowski, and Pronckietis were sentenced to 3 years in prison and deprivation of civil rights; James Sharnas, to 6 months in prison and deprivation of civil rights.

The Fate of the Archbishop

Archbishop Cieplak was put in isolation in the Butyrka prison in Moscow, except for when Father Zielinski from Saints Peter and Paul, arrested in 1923, was imprisoned with him for a time.[15] Father Zielinski later wrote to a bishop in Poland, after his release, that the uncertainty and isolation were a great torment to the archbishop, this at a time when Zielinski was responsible for the care of another twenty priests imprisoned in the city.

The archbishop was visited by Father Walsh in May 1923. He corresponded with other jailed priests, and received packages from the faithful Father Zielinski. In March 1924, he was transferred to the fearsome Lubyanka prison. From there, on April 9, he was removed in complete silence and taken to the train station. At the Soviet border with independent Latvia, he was released with an identification card, a piece of black bread, and a salted herring. The Polish conductor of the Latvian train bought the archbishop a ticket to Riga, where he stayed at the Church of Saint Francis.

Archbishop Cieplak eventually met with Pope Pius XI in Rome, where he was careful not to publicly criticize the USSR, for fear of worsening the prisoners' situation, and where he had the pleasure of enshrining Blessed Andrew Bobola's relics in 1924. Named Archbishop of Vilna (Wilno, Vilnius) in December 1925, he died of pneumonia in the United States on February 17, 1926, unable to take charge of his new see.

Monsignor Malecki was stricken by paralysis in the winter of 1923. Exarch Feodorov would never return to Petrograd, dying a lonely death in exile. A few of the priests, such as Father Rutkowski, were eventually allowed to emigrate or were forcibly expelled. The remainder who survived their terms and returned home died under Soviet rule, usually as a result of further jail terms and persecution.

In June 1923, after the prison terms began, Bishop Peter Mankowski of Kamenets was arrested, and exiled to Poland shortly thereafter. Save for the lonely Siberian bishop on the Pacific and the increasingly isolated incumbent of Tiraspol, all the Catholic prelates were in jail. Only the barest skeleton of the archdiocesan structure remained, with curial officials trying to provide direction from Petrograd, including a marriage tribunal. In Tiraspol, guidance came from the deans.

Emigration

In Petrograd, the great parish of Saint Catherine's declined from 29,000 faithful in 1914 to only 8,000 by 1925, and the Polish working-class parish of Saint Stanislaus's dropped from 17,000 to 3,000 over the same years. Immaculate Conception in Smolensk had only 100 parishioners in 1925. Although it should have had some 430,000 faithful after the establishment of new dioceses and vicariates in independent countries and Siberia, the archdiocese of Mogilev counted only 227,000 in 1925. Catholics abandoning their faith because of persecution and discrimination in the early 1920s accounted for an unknown, but probably small, part of this loss. Far more believers had died, fled, or been exiled, and with them had gone 151 priests of the Latin Rite,[16] as well as several of the Byzantine-Russian Rite, including the three exiled abroad by the State: Fathers Diodorus Kolpinsky and Gleb Verkovsky, exiled in 1918; and Father Vladimir Abrikosov, exiled in 1922.[17]

CHAPTER 16

Catholics in the Gulag

> The long suffering of those days and nights can never be told, only a few
> peaks and valleys of joys and disillusionment, of triumph and pain can
> mark the course followed.
> —Peter Leoni, SJ, and George Maloney, SJ, *Leoni: He Asked for It*

The prison complexes in the Russian Federation today hold only real criminals—Russian mafia, murderers—and no longer innocents. At least one
hopes they do. Empty prison buildings pockmark the Russian landscape, with
watchtowers and rusted fences around camps that have decayed. In the north,
one can find the camps frozen as they were when abandoned in the 1950s,
their Socialist-Realism posters on the walls exhorting inmates to ever greater
goals even as they starved beneath them. Rail lines pop out of swamps. Mine
entrances are boarded up. Canals are good only for recreational sailing. Piers
are rotting. And everywhere are overgrown cemeteries, their crosses and little
sign posts ruthlessly ripped down so that the relatives of *zeki* (prisoners)
buried there have no idea where their dead lie. Survivors estimate that between
World War II and the Gulag, one-third of Russian families lost members.[1]

Prisons, Camps, and Reform by Labor

From the start of the October Revolution, real and imagined opponents were
thrown into the former tsarist jails. As the opposition parties were outlawed,
religious persecution introduced, and supporters of the Whites captured, the
jails of old expanded into ever-larger prisons. Monasteries were converted to
prisons, as were churches and even secular buildings, such as the infamous
Lubyanka in Moscow. Then new prisons were built to hold the thousands of
prisoners pouring in. Camps were erected, and work projects using convict
labor begun. These projects had their own camps, sometimes scores of them,
entire colonies of poorly built barracks, enclosed by barbed-wire fences and
surrounded by armed troops and vicious dogs.

190

Prisoners were interrogated, tortured, put into solitary confinement, experimented on, and sent to work in factories. In later years, special "psychiatric" prison hospitals were established, where anyone believing in God or opposed to Communism could be declared insane and confined indefinitely—incapacitated, actually driven to insanity, or killed by the forcible injection of dangerous drugs.

Forced Deportations

The prison camp system was fed with hundreds of thousands of people during the various campaigns against religion, the so-called kulaks, real and imagined political opponents and members of the pre-Revolutionary political parties. Relocation became common after 1929, with peasants being sent en masse to the north and east, followed by "nonpersons" in the mid-1930s.

A massive forced relocation took place in 1937 in the oblasts of the Soviet Far East. In the fall and winter, the NKVD arranged for the arrest of the entire Korean population in those lands, for fear of possible loyalty on their part to Japan, which had ruled Korea since 1910 and which was then invading China. This exercise was carried out so quickly and efficiently that, when Japanese consular officials went to check on the Soviet Koreans, they were stunned to find that there was no one left. The Korean deportees came from city and village; army and navy; the Party itself. For good measure, the NKVD also rounded up Soviet Hungarians, Germans, Latvians, Lithuanians, Chinese, and Japanese living in the Far East.

On December 20, 1937, *Pravda* praised Commander Lyushkov for his role in the removal of more than 60,000 people. By 1939, the Korean population had been relocated entirely to Central Asia, especially to Kazakhstan, where they remain today. Almost one-third perished in the harsh new conditions, the population plunging from 250,000 in 1926 to only 180,000 in 1939.[2] This mass relocation of ethnic minorities deemed undesirable by the State paved the way for the mass removal of Soviet Poles, Balts, Germans, Kalmyks, Chechens, Ingush, Balkars, and Karakalpaks and of Crimean Tatars from the European Soviet Union in the years 1939–1949.

The Gulag

The forced labor camp system began under Lenin, and expanded tremendously under the auspices of the OGPU organization in 1930. With this "company" and others, the prisons and camps became part of the Soviet economy. Prisoners were ruthlessly exploited in coal, gold, and uranium mines with no protection; forced to fish in arctic waters with leaky boats, to harvest timber with the wrong tools, to raise massive cities in Siberia and the north, which still stand today, to construct and man factories for Stalin's fanatic industrialization drive of the 1930s, and vast agricultural projects in the steppe, to build new homes for their jailers. Imprisoned scientists were forced to continue their labors for the State that had jailed them; even when their findings were published, they remained in labor camps and prisons.

Even before the Great Terror began in 1934, 3.3 million prisoners had been confined in camps, prisons, labor colonies, and exile settlements. They included "kulaks," "former persons," members of former political parties, members of religious sects, people who had been denounced, real and imagined members of White armies, along with their spouses, children, and even grandchildren. There were special orphanages for the children of the "enemies of the people," with armed guards watching over the offspring of the prisoners, so that generations came to know life in the camps.

Under Stalin during and after World War II, the prison camp population climbed even more dramatically, peaking at more than 5.5 million persons in 1953, then declining during de-Stalinization to 1 million in 1958.[3] Over the entire Soviet era, an estimated 20 million people perished in these camps, in Bolshevik massacres, in "political" executions, and in State-induced famines. Even after the Khrushchev era, and into the period of glasnost, the Gulag and its many remaining prisons remained an active force in Soviet life, frightening believers with its fearsome reputation, although it is doubtful you could find any survivors whose "anti-socialist opinions" had been "reformed" by that system.

Foundations

However critical the Gulag became to the Soviet economy in mining, construction, and manufacturing, its prisoners were as often forced to work on utterly useless projects: the horrible White Sea Canal, rail lines and other canals that today are completely abandoned, some constructed simply to gratify Stalin's megalomaniacal whims. It was these and other grandiose projects that Stalin took great pride in showing off to naïve Western admirers such as Duranty, Shaw, and the Webbs and in telling them how the projects converted antisocial elements into productive members of Communist society.[4] These admirers never looked for the graves, or inspected the living skeletons beneath the flimsy uniforms, or picked up on cues given by desperate inmates in

Potemkin setups (when Gorky went to Solovetski, the newly washed prisoners held their newspapers upside down, but he was too excited about Soviet humanism to notice this dangerous protest). Even the productive projects killed or crippled thousands upon thousands, who were given no protection against asbestos, frostbite, dangerous machines, nor against the sadism of guards driven mad in a society that had itself gone mad in the 1930s.

Because there was no respect in the Soviet system for human life or for the human person, the "politicals" (peasants, merchants, the educated, clergy, presumed oppositionist Communists) and the criminals (murderers, thugs, and thieves) were grouped together under atrocious conditions. Rations were poor, medical care almost nonexistent (limited to what little the imprisoned doctors and nurses could do with practically no supplies). Many camps came under the control of the criminals, who were fully supported by the "legal" authorities. Here whatever "protections" were offered by the various Soviet constitutions and decrees were effectively abandoned.

Although the men who imposed these terrible conditions on their fellow citizens had themselves lived in tsarist jails (often comfortable places of exile, especially when compared to the Gulag), they had no intention of treating their victims with any sense of humanity. Stalin, Lenin, Trotsky and their exiled confederates had access to libraries, to private cabins, to letter writing, visitors, and good meals. Lenin even got married in the local Orthodox Church (which church did not survive Communist rule). None of this came to their prisoners.

Prison conditions worsened during the Great Terror, the Great Patriotic War (World War II), and afterward, when the Soviet Union was again swept by famine. Nationalists from Poland, Ukraine, and the Baltics were especially persecuted. Suspected spies and a host of foreign citizens were dragooned into the Gulag, including clergy from Axis countries. During famines, rations were cut in the camps, killing off still more "enemies of the people." Impossible quotas were assigned, and rations again cut to punish the prisoners for their "laziness." The only justice that the *zeki* saw was when their tormentors were themselves consumed in the Great Terror and imprisoned alongside them, or when sudden acts ascribed to divine intervention took place.

Solovetski

One of the earliest large camps—and ultimately the most feared—was Solovetski, originally a complex of monasteries in the White Sea founded by Saints Herman and Zosima in the fifteenth century. After 1918, when Solovetski was converted to a Soviet prison camp, some monks managed to continue a communal life, while others were dispersed or imprisoned. It was to Solovetski that the first large group of Catholic priests and parishioners was sent in the 1920s. Solovetski became infamous immediately. Because of its archipelago of islands, Solzhenitsyn entitled his massive work on the prison system *Gulag Archipelago,* using this as a metaphor for the vast stretch of labor camps across the whole of the USSR (not just in remote areas).

Although the great monastery had often served as a tsarist prison for individual opponents (and as an important defense base for arctic Russia in two wars), it had never seen such atrocities as it was to see in the Communist era. Eventually, 400,000 people would pass over its islands; although only 30,000 victims are buried there today, Solovetski's death rate was an appalling 85 percent. Ostensibly used for the construction of projects such as the Stalin Canal, it served primarily as a site for torture and punishment. In the 1930s, an escapee wrote how guards would strip prisoners naked and leave them tied to trees, exposed to the bites of thousands of mosquitoes, or tie prisoners to logs and roll them down staircases.

When Solovetski was reclassified from a camp to a prison in 1923, it was known as a "special purpose prison," whose acronym in Russian, STON, is spelled the same as the Russian word for "groan." Over the years, its chapels, churches, and abandoned monastery buildings decayed, although new prisons were built on some islands as late as 1987, well into the Gorbachev era.[5]

Magadan and Kolyma

In Matthew 15:39, Jesus crosses to a place called "Magadan." Biblical archaeologists have never been able to identify such a location anywhere in the Holy Land. Soviet believers interpreted the elusive place as being the hellhole built by Stalin in the arctic, and saw it as a prophecy that Christ would be with them even in that most abandoned of abandoned horrors.

Known as the "Gateway to Hell," the city of Magadan was the destination of shiploads of prisoners and exiles. It did not exist before the Gulag, but was constructed in 1932 by convict labor on the shore of the Sea of Okhotsk. So harsh were the conditions at the site that entire populations died in makeshift camps during its construction. But the losses meant nothing to the Soviets, intent on mining gold and other precious metals there. It is said that as many as 12 million people died in this wasteland, haunted still by empty guard towers, rusting wire, and abandoned rail lines. Although there are now real mines and real towns nearby, there was never any excuse for the atrocities committed at

Magadan, whose horror is captured in the prisoners' name for the highway that straggles out of it across northern Siberia: "Road of Bones": convict laborers were literally paved under its roadway where they fell. Temperatures here have fallen to 129 degrees below freezing.[6]

Evidence: Mass Graves

Some of the mass graves of people executed during the Great Terror were pits filled with innocents in forests, such as Kurapaty in Soviet Belorussia. Others were later covered with KGB summer homes, public parks, and children's camps: another sign of Communism's inhuman treatment of its victims.

The most famous of the Siberian mass graves is at Kolpashevo, on the Ob River near Tomsk. After a high flood in May 1979, Kolpashevo's riverbanks suddenly gave way, revealing to the horrified inhabitants the skeletons and bodies of their long-vanished loved ones. They had been taken by the NKVD to its riverside headquarters on various and fantastic charges. Their skulls showed where they had been shot, their bodies thrown down layer upon layer upon layer. The sunlight revealed skeletons and intact corpses alike, and processions of townspeople came carrying icons and flowers to the site.

The KGB tried frantically to cover up the scene by boarding up the land and expelling the residents, then spent two days having boatmen force the bodies into the Ob River again and dump gravel on them. This caused more trauma, and the situation worsened when the bodies, with their bullet-torn skulls, floated downstream to the other towns. To this day, the bones still surface through the KGB's gravel, grisly evidence of the crimes committed against Soviet citizens.[7] Graves continue to be found in Russia and the former Soviet Union. Many are under playgrounds, summer homes of the police elite, and parks. If this is what was done to the dead in the Brezhnev era, one dreads to find out what happened to the living in the Stalin-Khrushchev eras.

Catholic Religious Life in the Gulag Before 1939

And yet under the worst prison conditions, some found divine solace. Bishop Boleslas Sloskans wrote to his parents in 1928: "[D]uring fifteen years I have never received so much grace as during these last five months in prison. It is the best grace and most beautiful event of my interior life. I am very happy because now I am capable of loving all men without exception, even those who've not merited it, they are the most unfortunate." Bishop Sloskans was flogged until his blood poured out upon the floor, he was dragged through seventeen different prisons and camps, and yet he could love those who tortured him because of his meditations on the sufferings of Christ and the internal growth that resulted from this. Though he was long deprived of Holy Communion and locked in isolation and darkness for months, he did not succumb to despair but rather grew.[8]

Strong men could die quickly of despair in the Soviet prison system, whereas physically weak ones could survive their 25-year terms because of their stubbornness. In all accounts, however, religious faith is credited as being a mainstay of survivors.

Catholics entered the Soviet prison system quickly after November 1917, with the first arrests of clergy in Petrograd. As we noted in chapter 13, by the early 1920s, Mass was celebrated as often as possible throughout the system, using what bread was available, raisin juice in place of wine, glasses in place of chalices, and any location that was safe from the guards for the Sacraments. Altar stones and antimensia with relics of the Saints were replaced by a spiritual connection with the many martyrs buried at the prisons.

In the early days, religious prisoners were often jailed together, thus providing opportunity for clandestine ordinations and even elaborate celebrations at holidays. This changed in the latter part of Lenin's rule and throughout the Stalinist era, when clergy were subject to execution (Lenin) or to dispersal among the Gulag's general population on work projects (Stalin).

Some priests, such as Exarch Feodorov, were totally unable to exercise their ministry. If they were lucky, they were at least buried under a cross or with surreptitious Orthodox rites. Others, though dispersed, continued to receive parcels from relatives and friends. These priests were able to continue their ministry, using makeshift altars and wine made from raisins, and consecrating precious bits of bread for Holy Communion. The Western world's liberals ignored the situation of these men, but it was made known—to little avail—to Catholics. A French book published in 1934 lists the Armenian Catholic administrator and three of his priests as being imprisoned in the north at that time and laments the condition of the few remaining free priests and faithful in the Caucasus as "very precarious."[9] (The last of those priests were arrested during World War II. Only two Armenian Catholic priests would ever return home; all the others died in exile.)

Priests were generally subject to hard labor, and despised by dedicated Communists. They did not gain access to "light" work until after Stalin's death unless other Catholics and sympathetic prisoners protected them.[10] As a result, death rates were high among the clergy, except when believers held trusted positions in the camps and could get priests work in offices, kitchens, and hospitals, where there was warmth and the chance of a little extra food and the possibility of expanding their ministry to more people; or when a gang of criminals took a liking to priests and protected them.

The Modern Period

As the Red Army moved out of the Soviet Union's 1939 boundaries, the NKVD and the Ministry of Internal Affairs went to work arresting people. The Western Allies generously collaborated, turning over Soviet ethnic Germans who had successfully escaped to the Allied zones, and forcibly repatriating Soviet citizens who had no desire to return to their "Motherland." England and America sent back *Volksdeutsche,* Vlasov Men, Cossacks, and other anti-Communist Russian and Muslim fighters to certain death or imprisonment. Such behavior, of course, weakened the hopes of prisoners and deportees regarding their eventual escape from Communism or the end of Soviet rule by a new war. The West was obviously of no help to them (as would be proven in 1953, 1956, 1961, and 1968). Indeed, these atrocities only ended in 1947 after threatened mutinies by the Allied soldiers involved in the disgrace.

From 1945 to 1955, inhabitants of the "western lands of the USSR" (Poland, Czechoslovakia and the three Baltic States) who resisted collectivization or political repression, who sheltered partisans (even for an hour), or who happened to visit a friend on the wrong night all ended up in the camps.

Perhaps the saddest category of new prisoners was that of Spanish children sent by their Loyalist parents to the Communist Motherland during the Spanish civil war. These children never did fit into Soviet life, and many wanted to go back to Spain. Instead, they were sentenced to prison as American spies or as socially dangerous elements.

The Army engaged in massive orgies of rape, especially in Germany (which ultimately resulted in epidemics of venereal diseases among the troops). What had happened in occupied Poland and the Baltics in 1939–1941 now swept through Central Europe: the Red Army brought back entire factories, streetcars, telephone systems as war reparations, much of which was left to rust or rot because no one knew how to run it or because prisoners they also brought back sabotaged the machines in revenge against their captors.

With the influx of prisoners into the USSR from all over Europe, from as far as Sweden—which unconscionably sent back Baltic freedom fighters—and the Low Countries, the Soviets gained specialists who were forced to work on scientific projects, or who undertook to educate the poorly trained products of Soviet education, including doctors, in the camps or prisons.[11]

Medical care in the camps was always abominable, despite the work of conscientious Soviets and prisoners alike. There were simply never enough supplies allocated for the millions of prisoners. Prison fare was meager and of abysmal quality, which contributed to the spread of illness, especially scurvy. Starving prisoners would eat grass, leaves, and bark; they would even boil pine needles (these at least contained Vitamin C) to stave off scurvy. Lice and fleas were everywhere, spreading typhus and plague. Dentistry was nonexistent or unbelievably crude.

Mass Deportations from the Western Soviet Union

We have already described the terrible mass deportations of people from annexed territories in 1940–1941, and those in 1945 as Soviet rule returned to or entered new lands. Although uprooted, the Catholics among these people invigorated the Catholic networks with their enthusiasm, Catholic morality, Catholic education, and Catholic devotion.

Polish children who escaped with Commander Wladyslaw Anders's army wrote of their parents grabbing holy pictures off the walls and clutching rosaries in their hands when the NKVD came. When Russian believers would offer them food for these sacred images, the Poles, even though they were starving, refused to part with their Czestochowa and Ostrabama icons and other holy pictures, which remain with their descendants to this day. Soviet soldiers, like the Nazi troops in 1941, were impressed by the strict moral standards of the Catholic Ukrainian and Lithuanian girls, who fought against rape and refused seduction attempts—these were not at all like the girls brought up under the two totalitarian systems.

Solzhenitsyn tells us of the Lithuanian Catholic exiles who took precious pieces of bread out of their meager rations, soaked them in water, kneaded them into little balls, colored and threaded them, and thus made rosaries for themselves. While starving physically, they nurtured themselves spiritually.

A Ukrainian Catholic woman deported to Tobol'sk in 1940 resisted the advances of a camp officer, who punished her by sending her to cut reeds along the frozen Irtysh river. There, finding herself surrounded by Siberia's infamous wolves, she cried out to the Mother of God for help. She fainted, and when she came to, she was back in the camp, safe and sound. The officer, however, was attacked by the wolves that very night, and barely escaped with his life.[12]

The arrival of Archbishop Josef Slipyj in exile brought great consolation to the camp prisoners. His courage and fortitude in rejecting Russian Orthodox honors if he would abandon Rome, and his personal morality, gave new hope to those he met.[13] Although the camp authorities, wary of his effect on fellow prisoners, moved him around a great deal, this only served to increase his influence.

Foreign Catholics in the Gulag

Foreign Catholics resided in Soviet Russia from the early days of Communist rule. Priests who could claim Polish or Baltic citizenship to protect themselves were nevertheless jailed. Others who could have kept foreign citizenship, such as the Latvian Bishop Sloskans, but who took on Soviet citizenships to remain with their parishioners, were generally arrested as spies. Foreign workers, whether Catholic or not, were also rounded up, especially in the paranoiac 1930s, and sent to the camps. Ultimately, foreign citizenship was of no protection anyway.

Axis Prisoners

I saw the Russians kicking a German soldier who was a prisoner. He looked at me and murmured, *"Ich bin auch katholische"* [I am also Catholic].

—Father Orestes

A Ukrainian Greek Catholic priest, Father Orestes witnessed the suffering of many German soldiers, not just this one officer. Even so, the bond of religion surpassed that of enmity created during the war. Thus when Monsignor Josef Kasper was caught at Stalingrad carrying Holy Communion to the dying Germans and was captured by five Siberian soldiers, he made the Sign of the Cross over them with his hand and the Blessed Sacrament. The Siberians bowed and blessed themselves three times in the Orthodox fashion and said, "You will live," as they took him prisoner.[14]

In the course of World War II, millions of Axis troops and their chaplains were captured by the Soviets, from the terrible debacle at Stalingrad in February 1943 to the final conquest of Berlin in 1945. Besides Germany, Italy, and Japan, Axis countries included Vichy France, Hungary, Romania, Slovakia, and Bulgaria because of their alliances or associations with Nazi Germany in 1938–1945. Many Axis troops died of untended wounds, starvation, or in bloody massacres. Others were herded east and north, including a great victory parade in Moscow where Nazi standards were hurled down at the feet of the Great Stalin—but where old Orthodox women broke through the Red Army ranks to hand out crusts of bread to the starving survivors to fulfill the words of the Gospel: "When you do this to the least of my brethren, you do it to Me."

Of 3,740,000 German troops captured by the Red Army and sent east in the war, only 1.2 million survived to return home in 1946–56; hundreds of thousands had already died from forced labor. The priests among them joined in the clandestine Masses and celebration of the sacraments.

German civilians started returning as early as the autumn of 1945 on trains that passed other trains carrying others of their countrymen to the east. But it was an uneven trickle, not a great flood. Not until 1954 did the last Alsatian prisoner of war leave Siberia.[15] Of the 60,000 Italians captured, 47,000 never came home. Many died in the camps and mines; others were simply not allowed to leave the Soviet Union. I interviewed a Russian university student from Uzbekistan who spoke of his Italian grandfather, imprisoned by the Soviets in 1944. On his release from prison, the grandfather married a Russian Orthodox woman and was sent to the Uzbek SSR in the 1950s to work. The couple raised their children Orthodox, with respect for the Catholic Church of the husband, and in America, the grandson sought out both Churches.

Father Giovanni Brevi, with the Bersaglieri Division of the Italian Fascist forces in the USSR, was captured in January 1943 and sent to forced labor in Siberia, where his ministry included young Catholic women in the camps, an assortment of Balts, Ukrainians, and Poles. Italian prisoners in Siberia set up an entire chapel in one camp for their Armenian Rite priest, who served the Latin Mass for them. Atop the altar were a crucifix, chalice, and a monstrance for the Sacred Host made out of Red Army materials.[16] Italian prisoners of war were also at the other end of the country, working in the Belorussian SSR on urban reconstruction. After the war, many were put to work on rebuilding the city of Minsk, where they received the sacraments and rites of the Church at Saints Simon and Helena. (Only in the summer of 1991 were arrangements made to return to Italy the remains of the Italian POWs who had died in Minsk.)[17]

Foreign Catholics after 1945

Foreign priests in the camps came from the Baltic States, Poland, Hungary, Romania, Italy, France, and the expanded German Reich. All these men, priest and lay, reconnected pre-1939 Soviet Catholics with the outside world, with the Universal Church. They brought news of Pope Pius XII, of the Fatima message now seen to be so prophetic for Soviet Russia.

Although most Catholic prisoners from Central and Western Europe who survived either chose to be repatriated in the 1950s or were expelled, a number of Polish priests who could have emigrated after 1954 exercised the option given them to stay behind. At least one German Capuchin also remained behind. The former master of ceremonies to the primate of Hungary, Father Tibor Meszaros, OSB, celebrated daily Mass and heard confessions for all prisoners regularly until the last of the Hungarian prisoners were repatriated.[18]

Celebration of the Eucharist and Other Sacraments

As we have noted in detail, the first recorded celebrations of the Catholic Eucharist in the Soviet prison system took place at Solovetski. It was there that the problems of having neither relics in an antimension nor sacramental wine were resolved. It was there that priests heard confessions, without wearing a stole, while cutting trees or dragging in nets of fish. It was there that the practice began of distributing the Sacred Host in remote corners or prison camps, or of carefully carrying it in jacket pockets to Catholics scattered across forbidding landscapes constantly patrolled by atheists. And it was there that Latin and Byzantine Masses and Liturgies were celebrated using whatever bread was available when Latin-style Communion wafers and Byzantine-style prosphoras could no longer be smuggled in. Finally, it was there that such "necessities" as vestments, books, proper sacred vessels, altars, reserved chapels, and bishops' consecrated oils came to be seen as truly unnecessary, as long as the Sacred Sacrifice itself could be continually offered.

Mass continued to be celebrated in the camps. The hope was always to continue the practice of Solovetski, of daily Masses, in remembrance of Exarch Feodorov's words, "Our Liturgy may be the only Catholic Liturgy offered today in all of Russia." This was not always possible, especially in harsh camps where bread and wine had to be carefully rationed out for Sundays and holy days, but even then, priests would recite the prayers of the Liturgy.

Father Jean Nicholas, taken from Odessa, related that favorite places for the Eucharistic celebrations were in mine shafts after guards had been lured away, in the barracks, and in corners of offices where a priest had secured a desk job after 1953. The American priest Father Walter Ciszek said Mass out in the forests, away from prying eyes, sometimes with a server, and usually with a guardian keeping watch. Priests would then distribute the Sacred Host to the Catholics scattered throughout the camp.

Prayer was forbidden, and it was extremely dangerous to do anything remotely religious. Yet lay believers would make the Sign of the Cross over their miserable meals, and priests who had nowhere else to go would crouch in the crowded bunks at night to whisper the prayers of the Mass.[19]

When, in 1954, the Moscow foreigners' chaplain, Father Georges Bissonnette, went for Confession to Father Nicholas, finally being repatriated by way of Moscow, he wrote that Father Nicholas "heard it with the routine ease of one who has heard thousands of confessions."[20] In many camps, Catholic women would write down their sins on a piece of paper or tree bark with a number, which would be smuggled to the priests on the men's side. The priests would go along the fence and silently dispense absolution to the women, who held up their fingers to identify themselves, and smuggle penances back to them.

The Solovetski practice of men confessing to priest-prisoners in fairly isolated spots continued as well. Indeed, many men took great risks to make regular confessions and find strength in the Sacrament, surely a lesson to modern First World Catholics who have nearly abandoned that practice. Many Catholics returned to the practice of their religion in the Gulag.

Lithuanians seem to have invented Catholic camp marriages. Bride and groom would be on opposite sides of the fence, with the priest witnessing their vows. The faithfulness of these clandestine marriages endured into freedom.

In terrible conditions, priests would dispense absolutions en masse, instead of in individual confessions. Massacres of prisoners in revolts, or executions of the weak, were accompanied by whispered phrases of absolution in Latin and Old Church Slavonic. Sometimes priests used the vernacular to be sure the unfortunates understood they were being cleansed of their sins. Barely raised hands, quickly making the Sign of the Cross, might be all that was possible, but at least men and women died knowing they had not been abandoned.

The practice of ordaining men to the diaconate and priesthood dates back to the Solovetski prison. In the early 1920s, it was possible to actually obtain episcopal and priestly vestments for ceremonies in the Catholic chapels on the Solovetski Islands. Such "lenience" would later disappear.

Arrested in 1947 at the age of 21 for protesting against the dissolution of the Greek Catholic Church in Galicia, Pavlo Vasylyk was ordained a deacon in prison during his eight-year term. As a deacon, he held Catholic services, which resulted in continual movement across northern Soviet Russia and Kazakhstan, until his release in 1955. Ordained a priest by a secret bishop in Galicia in 1956, he began missionary work in his homeland. For this, he was resentenced and exiled to the far northern state of Mordovia. That exile backfired, however, on the authorities, because the young priest was able to connect with Archbishop Slipyj there.[21] Conditions were abominable, but religious life always went on.

Returns, Conversions, and Ecumenism

The presence of so many priests expanded the network of sacraments available to the prison and special settlement population. For some of the Axis military prisoners, the Gulag brought them back to the Faith, which they had abandoned under fascism or national socialism. For others who had remained Catholic, it was the Faith that kept them alive in those cold or hot desert places where they were trapped. There were also new Catholics—Communists, Jews, Muslims, and Buddhists baptized, sometimes at the morning washup or on a fishing expedition—after taking instruction from the priests. Giving instruction was dangerous: a priest did not know if the catechumen was sincere or an informant. In addition, the spread of Catholicism inevitably came to officials' attention. If a specific priest could be accused (on whatever basis), he risked solitary confinement, transfer to a camp where he was unknown and possibly in serious danger, extension of his prison term, or even execution. Yet priests continued to perform Baptism, or use Confession to reconcile apostates.

Many Orthodox bishops and priests became Catholics in the camps in the 1920s and 1930s. Their conversions were kept secret from the Church of Moscow by permission of the Holy See, both in the outside world and in the camp system. Eventually, uniting Orthodox with Rome took a second place to breaching past misunderstandings and prejudices on both sides. In pre-Vatican II times, this was a huge step. Like the Nazi concentration camps, the Soviet prison camps forced believers of different faiths to set aside their differences and focus on what they had in common. Even if they could not agree—and there were occasions when Catholics and Orthodox came to that conclusion despite months of fervent discussion—they could at least respect each other. Compared to what was going on elsewhere, that was quite remarkable.

A dramatic ecumenical moment is recorded when a large number of prisoners gathered to be repatriated. Those remaining behind assembled for an impromptu prayer service. Orthodox, Protestant, Catholic, Evangelical, Armenian Apostolic, Buddhists and Jews all sang the magnificent Te Deum in thanksgiving to God for the release of their companions. An old Orthodox priest prayed aloud, followed by a Protestant minister. The guards not only left them alone, but an Old Bolshevik guard told them to continue to pray, because "it seems there is still someone above who hears your prayers!" [22]

Nuns and Consecrated Women

Sisters were brought east as well. The Gray Nuns of eastern Germany, or Sisters of Saint Elizabeth; Pallotines, Nazareth, Family of Mary, and other orders came from conquered Poland and Hungary. Deprived of their habits, they still sought to live in community and remained faithful to their vows and an active prayer life while logging, sewing, nursing, and farming. Perhaps the most famous story of imprisoned Catholic nuns is the one oft told of a group of Greek Catholic Sisters from Ukraine who refused to do any work that would support the atheistic regime. They were dragged out into the center of their camp. When the commandant gave the order for the guard dogs to be set upon them, the Sisters were kneeling in the snow and singing hymns. To everyone's amazement, the dogs came to a dead stop and lay in the snow around the nuns. The Ukrainian prisoners burst into religious hymns, the prisoners were ordered to their barracks, and the commandant was shamed.

Male convicts showed great respect to the *monashki* (consecrated women) or to women imprisoned who held firm religious beliefs and consecrated themselves to God. This respect continued into the next generations of guards: Irina Ratushinskaya, imprisoned in the 1980s, relates that sexual advances by the guards against her ceased when she explained that she was an Orthodox believer and was suffering for her faith.

A priest related the story of a group of young female novices from a Soviet Catholic religious community collectively exiled to a logging camp in Siberia. One night a group of twenty men came to their little hut while they were praying and ordered the Sisters to open the door. With great fear they did so, only to be astonished at the request of the leader: "We have been told that you are nuns. Speak to us of God, of Jesus and of His Mother. We have been here for thirty years without a priest. Tell us something."

The Sisters' hut became a church in the camp, a center not only for prayer but for instruction in religion, baptisms, and marriages witnessed according to the Latin Rite. The convicts took on the novices' logging tasks in order to free them up for their apostolic work. [23]

In the Kolyma prison camp in the Far East, a group of Orthodox women from Voronezh asked to be dispensed from working on Easter. When their request was denied, the women refused to leave their barracks. They were taken out into the forest, where they began to sing the Resurrection service, then onto a frozen pond, covered with a thin film of water. When an Old Bolshevik intervened for the believers and threatened retribution from the government, he was shot at. The Orthodox women continued to pray barefoot in the freezing water. Agonizing over their comrades, the Communist women prisoners could not decide that night whether it was fanaticism or defense of conscience that drove these believers. And why didn't Communists have such courage? Not one of the Orthodox women became sick, and on Easter Monday they overfulfilled their work norm by 20 percent.[24]

Stories of Priests and Their Works

Soviet archives released in 1996 indicated that some 1,000 Soviet Catholic priests died in executions, the Gulag and internal exile before 1939. Some had been shot on the spot, or in prisons in the west. Ethnic Germans were slaughtered en masse in the camps in 1941 in retaliation for the Nazis' attack. The German Catholic priests had taken it upon themselves to instruct the parishioners in Baptism and in leading prayer services. Those who were not killed outright ministered to their fellow prisoners; those who survived their terms found work in areas where there were other Catholics, and continued to say Mass at night and make pastoral rounds. One Volga German priest became a shepherd on the steppes, an appropriate symbol for these men who truly were shepherds to a desperate flock. At Karaganda in Kazakhstan in the 1970s and 1980s, Bishop Chira often said that his pastoral work among exiles was made easier by the work of the Soviet priests who had preceded him, especially the German ones.

Priests always took risks, no matter what they did. The indomitable Father Peter Leoni went further, however, in his resistance to the "Dove of Peace" campaign in his camp in the Khrushchev era. This was a manifesto that all Soviet citizens had to sign, to show their support of world Communism (i.e., the USSR and its allies) and its ways for world peace against those of the warmongering United Nations. The government had the nerve to force prisoners to sign this manifesto, but when the officials came to Father Leoni's camp and gathered the men together, his strong voice rang out: "Anyone who puts his name in that book, signs his own death warrant." No one betrayed him, and the crowd began to laugh, then cheer, and finally walked away from the officials and their precious book.[25]

When Father Brevi was finally repatriated, he gave away religious medals and items to young girls who had been sent to Camp 3 at Stalino in the Donets

Basin of the Ukrainian SSR. In return, they gave him their message to Pope Pius XII:

> When you return to Italy, inform the Holy Father that our churches are empty, our bells are silent, our vigil lights in front of our tabernacles are extinguished, our priests have been deported. Nevertheless, we are certain that the time will come when our bells will ring again, our priests will return wearing the crowns of confessors, the vigil lights will glow once more, and we will again sing our religious hymns in our nations and our solemnly decorated churches. Christ conquers![26]

Glasnost

Soviet spokesmen would often declare, "We have no religious or political prisoners" well into the Gorbachev years. Technically, the spokesmen were right because religious and political dissidents were always sentenced under articles of the criminal code and therefore considered "criminal prisoners." But prisoners there were. Only in 1989 was the Ukrainian Catholic activist Pavlo Kampov released, after eight years in prison, labor camps, and prison hospitals. By then, he was going blind and had developed cardiac and pulmonary problems.[27]

CHAPTER 17

The New Economic Policy,
1921–1928

> We all want to leave this place.
>   —Letter of a German colonist, 1920s

The implementation of the NEP brought important changes to the USSR. Private business and industries were restored, and some people actually made money. Products that had been all but forgotten returned to the stores, and the standards of living finally began to improve. In the countryside, new methods of agriculture were enthusiastically followed, and private farms prospered. Stalin and Bukharin both encouraged the peasants, and 80 percent of arable land was cultivated. In 1925, the peasants were told to enrich themselves, and not to fear restrictions.[1] There was even restoration of old icons under Bolshevik supervision.[2]

Although the NEP brought relief, morality suffered grievously. Those who were financially successful often flaunted their wealth with free spending and dissolute behavior, perhaps because they feared the freedom would not last. The derogatory epithet "NEPmen" was directed at all who engaged in private commerce. (Under Stalin, repression that followed the NEP would instill in Soviet citizens a permanent fear of being prosperous, or of even making a profit in a private enterprise, a fear that persists in modern Russia.)

The State continued to aggressively introduce atheism into the schools. Divorce was liberalized, "free love" encouraged, and new laws against family life passed, such as the "Nationalization of Children." The new Bolshevik morality—which to the traditional population seemed more like immorality— was lauded by liberals in the West, which created new pressures at home.

Lenin's health declined due to serious strokes. In his codicil of January 4, 1923, he would warn the Party against the monster they had created and urge them to find an alternative to Joseph Stalin as leader of Party and State, someone "more tolerant" than his likely successor. His warning and appeal would

207

not be heard. At the Twelfth Party Congress in January 1924, Stalin denounced Trotsky and embarked on his campaign to eliminate all real and potential sources of opposition.

The congress ended on January 19. Two days later, Lenin's trusted cook
found his master choking out the words "I've been poisoned!" Torn by con-
vulsions that flung him out of his bed, Lenin soon died in agony. Sent to the
Gulag, as were so many of Lenin's coworkers, the cook would die there, but
not before revealing his terrible secret to another Old Bolshevik.[3]

When Lenin's body was embalmed, enshrined under glass in a special
mausoleum, and set up for public viewing, his widow was appalled, insisting
that her husband's body be buried by his mother in an Orthodox cemetery in
Petrograd.[4] Instead, Lenin's murderer elevated him to the status of an atheist
god with an incorrupt body (maintained by generations of scientists injecting
the corpse and treating it against decay). Historic names were dropped in
honor of Lenin; statues of him pointing the way forward appeared in cities
across the Soviet Union. In the schools, the icon corners that had been emptied were now filled with busts of Lenin. Banners bore his portrait. He had
begun to replace God. It was the beginning of the personality cult, one that
Stalin would use to anoint himself Lenin's successor. Even though the Communists had desecrated the bodies of the Orthodox saints, whether preserved
by God or by natural conditions, they allotted an enormous budget and created a special institute to study Lenin's brain and to keep his body incorrupt.

By contrast, when the tomb of Emperor Karl of Austria-Hungary, who
preceded Lenin in death on April 1, 1922, was opened fifty years later to begin
the cause of his beatification, his body was discovered to be miraculously incorrupt. Of Lenin's original body, precious little remains due to all the chemi-
cals. Of the emperor's body, all remains. Lenin's Communism has been
defeated everywhere but China, Southeast Asia, and Cuba. The Emperor's
faith and Church still go on.

Despite everything, the years 1923–1926 are remembered by those who
lived through them as among the calmest years in Soviet history. Political
machinations of the Communist Party continued. The death of Lenin
brought real grief to idealistic young people who had joined the Revolution
and Party, and also marked the ascendancy of Stalin.

Religion in the First Years of the NEP

After 1921 and the consolidation of Soviet power in the west, religion was
seen as the principal obstacle to the spread of Communism. Although the

NEP is often presented as a time of relief for the Churches, this is not true. Physical persecution had been violent during the civil war, as we have seen, but administrative persecution continued after the fighting ended. Intense persecution took place in the press, in meetings at work and neighborhoods, and on a national level.

In 1923, religious holidays were all abolished in the workers' state, and Sunday mornings were replaced with "voluntary" work, sports tournaments, and other secular events. (By 1929, the country would be known as the "Land without Sunday" abroad because the traditional seven-day week would be completely replaced by a rotating six-day week.[5] Sunday would only be restored in World War II, to enlist the support of Orthodox believers.)

Although the 1924 Constitution granted equal status to religious and atheist propaganda, the State continued to make rules for religious life; the secret police continued to infiltrate and harass the clergy. The enormously popular processions and religious gatherings outside of churches were banned in 1924: bringing an end to ceremonial blessings of the fields, outdoor Stations of the Cross and Rosary recitations, outdoor altars for Benediction, the blessing of streams and rivers—an integral part of Catholic parish life, and even more so for the Orthodox. Holy Communion and Anointing of the Sick was restricted to special areas of hospitals, could be given only at the request of the patient, and later only at the discretion of the doctors or Communist authorities at the hospital. Even funeral processions from church to cemetery were not allowed. Bell ringing ceased when bells were confiscated during the industrialization drive of the 1930s and after 1941. The Soviets tried to drive religion inside the four walls of the churches, then to do away with the churches themselves.

During the NEP, forcible church closings was generally replaced by "voluntary" closings on the basis of faked petitions, or on the grounds that there were no longer believers to use the churches. The Cieplak trial of 1923, the arrest and expulsion of the Latin bishops, and the imprisonment of the Exarch Feodorov were but one phase of the ongoing war against religion. Churches of all faiths continued to be shut down; clergy and lay religious teachers and committee heads, to be arrested. It was the belief outside the USSR that the government wanted apostates, not martyrs, after the Civil War had ended, and thus entered into the propaganda battles.[6] The year 1924 marked an escalation in antireligious repression, with growing numbers of Catholic priests expelled or arrested. Nevertheless, in 1924, the Soviets also traded, first, 117 Polish prisoners, including 7 priests, for 36 Communist prisoners; then, 208 Polish prisoners, again including priests, for 67 Communist prisoners. Those released to Poland included defendants from the Cieplak Trial: Fathers Juniewicz, Rutkowski, and Eismont. In 1925, two priests were released. There would be no more releases until 1928.[7]

Founded in 1925 under the direction of Emilian Yaroslavski, the Bezbozhniki, or "League of the Godless," put on blasphemous processions, participated in the desecration of the sacred, and were given exclusive access to the media and propaganda concerning religious beliefs.[8] In the schools, atheism was heavily promoted. As observed by Nicholas Brianchaninov, writing in 1929–1930, after the NEP and just as the worst of collectivization was beginning, the Soviets deemed it

> necessary to drive into the heads of the people the axiom that religion was the synthesis of everything most harmful to humanity. It must be presented as the enemy of man and society, of life and learning, of progress. . . . In caricatures, articles, *Bezbozhnik, Antireligioznik,* League of Militant Atheists propaganda, and films. School courses [were given] on conducting the struggle against religion (how to profane a church, break windows, objects of piety).[9]

The young, always eager to be with the latest trend, often responded to such propaganda. In Moscow in 1929 children were brought to spit on the crucifixes at Christmas. Priests in Tiraspol diocese were sometimes betrayed by their own young parishioners, leading to their imprisonment and even death, and tearing their families apart.

The last Orthodox church to be consecrated in the USSR before World War II was finished in 1921, Saint Nicholas the Miracle Worker, in Moscow, across from the Belorussky rail station. In 1922, the Catholic cathedral of the Holy Mother of God was finished in Vladivostok. Construction of other churches begun before 1914, such as the Tashkent Catholic Church by that city's large Polish community, was not allowed to continue. There would be no more construction of Orthodox churches until after World War II, and none at all of Catholic ones for many more years.

Cult of Lenin

With the death of Lenin on January 21, 1924, Communism entered a new phase. Over the objections of his widow, Lenin became the Communists' new God. In addition to embalming his body was and exposing it under glass for the veneration of the faithful, and to setting up statues of Lenin across the country, pilgrimages were organized to the important places of Lenin's life; his hometown of Simbirsk was renamed Ulyanovsk—and Petrograd renamed Leningrad—in his honor.

His widow, Krupskaya, was stunned, as were many Old Bolsheviks. Even more stunning was the supposed scientific revelation that Lenin's brain had "important peculiarities in the structure of the so-called pyramidal cells of the third layer." These were supposed to be the source of his brilliance in leading the Revolution, and elevated him above all other Bolsheviks of his time.[10]

Communism had gone from aping religious processions with great marches and placards to creating a new messiah, a messiah who was a super-man. At the same time, Joseph Stalin, murderer of millions, was evolving into "Father Stalin," the brilliant leader of the USSR.

Catholic Numbers in the USSR

The French priest Pie Neveu, who will figure in our story as the secret bishop in Moscow after 1926, was ministering to French nationals at Makyevka in the Donets Basin of the Ukrainian SSR—in the parish established in 1907 under the protection of Saint Joseph. By his count (and from population statistics confirmed by other researchers), the Catholic population of the new Union of Soviet Socialist Republics in the mid-1920s numbered only about 1.5 million, of which 367,277 were in the Tiraspol diocese. The archdiocese of Mogilev had about 85 priests (down from 473 in 1919) trying to serve 296 working churches (35 had been lost to the State). (Father James Zatko reports only 111 working priests in the entire north in 1924.)[11] Similar drops were experienced elsewhere: Neveu wrote to the Vatican that, by 1932, the Lutsk-Zhitomir diocese had only 26 priests (down from 200 in 1920); in 1930, the southern part of Tiraspol diocese had only 57 priests for 68 churches.[12] There was no hope of improvement.

Catholic Religious Life
in the European Soviet Union

Soviet Catholicism had become concentrated in the cities and among the rural Belorussian, Polish, and German populations. Despite the population losses, there were still Polish, Lithuanian, and German Catholic workers among the urban proletariat, people who were not allowed to leave or who had thought Bolshevism would pass. Emigration to Poland, the Baltic States, France, Germany was gradually restricted under Lenin. Under Stalin, there would be none.

The Catholics inside the USSR, therefore, made great sacrifices to keep their churches open, paying the enormous rents, taxes, and high utility bills assigned to all religious centers. As noted in chapter 3, these were the Catholics who had firmly adhered to their faith in tsarist times. Educated urban Catholics, whose faith was generally weaker, had to make conscious choices, and not all opted for the Church. For that matter, not all of the priests could stand the pressures either, and some did apostatize publicly.

The German ASSR was founded in the Volga valley, and a number of German national districts established in the RFSSR and in the Ukrainian, Georgian and Azerbaijan SSRs. Polish districts existed in the Ukrainian and Belorussian SSRs (the one at Kojdanow was renamed Dzherzhinsk in honor of the apostate head of the Cheka). In all of these areas, parishes continued to exist, though with diminished staff and not as many churches.

The Belorussian Soviet Socialist Republic (BSSR), which would become one of the "sovereign" constituent republics of the Soviet Union, was originally very small. From a core region around Minsk in 1920, the BSSR was expanded in 1924 and again in 1926, however, to embrace most of the Belorussian-speaking areas, and thus also significant Catholic populations in and around Polotsk, Vitebsk, Orsha, and Mogilev, in the first expansion, and around Gomel, in the second. Nevertheless, these expansions still left many Belorussians—and many Catholics—in the RSFSR. In 1926, the Belorussian SSR had nearly 5 million inhabitants, with many of the archdiocese's remaining faithful.[13]

Catholic Centers: 1921–1926

A number of priests in the archdiocese of Mogilev struggled valiantly to keep a curia going in Petrograd, trying to stay in touch with parish curates and even process marriage cases. In 1923, the archdiocese still had 250,000 Catholics, a big population. Interference from Bishop von der Ropp in his Polish exile made life complicated, though, on two counts: first, the bishop and his staff were increasingly out of touch with Soviet reality; and second, their presence in Warsaw fueled Soviet suspicions about Poles and exacerbated the perennial tensions between Poland and the USSR.

In the Minsk diocese of the Belorussian SSR, though 46 churches had survived the war and confiscations, only 14 priests were left to serve its 150,000 Catholics in 1923. In the Ukrainian SSR and southern Soviet Russia, Monsignor Teofil Skalski at Kiev and Bishop Anton Zerr at Selz and

Franzfeld began to emerge as significant figures for Polish and German Catholics, respectively. In addition, Monsignor Joseph Krushchinsky, who would be the "star" in a Stalinist show trial in 1930, tried to keep the Tiraspol diocese functioning from its new home in Odessa. In 1923, Tiraspol had more than 300,000 faithful with 90 churches with 100 priests; Kamenets, 300,000 with 100 churches and only 48 priests; Zhitomir, 350,000 with 107 churches and 66 priests.[14] Tbilisi remained the Catholic heart of the Caucasus for the Armenian, Byzantine, and Latin Catholics. In 1923, the Latin vicariate of the Caucasus counted 70,000 Catholics, with 30 churches and 30 priests; the Pyatigorsk and Tbilisi deaneries, 11 and 8 parishes, respectively, with Tbilisi initially placed under an Italian priest as administrator, until his expulsion in the persecution.

In 1923, the Armenian Catholic administration had more than 66,600 faithful with 47 priests, 45 churches, and 15 chapels headed by Bishop James Bagratian.[15] An Armenian Jesuit priest holding Italian citizenship, Father Pietro Alagiagian, established a base at Krasnodar (Ykaterinodar), from which he made a series of missionary journeys throughout southern Soviet Russia, the Georgian SSR, and northeastern Armenian SSR. He covered a territory that extended from the Armenian Catholic parishes of Crimea down to those around Alexandropol, and even was able to establish an orphanage in Krasnodar for victims of the civil war.[16]

Nine missionaries of the Georgian Congregation of the Immaculate Conception came from the tiny parish in Istanbul to establish the Georgian Byzantine Catholic Church in the Georgian SSR. By 1929, the Byzantine Catholic population had grown to 8,000, consisting mostly of transferred Latin Georgians who had returned to their ancestral rite, and perhaps converts from the national Orthodox Church. The Georgian mission was organized by Bishop Shio Batmalashvili, who had emigrated from the Russian Empire to study in Rome, then gone to Turkey, where he served the parish in Istanbul, and was now back in his homeland.

In the years 1918 to 1935, the Russian Greek Catholic exarchate had as many as 20 priests and deacons, both Ukrainians and Russians, under the exarch in Petrograd. Membership probably never exceeded 2,000. Parishes and missions existed in Petrograd, Moscow, Saratov and there was strong prounion sentiment in Vitebsk among the Orthodox and also among the "stubborn ones," who had entered the Roman Catholic Church in 1905.

The Ukrainian Greek Catholic parish at Kiev continued—miraculously—to survive with many resident western Galicians attending the church. Father Mykola Shchepaniuk, would serve his parish until the Great Terror.

The Parishes

Where parishes remained, sacramental life continued, but with a great difference. Sacraments were now taxed by the State; denied ration cards and civil rights (along with imbeciles and criminals), priests had to depend on the charity of the people for survival. Parish organizations were banned, save for choirs. Children were pressured by teachers and Komsomol (youth group) activists to stop serving at the altar, singing in choirs, or attending Mass. Komsomols disrupted church services and processions, with no fear of retribution by the police. Atheism was taught in the schools, and religious beliefs mocked.

Urban Catholics came under increasing pressure at work to stop going to Mass—what Pope Pius XI condemned in 1930 as moral blackmail. A parish needed twenty adults to be able to function: these adults were now known to the police and activists. Their "collaboration" with the priests would place them in danger in later years. The Catholic press soon disappeared—along with the rest of the non-Communist press.

The physical structure of the parishes was sharply reduced by 1924. Only churches, cemeteries, and rectories remained. Moreover, because the churches had been nationalized, the priests in the rectories, or in tiny apartments and rooms, had to pay high rents and taxes. Congregations had to pay a high rent to use the churches built by their ancestors. Only two parishes escaped being nationalized: Notre Dame in Petrograd and Saint Louis des Français in Moscow, both belonging to the French government. Attempts to place Saint Joseph's in Makeyevka under French protection, due to the presence of the Franco-Belgian colony of engineers and miners, failed.

Closing of Churches in the NEP Era

By the summer of 1923, many churches had been lost; many religious centers shut down. Some were able to reopen, including most of the Petrograd churches after the terrible trauma of the closings, once the contracts were signed by Church committees. Some were never restored to religious use. Many Catholic houses of worship met the fate of the Orthodox Church's Kremlin cathedrals in Moscow, which had been confiscated in 1918, and which remained secularized until after 1991.[17]

Chapels and churches in nationalized public buildings or in public complexes, such as the Catholic chapels in the Imperial Pages Building in Petrograd and the former Theological Academy, were permanently lost to Catholic worship. Additional closings took place throughout the NEP era. Exorbitant rents and taxes were assessed in some locales, and the church would be closed for nonpayment. A closing also meant the loss of statues, images, vestments, and all the remaining Mass vessels. All that could be legally removed by the priest or council was the Blessed Sacrament itself: the Sacred Host had to be carried out in a cloth or a container belonging to the priest personally.

The building where a community's baptisms, weddings, and funerals had taken place, where parishioners had gone each day for divine consolation, was transformed into a theater, club, warehouse, garage, or barn—or it was demolished altogether. Either way, the situation was causing pain to the remaining believers, pain that would worsen during collectivization.

Two Roman Catholic churches closed in the 1920s at opposite ends of the country will stand as examples. Nativity of the Virgin Mary at Borisov, Belorussian SSR, was closed after the parishioners could no longer pay the high "taxes." The church began a long career of misuse as a workshop and garage. When it was finally returned in the late 1980s in a hopelessly decrepit state, the Catholics of the region had to purchase it back and pay for its total restoration. The church in Novosibirsk, Siberia, which had stood so proudly atop a ridge overlooking the city, was torn down; not a trace remains today. The abused church building and the vanished church both were sources of sorrow.

Lay Participation

Many Catholics had belonged to lay associations: the Third Order of Saint Francis and the societies of the Sacred Heart, Immaculate Conception, and the Holy Rosary had all been popular before 1918. In Russia, German villages choirs had been well organized. In the NEP era and beyond, the discipline of praying together, reflecting on the faith, caring for the poor, working to bring back the fallen-away and family participation in such activities took on a new importance. Rehearsals and the teaching of hymns and responses to the Mass provided education in the Faith.[18] Although these sodalities and fraternities were all banned, some continued in secret for a long time and the practices were kept up for many years.

In Tiraspol diocese, many Catholics belonged to parishes where Mass had been offered only once a month, and in the Siberian parishes Mass had been even less frequent. On priestless Sundays and feasts, the laity had held services of prayer and hymns. In the Belorussian SSR, public recitation of the Rosary began to take the place of Mass in places from which all the priests were gone. In the northern part of Tiraspol diocese, many parishes had their own distinctive church music, which had been sung from memory, without written music. This helped Catholic knowledge to survive.

All these traditions now became important. Police restrictions impeded the movements of priests, and the new borders cut off new sources of clergy. Priests could no longer be assigned from Polish and Lithuanian seminaries. There was no organized training of new priests in the USSR; in fact, there was no legal religious education of any kind. Designated leaders of prayer, at personal risk, assembled people in priestless churches. In the northern Volga area of Catholic German settlement, the Holy Cross pilgrimage on May 3 at Köhler continued to attract thousands of people.[19] Discrimination against believers, atheistic propaganda in school, the press, and at work all meant that religious belief now had to be held out of conviction.

All indications are that most Soviet Catholics remained faithful. In this, they matched a national trend of increased religiosity.[20] Utopia had not appeared with War Communism, and the NEP did not bring it either. Even though churches were still being shut down, people continued to examine their lives and make religious choices. Catholic stalwartness can be seen in these examples. Very few Germans joined the atheistic Communist Party, and few subscribed to Communist literature: out of six German national districts having 140,000 people in 1931, only 324 people subscribed to atheist newspapers.[21] Armenian Catholics would keep their parishes open the longest of any group of Catholics in the Soviet Union (other than the French), and retain their Church affiliation to this day. Out of 500,000 Poles in Ukraine in 1926, only 3,000 belonged to the Party and 8,200 to the Youth League.[22]

Of those who abandoned the Faith, not all did so quietly. There were also active apostates, who turned in priests for breaking laws on religion, and who caused dissension in parishes. Such apostates became especially dangerous during collectivization and the fanatical years of the Great Terror.

Religious Education

Soviet law forbade the religious training of children under the age of eighteen, except by their parents. Religious books were few: Catholic schools had done most religious training, and their archives had been confiscated. For younger children, preparation for first confession and first communion was continued, illegally, in the rectories by the local priests.[23]

Instruction could be provided for adolescents and young adults for Confirmation, but this sacrament normally required a bishop or his delegate. Bishop Zerr was too frail to undertake a confirmation tour in Tiraspol diocese, and there were no bishops or appointed apostolic administrators with episcopal powers anywhere else in the west. It would seem that at least some priests were given the authority to confirm: the last known administration of Confirmation in the southern region was undertaken by Monsignor Jakob Feser (d. 1926), in the region of Vollmer, in the mid-1920s.

In those sad days, education of the faithful depended on the sermons of the priests who remained, use of prerevolutionary bibles and books, good memories, perseverance, and stubbornness in the face of persecution and betrayal. Indeed, it was because of such stubbornness that Catholics exiled to Soviet Asia remained faithful.

Seminaries and Priesthood

Catholicism is dependent on the ordained priesthood for the essential celebrations of the Faith: Holy Mass and thus Holy Communion, Confession, and the Anointing of the Sick.[24] Priests are the only celebrants of these sacraments. In the NEP years, there were few priests and ever fewer bishops to ordain new ones. Only the sacraments of baptism and matrimony could be kept up without priests. Baptism could be administered by a layperson using water and the proper formula invoking the Trinity. Latin Catholics could contract marriage by pronouncing their vows before two Catholic witnesses: Germans did this, but apparently not Poles. Without priests, there was no Mass, no Holy Communion, no Confession, no Anointing for the sick and dying.

The closure of the Theological Academy was devastating. Although the successful evacuation of professors, students, and books resulted in the foundation of the Catholic University of Lublin in Poland (the only Catholic university to survive Communist rule in all Eastern Europe), the graduates of this academy basically served outside the USSR. Under Soviet law, Catholics were absolutely forbidden to train new priests. Nevertheless, they continued to train candidates for the priesthood secretly in Moscow, Odessa, and Selz.

The Secret Seminaries

In 1919, Archbishop Cieplak reported 68 priests expelled from the archdiocese of Mogilev, already short of priests. Some had emigrated; some had been executed; some had fled to Poland and either did not return or were not allowed to return at the end of the Russo-Polish War. After the first arrest of Archbishop Cieplak in 1923, the Church considered providing at least a minimal number of pastors and preparing new priests for Soviet Catholics. There was correspondence between the archbishop, the primate of Poland, Cardinal Adolf Bertram of Breslau, the Vatican, and the Polish Ministry of State. In the hopes that the Soviets would respond favorably to Berlin's good offices as a result of the Rapallo Treaty, Archbishop Cieplak also sent a letter to Cardinal Bertram through the German vice-consul in Petrograd for the assistance in the form of at least five priests who could speak German and possibly Polish to take over the empty parishes in Siberia around Omsk. Because, however, both the Polish foreign minister and the cardinal primate felt that this would have a negative effect on Polish-Soviet relations, the archbishop's requests were turned down.

The refusal of Rome and the Church outside the USSR to provide new priests impelled the Soviet Catholics to look for new solutions at home. Basically, they entered into a conspiracy, setting up secret seminaries in direct defiance of Soviet law. In 1921–28, Bishops Zerr and Malecki reported ordinations in Leningrad, Volga Republic, and Ukraine. There were also ordinations at the Solovetski prison camp. Indeed, secret seminaries to prepare men for priesthood functioned in Soviet Russia and the Ukrainian SSR from 1922 to 1930.

In 1918, the Tiraspol seminary was moved underground and relocated from Saratov to Odessa, where antireligious oppression was not as bad as in Petrograd. The rector was Prelate Josef Krushchinsky, administrator of the Black Sea region, who would suffer grievously for his role in the secret seminary and as administrator of the diocese. The seminary lasted until 1924, with several deacons ordained.[25]

Founded in 1922, four years after the metropolitan seminary had been closed, and reported by Archbishop Cieplak in a letter to Cardinal Gasparri, the first secret seminary in Petrograd survived until 1930. Father Malecki, later to be a secret bishop, served as rector. The seminary had ten graduates, including four Russians, who worked in government jobs. Two became priests—Julian Cimaszkiewicz and Bolesław Jurewicz—by secret ordination at the hands of Bishop Zerr in April 1926. Both were arrested and sent to Solovetski: Father Cimaszkiewicz in 1928, and Jurewicz in 1929. The other eight graduates successfully escaped to Poland, where they were ordained.

A second secret seminary started by Bishop Malecki in Leningrad (as Petrograd was now called) in October 1926 had six graduates, but was quickly shut down: on January 14, 1927, the GPU arrested Father A. Wasilewskiego, the director of the seminary and all of the students. Two seminarians were sentenced to five years at Solovetski for conspiracy against the State.

A third secret seminary in Leningrad, which trained four young candidates for the priesthood in the evening with lectures on homiletics, Scripture, Latin, French, spiritual direction, and church history was shut down on May 14, 1930. Arrested by the secret police as part of a counterrevolutionary movement, all participants were sentenced to 3 years in the Gulag.

In Kiev, the Lutsk-Zhitomir diocese, under its administrator, the famous Father Teofil Skalski, and his successor, Father Casimir Naskrecki, a secret seminary survived until 1929, producing several graduates. Two were ordained in Leningrad on December 4, 1928; they were arrested in the Ukrainian SSR in 1929. Father Joseph Kowalski was sent to Solovetski, where he was executed in the massacre of 1937, and Father Andrew Rybałtowski to Siberia. A second secret seminary in Kiev was discovered by the Soviets in 1929: Two students were sentenced to Siberia, one to the camps for 3 years. In 1933, Father Boleslaus Blechman was also arrested in Kiev district and charged with giving information to the Vatican. He was shot in 1937.

At Solovetski, in a Byzantine Rite service on September 7, 1928, the exiled Bishop Sloskans ordained Donat Nowicki and Sergei Karpinskiemu. In St. Louis Church, Moscow Bishop Neveu ordained sixteen men for priesthood from 1922 to 1928, including a monk for Makeyevka in the Donets Basin. Ordained *pro sola missam* (for celebration of Mass) for lack of theological training, the group of new priests consisted of 9 Germans from Tiraspol, 5 Poles from different dioceses, 1 Russian, and 1 Frenchman. The Frenchman was expelled; the others went through the camps and prisons and some were shot. All had been told what to expect, but they persevered in their studies for the sake of the people.

Despite their ultimate fate, all had a tremendous impact on the Church in the Ukrainian SSR and Soviet Russia. Some of the new priests celebrated in both Latin and Byzantine Rites, especially Fathers Andronik Rudenko, Sebastian Sabudzinski, and Leonid Jurkiewicz. A few foreigners became priests in Poland and illegally crossed the Soviet border in 1920–1921 to work for the Zhitomir diocese, again to great effect.

Although the seminary started in 1922 at Vladivostok was quickly shut down by the government, at least one priest had been secretly ordained in Harbin in 1920–1921, Father George Oborowsky, who would minister until his arrest in 1932. Two priests were secretly ordained at Strassburg in May 1922: Father Ludwig Erk, who became a heroic missionary to Siberia in the Turgai and along the Trans-Siberian Railroad (see "Siberian Catholicism" below), and Father Michael Köhler, destined to be the last survivor of the

Table 3

Ordinations in Tiraspol Diocese after 1917

1918	1	1922	2
1918–1919	1	1924	5
1921	1	?[a]	6

Source: Schnurr, "Streiflichter."
[a] Ordination dates of these six priests are unknown, but they were ordained before 1925 and were all in the south.

Tiraspol diocese. Father Emmanuel Bader was secretly ordained sometime in 1924.

In that year, the last ordinations for Tiraspol diocese took place on May 13, at Blumenfeld in Beresan, where Bishop Zerr secretly ordained three young men who had been privately prepared: Fathers Johannes Nold, Christian Siske, and Adam Zimmermann. Their pastoral life was brief. Father Nold celebrated their tenth anniversary alone; both his classmates had been sent to prison. Even with the secret ordinations, however, the Soviet Catholic Church could not offset its losses through arrests, flight, and death.

Sisterhoods

Sisters from Austria-Hungary, led especially by Blessed Ursula Ledochowska, had been expelled in 1914, as had those from Germany. French Sisters had remained at their hospitals and schools until pressured to emigrate by the Soviets when all their institutions were closed. The convent in Blagoveshchensk, with its hospital, endured for a time but eventually was closed; the fate of its Sisters—indeed even the name of their community—is unknown. (They were likely arrested in the terrible purge of Siberian and Far East Catholicism of the 1930s.) The Sisterhood of the Russian Greek Catholic Dominicans, indomitable in its devotion and faith, was also ultimately destroyed. Sister Kamilla, a Dominican, who assisted Bishop Neveu until her arrest, was sent to Solovetski. (Stalin would personally initial her execution order in a weeklong massacre of religious leaders in 1937.)

The Franciscan Sisterhood continued to function in Leningrad itself, after Immaculate Heart of Mary Church was closed. Its twenty-three sisters, who were mostly Polish, continued their vocations in Leningrad throughout the

Table 4

Natural Attrition of Tiraspol Diocesan Clergy:
Deaths, 1920–1926

1920	4	1923	2
1921	1	1925	1
1922	2	1926	3

Source: Schnurr, "Streiflichter."

NEP era. (The convent would be liquidated by an administrative order in 1929 and all but the four eldest sisters arrested. Given the choice of destination, the thirteen Sisters would choose Kostroma, where six other Franciscan Sisters had been sent in 1928; four would choose Yaroslavl'.)

The novice Tekla Kazimiec, a factory worker who refused to sign the decree of exile despite pressure from the police, was finally arrested and taken to an unknown fate. The other Sisters, ranging in age from 60 to 85 and (one was even paralyzed) sold off their belongings and left for their places of exile, where they had to register with the police office. When the Polish government tried to intervene for these nuns, it was told that the Soviet government would "take care of them." [26]

Consecrated women in the German colonies, who were sometimes widows, sometimes young women who had never married, became the prayer leaders as the persecutions increased. They carried the teachings of the Catholic faith into exile.

A community of Third Order Sisters of Saint Francis was founded at Karlsruhe by Father Jacob Scherr to work in the Catholic orphanage there. Twelve young women took their vows in 1888–1889. They taught the children of the Karlsruhe orphanage, assisted in the parishes of the Black Sea and Volga German villages, and conducted charitable work among the poor. When the orphanage was closed in 1923–1924, their adjacent mother house was confiscated by the State as well. Five sisters went to work in the Landau hospital, and then to the town of Nikolaew. There they were arrested and sent into exile. When the parish churches were closed in the German settlements, the Sisters who were at liberty undertook leadership of prayers, catechesis of the children, and leading illegal worship services.

Under the leadership of Sister Helene Scherr, sister of the founding priest, and later Sister Gertrude Keller, sister of another priest, these Sisters led Communion services, distributing the Sacred Hosts left by traveling priests using specially made spoons so that their fingers would not touch the conse-crated wafers. They taught the Scriptures, baptized infants, led the Rosary, taught hymns, and organized Sunday worship services in barracks or in private homes. These Sisters and many lay women were responsible for keeping the Catholic faith alive under harsh circumstances among the Russia Germans, and later in other Catholic communities in exile.[27] Indeed, modern Russians who speak of religious activity in the past are sometimes asked, "Why do you say 'grandmothers' all the time? Where were your grandfathers?" Their answer is always the same: "We had no grandfathers: they were all dead or in prison."

Priestly Martyrdoms in the NEP Era

As we have noted, priests were arrested throughout the NEP years. At Batum, Father George Tatoian, a former associate of the Armenian-Italian priest Fa-ther Peter Alagiagian, was arrested in 1922. When Father Alagiagian had writ-ten him, in Latin and Italian, advising he exercise caution with the police, the letter had been seized upon as an example of an antigovernment conspiracy, and the fate of the young priest sealed.[28] Many priests were seized in the spring of 1924, and in August a priest of Saint Catherine's in Leningrad was shot. At the very outset of the NEP, in 1921, godless activists disrupted Christmas midnight Mass at a Russian Catholic parish; an unknown young engineer resis-ted them and was so badly beaten that he later died. Before he passed away, however, he wrote to his sister: "It is a most honorable privilege to be allowed to die for our Faith. We Russians, the most backward of all, seem to have this great honour now. May God be thanked."[29]

The priests who remained at liberty used every opportunity to preach, and the faithful listened. Church anniversaries, blessing services of fields or vehi-cles, funerals, weddings, baptisms—any occasion was used so that basic teach-ings could be passed on.[30]

The Continuing Exodus

Even though economic conditions improved and barely remembered con-sumer goods began to appear again, Communism was still the order of the day. As before, refugees, including many Russia Germans, continued to flee to the West, especially into Poland and the Baltic States.

Along the western border, where Catholic Poles and Belorussians were concentrated, the atmosphere degenerated to that of "a Wild West frontier." The Red Army would pursue refugees across the Soviet border, the Polish

Army would respond, and villagers in the area would get caught in the cross-fire. Although Poland finally formed a special frontier defense force, peace came to the region only after 1925.[31]

In 1922, 80,000 Volga Germans converged on Moscow, seeking to emigrate. About 10,000 Mennonites were permitted to leave; the rest were forcibly returned to the Volga German ASSR, or relocated elsewhere in the Soviet Union. Other Russia Germans tried to cross into Poland through the Belorussian SSR, with large groups going on foot or part of the way by train. One such band contacted the German Red Cross when it was leaving the country, and begged to leave with the other refugees. A certain number were allowed to come along, but the rest were left to cross the chaotic frontier on their own.[32]

Internal migration also took place. The Far East oblasts retained considerable autonomy until 1929, and encouraged new immigration and colonization. As a result, many German Catholics and Protestants left central Siberia and European Soviet Russia from 1926 on and established new colonies in the region above Manchuria. These colonies had more freedom.[33] (When the Stalinist repression began in 1930, tens of thousands would cross into China.)

Catholic Life in the Caucasus SSRs

As we have noted, the Bolshevik conquest of Georgia was accomplished in 1921, after the Georgian government fled by steamship from Batum just ahead of the Red Army. Independent Georgia surrendered on March 18. Ordzhonikidze rapidly and brutally Sovietized the country despite Lenin's fears of Georgian nationalist feelings and the possibility of a revolt. (Georgia remains strongly nationalist to this day, and voted for independence in 1991.)[34] Repression also took place in the Armenian SSR. Both Soviet republics experienced nationalist uprisings against the Bolsheviks, and in both cases the revolts failed.

The Church in the Georgian SSR

Sovietization in Georgia meant martyrdom for the Churches. As seen previously, the Latin Catholic administration served churches in the capital, as well as at Gori, Batum, and Kutaisi and in a number of villages for the Georgian, Polish and German faithful. Georgian Latin Catholics consisted of Georgians who had converted to the Church during the years when the Byzantine

Catholic Church had been banned. As we noted in chapter 3, Georgian Catholicism was especially tenacious.

After 1918, it had become possible for Georgians to worship according to their ancestral traditions, and yet be Catholic. Under the Menshevik Georgian Republic, the Georgian Fathers of the Immaculate Conception, founded in Constantinople by the émigré Father Peter Krischiaranti in 1861, had come to establish the Georgian Byzantine Catholic Church in its homeland.[35] This Church is usually estimated to have had a membership of some 5,000 people in the 1920s.[36] By 1936, the Byzantine Catholic Church of Georgia had two communities, served by a bishop and four priests, with 8,000 believers.[37]

All religion was repressed bitterly. The Georgian Orthodox Patriarch and four of his council were imprisoned in 1922 as part of the so-called famine relief, and one archbishop was shot. As in the other Soviet republics, if the majority Orthodox were suffering so, then the minority Catholics could not expect much better treatment. Catholic priests were publicly stripped and tortured. Foreign clergy were expelled,[38] including the Italian administrator, although he was replaced by Monsignor Stefan Demurof, from Baku, so that Catholics continued to have a central figure to turn to for guidance.

The Church in the Azerbaijan SSR

Although Azerbaijan was predominantly Muslim, there were areas and towns with Christian pockets, such as the Armenian Orthodox enclave at Nagorno-Karabakh (which would become famous in 1988) and a German national district.

The Roman Catholics had opened a new church in Baku, the capital, just before World War I, which stood on the second street in from the sea, north of the harbor.[39] When this church was eventually closed, parishioners were forced to hear Mass in the rectory, and after the rectory was confiscated, in the cemetery chapel. All of this would end in 1937, when the priest serving there was deported. The Russia German inhabitants who frequented this parish were all forcibly relocated to Kazakhstan in 1941. Catholics would remain in Baku, mostly Poles and Armenians, but a priest would not return to take up residence for sixty years.

Armenian Catholicism

The Armenian Catholics had two distinctions among Soviet Catholics: they had the longest continuous link with foreign Catholic clergy and the last parishes (apart from the French) to survive. Like the Georgian Byzantine Rite faithful, the Armenians had received clergy from abroad; unlike them, however, Armenian Catholic priests from the Catholic patriarchate entered the country not only during independence but also well after Soviet annexation. Although local ordinations were apparently impossible to undertake, missionaries are reported coming from Rome as late as 1927,[40] by which time the Catholic population was reported at 60,000, one-sixth of whom lived in Akhaltsikhe and Akhalkelek regions of the southern Georgian SSR. The majority of Armenian Catholic parishes continued to thrive along the Georgian coast and in the northwest districts of the Armenian SSR proper at Alexandropol (Leninakan Gumri), Parkin, and in the Stepanovan region.[41] (Catholic Armenians would be the last to have organized sacramental life in freedom in the USSR, and would do so to a minimal extent until 1940 with a handful of wandering priests.)

Chaldean Catholicism

The Caucasus region was home to the Chaldean Rite parish (mentioned in our discussion of the Tiraspol diocese), which served Catholic Assyrians, a minority among the 50,000 fleeing into the Russian Empire to avoid religious persecution by the Turks before and during World War I. Most Assyrians were Nestorian Christians, and all Assyrians were considered to be deeply religious. Sovietization collided head on with these people's deeply entrenched religious traditions.[42]

Siberian Catholicism

As in the rest of the USSR, the foreign bishops appointed by the Holy See were expelled, although Bishop Sliwowski remained at his post until 1932, and a very advanced age, under difficult circumstances. (Expelled from his parish in 1933 to a lonely cabin and barn, at his death, he would be buried in the woods by surviving Catholics.) Siberia's Pacific Coast population of 30,000 Catholics would soon face devastating persecutions.[43]

The deanery structure had empowered the Siberian Catholics to survive the civil war and the establishment of Bolshevik rule. But with the closure of the Theological Academy, and the withering of ties with Petrograd, the parishes that had lost priests had no replacements. The large church in Novosibirsk continued to hold Masses until 1923, when it was closed and began a long history of misuse as a storehouse and later as a chemical factory and garage. For the time being, though, most of Siberia's other churches continued to survive.

As mentioned above, the Far East retained much of its autonomy until Stalin. The oblast authorities encouraged the settlement of new immigrants from the western Soviet Union in order to strengthen the country's defenses against Japan and to exploit Siberia's natural resources. Much of this settlement occurred in the former Far Eastern Republic and Maritime Provinces. (Indeed, the Amur River is known as the "Green Ukraine" because it was so heavily colonized by free Ukrainians in these years.) From his cathedral church, Bishop Charles Sliwowski would serve the territory, even arranging a memorial to the territory's pioneer priest, and his young associate Father Yezhi Yurkevich, remembered still by the few survivors as "the handsome young priest," served until the Great Terror.

Although German colonies of small villages and private farms had long been established across Siberia in 1870–1900 the immigration of more Russia Germans into these colonies and Siberia's Maritime region would set the stage for a dangerous experiment by a brave young priest, Father Ludwig Erk. After the restoration of the hierarchy in 1926, he volunteered to leave his parish in Sulz for Siberia. Having studied medicine along with theology in Vienna, Father Erk used this knowledge to serve as a physician even as he ministered to his widely scattered flock. Arrested for his priesthood in 1930 when collectivization began, this missionary was charged with espionage and conducting secret religious ceremonies. He was memorialized as being not only a good priest anxious for the welfare of souls, but also as a good doctor.[44]

By 1936, there was literally no priest left to serve Siberia's free communities. Stalin's concentration of clergy in Siberia's labor camps and jails gave the region the highest number of religious services in the Soviet Union—all unavailable to the free residents.

Foreign Tensions and Their Effect

In 1925–1926, although the Faith was intact and worship was continuing, the Church's position in the USSR was precarious. Moscow feared a new capitalist alliance, between Germany and the other European powers, and was still deeply suspicious of Poland. Moreover, it viewed the Holy See's relations with the European powers, particularly with Poland, and the future of the Soviet state with growing concern.

The Vatican and Poland set up diplomatic relations in early 1925, and in response to Polish pressures the Church reestablished the Latin Catholic diocese of Pinsk[45] on the Polish-Soviet border in Polish Belorussia. Once again, the Soviets reacted with ambivalence: they perceived a Catholic threat, even as they also saw the possibility of Catholic assistance against their enemies. The "Neo-Uniate" missionary work of various religious orders in Poland (see Chapter 21: "The Crucifixion of Poland"), the official Polish persecution of Orthodox in 1924–1926, and the gradual Polonization and suppression of the Belorussian and Ukrainian minorities also antagonized the Soviets, who feared a resurgent Polish state.[46] After 1927, charging Belorussians with "espionage for the Poles" and with "dismantling Belorussian nationalism" would become a common pretext for arrests and executions.[47]

It was at this point that the leader of the Renovationist Church, which had split from mainstream Russian Orthodoxy, Metropolitan Vvendensky (who had betrayed his ordinary, the martyred Metropolitan Benjamin of Petrograd), invited Father Michel d'Herbigny of the Papal Oriental Institute, to visit Soviet Russia. The Berlin negotiations with the Soviets were going nowhere, the Vatican had no contacts left with Soviet Catholics, Bishop Zerr was getting older, and the chance seemed heaven-sent. Pope Pius XI granted permission for d'Herbigny to make the journey.

This forty-five-year-old Jesuit would become the Vatican's first secret agent in the twentieth century.

CHAPTER 18

Secret Agent and Secret Hierarchy

O my beloved Russia, you faithful souls of the Russian people . . . is a
season of flower and fruit dawning for you too after your winter?
—Bishop d'Herbigny, May 1926

Father Michel d'Herbigny was a French Jesuit, a member of the society so
feared by so many Russians. He was also a foreigner, from one of the Allied Powers that had actively intervened in the civil war against the Bolsheviks.
He would visit the Soviet Union three times: (1) October 4–20, 1925; (2) April
1–May 16, 1926; and (3) August 4–September 6, 1926.

His ministry took place during the NEP era, marked by relative liberalization on the one hand, and by the founding of the Union of the Godless in
1925, on the other. Atheist propaganda was greatly on the increase; blasphemous processions on religious feast days mocked all faiths; and gangs of godless youths disrupted services and attacked the churches. Exorbitant taxes
continued to oppress the parishes.

In 1925, fearful of capitalist attacks on the Revolution, the Soviets entered
into negotiations with the Holy See, in Berlin. The Vatican made use of the
opportunity to send in Father d'Herbigny.

The First Visit

This visit was brief and focused on the "Renovationist" Orthodox Church,
which was favored by the Soviet state. D'Herbigny was naïve enough to be impressed by Metropolitan Vvedensky, who invited him to attend the Living
Church's 1925 Council. The French and Soviet foreign ministries both worked
to pave his way: the French hoping for an improvement in relations with the
Holy See, the Communists diplomatic recognition from the Vatican. D'Herbigny wrote favorably of the Living Church movement as well disposed to reunion with Rome, and criticized the patriarchal (and majority) Russian
Orthodox Church.[1]

228

In late 1925, he reported that the northern Catholic parishes of Arkhangel'sk, Vologda, Yaroslavl', Kostroma, and Rybinsk—"an area nearly as large as . . . Italy"—had to rely on a single priest.[2] Although some churches had been permanently closed, others, whose committees had signed contracts, were functioning. Given the upsurge in religious feelings in the Soviet Union, and his own innate enthusiasm, d'Herbigny considered that there was a real possibility of the spread of Catholicism in the country. He also gave the Holy See its first eyewitness report on Soviet Catholicism since the end of the famine relief mission. In particular, he emphasized that, in the absence of Catholic seminaries, it was important to restore bishops to the European Soviet Union.[3]

Change in Tactics: 1926

The Vatican considered restoring the episcopal hierarchy in Russia, in the person of a French citizen working in the Ukrainian SSR. He would have to be ordained, however, and the ordination would have to be performed inside the USSR. Father d'Herbigny was willing to return for a second visit. The negotiations in Berlin were at a standstill; feeling less worried about capitalist encirclement, Moscow also felt less need for Vatican recognition. Nevertheless, because it still hoped for diplomatic recognition by London and Washington, a "blessing" from the Roman Catholic Church could only be advantageous. In 1926, that still would be important.

The moment seemed opportune from the papal viewpoint. France and the Soviet Union had recently opened diplomatic relations, France and the Holy See were finally on speaking terms again, and there was a French priest who could serve the needs of the Church in the Soviet Union: Father Pie Neveu, pastor to the French and Belgian mining colony in the Donets Basin, at the Church of Saint Joseph in Makeyevka. As a French citizen, Father Neveu would be spared arrest or prosecution, or so hoped Rome; as a long-term resident, he was conversant in the language and familiar with the situation.

On March 10, 1926, Pope Pius XI issued a personal rescript, *Plenitudine potestatis,* and a decree, *Quo aptius,* by which the Church in the USSR was to be totally reorganized. The power to do so was conferred on d'Herbigny.[4]

The Second Visit

D'Herbigny was able to obtain a visa to Moscow, supposedly to minister to foreign Catholics there during the Easter season. On March 29, 1926, he had been secretly ordained in Berlin by Nuncio Pacelli, in the chapel of the Nunciature, as titular bishop of Ilium (Troy).[5] He arrived in Moscow on Holy Thursday, April 1, and was quickly caught up in the difficult web of Vatican-Soviet-German-French connections.

The efforts of the French Embassy to bring Neveu to Moscow were thwarted, until the French lodged a protest at the Commissariat for Foreign Affairs and Neveu was at last permitted to board the Kharkov-Moscow train on April 21. At the capital, he made his way to Saint Louis des Français, where he was astonished to learn he was to be ordained as a bishop and named "Apostolic Delegate" in the Soviet Union with authority to ordain more bishops.

Because Saint Louis des Français was placed in plain view of Soviet secret police headquarters at the Lubyanka, the heart of the Red Terror instituted by Lenin, it was quite simple for secret police operatives to keep track of who entered the church and when. Nevertheless, d'Herbigny used this hopelessly compromised church as his center because it was under French protection.

The ordination was carried out in the presence of the sacristan of Saint Louis, Alice Ott, and Lieutenant Bergera of the Italian Embassy (a friend of the pope from his Warsaw days). Two more priests were designated for ordination as bishops: Fathers Boleslas Sloskans, an ethnic Latvian working in the Belorussian SSR with Soviet citizenship, and Alexander Frison, a Russia German and dean of Sebastopol in the Tiraspol diocese.[6] Alice Ott would later be sent to the Gulag for her activities in the Saint Louis des Français parish.

Neither of the new prelates was "clean" in Bolshevik eyes. The Bolsheviks had already imprisoned Father Frison in 1925 for distributing clothing to the poor without permission. Once the secretary of exiled Bishop Kessler, he was working in the Crimean parishes at the time of his ordination.[7] Father Sloskans had given up his protection by a foreign state—Latvia—so that he could remain with his parishioners in Vitebsk. Given the precarious state of organized religion in the Soviet Union, this was viewed with great suspicion by the police, who surmised he must be an agent of the "counterrevolutionary bourgeois" of the Latvian Republic, for why else would a religious worker willingly stay in a country where he faced certain imprisonment?

The New Latin Metropolitan

A member of the French Assumptionist missionary order, Bishop Neveu had a long record of work in difficult circumstances: he had ministered to Roman Catholics in the now-vanished Ottoman Empire as well as in Bulgaria. Arriving in Imperial Russia in 1906, he had managed to establish the French parish of Saint Joseph (1907) in the Donets Basin, territory of the Don Cossacks, with the permission of both the imperial government and the ataman of the Cossacks, to serve the French mining engineers and members of the Franco-Belgian colony there.

Although able to get results from the civil authorities, Père Neveu had not fared so well with the ecclesiastical. His attempts to preach in Russian had been firmly rebuffed by Bishop Kessler. Saint Joseph's Church had been described as "spacious" and lit by electricity, not dedicated until December 12, 1915 (new style). Within the space of the following four years, Père Neveu had ministered to his congregation under the rule of Imperial Russia, German military occupation, the Ukrainian Republic, Cossacks, the Volunteer Army, Makhno's anarchists, and finally the Bolsheviks. Although, through it all, Neveu had remained in his parish, even after the French military mission aiding the White Volunteer Army had been evacuated in the spring of 1919, he had never been able to gain French legal protection and ownership of the parish.[8] His endurance under such extraordinary conditions, his command of Russian and other languages, and his foreign citizenship had combined to recommend him, at the age of 49, as the first secret bishop. (He would serve as such until 1936.)

At his ordination in Moscow, Bishop Neveu was shown a map from the Vatican that delineated the boundaries of the new apostolic administrations. For security reasons, this map was entrusted to Lieutenant Bergera; it has not been seen since. Apparently, Bishop Neveu never showed it to any of the bishops or administrators. The GPU and NKVD made a point in their interrogations of asking Catholic clerics exactly what the delineations were of the ten apostolic administrations. Thanks to the bishop's precaution, however, they could honestly say they did not know.[9]

D'Herbigny's 1926 Tour

From April 22 through May 16, Bishop d'Herbigny was able to travel the country, contacting priests recommended by Bishop Neveu. His choices reflected the multiethnic character of the Church: French, Ukrainian, Russia German, and Latvian. In Kharkov, he conferred with Father Ilyin (who became apostolic administrator for the region); in Karlsruhe, with Fathers Augustin Baumtrog and Johann Roth, in Odessa, with Father Alexander Frison. On May 1, he circled up to Kiev and appointed Monsignor Theophilus Skalski as apostolic administrator of the Soviet portion of Lutsk-Zhitomir diocese. By May 4, he was at Notre Dame in Leningrad, where he met with the fifteen priests serving the region's parishes in a conference at Saint Catherine's. It was here that he informed Father Sloskans of his destiny.

On May 10, in Moscow, Fathers Frison and Sloskans were ordained as bishops, with the same two witnesses, at Saint Louis des Français. All three of the new bishops were forbidden to reveal their new status to anyone for six months. On May 12, d'Herbigny met with the Soviet executive for religious affairs, Peter Schmidovitch, proposing the installation of Father Neveu as a French-protected bishop in Moscow and the reestablishment of a seminary in Odessa. He neglected to tell Schmidovitch what was already being suspected by the police: that he had been busily setting up a clandestine—and thus unknown and uncontrollable—Church structure.[10]

On May 14, he left Moscow, the same day that a new government was established in Poland under Pilsudski, who had defeated the Red Army in the Miracle of the Vistula. The rise of a new Polish government endangered the Polish minority, and thus a large part of the Catholic Church, once again.

Purge of the Poles

Soviet fear of the revived Polish state focused attention on Polish Catholic activists in the Soviet Union. In June 1926, Monsignor Skalski, the pastor of Saint Alexander's Church in Kiev, was arrested and charged with counterrevolutionary activities. The apostolic administrator for the Lutsk-Zhitomir diocese was immensely popular with Ukrainian Poles. The "facts" of the case included his work with Polish youths, his sermons, and his private conversations with Poles of all ages dissuading them from Communism. He had also sent several Polish men to Poland for seminary training, with letters of recommendation.[11] In addition, priests of his diocese had reported to the Polish consul about attacks on the Polish churches in 1923–1924.[12] Although the priests had done so in the spirit of the Treaty of Riga, which guaranteed Polish minority rights, the Soviets saw it as diplomatic interference and as convenient grounds for leveling more charges. Accused of supporting counterrevolutionary activity and of being a Polish spy, Monsignor Skalski was not brought to trial until January 1928. He was sentenced to 10 years' imprisonment and to 5 years' deprivation of civil rights, and finally expelled to Poland in 1932.[13]

Threats, interrogations, and increased police surveillance became the daily lot of the clergy in the Ukrainian SSR. The remaining Polish priests were forced to sign loyalty statements, statements that were obviously fabricated by the secret police and filled with fantastic "confessions." Continued pressure was brought to bear on the faithful (although a 1930 Soviet publication would concede that Monsignor Skalski had at his trial and sentencing acquired "the nimbus of a martyr").[14] In October 1926, another of d'Herbigny's new administrators, Monsignor Vincent Ilyin, was arrested at Kharkov.[15] Although most of the 476,000 Poles in the Ukrainian SSR remained faithful to their suffering Church, the dwindling number of parishes had been rendered leaderless. D'Herbigny's network was collapsing. Meanwhile, on his return to Crimea, Bishop Frison had been arrested and interrogated. His "secret" status was already known.[16]

In the face of these arrests, Bishop Frison reorganized the Tiraspol diocese into four divisions: central (Odessa), north or Volga (Saratov), south or Caucasus (Pyatigorsk), and Tbilisi (for the Latin Catholics in Georgia). Also in June, d'Herbigny's status as bishop and as president of the Commission for Russia within the Oriental Congregation was publicly disclosed in Rome.

The Third Visit

On August 3, 1926, d'Herbigny arrived again in Moscow. He was now restricted to the RSFSR, alone, and thus could not travel to either the Belorussian or the Ukrainian SSR, where so many Catholics lived. Despite the rising panic over the ethnic Poles on the part of the Soviet government, Rome had decided to elevate the Polish priest Anton Malecki, a defendant in Archbishop Cieplak's trial, to the episcopacy. He was ordained as bishop on August 13, in Notre Dame, the French church in Leningrad. The reorganization of the Soviet Catholic Church was completed with the establishment of the new administrations of Leningrad and Mogilev-Minsk.

On the Feast of the Assumption, Bishop d'Herbigny celebrated the holy day Mass at Saint Louis des Français in Moscow in full episcopal garb. Although the Soviet media did not publicize his presence, the Catholic network spread the news, and thousands took to the trains for Moscow. D'Herbigny spent his days hearing Confession in French, Italian, German, and Russian, confirming hundreds of children and young adults in the Faith, administering Extreme Unction to the sick, and blessing rosaries, holy pictures, and candles.

Confirmation had been unavailable outside the Tiraspol diocese even before the expulsion of the bishops; in Tiraspol, the vicar general had made his last attempt at confirming children in 1925. Many realized that that this sacrament would never be available again. The foreign-produced devotional articles, besides being desperately needed, provided Soviet Catholics with a tangible reminder of the rest of the Catholic world, and the hope that they were not totally forgotten by Rome.

The crowds that descended on Saint Louis des Français and Saints Peter and Paul consisted of many Russian converts to the Faith, Catholic foreign specialists resident in Soviet Russia and the Ukrainian SSR, and members of the ethnic minorities. Soviet officials were definitely not amused. The audacious prelate was ordered out of the country by Saturday, September 4, eight days before his extension was to expire. Yet on that day, Bishop d'Herbigny handed Bishop Neveu his authorizations to install future apostolic administrators without consulting the Holy See, in case of vacancy through death or arrest, as long as there were never more than three other bishops in the country, and to serve as the Soviet Catholic Church's sole negotiator with the Soviet government: all other bishops had to defer to him. Also, the faithful of the Russian Catholic Exarchate (whose leaders were all in prison) came under the jurisdiction of the new Latin Apostolic Administration of Moscow, with the exarch serving as vicar-general on their behalf; and the ordinaries were granted extensive powers to receive Orthodox faithful, including members of the parish clergy and hierarchy (Bishop Bartholomew of the Russian Orthodox Church was one such secret convert) into the Catholic Church and to keep their conversion secret.[17]

The next day, Sunday, September 5, Bishop d'Herbigny introduced "Father" Neveu as the new pastor of Saint Louis des Français, then traveled the few blocks to Saints Peter and Paul. There he not only celebrated a Pontifical High Mass, but led a Eucharistic procession in the church courtyard complete with banners, male choir, and young girls strewing flowers before the elevated Host.

Profoundly impressed, the secret police promptly deported the bishop to Finland. He wrote: "[I]n May, when I was returning home [from the second trip], I could see only bare branches from the train; today I saw the beautiful Russian fruit."[18]

Changes in the USSR

Bishop d'Herbigny's naïve optimism was hopelessly misplaced: the NEP was already beginning to end in late 1926, rural taxes were hurting the peasant economy, and urban unemployment was up. Supporters of War Communism felt that the Revolution had been betrayed. In 1927–1928, there were shortages of food and especially grain supplies to the cities. The bureaucratic administration of the country was starting to break down. Internal struggles in the Party were to lead to Stalin's victory, and to the saddest chapter in Soviet history.

When finally, in 1927, Great Britain and the United States granted the Communist state full diplomatic recognition, the value of recognition by the Catholic Church of Pope Pius XI dropped dramatically. The USSR suspended all negotiations for a concordat with Rome, vowing instead to "resolve" Catholic "problems" internally.[19]

The New Bishops and Administrators

Despite their mentor's original strictures, the new bishops revealed themselves only gradually: Bishop Neveu appeared in miter at the Polish church in Moscow on Sunday October 3, one month after d'Herbigny's deportation. To the shock of the Poles, he preached in Russian, proclaiming the desire of the Church to serve all people. Bishop Sloskans appeared in miter at Saint Anthony's, in Vitebsk, on November 14.[20]

Despite a new law passed in October 1926, that no foreign religious body could exercise jurisdiction in the country or serve Soviet citizens, Bishop Neveu continued to serve as the head of the Soviet Catholic Church. Even as the hierarchy and parish clergy dwindled away, he continued in his dual role as pastor of the French parish and somewhat clandestine bishop.[21]

The Church's position grew still more precarious. When, in 1927, Easter prayers were offered for "Edward, our bishop," referring to Archbishop von der Ropp living in Polish exile, this again sounded to ever sensitive Soviet ears like a connection with Poland.[22] Also in 1927, Bishop Frison became the ordinary for Tiraspol; Monsignor Joseph Krushchinsky of Karlsruhe, the vicar general. The specifications for future bishops were that they must be "pious, attached to the Holy See, and holy": using these qualifications, Bishop Neveu designated Fathers Baumtrog and Roth as future bishops.[23]

The Persecution Intensifies

In January 14–15, 1927, there were major arrests of the Catholic clergy and lay activists in Leningrad. The focus of these arrests was to discover more about the secret Church hierarchy established the previous year, and how much authority Bishop Neveu had been given.[24] In May, Father Jean Amoudrou, a French Dominican working in Leningrad, wrote that the Communists had completely destroyed d'Herbigny's efforts to rebuild the Soviet Catholic Church.[25]

Although Bishop Neveu was protected by his French citizenship, he had to witness the brutalities suffered by his fellow clerics. Bishop Sloskans, so devoted to his flock that he had abandoned his Latvian citizenship, was arrested in 1927. (He would be shunted sixteen times from camp to camp and from prison to prison before finally being deported to the Latvian Republic in 1933.)[26] He was stripped naked, strapped to a table, and brutally flogged until he was covered in blood; he was chained to the floor in his cell under a floodlight, with ice water dripping down upon him; and, he was kept in a pitch-black cell for three months. Yet when he was asked by a guard, "Are you happy?" he replied, "Yes, because I am free and you are not."[27]

In 1928 the Byzantine Georgian Catholic Mission came to an end, when Bishop Batmalashvili was arrested and his priests murdered. At Minsk, Father Josef Lukjanin, who had tried to protect the body of Blessed Andrew Bobola, was arrested, eliminating the deanery for Catholics in the central Belorussian SSR. On February 2, 1930, Pope Pius XI sent an open letter in which he complained of the "horrible and sacrilegious outrages" being suffered in Bolshevik Russia: the lack of moral formation, persecution of believers, arrest and execution of the clergy. This was followed by a Mass on the feast of Saint Joseph (patron of workers) on March 19 at Saint Peter's, offered in expiation for these sacrileges and attended by 50,000 believers. It was followed by similar public Masses and demonstrations against the Communists throughout the Catholic world. The pope criticized the countries that had extended both de facto and de jure recognition to the Kremlin, and called on all Christians to unite against godless Communism. Deputy Foreign Commissar Litvinov responded by asserting that the Vatican would be the moving force behind every anti-Soviet crusade of the future. The Kremlin went on to condemn the Russicum and the Oriental Institute in Rome as staging grounds for the formation of a new White Army. Bukharin accused the pope of being in league with Wall Street and the exiled Kerensky.[28] Soviet Catholics would also bear the Soviets' wrath for the Day of Prayer of 1930 and for all subsequent "anti-Soviet" statements from global Catholicism. In the years to come, the pattern became such that both Catholics and Orthodox would plead for the Holy See to be more cautious in its condemnations and charges.

The Fate of the Soviet Catholic Hierarchy

After his arrest in Tbilisi in 1928, at the age of 41, the Byzantine Georgians' Bishop (Batmalashvili) was sentenced to 10 years at hard labor. He was shot at the Sandomorch Massacre in 1937.

Bishop Malecki, already a graduate of the Bolshevik prison system, was arrested in 1930 after the Day of Prayer, and spent four brutal years in prison. He was exiled to Poland, where he died in 1935, at the age of 70. Bishop Frison was arrested several times: in 1929 (collectivization), in 1930 (Day of Prayer), in 1935, and again in 1936 (the Stalinist Terror). He was shot in 1937.[29]

The lives, sufferings, and deaths of the bishops reflected the Church that they were trying to both serve and save. Foreigners such as Neveu had less and less influence with the Soviets and could provide less and less direct assistance. The Soviet Catholic Church benefited little from foreign aid or presence.

Natives faced increasing pressures, greater suffering, and, as Stalinism evolved, the ever growing prospect of death. Very few Soviet Catholics were able to emigrate abroad, to live in safety, or to die a quiet death assisted by the sacraments. Far too many were to join their bishops in the Gulag. And many who were there or were trying to stay out were hastened to their eternal reward by their privations.

Rome had succeeded in keeping a hierarchy of sorts present on Soviet soil, and did so until 1941. Of greater importance to worshipers on the collective farm, in the urban slum, or across the Siberian tundra was how the Faith was going to keep them alive, and how they were going to keep the Faith alive.

Religion had no place in Stalinism's "New Soviet Man." Catholic beliefs and Catholic minorities in the Soviet Union were doomed to being melted into this new creation.

The New Organization of the Soviet Catholic Church

Only two of the Latin Catholic dioceses survived, both on the border between Poland and the Ukrainian SSR; Kamenets, under Bishop Mankowski's successor, Monsignor Swidwerski, and Lutsk-Zhitomir, under Monsignor Skalski, successor of Bishop Dubowski. The rest of the Soviet Catholics were organized under the new structures.

Four of the new districts had bishops, as listed below. The others had administrators, who, though unable to ordain priests or confirm believers, could administer day-to-day life in the parishes, organize the priests, appoint officials such as deans, give answers to the vexing questions of the day, and provide focal points for the religious and ethnic aspirations of the Soviet faithful. The new arrangements were not published in the Vatican's annual yearbook, the *Annuario Pontificio,* until 1930.

The archdiocese of Mogilev-Minsk was divided into five apostolic administrations: Mogilev, Moscow, Leningrad, Kharkov, and Kazan'-Samara-Simbirsk. The Tiraspol diocese, whose bishop remained Monsignor Kessler in exile, was divided into five more administrations: those noted above (Odessa, Volga, Caucasus, Georgia) and separate Armenian administration, at Tbilisi, for all Armenian Catholics resident in the USSR. Initially, only Odessa received an apostolic administrator, in the person of Bishop Frison; the other districts continued to be headed by priests. The Georgian Byzantine Catholic Administration had lost its leader, but struggled on.

Final Changes

Two Tiraspol administrators became titular bishops: Augustin Baumtrog for the Volga, and Johann Roth for the Caucasus, both named on May 23, 1926. In 1931, the diocese's exiled bishop, Monsignor Kessler, died. In Tbilisi, Father Stephen Demurov continued to serve as vicar for the Latin Catholics in the Georgia SSR. The Latin diocese of Lutsk-Zhitomir was already decapitated, as we have noted, and its clergy persecuted. The Latin diocese of Kamenets suffered in turn. Monsignor Swidwerski was arrested in January 1930, imprisoned, and finally expelled to Poland in 1932. The priests in both dioceses simply carried on as best they could, with no leadership and no hope of replacement, isolated both from Rome and from the other Soviet Catholic jurisdictions. As is abundantly clear from the preceding text and from the listing below,[30] d'Herbigny's efforts and the Vatican's secret initiatives were all in vain.

Latin Apostolic Administrations

Seats of Bishops

Moscow. Bishop Pie Neveu (titular bishop of Citro), named in September 5, 1926, not allowed to return in 1936). Succeeded by Bishop Amoudrou (Leningrad), expelled in 1941, and by Father Leopold Braun, expelled in 1945. Seat vacant after 1949.

Moghilev-Minsk. Bishop Boleslas Sloskans (titular bishop of Cillio). Arrested in 1929, expelled to Latvia in 1932. Forcibly removed by retreating Nazis in 1944, died in Belgium in 1981. Seat vacant after 1932.

Leningrad. Bishop Anthony Malecki (titular bishop of Dionisiana). Arrested in 1930, exiled to Siberia at the age of 74, expelled to Poland in 1934. Died in January 1935. Seat vacant after 1935.

Odessa. Bishop Alexander Frison (titular bishop of Limira), arrested several times, shot in 1937. Seat vacant after 1937.

Seats of Apostolic Administrators

Kharkov. Monsignor Vincent Ilyin, named in August 15, 1926, arrested in 1926. Expelled to Lithuania in 1933 with eight priests. Seat vacant after 1926.

Kiev. Monsignor Teofil Skalski, last arrested in 1930. Expelled to Poland in 1932 along with fifteen priests as part of a prisoner exchange for Polish Communists.

Kamenets-Podolski. Monsignor Jan Swiderski, last arrested 1930, expelled in 1932 prisoner exchange. Seat vacant after 1932.

Kazan-Samara-Simbirsk. Monsignor Michael Iodakas, arrested in 1926, 1929, and 1933, sentenced to 10 years in camps at Pechora. Seat vacant after his disappearance in 1937.

Saratov. Monsignor Augustin Baumtrog, Volga region, arrested in 1930, sent to Solovetski. Seat vacant after 1930.

Pyatigorsk. Monsignor Johann Roth, Caucasus region, arrested in 1930. Seat vacant after 1930.

Tbilisi. Monsignor Stefan Demurov, Georgia. Arrested 1937. Shot in 1938. Succeeded by Father Emmanuel Wardidze, arrested in 1935, and sent to camps in 1936. Survived. Seat vacant after 1938.

Latin Dioceses

Kamenets. Monsignor Swidwerski, apostolic administrator, imprisoned in 1930, expelled in September 1932.

Lutsk-Zhitomir. (See Kiev, above.)

Armenian Adminstration

Monsignor Karapet Dirlughan, administrator, arrested in 1929. Dragged in and out of prison until his death at an unknown date. Succeeded by Father Denis Kalatazov (Mekhitarist Fathers) in 1929, arrested and exiled, year unknown. Monsignor James Bagratian, vicar general, arrested in 1930; died at Solovetski in February 1936.

Georgian Byzantine Administration

Headquartered at Tbilisi along with the Armenian and Georgian Latin administrations. The bishop was arrested in 1927. The work of the Immaculate Conception missionaries ended in the 1930s also with the execution of the priests.

Russian Catholic Exarchate

All clergy and faithful were placed under jurisdiction of the Latin Apostolic Administration of Moscow after the imprisonment and exile of Bishop Feodorov (1926–1934) and the destruction of the exarchate's parochial life.

Ukrainian Greek Catholic Church

Although there was only the parish at Kiev, the Metropolitan of L'viv still held canonical jurisdiction over Kamenets, also in the Ukrainian SSR, hence jurisdiction over both the Kiev parish, and any Greek Catholics who might be living elsewhere in the Ukrainian SSR. This anomaly allowed Archbishop Sheptytsky to undertake a bold experiment during World War II.

All of these dioceses and apostolic administrations remained vacant well into our time. Indeed, there were no bishops in those territories of the USSR until the 1989 appointment of a bishop as apostolic administrator in Minsk.

CHAPTER 19

The Destruction of Rural Life and the Great Change, 1929–1936

> You can't make an omelet without breaking a few eggs.
>
> —Stalin to Walter Duranty

As the NEP collapsed, Stalin tightened his hold on the Soviet Union. Foreigners continued to work there under contracts with the State; some even became advocates of Stalin's new campaigns. Other foreigners, well disposed to Communism or simply seeking to accommodate their hosts, made visits in which they lauded Soviet accomplishments (a pattern that would go on into 1980s among many Western liberals). Among these foreigners were such figures as the *New York Times* reporter Walter Duranty, who became Stalin's apologist, and the British sociologist couple Sidney and Beatrice Webb.

Bolsheviks had replaced the old elite; there was no political opposition from the fractured intelligentsia or the remnants of the parties.[1] Having gradually centralized its power, the Bolshevik government now controlled regional centers and could rely on a strong army and police. Lenin's Red Terror had taken away people's will to resist. In their drive to collectivize Soviet agriculture, the Communists also made sure to raise certain people to a new standard of living, thus giving them a vested interest in the Revolution's success. With rapid industrialization and forced collectivization, the full effect of Communism came home to the ordinary people. The NEP had provided a brief respite; now life became harsh and frightening again, with many people living in fear of arrest or persecution.[2]

The Cheka was replaced by the GPU, whose powers were expanded. In 1916, during the Great War, the tsarist government had 142,399 people in jail; in 1925, the Soviets had 144,000 prisoners, more than 40 percent of whom were peasants and workers. That number would soon grow beyond belief, into the millions.

In April 1928, a year marked by the Communists' "scientific" attack on religion, Stalin warned against "internal enemies" and the need to be vigilant. His charge was followed by the sensational Shakhty trial, in which fifty-three engineers and technicians were charged with attempting to "wreck" the Soviet economy. The defendants included German citizens. The trial lasted six weeks, and the Soviet people caught on that something against them all was definitely in the wind. In perhaps the saddest moment of the trial, the twelve-year-old son of one defendant asked that his father be shot. Life was truly not going well in the USSR.

The Great Change Begins

In April 1929, the Party purged anyone who had ever voted against Stalin. The purge was extended to everyone working in government institutions; special activists were directed to go over everyone's records. Effectively in control of the State, Stalin decided to implement "the Great Change" that would bring Soviet Russia out of its backwardness through rapid, heavy industrialization and the collectivization of agriculture.

In 1929, the Smolensk OGPU reported that the workers were becoming more religious, and that the churches were overcrowded. Religious attitudes had endured even among Party members and atheist activists, who continued to baptize their children, get married in church, hang icons at home and attend church services.[3] There were similar trends across the Soviet Union.

With the Law on Religious Associations, published on April 8, 1929, and the related instruction that followed in October, the State became intimately involved in religious life, breaching the boundaries of the 1918 laws and later decrees. The Council of Religious Affairs (CRA) established itself locally and nationally. Religious associations had to register again with their *dvatstaka;* the CRA could remove members from the church councils.

All contact with the young was banned; all church social welfare work was banned; all church educational work was banned, and catechetical books could not be kept on church property. Priests could only serve one parish, creating terrible difficulties as more and more were arrested. The remaining Orthodox and Catholic institutions serving the old, orphaned, disabled, and mentally ill were confiscated. Sacraments could not be celebrated outside a church, except for Anointing and Viaticum (and even this would soon be restricted). The remaining clergy and monastics were forbidden to wear their habits and cassocks in public, making life increasing secular. (This law would become the norm for the USSR from then on, and all religious policy—whether strict or relaxed—would reflect it and its three revisions under Stalin, Khrushchev, and Brezhnev.)[4] In a scrap metal drive announced as part of Stalin's industrialization campaign, church bells were confiscated across the country. Where bells escaped destruction, ringing them was forbidden as being "injurious to health and society." Before 1929, a visitor to Moscow on Easter Sunday could go temporarily deaf from the enormous number of chiming bells. Now the bells were silenced. Surely it is not coincidental that the Virgin Mary appeared to the sole survivor of the Fatima apparitions, Sister Lucia, in her cell in June of 1929, and told her it was now time to consecrate Russia.

In the context of the Great Change, religion suffered directly during collectivization. In villages across the Soviet Union, tens of thousands of churches, mosques, synagogues, and temples were taken over for use as clubs, soviet meeting halls, theaters, cinemas, dance halls—or were simply leveled. Often, several villages would be merged into a single collective. All the inhabitants would be forced into a central location; families would be forced into apartments, where the commissars could spy on them. And of course no church could be built, which left the old churches to sag into ruin. The antireligious antagonism and hostile actions of local officials alienated the believers, whose hostility to the government increased throughout the 1930s.

In 1930, Metropolitan Sergei announced that the Orthodox churches could no longer offer prayers on behalf of arrested parishioners. With the loss of leadership, the loss of churches and services, and the loss of priests, the Orthodox religion went underground,[5] as Soviet Catholicism already had.

Once a religious building was confiscated by the State, it was not returned.[6] The practice of levying excessive taxes on so-called kulaks and independent farmers was used against the churches as well. No tax payment, no religious services. Because religious worship was strictly limited to within church walls under the 1929 law, those who held prayer services in their homes were subject to arrest and removal.

Atheism was the only acceptable form of belief, and the mass media were given over to continual assaults on religion. Moreover, to publicly counter such propaganda was to violate Soviet Law and the Soviet constitution. The process of reducing religious influence in Soviet society at large was well under way. Even so, by 1932, there were already hints of a religious revival in the remaining churches.[7] Belief in God was not going to simply vanish. Half the Soviet population still believed in God, even though religious institutions were being devastated: of the 163 Orthodox bishops claimed by the Moscow

Patriarchate in 1930, only 4 were in office in 1939. Of 30,000 Russian Orthodox churches reported in 1930, 4,225 were supposedly working in 1936.[8] By
1939, there would be fewer than 300.

In 1932, Stalin declared that, in five years, religion would be extinct in the
USSR.[9] Significant religious monuments were disappearing, regardless of
their place in Russian or Ukrainian history: in Moscow itself, the Church of
the Iberian Virgin at the Kremlin Gates and the Cathedral of Christ the Savior
were destroyed; in Leningrad, the Kazan' Cathedral became a museum, along
with Saint Isaac's Cathedral. Inside the Kremlin, some of the oldest surviving
churches were deliberately destroyed and replaced by office buildings. In Kiev,
a massive campaign was launched to secularize the "city of churches." Complexes of Orthodox monasteries, shrines, and sanctuaries were blown up, their
precious metals melted down for foreign exchange, and their priceless icons
and frescoes destroyed. Even the city's cemeteries were plowed under, all in
the name of progress, to make Kiev a "Socialist Capital."[10] Kiev's Ukrainian
Greek Catholic church was closed in 1934; its priest arrested in 1935; and the
church destroyed the same year. The most valuable monuments of Rus' fell to
Bolshevik work crews armed with pickaxes, dynamite, and ropes to pull down
domes.

Collectivization

Peasants were forced to surrender their livestock and tools to a central (collective) organization. They lost title to all their land and were allowed to keep only
small garden plots and sometimes their homes. At the heart of collectivization
was the Machine Tractor Stations (MTS), which served also as a political center. These stations were to be home to both tractors—to replace "antiquated"
horses and oxen—and political activists.

In this terrifying drive, inaugurated in late 1929, Communist activists descended on villages; with no knowledge of rural life, they created chaos. Many
intellectuals had long felt, even before the Revolution, that the peasants were
holding Russia back. Tapping this latent reservoir of antagonism, the Bolsheviks combined it with the naïve enthusiasm of young Communists and the
ruthlessness of Stalinism.

The casualties were enormous among people and animals alike. In many
villages that resisted, and the Red Army would be called to kill and burn. In
others, the farmers themselves would slaughter their stock rather than turn the
animals over to the State. Colossal mismanagement by Party men led to need-

less shortages of food and seed, and to the needless deaths of more animals due to improper housing and care.

A partial picture of the losses can be seen in the destruction of animals: from 1929–1934, 149.4 million head of livestock and 8.8 million horses were lost, together with all their products and power; there were only 380,000 tractors available, not enough to farm the land.

In the Belorussian SSR, 9 percent of the rural population was forcibly deported to the arctic regions as "kulaks," and between 3 and 6 percent were removed to Siberia as "middle peasants," causing the BSSR to lose some 15 percent of its best farmers. In the famine of 1931–1933, another 3 to 5 percent of the population perished, with casualties highest among the urban poor, the elderly, children, and the peasants who had resisted collectivization, which was only completed in 1937.[11]

The forced relocations that began in 1929 and continued through World War II created a vast Diaspora of Catholics across territories that had previously been Orthodox, Muslim, or Orthodox-shamanist. Tens of thousands of Soviet Poles, Germans, Lithuanians, Latvians, and Georgians were scattered in these relocations. The practice of priests at liberty to instruct their parishioners in the basic dogmas, prayers, rituals, and sacraments of baptism and marriage took on increasing urgency in the 1930s. (The labor of these priests would bear fruit in the last thirty years of the USSR, and in the successor states of the 1990s, as secret Catholic communities gradually made themselves known.)

Stalin's decision to forcibly collectivize agriculture took an enormous human toll. The hardest-working, most productive farmers were condemned as "kulaks," and executed or removed to prison camps, sometimes with their entire families. Those left behind learned their lesson well and worked only as hard as they had to. For if they did not produce enough, they could be condemned as "wreckers" and suffer the same fate as the "kulaks." The rural economy collapsed.

In December 1932, internal passports, so hated under the tsars, were reintroduced, effectively binding peasants to their localities, and preventing priests from ministering beyond the bounds of their districts. The passports also trapped those who wanted to flee to the towns to escape famine and the growing chaos.

The forced relocations of "kulaks" to the north and east deprived farm villages of workers, killed at least 3.1 million with massacres and executions claiming more, and led directly to famine, including the horrible Terror

Famine in the Ukrainian SSR and the Volga German ASSR in 1932–1933. The population level dropped drastically across the whole Soviet Union. When the 1937 census showed the population well below what it should have been according to demographic norms by 13 million, the census takers were condemned as "wreckers" and shot, adding to the death toll.

The Challenge to the Church

Collectivization was meant to break traditional rural life and its attachment to religion, ethnic customs, and local leaders. The Party was to be supreme, and political background or attitude, not farming knowledge, determined who would lead these new agricultural complexes. Collectivization was also seen as an invitation to close the churches: as it transformed social life in the USSR, it also dramatically changed the religious complexion of the country.

There were already intergenerational tensions over religion in Soviet villages in 1929. Komsomol members far outnumbered Party members, and they mocked religious ceremonies and harassed priests and believers. So focused had Communist efforts been to establish atheism, and so successful in many places, that the new Soviet cities were "godless."[12]

The principal victims were the so-called kulaks and the religious. "Kulaks" were first defined as rich peasants, peasants who could afford to hire labor and who had built up good-sized farms and collections of livestock. Few of the truly wealthy peasants were included in this category. Most of the condemned "kulaks" were people who had worked hard during the NEP to produce food for the Soviet state and who had followed the new scientific methods. According to Stalin's and the activists' whims, more and more of the good farmers and leaders were branded "class enemies" and taken away. Many villages had to be abandoned, and rebuilt in a new location and new style, which of course meant no church.

In 1928, there were still many active Catholic parishes in the countryside. In the Volga German ASSR, there were 45 open parishes with 32 priests. In the Ukrainian SSR, there were 69 surviving parishes among German Catholics, again with 32 priests serving.[13] Mass continued to be celebrated across the USSR, as far as Vladivostok, and the country had an estimated 110 working Roman Catholic priests.[14] If a church had been lost, then Masses and sacraments continued in rectories, cemetery chapels, or outdoors (which was illegal of course). There were still also urban parishes, though a number of cities might be served by the same traveling priest. (This, too, would end after 1929.)

Communist activists would enthusiastically enter the few remaining churches to smash icons and statues and drag out furnishings to be destroyed or used elsewhere. Once again, soldiers fought the faithful as the last of the belltowers were torn down. Great pressure was put to have the locals "spontaneously" declare that they wanted their church closed. Where church buildings survived, they were converted to secular and profane uses. Lay believers who resisted were arrested and sent away to prison camps in the north or Siberia. A church council would be dissolved, only to be replaced by twenty more valiant people, who would in turn be arrested, until finally no one would sign up for the "religious association" (parish committee) and the church would be closed. Nevertheless, in the face of deep resentment by the Communist activists, the few surviving priests at liberty refused to support class warfare and instead called on their parishioners to exhibit the quality of mercy, and to extend charity to the dispossessed and starving families of the exiled men.

Casualty List

In 1995, the Russian Commission for Rehabilitating Victims of Political Oppression reported that over the Soviet era, some 500,000 priests, monks, and nuns were jailed, forcibly relocated, or deported. Executions recorded in the NKVD and KGB files detailed horrendous atrocities. Although most priests were either shot with the "traditional" Chekist bullet to the head or hanged, others were stripped naked, soaked with water in freezing weather, then crucified on church doors and left to die. By the time of the wartime "concordat" with the Orthodox Church, less than 20 of the 200 Orthodox bishops could be found alive, and only 4 were actually free. According to the commission, approximately 1,000 Catholic clergy were arrested, and practically all of the 614 Catholic churches closed. Stalin took Lenin's 1922 policy of shooting as many clergy as possible, and expanded it into a genocidal campaign.[15]

The repression reached its worst levels in the two border SSRs of Belorussia and Ukraine, where Stalin most feared contamination from the West. The Poles, Germans, Balts, and Finns who lived here were all rounded up and sent to the east and north. By 1935, a depopulated zone 10 to 50 miles wide ran from Karelia down to the Black Sea, which meant of course the complete elimination of the old Catholic parishes.[16]

In the RSFSR, itself, mission work ended. Father Antoni Dzemiew-kewicz, who was serving the churches at Kazan', Vladimir, and Nizhni Novgorod, was arrested in 1929, and the churches closed. Like so many Catholic priests in these years, he was sent to Solovetski.[17] Father Ludwig Erk's Siberian mission came to an end, which also signaled the imminent closing of all of Siberia's parishes.

In the collectives, the priests were condemned for trying to keep religion alive. In particular, the clergy preached mercy, saying that class warfare was evil and that pity should be shown to those designated as "kulaks." Their sermons emphasized that Christ did not differentiate between the classes. In addition, the priests continued to preach loyalty to the Pope in Rome, and devotion to the truths of the Faith.[18] The teaching of mercy resonated well with the people, who were increasingly appalled at the scandalous treatment being meted out to their neighbors and relatives.

In Father Rafael Loran's last will and testament, he urged his parishioners to remain "steadfast in the Faith" and to keep up the religious customs in their homes. Copies were distributed throughout other parishes and were treated "with the reverence worthy of the epistles of St. Paul." This became a common practice with the priests as their numbers dwindled.[19]

Atheist propaganda proliferated, especially in Polish and German, with little apparent success. The example of Pavel Morozov, the child who betrayed his father to the Party, was constantly shown to Soviet children. Religion was continually belittled; minority nationalities were constantly threatened.

The police used any excuse to arrest priests and take them away. Father Peter Weigel was on a Vatican fact-finding mission among the Volga Germans, having worked abroad for the Secretariat of State of the Holy See. Such foreign experience proved deadly: he was arrested in 1930 and, despite a direct appeal by the pope through the Red Cross, sent to Solovetski, where he died in 1937.[20] Three priests in the Volga German ASSR who went into hiding to minister secretly, Fathers Josip Paul, Adam Belendir, and Aleksi Kappes, were finally caught and sent to Solovetski. Father Kappes broke down under torture, and named innocents as his collaborators in spying for Germany, although he later recanted. Condemned by the NKVD for continuing to say Mass in prison camps and for attracting Catholics and other believers with his sermons and prayers, he was shot, along with his two companion priests, during the Sandomorch massacre in 1937.[21] In 1932, alone, the USSR deported eighteen priests, most from the Ukrainian SSR, to Poland.

In the cities, the workers for whom the Revolution had been fought were

Table 5

Arrests of the Clergy in the Tiraspol Diocese, 1928–1936

After 1928	52[a]	1933	2
1929	1	1934	1
1930	5	1935	8
1931	1	1936	1

[a] These priests were working in parishes in 1928, but disappear from the records when collectivization began: many clergymen were arrested in the winter of 1929–30.

not spared. Churches continued to be closed. The premier Leningrad parish, Saint Catherine's, was closed again, this time permanently, in January of 1930.[23] The Franciscan Sisters' convent was closed that spring. From then on, religious life in Leningrad would focus on Notre Dame and its French priests and the handful of remaining parishes.

Since the first mass imprisonment of the Catholic clergy in 1923, it had been possible to send items for the celebration of Mass to the priests and bishops in prison. Relatives and friends regularly shipped vestments, sacred vessels, altar wine, and books. This stopped in 1931, and believers could be arrested for this charitable act.[24] Conditions at Solovetski deteriorated, with Marina Osipova reporting 23 priests forced to "sleep like sardines" in a 40-square-foot room.[25]

Bishop Anton Zerr, who had obtained American citizenship during a visit to the Holy See in 1924, continued to live in Selz with relatives and friends. Although he could not ordain any more men to the priesthood, he spent his last years living giving out money sent from America to the poor and starving. Tipped off by an informer, the NKVD began to interrogate Zerr on a regular basis, but his housekeeper hid the money where the police could not find it. The bishop finally died on December 15, 1932, at the age of 83, outliving most of his priests despite his chronically poor health. Bishops Frison and Roth were able to concelebrate his Requiem Mass, joined by 15 priests and over 2,000 lay believers in the huge Selz church. The bishop's housekeeper, arrested in 1933, was forced to turn the last of the American money over to the police in 1934.[26] It is safe to assume that none of it ever found its way into the hands of the poor. In 1933, nearly 1.5 million people—"former persons," known dissidents, Orthodox clergy and their families, Catholics of both Latin and

Byzantine Rites—were forcibly removed from Moscow (800,000) and Leningrad (650,000).[27]

Closing of Catholic Churches

In 1930, there was a massive arrest of Poles in the Zhitomir diocese, including two priests in the city, where Saint Joseph's Church was closed. Churches were subject to looting or incredible taxes, such as the "White Church" in Volhynia region of Ukraine charged 1,127 rubles. Polish diplomats continually sent reports to Warsaw of churches being closed because the taxes could not be paid. Saint Catherine's in Leningrad was assessed 270,000 rubles! After the Minsk Cathedral paid its tax of 4,000 rubles in 1936, the levy was raised to 7,800 in 1937. When these ever-rising taxes were somehow paid, "committees of workers" would call for the local parish to be shut down. The Catholic *dvadtstatka* members were repeatedly arrested, or were disappearing in the "kulak" arrests.

The forms of legality were kept of course, as in all dictatorships. Saint Barbara's Church in Berdichev, Ukrainian SSR, was first subjected to inspection by a committee and then closed. Some Catholic churches, like some Orthodox ones, were declared "historical treasures" or converted to "museums of atheism."

The Cathedral of the Assumption in Odessa was closed in 1931, and subjected to four years of progressive desecration. Like so many churches, it was used as a warehouse. Then it became a horse stable, and finally a military depot. The painting of the Assumption, donated by Ludwig I of Bavaria was replaced by a huge portrait of Stalin and the altars were removed.[28]

Father Zmigrodzkiego was arrested in Kiev at Saint Nicholas's in 1930 by the GPU. The great Gothic church was ordered closed "at the request of the workers," complete with a resolution condemning the "clerical agents of fascism." Saint Alexander's survived only because the diplomatic personnel attended Mass there.[29]

Churches throughout the German colonies in the Ukrainian SSR and the Volga German ASSR were shut down, especially once the priests were arrested, or the elderly priests died and could not be replaced. *Wehrmacht* photographs from World War II of the Black Sea region depict every church as having lost its towers, its interior decorations, sometimes even its gateway.[30] Active parishes in the Belorussian, Georgian, Armenian, and Ukrainian SSRs and in the RSFSR, itself, were reduced to a tiny handful, all of which would vanish in the Great Terror.

Caucasus SSRs

The repression of religious life in the Caucasus SSRs, although brutal on the "normal" level of Soviet campaigns, was also marked by local excesses. In the Georgian SSR, Catholics were forced to watch some of their devoted priests being publicly tortured and strung up in the streets of the towns, and by 1930, not a single urban church was left, and all of the priests were dead or imprisoned or forcibly converted to Orthodoxy, a religion that itself was being persecuted.[31] In the German villages of the Caucasus region, a desperate effort was made to keep the Church alive and active, a result of d'Herbigny's mission being the center at Pyatigorsk under Monsignor Johann Roth. Collectivization took a serious toll on the Assyrians, whose population was cut in half by 1939 (the Chaldean parish vanished somewhere in this era, never to be restored).[32] Yet Assyrian religious resistance, both Catholic and "Nestorian," continued throughout. (By 1940, Communist persecution would lead to the arrest of every single priest, and the closure of all of the churches and chapels, in both the Georgian and the Armenian SSR.)[33]

Kolarz noted that the small Armenian Catholic Church was treated much more brutally than the Armenian Apostolic Church, which lost nearly all of its parishes and centers:[34] the Armenian Catholics' religious activism, political anti-Communism, and foreign contacts may explain why. Yet the Faith was kept alive in families, and Armenian Catholics remained faithful even when isolated and priestless.[35]

The little Byzantine-Georgian mission was doomed to extinction. Four priests of the Congregation of the Immaculate Conception were shot around 1928. As we noted in chapter 3, there had been Catholics in Georgia for over 600 years. By 1937, however, it seemed certain that this history was drawing to a sad close. Yet the believers in the Georgian towns and villages remained Catholic.

Even when forcibly collectivized in the 1930s, the Caucasus Germans of the Georgian SSR maintained their communal existence. Although most Caucasus Germans were Protestants, there were a number of Catholic colonies that endured in scattered districts. Catholic centers still existed in Vladikavkas, Ykaterinodar, Grozny, and Pyatigorsk, the last one becoming the seat of Bishop Johann Roth as apostolic administrator in 1926. Priests had traveled out of these centers to minister to six large villages and several smaller ones since before the Great War,[36] but this ended during the persecutions of the 1930s. Monsignor Roth was arrested in 1930 in response to the papal World Day of Prayer,[37] and whatever priests were still left working were taken away seven years later in the great roundup of clergy.[38] Unknown to the remaining German laity, who were struggling against both the "kulak" persecution and the religious one, even worse days lay ahead.

The Papal World Day of Prayer: 1930

Pope Pius XI wrote an open letter about the worsening persecutions in which he protested the murders of priests, the moral corruption of children, the moral blackmail of Catholic workers, and "the horrible and sacrilegious outrages being perpetrated against the Catholic Church." Moscow's response was to claim that the Vatican, with its allies the Wall Street capitalists and Kerensky, was planning a holy war.[39] A special mass held in Rome on the feast of Saint Joseph, March 19, 1930, was attended by 50,000 people, including non-Catholic Christians and Jews. (It would be remembered forty-three years later by the Soviet cyberneticist Mikhail S. Agursky writing in support of Sakharov and Solzhenitsyn.) The Kremlin issued repeated threats in response to the pope's denunciations, and even approved a resolution on March 15 applauding the horrendous destruction of churches and mass arrests of 1929.[40] The West, however, was well into the process of accommodation and excusing Communist atrocities. None of the diplomats accredited to the Holy See from countries recognizing the USSR attended the special Mass, although the papal protests and Catholic public opinion in the West did succeed in getting Stalin to tone down his rhetoric in 1930.[41] Nevertheless, as a result of the "March Mass," the Soviet government moved against Catholic bishops and parishes alike. In Soviet Russia, the Catholic churches of Samara, Kazan', Nizhni Novgorod (Gorki), and Smolensk were all closed in 1930. More were closed in 1933. In a large purge of the Belorussian SSR's Catholic churches, the Polish Autonomous District at Kojdanow (Dzherzhinsk) lost its parishes.

By May 1930, in the Latin Catholic Church, Apostolic Administrators Monsignors Swiderski (Kamenets), Baumtrog (Volga region), Roth (Caucasus region), and Malecki (Leningrad) had all been arrested, with no possibility of replacing them. Of the bishops, only Neveu (Moscow) and Frison (Odessa and Crimea) survived, and Frison was subjected to ever more restricted house arrest and to repeated imprisonment. Mission work was becoming harder and the number of martyrs was steadily rising.

In the Armenian Catholic Church, directly as a result of the Pope's Day of World Prayer on behalf of the Russian Church,[42] Bishop Bagratian and his associate, Monsignor Karapet Dirlugian, were both arrested in the late spring of 1930 and sent to the dreaded Solovetski concentration camp, home of so many bishops and priests. (Bagratian is reported either to have died in 1936 or to have been shot in 1937.) Yet in 1936, during the Great Terror, religious beliefs in the country would once again be resurrected—only to be brutally crushed.[43]

The American Priest

In 1933, while the Great Terror was devouring victims, America extended diplomatic recognition to the Soviet Union. As part of the deal, the Roosevelt-Litvinov Agreement guaranteed that the Americans living in the USSR would have clergy available to minister to them. Because the Catholic bishop residing in Moscow, Monsignor Neveu, was an Assumptionist, the Holy See asked Washington to send an American member of the order to fulfill the agreement. This was Father Leopold Braun, who began a difficult ministry in 1934 with Bishop Neveu at Saint Louis des Français. The Catholic Church used the agreement to allow Father Braun to follow Bishop Neveu's practice of ministering to Soviet Catholics, both at Saint Louis and in the regions around the capital.[44] Nevertheless, neither the agreement nor Braun's arrival led to any relaxation of the persecution of Catholicism in the USSR.[45]

The Crisis of Fascism

Hitler's successful coup in Germany after the 1933 elections stunned Moscow. Despite the concordat the Nazis had signed with the Holy See, however, they were quick to persecute the German Catholic Church for its antifascist stance.[46]

Eyewitness Reports from Survivors

In November 1932, the Polish government was able to arrange for the extradition of sixteen Roman Catholic priests. When the priests arrived at the border, according to eyewitnesses, they looked like living ghosts. They and other exiles were dumped out of two dirty boxcars, whereas the Soviet prisoners being sent back by the Poles left in Pullman passenger cars with all their belongings.

Among the extradited priests were Administrator Skalski of Zhitomir, who knelt on the Polish side of the border to make the Sign of the Cross over the USSR, and Father Swiderski, who related how he had been beaten into unconsciousness, then imprisoned without even the farce of a trial. Father Casimir Naskrocky had been dragged from the altar and jailed for four years.

The parish priest of Vinnitsa, Father Liliewsky, who had long endured atheist assaults, was arrested in January 1930, hauled before a GPU court as part of a show trial in March (27 of his codefendants were shot), and shipped off to Arkhangel'sk, where guards stole his shoes, and he was forced to go barefoot in the arctic cold. Father Francis Andruskiewicz had been jailed for five years; both his hands were broken from torture.[47] Just before this transfer, however, the NKVD had seized thirty-five Catholic priests in the Ukrainian SSR alone, ethnic Poles and Germans, on charges of spying for the Vatican and Poland and of engaging in anti-Soviet agitation. They were all sent to Solovetski.[48]

CHAPTER 20

The Great Terror and
the Annihilation of the Church,
December 1934–September 1, 1939

> We know that not a few of them [the peoples of the Soviet Union] are
> groaning under the hard yoke inflicted upon them by men who are
> predominantly strangers to the true interest of the country.
> —Pope Pius XI, *Divini redemptoris,* 1937

The Great Terror is said to have begun with Stalin's arranged assassination of Sergei Kirov, Politburo member and Party secretary in Leningrad, in December 1934. Immediately, a large-scale campaign of arrests, torture, executions, and forced labor imprisonment engulfed the entire nation. The sciences, all of the military branches, industrial technology, and the arts were all devastated. Any possible political opposition was eliminated. Traditional targets—the Churches and national minorities—were swept up in the tragedy.

The Census of 1937:
Effects of the Terror on Population

Soviet planners had projected a population of 177.3 million by 1937. The census of that year reported only 164 million people in the country, a shortfall of more than 13 million. *Pravda* declared that "traitors" in the census bureau had conspired to underreport the nation's population.[1] That eleven million had died in collectivization and famine, and another 3.5 million in concentration camps, could not possibly be a factor in the declining Soviet population. The census takers were shot or sentenced to forced labor in the north.

Collectivization, "dekulakization," famine, executions, forced labor under intolerable conditions combined to kill more than 20 million Soviet citizens, more even than would die in all of World War II. It was Father Stalin's terrible legacy to his children.

On January 1, 1935, a security zone of 10 to 50 miles wide was declared along the western border. This affected all of the western-oriented national minorities from Romania to Finland. The deportation of Ukrainian Poles and Germans was joined by that of the Ingermannland Finns in 1936.[2] The entire German population of Zhitomir diocese, which had lost all of its churches and priests, was rounded up and relocated to Murmansk, in the far north.[3]

Mail service between the minorities and their relatives who had emigrated abroad or were on the other side of the border after the civil war was terminated—the Soviet people were completely cut off from the outside world. Those who had received money and food parcels from abroad (which may have saved their lives during the hard times) or even ordinary letters now faced the real risk of arrest.[4]

"Former persons" (nobles, imperial officers, leaders of the former political parties) and their families, clergy, and intellectuals were removed from Leningrad. Many Catholics were among this great wave, and they were dispersed to Central Asia or to the north. Families were separated and scattered, and there were no priests to minister to them.[5] From July through December 1937, Father Braun of Moscow wrote, some 300 to 400,000 people were forced to leave under terrible conditions.

The charge of espionage for foreign powers was used liberally. In 1937–1938, the GPU arrested more than 21,000 "Polish agents." Of these victims, nearly half were Belorussians; several were priests, including Fathers Andrekus Homla and P. Awgło from Mogilev and J. Borowik from Minsk. The NKVD started sentencing people to death in the Belorussian SSR in 1937, and mass graves were dug.[6]

Saint Louis des Français in Moscow, located as it was so near the headquarters of the secret police at the Lubyanka, symbolized the perilous position of the Catholic faithful and their priests: firmly under the thumb of the Chekists and subject to arrest, execution, or imprisonment at any time. As one victim put it, the purge was directed against "the few real friends of liberty and against the many who—Stalin and his GPU feared—might become friends of liberty."[7] In these terrible years, only the French diplomats could save Saint Louis and the small French church of Notre Dame in Leningrad. Polish protests went unheard. Treaties guaranteeing Polish and Italian diplomats and foreign workers access to the sacraments were ignored. Religion must be totally destroyed.

Table 6

The Decline of the Catholic Church, 1917–1940

Jurisdiction		1917	1926	1932	1935	1940
Mogilev-Minsk	Churches	331	296	*	30	2
	Priests	473	85ᵃ	*	16	2
Tiraspol	Churches	233	*	North: 49 South: 4	North: ? South: 4ᶜ	All closed
	Priests	181	North: 68 South: 57ᵇ	*	*	North: 0 South: 1
Lutsk-Zhitomir	Churches	582	*	Few	0	0
	Priests	200	Lutsk: 26 Zhitomir: 1	0 0	0 *	0 *
Irkutsk-Tashkent	Churches	35		2?	0	0
	Priests	12		2?	1?	0
Central Siberia	Churches	36	6	2?	1	0
and Vladivostok	Priests	26	5	2?	1	0
Eastern Catholics						
Armenian	Churches	60	*	*	4	0
	Priests	47	*	*	6?	4ᶜ
Chaldean	Churches	1	1	1	0	0
	Priests	1	0	1ᵈ	0	0
Russian	Clergy	20	3	1	0	0
	Bishops	1	2	1	0	0

Sources: 1935 report of Bishop Neveu to Monsignor Pizzardo in Wenger, 495–7; Lorenz, *Römisch-katholische Kirche;* Kolarz; Galter; Ledit; *Vladivostok Sunrise,* no. 3 1992.

* Indicate no information available.

ᵃ Of the 473 priests in 1917, 151 had been forced to emigrate to Germany, Poland, Romania, and the Baltic States; 18 were doing study abroad; 11 priests had been jailed; and 208 had been shot by 1926.

ᵇ Of the 181 priests in 1917, 69 were working at forced labor; several had been exchanged for Soviet spies caught abroad; one priest was working in Siberia; 13 died of natural causes; several had emigrated.

ᶜ As noted, the remaining priests had been deprived of passports and were living as vagabonds: there was no information as to how many were still alive in the region.

ᵈ This was the same priest, provisionally freed.

Historical Catholic churches were dynamited in Satanów, Solobkowce, Dunajowce, Mogilev-Podolski, and Grodek-Podolski—some of them over 300 years old. Others (Saints Peter and Paul, Moscow; Saint Mary's Cathedral, Minsk) were so secularized that their exteriors no longer resembled church buildings, as towers were pulled down and the interiors carved up into offices or apartments.

Prison and Humiliation

People who were dragged into prison were deprived of their basic dignity immediately: collars, suspenders, and belts were taken away, so that men were disheveled and had to hold their trousers up with their hands. Prisons that housed hundreds under the tsars were now crammed with thousands; there was not enough food, clothing, soap, water, or lavatory space, but plenty of lice, dirt, rats, and roaches. Although appeals to constitutional rights were occasionally heard, most legal rights were lost in prison: people were subjected to "conveyer belt" interrogations, deprived of food and sleep, beaten, and psychologically abused. Cases were heard, if at all, in orchestrated show trials, never before a genuine court. In 1937–1939, although the number of "criminal" prisoners dropped, "socially harmful" prisoners nearly tripled, and "political" prisoners quadrupled.

Death of a Nation

Many people did not survive their arrests. Mass graves uncovered in the Belorussian and Ukrainian SSRs in the 1980s confirmed what the Vinnitsa discovery in World War II by the Germans had suggested: hundreds of thousand of Soviets were massacred by their own government. One grave found in 1989 in mines near Chelyabinsk yielded the remains of 300,000 people, including small children, pensioners, and factory workers. A grave outside Minsk filled with several thousand bodies revealed workmen carrying their lunches, secretaries in summer finery with purses in hand: people who had disappeared from the streets and, in another bitter Stalinist irony, had been sentenced to "ten years without the right of correspondence." The Kuropaty graves near Minsk contain from 250,000 to 300,000 bodies, buried there from 1937 to 1941. A grave in Volhynia holds 15,000 bodies, found in October 1997, and there are still other graves yet to be excavated.

Because relatives who survived those killed had associated with known "enemies of the people," they had no right to know that their loved ones were dead, let alone where the dead were buried. The Great Terror devoured the last of the Catholic clergy, and practically obliterated sacramental life of Catholics and Orthodox alike, outside the camps.

Stalin personally initialed the orders for arrests, camp internments, and executions. In 1937, he authorized a weeklong massacre at a place called San-domorch, 150 miles north of Leningrad. From January 1 through December 10, surviving prisoners from Solovetski were brought here to be shot in the head and thrown into a vast grave. The majority were slain on March 11, and another group on August 12.[9] Among the Catholic dead were Georgian Byzantine Bishop Batmalashvili, Armenian Bishop Karapetian, an unknown laywoman, who had given birth to a son just a month before, Sister Kamilla Krushenyckaya—one of the last nuns in the USSR—of Moscow, and thirty-two priests. They were joined in death by four Russian Orthodox bishops, Archbishops Damian of Kursk and Peter of Samara, and Bishops Nikolai of Tambov and Aleksi of Voronezh. The massacre claimed the head of the Baptist Union, Muslim imams, 300 Ukrainian intellectuals, 20 Gypsy and Tatar leaders, and scores of scientists, writers, poets and artists. The grave eventually held 1,111 bodies.[10]

Victims of the 1937 Sandomorch Massacre also included Father Kappes, the Armenian vicar, the Siberian missionary Father Erk, and Father Jurewicz, who served for such a short time in freedom as a priest. Although these four men are only a few of those killed, their deaths underline the truth of the statement "all the best were murdered," a statement one hears again and again in Russia and the successor states.

The Stalin Constitution

In the midst of this terrible suffering, Stalin promulgated his new constitution, which would remain in force until 1977. Article 124 granted freedom of religious worship and antireligious propaganda. The 1925 right to "confess" religious beliefs was repealed: in a new clause, believers could only engage in ritual worship. This clause sealed the fate of Catholicism in the country; it was used throughout the Great Terror and after to imprison priests and to close churches. Of 50 Latin Catholic priests at liberty in 1936, 40 were arrested in 1937, and another 8 by 1939.[11] All hopes in Rome of sending missionaries from Poland or elsewhere evaporated.

Moscow and the Holy See: The Communist International

In 1936, the Communist International (Comintern) backed off on its antireligious campaign to enlist the participation of believing workers against the Nazis and other fascists, even as Soviet agents infiltrated Catholic organizations to spread atheism. Still, by 1936, the Kremlin abandoned its international anti-Catholic campaign, and the French, Belgian, and German Communist parties followed Moscow's new policy of "the extended hand" to the Church. Germany had remilitarized the Rhineland; Spain was torn by bloody civil war between Republicans and fascists; Italy had conquered the Ethiopian Empire; the Axis Powers had signed Anti-Comintern Pact; and Catholicism in Germany was coming under worsening pressures.[12]

Divini Redemptoris

In March 1937, Pope Pius XI published two encyclicals, *Mit brennender Sorge* (March 14), condemning Fascism; and *Divini redemptoris* (March 19), condemning Communism and the Comintern's policy of a so-called Popular Front against the Fascists and Nazis. This left the Kremlin, which had portrayed the Holy See as a handmaiden of Italian fascism, somewhat at a loss. It quickly recovered, however, accusing Rome of craven pacifism before the fascist menace, of supporting Japanese militarism (which explained why most Catholics in the Far East were accused of being Japanese spies), and even of conspiring with Trotskyites.[13]

Divini redemptoris condemned Communism, its atheism, and its totalitarianism. The pope had become more hostile to the dictatorships taking over much of the world, and had seen bitter persecution of the Church by Communists and Marxists not only in the USSR, but also in Mexico and Spain. In his encyclical, Pius XI defended human dignity and worth against the claims of the State, and wrote that "the arrogant claim of the Communists to substitute for divine law, based upon the principles of truth and charity, a political program inspired by hate and devised by the wit of man, is beyond all doubt a most unjust and iniquitous usurpation."

Further, Pius wrote, "Communism is perverse through and through and no one who wants to preserve Christian culture can engage in any kind of cooperation with it." Diplomatic niceties went out the window, so to speak. At the same time, the Vatican firmly refused to bless the Fascists' Anti-Comintern Pact, showing that it had no illusions about the Nazis either.

The Devastation: The Latin Church

As seen, closed churches met a variety of fates, from complete demolition, to secular and often degrading misuses, to simply falling to ruin because no one was allowed to fix them. All too often, churches were replaced with statues of Lenin and Stalin, the new gods, or with vast squares designed to diminish the people using them.

(By the time the USSR finally collapsed in 1991, the vast majority of Catholic parish churches had either vanished or were practically beyond repair. The descendants of Russia German émigrés have discovered bridges in Ukraine where the supports are Catholic tombstones. Although some Catholic cemeteries have survived, under the care of Russian Orthodox, most are grasslands or wilderness, such as those in the depopulated Volga and Crimea German villages. When Lenin's statue came down in L'viv, Ukraine, its base was found to be made of tombstones; indeed, the streets of the Armenian Quarter around the Armenian Catholic Cathedral in that city were all paved with the tombstones of the Armenian nobility and merchants.)

In Moscow, throughout the Great Terror, hardy parishioners of Polish, Lithuanian, German, and Russian descent, most of whom had spent some time in prison, continued to attend Mass, along with the diplomats. There was still dialogue with the Russian Orthodox and numerous clandestine conversions of priests.[14] Bishop Neveu was permitted to leave for medical treatment in 1936 in France, but his permission to return was revoked. (He would not again be permitted to return until after the Soviets learned of his death in 1946.) His successor, Father Leopold Braun, arrived in Moscow on September 6, 1936, just after the execution of Lev Kamenev, former Politburo member and former member (with Stalin and Zinoviev) of the triumvirate that succeeded Lenin in 1924, when the Great Terror was in full force.[15]

Saints Peter and Paul suffered the final loss of its pastor, the long-suffering Father Michael Tsakul. Ordered by the Polish Ambassador to celebrate a Mass in honor of the republic's independence, he was almost immediately arrested, on May 3, 1937.[16] His arrest also doomed the Church of the Immaculate Conception. All that Father Braun could remove from the two churches when they were closed in July 1938 was the Blessed Sacrament, and that in a handkerchief because all religious objects had been confiscated by the State, and because Father Braun, who was receiving requests for help from parishes in Mogilev, Tbilisi, Rostov, Krasnodar, Saratov, Briansk, and Smolensk, did not want to be accused of breaking any laws. He was most distressed that the Polish ambassador was indifferent to the loss of the Moscow parishes and the removal of the sacred vessels for Mass to museums.[17] (By the end of July 1938, Father Michel Florent in Leningrad, fearing deportation, authorized Father Braun to say Mass at Notre Dame.) The Alsatian sacristan Al-

Former Saints Peter and Paul's Church, Moscow. Closed in 1937; converted to office building. Courtesy of Mark Sevachko.

bert Ott was imprisoned in 1938 for having witnessed secret ordinations in 1926. His wife's letters were returned unopened.[18]

Conditions in Moscow continued to worsen: the NKVD demanded that Madame Ott give them a list of all Soviet citizens who went to church regularly. This was an attempt to close the church based on the 1929 law that allowed only local residents to frequent a church. Saint Louis des Français received Catholics from all over, which was against the law. The parish was spared, but only because of the Roosevelt-Litvinov Agreement.[19]

The fate of the Catholic Church in Leningrad was foretold by the fate of Orthodoxy there. In 1930, there were still over one thousand Orthodox priests working in the Leningrad region. In 1937, there were only 15 priests, 1 deacon, and Metropolitan Alexi. In 1938, the deacon died, and the Metropolitan served the Liturgy, as the numbers of priests dwindled.[20]

The Catholic churches in Leningrad were steadily shut down. Sacred Heart, partially burned on June 12, 1936, was closed on July 21, 1937. The church in Luga was closed on the Nativity of the Virgin, September 8, 1937; the church in Kolpino, where the ill-fated Corpus Christi procession had taken place back in 1920, on September 16. It became impossible for the priests in Leningrad to communicate with the surviving parishes at Pushkin (Tsarskoe Selo), Gatchina, and Lesnoy. Permission was refused to say Mass at Luga. There were five priests in the city at the beginning of the Great Terror: Fathers Amoudrou (French), Jan Vorslav, Epifani Akoulov (Byzantine-Russian), Michaelev (Latin-Russian), and Michel Florent (French). At the end of 1937, there were two. Father Michaelev was removed in May 1935 to Taganrog, where he served for a time as Bishop Frison's vicar; Father Akoulov in July, to forced labor at Kolyma; and Father Vorslav in September and shot.[21]

Ordination of Bishop Amoudrou

Father Jean Amoudrou, a Dominican, continued to successfully minister in the capital of the revolution for thirty years. He served at Notre Dame Church because all other churches in and around Leningrad had been closed by 1937. In January 1935, he was joined by another Dominican, Father Michel Florent, who was allowed to settle in the city on the condition that he not preach in Russian. At the instruction of the Holy See, Bishop Neveu ordained Father Amoudrou as bishop at Saint Louis des Français in May 1935. The NKVD of course found out, as they had about all the other bishops, and pressured the French to pressure the Holy See to "transfer" the new bishop. The "secret" ordination destroyed this heroic priest's ministry: his appointment was for naught. A farewell Mass was sung for him with the Polish, Baltic, French, and Russian parishioners gathered to weep at his departure. "Good-bye, my dear children,' he told them, "until we meet in heaven." He would never return to the USSR, dying in France in 1961.[22]

The hardiness of Soviet Catholic believers was well borne out in the Leningrad oblast, although marriages declined in the face of continuing arrests and surveillance. In 1937 there were 150 first communions and 200 confirmations; 200 Catholic children took part in an outdoor procession authorized by the Leningrad soviet. The German Catholic colonists of the oblast were especially steadfast, instructing their children in the Faith, and regularly attending church.

Even so, the situation was somber. Members of the *dvadtsatki* in cities and villages alike were being taken away, and believers increasingly had to make do without churches, without Mass, and without sacraments.[23] In 1936, several churches in Soviet Belorussia were closed under the pretext of a flu epidemic. The cathedral of Mogilev was finally lost. The last Protestant chapel in Moscow was closed, despite foreign protests, as was that last Catholic church in Siberia, at Irkutsk.[24]

Zhitomir and Kamenets Dioceses

In the diocese of Zhitomir, the once dense Catholic concentrations in Volhynia and Podolia (527,000 faithful in 1914) were being systematically eliminated. In wave after wave of deportations, people were removed from the borderlands and sent to work on canal and railroad projects around the country. What few priests survived by 1935 were deprived of their passports and forced into a vagabond existence in the regions above the Dnieper. Polish and Italian consuls in Kiev were barred from attending Mass, despite treaties that guaranteed their access to the sacraments. Saint Alexander's was confiscated in 1937 for use first as a "museum of atheism," then as a library, and finally as an observatory;[25] Saint Nicholas's had already been turned into an organ recital hall; a priest, who was still in Kiev in 1937, could only celebrate Mass in private.

In Zhitomir, an elderly and ill priest, Monsignor Stanislaus Yakhnevich, former administrator of the diocese, was put in prison; his auxiliary was already dead.[26] One church was converted to use as a "house of culture" and the Cathedral of Saint Sophia was closed.[27] All the churches in the city of Zhitomir were also closed in 1937; and the faithful met for prayer in the cemeteries.

The border diocese of Kamenets, after five and a half centuries of service, the Cathedral of Saints Peter and Paul was finally closed down in 1937—and converted into a cinema. In this and neighboring Lutsk diocese, there were now no churches left open. Catholics met, secretly and illegally, in private homes for prayer.

Yet, in the late 1930s, *Antireligioznik* would report that three secret Roman Catholic monastic communities had been uncovered in Zhitomir diocese: one, called Sertsano, was operated under the cover of a communal cafeteria by Father Casimir Naskrenski; the other two, organized by Father Budnitsky, were based in Kiev and Zhitomir.[28]

Tiraspol Diocese

In Bishop Neveu's 1935 report, the number of priests in the Tiraspol diocese had plunged from the 181 serving in 1917 to only 61. In the north, there were only 4 Soviet priests left at liberty; in the south, 57, with 68 working churches where there had been 233 only twenty years before. In 1935, most of the diocese's priests were arrested and sent away to forced labor, as were "an incalulable number of Germans," including many Catholics, in the Volga basin during Stalin's drive against the peasants.

On the feast of the Assumption, August 15, 1935, Bishop Frison was arrested one last time, never to be released. In addition to the many priests rounded up for the show trials of Father Joseph Krushchinsky and of the clerics from Tambov, Fathers Johannes Albert (Kandel), Johannes Thauberger (Karlsruhe), Laurenz Wolf (Elsass), and Josef Wolf (Selz) were also arrested.

In the Odessa districts, lay committees were no longer able to keep their churches open. Except for Saint Peter's in the city (still known as the "French church"), every single Catholic (and all but one Orthodox church) church was shut down—some converted to dance halls; others to social clubs or storehouses.[29] Their steeples were toppled and their bells melted down. The church in Landau was converted into a parachute-jumping platform. Rectories, outbuildings, and parish lands were given over to collectives or to the Party for secular use. Even the cemeteries were desecrated: their walls were pulled down for use as construction material, and cattle sent in to graze among the few tombstones and crosses that survived.[30] At Rosenthal, the church was to be converted into a dance hall. When the authorities ordered the cross torn down, however, no one would do it, the workers denouncing it as a sacrilege. Finally, a Russian was hired to do the deed.[31] At Baku, after the Catholic church was seized, Mass was celebrated in the rectory until the priest was arrested in 1937 (it would not be celebrated again until 1997).

Yet even so, faith survived. Father Johann Hermann of Saratov submitted his last report to Bishop Neveu in 1936: in the previous year, he had heard 5,400 confessions, distributed 11,000 communions, received 107 converts from the Lutheran and Orthodox faiths, baptized 800 children, and blessed 200 marriages. He was caring for people from the cities of Saratov and Stalingrad, as well as five German colonies whose churches had been closed.[32] The priest who arrived in Baku in 1997 found an old Catholic woman who was hoping beyond hope that she could die with the sacraments. Such was the faith of that generation, oft rewarded.

Soviet Russia

By the end of 1937, the last Roman Catholic parishes in Soviet Russia outside the two capitals had been shut down. Holy Mother of God Cathedral in Vladivostok was closed in 1933; its priest arrested the night before the last wedding was scheduled to take place. (The couple would not have their marriage blessed until 1991 when a priest could finally come to the city.) Saint Anthony's in Vitebsk was closed in 1936; its priest deported. Immaculate Conception Church in Smolensk was closed in 1937—and converted to archives for the NKVD. Father Adam Desch, the pastor of Astrakhan imprisoned in 1934, died of stomach cancer in October 1937.

Karlsruhe Show Trial

Autumn 1937 saw the show trial of Monsignor Joseph Krushchinsky (Karlsruhe) and eleven codefendants on charges of anti-Soviet activity, held in Karl Liebknecht Raion in the Ukrainian SSR. The priests were nicknamed the "Twelve Apostles" by the Catholics; besides Monsignor Krushchinsky, they included Fathers Michael Köhler (Speyer), Anton Hoffmann (Landau), Valentin Greiner (Katharinental), Raphael Loran (Sulz), Michael Merklinger (Rastadt), Anton Fröhlich (München), and Peter Eisenkrein (Blumenfeld). It was in Monsignor Krushchinsky's rectory at Karlsruhe that Bishop d'Herbigny had designated Fathers Baumtrog and Roth as future leaders of the Soviet Catholic Church. Monsignor Krushchinsky had been serving as apostolic administrator in the southern UkSSR since 1924, secretly instructing young men for the priesthood. Fathers Landgraf (Kutschurgan region), Johannes Nold (Ponjatowka), Jakob Warth (Heidelberg), and Adam Zimmerman (Klosterdorf), ordained in 1924 by the aged Bishop Zerr, were most likely products of his little seminary.

The show trial was held at the new theater in Landau, built on the site of the Russian Orthodox church and its cemetery, both of which had been destroyed. Monsignor Krushchinsky gave an eloquent defense in Russian, but as in all such trials of the time, the verdict was a foregone conclusion, and all twelve priests were declared guilty.

Of the twelve, only Father Greiner was spared, on account of his great age and infirmity (he was then 73 and had gone blind in 1932–1933). The remaining eleven priests were all sentenced to forced labor in the far north, Siberia, and Kazakhstan; of them, only Fathers Warth, Loran, and Köhler were destined to survive to work again as priests.[33] Monsignor Krushchinsky died of a heart attack on his way to Solovetski; Father Nold died in prison in 1936.[34]

The trial effectively eliminated sacramental ministry in a vast region, affecting twelve parishes with filial churches that relied on these priests. As for Fr. Greiner, he eventually took up residence in a single room in Landau, where, despite continual harassment by German Communists, he secretly performed baptisms and marriages straight through until World War II.[35]

Soviet Ukraine and Belorussia

In 1936, some 18,000 rural Poles and Germans were removed from these border SSRs; an even greater number in 1937–38. At the same time, the national minority districts and courts were abolished, as pressures on non-Russians increased.[36]

By 1935, in the Ukrainian German parishes, every single Catholic church had been desecrated. After the last wave of arrests in 1937, only three priests remained at liberty: one was very old, one was blind, and one was mentally unbalanced from his sufferings. The others were either at forced labor, in internal exile, in prison, or under strict surveillance.[37] A number of priests were deported to their countries of origin: Latvia, Lithuania, and Poland.

Religion and the 1937 Census

Religious belief also figured in the 1937 census, apparently at Stalin's insistence. To obtain as much information as possible not only on belief in the supernatural, but also on the 470 possible religions, churches, or sects still existing in the Soviet Union, all adults (ages sixteen and up) had to answer question 5.

The census took place on January 6, Orthodox Christmas and Catholic Epiphany. It would show, trumpeted *Pravda,* that religion, "one of the strongest survivals of capitalism," had been rooted out.[38] There was panic in the country. Some believers feared they would be arrested and sent away to forced labor, and their children taken out of school. Others thought they would be thrown out of the *kolkhozy* (farm collectives) or factories and left to shift for themselves. Still others, however, hoped that if enough believers registered, their churches would be restored or new ones built.[39]

Despite all that had taken place, more than half of the population continued to believe in God. There was a massive media campaign denouncing be-lievers as "fascists," "Trotskyites," and "accomplices in the repression of free-dom in Ethiopia, Spain, and China." Particular attention was paid to Catholic believers because of their "foreign origin" in other countries and their inter-national center at Rome.[40]

The census results would not be published until the closing years of the Soviet era. Slightly more than 56 percent of adult Soviet citizens (nearly 55.3 million) registered as believers in 1937. The number of believers among young people, who had lived their entire lives under Communism, had dropped (only 35 percent of citizens aged 16–19, versus 93 percent of those older than 70). For every young believing Catholic, there were 2.38 believing older adults (for every young believing Orthodox, 2.42 believing older adults); a total of 484,731 adult Catholics registered.[41]

Although very likely within normal parameters of statistical error, the cen-sus was declared invalid on September 25, 1937, and the census officers purged, along with church leaders.[42] The government responded to the religious statis-tics with a final burst of repression against believers before war came.

Repression of 1937

The arrests of Catholic clergy in 1937 became known as the "final blow."[43] Al-leged nests of saboteurs and spies directed by "holy Catholic priests" were un-covered and their members arrested.[44] On March 17, 1937, Bishop Alexander Frison, imprisoned since 1935, was executed at Simferopol, after a typical Stal-inist show trial of nine days' duration, in which he was accused of spying for foreign powers. Like that of his papal predecessor, Saint Clement, who had been martyred in Crimea, his body was disposed of (either thrown into the Black Sea or quartered and hurled into a ravine for the wild animals)[45] to pre-vent the faithful from obtaining relics or making pilgrimages to his grave.

In the Belorussian SSR, the last of the parishes were taken over. In Orsha, Saint Joseph's (founded 1819), in Minsk Saints Simon and Helen (1910), in Borisov the Church of the Virgin Mary (1642), in Lohosk Saint Casimir's (1813) were all shut down in 1937, and converted into theaters, garages, and other uses.[46] Catholic sacramental life ended in the BSSR.

Outside of prayer groups and the Church of Saint-Pierre in Odessa, or-ganized Roman Catholicism was also extinguished in the Ukrainian SSR. (Al-though the church had no priest, the *dvadtsatka* was allowed to keep it open and pray there, perhaps because it had been the French church for so long.)

Siberia and the Far East

On the grounds that there were no longer any Catholic priests or believers in the provinces, practically all of the remaining Catholic churches still functioning were closed down by the authorities in 1936, and the survivors were driven completely underground in their religious practices. Handwritten prayer books were used to keep the teachings alive. (Throughout the 1990s, Bishop Josef Werth would often remark that it was the regular practice of daily prayer and meditation that kept Catholicism alive in Siberia.)

At Khabarovsk, the two Catholic parishes and school were shut down; one church was destroyed, the other converted to a hospital for venereal disease patients.[47] In Blagoveshchensk (a city named for the Annunciation), the parish church became a stable and the hospital was taken over by the state medical service; no one knows what became of the isolated nursing Sisters there.[48] The remaining priests were arrested and removed, deported, or executed. Hillsides above Vladivostok are dotted with mass graves, including large numbers of the city's remaining Catholics.

Despite the massacres, however, there were still Catholics; one priest was successfully hidden in the Far East by a Polish farming family named Sliparski. Enraged that one of his sons, Dmitri, left the Faith and joined the Party, his father made him sleep in the barn instead of the house—a risky act in those days.[49] Though his brother was executed as a Polish spy, Dmitri's Party membership saved the other family members.[50]

Father Yuri Yurkevich, the handsome young priest from Vladivostok, was arrested and taken away. A parishioner later encountered him at the prison camp in Dudinka, where the priest had lost an eye (as presumably later he would his life). A survivor of the parish recounts that, in 1938, her parents and a brother were taken for questioning, executed on the Feast of the Assumption, and their bodies thrown into a mass grave atop those of parishioners killed earlier.[51]

The cemeteries were turned into dance halls and amusement parks. Orthodox churches were either torn down (the cathedral in Blagoveshchensk) or converted into public toilets and barns. Very few Orthodox churches survived in the region. Holy Mother of God Catholic Cathedral was the largest.

In the middle of 1937, some 60,000 Chinese and non-Korean Orientals, Hungarians, Germans, Latvians, and Lithuanians, including many Catholics, were taken away.[52] More Catholics were taken that December, when Poles were added to the list.[53] In a final massive purge of the Siberian parishes, Catholic lay leaders were arrested as spies for the Vatican and Japan.

Holy Mother of God Cathedral, Vladivostok. Closed in 1935; used as state archives.

Soviet-Polish Tensions

In June 1938, the relics of Andrew Bobola, canonized by Pope Pius XI earlier that year, were solemnly enshrined in Warsaw, despite the earlier promise never to return them to Polish control.[54] The enshrining of the Polish Jesuit saint served to further antagonize the Communists and to provide a symbol of opposition.

Poland also engaged in a bitter campaign against the Orthodox Church in its eastern provinces, destroying parish churches or converting them to Latin use. Metropolitan Sheptytsky issued a pastoral letter in July in which he protested strenuously against this foolish policy, but to no avail. As he wrote, "the events in the province of Kholm are ruining the very thought of the possibility of reunion. . . . A new gulf has been dug."[55] The Bolsheviks, who had reduced the Orthodox Church to utter ruin in their own country, used this campaign to claim the right to defend Poland's Ukrainian and Belorussian Orthodox.

Russian Catholics

The patriarch of this tiny, much-persecuted community, Father Alexis Zerchaninov, died in Gorki (Nizhni Novgorod) at the age of 85, in 1933. A fellow prisoner murdered Father Ivan Deibner. Another priest, known only as "E.A.," was arrested in the 1930s and disappeared without a trace. Father Peter Emilianov died working on the Murmansk railroad in 1937. Father Serge Soloviev was driven to the point of mental and physical breakdown. Although dispersed, the nuns did not lose their faith, and continued to minister: indeed, the Sisters are credited with instructing pagan Siberian fishermen in one place of exile, and arranging for their baptism by Father Alexis Zerchaninov while he was imprisoned at Tobol'sk.[56]

Only two of the exiled Russian Catholic figures managed to go beyond Poland: Father Abrikosov, as seen, was expelled. He lived and worked in Rome for many years, still in love with his dear wife who was martyred, and ended his days in Paris. Julia Danzas was released from Solovetski through the intervention of Maxim Gorky in 1933. She returned to Leningrad. Ransomed by her brother, who lived in Berlin, for 20,000 francs, she was able to emigrate to France in 1934, where she wrote extensively on the Russian Catholic martyrs.[57] Russian Greek Catholics, both secret and open, remained incredibly loyal to the Church. Sergei Filatov encountered very old monks in the late 1990s who still kept the Faith.

Dominican Sisters

The community of the Third Order Dominicans, under Mother Catherine, continued to grow in the 1920s. New Sisters were received, from Roman

Catholic, Orthodox, and Jewish families, and they conducted a small school in Moscow which included illegal religious instruction. In addition, many lay people joined the Dominican Association while living in the world. Mother Catherine led the nuns in making a vow of offering themselves as to save Russia in October 1922. Several of the nuns were known among the Russian Catholics as being true mystics; Sister Julia Danzas, OSBM, came from Petrograd occasionally and saw moments of spiritual ecstasy in the chapel. Sister Catherine of Siena conducted relief work for Roman and Byzantine Catholic exiles and was arrested and deported to Solovetski.

Arrests were conducted in late 1923 and in March of 1924, with seven of the nuns and Mother Catherine being thrown into the Butyrka prison and the Lubyanka. Those in the Lubyanka were totally isolated from the outside world and kept in their cells; those in the Butyrka were kept in filthy conditions; all were under great pressure. To prevent their mental collapse, the Sisters devoted themselves to theological and academic studies, reciting the Rosary by using their fingers to count the prayers, and performing deep prostrations while saying the Jesus Prayer. Indeed, Sister Philomena Eismont, a convert, completed her novitiate while in the Butyrka prison, under the direction of Sister Osanna, another convert. Mother Catherine and all of the nuns were finally reunited in the Butyrka in one large cell. The Roman Catholic nun, Mother Lucia Czechowska of the Holy Family Missionaries, was later repatriated to Poland and described how the Dominicans faithfully followed their Rule, the Byzantine Rite Divine Office, and recitation of the Rosary and the Way of the Cross in this prison cloister. Three Sisters made their Final Profession in the cell on April 30, 1924, and the nuns celebrated the Resurrection Matins for Easter Sunday.

The nuns were finally tried in absentia and sentenced under Articles 61 and 66 as being part of the international bourgeois counterrevolutionary conspiracy, for conducting an illegal religious school, maintaining contacts with foreign diplomats and the Papal Mission, and belonging to their Sisterhood. Mother Catherine and Father Nikolai were sentenced to ten years each; the others received terms ranging from three years to eight years imprisonment or exile. They were dispersed to Solovetski, Tobolsk, Irkutsk, and other Siberian locales. Some of the Sisters were able to work, and sometimes they were in places where there were exiled priests, especially Father Zerchaninov, or Roman Catholic parishes (although some of those churches no longer had a priest). Mother Catherine was put in with ordinary criminals, who ended up treating her with great respect, and as a result she was moved into isolation for six years. She did, however, meet occasionally with Father Teofil Skalski for Confession while imprisoned at Yaroslavl.[58]

In Moscow, the other fourteen Sisters carried on with their prayer, worship, work, and studies. Sister Catherine Ricci suffered greatly from serious illnesses and surgeries, and was allowed to live in the Abrikosovs' former apartment with two Sisters to nurse her, until her natural death from a brain tumor in 1926. In 1927 the acting Superior, Sister Catherine Ricci of Jesus, was arrested. Sister Jacinta assumed leadership of the community members still in freedom. Twelve OGPU agents harassed the members relentlessly and tried to force them to renounce Bishop Neveu. Even so, Sister Nora Rubasheva, a convert from Judaism, was received in 1929, and gave herself completely to the service of Christ, and the nuns continued to work among the poor and prisoners. All of the Moscow nuns were arrested in February 1931; Sister Jacinta was deported to Siberia in the summer of 1932. The sisters were convicted of espionage, engaging in illegal religious activity, and receiving converts into the Catholic Church.

Some of the original eight prisoners were released in 1931 and allowed to live in exile in small towns, and Mother Catherine was released in 1932 because of breast cancer. She was periodically allowed to go to Moscow for treatments, where she would attend Mass and receive Holy Communion daily during her treatments. She was rearrested in 1933 due to her work with another Russian Catholic, Kamilla Krush'nitskaya, in giving religious instruction to a number of Komsomol members. All of the Dominican Sisters who had been released were imprisoned again after the rearrest of Mother Catherine. She died in 1936 of cancer of the face in the Butyrka prison hospital; she was denied the right to receive the last Sacraments, and her body was cremated to prevent anyone from visiting her grave or collecting relics. Sister Imelda was shot at Solovetski in 1937. Sister Kamilla Krush'nitskaya worked for Bishop Neveu among prisoners and exiles until her execution in 1937. Seven Dominican Sisters survived the camps, only to be arrested yet again in 1948. Only Sisters Nora, Philomena, and Rosa of the Heart of Mary survived the Gulag.[59]

Tambov Show Trial

In November 1935, three Latin Catholic priests and three Russian Catholic Dominican nuns from Tambov, were accused of espionage on behalf of foreign powers, were "tried" in Voronezh. The priests were Father Adam Garreis, of the German Catholic parish in Voronezh, and Fathers Johann

Beihman and Alexander Staube. The nuns were Sisters Antonia, Stephanie, and Rose of Lima. The last was a Polish Roman Catholic who had transferred to the Byzantine-Russian Rite when she joined the order in the early 1920s. She had already been imprisoned at Irkutsk, Tobol'sk, Tyumen, and had refused to be repatriated to Poland in 1933 in order to remain with the other Dominican Nuns in the USSR.

Catholics in the Tambov area consisted of both locals and those relocated there. They had received money from Bishop Neveu to help them survive the food shortages. The priests were subjected to "conveyor belt" interrogations, and forced to confess to receiving money and instructions from Bishop Neveu in Moscow, and to implicate the nuns. Father Beihman had previously been interrogated by the GPU, and as a result implicated others, although he recanted his testimony in a letter to the Central Committee in Moscow. He had been sentenced to Butyrka and then sent to Tambov; as the Great Terror began, he was once more brought to the attention of the police. Father Staube had already been investigated because he had received Mass stipends, but had provisional freedom. Rather than tell the police that the stipends had come from Bishop Neveu, he had said the money was from local Catholics. This became the pretext for an investigation of the believers for proof of a conspiracy, which focused on the German colonists and Fathers Beihman, Staube, and Garreis. Preying upon his fear of execution, the GPU coerced Father Garreis into betraying the colonists, other priests, and Bishop Neveu. The stipends from Moscow were now construed as "anti-Soviet agitation," and providing information to the Bishop as "spying for foreigners." Following "conveyor belt" interrogations, Fathers Garreis and Beihman both signed affidavits against their fellow Catholics. In classic Stalinist form, they were forced to denounce the Catholics as having held anti-Soviet ideas and being engaged in illegal transport and receipt of currency. Stalinist paranoia of foreign contacts came into play as well. Bishop Neveu's trips abroad to France and the Vatican were transformed into espionage expeditions, and the extension of charity through the bishop and Moscow Catholics who acted as his representatives to other Soviet Catholics as further excursions into espionage.

The Dominican nuns were thrust into cells that were overcrowded and filled with criminals and prostitutes, along with countless vermin. Although, to resume community life, they agreed to move into the cells designated for women with contagious venereal diseases, on the Nativity of Mary, September 8, they were again dispersed into different cells and isolation.

The priests' depositions stunned the nuns who wrote, "[I]t was horrible to think that the priests to whom we gave the name of 'Father' had betrayed us and sold out their bishop.' " Equally stunning, however, were the priests' public recantations at the trial. The physical appearance of the priests as miserable and weakened brought great sympathy from the Sisters.

A secret trial was held during mid-November. A fourth priest, Father Joseph Verbitsky, was added to the case. Sister Stephanie gave a stirring testimony of faith at the trial and in a letter to Bishop Neveu. She noted that although there were apostates and traitors, there were still many Catholics who were proud of their faith. The priests were convicted and sentenced, although the military tribunal acquitted the nuns, a miracle attributed to the intercession of the Carmelite Nuns of Lisieux, France, home of Saint Therese. When the State appealed the verdict,[60] however, it was overturned; all defendants were sent to prisons or labor camps. Staube survived his imprisonment, ending his days in the German suburb of Maikutok, in Karaganda, where he died in 1961.

Bishop Neveu wrote that the three Dominican Sisters gave a powerful witness to their devotion to the Church and loyalty to the pope. They were instrumental in the conversion of many Russians and Jews, all of whom became fervent believers. "What would they not be able to do," the bishop asked, "if we in Russia had a little bit of liberty?" They remained faithful to their vows in prison and labor camps. They gave a further "catholic" witness in that, though they were part of the Byzantine Rite, they frequented the Latin priests and churches for the sacraments, a practice followed by the Russian Catholic laity.

The National Minorities

Russification had become official policy under Stalin, with a steady diminution of national districts, national languages, national cultural organizations, and with the organized destruction of the national elites.

Members of national minorities were accused of being spies for, or of agitating for union with, foreign powers, ranging from Afghanistan to Nazi Germany to the Japanese Empire. A whole Finno-Ugric tribe was arrested on the charge of planning to unite with Finland—even though Finland was 600 miles away. Soviet Bulgarians and Greeks were charged with planning to unite their coastal districts with their ancient homelands, which were far across the Black Sea. In Ukrainian German colonies, the men were taken from the fields and the women from the houses, and they were sent to "voluntary colonization" in the north, with their small children farmed out to Russian families in other territories.[61]

In the Far East, the entire Korean minority was seized in the fall and winter of 1937. No one was spared: 180,000 Koreans were taken away, with 2,500 being arrested for resistance.[62] When Japanese police and diplomatic representatives (who were responsible for Koreans because Korea was then part of the Japanese Empire) went into the Far East oblasts, they could not find a single Korean left. Practically all were sent to Kazakhstan and Central Asia, where they remain today.[63]

In January 1939, the Great Terror eliminated national minorities in the cities. Many minority congregations had already been shut down when Armenian, German Protestant, and Finnish Lutheran churches in the cities had been closed and their clergy arrested. Now, Stalin moved against the remaining lay believers of those congregations: the German, Bulgarian, Armenian, Latvian, Polish, and Greek populations in the cities of Soviet Russia and Ukraine were devastated. The Austrian Communist prisoner Alexander Weissberg, who, like many Reich Communists, had fled to the "safety" of the Communist Motherland and then been arrested as a spy, was put into a mass cell in 1940. He reported that there were 22 national minorities represented among his 260 fellow prisoners, and that the urban minorities had been "ruthlessly liquidated."[64] Among the Catholics, this affected mostly Soviet Poles and some Soviet Armenians and Germans.

The Blue Light of 1938

An unusual aurora borealis took place in Europe in 1938, remarkable for its strange and widespread lights. This was interpreted later by Sister Lucia as the fulfillment of the prophecy of Fatima by Our Lady: "When you see a night lit up by an unknown light, know that it is the sign God gives you that He is about the punish the world for its crimes by means of war, hunger, and persecution of the Church and the Holy Father." Mary told the three children that war would break out during the pontificate of Pius XI. When she was queried on the accuracy of that prophecy, with the questioners pointing out that Germany invaded Poland in 1939, she replied—quite rightly—that the war really began with the annexation of Austria and the dismemberment of Czechoslovakia the year before. Pope Pius XI would die February 10, 1939, despairing of peace, and be succeeded by his secretary of state, Cardinal Pacelli, who would become Pope Pius XII.[65]

The Situation in 1939

According to an official 1995 report by the Russian government, by 1939, an estimated 1,000 Roman Catholic priests had been killed outright, imprisoned, interned, or deported, and 614 parishes had been closed.[66] Of those priests arrested and interned, a grand total of *twelve* would survive the Gulag. All of them would go back to work as priests either in their home territories or in the Catholic diaspora, and they would work until they died. The survivors were

Father Josef Borodziula (d. Rydze, 1983)
Father Władysław Dworzecki (d. Kamenets-Podolski, 1947)
Father Roman Jankowski (d. Zhitomir, 1987)
Father Jozef Kozinski (d. Berdichev, 1967)
Father Alexander Samosenko (d. Zhitomir, 1956)
Father Michael Köhler (d. Frunze, 1983)
Father Rafael Loran (d. Kazakhstan, 1948)
Father Josef Neugum (d. Kazakhstan, 1955)
Father Alexander Staube (d. Kazakhstan, 1961)
Father Konstanty Sapariszwili (d. Tbilisi, 1973)
Father Emmanuel Wardidze (d. Tbilisi, 1966)
Father Jakob Warth (d. Kazakhstan, 1970).[67]

As for the majority Orthodox faith, by 1939, there were less than 300 Orthodox churches open in the entire Soviet Union, of which 150–200 were in Soviet Russia. There were less than a dozen Orthodox churches in the Ukrainian SSR, a few more in Central Asia and the Caucasus, and none in the Belorussian SSR. According to the same report, 200,000 Russian Orthodox priests, monks, and nuns had been slain and another 500,000 imprisoned or interned in labor camps; 54,000 Orthodox churches had been closed on Soviet territory before World War II.

By 1939, the parishes we have come to know so far had disappeared many never to be restored. (Others would open briefly during the German occupation, but most of those were closed again until just before the collapse of the Soviet Union. Only a fraction would be restored to Catholic use before 1989.) Within the space of two years, hundreds of thousands of Soviet Catholics still living in their hometowns or villages were to be uprooted by their own government and subjected to imprisonment, forced relocation, deportation, or execution. Just as many were to experience the full horror of Nazi rule.

Gasparri, the Holy See, and the Coming War

In early 1916, Cardinal Gasparri had been stunned to learn that the Allies intended to dismantle the Austro-Hungarian Empire and to establish a series of small states instead. Gasparri predicted that, if such was done, "in a matter of years the Slavs will have swallowed up half of Europe [and] the Catholic religion will be under constant attack in all the countries of Eastern Europe."

When the Treaty of Versailles only confirmed the Allies' intentions, the Holy See, in 1922, publicly warned of the impending danger regarding the new states: "These are bound sooner or later to come under the domination of Russia. They will form a Russian confederation stretching from the Carpathians to Constantinople, from Danzig to the Adriatic. Austria itself is being reduced to a rump, which will be incapable of holding its own against a hundred million Germans."

The accuracy of this prediction is uncanny. For the Western powers continued to dismantle empires and to set up little countries, which then became tangled in a web of conflicts—and which did nothing to stop either Bolshevism or National Socialism. Hitler continually expanded his power, into the Rhineland and the Saarland, taking Austria, as predicted, and crippling Czechoslovakia, all by 1938. The Second World War would end with all the territories included in the prediction under Soviet control, and with Catholics there under bitter attack.[68]

PART THREE

1939–1945

CHAPTER 21

The Crucifixion of Poland

> With the Germans we run the risk of losing our liberty. With the Russians we will lose our soul.
>
> —Marshall Edward Rydz-Smigly of Poland,
> Spring 1939

> Get used to it or you'll croak.
>
> —Red Army soldiers to Polish civilians

Poland, of course, was the nation whose death marked the beginning of World War II and the end of the traditional divisions of Europe. By the time Germany surrendered in May 1945, Europe had been transformed. For Catholics, the Molotov-von Ribbentrop Pact, announced on August 24, 1939, and the Soviet-Nazi agreements that followed the occupation of Poland had serious consequences. The pact, which established mutual assistance, trade, and peace between the Soviet Union and Nazi Germany, two hitherto bitterly opposed totalitarian dictatorships, shocked the world. It was very much a case of Pilate and Herod becoming friends over the body of Jesus Christ—and the image of Poland Crucified was a familiar one in Polish history. According to secret protocols, Warsaw was to be divided (as Berlin would be after 1945) and Germany given control over Lithuania, the Galician oil fields, and the city of Lwów (L'viv). The USSR was to take over Bessarabia (from Romania), Estonia, Latvia, western Belorussia, and the rest of Galicia.

The German Invasion

At 4:45 A.M. on September 1, 1939, Germany invaded Poland, launching World War II. (In June 1941, Hitler would also invade the Soviet Union before dawn, with the surprise attack only adding to the shock of betrayal.) The desperate Polish army was forced to retreat eastward. But the bravery of the Polish cavalry[1] and the tactics of moving toward the Pripet Marshes were all for naught: Poland's allies, Britain and France, did nothing to help it in the west, and Stalin, breaking his 1934 nonaggression treaty with Poland attacked it from the east on September 17. Despite all this, the Republic of Poland survived for thirty-five anguished days, longer than most of the western nations invaded by Germany in 1940.

The Soviet Invasion

As the TASS news bulletin on the Soviet invasion explained (ignoring the presence of the Polish government at Lwów and its still-fighting army), the Polish state had "disintegrated." The Soviet Union was therefore obliged to intervene to provide assistance to the struggling Belorussians and Ukrainians, and to deliver the Polish people from the folly of their masters.

Although Warsaw, a tiny Polish outpost near Danzig, and the Modlin Fortress held out valiantly for as long as they could, they were eventually overrun. The Red Army, which by then had occupied all the territory allotted to the Soviets in the east, with only 737 dead and 1,800 wounded. Stalin immediately began to change the secret protocols; he abandoned the four-river line, turning over to Hitler the central core of the Polish and Jewish populations; the two dictators agreed that there would be no Polish buffer state between them. Lithuania passed under Soviet control (thus denying the Germans a direct invasion route and increasing the Soviet warm-water coastline), as did all of Galicia (with the provision that the Galician oil fields would export their product to Germany), and all of western Belorussia.

The result for the Church was that a host of Latin Catholic dioceses and administrations from Estonia on the Baltic down to Romania, the entire Ukrainian Catholic Metropolia, the "Neo-Uniate" parishes of northeast Poland, and the Armenian Catholic Metropolia, with a Catholic population of some 10 million people, came under Communist control, whether through occupation or outright annexation.

Changes in the Soviet Zone

Both the Soviet soldiers who entered Poland and the general Soviet public were told that the USSR's purpose in invading Poland was to deliver the Ukrainians and Belorussians of eastern Poland, as well as the Baltic peoples, from capitalist oppression—to give the Poles and them a chance to truly prosper under Communism.

Of the 13 million Polish citizens in the Soviet occupation zone, only 5.2 million were ethnic Poles. The rest were Ukrainians, *Latynnyky* (Roman Catholics of Ukrainian or Polish origin with a mixed national consciousness), Jews, Belorussians, Galician and Volhynian Germans, Armenians, Karaites, and Tatars. Eastern Poland had suffered from the right-wing Polish chauvinism of the Sanacja regime, oppression of the non-Poles, nationalism on the part of some Polish Catholic clergy, and rising anti-Semitism:[2] there were serious divisions between the nationalities, the Churches, and within the Catholic Church.

Poland had persecuted the Eastern Orthodox of Volhynia and Podolia, pressuring many people to convert to Latin Catholicism and thus to a Polish or pro-Polish national identity. Churches and properties that had once belonged to the Greek or Latin Catholic Churches but had accrued to Orthodoxy under tsarist Russia were confiscated for Latin Catholic use or pulled down, and even the Greek Catholics and "Neo-Uniates" were denied use of their former churches. The Polish government did not grant Orthodoxy legal status until 1938, and even then stood by as 120 Orthodox churches were vandalized and destroyed.[3] "Voluntary" conversions of Orthodox throughout Volhynia and Kholm were conducted, especially along Poland's frontiers with the Soviet Union, under the threat of deportation, prompting Metropolitan Sheptytsky's public defense of the Orthodox in July 1938. In addition, he protested against the confiscation of Orthodox church buildings and properties for Latin Catholic use, but without effect. Although few Latin Catholic priests participated in the conversion campaigns, they still took possession of the "recovered churches" and their parish registers for the Latin Rite.[4]

Many Ukrainian Greek Catholics found themselves forced to become Latin Catholic (and thus implicitly Polish) in order to gain land when the estates were broken up, or to find work on the railway or in Polish-owned factories or in state industries. In 1921, a recommendation had been made by a nationalist committee in Galicia that Polish Latin Catholic priests "convert" Greek Catholics children of mixed marriages, Greek Catholics attending Latin Catholic schools, those whose ancestors had been Latin Catholics, those who wished to buy land from Latin Catholics, those who sought employment or aid from the state agricultural commission, or who sought to have a Latin Catholic sponsor their child at baptism. Though not official state policy, the campaign was widely pursued in Galicia up to 1939 with the cooperation of nationalist officers and officials.[5]

In addition, in 1918–1922, from the great mass of Polish refugees fleeing the Bolsheviks and overcrowded provinces elsewhere in Poland, settlers established pure Polish villages with Latin Catholic churches and schools in non-Polish regions. The men worked as farmers, foresters, and auxiliary border police. Their presence angered the non-Poles and further soured the tense relations between the minorities and the "old" Poles whose families had lived in the borderlands for many generations.[6]

Efforts in Polish Belorussia to unite the Orthodox with Rome under the "Neo-Uniate" Church were obviously frustrated by both Polish ethnic chauvinism and religious prejudice. So divisive and inflammatory were the anti-Belorussian, -German, -Jewish, and -Ukrainian measures taken by the Polish police, army, and government that, in December 1938, Pope Pius XI was moved to speak out, through his nuncio to Poland in Lwów (L'viv):

> [H]aving learned with uneasiness and profound sadness of the antagonisms and struggles that rend the sons of those [nations], as a common Father [I] heartily exhort[] the three communities, the Polish one, the Ruthenian [Ukrainian Greek Catholic] one, and the Armenian one to peaceful co-existence and to mutual understanding and charity.[7]

Absolutely no reconciliation had taken place between the communities by 1939, and the war only exacerbated their divisions.

The Soviet invasion saw a bitter increase in ethnic enmity. Many Belorussians and Ukrainians responded to Soviet propaganda to turn on Polish officers, settlers, and merchants. The retreating Polish army retaliated by burning non-Polish villages and executing suspects. It was Catholic against Catholic, Christian against Christian.

Communist sympathizers among the Jews cooperated with the Reds at all levels, even organizing militias. National minority militias were also formed. Despite the fears of older Jewish people who well remembered the Russo-Polish War of 1920–1922 and Bolshevik behavior, many small groups welcomed the Red Army with bread and salt and floral arches. In addition, Jewish Communists were especially recruited by the new Communist administration in the Soviet-occupied zone to implement decrees and rules. Their collaboration would later be exaggerated by anti-Semites to provide a "reason" for collaborating in the Nazi persecutions and extermination of eastern Polish Jewry.

The result was that "the gap between the Poles and the other nationalities . . . widened into an abyss."[8] All this infighting and confusion only increased the divisions between fellow Catholics of different ethnic groups.

Who was to be "liberated"? And from what? In the words of a Red Army soldier in occupied Poland, "They lied to us, the bastards. They all lied to us.

This isn't the West they told us about!" (The social changes and fraudulent political "choices" engineered in Soviet-occupied Poland would be repeated elsewhere as Stalin's empire grew. What happened in Poland would also happen in the Baltic States, Bessarabia, and Bukovina.)

The Red Soldiers' Surprises

Everywhere, the Red Army discovered that the people being "liberated" were better fed, housed, and employed than the people of the USSR.[9] Eastern Poland was one of the poorest regions of Europe, but to the Red soldiers' eyes, it was a paradise. Stores were well stocked with consumer goods, workers lived well, peasants were prosperous, and life in the cities and towns was obviously pleasant. Churches of all denominations as well as synagogues and Tatar mosques were open and full. The Soviet soldiers looked in vain for oppressive capitalists. They decided that the victims were to be found in jail, a logical conclusion for graduates of Stalinism, and so they opened the prisons, releasing hordes of criminals on a defenseless populace, or enlisted the aid of these criminals in taking over eastern Poland.

The ignorance and deprivation of the Soviet occupiers became obvious to all. Soviet women appeared at the opera in nightgowns; Soviet soldiers bought up stores' whole stocks of sausage, bread, and fruit to send home, with exclamations of not having seen such things ever or at least not in a very long time. In conversations with Red soldiers, Russian-speaking Ukrainians and Poles in Lwów discovered that many thought oranges were made in factories, and that Greta Garbo was the name of a factory item.

The local people put away their good clothes: it was dangerous to appear prosperous. Casual conversation on the street ceased: the commissars feared plots everywhere. Religious objects disappeared from schools and public buildings. Public religious and civil shrines often were vandalized or destroyed. National symbols and flags disappeared from sight. There were constant meetings exhorting the people to build Communism and embrace their Soviet "elder brothers" who had brought "true freedom." At the meetings, staged questions were presented from "plants" in the audience, so that the Communists could proclaim the "truth" about Communism and Communist freedom, including the destiny of religion. Soviet commissars, officers, and ordinary soldiers were billeted in private homes and apartments, sometimes occupying entire blocks of residences, creating refugees everywhere. Furniture, factory machinery, electrical systems, livestock, even pet dogs were hauled away in trucks and trains to the Communist Motherland, which obviously was out of everything.

Hordes of refugees from the German zone crowded into the Soviet one. Although some were simply returning home, others were hoping to pass through to Romania or Hungary and reach the Free Poles in the West. Many were Jews, fleeing the beginnings of Nazi persecution. When they joined those who had been bombed and burned out and evicted by the Red Army, the cities and towns were crammed with the homeless.

The Plebiscites of October 1939

By no Western standard could the plebiscites held in western Ukraine and Belorussia be called "free and open." People were forced to vote, often with numbered ballots corresponding to their numbers on the voter lists. Red soldiers and Communist sympathizers went to apartments and offices to pressure voters; soldiers were visible at the polling stations—sometimes voting themselves.

Even though whole villages refused to take part in the plebiscites, and even though many people voided ballots or escaped the "privilege" of voting the outcome was yet another foregone conclusion. According to the "official" count, virtually all the votes were for union with the USSR. On October 26 and 28, the two puppet legislatures set up for western Ukraine and Belorussia nationalized lands owned by the Church and nobility, nationalized all banks and major industries, and petitioned for union with the adjoining Soviet republics. On November 1 and 2, the Supreme Soviet "graciously" consented to the annexations.

Sovietization Begins

After the plebiscites, Stalinism showed its true colors. The oft-repeated warning by Red Army soldiers—"Get used to it or you'll croak"—proved all too prophetic.

Although relatively few churches were permanently closed, churches and religious institutes were nationalized, and heavy taxes were assessed on the church buildings themselves. Jesuit parishes were especially vulnerable. Priests were allotted tiny spaces for living, and their rectories turned over to soldiers and other Soviet immigrants. The houses of many religious orders were shut down and their members forced into smaller quarters or expelled altogether. Crucifixes were removed from classrooms and public buildings. Religious buildings other than churches were subject to new and onerous taxes or confiscation. Connection with the Vatican was slowly choked off. Many priests were arrested and shipped off to Soviet Russia. Generally speaking, Greek Catholics suffered more than Latin Catholics, except in the Pinsk diocese, which was especially brutalized.

All Church schools were secularized; atheism and Marxism-Leninism were aggressively introduced into all areas of education. Teachers were pressured to become Communists, and "corrupt" books were destroyed. Independent faculties of theology and philosophy were eliminated from the universities, and atheism promoted through crude exercises such as one repeated in thousands of elementary classrooms. Children were told to close their eyes and pray to God for candy and presents. When they opened their eyes, nothing new was present in the room. They were then told to close their eyes and ask the Great Stalin for candy and presents. Now when they opened their eyes, great heaps of goodies appeared on the teacher's desk. Such "exercises" did not always succeed, however. As one little Ukrainian boy told his parents, "I peeked and saw the Russians bring in the baskets with everything in them. But I didn't tell anyone what I had seen; I didn't want to get into trouble." [10] Even the children were learning how to be cautious in the new system.

All independent organizations were banned and replaced with Soviet ones. Polish army officers and enlisted men remained in Soviet prisoner of war camps and those who had been released were rounded up in 1940–1941 and shipped off to new camps. The budding nationalism of the minorities was quickly nipped as Russification intensified. All non-Communists capable of leadership were systematically removed and either executed or sent to Soviet concentration camps. Over bitter opposition, all the peasants' farms, both new farms and those existing before the war, were collectivized.

Persecution of the Latin Catholic Church in Former Eastern Poland

After October 10, 1939, all or part of six Latin Catholic dioceses once in Poland were now inside the USSR (Lithuania annexed the city of Vilnius and part of its district). The archdiocese of Lwów (L'viv) and the Pinsk, Lutsk, and Łomża dioceses were totally under Soviet rule. The archdiocese of Vilnius (Vilna) and the Przemyśl diocese were divided between the Soviets and the Nazis. Latin Catholics numbered 6.5 million in 1939; although most were ethnic Poles, many were ethnic Belorussians who had adopted Latin Catholicism when Greek Catholicism was banned under the tsars. Others were ethnic Germans or Polonized Armenians, Germans, Belorussians, or Ukrainians.

In Galicia, perhaps as many as 35 percent of the Latin Catholics were *Latynnyky*, ethnic Ukrainians who had switched from the Greek Catholic to the Latin Catholic Church because of social, economic, or governmental pressures (see "Galicia" below). Nearly all the Ukrainian gentry, for example, had become Latin Catholics by the early 1930s. Thus, although Metropolitan Sheptytsky, head of the Ukrainian Catholic Church and descended from a noble family, and his brother Klement had returned to the Greek Catholic Church of their ancestors, most of their relatives remained faithful Latin Catholics. Some of these non-Polish Latin Catholics retained a non-Polish ethnic awareness, but most were becoming Polish in their orientation.

The Polish Latin Catholic monasteries and convents outside Galicia were attacked first, with Red Army soldiers being billeted there and with monks and nuns expelled to find other quarters. When, for example, Red soldiers confiscated the Jesuit seminary in Albertyn, Father Walter Ciszek wrote, "they hit the seminary like old October revolutionaries storming the Winter Palace." Library books were thrown out the windows to be ground into pulp; priests were crowded into one room, with refugee families put in the other rooms; a statue of the Sacred Heart was destroyed; and religious ceremonies were disrupted.[11]

After the plebiscites, churches could be used for worship only if their congregations could pay the heavy taxes. The extensive network of Church schools was secularized, and religion could not be taught in any schools. Religious newspapers and magazines were shut down, and antireligious propaganda and slanders were promoted. It became increasingly difficult for Catholic bishops to have any contact with the Holy See. Many Latin Catholic rectories were confiscated, and the priests forced to look for new lodgings in towns filled with refugees and homeless. Although some Latin Catholic seminaries were shut down, others were spared, according to local circumstance (see "Galicia" below). The Latin Catholic seminary in the Przemyśl diocese, for example, was untouched, the churches still open, and Mass celebrated in November 1939, apparently because the bulk of the diocese was in the German zone and the Soviets wanted to keep the people calm.[12]

Belorussia

In the Belorussian part of eastern Poland, three dioceses came under Soviet rule here: Pinsk, Łomża, and Lutsk. In October 1940, the papal Nuncio wrote that all of the seminaries and monasteries had been closed and given over to use by soldiers, and all of the churches nationalized.[13] In 1939, the archdiocese of Vilnius lost 890,000 Catholics in 238 parishes, 53 monastic churches, and 136 chapels to the Soviets. Nearly all of these were of the Latin Rite. Łomża diocese lost 7 parishes to Soviet rule.[14]

The Pinsk diocese suffered the harshest persecution of any Latin Catholic community in the Belorussian part of eastern Poland, because it was so far to the east, and so isolated from any foreign presence. Furthermore, Bishop Casimir Bukraba was incapacitated by illness, and his auxiliary, Bishop Charles Niemira, was trapped in German-occupied Warsaw.

In 1939, the Pinsk diocese had 126 parishes, 119 chapels, 35 monastic and private churches, nearly 243,000 Latin Catholics and more than 11,000 Byzantine Catholics.[15] Strapped with astronomical taxes, its churches faced mass closure and conversion to secular use; moreover, its largely Catholic population suffered from mass relocations as well.[16] In the city of Pinsk, the Jesuit novitiate and juniorate were both devastated and the cathedral severely damaged.[17] When the Red Army occupied the city, gunners used the cathedral's great towers for target practice. One Polish woman claimed she saw Saint Andrew Bobola (who had been buried in the cathedral) appear above the flames in agony.

Of the sixteen priests arrested and jailed or shipped off to Soviet concentration camps, four died.[18] The curate at Pruzana, Father Casimir Swiatek, was taken on charges of being anti-Soviet and was sentenced to death: he miraculously escaped execution during the German invasion in 1941.[19] At Albertyn, the Jesuits maintained two churches for the Latin Catholics and "Neo-Uniates." Father Ciszek was named superior because of his American citizenship, the United States still being neutral. In spite of that precaution, the entire mission was damaged and looted. The Greek Catholic chapel was shut down in October 1939, shortly after the town fell to the Red Army. As for the Latin Catholic parish, Father Ciszek wrote that, as a result of Soviet intimidation, and interference, the work of the Jesuits was destroyed in a matter of weeks.[20]

Galicia

The counties that made up the traditional Ukrainian region of Galicia had been experiencing some of the worst of the difficulties in the 1930s. Galicia was home to over 5.8 million people in 1938.[21] According to statistics assembled by émigré Ukrainian demographer Volodymyr Kubijovych, who worked with prewar Polish census figures, In January 1939, more than 3.7 million Galicians were ethnic Ukrainians (64 percent). "Old" Poles numbered 875,000 (15 percent); Jews, 570,000 (10 percent); *Latynnyky,* 515,000 (9 percent). The balance of the population consisted of Polish colonists, 72,250; Ukrainians using Polish language, 16,405; and "others" (ethnic Germans, Czechs, Armenians, Karaites, and Russians), 49,040.[22] Most of the "others" were ethnic Germans, living in a variety of colonies that dated back to three waves of German settlement, in 1781–1785, in 1802–1805, and in 1810–1848, and coming largely from the Latin Catholic regions of Austria, Bohemia, and southwest Germany, although Kubijovych reports many Evangelicals as well.[23] Both ethnic Germans and Czechs were subjected to intensive Polonization, as well as to Ukrainianization, but on a smaller scale.

Although Galicia was the Ukrainian stronghold in Poland, the Polish population had a long history here. In 1931, in the capital city of Lwów (L'viv) over 50 percent of the residents were Latin Catholics, less than 16 percent were Greek Catholics, and the remaining 34 percent were Jews (with a few Armenians).[24] Because Poles had settled in eastern Galicia from the thirteenth century, the province was as much their home as it was the Ukrainians'.

Overall, the Greek Catholics made up 72 percent of Galicia's Christian population, and the Latin Catholics 27 percent. Over one-third of the Latin Catholics were *Latynnyky,* a sore spot with the Ukrainian Greek Catholic Church.[25] Because young *Latynnyky* were steadily dropping Ukrainian in favor of Polish in the 1930s, this population seemed destined to be lost to the Ukrainian nation entirely. Government-sponsored Polish chauvinism in Galicia had exacerbated the ethnic tensions between the two nationalities and the Depression had hit hard.

Thus, entries such as this for Drohobych County are common in Kubijovych's exhaustive text: "These had all been strictly Ukrainian villages, until the development and growth of the petroleum industry. . . . Under Polish rule only Ukrainians who converted to Roman Catholicism were hired."[26] Notations such as "These were former Greek Catholics who changed rites during the 1930s as a result of efforts of the gentry" or "This includes members of the Ukrainian gentry who changed rites in order to obtain work" or "They were Ukrainians who converted to Latin Catholicism to take part in the land parcelation" can be found on every single page describing the population of the Galician villages. It is especially sad to read that Latin Catholic monasteries and Church estates repeatedly induced people to abandon the Greek Catholic Church, either through local influence or in order to obtain employment, a practice dating to the Dominican missions of the 1200s and one condemned by a succession of popes since that time.

Throughout Galicia, Ukrainian hereditary leadership had given way to

Latin Catholicism and Polish identity, and there were continual pressures on ordinary worker and peasant Ukrainians to become Latin Catholic and ultimately Polish in order to secure their fair share of jobs and land. These pressures, and growing Ukrainian national pride, gave rise to serious divisions between the Latin and Greek Catholic Churches and between Polish and Ukrainian nationalities, divisions that would lead to fratricidal bloodshed during World War II.

Although Latin Catholics experienced persecution at the hands of the Soviets here as in the north, they were deliberately treated less harshly than the Greek Catholics. The Latin Catholic seminary in Lwów (L'viv) was pointedly spared, whereas the Ukrainian Greek Catholic one was not.[27] The Soviets were working hard to exploit the Polish-Ukrainian divisions mentioned above.

At the same time, life was not easy for the Latin Catholic Metropolia either. The Latin metropolitan, Archbishop Boleslaw Twardowski of Lwów (L'viv), reported in 1943 that 10 priests and 6 monks were murdered during the Soviet occupation. All Latin Catholic churches were heavily taxed; all Church hospitals, orphanages, monasteries and schools nationalized; and all archdiocesan and parish records and archives confiscated. Archbishop Twardowski and his auxiliary, Bishop Eugene Baziak, were evicted, and their episcopal residences vandalized. Although the seminary was not closed, its faculty and students had to find separate housing in the overcrowded city.[28] During the withdrawal of the Red Army from Galicia, soldiers took the time to attack the Dominican Monastery in Czortkow/Chortkiv, on July 2, 1941. Father Hieronymus Longava, who was known in the region as being filled with the "light of unending love" was brutally attacked in his sick-bed and burned alive. Fathers Yacer Misyuta, Ustin Spirluc, and Anatoli Znamiroskiy were taken from the monastery and murdered on the banks of the Siret River. Finally, the soldiers tortured and then killed four Brothers; Andriy Boyanovsky, Reginald Chervonka, Karol Ivanishiv, and Josef Vincentovich. One victim was eighty-four years old; none were a danger to the retreat of the Red Army. It was a parting blow for the Catholics in Galicia.[29]

In the city of Lwów (L'viv), where the old Jesuit college and Saints Peter and Paul's Church had both been damaged by air raids, the Jesuits carried on retreats and helped Polish and Jewish refugees. On the pretext that it was an arms depot for anti-Soviet partisans, Red soldiers tore down the college church. In Ternopol' (Ternopil) the Jesuits were expelled from their house, and their church was confiscated.[29]

The bulk of the Galician Germans including many Latin Catholics, were forcibly relocated to Germany and to the Warthegau in Nazi-occupied

Poland.[30] The removal of the Galician Germans effectively depopulated entire communities: for example, in 1934, in Kolomya County, in the cluster of villages around Catholic Mariahilf, 1,427 of the 1,497 residents were German; in Stryj County, 250 of the 300 residents in Annaberg were German, as were 935 of the 1,030 in Brygidyn, and 680 out of 730 in Feliziental.[31] The Soviets forcibly removed virtually all 72,000 Polish colonists—who were active Latin Catholics—from Galicia, as well as many of the "Old" Poles and *Latynnyky*.[32] Thus thousands of Galician farms and village and town homes were left abandoned and desolate.

The Ukrainian Greek Catholic Church

Home to some 3.4 million faithful in one archeparchy (Lwów, L'viv) and two eparchies (Stanislav and Przemyśl), the Ukrainian Catholic Metropolia was not only the primary organization for Byzantine Catholics in the Republic of Poland in 1939, but was the principal supporter of Ukrainian national identity, having sponsored the growth of national awareness under the Austrians,[33] and having defended both the Ukrainian national ideal and the Ukrainian Orthodox minority during Polish persecution.[34] It was headed by Metropolitan Andrei Sheptytsky, revered by all the Ukrainians and a stalwart figure who commanded the respect, if not the affection, of the Communists as well. He served from the symbolic heart of Ukrainian Catholicism, the baroque Cathedral of Saint George in Lwów (L'viv).

Prewar Divisions in the Greek Catholic Church

In the 1930s, the Greek Catholic Church was experiencing conflict over its identity: Was it a Ukrainian Catholic Church or a Slavic-based Greek Catholic one? Along with that conflict went serious issues concerning the life of the Church.

Against the ancient tradition of the Eastern Catholic Churches, clerical celibacy was introduced into two eparchies (Przemyśl and Stanislav). Although celibacy was seen by some as a enabling smaller and poorer parishes to support a resident pastor (nearly 30 percent of the archeparchy's parishes did not have a resident priest in 1937), the married clergy had been a strong source of Ukrainian religious and national culture,[35] and a celibate parish clergy was an obvious imitation of the Latin Catholic Church. The bishop of Stanislav favored the introduction not only of clerical celibacy, but also of the Gregorian calendar and "anything to strengthen ties" with the Western Church, while keeping Byzantine liturgy. Thus, although 80 percent of the archeparchy's secular clergy were married, only 63 percent of the Stanislav eparchy's were—and a mere 2 percent of the Przemyśl eparchy's.[36]

Liturgical reform—aimed at eliminating the many Latinizations that had crept into the Divine Liturgy, church services, and church decoration, and into popular piety from the Polish Latin Catholics—aroused passionate feelings. The Oriental Congregation had written to the Ukrainian Catholics back in 1923 asking that they eliminate all the "alterations" (Latinizations) sanctioned by the Synod of Zamość in 1720.[37] Dissension arose not only at the parish level, but at the highest levels of the Ukrainian Catholic Church. The Metropolitan's "purified" *Liturgikons* (for the celebration of the Eucharist) published in 1929 and 1930 were opposed by his own bishops. Bishop Hryhorii Khomyshyn, for example, perceived "Byzantinisms" as anti-Catholic. Although, to improve the chances of Orthodox union with Rome and to retrieve an authentic East Slavic Catholic spirituality, Sheptytsky worked at restoring authentic Byzantine-Ukrainian usages in place of Polish Latin Catholic ones, he was also keenly sensitive to the pastoral needs of parishioners for more participation in liturgical services and their hunger for spiritual growth. In 1938, after years of acrimonious debate, Rome was just beginning to coordinate compilation and publication of new service and prayer books for all the Byzantine-Slavic Catholics of Europe.[38]

The metropolitan had no illusions regarding Communism, or the fate of Poland. In 1930, he had predicted the war, occupation, and persecution, and had warned his Studite monks to prepare themselves for the inevitable. In 1936, he again warned the monks to prepare for "difficult times" and for the coming martyrdom.[39] Some in Poland heeded his warnings; others dismissed them. The divisions between factions of clergy were exploited by the Soviets in 1939–1941 and again in 1945.

The Occupation

The Ukrainian Catholic Metropolia counted 2,190 parishes, 3 seminaries, 1 theological academy, 29 monasteries, and 120 convents in 1939. Most of the faithful and institutions came under Soviet rule. Only the Apostolic Administration of Lemkowczszyna (129 parishes with 128,000 faithful) and the western part of Przemyśl eparchy (136 parishes, with 216,910 faithful) were in the German occupation zone. There was also an old Ukrainian Catholic colony of miners and laborers in Germany itself, with administrative headquarters at Berlin, dating to 1908 and forming a separate jurisdiction under Lwów (L'viv) since 1927. With the expansion of the Third Reich through the annexations of 1938–1940 and the voluntary and forced migration of workers from Galicia, the Berlin administration grew to a membership of 800,000 in Greater Germany. Together with the more than 300,000 Greek Catholics in the southern part of the German occupation zone, there were about 1.1 million Greek Catholics (Ukrainian, "Neo-Uniate," Russian Catholic émigrés) under German rule in 1939. There were 3.2 million in what became the western Ukrainian SSR.[40] Thus most of the lay believers and clergy of a Church seen as "the last major bastion of Ukrainian nationalist resistance"[41] and known to be both devoted to Rome and firmly opposed to Communism now came under the control of the Russifying, anti-Greek Catholic Soviet regime.

As in the Latin Catholic dioceses, churches were nationalized and heavily taxed, religion expelled from the schools, and children pressured to accept atheism in the Greek Catholic eparchies. The Greek Catholic faithful were also deported: 200,000 from the eparchy of Lwów (L'viv) and another 200,000 from the other eparchies.[42]

Persecution

In other areas, however, the situation of the Greek Catholic eparchies was worse than that of the Latin Catholic dioceses. The Soviets, like their tsarist predecessors, were definitely opposed to the "Uniates." Within days of the Soviet occupation, all Greek Catholic publications were shut down; all reading rooms, bookstores, schools, and libraries purged of religious books, which were destroyed; all teacher colleges, vocational schools, foster homes, shelters, kindergartens, and nurseries nationalized; all seminaries, religious and monastic novitiates and juniorates closed or placed under severe restrictions. Candidates for the priesthood or monastic life had to postpone taking permanent vows, and new vocations were discouraged due to the unsettled conditions.

All the secular Ukrainian Catholic organizations and societies were banned, and all of the property held by the metropolitan, the eparchies, and the religious orders confiscated, as were the monastic archives. All of this was accomplished even before the puppet "People's Assembly" convened.[43] Latin Catholics would not encounter such rapid Sovietization until after annexation.

As under the tsars, all monasteries and convents were closed, as were all seminaries, and the monks and nuns dispersed. The buildings were occupied by Red Army troops. In Lwów (L'viv), only twelve student priests could be accommodated privately with secret classes; the rest were sent home. Many priests were expelled from their rectories, even in Lwów itself.

The forced relocations of 1941 cost the metropolia's priests dearly: 20 from the Przemyśl eparchy, 8 from the Stanislav eparchy, and 30 from the archeparchy of Lwów were sent east. The Soviets killed three priests outright in Stanislav; they tried to poison Bishop Khomyshyn and his auxiliary, Bishop Ivan Liatyshevskyi. Some priests from that eparchy were also drafted into the Red Army. The Vatican estimated that some 70 Ukrainian priests were deported and that several of these were "barbarously murdered." Two Studite monks were tortured and shot; at Kropynva, the Studite priest Father Januarius was dragged behind a horse and bayoneted to death; three other priests were murdered, including one who served as a chaplain to the Ukrainian resistance.[44]

Believers were confronted with direct intimidation. Mother Superior Iosyfa Viter of the Studite Nuns in Lwów, was interrogated forty-seven times by the NKVD and tortured to try to force her to denounce the Metropolitan as a Ukrainian nationalist traitor. Lay believers and priests alike were pressured to spy on the bishops, and subjected to blackmail and random arrests, as well as psychological and physical torture.[45]

First Attempts at Schism

Again as under the tsars, the government attempted to create a separate National Greek Catholic Church, and to introduce Orthodoxy into an almost exclusively Greek Catholic environment. Although the Orthodox had only one parish in the city of Lwów (L'viv), at the Church of Saint Nicholas,[46] with the connivance of the Kremlin, a Russian Orthodox bishop was appointed to take up residence there in March 1941 (he was prevented from doing so by the German invasion) and a new Orthodox eparchy founded. Playing upon the divisions caused by the liturgical reform movement and imposition of celibacy, and by the resentment of many Ukrainians toward the Vatican's policies regarding their Church, the Soviets hoped to create a schismatic Catholic Church. Father Havriil Kostelnyk, a leading priest in the city of Lwów and the chief spokesman for de-Latinizing the life of the Church, was pressured to lead the new Church. Though the Soviets arrested his son, he refused to cooperate.[47] (The situation would change in 1946.)

Expansion of the Hierarchy

Seeking to strengthen his Church against the day of full-fledged persecution, on October 10, 1939, three weeks after the occupation began, Metropolitan Sheptytsky wrote to Rome to organize his succession and to confirm the powers given him by Pope Pius X. On December 22, Josef Slipyj—future cardinal and Confessor for the Faith—was secretly ordained as Sheptytsky's coadjutor with right of succession. The ordination was performed by Bishops Budka and Charnetsky, both destined to die as martyrs. The new bishop was given the wooden staff, ring, and missal that the Metropolitan had used when he was a prisoner of tsarist Russia in the secret ordination of Bishop Josef Botsian in 1914.[48]

Under the authority granted him by Pope Pius X in 1907 regarding the lands of the Russian Empire, the Metropolitan expanded his Church's hierarchy and extended its area of administration. By September 1940, he had named four apostolic exarchs for the USSR: one for Belorussia, Anton Niemancewicz, SJ; two for Ukraine outside Galicia: Mykola Charnetsky for Volhynia and occupied Poland (already serving as apostolic visitor to the "Neo-Uniates" in northeast Poland) and Josef Slipyj for Great Ukraine (the territory to the east of Galicia); and his own brother, Klement, for Great Russia and Siberia. By this move, Sheptytsky covered the territory inhabited by Greek Catholics who were part of the old Greek Catholic patrimony as well as that to which believers were being deported on a regular basis. In addition, he gave his Church more bishops to ordain new priests (and thus provide more parishioners with sacraments) and to administer Church life.

The Reverend Doctor Peter Verhun, who had been a pastor and professor of Church studies in Berlin, was elevated to exarch of Germany. He now became the apostolic administrator for the Ukrainian and Russian Greek Catholic émigrés and laborers in Germany, with jurisdiction over all of the old German Reich.[49] (The faithful in Berlin continued to meet in the Latin Catholic parish of Holy Family Church in Prenzlauer-Berg.)

Unbeknownst to Metropolitan Sheptytsky, however, Pope Pius XII had restricted his authority to Galicia on May 30, 1940. When Rome learned of his appointments, a restrictive letter was sent converting the exarchs to temporary apostolic administrators. This was done to placate the Polish Latin Catholic bishops because there had been no Greek Catholic bishops in their territory.[50] The exarchs turned apostolic administrators wrote back to Rome that they were resolved "to continue to adhere to [their] obligations with respect to the union of churches . . . as far as the situation in Soviet Russia will allow this."[51] To that end, Sheptytsky convened two synods, in September 1940 and in May 1941.[52] The synods emphasized preparation for union of the Orthodox with Rome, rules for the guidance of the dispersed monks and nuns, catechesis, and liturgical life. The 1941 synod, in particular, emphasized the removal of

Latinizations and the bringing of greater uniformity into parish worship so as to hasten union of the Orthodox with Rome.

When the Communists confiscated the metropolitan's mimeograph machine, he summoned all the priests in the city of Lwów once a week and dictated pastoral letters to them. They wrote several copies each, and then distributed them to neighboring parish priests, who repeated the process until the entire archdiocese was covered.[53]

Religious Renewal

Thirty seminarians in the Lwów metropolia were allowed to continue their studies. The churches of the 1,267 parishes remained open and were packed. Priests' personal possessions and the churches themselves were guarded by the faithful.[54] Because the confiscation of Church lands left the parishes and priests without a solid base of financial support, the survival of the priests and the maintenance of the churches and their use for religious purposes now depended entirely on the offerings of an increasingly impoverished laity. As for the farmland, even the very poor peasants were reluctant to take Church land over for their use from the authorities. Those who appropriated land were subject to excommunication, and many people just felt it improper to use lands that had been given over to produce income for their parish.[55]

Furthermore, the Metropolitan emphasized the need for continued renewal in the parishes and among the faithful. Letters of exhortation encouraged parents to teach the Faith at home and priests to organize religious circles for students both in church and private homes. The recruitment of catechists and evangelists was emphasized. Significant changes were introduced into parish life: to increase popular understanding, Old Church Slavonic was replaced with vernacular Ukrainian in the Scriptures and parts of the Divine Liturgy; because people were now forced to work on Sundays and holy days, Divine Liturgy was offered in the evening on those days; and popular singing was ordered to be introduced in place of choirs so that more people could participate in the services. Religious services could be offered outside of church buildings, and priests were allowed to administer the sacraments secretly to believers in hospitals under atheist control.[56] (These measures would not only strengthen the Church during the war, but also prove invaluable after the final Soviet annexation in 1945.)

The "Neo-Uniate" Greek Catholics

As we have seen, even though the Belorussian Greek Catholic Church was forced into the catacombs after 1839, the idea of Church union had endured. Thus former Greek Catholics and their descendants had accomplished the "great return" of 1905–1907. The deep-rooted nature of the union in Belorussia had been demonstrated by the effect of Exarch Feodorov's 1922 visits to Mogilev, Sophiisky, and Vitebsk, where he was greeted with the exclamation "The Union has returned!" In Poland in 1939, the old Belorussian Greek Catholic Church had some 40,000 faithful under Latin Catholic administration. Its resurrection and difficult history in the Republic of Poland are worth recounting here.

Now in the newly expanded Belorussian Soviet Socialist Republic (BSSR), the government suddenly faced a large Byzantine Catholic population connected with the old *uporstvuyushchie*.[57] Dubbed "Neo-Uniates," the "stubborn ones" had initiated their movement in northeastern Poland for a variety of reasons. Many older followers genuinely longed for the restoration of the Greek Catholic Church; they "remembered the days when the entire population belonged to the Uniate Church," as the mayor of BiaŁa (Bielsko-BiaŁa) wrote to the governor in Lublin in 1927. Many resented the pressured conversion of many Orthodox to Latin Catholicism in 1919–1920; they were very much aware of the serious shortage of Orthodox priests and chaos in the structures of the Orthodox Church in Poland, on the one hand, and of the growing availability of united rite or bi-ritual Latin priests to serve the "Eastern Rite" Slavic faithful on the other. Some followers sought to achieve an easier political or social life as a Catholic.

The "Neo-Uniates" in 1939

The "Neo-Union" had not been accepted by the bulk of Polish Belorussian faithful by 1939. Its success was hampered by chauvinism on the part of Polish Latin Catholic bishops and priests; by a determined resistance among many young Orthodox believers, especially in the region across the Bug River ("We know that our fathers were beaten with the knout of Orthodoxy [by the tsars,] but we were born Orthodox and will remain so" in the words of a man in Sobibor); and by the intransigence of the Polish Catholic civil authorities, who refused to allow for the establishment of a Byzantine Catholic diocese in the northeast and who harassed all Belorussian religious activity. The situation became so bad that Byzantine Catholic Belorussian priests and students of the

Marians of the Immaculate Conception were expelled from their college at Druja in June and July 1938,[58] forced to emigrate to Harbin, China, where they would serve the local Byzantine Catholics. The Belorussian Catholic newspaper mourned their departure for a far land, when Belorussians were in such need.[59]

The Soviets, for their part, viewed union of the Orthodox and Latin Catholic Churches, and thus the "Neo-Uniate" Church, as a way to Polonize non-Polish Slavs and as designed "to form a single clerical front against the Proletarian Revolution."[60]

The Polish government, which had confiscated Orthodox properties belonging to the old Latin and Greek Catholic Churches (but turned all of them to Latin Catholic use only), also did not approve of the "Neo-Uniate" Church. Marshal Jósef Piłsudski, though a Catholic, favored the creation of an autocephalous Orthodox Church of Poland, headquartered in Warsaw, to serve the Ukrainians and Belorussians. Piłsudski refused to grant state recognition to the mission, and authorized Count Michael Lubienski to publish a book critical of the methods used in the mission in eastern Poland, which in a turn led to creation of a row involving the Church and the Polish press.[61]

Nevertheless, the "Neo-Uniate" Church—using the pure Russian Rite[62]—persisted and even spread, starting from Pinsk, especially Pinsk, Slonim, Brest-Litovsk, Baranovichi, and Zhyrovitsi, the home of the famous icon, and Hola. The Church's first superior, French Jesuit Charles Bourgeois, had been forced to leave the country by the Polish bishops because he would not require Orthodox converts to abjure their former faith. But he had been replaced in 1926 by a Polish Jesuit superior, Wolozimierz Piatkiewicz, who had become a great defender of the "Oriental Mission," the priests, and the faithful. Also in 1926, the Jesuit monastery and novitiate had opened at Albertyn, and two more "Neo-Uniate" parishes had been founded. Father Antoni Dabrowski, who ran the mission from 1933 to 1940, was noted for working to keep the "Neo-Uniate" liturgical life pure and free of Latinization. A particular source of the mission's success was that its Jesuit clerics preached in Belorussian, the language of the peasants. In Vilnius (Vilna), children were taught the old Belorussian hymns; at Albertyn, Belorussian history—considered radical innovations for the time.[63]

The mission's forty parishes in the Latin Catholic dioceses of Pinsk, Lublin, Lutsk, Vilnius, and Siedlce were healthy centers of religious life for Belorussians and Ukrainians. The Liturgy was celebrated regularly, with sacraments dispensed to the faithful, who made serious efforts to observe the feast days properly. A "Neo-Uniate" seminary was founded at Dubno, under the direction of the Jesuits, and produced fine priests. Although the mission had no diocese, Rome was able to nominate an apostolic visitor, Ukrainian Greek Catholic Bishop Mykola Charnetsky, CSSR, ordained in 1931 by Metropolitan Sheptytsky.[64] (Charnetsky would die as a Confessor for the Faith in Siberia in 1959.) At the church in Albertyn, "Neo-Uniates" venerated an icon of Our Lady of Zhyrovitsi as a symbol of their connection with the old Greek Catholic Church.[65] At the same time, some of their churches were considered chapels of the local Latin Catholic parish; their clergy were subject to the Latin Catholic bishops and even deans; and they were not allowed to communicate with the metropolia in Galicia[66]—none which, of course, fostered union with Rome.

On the other hand, the "Neo-Uniates" also scored important successes among Polish Latin Catholics. A few bishops did offer continued support. Notable were the Archbishop Romuald Jałbrzykowski of Wilno (Vilnius, Vilna) and Bishops Zygmunt Łozinski of Minsk (exiled), Bukraba of Pinsk, and Henryk Przezdziecki of Siedlce. Many priests of important Latin Catholic Religious Orders, such as the Jesuits, Redemptorists, Pallotines, Capuchins, Basilians, Marians, chose to work in the Byzantine-Slavic Rite, and in the Siedlce diocese the Greek Catholic Studites and Latin Catholic Oblates took a share of pastoral work. A congregation of nuns, the Missionary Sisters of the Sacred Heart,[67] was founded at Warsaw to work among the Belorussians. The principal centers were at Kovel (Redemptorists), Druja (Marians), Albertyn (Jesuits), and Dubno (secular seminary).

Members of these religious orders did much to break down prejudices not only by serving in the parishes, but also by publishing important journals, books, and pamphlets, and by establishing Byzantine-Slavic Rite monasteries and convents. It was this kind of successful work that would bring harmony among Latin and Eastern Catholics and thus increase feelings of unity so worrisome to both Nazis and Soviets.

Especially noteworthy were two "Neo-Uniate" centers: Druja, where the Marian Fathers of the Immaculate Conception produced Bishop Ceslaus Sipovich, who ministered in the Byzantine Rite from 1942 to his death in 1981 and who was much revered by all Belorussian believers;[68] and Albertyn, the home of the American Jesuit Father Walter Ciszek, who became a Gulag prisoner and missionary to Soviet Catholics after 1939. (Another important Jesuit devoted to his Belorussian flock, despite Polish opposition, was Father Anton Nemancevic, whom we met in Petrograd when he was imprisoned and finally expelled from the USSR.)

Soviet Persecution

The Soviet occupiers absorbed all or part of 6 Polish Latin Catholic dioceses; 24 of the 40 "Neo-Uniate" parishes, from Lutsk and Pinsk dioceses, now lay in Soviet territory.[69] As in Galicia, Soviet religious persecution fell harder on the Greek Catholics than on the Latin Catholics,[70] particularly in early 1940 when the Soviet government began to consider an alignment with Russian Orthodoxy, Western pressures opposing persecution relented, and Sovietization pressures increased. The Moscow Patriarchate was allowed to name a Patriarchal bishop in Volhynia, home to three dioceses of the autocephalous Polish Orthodox Church and to the "Neo-Uniate" administrator, with the prospect of integrating both the Orthodox and Greek Catholic faithful into Russian Orthodoxy.

Sufferings in Pinsk and Albertyn

Religious persecution of both Latin and "Neo-Uniate" Belorussian Catholics took its harshest form in Pinsk. When Bishop Bukraba, a supporter of the "Neo-Union" and one of the few bishops to regularly attend conferences on the movement,[71] was hospitalized in Lwów (L'viv) and his auxiliary bishop was trapped in German-occupied Warsaw, this most eastern surviving diocese in Catholic Europe was left leaderless. The Soviets imposed "impossible taxes" of 100,000 rubles on each church in the diocese, constantly interfered in its affairs, and subjected its lay believers to mass relocations. In spring 1940 ten "Neo-Uniate" parishes in the diocese were suppressed,[72] a move that affected a quarter of the pre-1939 Polish total. Although the Soviets, fearing that the rapid fall of capitalism might mean Nazi invasion, when the Western powers fell back in the face of the German offensives, relented in their persecution, there was no restoration of the closed churches.

The "Neo-Uniate" Church of the Assumption in the Jesuit compound at Albertyn continued to function after the town was occupied on October 17. Father Ciszek preached a particularly strong sermon on the text "The fool hath said in his heart there is no God" (Ps. 41:1) when Red Army soldiers intruded into the church. Although he confounded the soldiers, he paid a heavy price: a few days later, the church was desecrated, with soldiers using the church attic as a latrine; the "Neo-Uniate" mission was permanently closed and all worship restricted to the Latin Catholic church building.[73]

The Jesuits were forced to flee: Father Ciszek started his epic journey to the Soviet interior, accompanied by Fathers Nestrov and Makar, by going first to see Metropolitan Sheptysky. Foreign missionaries working among the "Neo-Uniates" were expelled; Polish and Baltic citizens were sent back to their home monasteries. In the winter of 1940, the great Capuchin library of Eastern Christian materials so laboriously created was burned for fuel by occupying soldiers.

Naming the Hierarchy in 1940

Metropolitan Sheptytsky's nominations of apostolic exarchs affected the "Neo-Uniates." The Apostolic Visitor Charnetsky became the exarch of Volhynia and occupied Poland; the Belorussian SSR received its own resident Greek Catholic bishop, the first since 1839, in the person of the Jesuit missionary Anton Nemancevic, named exarch for the Ukrainian Catholic Church in 1940 at the age of 43. Upon his release from prison in Soviet Russia, he was repatriated to eastern Poland, where he became famous for his work among the "Neo-Uniates."[74] He was captured in 1939 by Red Army soldiers, imprisoned once again, then finally released. He chose to be based at Dubno, with Fathers Jerzy Moskwa and Victor Novikov at the persecuted Oriental Seminary.[75]

The pope's decision of May 10, 1940, to name Charnetsky and Nemancevic as apostolic administrators presented the Soviets with two Greek Catholic bishops able to minister to believers in an SSR with strong pro-union sentiments in its eastern part. After all, the triumphant Mogilev and Vitsyebsk visits of the late Exarch Feodorov had taken place only seventeen years before. The Soviets knew their history: closed churches did not mean an end to religious life for these stubborn people. Although no statistics on forced relocations of Belorussian Greek Catholics are yet available, the western Belorussian SSR was not spared.[76]

The Armenian Catholic Metropolia

Armenian Christianity had come to Galicia in the 1200s by way of Crimea and refugees from devastated Kiev. A lively Armenian colony of merchants and jewelers was founded in Galicia. By 1500, there were colonies across the southern Ukraine, in Lutsk, Lwów (L'viv), Zamość, Sniatyn, Stanislav (Ivano-Frankivs'k), and Kamenets. They concentrated themselves in doing fine embroidery, miniature paintings, importing valuables from the East, and other aspects of commercial trade.

In 1763, Armenian Catholics had numbered 3,241, with 41 priests and 22 churches belonging to their archdiocese.[77] After the 1772 partition of Poland, most of the Armenians withdrew from mercantile life and began to acquire land, while remaining a mostly urban population.[78] Although most Armenians in Galicia were Catholic, there were still about 1,000 Armenian Apostolic faithful to the south, in Bukovina.[79] The archdiocese, though not part of the structure of the Armenian Catholic Patriarchal Church, was immediately subject to the Holy See; the archbishop was named by the Vatican, but in accord with the wishes of the Polish government.[80]

The Armenian Cathedral of Lwów had been built in 1363 and was the seat of Armenian Catholic and Apostolic archbishops from 1365 to 1412 and of the Armenian Apostolic archbishop from 1516 to 1630. Bishop Nikol Torosovich accepted union with Rome and, after a long struggle, established the Armenian Catholic Archdiocese (1630–1635).[81] In 1635, the archdiocese had two suffragan dioceses of Armenian Catholics in Russia, at Kamenets and Mogilev. In 1808, however, the archdiocese's jurisdiction was limited to Galicia and Bukovina in the Austrian Empire.[82]

Although the Armenians prospered under Polish rule, because their numbers were not replenished with immigration, they steadily assimilated to both the Polish culture and religion. Indeed, Austria abolished their separate status in 1784;[83] according to one source, by 1900, there were only 1,500 registered Armenians in eastern Galicia,[84] although the Armenian Catholic Church counted 4,000 faithful in 1910.[85] Polonization of the Armenian community continued after the First World War; unlike the Ukrainians, however, the Armenians did not complain.[86] Although Armenian Catholic priests celebrated the Eucharist in Classical Armenian, their congregations sang the accompanying hymns in Polish.[87]

Polonization proceeded naturally an inevitably to the point where, despite the independence of its Church, the Armenian Apostolic community in Bukovina lost its national character.[88] The Armenian Catholic Metropolia continued to exist, however, and there were still people who identified themselves as "Armenian Catholics." In 1919, the metropolia embraced faithful in two countries, Poland and Romania, where the Armenians of Bukovina province were not incorporated into the Armenian Catholic Apostolic Administration of Gherla (Armenierstadt), which served the 36,000 Armenian Catholics in five parishes in Transylvania and elsewhere in Romania).[89]

In 1925, there were 3,609 Armenian Catholics in Poland, and 1,374 in the Bukovina vicariate in Romania. The Armenian Catholics maintained 6 parishes in Galicia and 2 parishes in Bukovina.[90] with 16 priests (celibate following the dictates of the Synod of 1691) working in the metropolia: 7 at the cathedral (3 canons and 4 vicars) and 9 in parishes outside Lwów (L'viv) Armenian Catholics of the archdiocese supported 20 churches and chapels, all open for worship on Sundays and feast days, and 1 lay organization, the Pious Union of the Death of Saint Joseph.[91]

Polish Armenians were concentrated in Lwów (L'viv), with small clusters of about 200 in the southeastern counties, most notably those of Kolomya, Kosów, Stanislav, and Sniatyn. Half lived in Sniatyn and Lysec, with the rest living in a half-dozen small towns.[92] Even in places such as Stanislav, where the Armenians were still in the process of Polonization and conversion to Latin Catholicism,[93] the community was solid enough, in 1925, to fund an extensive restoration of the cathedral.[94] Indeed, the pastor of the Church of the Virgin Mary of Mercies there served as vicar general for the archdiocese.[95]

In the city of Lwów, the heart of the Armenian Catholic Church was at the Assumption Cathedral on Armenian Street. The cathedral complex consisted of the ancient cathedral church, built in classical Armenian style with later additions, a nearby convent, two outdoor shrines (to Saint Christopher and the Crucifixion), the medieval cemetery, and the archbishop's residence and curia offices.[96] The archdiocese also boasted the Torowsiewicz School and a diocesan bank, as well as a museum and library containing valuable and precious antiquities.[97]

The tenacity of Armenian Catholicism in eastern Poland is well illustrated by the history of the cathedral convent, home to Armenian Nuns of Saint Benedict, who traced their community back to three ancient groups of devout Armenian women that had prospered in Kamenets and Jazłowiec, and Lwów itself in seventeenth-century Poland. During the struggle over the Church union, the pro-Catholic Lwów nuns had gathered at Kamenets in 1630, and been forced to flee all the way to Macedonia. Upon returning home, they joined with the Jazłowiec Sisters to establish an Armenian Catholic convent at Lwów in 1680; and in 1690, the community was given the Rule of Saint Benedict by Archbishop Nicholas Torosovich and Pope Alexander III. With 15 nuns and 4 novices in 1932, based in their motherhouse at Skarkosska Place in Lwów, they conducted two schools: a primary school founded in 1785, and a secondary school founded in 1928.[98]

In Bukovina, Armenian religious and cultural life focused on the provincial capital of Czernowitz (Chernivtsi), where the Armenian Catholic Church dated from 1870. With 900 faithful before World War I,[99] Czernowitz was home to most of the province's Armenian Catholics, the rest belonging to the parish of Suczawa, the province's other principal town.[100]

Tragically for the Armenian Catholics, their distinguished and widely respected archbishop, Josyf Teodorowicz, died on December 4, 1938, less than nine months before the crucifixion of Poland. Nominated at the age of 37, he had served as archbishop for thirty-six years, working for solidarity of all citizens. In testimony to his work, the archbishop's funeral at the cathedral was attended by more than 100,000 mourners from all ethnic and religious groups in the city.[101]

In January 1939, the priests of the archdiocese gathered to vote for three candidates from which the Holy See would choose a new archbishop. The Polish government was known to favor the pastor from Czernowitz, Monsignor Lukasiewicz. Pending word from Rome, the vicar capitular, Monsignor Dionysius Kajetanowicz, continued to administer the Church. Because the Holy See had not acted by September 1, there was no archbishop in place for the Armenian Catholics when the war came.[102]

In 1940, the entire metropolia came under Soviet rule. In 1940–1941, about 2,500 Armenian Catholics, half the membership, were shipped off to Siberia; in Lwów, the seven priests were arrested, and heavy taxes were levied on the cathedral complex so as to force its closure. By making heavy sacrifices, however, the Armenian Catholics who remained in western Ukraine were able to pay these taxes. The Oriental Congregation reported that they were "decidedly firm in the profession of their faith."[103]

Mass Deportations from Eastern Poland

They told us to get ready and said that we are going to another oblast in
Russia. They didn't let us take anything away, only what we were wearing.
. . . It was very cold. . . . They gave very little bread and it was impossible to
eat the soup. They didn't let us out of the cars nowhere. . . . That's how we
went for 3 weeks.

—Polish girl, age 14, Lida County

We ate snow like madmen because it was much better than the white
frost on frozen nails in the car. Riding for over two weeks . . . we twice
got a loaf of bread for the family and twice soup with rotten cabbage. . . .
Everywhere one heard groans and crying.

—Polish boy, age 13, Baranovichi County

These children's firsthand accounts capture something of the horror that befell some 1.2 million Polish citizens in 1940–1941. Not one person taken was a criminal. All were taken because they were seen as either being potentially hostile to Soviet power or because they were related to someone who might be. Included among the 14 categories of persons slated for forcible relocation from Vilnius (Vilna) were refugees from the Soviet Union, policemen, ex-Communists, foreigners, Red Cross workers, government employees, business owners, nobles, student activists, military officers, clergy, parish secretaries, parish leaders, people who had been abroad or who had contact with foreign governments, and people who collected stamps or studied Esperanto.[104] The last category reflects Stalin's paranoiac fear of any connection with the outside world. Removed with these people were spouses, parents, children, close friends, and even overnight guests.

Most were awakened by the pounding of rifle butts on their door. The mass deportations were scheduled for early hours of the morning so as to catch people when they were deep asleep, and thus easily disoriented. They had as little as thirty minutes but never more than an hour or two to gather up clothing, bedding, and food. No one in a household was spared, and neither age nor physical condition could prevent someone from being removed: soldiers and Party activists carried out the sick, the elderly, and the pregnant along with the others. Like the Nazis with the Jews, the Communists wanted to make a clean sweep.

Brought to rail yards, the victims were herded into wooden boxcars, 60–80 people to a car. Although some cars had stoves and hastily built bunkbeds, many had only straw. A hole in the floor or a single bucket served as an open lavatory for everyone. The doors were slammed shut and locks put on, the soldiers and NKVD officers climbed aboard, and the trains headed east.

> The conditions in those trains defy coherent language . . . sealed, windowless, and unheated cattle-wagons, for a winter journey of three, four, five, or even six thousand miles . . . derangement, frostbite, starvation, infanticide, even cannibalism. . . . [T]hose who survived the trains often faced further journeys in the holds of riverboats, or on the backs of open lorries, to the farthest recesses of the Soviet wilderness.[105]

Just as the Nazis committed badly needed rolling stock and troops to the transportation and extermination of Jews during the war, so did the Soviets. Forced depositions from eastern Poland and the Baltic States continued during the German invasion in June 1941, and soldiers who should have been fighting at the front were guarding helpless civilians. Indeed, just as the Nazi concentration camps continued to function until the collapse of the Third Reich, so did the Soviet concentration camps. People continued to be arrested and young soldiers continued to serve as guards throughout the war years. Had the Germans not invaded, and respected their treaty with the Soviets, God only knows what would have happened to the Polish nation under Communist rule.

A large portion of those removed were Catholics: practically all of the ethnic Poles, most of the Ukrainians, and many of the Belorussians. These believers brought their Catholic religion into the spiritual wasteland of the Gulag Archipelago. The depth of their faith is obvious from what they carried with them. Though awakened in the middle of the night, and given at most an hour or two to pack a lifetime, they made sure to include holy pictures, bibles, prayerbooks, rosaries, and holy medals in their pitiful sacks of belongings.[106]

Indeed, among believers of all faiths, prayer became more important than bread itself. The Catholic, Orthodox, Protestant and Jewish clergy among those removed in the mass relocations organized services and provided emotional and moral support. Although priests who tried to join the convoys voluntarily were forced out by the NKVD, many were later arrested anyway and began their years of underground ministry. These priests joined the Soviet Catholic tradition of secret Masses, confessions, conferences, and conversions. They were exposed to terrible dangers, not only from the miserable conditions but from Catholics whose faith was not strong enough to withstand the brutal change and who apostatized: one priest was betrayed to the police by his friend and former organist.[107]

For believers faced with starvation, ill treatment, atheistic propaganda, constant abuse, and a death rate as high as 50 percent, Catholicism became the only force that could sustain them. This same Catholicism slowly changed the lives of their Soviet neighbors outside the Faith.

The Losses

Four giant convoys took more than a million people away in February, April, and June 1940, and again in June 1941. These convoys removed 500,000 from Belorussia (300,000 from the northern counties and 200,000 from the southern) and 550,000 from Ukraine (150,000 from the northern counties and 400,000 from the southern). In addition 150,000 were drafted into the Red Army, 180,000 were taken as prisoners of war, and 20,000 were sent to work in Russia as laborers. Slightly more than 50 percent were ethnic Poles, 30 percent were Jews, and 18 percent were ethnic Ukrainians and Belorussians. One out of three were peasants and workers; one out of four were children under the age of fourteen. Half the people were sent to labor camps and prisons, and the others were scattered in settlements across the Soviet Union stretching as far as the Pacific Ocean.[108]

Nearly all the Polish colonists who had been settled in the east as a reward for their military service to the new country in 1918–1922, were removed,[109] as were nationalist leaders of all parties, including local Communists, who were not trusted because of both their time under capitalist rule and their surprise at the terrors of Soviet administration. The people left behind in western Belorussia and Ukraine found themselves leaderless, traumatized, and impoverished by the summer of 1941. When the Red Army was forced to retreat in June and July, countless innocents were put to death by the NKVD in a series of horrendous massacres. The advancing German army found a greatly relieved population with no idea of what horrors awaited it at the hands of its supposed deliverers.

CHAPTER 22

The Great Patriotic War

When elephants fight, it is the grass that suffers.

—African proverb

O n June 22, 1941, Germany invaded Soviet territory. Against an ill-prepared enemy whose leader could not believe the betrayal, the Germans threw 153 of their own divisions, plus troops from Finland, Romania, Italy, Slovakia, Hungary, and Spanish volunteers, along with *Waffen-SS* forces. Millions would die in battle, from wounds or starvation on the infamous Eastern Front; millions more in Soviet camps.

Military and civilian losses of the USSR to the Nazis were about 19.25 million, many of whom died because Stalin failed to prepare his country's defenses or died in battles, massacres, or in such horrors as the siege of Leningrad. But an estimated 13 million people are thought to have died as a result of Stalin's policies;[1] in particular,

1. *scorched-earth withdrawal,* which destroyed towns and villages and condemned millions to flight without prospect of securing food or shelter.

2. *mass relocation of nationalities* under conditions so brutal that one author entitled his work on those responsible *The Nation Killers.* Whole nationalities were deprived of their ancestral homelands.

3. *imprisonment in the Gulag* of Soviet citizens and hapless victims of the annexed territories. Even as the USSR was fighting for its life, it dispatched one million souls to the camps each and every year of the war. The victims included not only the Poles, Balts, and Romanians discussed later, but anyone considered to be a dissenter of any sort, especially from 1943–1945. Wartime worsened the already bad conditions, and huge numbers died of starvation, exposure, illness, torture, and physical abuse. Like the Nazis who continued to use precious trains and soldiers to transport, guard, and kill Jews and other "undesirables" throughout the war, Stalin continued to use trains and trucks

and badly needed Red Army troops to transport, guard, and kill his own "undesirables." Catholics were victims in all of these areas.

Rapprochement with Orthodoxy

With the rout of the Red Army by the invading German forces, Stalin desperately needed to mobilize Soviet defenses. In October 1941, while the government evacuated to Kuybyshev (Samara), Metropolitan Sergius and other Orthodox prelates were removed from Moscow to Ulyanovsk (Simbirsk), Lenin's birthplace, where every Orthodox church had been obliterated, save two that were in ruins. Sergius established a "pitiful outpost" there. His band moved into the former Catholic church and rectory, and renamed it "Our Lady of Kazan' Cathedral," in honor of the the Virgin of Kazan', one of Russia's holiest icons, credited with saving the country from foreign invasion and annihilation. This cathedral would become the Russian Vatican."[2]

The war effort required spiritual as well as material mobilization if the Soviets were to defeat the enemy. Russians and other peoples responded to the invasion with a revival of religious feeling. Stalin moved quickly to turn the upsurge among believers to his ends. The new official promotion of Russian nationalism, of reverence for the elderly and the qualities of the peasant was especially well received by Orthodox believers. Stalin entered into what amounted to a concordat with the Russian Orthodox Church, and into accommodation with the other Soviet religions. The Orthodox, appalled at reports of Nazi barbarism,[3] fervently wanted to save their homeland. Official toleration was extended to Muslims and to a lesser degree to other faiths, but believers of all faiths were expected to support the war effort.

"Restoration" of Russian Orthodoxy

The Orthodox Church had gained millions of believers when the Soviets expanded their borders in 1939–1940. The Communists used two of the four surviving Orthodox bishops to conduct Russification and Sovietization campaigns among the Ukrainian, Belorussian, Estonian, and Latvian Orthodox: the local autonomous and autocephalous Churches were eliminated, and Russian ritual and language imposed on all parishes that escaped being closed. When Hitler invaded in 1941, a well-documented revival of Orthodoxy began in the occupied zones. Although the people turned against their German occupiers because of Nazism and its cruelty, thousands of churches and many monasteries and convents were reestablished.

In Soviet Russia, itself, a few dozen Orthodox churches were opened in 1941, and some new bishops were finally ordained. Metropolitan Sergius condemned the German invasion, and called on believers to rally to the defense of the Motherland. In 1942, the Orthodox hierarchy was enlarged to three metropolitans and eight bishops. In 1943, as the Red Army retook territory where Orthodoxy had revived and where the Greek Catholic Church was large and strong, the Patriarchate was permitted to establish a bank account; that September, Stalin met with the metropolitans in Moscow, and authorized an Orthodox Church Council to elect a new Patriarch, reopen seminaries, establish church shops for candles and icons, ordain bishops and priests, and open new churches. Stalin's "concordat" with the Orthodox Church provided a way, not only to mobilize believers for the war effort, but to stabilize Soviet rule and prevent underground religious movements from taking root.

Again, autocephalous Churches were suppressed, and a campaign launched against the Soviet Catholics. Stalin knew that to obtain troops, military aid, and the opening of a second front, he needed to convince the Allies that religious freedom was being restored, and that democracy was part of Soviet life. His moves regarding the Orthodox greatly helped the "Red Dean" of Canterbury and the Archbishop of York promote this vision to the world. By March 15, 1944, the Russian Orthodox Church had 29 bishops, perhaps 23,000 restored churches, and parishes in the occupied lands of eastern Poland, Romania, and the Baltic States.[4]

Improved Foreign Relations

The "concordat" of the war years helped Stalin gain support, not only in the Allied camp, but also in the Balkans, Eastern Europe, and the Middle East. Balkan Orthodoxy was devastated by the Nazis, and Moscow began to emerge as the logical center for its restoration. Patriarch Sergei began to address the Orthodox of Yugoslavia, Czechoslovakia, Greece, and Bulgaria as his "beloved brethren" in 1943 radio addresses.[5]

The 1944 council that met in Moscow to elect Patriarch Sergius' successor "clearly illustrated the fact that Moscow [had] now become the center of the Orthodox world."[6] Pro-Soviet feeling grew among the Orthodox of the Near East, especially in Lebanon and Palestine, with the Soviets being seen as arbiters between France and Lebanon-Syria and between Greek clergy and Arab laity or as guarantors (the Greek clergy vis-à-vis the Arab laity). A Russian Orthodox chapel was opened inside the former Soviet embassy building in Istanbul (Constantinople), now used as a Soviet summer residence.[7]

During the war it became clear that, in the Orthodox Church, Stalin had a reliable ally to limit the influence of Catholicism. In February 1945, the Orthodox Fathers of the Council went so far as to brand the Vatican as a "shield of Nazi Germany" used to cover up the crimes of the fascists.[8]

As part of his "concordat," Stalin ordered that all the churches turned museums of atheism outside Moscow and Leningrad be closed or transformed into general museums of history[9] (none of the closed churches was returned to religious worship). Although Marxism-Leninism and materialism were taught throughout the war, "overt" atheistic education in the school was stopped. Nevertheless, by 1944, as reflected in the press the Central Committee had committed the Party to teaching the people that the war was being won by Communism, not by "mystical interpretation of life" and "superstition." Although press reports did not directly attack religion, it was obvious that the Party was not going to abandon its antireligious stance. Thus reporters could not mock, at least not in print, Red Army men who wore crosses and said prayers, but they were free to laugh at them. Thus, too, subscriptions by laity to the *Journal of the Moscow Patriarchate* were canceled in September 1944, not for official antireligious reasons, but because of a "paper shortage."

Orthodox Attitudes to the Vatican

In the April 1945 issue, the journal denied that the Pope was Vicar of Christ on Earth. Here Stalin and the Patriarchate were of one mind: Stalin also denied papal authority over his subjects.[11] Metropolitan Alexei (later Patriarch Alexei) condemned the Roman Catholic Church for encouraging crusades of the Swedes and Teutonic Knights.[12]

Fate of Polish Citizens under Soviet Control: Removal, Amnesty, and Recruitment

It is a hard destiny to be Polish.
—Diary of Major Adam Solski, murdered at Katyn, 1940

For Polish citizens who had escaped execution and who had survived forcible removal by their Soviet occupiers, the German invasion would mean an amnesty for the crimes they had been falsely accused of. They would elude, at least for a time, the Soviet genocide that had eliminated their natural leaders—the career officers, educated professionals, and priests who died in the massacres at Katyn and near Miednoye and Kharkov—the genocide that had already killed half the innocents removed in 1940–1941.

On the eve of that amnesty, 1.7 million Polish citizens were sent to

1. concentration camps in former eastern Poland (99 camps) and the prewar Soviet Union (51 camps), under atrocious conditions without medical care and adequate food; 100,000 Polish troops;

2. Northern European Russia; 220,000 Polish citizens forcibly removed in February 1940;

3. Kazakhstan; 320,000 Polish women and children forcibly removed in April, 1940;

4. Arkhangel'sk, Sverdlovs'k, Novosibirsk, Krasnoyarsk, and the Bashkir and Mari ASSRS: 960,000 Polish citizens fleeing the German invaders, rounded up in the summer of 1940;

5. across the entire Soviet Union: 100,000 Polish residents of Wilno (Vilnius, Vilna) forcibly removed in June 1941.

Of these 1.7 million people forcibly removed and subjected to deprivation, humiliation, starvation, abuse, and torture, 850,000—or one-half—had died by the time of the amnesty. Shortly after the German invasion, on June 30, 1941, the survivors were granted amnesty for crimes they had never committed. On July 14, the Polish government signed a military agreement with Moscow to raise 100,000 troops from the Polish internees under the leadership of General Wladyslaw Anders. A Polish Protestant, Anders had suffered torture in the Lubyanka prison. He demanded the right to organize his army on the basis of the old laws of the Republic of Poland, which meant that there would be religious chaplains and women's units (these became refuges for many nuns). Chaplaincies were established for Catholics (under Father Cienski), Orthodox, Jews, and Protestants. A Polish Mass for the survivors was held at Saint Louis des Français in Moscow on September 7. By October, 36,000 men had reported for the "Anders Army," malnourished and physically weak, but filled with a proud spirit.

On December 4, 1941, Stalin announced that the new recruits would be moved south and fed; that all surviving Polish internees would be freed; that as many as 100,000 could serve in the army; and that Bishop Josef Gawlina could come to the USSR and visit the army. Release of civilians was painfully slow. Ethnic Belorussians, Ukrainians, Lithuanians, and Jews were claimed by the USSR as Soviet citizens and detained, sometimes permanently. Despite NKVD resistance, however, Polish army officials were able to admit at least some Polish Jews into the army and civilian centers; Bishop Gawlina secured the release of two rabbis, their families, and children from a Jewish orphanage in the Soviet Union in the summer of 1942.

For all Stalin's promises, the Polish forces were denied adequate rations and medical supplies. Forced to set up their military camps in unhealthy areas, half became ill in epidemics.

Restoration of Catholic Religious Life in the Polish Army Gathering Centers

Priests were needed for pastoral work, and over the objections of some Red Army generals, were assigned to provide spiritual and moral education and religious services for the Polish soldiers and for their families in the gathering centers: there were children to be baptized and instructed, weddings to be held.[13] Orphans were attached to the army, and instructed by the nuns in the women's auxiliary. Pastoral care was also extended—at great risk—to released Polish internees not attached to the army.

Bishop Gawlina's vicar general reached the headquarters of General Anders's army in November 1941 and preached in the new chapel. Soldiers from Kozelsk camp brought their carved image of Our Lady of Kozelsk with them, which became Our Lady of Victory. The army and its hospitals, schools, civilians, and troops were then scattered across the southern republics, amid Muslims who did not understand them and who feared them. It was the Poles' fervent celebration of Lent and Easter that finally moved the locals to assist them. Indeed, the public Palm Sunday processions of 1942 included many Muslim participants, along with Russian Orthodox. Although the Muslims resented the Red Army, Orthodox missionaries, and Russian atheists, they came to like the Catholic Poles.

Bishop Gawlina continued to send the exiled Poles crucifixes, portable altars, prayerbooks, and other religious supplies. In April 1942, the bishop was finally allowed in for a brief visit. Hounded by NKVD agents and Polish traitors, he continued to celebrate Mass, administer Confirmation, and wept over the conditions of the starving children. On June 27, he received General Anders into the Church: the general had been deeply moved by the faith of the Catholic chaplains and soldiers. Muslims welcomed Bishop Gawlina as "the great Polish mullah," with processions and attendance at Masses. The bishop ordained three seminarians among the troops in Yanigyul', and removed two unworthy priests from the ministry. He asked permission to stay permanently in the USSR and to establish regular missions with 20 of the 39 Polish priests who had been released (50 were still in prison).

But times were darkening. On June 11, Britain and the USSR signed a mutual assistance treaty, and the western powers promised aid to Stalin. Shortly afterward, General Georgii Zhukov forbade the establishment of permanent Catholic missions to exiled Polish civilians, and in August 1942, religious shipments from abroad for Catholics in the Soviet Union were stopped. Religious freedoms were once again denied: the NKVD resumed its strict surveillance and even its arrests of Polish priests, all the while complaining that the benefits of Gawlina's two months in the south would take twenty years to undo.

The Polish government and military officials came to realize that not only were they not going to get all their citizens released, but that vast numbers had already perished. Attempts to receive a reckoning of what had happened failed. As Stalin observed with brutal irony, "The people of the Soviet Union are well disposed towards the Poles. But officials can make mistakes." [14] On April 12, 1943, one of those "mistakes" would come to light.

Katyn

> The victim's hands were first tied behind his back . . . the cord was
> passed down the back, looped around the bound hands and tied again at
> the neck. . . . Every move of his arms only tightened the noose around
> his neck.
> —Rudolph Chelminski, "Katyn: Anatomy of a Massacre"

Among those who perished under Stalin's rule were over 15,000 Polish officers. The USSR had taken 250,000 Polish soldiers as prisoners of war. The enlisted men were sent to slave labor or shot, and the officers interned in special camps. Of the 15,570 officers interned, only 448 were recruited to the Communist line and the USSR's so-called army of liberation. When the head of this army asked for his comrades, he was told by the deputy head of the NKVD, "No, not those, we made a big mistake concerning those."

The missing officers had resisted all Communist influence. Their barracks in 1939–1940 were home to Masses held by the priests imprisoned with them, to prayer meetings, and to the singing of the banned Polish national anthem: "God Save Poland." Interned at the special camps of Kozelsk, Ostashkov, and Starobielsk in western Soviet Russia, near Smolensk, very few survived. Of 5,000 who refused to accommodate themselves to Communism at the Kozelsk camp, for example, only 225 were spared. From another such group at another camp, only one man is known to have survived, simply because he was transferred to Moscow for interrogations at the time that the men were being removed from his camp. Virtually the entire Polish officer corps disappeared into the mists of Stalinist lies: no family received a letter after May 1940, and Polish government appeals were met with denials and brush-offs.

The Poles at Kozelsk embodied the qualities of Poland that Stalin feared: education, independent thought, religiosity, and outreach to Soviet Catholics. The 5000 prisoners were placed in a former Orthodox monastery. The upper ranks, all of the intelligentsia, were put into the main monastery, with the lesser ranks put into the former hermits' huts in the monks' settlement around the monastery and church.

Only the prisoners knew the priests; the Soviets knew that there were priests, but could not discover who they were. In the face of absolute prohibitions, the Poles nevertheless continued to conduct their religious life. A wood carving of a crowned Madonna and Child was made and titled "Our Lady of Kozelsk," and a Nativity set was created for Christmas 1939. Confessions were heard while walking in pairs; Mass was celebrated at 9 P.M. at the monastery using wine made from fermented raisins and wafers made from miraculously procured flour. When a second lieutenant had asked the camp cook for flour in Russian, but had blurted out in Polish "to make *oplatki*" (special Christmas wafers that resembled the Sacred Host), the cook had replied by reciting the basic prayers of the Rosary—the Our Father, Hail Mary, and Glory Be—in flawless Polish with an eastern Polish accent, concluding with "Mary Queen of Poland, intercede for us," and had then given the lieutenant the needed flour. Here was living proof of the success of efforts to preserve the Faith in those priestless times. Shortly after the cook was removed.[15]

The quality of life in Kozelsk was marked by Christian charity. Though brutalized behind barbed wire, and roughly treated by guards who would even kill a stray dog that had befriended the Poles, the prisoners countered hate with love; they shared their rations and gave each other support after interrogations. As for the second lieutenant, he and 224 others escaped questioning: the German invasion of 1941 brought them liberty with the Anders Army. (He went on to be ordained a priest, and to return to Katyn to celebrate a graveside Requiem Mass for his lost friends on All Saints Day in 1988.)

The site of the Katyn Massacre was uncovered in 1943 by an anti-Communist peasant, Ivan Krivozertsev, who informed German officers in the area. The NKVD's infamous Black Ravens had driven some 4,300 Polish officers into the forest, to a spot called "Goat Hill." Nearly all were executed in the classic Chekist way: one shot in the back of the neck, exiting at the forehead. The slaughter required six weeks, and an army of killers. Despite their bindings, many of the 4,321 victims resisted, only to be stabbed with bayonets.[16]

Were the priests able to whisper words of absolution to their comrades before they died? As rank after rank of victims fell into the yawning pits, what thoughts of family and God soared heavenward? What cries of anguish and abandonment rang out in this brooding forest?

And what became of the other 11,100 officers? Though there were persistent rumors among Polish exiles and Soviet Gulag prisoners that they were put on barges in the White Sea and drowned when the barges were bombarded by the Soviet navy, no trace was found of these men. (At least not until 1990, fifty long years after their slaughter. The 6,200 officers from the Ostashkov camp were murdered 90 miles north of Moscow, again in a forest, near Miednoye. The 3,900 from Starobielsk were murdered outside of Kharkov; their mass grave became a park and recreation area for KGB officers and their families.) [17]

The Germans made good propaganda out of the massacre: one Ally had wiped out nearly half the officer corps of another. The repatriation of Polish prisoners and exiles and the reconciliation between Poland and the Soviet Union came to an abrupt halt with the discovery of the mass grave. Moscow broke off all relations with the Polish government in exile, and General Anders's army was forced to leave thousands of Polish survivors behind.[18]

The Polish government in exile demanded an impartial investigation of the Katyn atrocity by the Red Cross. Stalin used this as a pretext to break relations off with Poland. The Western Allies found Poland to be an embarrassment; in agreements at Tehran, Yalta, and Potsdam, they handed eastern Poland over to Stalin and guaranteed Soviet domination of what remained.

General Anders's army was able to evacuate only a portion of the Polish survivors. Some 4,000 Polish Jews and nearly 66,000 ethnic Poles and others were successfully evacuated to Persia, though they were ill and starving; 500 Polish orphans were rescued and taken to India with a Polish priest. Bishop Gawlina left the USSR with the second group escaping to Persia.[19] The remainder of lay and clergy internees were relocated to towns in the eastern Soviet Union, where they constituted new Catholic communities.

Soviet Catholics in Moscow and Leningrad

In Moscow, Father Leopold Braun continued to minister at Saint Louis des Français, which was subjected to a series of robberies and vandalism from Christmas 1940 to February 1941. After the third robbery, the Soviets billed the beleaguered priest several thousand rubles for the missing church items, which were state property. At that point, the good Father lost his temper and went to the United States Embassy and the Associated Press bureau for help. With their support and the support of other foreign embassies, Saint Louis was spared further serious troubles, except for the "normal" police surveillance.[20]

After the German invasion, and particularly after he was interviewed by Averell Harriman, in Moscow to discuss Lend-Lease shipments, conditions for Father Braun improved. In the fall of 1941, as the front drew closer to Moscow, police surveillance ended, and he was able to minister freely to his congregation, effect repairs to Saint Louis despite wartime shortages, and even administer the sacraments to Red Army men. The parish grew substantially.[21] Soviet citizens were traveling up to 300 miles to go to Moscow for Confession and to have their children baptized, and the police did not interfere. Father Braun was even allowed to take the sacraments to the wounded in hospitals, and was shown "the greatest courtesy,"[22] although permission was denied Father Laberge to assist him.[23]

This hiatus lasted until late 1944, when Father Braun was subjected to intense pressures once again. By then, as the Red Army rolled across the Baltic and Central Europe, the USSR was resuming anti-Catholic policies. At Yalta, Stalin personally asked for the removal of Father Braun, who was replaced shortly after Christmas 1945 by another American Assumptionist, Father George Laberge.[24]

In the last years of Father Braun's pastorate, Saint Louis des Français had developed an impressive liturgical life. On Sunday there were three Masses: at 9 A.M. for English-speaking foreigners, at 10 A.M. (High Mass) for the Muscovite faithful, and at 11:30 A.M. for French-speaking foreigners. Daily Mass was offered early in the morning for the workers. Though many of the faithful were ethnic Poles or Lithuanians, Saint Louis carefully maintained all of the traditional French hymns, decorations, and traditions, for it was strongly felt these helped to keep the parish open.

When Father Charles Bourgeois arrived in Moscow in the fall of 1944, he was warned by Father Braun not to consider celebrating in the Byzantine Rite he had used in Estonia, as "one Eastern ceremony in the church . . . would be enough to have it closed." Father Bourgeois found great inspiration in the Moscow congregation. Many of the Soviet parishioners had been in prison, and all were living in impoverished and overcrowded circumstances. Catholic families lived side by side with atheist or religiously indifferent families, three or four families to an apartment. Children were taught their prayers, but in secret. There were no missals (save ones that predated the Revolution), no access to Catholic literature, no social gatherings of any sort. Denunciation in these Stalinist days was seen as a public service, and the Catholics were generally spied on. One woman who had been jailed for her religious beliefs told Father Bourgeois that she had fallen into a deep depression while in prison, but had been saved by her meditations on Christ's agony in the garden of Gethsemane and by the constant refrain "Thy will be done." Encounters of this sort convinced him of the deep spirituality that was present in Catholic Moscow.[25]

Sadly, in July 1941, Leningrad's Father Michel Florent was expelled from the Soviet Union as a subject of Vichy France. He eventually arrived at Beirut, with the other expelled French diplomats and citizens. Monsignor Angelo Roncalli, the future Pope John XXIII, who was nuncio to Turkey, asked that Florent be sent back to the USSR, this time as a representative of the Free French government of General Charles de Gaulle, but his request was turned down as too risky for the Holy See.[26] Notre Dame was left without a priest for the first time in its history. Throughout the 900-day siege of Leningrad, the laity kept the church open, under the direction of an elderly Frenchwoman, Madame Rosa Souchal, respected both by the Leningrad Catholics and by the NKVD. Every Saturday night and Sunday morning, no matter what, a congregation made its way to Kovensky Lane for the recitation of the Rosary and collective prayers. Although German shells would destroy one of the towers of the church, and although death and evacuation would take their tolls, the church was never abandoned.

When Father Bourgeois was able to visit Leningrad for ten days, he contacted Madame Souchal. He celebrated Mass twice daily in Notre Dame, once in the morning and once in the evening by special dispensation at 6 P.M. He was amazed by the resiliency of the local Catholics. For Mass, he had altar servers, choir, sacred vessels, and candles, and preached to a packed church. After ten days spent baptizing and administering other sacraments, however, he was finally expelled from the city by the NKVD.[27] For her years of service to the French community and her role in preserving the church building and parish, Madame Souchal was decorated by the Free French government.

The Allies' View of Religious Freedom in the USSR

The Allied Powers seemed willing to delude themselves that the situation of believers in the USSR was improving, based on Stalin's "concordat" with the Russian Orthodox. The American Ambassador, Joseph Davies, was especially naïve, characterizing Father Braun in 1942 as a good man, but simple and "difficult" regarding the campaign against religion.[28] Stalin was pleased, of course, because Axis Forces were nearing Moscow at that time, and he needed friends in the West.

Hopes for Improvement in the Situation of Soviet Catholics: 1944

The American priest Father Stanislaw Orlemanski, who visited Moscow in 1944, reported that Stalin was against persecution of the Catholic Church. (The OSS assessment of Orlemanski as "rather eager" to believe Stalin would be borne out later.) Nevertheless, based on developments in Soviet- "liberated" and -reconquered areas, there was hope for a Soviet-Catholic rapprochement in 1944: the bishop of Lutsk-Zhitomir-Kamenets diocese (the three dioceses were one again) was restored to his palace in Lutsk; Archbishop Romuald Jałbrzykowsy was freed from a Nazi prison in Vilnius; and the seminaries in Vilnius (Vilna), Kaunas (Kovno), and Riga were allowed to reopen so that priests for Soviet Catholics could be trained at home. Moreover, the chairman of the Council of Religious Affairs told the *New York Post* that priests could now instruct the children of Catholic believers in groups, and that Catholic parents could instruct their own children. Although such concessions were less than the Orthodox had at the time, they were far more than the Catholics had before the war.[29]

There was even consideration given to restoring communications between Soviet Catholics and the Holy See, a sign of Stalin's willingness to acknowledge some papal authority in the country, although not one that would please Rome. (As the 1944 OSS report prophetically concluded, "the course of Soviet-Vatican relations is likely to be far from smooth.")[30]

Mass Deportations in the USSR During and Immediately After the War

We have already seen how the policy of forcibly relocating nationalities had begun in 1937, building on the mass internment of millions of innocents in the Gulag. During the Soviet phase of World War II (1941–1945) and immediately after it, specific nationalities were singled out for forcible relocation. Mass relocations of Russia Germans, including many Catholics, occurred from 1941 until 1948; mass relocations of Balts continued until the German conquest of the Baltic region in 1941; mass relocations of Finns from Leningrad and its environs occurred in 1942.

In territory recovered by the Soviets, Germans who remained behind or were caught in flight were also shipped east. As the Axis forces were repulsed in 1943–1944, mass relocations began anew out of the northern Caucasus: Chechens, Ingush, Karachai, Balkars, Turks, Kurds, Khemshils, Meshketians, and Kalmyks were forcibly removed. When the Red Army "liberated" Crimea, the Crimean Tatar ASSR was dissolved, and the Crimean Tatars (some 183,000) removed along with the Crimean Greeks, Bulgars, and Armenians (some 45,000 in all),[31] effectively destroying what remained of Armenian Catholicism on the peninsula.

Mass Executions and Mass Removals of Russia Germans

Russia Germans formed the largest single group of Soviet Catholics subjected to wartime removal. Although the Nazis planned to "liberate" and "incorporate" these Germans into the Third Reich, their invasion directly prompted the Soviets to execute tens of thousands. The entire ethnic German population of the European Soviet Union (1.1 million) was scheduled for forcible removal to the north and east.

On the night of the German invasion (June 22, 1941), all the Volga Germans in a Komi concentration camp were put up against a wall and shot. Russia German prisoners, officials, and leaders would be executed elsewhere in the Volga region throughout the summer. In July, the NKVD occupied the capital and all the principal towns of the Volga German ASSR. All surviving Germans in official positions were removed and replaced by NKVD personnel: none have ever been seen again; the Volga Germans interned in labor camps were also subjected to mass executions.[32]

Before collectivization, the Ukrainian SSR had counted more than 393,000 Russia Germans; the Caucasus SSRs, 25,000; the Belorussian SSR, 7,000; and European Soviet Russia, nearly 657,000, concentrated in the middle and lower Volga, northern Caucasus, Crimea, Leningrad-Karelia, and the central industrial zone. In 1938, the Volga German ASSR counted 398,000 Russia Germans, far fewer than should have been, as a result of the deaths during collectivization, the purges, and famine.[33]

In the wake of the August 28, 1941, decree legalizing the NKVD executions and removals, "tens of thousands" were denounced as "spies" and "wreckers" of the Soviet economy.[34] Russia Germans who escaped execution and who survived mass removal went on to found many of the Catholic parishes of Siberia and the Soviet Far East. As their fellow Catholics removed before them, despite short notice, they made a point of packing missals and bibles, along with the holy pictures that had been venerated in each home's *HerrGottseck* (Lord God's corner), testimony to the persistence of Catholic belief and practices in the absence of religious services.

Western and Southern Ukrainian SSR

The Soviets removed all males aged 17 to 60 from those Russia German communities not immediately occupied by the invading Axis forces. In late June and the first half of July, the men were sent to drive herds to the east or to work on defensive fortifications, away from the *Wehrmacht*. Russia German women were also put to work on digging trenches and tank traps. Villages were placed under guard, people were arrested, and ultimately, the remaining women, elderly, and children were evacuated. Only in the territory of "Transnistria" between the Dniester and Bug Rivers, given by Germany to Romania on August 30, 1941, were the Russia German men spared, due to the rapidity of the Axis advance. Some 129,000 Russia Germans were found there. Another 100,000—without their men—were found in the Dnieper Bend. Beyond the Dnieper River, nearly all the Russia Germans were gone.

Eastern Ukrainian SSR

In the Donets Basin and the villages that dotted the region north of the Sea of Azov, the Russia German population was evacuated from August 31 through late October, with all the men removed by train or on foot. Most villages were emptied. The Axis advance killed some evacuees in air raids, when trains full of women and children were bombed, and freed others, when train yards filled with evacuees were captured. Relatively few Russia Germans were left around Kharkov and Berdiansk; the whole Catholic colony from Chernigov region had been removed as early as June 1941.

Volga German ASSR

Its leaders executed, the ASSR was further traumatized by staged incidents of supposed German parachutists seeking refuge in Volga villages. Whenever a village was alleged to have given them sanctuary, its entire population was slaughtered or forcibly removed. Houses were searched, and German flags distributed by the Soviet government in 1939 after the Molotov-von Ribbentropp Pact were used as grounds for more shootings. German Communists were executed for their alleged failure to root out spies.

On August 8, 1941, the Volga Germans were officially accused of collaborating with the enemy, and the forcible removals begun in earnest—with little or no warnings.[35] In the Marxstadt and Pokrovsk train yards, crowds of Russians and Kirghiz came to say good-bye to Russia German friends and relatives, who were loaded into cattle cars, with two passenger cars per train for the NKVD troops, pregnant women, and the sick.[36]

In August and September, 400,000 people were forcibly removed: fathers, sons, and brothers aged 15 to 50 were taken from their families and impressed into the forced labor army; the rest were packed into the trains without adequate food or heat (despite the early onset of cold weather). Though told to take food for six weeks' journey, many were not able to obtain such supplies on such short notice. There was no drinking water; the cars roasted in the day and froze at night. Whenever the trains stopped, the prisoners buried their dead alongside the tracks.[37] Even Volga Germans living as far away as Moscow were rounded up and removed, most to Siberia. On September 7, the Volga German ASSR was formally dissolved.

Crimea

The Crimean Germans had suffered brutally from collectivization: many survivors had moved into the cities, where they tried to disappear into the urban working class.[38] Because of government registration, however, their locations were all known. Younger sons of these folk had remained in the countryside with their families in mostly German villages, or as strangers in non-German villages. When townspeople removed on August 20, 1941, passed through these villages, only dogs and chickens were left. As in the north, people and baggage were crowded into railroad cars, although in many areas, workers were given their wages and families had time to prepare food and pack calmly.

Few Crimean Germans were left behind to be liberated by the *Wehrmacht;* most were removed to the North Ossetian ASSR, where they were used to bring in the wheat harvest. In October, 1941, the unmixed German families were removed once again, mostly into Kazakhstan, where they suffered a high death rate, especially among the children and young men drafted into the forced labor army. The mixed families were left behind.

South Caucasus SSRs

An estimated 20,000 Russia Germans lived here in 1941.[39] In mid-October, NKVD troops began to occupy the German villages, advising residents to gather up a month's supply of food, as well as bedding and basic clothing. Some villages had as long as a week to prepare. Removed in trucks, they were put on trains to Baku, then transported across the Caspian Sea to Krasnovodovsk.

The multiethnic city of Tbilisi was devastated by the removal of its Russia Germans, many of whom were doctors, or other professionals. Members of the city's many nationalities crowded into the train yard to say farewell, give out jewelry to be used for barter in exile, and affirm friendships. Although some German men with non-German wives (other than Armenian or Georgian) were allowed to remain behind, German women with non-German husbands had to leave.

The city people joined the farmers at Krasnovodovsk, where all embarked on a "descent into hell." Crammed into hot cattle cars, they were forced to travel across the desert without water. Most of the older people died, and their bodies were buried in the sand in unmarked graves. The survivors were scattered across Kazakhstan, from Alma-Ata in the south to Tselinograd and Semipalatinsk in the north. In the fall of 1941 and the summer of 1942, all men and women from 14 to 40 years of age were removed for the forced labor army. For those who remained behind, conditions were atrocious: working women came home exhausted to find that their children had died of starvation.[40]

Belorussian SSR and European Soviet Russia

Although almost all Volga Germans living outside the ASSR were also removed, the *Wehrmacht* found several thousand exceptions—descendants of Volga Germans who had moved to Minsk in 1928. Elsewhere in the Belorussian SSR, it found a few hundred Russia Germans, in Borisov, Bobruysk, and Vitsyebsk; in European Soviet Russia, another few hundred in Smolensk, Orsha, Mogilev, and Pskov. The very old German colonies around Leningrad, whose ardent faith had so impressed Bishop Neveu and Father Amoudrou, had been virtually depopulated of their men in the summer of 1941. The *Wehrmacht* found only 2,800 ethnic Germans south of Leningrad, and another 1,000 in Ingermanland.

In Leningrad, itself, the 20,000 Russia Germans in the Petrovskaya Slavyanka district were completely isolated from the rest of the populace throughout the Great Siege. Those who survived the siege were deported to Siberia on March 16, 1944; not even their participation in the life of the "Hero City" could spare them this fate.

By 1945, the NKVD and the Red Army had forcibly removed 948,289

Russia Germans and relatives; of these, 446,480 from the Volga German ASSR. In the next three years, they would remove an additional 120,192 Russia Germans, who would constitute the largest single minority nationality forcibly removed to labor camps or special settlements or exile.[41]

Mass Executions and Mass Deportations of Poles, Belorussians, Ukrainians, and Balts

The pace of executions and deportations dramatically quickened with the Axis invasion. In eastern Poland, there was a fourth (200,000 people) deportation even as the Germans were advancing; this one included children snatched from summer camps and orphanages.[42] In Lwów (Lvov), 3,500 prison inmates were mutilated and slain; elsewhere, prison cells were "cleared" by throwing grenades into the mass of prisoners. In Dubno, 500 women and children were slain; at Chervene thousands of Poles, Belorussians, and Ukrainians were killed. Jewish Communists were deliberately used to carry out the last arrests and executions so as to inflame anti-Semitic passions. Victims were executed the traditional way, with a shot in the back of the neck, often after prolonged torture that included mutilation of tongues, eyes, and genitals; they were burned or buried alive; or their skulls were crushed in vises.

The Soviet retreats from the Baltic States was accompanied by horrendous massacres, equal to what took place in eastern Poland. Many were slaughtered in forests, away from public view; many others were butchered in the prisons of the cities. Kaunas, Telsiai, Panevezys, and Kretinga (Lithuania); Riga, Rezekene, the Holy Cross Church of Litene (Latvia); Tallinn, Tartu, Viljandi, and Keiressare (Estonia)—all had yards and cells filled with the dead. From Estonia, which remained Soviet until October 1941, 42,649 young men were forcibly removed to arctic concentration camps. Nearly one-fourth of the Baltic population was directly affected by executions and deportations.[43] When the Soviet Russians and their henchmen were finally gone, survivors emerged "with tear-stained faces. Everybody had somebody to mourn."[44]

Soviet Attitudes Toward the Vatican During the War

The USSR and its propaganda machine were caught in a quandary during the "Great Patriotic War." The Catholic Church was obviously an impediment to Sovietization of the European territories occupied in 1939–1941, and as such fair game for Stalinist liquidation. Yet because of the Church's great influence in the world at large, the Kremlin wanted to impress the Vatican with its "tolerance": the Soviet Ambassador to Germany came to the Holy See in January 1941 insisting that the Church was not being persecuted; Lithuanian priests were ordered to send Rome favorable reports. Indeed, in early 1941, Soviet persecution of the Church abated somewhat, at least until the mass relocations resumed in June 1941. Even so, the Kaunas (Kovno) seminary, Lithuania's last, was closed in January 1941; an Orthodox bishop was sent to Lwów (Lvov) to threaten the Greek Catholics in March; in late spring, a campaign of terror was reinitiated against the Catholics; and from December 1941 through February 1942, Saint Louis des Français in Moscow was subjected to robberies and vandalism, and its pastor, Father Braun to harassment.[45]

With respect to the Soviet Far East, the Kremlin's anti-Catholic feelings were mixed with its fear of Japan's aggressive designs. At the same time, the Kremlin could ignore neither the Vatican's refusal to bless the Axis invasion of the USSR as a "crusade" against Communism, nor its delicate balancing act vis-à-vis the Japanese. For when Tokyo's ambassador came to Rome, so did a representative of Nationalist China, the country invaded by Japan in 1937. The Holy See refused to grant recognition to the Japanese puppet government in Nanking.[46] Having installed a representative in the Japanese puppet state of Manchukuo, the Holy See opened diplomatic relations with Tokyo in March of 1942, causing a great scandal in America and elsewhere. (That this had followed lengthy negotiations begun before the Japanese attack on Pearl Harbor in December 1941 and that the pope wanted to be able to communicate with the Catholics under Japanese rule and to assist Allied prisoners of war and civilian internees was simply not accepted by the Allies.)[47]

Vatican Attitudes Toward the Soviet Union During the War

Monsignor Domenico Tardini, the papal secretary of state, refused Italy's repeated requests that the Holy See reaffirm its condemnation of the Communists, pointing out that if it were to do so, it would also have to reaffirm its condemnation of the Nazis, who were no better. Tardini told the Italian ambassador that Germany would probably end up treating religion just as badly as the Communists in the near future (he was, of course, correctly interpreting Hitler's goals for the Churches). Further, it was the Axis diplomats who had claimed cooperation with the Soviets was beneficial by their support of the infamous Molotov-von Ribbentrop Pact of 1939.[48] Finally, the apostolic delegate in Washington instructed the Archbishop of Cincinnati to state that the war against Nazi Germany changed the prohibitions against giving aid to the Reds, as was specified in *Divini redemptoris* and to which prohibition 90 percent of American Catholics firmly adhered in 1941. Thus, indirectly, Communism was condemned, but not aid to the Soviet people.[49]

Indeed, the Vatican would never extend the Kremlin the kind of support it would receive from the likes of the Church of England and its clergy, who touted the freedom of religion in the Stalinist empire and who pushed for the "suppression of all anti-Bolshevik movements." Pope Pius XII were not fooled when President Roosevelt told Monsignor Tardini that the elimination of the Third International meant that the USSR had changed its course. The papal diplomat replied that Stalin's word was worth as much as Hitler's.

The Vatican lamented the naïveté of the Allies, who throughout the war held that Stalin and the Soviet Union had changed. As the Axis fell back in 1942, and as Germany faced in 1944 the prospect of unconditional surrender to the Allies, Monsignor Tardini was dismayed at the Americans' lack of understanding of what was really coming to pass in Europe.

Regarding the USSR itself, the Vatican took two courses. One was to (fruitlessly) warn the Western powers about Moscow's true intentions. Those powers believed that Rome was still harping on the USSR's past antireligious policies, which Stalin had supposedly altered; they perceived the Vatican's continued anti-Communism as being pro-Nazi. The second course was to strengthen the Church in Soviet Belorussia and Ukraine and to try to send missionaries into these Nazi-occupied territories.[50] This second course is detailed in chapters 26 and 27, on the religious revival in Soviet Belorussia and Ukraine.

CHAPTER 23

The Baltic States, Bukovina, and Bessarabia, 1940–1941

> We will make all your churches and prayer houses into clubs, theaters and magazine rooms.
>
> —Soviet officers to Bessarabians, 1940

In 1940, as the Western powers collapsed and Germany rolled across Western Europe, the destiny of Eastern Europe was being written in the Kremlin.

To the north, the Winter War, marked by the Soviets' strafing civilian refugee columns and blinding Finnish POWs, had come to a bitter close, with Finland forced to surrender on March 12, 1940. The elimination of the Finnish front had freed up Soviet forces in the north. One of eight Finns lived in the territory that Stalin annexed: 415,000 Finns had been evacuated west in only 10 days.[1] There were no illusions in Finland as to what Soviet rule would mean.

In 1940, Germany seemed unstoppable. Hitler's troops swiftly overran Denmark, Norway, and the Benelux countries. France collapsed in June 1940, and Britain was left to fight on alone. For its part, having issued ultimatums to all its western neighbors, the USSR occupied Lithuania on June 16, Latvia the next day, and Estonia on June 17–18, invading northern Bukovina and Bessarabia (in the Kingdom of Romania) on June 27–28. In eastern Poland, yet another surge of refugees from the German-occupied zones was gathered in by the dragnet of Soviet paranoia.

The Molotov-von Ribbentrop Pact gave Stalin direct control over a vast area, allowing for the ultimate annexation of eastern Poland and the Baltic States, and for influence in the southeast, over Romania.

Under Article 3 of the pact, anyone with one German grandparent or any non-German with a German spouse was allowed to emigrate from the Baltic States or Soviet-occupied Poland to the Third Reich. This provision enabled not only most ethnic Germans but also many non-Germans to leave Soviet-held territories (some 750,000 people, all told).[2] Thus an estimated 5,000 non-Germans left Lithuania, with the assistance of the German consular staff there; an estimated 20,000 non-Germans emigrated from Bukovina.

On the other hand, because the SS controlled the evacuation of real and alleged *Volksdeutsche,* it later forced many young men to enroll in its ranks. The pact also required all Third Reich citizens to abandon the region, and all foreign diplomatic personnel to leave as well. These provisions hurt the Church badly. The first crippled the missionary work of the religious orders that had recruited heavily from Germany and Austria; the second cut off all contact with the Vatican, as papal diplomats returned to Italy.

Soviet Annexation of the Baltic States

Forced to cede both inland and coastal bases to "fraternal" Red Army forces, the Baltic States knew they were being hopelessly isolated from any outside assistance. Elections to decide their destiny were held July 14–15, 1940. Like voters in Soviet-occupied Poland, Baltic voters were allowed to choose only from a slate of Communist-approved candidates to form new legislatures; they were subjected to police intimidation and terrorism. Refusing to vote meant not receiving the stamp on one's papers that showed one had cooperated, yet many took that risk rather than participate in the sham; others voided and defaced their ballots. To no avail: the "official" count showed 99 percent or more of the Balts had voted "properly." The puppet assemblies quickly petitioned the great Communist Motherland for annexation; Moscow "graciously" acceded.

The three Baltic States now came under Soviet rule by terror. Thousands of innocents were arrested and thrown into prison, where they were subjected to psychological and physical torture, and where many people died or were cruelly murdered. Furthermore, Stalin engaged in mass deportations modeled on those in eastern Poland. The sheer extent of the 1940–1941 Baltic operations made his goal abundantly clear: the Baltic nationalities becoming minorities in their own countries. As in eastern Poland, all political activists, nobles, army officers, relatives of Soviet émigrés, diplomats, and public leaders were quickly removed, and the believers' turn came swiftly.

Status of the Catholic Church in
the Soviet-Occupied Baltic States: 1940–1941

Estonia

Estonian Catholicism formed the smallest and weakest, yet also the most diverse, of the Baltic Catholic Churches.[3] In 1939, in a country of 1.1 million, there were about 3,500 faithful, of mostly Polish, Polish-Estonian, Lithuanian, German, Latvian, and French extraction. Most Estonians were Lutheran, and 210,000 were Eastern Orthodox. There were very few unmixed ethnic Estonian Catholics; all Catholics here were converts or children of converts. Thus Estonian Catholicism was very clearly perceived to be "foreign."

The entire country was covered by a single apostolic administration headed by a German Jesuit missionary, Archbishop Eduard von Proffitlich, who was responsible for 6 parishes and 14 priests in 1939. Appointed in December 1931, and ordained as bishop in 1936, von Proffitlich worked hard to counter the widespread perception of his Church as "foreign." Sermons were preached only in Estonian, not in Polish or German, and Estonian was used for a new prayerbook, catechism, and Catholic weekly paper.[4]

At the same time, energetic missionary work was undertaken in connection with the Estonian Orthodox Church. Two centers at Esna and Narva served the Byzantine Rite in Estonian; Greek Catholic nuns from Poland ran a kindergarten at Narva; and there were churches at both centers. Although Archbishop von Proffitlich gave great support to the nascent Byzantine Catholic community and its priests, and although many Estonian Orthodox leaned toward union with Rome, Estonia's Russian Orthodox Church firmly opposed any Church union.

Of the Catholic priests working in Estonia, half were German, and thus vulnerable to the power politics of the day, and the remainder were French, Lithuanian, Luxemburger, and English. Several missionaries, among them the intrepid Jesuit Father Charles Bourgeois, having been authorized to minister in both rites by the papal nuncio in 1940, served Estonia's tiny Byzantine Catholic community. Missionary efforts among the Russian Orthodox in Estonia proved unsuccessful, and energies were directed to the Estonian Orthodox clergy and faithful, although also with little success.

In October 1940, Archbishop von Proffitlich wrote to Rome for guidance now that all ethnic Germans and foreign nationals were being forced to leave Estonia. Also in October, the Estonian ambassador to the Holy See reported that the Baltic Germans were being pressured to either emigrate or take Soviet citizenship and risk forcible removal to Siberia.[5] The sources differ as to the Vatican's reply but agree on the result: the archbishop gave up his German citizenship, which both protected him and exposed him to forcible exile back to Germany, and took on Soviet citizenship.[6] At his trial in November 1941, he testified that the Pope had ordered him to remain in Estonia with his flock.[7] By then, he had lost most of his priests and nuns.

The Estonian Communist activists called up in June 1941 were told that the bourgeoisie and all potential enemies of the Soviet state had to be destroyed to enable the Revolution to take place.[8] In the mass relocation of June 1941, no one was spared. Of the 10,157 persons forcibly removed, less than 22 percent were men aged 20–49, that is, males who could be reasonably expected to fight; more than 45 percent were under 14 or over 50. In addition, many politicians and civil servants and 150 military officers were arrested before the great deportation, on the ground that they *might* act against Soviet power. Ultimately, 67,000 of the Estonians were shipped east and 77,000 were killed, of an original population of only 1.1 million.

For Estonia's Churches, the devastation was thorough: 4 bishops were removed, 2 from the Lutheran and 1 each from the Orthodox and Catholic Churches; they were joined by 6 Lutheran deans, as well as 26 Lutheran pastors and 163 members of Lutheran parish boards. Many were removed with their families. None of the clergymen returned, though some of their family members did.[9]

The Catholic network of six parishes so carefully built up "simply ceased to exist."[10] All of the German priests, except for the archbishop, who had taken Soviet citizenship, had been forced to leave. Both Catholic papers were closed, and the printing of the first Catholic edition of the New Testament in Estonian came to an abrupt halt. After the removal of the archbishop and one other priest, only four priests were left, and they were subjected to repeated interrogations, torture, and imprisonment.[11]

Despite its small size, the Estonian Catholic Church "was the target of the most intense Communist hate."[12] Except for services held by the four remaining priests, all Catholic activity was abruptly halted. In 1942, Estonian Catholics numbered only 2,340: one-third had been lost.[13]

Shortly after the German invasion, on June 27, 1941, officers of the NKVD surrounded Archbishop von Proffitlich's rectory; with pistols drawn, they accompanied him into his church, where he was to bid good-bye to the Lord in the Blessed Sacrament.[14] Then, like so many of the faithful he had served and loved, he was taken away, and sent to a concentration camp in the Urals. Although the Holy See received word in September 1941 that he was alive, following the German defeat at Stalingrad in February 1943 all trace of the archbishop was lost for decades.[15] He was subjected to a cursory trial, where he, accused of having received secret Vatican instructions at his audience with Pope Pius XII in 1940, which he denied, was sentenced to death for "counterrevolutionary activity and agitation in church and prison." He was executed on February 22, 1942, in a prison at Kirov.[16]

So brutal had Soviet rule been that Estonians, despite their bitter resentment of Baltic German overlordship before 1919, willingly assisted the invading German armies. Even as the Soviets retreated before the Axis forces, however, they continued to arrest and remove or execute their Estonian victims, engaging as well in wholesale massacres of prison inmates.

Latvia

Although Lutheranism was the dominant religion among the ethnic Latvians, the Catholic Church had kept the loyalty of the Latgalians (a transitional group between Latvians and Lithuanians, still in the process of assimilating into the Latvian majority), of the ethnic Latvians who lived in areas adjacent to Latgalia and Lithuania, and of the ethnic Poles. Of a total population of 2.1 million in 1940, Lutherans numbered about 1.1 million (53 percent); Catholics, about 525,000 (25 percent); members of the autonomous Orthodox Church, about 252,000 (12 percent), more than one-third of whom were ethnic Latvians); Old Believers (all ethnic Russians), about 100,000; Jews, about 93,000; and Byzantine Catholics, about 13,000.[17]

In 1918, the Republic of Latvia was formed from all and the western part of two Russian provinces (Courland and Vitebsk, respectively). In September 1918, Rome reestablished a diocese at Riga, the Latvian capital, and named a refugee priest from Petrograd, Monsignor Edward O'Rourke, whom we earlier met in Saint Petersburg as its first bishop.[18] Although the Catholic presence in Riga before independence had been weak, it had shown signs of growth. The Church of Saint James had been consecrated in 1785, at the end of Great Castle Street, when open practice of the Faith returned to the city; it had served as the only Catholic parish until the Gothic Church of Saint Francis was opened in Riga's "Moscow" suburb in 1892, a district inhabited by the poor. A third parish was opened at Mitau in 1903, Saint Albert's. These three urban parishes had been united with the Estonian parishes to form a deanery separate from the rest of Latvia. Latgalia's Catholics had weathered the storm of tsarist persecution also: the rural deaneries of Daugavapils counted many faithful; a new church had been built in the Latgalian center of Rezekne in 1893.[19]

A year after the Concordat of 1922 was signed, the Church of Saint James became Riga's cathedral. In 1938, Latvia was formed into an ecclesiastical province, with Riga as a metropolitan archdiocese, under Archbishop Anthony Springovics, and with a suffragan diocese in Liepaja. A third ordaining bishop was designated to live in Riga; in addition, Bishop Boleslas Sloskans continued to reside in the country after his expulsion from the USSR in 1933.

In 1939, the Latvian Catholic Church counted 150 parishes, with 250 churches served by 180 priests. In the east, the great shrine of Our Lady of Aglona still drew huge crowds of pilgrims. A major seminary had been founded at the shrine after independence, and this was moved to Riga in 1924; a separate faculty of theology was established at the national university there in 1938.

In 1939, Latvian Catholicism formed a large and vibrant Church: there were a number of religious orders at work in the country; some ten Catholic newspapers and magazines were published; and there were a wide variety of Catholic lay associations. On Sunday, Mass was broadcast on the radio, and Catholics had allotted time for religious instruction in the State schools. In addition, they ran several schools, libraries, and reading rooms. All of this activity was doomed with Soviet occupation and annexation.

In 1940, the Riga seminary, the two high schools, and Catholic youth organizations were closed down; broadcasts of the Mass were stopped; and Catholic books were removed from the shelves of libraries and stores.[20] By Christmas, all religious orders except the Poor Servants of Our Lady had been dissolved, and the various monasteries and convents confiscated. Members of the orders were forced to return to their families and to pursue secular vocations. Early in the Soviet occupation, several churches were seized for secular use or desecrated by troops: the Church of Saint Mary Magdalene was used as a theater for the Red Army, the church at Ozolmuiza for an airport, and a number of rural churches were plundered.[21]

The first mass relocations removed as many as 40,000 Catholics and Lutherans from the country, including 6,000 of the Catholic intelligentsia. Several priests were arrested on false charges, tortured into making "confessions," and imprisoned; many others were shot or removed. After the German invasion, still more priests were arrested or removed, and eleven were tortured to death.[22]

Among the deported priests removed were Father Jazeps Pudans, SJ, who was martyred in 1941,[23] and Fathers Stanislaus Kapacs, Edvards Bekers, Kazimirs Strods, Peters Aspiniks, and Janis Zuks, who were all exiled to Siberia.[24] Those who remained suffered as well: the Dutch Jesuit Father John Peeperkorn, for example, was given up for dead in 1947. In all, some 100,000 Latvian citizens were removed, including 10,000 Catholics; 30 priests were taken away in the Soviet retreat. Only churches with attached cemeteries were spared looting; the remaining priests and bishops were forced to live in smaller quarters or with the laity. Due to the closures of the seminary and theological faculty, only four new priests were ordained during the Soviet occupation.[25]

Lithuania

In 1939, of Lithuania's 2.9 million citizens, some 75 percent were Catholic, including most of the ethnic Lithuanians, Poles, and Belorussians. The Lithuanian Catholic Church had 6 dioceses and 1 prelature nullius, with more than 1,000 parish and mission churches, public and monastic chapels, 37 monasteries, 85 convents, and 4 seminaries. In addition, Lithuania also had a large Russian Orthodox and Old Believer population, as well as a strong Jewish community.

Given that the Church had opposed the Smetona government, some Catholics hoped for an accommodation with the Soviet state. In the 1940 memorandum of Father Mykolas Krupavicius, approved by the papal nuncio and the hierarchy, the Lithuanian Church set forth its position in favor of social reform and spiritual freedom. The memorandum was simply ignored. Bishop Vincentas Brizgys, who lost some of his relatives to Soviet prisons, vainly tried to save religious education. Between July and August 1940, however, Catholic and Jewish schools were nationalized, the Catholic press (with a circulation of 7.5 million) shut down, religious holidays abolished, and Lithuanian society forced to secularize.[26] In September 1940, anti-religious pressures suddenly increased, apparently at the behest of Stalin.

On June 14, some 35,000 people were arrested and removed in one night. A Communist defector involved in the mass relocations reported later that the Soviets had planned to remove some 25 percent of the Lithuanian population (700,000 people) and would have done so had the Germans not invaded.

Outside Vilnius (Vilna), seminaries, monasteries and churches were plundered; only the Kaunas (Kovno) seminary was spared closure in 1940, and that was shut in January 1941. Among leading Catholics arrested and either removed or murdered in prison massacres were 58 priests (40 removed; 18 murdered); some 40,000 lay believers were also removed.[27] Of the Jesuit clerics removed, 6 were priests, 4 scholastics, and 5 brothers.[28] Although 15 priests scheduled for deportation managed to escape in the chaos of the Soviet retreat,[29] others were not so fortunate: nearly 6,000 people were executed in massacres across the country.[30] In Vilnius, itself, the archdiocese lost another 15 priests and 100,000 lay believers to forcible removal; 6 more priests were "barbarously murdered" in the Soviet retreat.[31]

Yet in October 1941, the Lithuanian archbishop of Kaunas (Kovno) reported to Rome that, despite arrests, mass removals, and murders of Catholics, and despite the danger of associating oneself with the Church, Lithuanian Catholicism had experienced a revival. Lapsed Catholics had returned to the practice of their religion, and young scholars, who faced strong atheist pressures, "revealed a strong faith."[32]

Status of the Catholic Church
in Soviet-Occupied Northern Romania: 1940–1941

As the German armies advanced westward, Stalin turned his eyes south, to Bessarabia and Bukovina, provinces that formed one-third of the Kingdom of Romania. The Molotov-von Ribbentrop Pact had given Stalin a relatively free hand in the southeast, and he took advantage. Hitler raged at the Soviet expansion, but to no avail.

On June 28, 1940, the Red Army occupied all of Bessarabia and the northern part of Bukovina. Southern Bukovina, which had about 29 percent of Romania's Ukrainians in 1940, was spared Soviet rule,[33] although the town of Hertza and a host of surrounding villages were also seized, and more people lost to the Communists through "ignorance, theft or mistake."[34] The Soviets now occupied an area that included the Danube delta and that ran all the way to the Carpathians; they could place an army in striking distance of the Romanian oil fields at Ploesti. Without a shot fired, they had taken territory with nearly 4 million more hapless victims.

Bessarabia

Once part of tsarist Russia, like the Baltic States, Bessarabia was doomed by the Molotov-von Ribbentrop Pact to become part of the USSR. For many of Bessarabia's inhabitants, it was a moment of special tragedy: they had watched their relatives die in the famines across the border, heard the shots of Soviet border guards at would-be escapees, listened to refugees who had made it over the Dniester, thus knew full well what to expect from their Soviet occupiers.

Russia had annexed eastern Moldavia under the name of "Bessarabia" in 1812, and removed its autonomy in 1829. On January 24, 1918, Bessarabia became an independent republic, and on March 27 it united with the expanding Kingdom of Romania.[35] It was this legacy of Russian colonial rule that impelled Stalin to reclaim the province.

Bessarabia was predominantly Romanian, although Stalinist nationality policies defined these Romanians as "Moldavians," who were to be reunited with their kinsmen in the small Moldavian ASSR. Of Bessarabia's 2.8 million people in 1930, only 23.3 percent were ethnic Russian and Ukrainian, whereas 56 percent were ethnic Romanian;[36] in addition, the province was home to sizable populations of Jews (7.2 percent) and Germans (2.8 percent), with Poles and a host of smaller minorities such as Christian Gagauz, Bulgarians, Armenians, and Muslims making up the remaining 10.7 percent.

In 1940, the Latin Catholic diocese of Jassy had nine parishes in the province, with churches also in Bendery, Belt'sy, and Rashkovo, along with stations in ethnic Polish villages. Catholics were found among Romanians and three minority groups: Armenians, Germans, and Poles.[37] The Armenian population was very small, but very old, and contained both Gregorians and Catholics. An Armenian cemetery church still survives in Kishinev to this day. Bessarabia's Poles were overwhelmingly rural; its Armenians urban. There were a few Greek Catholics to be found among the Ukrainians, concentrated at Bendery.

Bessarabia's Germans had sixteen colonies, with names like Jakobstal, Leipzig, and Teplitz. There were also urban Germans in the capital at Kishinev and in the northeastern city of Tiraspol, the city from which the old Diocese had taken its name.[38] Most of the Germans were Lutheran; German Catholics were concentrated in Kishinev and its suburbs, and the colonies of Krasna, Emmental, Larga, and Balmas.

In 1940, some 100,000 "Moldavians" were removed to Soviet Russia. In two later mass removals, in the spring of 1941, hundreds of thousands more were taken, along with livestock, farm equipment, and machinery for "resettlement" in the Urals, Kazakhstan, and Siberia or forced labor in the Karaganda coal mines. Many of those removed were young adults and adolescents. The city of Belt'sy lost nearly one-half (25,000) of its residents in the space of nine days. Moreover, young men from throughout Bessarabia were drafted into the Red Army. By the summer of 1941, when the Soviets were forced to retreat, mass graves had been filled with the bodies of thousands of executed victims, the cities, factories, and railroads had been dynamited, and the province spiritually and economically devastated.[39]

Repatriation of the province's *Volksdeutsche* began during the first months of Soviet occupation. Several hundred treks of covered wagons crossed the Prut at Galati, whence the evacuees were taken, without their livestock, to German-occupied Austria and to southern Germany. Some 93,000 people (including non-Germans) were resettled in Germany. Of these, 8,000 were Latin Catholics. In the course of the war, virtually all Germans were evacuated from the province, either in 1940–1941 or during the German retreat westward in 1944.[40] They had little consolation in their departure: as Soviet officers bluntly told the evacuees, "We will soon be marching on Berlin."[41]

Bukovina

Bukovina had been a crown land in the old Austro-Hungarian Empire, one where many nationalities had lived together in harmony. After 1918, it became Romanian, but remained a multiethnic province. In 1930, Bukovina had 853,000 residents, with the highest population density of any province in Romania; Romanians constituted 44.5% and ethnic Ukrainians/Ruthenians 27.7 percent, with Jews, ethnic Germans, Poles, Magyars, Serbs, Bulgarians, Armenians, and Tatars making up the remaining percent.[42] Ukrainians, settled under Austro-Hungarian rule, were mostly in the northern districts; it was these districts which Stalin claimed as part of the "Ukrainian homeland." Catholics were found among the ethnic Germans, Magyars, Poles, Romanians, and Ukrainians/Ruthenians.

Romania had pursued a nationalist policy in the province, using only Romanian in public life and harassing minority schools, newspapers, and theaters. Most of those who had been civil servants under the Austro-Hungarian Empire were dismissed or, if they proved themselves competent in Romanian history, transferred outside Bukovina. The kingdom attempted agrarian reform in 1918 and 1921, to relieve the plight of the small farmers. In 1918, one-fourth of Bukovina's farmers had holdings greater than 250 hectares (about 620 acres), whereas nearly one-half had less than 25 hectares (about 60 acres). The reforms failed: among ethnic German farmers, fully 80 percent had tiny holdings of less than 2.5 hectares (about 6 acres), and many farmers of other nationalities fared no better. Bukovina, then, was experiencing a high rate of emigration, overcrowding, and stress on the traditional agricultural way of life. Soviet absorption of the north affected 500,000 souls, and created new problems.

The religious life of the province reflected its ethnic composition. Bukovina had been home to a diocese of the autonomous Orthodox Church of Cz-

ernowitz until 1925, when the diocese became part of the Romanian Orthodox Patriarchate. Eastern Orthodoxy was the faith of most of the province's
Romanians and Ukrainians, as well as of all its ethnic Serbs and Bulgarians: in
1937, Eastern Orthodoxy accounted for 500,000 believers in the entire
province.[43] Catholics of three different Churches, Latin, Byzantine, and Armenian, formed the second-largest religious community. There were also German and Hungarian Protestants, as well as Jewish, Muslim, and Armenian
Apostolic believers.

Under the archdiocese of Lwów (L'viv), the Armenian Catholics had two
parishes in the province, with three priests: two in Czernowitz and one at
Suczawa.[44] In northern Bukovina, Armenian Catholics worshiped at the main
church in Czernowitz and at three chapels.[45]

The Greek Catholic Ukrainian population worshiped in sixteen parishes
and one mission, which had formed part of the eparchy of Stanislav until
1919, when they were incorporated into the Romanian Greek Catholic
eparchy of Maramoros.[46] By virtue of the Concordat of 1929 between the
Holy See and the Kingdom of Romania, the Ukrainian Greek Catholics were
part of a separate international vicariate, under Monsignor Appolon
Simovych (of Kotzmann) as the Bukovina's superior,[47] with two deaneries,
one for the north at Czernowitz and a second for the south at Suczawa, with
twenty-two priests, serving some 40,000 faithful in 1940.[48]

In 1914, as part of the diocese of Jassy, the Latin Catholics had 31 canon-
ical parishes, with three deaneries, at Czernowitz, Radautz, and Suczawa.[49]
They came principally from the German, Polish, Hungarian, and Slovak mi-
norities. Although relations were strained between the German and Polish
Catholics, they were good between Latin and Greek Catholics: at Radautz
(Rădăuți), the Latin Catholic church had a "Ruthenian altar" for the use of the
Greek Catholics until they had their own church.[51]

After the Kingdom of Romania absorbed Bukovina in 1919, and incorporated eastern Hungary in 1920, the Latin Catholics hoped for their own
separate diocese, as the Romanian Catholic Church was being reorganized.
For a time, it was made an apostolic administration of the archdiocese of
Lwów (L'viv); at the end of 1929, pursuant to the Concordat of 1929 between
Romania and the Holy See, it came under the diocese of Iasi (Jassy), Moldavia,
as announced and enacted at the Assumption pilgrimage at Kaczyka in August
1930 by Bishop Michael Robu.[52] Although an ethnic Romanian, Robu spoke
German well, and preached in German at Confirmation ceremonies in the
ethnic German parishes. He appointed a separate vicar general to administer
the new Bukovina vicariate.

Bukovina had three men's religious orders: Jesuits, in Czernowitz (Germans and Poles), Vincentians, at Kaczyka (whose community superior had been the first vicar general; see below), and Trinitarians, at Augustendorf (Germans). Three orders of nuns were serving in the province: Felicians, Sister Servants, and Family of Mary, all at Czernowitz.[53]

The Catholics experienced a strong religious renewal, with energetic work by the priests on behalf of all the believers, in particular, by Father George Goebel, whom Bishop Robu had recruited from Germany. Goebel came to Czernowitz in 1931. Under his directorship, Bukovina's multifarious societies and youth groups were restructured and experienced a strong renewal. Popular missions, which emphasized devotion to the Church and internal renewal through return to the sacraments, were also preached by the Jesuits and other priests from Germany, and kept up by the Jesuit community in Czernowitz.[54] Once again, the faithful were being strengthened for the trials they would have to suffer.

There were 65 Roman Catholic priests in Bukovina in 1940: 41 Germans, 16 Poles, 5 Hungarians, 2 Slovaks, and 1 Romanian (convert from Orthodoxy). Of the German priests, 28 were from Bukovina and 13 were from Austria or the Third Reich.[55] Although some 80 percent of Bukovina Catholics were ethnic Germans, never before had Germans predominated among the parish clergy.[56]

Their loss to resettlement in the Third Reich in 1940–1941 would weaken the Church, as had the loss of its leader, Vicar General Father Adalbert Grabowski, who died in July 1939. A Pontifical Mass for the funeral had been held, the last big Catholic event before the war, on July 22 at Czernowitz. Like the burial of the Armenian Catholic archbishop in Lwów, Father Grabowski's funeral was a rare moment when leaders of all of the religious, civic, and royal groups and offices were able to unite in peace in one location. His successor, Monsignor Johann Reitmaier, would preside over the Church during the first months of the Soviet occupation.

When Poland was invaded and partitioned by Germany and the USSR in September 1939, refugees flooded into Romania, including members of the Polish government, armed forces, and ordinary civilians. They brought tales of atrocities, mass arrests, and forcible removal to the unknown Soviet Far East. The following summer, the Red Army invaded Romania, immediately threatening the entire Catholic community. As in eastern Poland, Catholic schools were secularized, atheist propaganda introduced, and Church life subjected to state interference. Seminary training ended with the "socialization" of the theology and philosophy faculties at the University of Czernowitz on

August 4; two weeks later, Church land and property were nationalized in both northern Bukovina and Bessarabia.[57]

With the consent of the Romanian government, evacuation was also offered to the ethnic Germans in the "isolated fragment" of southern Bukovina. Nearly 100,000 people accepted: 72,900 Germans and 20,000 members of other nationalities, who (as in Lithuania and Bessarabia) were able to obtain the necessary forged documents. To allow as many people as possible to escape, the Reich Commission had granted exit permits to anybody who could document one German grandparent.[58] Only 7000 ethnic Germans remained behind. [59]

The northern Bukovina exodus included several thousand Romanians, who hoped to be able to return to their homeland, several thousand Ukrainians, and 16 Catholic priests. The southern Bukovina exodus commenced in November and December 1940: 13 parishes were emptied, and 23 German priests left. In the spring of 1941, 13,000 ethnic Hungarians and "Szeklers" were resettled into Hungary, nearly all of them Latin Catholics.[60]

Among the Greek Catholics, only one priest was able to leave, Father Worobkiewicz from Radautz (Rădăuți), who had a German wife. The couple was ultimately sent to Łódź in German-occupied Poland, where he served for a time as pastor to the city's Ukrainian Greek Catholics. In 1942, he returned, first to the Maramoros region, and finally to Sereth.[61] Although, as in Soviet-occupied Poland, there were no moves to force the Greek Catholics into Russian Orthodoxy, they escaped neither antireligious propaganda nor the ever-present threat of removal to the east.

In northern Bukovina, Father Viktor Skrabel became the pastor of Czernowitz, when Monsignor Reitmaier chose to leave.[62] The nine parishes that remained were served by twelve preists, including two Polish refugees and two priests from the now-closed Catholic schools.[63]

Sacred Heart Church in Czernowitz was staffed by German-speaking Jesuits. The church was desecrated by the Soviets, but the community remained in the residence. Father Raphael Haag continued to minister to those German Catholics who remained, and the Superior of the Jesuit community, Polish Father Władysław Kumerowicz, continued his work among Jews.[64] In 1941, after the liberation of northern Bukovina by the Romanian army, Bishop Robu named him the new vicar general for the entire province.[65]

Annexation of Northern Romania

No elections were held in the former Romanian territories. Instead, in June 1940, a delegation of "working people" appeared before the Supreme Soviet in Moscow with their petitions to become part of the USSR. In the course of the summer, these petitions were acted upon. Bessarabia was partitioned, with the part bordering the Black Sea, annexed to the Ukrainian SSR (despite its Romanian population), and the remainder annexed to part of the Moldavian ASSR to form a new constituent republic, the Moldavian SSR (the remainder of the ASSR was incorporated into the Ukrainian SSR. Northern Bukovina and Hertza were also incorporated into the Ukrainian SSR, as the Chernovtsy oblast. The two territories remain part of independent Ukraine and Moldova to this day.[66] In the late summer and autumn of 1940, the so-called "exploiting classes" were "liquidated" with the forcible removal of 100,000 people.[67] "Official" results of elections held on January 12, 1941, in the new Moldavian SSR were dutifully reported in the press: 99.5 percent of the votes cast (with 99.6 percent of all eligible voters participating) were for Communist delegates, despite "widespread opposition by reactionary elements."[68]

The Kremlin and the Vatican in the Occupied East

Notwithstanding Stalin's quip about the "Pope's divisions," the Kremlin recognized the growing importance of the Vatican in world diplomacy during the war. Early on, the Vatican took advantage of strains in the Nazi-Soviet alliance. Pope Pius XII directly confronted von Ribbentrop regarding the German alliance with atheist Communism, and the Church as a whole continued to remonstrate against the Molotov-von Ribbentrop Pact. As early as June 29, 1940—just when the Soviets were devouring northern Romania—the Vatican diplomatic corps had reported on the growing likelihood of a German invasion.

The Vatican also actively reminded the Americans that the Soviet Union was still atheist. Radio Vatican did not let up on reporting and condemning Soviet aggression and persecutions. Indeed, so strident was its reporting that appeals came from suffering Lithuanians to tone down its Lithuanian-language broadcasts.[69]

Why were the Soviets so brutal twoard Catholics? Dennis Dunn suggests three principal reasons:

1. Faced with the need to enlist the long-suffering Russian Orthodox

Church to rally the masses and bolster support for the government, on the one hand, and the need to demonstrate atheist power over religion, on the other, the Kremlin attacked the traditional religious "enemy" of Church and State in Russia—Catholicism.

2. Faced with the need to defend its vast new buffer zone against German expansion, the Kremlin turned to confiscation of Catholic churches, monasteries, convents, and institutes to billet troops, and to mass removal of Catholics to reduce the number of inhabitants deemed "politically unreliable."

3. Faced with the need to Sovietize the nationalities of the countries of Eastern Europe, on the one hand, and with Catholicism as the incarnation of national identity in those countries, on the other, the Kremlin moved to break the Church's hold on Eastern Europeans.[70]

By January 1941, the Russians were seriously concerned about the growing power of their Nazi "ally." They began to seek a rapprochement with the Holy See—despite their treatment of Catholicism in Eastern Europe. They did so in three principal ways:

1. Lithuanian priests (under Soviet coercion) sent reports to Rome that religious conditions were fine, and that Radio Vatican should stop its broadcasts of persecution.

2. The Soviet ambassador to Germany informed the papal nuncio to the Third Reich that the Catholic Church in Soviet-occupied areas was "unharmed."

3. The Soviets restrained the level of Catholic persecutions in those areas (at least until the German invasion in June 1941).[71]

By the summer of 1941, Germany was in firm control of most of Europe. The Balkan States had all been conquered (or had joined the Axis); the British had been soundly defeated in the Mediterranean. Stalin expelled the ambassadors of Yugoslavia, Norway, and Belgium in May, and took over the Council of People's Commissars. The Holy See was isolated on a continent dominated by Nazis and Fascists, and the Communists were waiting in the wings.

CHAPTER 24

Catholic Life in the
Nazi-Occupied Baltic States

Estonia, Latvia, and Lithuania were forcibly incorporated into the USSR in 1940, under the same chicanery used in eastern Poland. Each country became an SSR; each was occupied by the Red Army; each was terrorized by the NKVD; each saw religious and cultural life severely restricted, if not altogether extinguished.

Although all three Baltic States expected to reestablish their independence upon their liberation from the Soviet Union, the efforts of their provisional governments toward that end were thwarted by the Nazis, who, acting through pro-German councils, allowed them to restore only bits and pieces of independent public life. Throughout the three states, the SS followed the *Wehrmacht,* butchering Jews and Communists en masse in cities and villages alike. Although some Balts also participated in these massacres, others tried to shelter Jews during the Nazi occupation (see appendix A: "Catholics and Jews in the Nazi-Occupied Territories").

Estonia

Precious little remained of the tiny Estonian Catholic Church. The number of faithful was reported at 2,340 in 1942, a drop of one-third from the 1939 estimate of Father Bourgeois. Although the Nazi occupiers allowed Father Henry Werling, SJ, to serve as administrator of the parishes, and four surviving priests, they did not allow any more priests to return to the country. Nor did they allow the Church to recover its losses under the Soviets,[1] hence to resume its work with Byzantine Catholics or the destitute or its religious publishing.

Latvia

As in Estonia, the Church did not recover lost property in Latvia, hence could not resume publishing. Although the Nazis, like the Communists, banned outdoor processions, they permitted full ceremonial life to resume *inside* the church buildings, and religious education to be at least in part, restored, in Latvia's schools, excluding, however, the Old Testament from all official catechesis.[2]

In October 1944, the Germans forcibly removed important Latvian religious leaders, most notably Bishop Boleslas Sloskans, the hero of the Gulag, who had been working in Latvia since 1933. He was dragged off, under protest, to Germany, ending up in the Western zone of occupation. (He would not die until 1981, at the age of 88, still willing to return to the USSR.)[3]

Lithuania

In Vilnius (Vilna), the Discalced Carmelite monastery was raided in 1942, and all of the monks sent to concentration camps. The monastery became an orphanage, and then a hospital. All the activities of Carmelite confraternities of laity were suspended as a result, and a Lithuanian diocesan priest served at the Carmelite church from 1942 to 1944 in place of the Polish Fathers. Under the Nazi occupation, because the chapel was under the care of the Carmelites, pilgrimages to the Ostrabama icon had to cease.[4]

Liberation from the butchery of the Reds had seemed a blessing to the beleaguered Lithuanian hierarchy in 1941. As late as March 4, 1943, the Archbishop of Kaunas (Kovno) declared that "Today we celebrate St. Kasimir's day and pray to God for deliverance from the return of Bolshevism to Lithuania!"

In April, Bishop Vincent Brizgys warned the Lithuanians to sacrifice part of the fruits of their labor for the struggle against the Muscovites.[5] Such attitudes and statements pleased the Nazis, but they also noted that the bishops did not pray for a German victory. Seminaries were reopened, some Lithuanian priests were allowed to accompany the young Lithuanians forcibly removed to Germany for labor, and religious education and a few properties were restored. But the Nazis removed Archbishop Romuald Jałbrzykowski and Polish priests and nuns to rural areas or to forced labor in Germany; Catholic-Nazi relations steadily deteriorated, with the 1941 Jewish massacres, the 1942 arrest of Lithuanian officials who protested these atrocities, the resettlement of the ethnic Poles, and the 1943 attempt to kill the disabled.[6]

Anti-Soviet Resistance

The problem faced by all three Baltic States was this: very few Balts were actually pro-Nazi, but everyone was anti-Soviet. The Balts wanted their independence restored, but obviously neither of the two great powers in the east were about to do that. So how could they resist the Nazis without bringing destruction upon themselves and without inviting the return of the Red Army? Would the Western Allies hold to their declarations that Baltic independence would be restored?

In all of the Baltic States, autonomous anti-Soviet units began to form as the Eastern Front steadily approached their borders. These became the source of the "forest brethren", nationalist partisans in the three countries who fought against Soviet reoccupation and hoped for an American intervention on their behalf.

In southern Latvia and all of Lithuania, the resistance of these partisans would inevitably affect the Church after the Soviet reoccupation in 1944. The restoration of Communism would drive tens of thousands of Balts from their homes in a desperate exodus to the West, detailed in chapter 28: "The Flight to the West."

CHAPTER 25

Catholic Revival in the Nazi-Occupied Soviet Union

T he widespread Russian Orthodox revival throughout the Nazi-occupied territories of the Soviet Union (pre-1939 borders) has been well documented. What mattered to the masses of believers under the Nazi occupation was whether churches could be opened and religious life resumed. A revived Orthodoxy was somewhat favored by Nazi policy as a vehicle to encourage anti-Soviet feeling and reconcile the populace to German rule.

Unknown, however, is the smaller, but equally widespread Soviet Catholic revival throughout these same occupied territories. Restricted by anti-Catholic Nazi ideology, feared and hated by many Nazi officials, it nonetheless took place, thanks most of all to the tenacious faith of the laity, but also to the courage and dedication of German and other clergy who accompanied or followed the invading Axis forces, on the one hand, and of the Polish and Ukrainian priests who were able to enter the occupied territories, on the other.

The Role of the Soviet Laity

As seen previously, though sacramental life had ceased in the western Soviet Union by 1939, religious practice had not. Atheism had not conquered the souls of the USSR's millions, and Catholics were no exception. This and the following two chapters will describe the extent of the revival among the Latin Catholic Belorussians, ethnic Poles, and Black Sea Germans, among Greek Catholic Belorussians, and among Catholics of either rite in ethnically mixed communities in Ukraine and Belorussia.

Catholic families had often kept up a quiet devotional life, usually centered on the Rosary and Litanies of the Virgin or saints. In a village where most people were Catholic, there were also prayer meetings. At these, the Rosary was also central, but there would be singing of hymns in Latin and the vernacular, administration of Baptism, and prayers to certain saints. Despite betrayals by apostates and infiltration by the NKVD, religious life had gone on. Holy pictures were hidden behind pictures of Stalin, or buried under linens to be brought out for common prayer.

The Role of the Axis Military

Although Hitler and Nazi Party theorists were bitterly opposed to independent-minded Catholicism (priests were reviled as "black beetles" to be smashed), for the soldiers of the *Wehrmacht,* the invasion of the USSR was truly a crusade against godless Bolshevism, and the Soviet believers who came forward asking permission to restore the devastated churches inevitably impressed them. Moreover, priests and seminarians were present in the German armed forces, both as official chaplains and as medics; chaplains also served with or followed the Hungarian, Italian, and Romanian armies, Slovak partisan units, and Spanish volunteers.[1] In either role, they carried great weight with young soldiers facing death. Axis soldiers, chaplains, and priest-medics helped Soviet believers reopen closed churches, both Catholic and Orthodox, throughout the occupied Soviet territories, clearing out rubble, restoring roofs and doors, or removing secular items from churches that had been used as garages, barns, and so forth.

The priests accompanying Axis soldiers on the Eastern Front were constantly confronted with theological and liturgical problems for which they were unprepared. Although the Catholic world of the early 1940s was locked in rigidity, the profound experience of the European war would break several areas of that rigidity.

Ecumenical Latin Catholic Ministry to the Orthodox

In town after town, crowds of Orthodox believers would approach the German priests, asking for the sacraments. They did not care that they were Orthodox and the clergy Latin Catholic: what mattered was that here were validly ordained priests who could baptize, marry, and bury, and who could offer Holy Communion again.

The level of theological awareness surprised the priests. In one Russian town, when Father Bernard Häring expressed his reluctance to baptize, the Orthodox pointed out that they knew that "Peter and Paul lived in Rome and died there, and of course we know that the bishop of Rome is the successor to Peter."[2] Peasants saved wounded German soldiers and specifically told the priests that they did so in fidelity to the Gospel. Prayer groups had survived, led by grandmothers who guided people in discussions of the faith.[3] Sometimes Orthodox presented their unbaptized children and youths to the priests; other times they sought validation from them of what had been done by laity years before. Slovak priests working with partisan units inside the USSR in 1944–1945 told of columns of parents "coming to the priest on bare and bleeding feet" to have their children baptized, parents who had been born and raised under Soviet power and had supposedly rejected God.[4] The phenomenon was equally true of Catholics and Orthodox.

The Sacred Congregation of the Holy Office in Rome had strictly forbidden the administration of Baptism to children of Orthodox parents unless the parents would promise to raise their children as Catholics.[5] Nazi Germany had officially banned its military from helping with the religious life of occupied territories. Although many German chaplains refused to minister to anyone outside the Axis armed forces, and even interfered with priest-medics who ministered "illegally" outside the troops,[6] other German, French, Italian, Hungarian, Slovak, and Romanian priests chose to administer the sacraments to all believers who asked for them. In this, they were often aided by soldiers: the *Wehrmacht* particularly disobeyed the ban in Ukraine throughout 1942.[7] These activist priests ran the risks of imprisonment or even execution.

Ecumenical Latin Catholic Ministry to Eastern Catholics

German Latin Catholic seminarians had been told it was a mortal sin for them to celebrate Mass atop an Eastern Rite antimension (although the requirement for either antimension or altar stone had long been abandoned by Soviet Catholics, as we have seen, the use of altar stones was strictly in force outside the USSR in the Latin Catholic Church). In the occupied territories, they often had no other altar available to them, yet the injunctions of seminary training were strong. By the same token, Latin Catholic priests were reluctant to use Greek Catholic churches for their services, or religious items from Greek Catholic priests. Only pointed reminders that the Axis soldiers faced the risk of dying without the benefit of sacraments would impel these chaplains to break the rules.

Ecumenical attitudes had to take root inside the Catholic Church at a time when the Latin Catholic majority had little to do with the Eastern minority, and Eastern Catholicism was viewed by many as an unequal partner in the Faith. During the war, Latin Catholic priests learned to celebrate Mass in Eastern Catholic churches, to accept concelebration with Eastern Catholic priests, and to accept material and spiritual assistance from them. None of this was typical of the day outside the occupied territories.

Common Characteristics of the Revival in the USSR

Everywhere that the Axis armies entered, Catholic believers came forward. In some areas, there were priests available, men who had either been in prisons whose inmates had survived the NKVD massacres that accompanied the Soviet retreat from the Axis invasion or who had completed their terms and were living under police surveillance.

Families had kept the Faith alive in secret, and they presented children, adolescents, and young adults to be baptized, couples to have marriages blessed, and all to receive First Confession and First Holy Communion. Father Nikolaus Pieger wrote that in every German village in the Black Sea region he had the same pattern: celebrate Mass in a cleansed and barren church, bless the graves of all who had died since the last priest was taken away, and celebrate collective baptisms, weddings, and communions. That the Faith had been successfully passed on in the family circle was miraculous, given the aggressive promotion of atheism at school and the exaltation of the "ideal" of turning in "enemies of the Party."

Just as they had with the imperial German forces in 1915–1918, Soviet civilians came forward with bread and salt and fed the exhausted troops of the invading armies. The Germans were seen as liberators from Communist terror. Their heartfelt welcome turned suddenly sour when, in the fourth week of the Axis campaign, the SS took over. Soviet prisoners were slaughtered or starved to death; Jews and those married to Jews, Communists and those married to Communists were massacred; the Soviet wounded and sick—soldiers and civilians alike—were refused medical treatment. After such horrors, the civilians would trust only the soldiers they had known. The *Wehrmacht* troops were deeply affected by these sights.[8]

CHAPTER 26

Revival in Belorussia

The entire Belorussian SSR came under Nazi occupation by October 1, 1941. In less than four months, the commissars of Stalin had been expelled. Like other Soviet peoples swept up in the Axis invasion, the Belorussians initially welcomed their conquerors.

The Nazis divided Belorussian territory into three areas:

1. BiaŁystok (Belostok) province became an administrative district of the German government.

2. The bulk of Polish Belorussia (Polesie and the town of Nowogródek), along with the Baltic SSRs, became part of the *Reichskommisariat Ostland,* under the civil administration *(Ostministerium)* of the hated Alfred Rosenberg, of mixed Baltic-German, Latvian, and Russian parentage, who taught and inspired Nazi racist ideology.

3. Central and eastern Belorussia came under German military rule.

In late 1941, the Nazi administrators agreed to the creation of the Samapomach, a Belorussian nationalist group that hoped eventually to establish an independent, self-governing Belorussian state; they permitted the group to organize schools and a defense corps. A Belorussian national revival in literature, drama, and education was followed, in 1942, by proclamation of the Belorussian Autocephalous Orthodox Church.[1] Nevertheless, the Nazis controlled everything of importance, and their atrocities against Jews, prisoners of war, and Christian civilians soon turned the people against them.

Massacres of Belorussian Jews and then of German Jews imported from the Nazi Fatherland stunned the Christian Belorussians, whose relations with their Jewish neighbors were generally very good during the occupation. Nor were Christian Belorussians spared. Attacks by Belorussian partisans against the German occupiers were met with harsh reprisals: entire villages were rounded up, herded into churches, and executed. Villages and cities were left empty and abandoned as residents fled to the woods and swamps. Silent streets welcomed the return of the Red Army: cities throughout the BSSR were almost entirely destroyed by 1945.

Having lost one-half million people to Soviet forced removals, the Belorussian SSR would lose many times that number by war's end. Some 4.2 million of its citizens were lost to massacres, mass resettlements, forced labor in Germany, and casualties of warfare: 1.5 million ethnic Belorussians, 1.5 million ethnic Poles,[2] and 1.2 million Jews.

The Nazis' Attitude Toward Catholicism in Poland and the BSSR

Like the Soviets, the Nazis viewed Catholicism as "the Polish religion"; indeed, they feared it as the most likely standard-bearer of a Polish revival and the defender of Polish culture. Despite the forced removals of ethnic Poles from the border oblasts of the BSSR in the late 1930s, there was still a large Polish minority. Moreover, before 1941, Polish and Belorussian Latin Catholics had been served by an overwhelmingly Polish clergy. The Nazis therefore imposed a strict ban on Polish priests from German-occupied Poland wishing to follow the *Wehrmacht* eastward. The German Secret Service reported that Catholic influence among the citizens and Great Russian immigrants of the BSSR posed "a political danger in the East."[3]

The Clergy

The few Catholic priests who survived the Stalinist purges were overwhelmed by work. Father Weliszynski, who worked as a street sweeper in Bobruysk on his release from prison, was finally able to resume his ministry, along with two other resident priests: Father Mieczysław Malynicz at Slutsk and Father Viktor Szutowicz at Borisov.[4]

Despite the ban, a few Polish priests, to include Valerian Chwałkowski, D. Malic, and Antoni Swiatospelk-Mirski,[5] did succeed in entering the BSSR through the assistance of local German officials, who thought that their presence would reconcile the people. Both native priests resident in the region and Polish migrants were restricted in their travels.[6] Jesuits were able to return to their historic territory: Father Antoni Swiatospelk-Mirski ministered to 10,000 people from Saint Josaphat's Church at the old College in Polotsk. Father Adam Sztark ministered at Slonim.[7] The Polish Carmelite Fathers Fidelis Krawiec and Gracjan Głowacz took over two abandoned parishes outside the city of Vitebsk in the autumn of 1941, only to be murdered in July 1942.[8]

Father Vincent Hadleushki, descended from the *uporstvuyushchie* and persecuted by the Poles under the Republic of Poland, returned from Vilnius

(Vilna). He became an active patriotic leader, working with the underground; he was shot in the summer of 1942 for his efforts.[9]

The Nazis shot 56 priests in the Pinsk diocese, and 25 more died naturally or in the fighting.[10] In 1942 they shot Father Sztark in Slonim; in 1944, Father Stanisław Sowa, SJ, in the concentration camp at Szaltupie.[11] They decimated the Greek Catholic clergy, executing the bishop himself. For a Church that was already short of priests, the losses were devastating. A Slovak chaplain, Father Jan Kelner-Brinsko, and another Polish priest, Father Jerzy Moskwa, were shot "in the early 1940s" after crossing into the occupation zone in response to the Vatican call for missionaries.[12]

In July 1943, at Nowogródek, the Gestapo executed eleven Sisters of the Holy Family of Nazareth out of hatred for the Faith.[13] They had offered their lives to God if the Germans would spare the men of Nowogródek who had been rounded up. The Sisters were butchered; the men were all safely returned to their families.

Church Restoration

To restore a church building that had been converted to secular use was an enormous undertaking. The building itself often had to be completely gutted: all intrusive secular objects removed and hauled away, artificial walls pulled down, electrical wiring either removed or rerouted, and floors and ceilings scrubbed or even replaced.

Usually, the stained-glass windows were long gone, as were the altars, communion vessels, tabernacles, statues, holy pictures, Stations of the Cross, vestments, books, candlesticks, candles, holy water fonts, candle racks for shrines, communion rails, pews, pulpits, and organs. Although some things had been hidden away by the faithful or were still in the church buildings, most were lost. The territories along the Eastern Front were absorbed in a bitter struggle, with food strictly rationed and almost all construction materials designated for the German forces. People were hungry, cold, and without resources, and they were supporting a Church that did not have the blessings of the governing powers. It seemed impossible to restore Catholic worship again. And yet restore it they did.

Revival in the Central BSSR

Occupied in the first weeks of the Axis invasion, the central Belorussian SSR was home to a host of devastated churches that were soon cleaned up and restored. In Minsk, the venerable Saint Mary's Cathedral, which had been turned into a municipal garage, and the Church of Saints Simon and Helen (built only in 1910),[14] which had been converted into a theater, were both restored for Catholic worship, as were churches in Bobruysk, Dzerzhinsk (Kojdanow), Timkovichi, Uzda, Logoisk, Borisov, Slutsk, Zaslavl', and "many others of which we know little."[15]

Revival in the Eastern BSSR

Catholic military chaplains with the Axis forces held public Masses in Baranovichi, Vitebsk, and Smolensk. The local commanders also turned over empty churches to surviving local priests.[16] The Mogilev cathedral, one church in Polotsk, and churches in Bykhov and Shklov are known to have been restored to public worship after the occupation began.[17]

Father Häring was the first priest in the area around Gomel since 1923. Asked to perform large numbers of baptisms, he resorted to a collective baptism that he called "one of the most wonderful liturgical experiences in my long priestly life." There had been little time for preparation, but it was a moment of genuine evangelization. Deprived of books, and unable to recall the Latin texts, Father Häring celebrated entirely in the vernacular, in an especially solemn service. The gathered believers wept much "so full were their hearts," and the ceremony had to be stopped frequently.[18] Though the baptism ceremony was performed for Russian Orthodox, it could easily describe the Belorussian Catholic experience elsewhere at that time.

Polish priests working in the heart of the Minsk diocese reported that 4,000 believers between the ages of 7 and 30 received First Communion in the diocesan seat alone. One priest reported baptizing 3,000 people in Minsk and its environs. Holy days were publicly observed, and a procession of 200 children marked the feast of Saints Simon and Helena.

Belorussian Greek Catholics

The Greek Catholic Churches of both the Belorussian and Ukrainian traditions were particularly feared by Rosenberg and his minions in the *Ostministerium*. The priests were not amenable to Nazi manipulation, and fostered local nationalism. In Belorussia, the Greek Catholic clergy would only give thanks for German rule when it was demanded of them and they were pressured to do so.[19]

The Nazis inherited the forced union of Polish and Soviet Belorussia and, with it, the "Neo-Uniate" Church's parishes. The exarchate established by Sheptytsky for the "Neo-Uniates" demonstrated the deep roots of the union among the Belorussian faithful. Bishop Anton Nemancevic's mission parishes came to include 30,000 faithful in a few months, as people flocked to attend Greek Catholic services and hear sermons preached in Belorussian.[20] Although Metropolitan Sheptytsky's attempts to send missionaries into Belorussia to assist in this revival failed, the Byzantine Catholic Liturgy was celebrated in Polotsk and elsewhere.

The Jesuit Belorussian Exarch Anton Nemancevic was arrested in Minsk and martyred in 1942, dying from either typhus or an executioner's bullet in a Nazi concentration camp.[21] The Gestapo martyred nine of his priests. (Two others, Fathers Novikov and Walter Ciszek from the Albertyn mission, were captured deep inside the USSR by the Communists. Bishop Charnetsky was still alive and free in Volhynia, where worship life continued, without any organizational structure left to coordinate the forty parishes from prewar Poland and the new parishes in the prewar BSSR.)

CHAPTER 27

Revival in Ukraine

The weeping was such that I shall never forget it my whole life long.
—Father Nikolaus Pieger, referring to the Russia
German Catholics who greeted him in Ukraine

Father Pieger was a German military chaplain who entered the southern Ukrainian SSR with the *Wehrmacht* in 1941 and was able to minister to the few surviving Catholics there. The poignancy of that moment, in Baden, epitomizes the Catholic revival in Ukraine.

Unlike Soviet Belorussia, Soviet Ukraine had virtually no Catholic priests left in 1941. Father Valentin Greiner was 80 years old, living in his tiny room in the Katharinental School. Father Johannes Schneider was still living in Strassburg. Father Franz Rauh, who had been arrested in Rothammel in 1928 and released in late spring of 1941, just before the invasion, was assigned to office work under police supervision.[1] Father Johannes Schönberger, ordained in 1911, and last known as pastor in Hildmann, was also in the region.[2] These four were the only priests remaining in the territory of the old Tiraspol diocese, and by 1941, none of them was able to exercise his ministry.[3]

The small Eastern Catholic communities at Kiev and in Crimea no longer existed, although there were still some Armenian Catholics in Crimea. The NKVD would disrupt that community after "liberation."

German Colonies

The extent of Soviet devastation in the Nazi-occupied Black Sea German colonies can be glimpsed in *Wehrmacht* photographs of church services. In one picture of a double wedding Mass in Kleinliebental, the woman's side of the church is packed, but the men's side has fewer than thirty men in isolated clusters. Saddest witness of all, a little boy is standing all by himself. What had become of his father, his brothers, his uncles?[4]

"South Russia"

The ethnic Polish community of the Ukrainian SSR had been devastated by the forced relocation of the border communities and urban minorities. Still, here as elsewhere, German chaplains' public Masses attracted both Catholics and Orthodox. Father Bernard Häring celebrated Mass in a theater near Kiev's Kreshchatyk Boulevard to huge crowds of German soldiers, inevitably attracting many civilians as well.

Although German chaplains such as Father Häring did volunteer work among the Orthodox and Catholic civilians, due to the opposition of Nazi ideologists and fanatics, there was no organized Catholic mission. The situation was different in the Romanian-occupied zone of the UkSSR.

Transnistria

When the Axis forces occupied southern Ukraine, Romania took on the administration of a vast region called "Transnistria" (Across the Dniester), from the Dniester to the Bug River, that still included many Catholics.[5] Invaded by Romania on July 17, 1944, all of Transnistria came under Axis control by August, except Odessa, which fell on October 16, after a long and bloody assault by combined Romanian and German forces.

At the request of the papal nuncio in Bucharest, Father Pieger enlisted the aid of a medical orderly, Father Joseph Arnold, and together they undertook an investigative tour from August 20 to September 10, 1941. A Reich German who had long served as spiritual advisor to German Catholics at Bucharest, Father Pieger was familiar with the *Volksdeutsche* of southern Ukraine. The following information is based on the report he sent to Rome at the conclusion of his tour.

Black Sea Colonies

Due to the rapidity of the Axis advance in the first weeks of the war, a large number of Black Sea German colonies were not evacuated at all by the Soviets. In other colonies, where the men had been drafted into the Red Army, the women and children were still at home when the Soviets retreated. The priests fell into a steady pattern of work: meeting with a community, blessing holy water, then blessing the church. Mass would be offered for all those who had died since the removal of the last priest, and their graves blessed. Then came the baptisms, confessions, First Communions, marriages, Anointing.

At Strassburg, there was great desolation. The town, which had suffered an earthquake in 1940, had been taken after bitter fighting. Some 2,500 believers attended the first Mass; in a church bereft of altars, statues, bells, and tower, the choir sang the responses to a Requiem Mass, a Te Deum of thanksgiving, and the *Salve Regina* to Our Lady, all in Latin: living proof of the tenacity of the Black Sea Germans' faith and tradition. The last Mass in Strassburg had been celebrated in 1932; the church had been converted into a dance hall and theater. Father Pieger baptized 300 children, only to find another 100 waiting.

In Baden, 2,300 believers attended Mass, asking that their church be consecrated and that requiems be held for their dead. They also asked Father Pieger to consecrate a new cemetery and to bless the graves in the old one. A former seminarian from the long-closed institute in Saratov, who had served in the dangerous ministry of religious leader for the colony, told him that the day of the reconsecrations was the most beautiful of his life.

In Munich, the most religious of the Black Sea German colonies, there were 1,200 Catholics and not a single Communist. Before Mass was to be celebrated in the church, the people went to the blacksmith's, where they proceeded to unearth the sacred items buried for protection from the Communists. A gold pyx with Consecrated Hosts, the altar stone with the relics of the saints, the monstrance (minus its base), and the crucifix from the cemetery had all been buried in the blacksmith's yard, and the vestments beneath his stables. A wooden base was fashioned for the monstrance (miraculously unblemished after its years of hiding), and Father Pieger placed the Sacred Host inside for exposition. At this, the joy of the faithful was boundless: "Now everything will go well; because we can see our Lord God again."

In Karlsruhe, the site of the illegal seminary and the show trials of so many Soviet Catholics, the biggest church of the Black Sea German colonies was desecrated but still standing. Though there was no religious organization of any kind left in this community of 2,550, "the participation of those in attendance was no less fervent." Here was another recovery of sacred objects. When the church had been closed, a Sacred Host had been walled up inside a house to save it from desecration, along with the relics of the altar stone, in sort of a tabernacle. After Mass, the woman from that house told Father Pieger the story, and a festive procession was held through the streets with the liberated Christ and relics.

At Katharinental, Father Pieger met the heroic Father Greiner, who was 81 years old, blind, and frail, and who told him the entire history of the destruction of the institutional Church. All of his conferees had been taken away. Not one had apostasized: every one had been a martyr.

In Speyer, which had the unhappy distinction of having the most Communists in a Catholic parish, every place in the church was taken for the first mass, and, as at other churches, the day was filled with sacraments. In Sulz, the cemetery blessing was all the more emotional because there were so many fresh graves of newly executed victims.

In Josefstal, 1,573 believers (95 percent of the colony's residents) attended and sang High Mass and Vespers for the Dead. In Franzfeld, all but 30 in the town's 1,005 survivors were still Catholics. One Catholic man had been shot in the street for tearing up an atheist petition. The parents here begged for religious materials for their young people to learn the Faith better. At Kleinliebental, Father Pieger learned what became known as the legacy of the Black Sea German priests. The last priest had divided his parish into sections, and appointed a woman in charge of each section (there were virtually no men left); he taught these women how to baptize, witness marriages, and recite prayers for the dead for funerals. When the women were forcibly removed, the legacy endured both in the colonies and in the diaspora. In Mariental, he found that the martyred priest Father Johannes Nold had organized everyone into a living rosary confraternity before his arrest. Every child was baptized, and there had been no Communist secular ceremonies in the colony.[6]

When Father Pieger sent his report to the pope, he requested that a priest from the old Tiraspol diocese, Doctor Martin Glaser, then a professor at the Jassy seminary under Bishop Robu, be sent into Ukraine and south Russia. Accordingly, the Catholic Mission of South Russia was formally founded, and Doctor Glaser was sent as apostolic visitor to Transnistria. Father Pieger undertook several tours of the different Russia German colonies, with the aid of Father Walter Kampe, German military chaplains, and priests from the Latin Catholic dioceses in Romania.

A number of clergy entered the region despite the German ban. Doctor Glaser coordinated the work of Italian, Romanian-German, French, and Reich German priests ministering to the traumatized Catholics of Nazi-occupied southern Ukraine, and based at the former diocesan center of Odessa, which had fallen to Romania in October 1941. In 1943, Doctor Glaser became the bishop, and Fathers Pieger and Kampe were named to the diocesan curia, Father Pieger being the vicar general.

Odessa

In 1941, Odessa had a Catholic population of about 8,000, according to the German Jesuit Father Egon Sendler. Only the Church of Saint Peter, once in the care of French Assumptionists, still survived in respectable shape: a community of laity had administered it ever since the last priest was removed, and when the Assumptionists returned, they found the church intact.

Assumption Cathedral had been made into a stable for horses and a military depot. The altars were gone, the windows were without glass, and in place of the altarpiece was a huge portrait of Stalin. Once Odessa had been occupied by the Axis, the Catholics had begun clearing out the mess to prepare for restoration of worship. Doctor Glaser began daily Masses as soon as possible there, blessing the church at All Saints Day (November 1) in the presence of 1,000 faithful.[7]

A poor Polish couple gave a room to the German Fathers who came there in 1941. The altarpiece, a painting of the Assumption of the Virgin, was discovered in a local museum, and people went to work restoring the church to its former splendor. It became the center of religious activity and of priestly community, with Catholic priest-medics from the *Wehrmacht* coming to the church. Daily Masses were offered during the week, and on Sunday there were three masses and vespers, all sung in Latin by the faithful of the city with hymns in German and Polish. The former organist of the parish had organized an excellent choir as well for Sunday and holy day services. In 1942, the Assumption cathedral was site of the city's first class for First Holy Communion in many years. The joyous cries from the crowd of "Great God, we praise Thee!" could be heard in the streets.[8]

Yet, even in a setting such as this, the priests were not safe. In that same year, the SS tried to arrest Father Pieger because he spoke the truth in public. One of the Catholic schoolgirls was told by her distraught sister, who worked in the SS offices, and early in the morning she rushed through the empty streets to warn the priest. He heeded the warning, and was hidden away until he could escape to Bessarabia.[9] Still, he and the others continued their work in southern Ukraine until the Axis withdrawal.

Two other Odessa missionaries were Fathers Jean Nicholas, a French Assumptionist, and Pietro Leoni, an Italian Jesuit. They served Saint Peter's and also a new Byzantine Catholic parish that they founded after their arrival in September 1943. (Like some other foreign priests, they did not withdraw with the Axis forces, but remained in Odessa after its surrender to the Red Army in

April 1944. In their churches, they "proclaimed the existence of God, the Catholic Church, and the primacy of the Pope."[10] They continued to minister for a year to both Catholics and Orthodox,[11] until their arrest—they were said to have been denounced by the restored Russian Orthodox bishop. Both were interned in Siberian labor camps, being repatriated only after 1950.)

Fate of the Mission

From January to July 1943, some 10,500 Russia Germans were removed for the Reich's labor service. After October 1943, the *Wehrmacht* evacuated the remaining 350,000 Russia German civilians from Ukraine and Transnistria, ostensibly to be sent to the so-called Warthegau as agricultural settlers, but in fact to be conscripted as soldiers in the *Wehrmacht* or *Waffen SS*. The survivors were scattered into central Germany, whence 200,000 were captured by the Red Army. About 110,000 escaped into the western zones, but 45,000 were forcibly repatriated back to the Soviet Union from 1945 to 1946. Many committed suicide rather than go back.

(The Assumption cathedral functioned fitfully until 1949, when it was finally closed until 1990. The Church of Saint Joseph in Nikolaev was reopened only in 1990, and Saint Peter's was the only church to remain open. It was closed after the arrest of the missionaries, but was restored to religious use in 1947 with Father Butyrowicz serving as the first priest under Soviet rule since the early 1920s.[12] None of the other parishes was restored.)

Bishop Glaser left Transnistria in 1944 with the refugees. He settled again at Jassy, where he became the coadjutor bishop and was arrested by the Communists. (He died in prison in 1950 of a heart attack brought on by interrogations.) Father Pieger accompanied the refugees and was caught in August 1944 by the Reds. He was repatriated to Germany two years later, and later provided the religious supplement to the Russia German newspaper. Father Kampe survived to become the auxiliary bishop of Limburg in West Germany.[13]

Central Ukraine

Roman Catholics in the territory between the pre-1939 Soviet border and Kiev were still present in the oblasts when they were conquered by the Axis in 1941. They had maintained their faith despite the loss of every single church and priest. With great sacrifices, they restored numerous churches dating from the sixteenth and seventeenth centuries and Catholic worship was held once again.

Zhitomir Diocese

The church in Slawuta was reopened during the Nazi-occupation, but closed after the war ended.[14] The Cathedral of Saint Sophia in Zhitomir itself was restored during the war, and continued to remain open under Father Alexander Samosenko.

Kamenets Diocese

Parishes were reopened during the occupation at Brahilow, Bratslav, Chmielnik, Deraznia, Dunajowce, Felsztyn, Gniewan, Granow, Grodek Podolski, Jarmolince, Kopijowka, Minkowce, Mohylow Podolski, Mukarow, Satanow, Skazince, Smotrycz, Solobkowce, Struga, Szarawka, Tarnoruda, Tynna, Uszyca, (closed in 1945), and Czerniowce Podolskie (closed in 1947).

Holy Trinity church in Manikowce was reopened and closed at "liberation" (it would be reopened successfully in 1948). Saint Michael's was opened in the war years (receiving a priest in 1953), as was Our Lady of the Angels Church in Vinnitsa, (which stayed open, receiving a priest in 1948.)

Greek Catholics

Metropolitan Sheptytsky held two synods of exarchs, in September 1940 and again in June 1942, at which plans were laid for future missionary work in the east. At the first synod, it was with the hope that the door would be opened again in Russia in the course of the war. The second synod dealt with work in the Nazi-occupied territories of the Soviet Union.[15] Sheptysky's missionaries were generally captured and sent back to Galicia, although two priests from Lwów (L'viv) succeeded in establishing themselves in Kiev, where they restored the Greek Catholic parish there, closed in 1934 (the church had been demolished). Again closed, in March 1942, the parish was briefly allowed to reopen when rumors spread around the world that Stalin was seeking an accommodation with the pope.[16] No trace was left of Greek Catholic missionary work in central Ukraine. (The Church would be reestablished only when western Ukrainian Catholics moved or were moved there after the 1950s.)

CHAPTER 28

The Flight to the West

W ith the decisive German defeat at Stalingrad in February 1943, the tide of the war turned. The great tank battle at Kursk in July of that year marked the beginning of the Soviets' tortuous advance toward Germany, which would engulf millions in yet another bloody phase of the war.

Kharkov fell on August 23, and by September 7, the Nazi retreat from Ukraine had begun. A lull in October was followed by further Soviet advances, with Crimea being isolated, and Kiev falling on November 6. By the end of the year, the Red Army was in Zhitomir. Catholic-inhabited areas were already again under the Soviet flag. By the summer of 1944, all Soviet territory had been liberated. By August 17, the Red Army was on the border of East Prussia and pushing deep into Romania.

On September 4, Finland withdrew from the Axis, freeing up Soviet forces. On September 15, 1944, Hitler finally allowed his beleaguered forces to withdraw to the Dnieper. The withdrawal degenerated into a rout, however, and by September 30, the Red Army had established five bridgeheads across the river. It entered the Reich on October 16, penetrating into the outer reaches of East Prussia. The Germans' painful retreat would end only in the ruins of Berlin, and would embroil many of the Catholics we have been studying.

In the north, *Volksdeutsche* from Warthegau, Reich Germans from Danzig, East Prussia, and eastern Germany itself, and Estonians, Latvians, and Lithuanians from the Baltic States fled west before the advancing Red Army. In the south, they were joined by Ukrainians, including many Ukrainian Catholics, *Volksdeutsche,* Romanians, Hungarians, and others.

Soviet propaganda had encouraged the Red Army soldiers to take their vengeance on all people of German descent and on any who had allegedly collaborated with them. Many soldiers also had personal scores to settle. The butchery of Slavic innocents by the *SS Einsatzgruppen* now reaped its bitter harvest. In the Soviets' 242d Rifle Regiment, for example, 158 soldiers had relatives who had been killed or tortured; 56 had lost their families to Nazi concentration camps, and 445 had had their homes destroyed. Gasoline was poured on the fire of Soviet revenge with the discovery of comfortable German quarters right beside the appalling concentration camps.[1] As soon as Germany proper was entered in January 1945, the Red Army soldiers went on a rampage of looting, rape, and slaughter of civilians and animals in refugee columns. The Red Army's marshals were appalled by these atrocities, and consigned the leading offenders to the labor camps, but the atrocities continued until after the German defeat.

The *Volksdeutsche* resettled in Warthegau from the USSR, Romania, and Poland had known Soviet rule for varying amounts of time, and had no intention of being restored to it. The Balts also had no desire to repeat what had happened in 1940–1941. Enormous numbers headed south on foot with the retreating *Wehrmacht* or boarded ships or boats to cross over to Sweden.

The Germans had learned in 1944 where the Allied occupation zones were going to be. As a result, the *Wehrmacht* fought on in the West so as to keep the lines of retreat across the Elbe open as long as possible. Civilians also learned where the zones were to be, and when the scope of the Soviet terror became known, great masses of people in the east pressed on to reach the territories allotted to the Western Allies.[2]

As the war drew to a close, the *Wehrmacht* sought to hold the line against the relentless onslaught of the Red Army. Under pressure from the other Allies, the Americans halted their headlong advance and ceded the prize of Berlin to the Soviets, which prolonged the fighting. For the Soviet Catholics caught up in this awful scene, Death seemed a better deliverer than long-forgotten Peace.

The North

> My mother and I were on the last train to leave Danzig. We had nothing, not even a suitcase. The train was filled with wounded, and the planes were shooting at us. So many people I lost. But I thank God we were on that train. I was only a little girl, but I know what those Russians would have done to us.
>
> —East Prussian refugee

All accounts agree that the drive of the Red Army into the Baltic region and the Prussian provinces inspired mass terror. For the Balts, the return of the Soviets meant a return to the Stalinist horror of 1940–1941. As the *Wehrmacht* retreated south or toward the coast, many young men took to the forests, and carried on a partisan war behind the lines. Tens of thousands of ordinary people fled across the sea or with the *Wehrmacht* soldiers who stood as their last defense against Communist rule. Although these people anti-Nazi as well as anti-Bolshevik, they saw their only hope of freedom in fleeing west with the soldiers of the same government that had betrayed them by not restoring their independent states in the summer of 1941. Even Allied prisoners of war did not want to wait for the Soviets, and fled west with the civilian refugees.

The flight of 200,000 civilians from the Baltic States and the northeastern edge of Germany took place by sea, to Sweden and Denmark, and by land and sea, to Germany via Memel (Klaipéda) and across East Prussia. Estonia lost 60,000 people, Latvia 90,000, and Lithuania 50,000. Flight across the Baltic Sea was perilous. Soviet submarines and planes made a point of sinking refugee ships heading out of Baltic and German ports. Some 15,000 lives were lost in the deliberate sinking of only two of the many refugee ships they destroyed, the *Wilhelm Gustloff* and the *Goya* in January and April of 1945.

On land, waves of refugees and soldiers poured into East Prussia, and they were joined by more tens of thousands of civilians from eastern Germany who took to the roads.[3] The Soviet revenge for the rape of Mother Russia was horrendous. The little village of Nemmersdorf was the first Reich German locale to be conquered, and the stories of the massacre of its inhabitants provoked a wholesale exodus of refugees. That incident became the first of thousands. People fled in great treks of wagons, cars, on horseback, and on foot. Soviet atrocities included crucifying their victims, raping women as their families were forced to watch, and running over columns of refugees with tanks. Massacres took place in farmhouses and villages alike. The Soviet Command finally intervened, but as the front progressed, so did the "elemental tide with pity for no one."[4] This raging force of terror impelled Reich Germans and *Volksdeutsche* alike to wrap up babies and old people in blankets and set out in the dead of winter as the front continued to move westward.

Hitler's insane conduct of the war doomed the German soldiers and civilians. Local Nazi officials would not evacuate a town until the Soviets were too close (they made sure they were the first ones out). Soviet, Polish, and Baltic prisoners of war and slave laborers would intervene for Germans who had acted properly toward them, and try to protect them against the Red Army soldiers.

A special hell existed on Germany's Baltic border at Memel (Klaipéda). The city was swamped with Lithuanians, Latvians, anti-Communist Russians, with English and Canadian prisoners of war and with East Prussians who had been forced to flee north when their escape route was cut by the Red Army.

The name of Memel evoked salvation for all these people, who hoped to be evacuated from there by the German navy. Soviet tanks surrounded the city on all sides. As naval and civilian vessels pulled up to the docks past sunken ships to pick up the refugees, however, Soviet aircraft repeatedly flew through heavy antiaircraft fire to strafe and bomb these columns of helpless people. Fog-shrouded, in flaming ruins, Memel hung on, with young girls caring for the wounded soldiers, and with civilians of all ethnic backgrounds and both sexes joining in with the troops to try to hold some sort of defensive line against the Soviets, while ships and boats of every description tried to save as many as possible. Miraculously, almost all of the refugees were safely evacuated while the *Wehrmacht* troops fought on: only then did the Germans begin to evacuate their own wounded troops, all the while fighting a losing battle.[5]

The masses of refugees, wounded, and those troops who escaped landed at places such as Pillau, which quickly became cut off or surrounded, or if they were lucky, made it all the way to Danzig, and some even went to occupied Denmark. Although Danzig was also doomed, at least from there land and sea routes were still open in late 1944 and early 1945 to the rest of the steadily shrinking Third Reich. As the Red Army closed in, frantic people crossed the frozen Frisches Haff, the vast lagoon that bordered the coast of East Prussia. The temperature dropped to five degrees below zero, killing the wounded, sick, and malnourished. Hopelessly lost children, whose parents had died in the crossing or before, in village massacres, wandered through the crowds of refugees. A huge metal cross, covered with frost, was raised upon a small hill, where priests encouraged the faithful to continue their struggle: "It looked like a huge sword, thrust into the breast of catastrophe."[6] Balts, Germans, and prisoners of war crossed the frozen lagoon despite the danger of Soviet bombs, which would shatter the ice and send people, animals, autos, and wagons to a frigid watery grave, to reach a long, narrow strip of land that eventually led to Danzig.

Civilians had no food; soldiers got two handfuls of flour and a cup of hot water with a tiny bit of tea. Children were freezing to death, horses strained to pull carts loaded with the wounded and dying, and still they came. The horror of Soviet rule and the unbelievable atrocities against the East Prussians impelled German and Balt alike to push on.

The *Volksdeutsche* colony of Warthegau was centered around the former German city of Posen (Polish Poznan in 1919–1939 and today). Its Nazi leader, a German native of Posen, had put all his trust in Hitler, and so made no plans to evacuate the territory until January 20, when he was ordered to come to Berlin. People in the eastern province were simply abandoned to the

Poles and Russians. The Posen citadel held out until February 22, but by then the armies had long since swept past.[7]

When the *Wehrmacht* blew up the bridges across the Oder River to halt the Soviet advance, they trapped refugees on the other side. Frantic people crossed until the last possible second. Behind them were scenes from hell: women and girls raped before their spouses and parents, who were forced to watch and then butchered, Soviet tanks plowing through columns of refugees, and endless looting. The screams alone were enough to impel refugees to take any chance at deliverance.[8] Finally, in March 1945, the tragedy in East Prussia came to an end. Kolberg fell on March 18, after everyone had been safely evacuated, Gdingen (Gdynia) on March 28, and Danzig on March 30, with helpless refugees still trapped. Some two million had escaped; perhaps as many had died.

A large *Wehrmacht* force continued to fight on in Courland, the southern part of Latvia, in yet another of Hitler's ridiculously termed "Fortresses." Supported by Latvians and Lithuanians, the hope of all three groups was that their independent presence would force the Western Allies to intervene against Stalin. The Soviets considered the Balts to be their citizens, and so would shoot captured Latvian nationalists as traitors. Here, too, some German officers assisted in civilian evacuation along with the flight of their soldiers. But the war ended too quickly for all these people, and the Western Allies did not intervene on behalf of the Baltic States or the trapped civilians and German military.

When Germany surrendered on May 8, 1945, they were all still trapped there. The Flensburg government of defeated Germany was able to evacuate 120,000 of them after the surrender, but the *Wehrmacht* group itself numbered nearly 300,000, which meant that most soldiers did not make it out. Rather than surrender to an uncertain fate, many Germans joined local guerrilla forces in their struggle against the Reds. Again, most people expected a war between the West and the Soviets, and so there were high hopes for eventual liberation.[9] (Real and imagined Balt-German cooperation against the Soviets would be used to exact an awful toll on the Baltic population from 1945 to 1955.)

The Baltic refugees pass out of our story, into the vast mass of displaced persons found inside the destroyed Reich at the end of the war. Very few of those who were in the Western zones in 1945 voluntarily returned to their homelands, although Sweden forcibly repatriated refugee Baltic soldiers in 1946.[10]

The South

> Oh my God, it was so awful. The bombs, the fires, the killing. We were so
> scared all the time, so afraid the Russians would catch us. I never saw
> some of my family again, I don't even know where they died. But it was
> worth it, I would do it again. Never would I live under them again after
> what happened to us in 1940, never.
>
> —Ukrainian refugee from Bukovina

Conditions in the south were not much better. The *Wehrmacht* ordered the
evacuation of the ethnic German population in the summer of 1944 as they
began their retreat from Ukraine. Because many of the Slavs believed Soviet
propaganda that there would be no reprisals, the evacuation of the German
colonies was often sabotaged by local residents to save their villages and towns
and to establish their credentials as antifascists upon the return of their old
rulers.

Those who lived in the Donets Basin and had experienced the return of
Soviet rule in the winter of 1943–44 had no desire to repeat the experience,
and they joined the collaborators and residents of destroyed areas in a flight of
600,000 Ukrainians (10 percent of the affected population), of whom only
280,000 actually made it across the Dnieper.[11] When the Ukrainian cities were
surrendered, large numbers of intellectuals and professionals fled with the retreating *Wehrmacht;* indeed, they ranked as the largest category of voluntary
refugees out of the USSR.[12] Thus, as the front pushed across Ukraine, the
number of refugees grew.

The Catholic population of the South was affected by three events: (1) the
evacuation of the German colonies of the Black Sea and Beresan regions; (2)
the flight from Galicia; (3) the flight from Bukovina.

Flight from the Black Sea Coast and Volhynia

The evacuation of the Black Sea, Beresan, and Volhynian Germans affected
some 300,000 people. Their treks headed west across Romania and Hungary,
or across Nazi-occupied Poland. Some were ordered to settle in Warthegau, a
German colony in Poland where the Bukovinan, Bessarabian, and west Volhynian Germans had been forcibly resettled in 1940–1941 in place of Polish
natives. They experienced the same misgivings and fears of those earlier settlers. The others went on a seemingly endless march, finally ending in Austria

or southern Germany as the Reich collapsed. As in the north, they were subjected to hunger and fear, their long wagon trains defenseless against attacks from the air. Their flight inspired fear throughout Central Europe, as people began to think that such would be the fate of everyone, not just of Germans.

Flight from Galicia

In July 1944 pressure began to build on German defenses in western Ukraine/Galicia. The battle broke out on July 13, and by July 27 the Red Army had retaken Lwów (L'viv). Nearly 300 Greek Catholic priests joined the exodus of Ukrainian refugees from the province, despite the metropolitan's orders to remain in their parishes, out of fear for their lives. The Home Army (AK) and Ukrainian Insurgent Army (UPA) continued their fratricidal warfare, while fighting the Red Army as well as remnants of the German forces pulling out for the west. Helpless civilians, devastated in continual battles and raids, begrudgingly welcomed the reestablishment of Soviet rule, which at least reduced the amount of fighting.

On August 8, a new front command took charge of *Wehrmacht* operations in the Carpathians. A bitter battle developed for the passes through the mountains, with town of Dukla falling on September 20. Bishop Theodore Romzha of the Greek Catholic eparchy of Mukachevo prevailed upon the German commander to rescind his evacuation order, fearful of the chaos that would engulf his parishioners in the maelstrom of air raids, partisan attacks, and full-scale battles of Central Europe. Ethnic Germans were to be evacuated, but the Slavic and Hungarian populations were allowed to remain at home.

In Carpatho-Ruthenia, only some of the *Volksdeutsche* were successfully evacuated west; most were overtaken by the Soviet advance. The Soviets deported the Germans from Teresiental and the villages around Mukachevo to Tyumen or labor camps in Siberia.[13] Others were allowed to remain in their traditional villages but with no civil rights.

Flight from Bukovina

The Soviets breached the German defenses at Kamenets on March 23, 1944. This created panic and flight from both portions of Bukovina. Several German priests who gathered together for this purpose held the last big Easter services at Kimpolung-Dornawatra.

The collapse of the German resistance to the north meant that Romania's turn was obviously next. On August 20, the Red Army struck above Jassy, encircling both German and Romanian forces in the field. Throughout the summer, the *Wehrmacht* had begun to organize transports for the civilians, and the last trek had headed out on August 9. One priest, Father Kaminski, went with the refugees to Bavaria. The other Latin Catholic priests fled into Transylvania, as did Bishop Ioan Robu. The Catholics who remained in southern Bukovina were "without shepherds and soon without a Chief Shepherd," for the bishop died on September 27.[14]

A popular uprising on August 23 had resulted in Romania's leaving the Axis, and in King Michael's surrendering unconditionally to the Allies. Even so, the Soviets pushed on and occupied Bucharest at the end of the month. Their victory meant that northern Bukovina would once again be part of the USSR.

German retreat prompted Ukrainian flight. Entire villages hid in the forests, and then set out for Austria. Unlike the Western Allies, these people had no doubts about Stalin. The Red Army captured some of the Ukrainian treks, and the refugees were sent back home or shot.

At rail junctions, all the refugees had to abandon their wagons and livestock. Jammed into boxcars, they headed west, hoping their trains would not be forgotten on a siding or strafed by the Reds. Those who survived were unloaded into detention camps that were being bombed by the Western Allies. Families were split up in the chaos, finding each other only years later through the mails.

Evacuation became the order of the day for these helpless pawns in the spring of 1945 as central Poland was liberated, and once again they took to the roads to flee west. The Red Army again caught many treks; wagons and occupants were deliberately crushed under Soviet tanks; men murdered after being forced to watch their women being raped; those who survived were rounded up and put on trains to be removed to the USSR.

The Repatriations of Russia Germans to the USSR

Of the *Volksdeutsche* who made it into the west and who evaded the Red Army, only 50,000 were allowed to remain behind by the Allied Powers. All of the rest were sent back. Indeed, out of 8,346,000 Soviet citizens in Germany at the end of the war, only 375,000 were able to stay abroad: all the others were sent back to executions or to slow deaths in the Gulag.[15]

Conditions on the trains to the forced labor camps were horrific. German children were taken from their mothers and given to Poles. People died from starvation, dehydration, and disease; their bodies were thrown out along the rail tracks. Women were raped repeatedly; men were tortured. Those who survived arrived weak, sick, and hungry, and yet were immediately pressed into heavy labor with no medical care. Frostbite claimed hands and feet; epidemics of dysentery, dropsy, and malnutrition killed thousands. At the Alshevsk camp in the Donets Basin, 1,100 of 1,600 people died in the first six months. Reich Germans who were eventually repatriated (from 1948 to 1956) were deprived of addresses of their friends and relatives left behind to prevent them from maintaining contact.[16]

CHAPTER 29

Catholicism and
Soviet Expansion into Europe

Western naïveté about the USSR during the war apparently knew few limits. In September 1942, when Hitler sent out peace feelers through the papal nuncio in Turkey (the future Pope John XXIII) by which Germany would end the war but keep much of what it had conquered, Roosevelt responded in a message to the pope that the Western powers had good relations with the USSR and expected Soviet cooperation in restructuring the world, and that he believed the Soviet Union had changed from a totalitarian state. The Casablanca Conference of the Western powers in 1943 sealed the fate of Eastern and Central Europe; the Yalta Agreement, in which the Allies committed themselves to force Germany and the Axis into unconditional surrender, simply ratified that development.[1] The Anglican archbishop of York declared that there was nothing separating Communism and Christianity, whereas Fascism had to be destroyed, and the "Red Dean" of England claimed that churches were opening in the USSR. Indeed, the Anglican bishop of Chelmsford went so far as to consider the destruction of anti-Bolshevik movements a top priority.[2] All the books written by escapees, all the tragic letters printed in émigré newspapers, all the speeches given by moderates who were not fascists but wary of the dangers of Communism, all these fell on deaf ears. At least in the early 1920s, those who believed the likes of Shaw could defend themselves that they had no knowledge of what was really going on in the USSR, but no one could claim that defense in 1942, especially not those in the governments of the Allied Powers of the West. Their naïveté, their rank obtusiveness, stunned the Holy See.

Stalin's campaign to regain the tsarist empire and all Soviet losses accelerated as the war raged on, and after it ended. In Asia, the USSR annexed the Republic of Tannu Tuva on the border of Mongolia; in Europe, Soviet-Finnish frontier of 1940 was restored, the Baltic States and eastern Poland were forcibly reincorporated, and the Romanians were forced to return hapless Bessarabia.

This caused great anxiety to the Holy See. Roosevelt wrote the Pope in 1943 that he believed religious freedom would be restored in the USSR after the war. The British and Americans both behaved as if Stalin's vast empire was a democracy, or at least well on its way to becoming one. The Vatican was appalled and alarmed by such gullibility—and rightly so. Soviet reincorporation of the the the Baltic States, the partitioning of Poland, and the installation of the Red Army throughout the Balkans directly contravened what the Atlantic Charter had proposed for a free Europe. The Pope rejected Stalin's claims about religious freedom. The Holy See wanted action, not propaganda phrases.[3] Unfortunately, what the Vatican feared came to pass, and Catholicism entered into a period of persecution unsurpassed in Christian history.

Postwar Soviet Annexations

Ruthenia

Czechoslovakia was forced to cede to the Soviets the strategic province of Ruthenia, which was incorporated into the Ukrainian SSR as Zakarpatska oblast, many of whose 800,000 inhabitants were Greek Catholics, and which had been part of Hungary for a millennium and of Czechoslovakia for less than a generation (see also "Eastern Czechoslovakia" below). The annexation, allegedly to "reunite" the inhabitants with Greater Ukraine, placed the Red Army in control of the Carpathian mountain passes leading directly into the Hungarian plain and created a common Soviet-Hungarian border[4] (to prove advantageous in 1956 during the Hungarian Revolt). Throughout Czechoslovak, rule there had been bitter debates as to exactly what the national orientation of the non-Slovak Slavic inhabitants was. Thousands of Carpathian inhabitants fled into Czechoslovakia after the war. Many were caught by Soviet occupation soldiers and sent back; others were resettled in the Sudetenland to replace the Germans expelled under atrocious conditions in 1945–1948.

The Latin Catholics of Ruthenia came from three populations in 1945: ethnic Germans, Hungarians, and Slovaks. The ethnic Germans were descended from colonization in the 1600s (2 villages), in 1736–1763 (7 villages), and in 1807–1878 (8 villages). The majority of the immigrants came from Bohemia and Sudetenland. Although 2 of the 17 villages were half Rusyn, half German in 1939, the other 15 were completely German.[5] The isolated German colonies at Nemecka Mokra, on the Mokrijanka River, and Koenigsfeld on the Torec River were mixed; less so the German settlements south and west of Mukachevo, especially at Palanka, a large Catholic village, and Sofiendorf. Although some of the Carpathian Germans were evacuated during the retreat of the *Wehrmacht,* the difficult terrain and quick retreat meant that a large population remained behind. These Germans were unique in the western Soviet Union: most were not removed from their ancestral villages by the victorious Soviets and remain there to this day.

Ruthenia's Hungarians and Slovaks came from much older settlement, as a result of the province being part of the Kingdom of Hungary for so many centuries. Some were Protestants, who lived throughout the region, especially in the towns. All of the Latin Catholics in Ruthenia were dependent upon the Greek Catholic bishop, an unusual situation in the Church at the time.

Eastern Poland

The USSR was allowed to annex all of Poland's historic eastern provinces, although the region around Białystok was restored to Poland in 1946, much to the relief of its 500,000 inhabitants. Repatriation to Poland was offered only to ethnic Poles, who had no "right" to Soviet citizenship. The atheist Soviets determined ethnic eligibility by membership in the Latin Catholic Church; as a result, this repatriation weakened the Church in what was now the western Belorussian SSR. Forced exchanges were made between Poland and the USSR of ethnic Ukrainians and Poles.

Northeastern Prussia

Historic eastern Germany was dissolved to accommodate Stalin's appetite. Most of the provinces were given to Poland, and the majority of the remaining Germans expelled under barbaric and murderous conditions. Stalin demanded the northern half of East Prussia, allegedly to have yet another warm-water port. Although adjacent to Lithuania, this became part of the RSFSR, with the ancient German city of Königsberg renamed Kaliningrad and Tilsit renamed Sovetsk. German inhabitants who had survived the war were removed to the east to work in the Urals. (Survivors were later repatriated to West Germany.) The new Kaliningrad oblast was completely Sovietized. (As late as 1988, there were no working churches of any religion in this area.) Memel, scene of horrific battles in 1945, was "restored" to the Lithuanian SSR under the name "Klaipėda." (Some 8,000 Germans who had returned to the district in or after 1945 or had never left were repatriated to West Germany between 1950 and 1965.)[6]

Northern Bukovina and Bessarabia

During the temporary restoration of northern Bukovina to Romania, the Latin Catholics had been able to reorganize. Where parishes had been greatly reduced by the German-Hungarian evacuations, they were merged with those which still had resident pastors. Every effort was made to continue a full sacramental life. With the reincorporation of northern Bukovina into the Ukrainian SSR came persecution of the Church. Bessarabia, which had become Transnistria during the war, was reincorporated into the Moldavian SSR.

Latin Catholics. The vicar general, Father P. Kumerowicz, SJ, had remained in Czernowitz (Chernivtsi) after the Red Army retook northern Bukovina. He was arrested on March 30, 1944, and removed to the Gulag. With him were taken Father John Nowacki and the Polish pastor from Sadagura (now part of Czernowitz), Father Alexander Chrzanowicz. The Polish pastor escaped on the way to Siberia; Father Nowacki was released in the late 1940s; but Father Kumerowicz was not freed until 1955, when he was deported to Poland, not returned to Bukovina.

The Slovak pastor, Father Kostka, SJ, was deported to Czechoslovakia, where ultimately all the Jesuits were imprisoned. Seven other priests and a majority of their parishioners were deported to Poland in 1945–1946. Only two priests were spared; of these, father Josef Jedrzyiewski was allowed to become pastor in Czernowitz. Sacred Heart Church was converted into an ammunition dump (it was returned to Catholic worship in 1945, and until 1989 remained the only surviving Catholic church offering the Mass in the entire province), and all the other churches were given over to secular uses.[7]

Northern Bukovina's ethnic Poles were reduced from 29,000 in 1940 to barely 3,000 by 1946, as a result of Soviet "resettlement": they were fortunate, however, in being deported to Poland, not removed to Siberia. Two-thirds lived in Czernowitz, forming the base for the parish there;[8] the balance lived in three settlements: Althütten (Krasnoilsk), Dawideny (near Augustendorf/Mesteceni), and Storozhynets.

Because of the removal of the different ethnic groups, a number of northern Bukovina's parishes had ceased to exist by 1946. There were no Catholics left in a host of villages and small towns; indeed, some had no people at all. The Czernowitz priests were limited by the police in what territory could be served. The parish of Althütten remained vacant, as it had been since the death of its Polish pastor in 1943: there was simply no one to send there, despite the presence of some 2,500 ethnic Poles, following the evacuation of the Germans. When, predictably, the Soviets forbade the installation of a new pastor, the congregation gathered in the Althütten church "to pray the holy Mass" by themselves, as did the Catholics of Dawideny, in the filial church there. Divine services led by lay persons also became the norm in the filial church of Panka, once part of Storozhnyets parish.[9]

Greek Catholics

The return of Stalinism meant destruction of the Greek Catholic Church in northern Bukovina and Bessarabia. Nine of the parishes were in the north. During the war, Father Vendelin Javorka, a Slovak missionary, had moved to Czernowitz, where he had worked with Byzantine Catholic Ruthenians in Bukovina. In April 1944, he had been removed to Siberia as a prisoner of war,[10] a status forced on him due to Slovakia's becoming a Fascist ally and puppet state. He would die in Siberia.

All of the Greek Catholic churches were given over to Russian Orthodox use, although, as elsewhere in the Ukrainian SSR, this did not guarantee their survival. The important church in Czernowitz, which once had three priests on its staff, was destroyed shortly after the "conversion."[11]

The restoration of Soviet rule in Bessarabia and northern Bukovina meant an extension of the Soviet coast along the Black Sea; the Ukrainian SSR was enlarged to include the coast, despite the small size of the Ukrainian population in the coastal area. Romanians were informed that they were Moldavians. About 1,000 of the ethnic German refugees from the area were forcibly repatriated from the West as "Soviet citizens." They ended up in the Tadzhik SSR (now Tajikistan). Churches were quickly closed here. The Armenian Catholics left for Poland.

Baltic States

Not only were these states not restored to freedom, but their borders were adjusted in favor of the RSFSR and the Belorussian SSR. Still more Balts were forcibly removed to the east. As the Cold War and Sovietization proceeded, guerrilla resistance grew.

Deportations of 1945

Within the pre-1939 borders of the USSR, seven more nationalities besides the Russia Germans were subjected to mass deportations in 1943–1945: the Crimean Tatars; the Kalmyks from southern Russia; the Meshketians, Chechens, Ingushi, Balkars, and Karachai out of the northern Caucacus; and the Greeks and Bulgarians from along the Black Sea coast. Millions were sent east as collective punishment for alleged collaboration with the Nazis. The Baltic SSRs were purged once again with wave after wave of mass removals as were the Belorussian SSR and the western Ukrainian SSR.

Foreign Catholics abounded among those dragged back from Europe by the Red Army as prisoners of war and slave laborers, and of course many of the inhabitants of the western Soviet Union were Catholic as well and included clergy and members of religious orders. For these Catholics, the mass removals and Sovietization would bring great suffering and disruption.

Orthodoxy in the Baltic States

Although the Orthodox Church was favored elsewhere in the USSR immediately after the war, this was not the case in either the Estonian or the Latvian SSR because these Orthodox Churches, like the Catholic, were not Russian-oriented. In the Estonian SSR, the surviving Orthodox bishop was removed to Siberia (where he died in 1948), and most of the Estonian Orthodox priests were similarly removed, or reassigned to territories outside the Baltic SSRs. The Estonian Orthodox diocese was reduced from 156 parishes to 98 and was heavily taxed.[12] Catholic-Orthodox cooperation ceased, and the nascent Byzantine Catholic community was not restored. (In 1990, this diocese would give the Russian Orthodox Church its first non-Russian Patriarch with the election of Metropolitan Alexei Rudiger to the Moscow See.)

In the Latvian SSR, the diocese of Riga came under the Orthodox archbishop of Vilnius (Vilna). Several of the Latvian priests were arrested in 1944–1945. Many of the Orthodox churches were closed. Latvian was replaced with Church Slavonic and many Slavic priests brought in to serve in the remaining ones.[13] (A Russian bishop was installed to lead the Latvian Orthodox in 1947.)

Alone among Baltic religious bodies, the Lithuanian Orthodox Church prospered under Soviet rule. This Church had always supported the jurisdiction of the Moscow Patriarchate, and was almost exclusively Russian or Belorussian in membership. Although Vilnius (Vilna) was a predominantly

Catholic city after the war, its Catholic churches were steadily closed, as will be seen, whereas the city's small Orthodox minority had seven churches available for worship.[14]

Eastern Czechoslovakia

As we have seen, Czechoslovakia lost Ruthenia to the USSR; as Zakaraptska oblast, it was made part of the Ukrainian SSR. Ruthenia was yet another Eastern European province in turmoil. Its incorporation into Czechoslovakia after World War I had brought mixed blessings. Although there had been advances in education and sanitation advances, it had not achieved political autonomy, and the Depression had crippled economic growth of what had already been considered one of the poorest provinces in all Europe.

The Slavic residents were divided among themselves as to whether they were Russians, Rusyns, Ukrainians, or Hungarian Rusyns. Even within the groups, there was division over which dialect to use. Other residents were Hungarians, whose country had ruled the Carpathian Mountains for over a thousand years, Carpathian Germans, Jews, ethnic Slovaks, and ethnic Russians (many of them refugees).

In 1918, 97 percent of Ruthenia's Slavic population had been Greek Catholic. In 1921, Czechoslovakia reported that the province's Greek Catholics (with some Armenians) constituted nearly 55 percent of the province's total population and the Orthodox slightly more than 10 percent. In the 1930 census, the totals of the province's Latin Catholics, Protestants, and Jews remained relatively stable, but the Orthodox had grown to more than 15 percent, and the Greek Catholics had dropped to slightly less than 50 percent.

The Greek Catholic Church in Ruthenia was less Latinized than its sister eparchy in Slovakia, and far less so than the Ukrainian eparchies to the north. The Byzantine Rite was generally considered to be purer in Mukachevo eparchy, and thus there had not been as much debate over ritual matters as there had been in Galicia. This was altered, however, after 1918, when priests imitating Hungarian culture and Latin Catholicism began to impose Latinizations such as statues, organs, moving the Feast of the Immaculate Conception from December 9 to December 8, and even removing the icon screens. The imposition of double taxes on already poor parishioners to support the Greek Catholic priest and his family aggravated the spiritual predicament. Returning emigrants from America brought the news of the formation of Ruthenian Orthodox parishes in the diaspora to resist such changes, and the Orthodox population grew from a little minority before the Great War, to nearly 61,000 in 1921, to an astounding 112,000 in 1930.[15] The "Orthodox movement" proved a source of tension before 1939, but under Soviet rule it accelerated into a crisis.

In the chaotic years of 1938–1939, the province was partitioned between Czechoslovakia and Hungary. Although, at one point, autonomy was achieved under Monsignor Augustin Voloshyn, a pro-Ukrainian Greek Catholic priest who engaged in fascist methods of control against his opponents, his connection with the National Ukrainian Union would later prove deadly to the Greek Catholics under Soviet rule.

Death once again claimed a Catholic bishop at a difficult moment. The Greek Catholic bishop of Mukachevo, Alexander Stojka, died suddenly on May 31, 1943. His prewar career had been a checkered one, reflecting the tensions that tore at the Greek Catholic Church in Ruthenia. On the one hand, he was devoted to the relief of the poor and hungry, especially during the Great Depression; the bishop devoted much effort to regaining churches lost to the Orthodox (whose poor he also helped); his personal devotion to the Mother of God had been the impetus behind a strong Marian devotion that swept the eparchy in the 1930s. On the other hand, Bishop Stojka had aligned himself with pro-Magyar parties and pro-Hungarian priests, while promoting the use of the local Rusyn dialect in the diocesan newspaper; he had supported Hungarian political leaders in 1938–1939 in hopes of achieving autonomy for the Carpathian region. These hopes failed, under the two partitions of Carpatho-Ruthenia, with the bishop being driven out of parliament with boos and hisses. The Hungarian government launched a Magyarization campaign to eliminate Slavic nationalism in the Catholic Churches and society. The Uzhorod Greek Catholic seminary experienced interference, and the Hungarian-language schools expelled all pro-Slavic students.[16]

As for the Orthodox, an eparchy of Mukachevo-Presov had been established in 1929 as part of the Czechoslovakian Orthodox Church, under the Serbian Patriarchate. Emigrants returned from North America with stories of Latin Catholic persecution. Greek Catholic traditional life had been eliminated there, they said, and an independent Carpathian Church jurisdiction created there. Pro-Russian nationalist sympathies combined to lead many people in Ruthenia to join the Orthodox missionary movement. From 1939 to 1944, however, the Hungarian occupation authorities had prevented the Orthodox bishop from serving, and there was no organized leadership at the time of the Soviet invasion.[17]

Bishop Stojka concentrated his energies on the eparchy, totally under

Hungarian rule after March 16, 1939. He intervened in behalf of Monsignor Alexander Chira, who had been persecuted by the Hungarian forces, and obtained the release of over 200 Slavophile students and seminarians from concentration camps. Further, the bishop kept the seminary out of the control of the Hungarians. Reemphasizing his work among the poor and returning to active pastoral ministry among the Carpathian residents, the bishop was able to recover popularity for himself and the Church.

On the Nativity of the Virgin, September 8, 1944, Rome appointed an energetic and devout young priest, Father Theodore Romzha, as auxiliary to Bishop Stojka's temporary successor, Bishop Nicholas Dudash, with explicit orders to become the ordinary if Ruthenia was occupied by the Red Army. Father Romzha became the de facto administrator of Mukachevo eparchy in October, when the occupation took place. On November 26, the military government summoned a congress of people's soviets in Mukachevo. This congress called for secession from Czechoslovakia and asked to "reunite" with Ukraine (rather difficult because the territory had never been part of Ukraine). In June 1945, this annexation was achieved, and the entire province east of the Uzh River was annexed.

About 100,000 residents of Ruthenia fled into Czechoslovakia after the annexation was announced, and were eventually resettled in the former Sudeten German villages of western Bohemia.[18] They were temporarily able to practice their Greek Catholic religion (served by priests from the church in Prague until Czechoslovakia suppressed the Church in 1950).

CHAPTER 30

Drawing in the Great Net of Stalin, 1945

> All you who have been delivered by the victorious Allied armies now are
> free to return to your own free countries, that you may build a new and
> better life on the ruins of tyranny and evil. . . . O Lord, who has so
> miraculously created the dignity of human nature, grant us faith in
> reconciliation, assure the triumph of love.
>
> —sermon for liberated prisoners distributed by SHAEF, 1945

For the prisoners freed from death camps and slave labor in 1945, for the
anti-fascists of all nationalities, these words summed the shining hopes
held by so many. After such a wrenching cataclysm, freedom and democracy
must triumph everywhere. There were 60 million displaced people in Europe
at the war's end that had experienced the enormity of the war. Millions of soldiers were tired of the bloodshed. Millions of families had been disrupted.
Surely, now the prayers of all would be answered?

Forcible Repatriation

> This is not what we fought the war for!
> —British soldiers involved in process

> You have given us more than we expected.
> —Soviet police at repatriation center

Sadly, those prayers would not be answered for anyone caught in the Stalinist
dragnet sweeping Europe. The Yalta Agreement called for the repatriation of
anyone holding Soviet citizenship.[1] Stalin was terrified of the possibility of a
large anti-Soviet emigration movement. At war's end, more than 8 million Soviet nationals found themselves in the West: those who had been freed from
concentration camps and slave labor centers, those who had fled in great treks
westward with the Germans, and those who had fought alongside the Germans in the anti-Soviet forces of the Vlasovite Army, of the Cossacks, of the

Muslim Caucasians and Turkomans, and of others in hopes of freeing their homeland from Soviet rule. Of 8,350,000, 7,975,000 of these nationals were given by the Allies back into Stalin's bloody hands.

The Yalta Agreement called for repatriation of only those people who had been Soviet citizens in 1939. In effect, however, its terms were broadened to include émigré White Russians and Cossacks who had left Russia from 1918–1922, their children, and even their grandchildren, even though they held foreign citizenship or Nansen stateless documents. The leaders of the Cossacks, who had emigrated in 1918, were handed over by the British. Efforts were also made to include non-Poles who had been Polish citizens in 1939.

Despite the frantic pleas of the victims, despite suicides and the murder of children by desperate parents—and even though Allied soldiers could hear the machine guns firing on the men and women they had forcibly sent back— Great Britain and the United States sent back millions of people in the spring and summer of 1945. Distraught soldiers came to the point of open rebellion at the scenes of screaming, bloodied mothers and children being hauled away.

The fate of the whole can be guessed from that of the White Russians forcibly repatriated from Judenburg: of nearly 1,000 sent back in 1945, only 31 survived to be released in 1955–1956—released, moreover, because of their foreign citizenship, which should have spared them in the first place.

The Soviet Catholics

Though granted German citizenship, this did not save all of the Russia Germans. Of 350,000 who had fled, only 100,000 were able to stay in the West. The others were taken prisoner by the Red Army in Warthegau or eastern Germany, or forcibly removed from the western zones to the Soviet one, and thus many were shipped back to the USSR on the infamous cattle trains. There they were scattered under atrocious conditions across the north.

Reich Germans who were forcibly deported to the Soviet Union included the inhabitants of northern East Prussia, which became the Kaliningrad oblast of the RSFSR. They continued to be sent east, where most died, until 1948, when the province was entirely emptied of Germans.

Survivors of the Red Army

Five million Red Army troops had been captured by the Axis. Stalin considered all Soviet prisoners of war—even the wounded, including his own son, Yakov—to be traitors to the Motherland. Furthermore, by being in the West, they had been contaminated. The precedent for their treatment had been set in the Winter War, when 30,000 wounded soldiers returned by Finland after medical care were immediately sent east to the Gulag. Of the Red Army soldiers interned in Nazi concentration camps, only 20 percent survived. When they were "liberated," the question asked was, *"Why* have you survived?"[2] Nearly all were sent off to Soviet concentration camps.

Baltic Catholics

Although the Allies did not push at all for the restoration of the Baltic States, Balts who had made it to western Germany or Sweden were generally safe (although the Swedes did send some back). Although a permanent loss to Estonia, Latvia, and Lithuania, these émigrés would spend the next forty-six years agitating for freedom for their homelands.

Arrests of People from Europe

The USSR forcibly removed 7.5 million of its own citizens to resettlement areas; an estimated 500,000 people from Germany, Romania, Hungary, Poland, Austria, Czechoslovakia, and the Balkans, including foreign diplomats, military, civilians, and prisoners of war were also sent to the east. (Some returned home as late as 1968, many never returned, many were never acknowledged, or reported dead only to be "resurrected" later.)[3]

When Budapest finally fell to the Russians in January 1945, the city was one-third destroyed. Even as their soldiers indulged in the now-traditional looting, raping, and killing, the Soviets forcibly removed thousands of Hungarians to the USSR.[4]

The classic example of those removed from Central Europe is Raoul Wallenberg, the Swedish diplomat who saved thousands of Jews in Hungary. Kidnapped in 1945 by the Red Army, he disappeared into the maw of the Gulag. (Survivors reported seeing him alive as late as the 1980s; the Soviets denied they had him; then said he was dead; then finally returned his personal effects to his survivors in October of 1989 as a belated acknowledgment that he had indeed languished all those years as a victim of their paranoia.)[5]

Among those forcibly removed from Europe by the Soviets were young people sent to work in the mines and factories of the Don Basin; Axis diplomats and prisoners of war; people who happened to be of German ethnic extraction; or people who were simply on the wrong list. (Some were returned home as early as 1946 due to illness, many people did not come home until after 1950 and especially after Adenauer's 1955 visit to Moscow, and many more died in the terrible conditions.) A number of Catholic priests and nuns were among those removed from Central Europe, including Italians and French, and they became part of Catholic religious life in the Gulag and in the diaspora itself.

Taken by the Red Army in 1945, Father Pieger, the Reich German vicar general of the mission in "South Russia," languished in Soviet prison until 1946, when he was repatriated.[6] In April 1945, Fathers Pietro Leoni and Jean Nicholas were both arrested in Odessa and charged with "espionage on behalf of a foreign power."[7] To the paranoid Stalinists, that could be the only possible reason two foreigners would have stayed behind: anyone who was *not* a spy would surely have fled. Thus Father Walter Ciszek's explanation that he had voluntarily gone to the Urals in 1940 fell on deaf ears. He was kept isolated in the Lubyanka prison, trying to keep his faith and sanity, until 1946.

The Catholic Church in the Expanded Soviet Union

By 1952, the Soviet Union had incorporated the territory of 5 ecclesiastical provinces and 24 archdioceses and dioceses; killed or deported 27 bishops; arrested or executed some 7,000 priests; destroyed or secularized some 8,000 parish and monastic churches; secularized some 3,000 convents, monasteries, seminaries, and academies; dispersed religious communities of men and women having some 10,000 members; secularized all Church hospitals, colleges, and universities, all parish schools, all Church welfare agencies; and suppressed all religious newspapers, magazines, and journals. Of the millions forcibly removed to Siberia and Central Asia, it was estimated in 1954 that as many as 5 million came from traditionally Catholic populations.[8] Yet even such statistics as these, and the silence that blanketed the West's view of Catholic life in the Soviet Union, could not eradicate the Faith.

CHAPTER 31

The War to Destroy the
Latin Catholic Church, 1945–1953

When the "Great Patriotic War" ended in the defeat of the Nazis in May 1945, and the Allies crushed the Japanese Empire in August, the vast majority of people in the USSR expected that life would improve. Fascism had been defeated, Communism and the capitalist powers had been allies in a bitter war, and a terrible force had been eradicated. Soviet troops had liberated— and occupied—nearly all the Balkans, all of Eastern and Central Europe, and were patrolling the streets of Vienna and Berlin. Russian power had never been so far west in history. Surely, after famines, terror, and warfare, Soviet citizens were entitled to reap the benefits of Communism?

In the years right after the end of the war, many Orthodox religious folk felt that times were almost tranquil for them, compared to the 1930s. By 1950, Russian Orthodoxy maintained, not only more than 14,200 churches, but also monasteries, convents, seminaries, and academies. Many of these were in the western Soviet Union, among Orthodox brought under Soviet rule because of the war, among Orthodox who had revived their church life under the Germans, and among the Greek Catholics who had been forcibly incorporated into the Patriarchate. Churches were renovated, parishes were registered.[1] The Orthodox hierarchy cooperated with the State on the international front (see below), and there was hope of a reversal of the past sufferings.

Unfortunately, this did not happen. Though the Potsdam Agreement in 1945, by sealing the infamous Yalta pact, allowed the USSR to consolidate its stranglehold on much of Europe, and though the Allies and the Red Army forcibly returned or removed millions of helpless people to the USSR, where they faced execution or internment in the Gulag, Stalin sank deeper into paranoia. The Cold War began very quickly after the end of the war against Fascism, and tensions between East and West rose over

1. the establishment of Communist governments from the Baltic Sea to the Mediterranean by 1948;

2. the capitulation of the Republic of China in 1948–1949 to Mao's Red Army and the resultant upsurge of interest in Communism and the USSR throughout the new nations of Asia;

3. the Soviets' race to develop their own nuclear, and later thermonuclear, devices, with espionage in the Allied countries leading to a Soviet atom bomb in 1949 and hydrogen bomb in 1953;

4. the North Korean invasion of South Korea in 1950, which brought the world closer to yet another great war;

5. a series of crises in Eastern Europe: the Berlin blockade by the USSR and airlift by the United Nations in 1948; the flood of refugees fleeing the new Soviet bloc after 1945; Yugoslavia's defection from that bloc in 1953; uprisings in East Germany and Poland in 1953 after Stalin's death, followed by the Hungarian revolution in 1956 (and ultimately the Berlin Wall in 1961);

6. the creation of NATO to protect Turkey and Iran against the Soviets, and the expansion of the new alliance across Western Europe.

Stalin perceived the Vatican as being part and parcel of these tensions, and Pope Pius XII and the Church were both demonized in the Soviet press.

The Soviet economy was in ruins, the birthrate in decline, millions languished in prisons and labor camps, and the country was wracked by famine and insurrection. Soviet collectivization of farms in the Baltic States and the annexed regions of Poland, Czechoslovakia, and Romania, as it had in the Soviet Union of 1929–1932, met with anger and resistance—and resulted in famine, which affected the whole country in 1947. Nevertheless, the government pushed ahead with collectivization, as a means to forcibly Sovietize the population, break the resistance movements, and weaken the Church in rural areas.

It also stepped up industrialization, which reached new levels (and which would later result in ecological disasters), but the people saw few benefits. Medical care was abysmal; the economy was shackled by Moscow's preposterous five-year plans; distribution of goods and materials was hopelessly mismanaged.[2] Driven by Stalin's diseaseed fantasies, oppression escalated into such episodes as the "Doctors' Plot"; the Gulag camps were kept full.

Western Credulity

The pattern of fellow travelers that emerged in the 1930s worsened after the war, with Communist sympathizers and spies alike promoting the Soviet system in the West. There were all too many Westerners who believed in "Uncle Joe" Stalin's claims of democracy and toleration. Inevitably, these people worked to discount or discredit reports of religious persecution and political oppression in the USSR. One could bemoan the horrors of Nazism, but criticism of Communism and its horrors became restricted to the "right wing" and was socially unacceptable in many Western circles into the 1980s. This meant that Catholics in the West studiously ignored the plight of the Soviet Catholics. Many Catholic activists focused their work against the totalitarian states of Latin America and Africa, but not against the "socialist" and "people's democracies" elsewhere.

Many of these well-meaning foreign Catholics were deluded by the Peace Campaign, headquartered in Prague but orchestrated by Moscow. Their fear of nuclear war (understandable after Hiroshima and Nagasaki) made them easy targets for manipulation. With Vatican II, dialogue with atheism was officially promoted by the Catholic Church, partly to improve the conditions of Iron Curtain Catholics; it soon degenerated into a farce. Although the Soviet invasion of Czechoslovakia in 1968 put an effective end to this "movement" in the West, it continued in the USSR, with heavy taxes on all churches to "spontaneously support" it.

Propaganda Against the Latin Catholic Church

The Latin Catholics of the USSR did not experience much of a respite after the war. Catholics were identified with "dangerous" national minorities, and the Vatican seen as a tool of Western imperialism. Catholic clergy and lay believers alike were shipped off to the Gulag in the last years of Stalin's reign, and the camps were filled with Latin Catholic believers.

By the spring of 1945, intimidating editorials began to appear in Ukrainian papers, as well as in *Pravda* and *Izvestia,* denouncing the Holy See and Greek Catholics as collaborators with the fascists. (This would become a hallmark of Soviet propaganda in Ukraine for the next forty-five years.) The local sobor of the Russian Orthodox Church in January 1945 charged the Vatican with wanting to keep fascism alive and trying to protect "Hitlerite Germany." Despite wartime paper shortages, anti-Catholic books and literature poured out of Moscow. The Vatican responded by warning the Allies of Soviet duplicity, and urging a separate peace with Germany. When that was refused, Pope Pius XII pushed for American forces to be stationed across Europe, especially in Italy and as far east as the Baltic States, to prevent the success of Communism. All of this was in vain.[3]

As the Cold War set in, anti-Catholic propaganda escalated, and all lines of communication between Rome and the Soviet Catholics were cut. The Soviet propagandist M. M. Sheinman condemned the Vatican for the Ustashe massacres of Serbs, for protecting Nazi war criminals, for being an ally of America, for supporting fascism around the world, and ultimately (in 1952) of planning to conquer the Eastern Churches and dominate the whole world. In an atmosphere like this, the Latin Catholics inside the USSR could not expect very much.[4]

Promotion of Schism

In 1944, even before the war ended, there were efforts to form a "Latin Orthodox Church" subject to the Moscow Patriarchate, on the order of the French Western Rite Orthodox parishes, throughout the borderlands, from Odessa up to the Baltics. The efforts were intensified after Pope Pius XII threatened excommunication for Catholics who belonged to the Communist Party or who voted for the Communists in Italy.

The State also attempted to create a National Lithuanian Catholic Church, although not a single Latin Catholic priest accepted the State's offer. Priests were summoned in 1949 to police offices to denounce the pope as "a satan of the war spirit" and thus provide an excuse for the Lithuanian Latin Catholics to go into schism from Rome. The priest who was offered the position of Lithuanian pope refused, despite being offered amnesty from his jail term of twenty-five years, the rectorship of an important church in the capital, and a bribe of 100,000 rubles.[5] This failure prompted the Soviets to push for pliant administrators who would cooperate with the so-called peace movement, and to manipulate the sole bishop left, the elderly Casimir Paltarokas. These administrators had to attend conferences, preach on the theme in the churches, collect signatures on "petitions," and praise Stalin in speeches.[6] It was a sad time.

Policies in the Baltic States

The genocidal campaigns that had been initiated in the Baltic States were resumed after the war, indeed, as soon as Communist control was reasserted in provinces. The Balts were subjected once again to forcible removals, as well as to forcible collectivization of agriculture, with those who did or might resist also removed to the east, to mass closing of churches of all faiths and Russification of the native Orthodox Churches, and to forced resettlement of Russians and other Slavs in their Baltic homelands.

In 1980, an Estonian researcher wrote that the mass removals of March

1949 qualified as genocide because their objective was to remove the most active and skilled social groups of these states. Most of those removed would never return, nor would their descendants, who were considered to be "children of kulaks" or to have "anti-Soviet tendencies." The three Baltic SSRs were terrorized by the collectivization and the recurring battles between Baltic partisans and the Red Army. As in 1929, collectivization was hurried and brutal, and farm production plunged. The people saw Great Russian hegemony as the Soviets' goal; indeed the native Balt populations steadily lost ground to resettled Soviet Russians.[7]

Forest Brethren: The Latin Catholic Church and Armed Resistance

Forced relocations from all three Baltic States continued into the early 1950s, and the Soviet response to the guerilla warfare was fierce and unremitting. Anti-Soviet partisan forces, called the "forest brethren" because they used the woods as their bases, fought especially hard in 1944–1948 in active campaigns to pressure the Soviet Russians to withdraw and to impel the West to intervene. Although some matériel was smuggled in to these forces, for the most part, they relied on captured German stores and what they won in battle; their ranks were joined by German soldiers stranded in the Courland pocket and elsewhere. Lithuanian partisans fought until 1952, and in Estonia active fighting went on until 1956, with the last of the partisans being killed only much later (in an ambush in 1978).

The constant warfare took its toll. A farmstead or village suspected of harboring or feeding the guerrillas was subject to burning and those who lived there, to forced removal or even massacre. Baltic Communists faced the same fate from the guerrillas. The partisan forces received many recruits from farm families who fled into the woods and marshes during collectivization. The KGB estimated that Lithuanian civilian casualties of the fighting reached 50,000, with 150,000 people imprisoned, and that, overall, the Baltic partisans numbered 30,000 men at their height.

One casualty of the war was religion. The Lithuanian and Latvian bishops refused to condemn the partisans, although a fraudulent letter was published by the government, claiming to be from the archbishop of Vilnius and offering amnesty. The bishop of Telsiai was executed in 1947 and other bishops jailed or exiled. All signs of national loyalty at church services were forbidden, and many priests followed their bishops into exile.[8]

In 1945, Archbishop Mecislovas Reinys issued a pastoral letter, "Thou shalt not kill"; that applied to both sides, hardly appeased the Communists. The parish clergy were caught in the middle: the partisans came from Catholic families and expected the sacraments and pastoral understanding, whereas the Communists wanted the priests to turn the partisans in and to refuse any connection with them at all. Although fewer than two dozen priests are known to have been involved in actively supporting the partisans with material aid or as organizers, and only one took up arms, all Latin Catholic priests were suspected of being engaged in the guerilla movement. Only after every bishop had been removed or killed, did the government succeed in getting apostolic administrators to cooperate on the partisan issue.[9]

Estonian SSR

The devastated Estonian Catholic Church was reduced to two working parishes after the war, in Tallinn and Tartu. Of Estonia's fourteen priests in 1939, nine, all German citizens, had been expelled in 1940 (Monsignor von Proffitlich and one other priest had been exiled to Siberia and would never return. Of the five remaining priests, all jailed and interrogated throughout the first Soviet occupation, one priest went back to Austria in the German withdrawal; the Capuchin missionary Father Ruszala died on January 30, 1945, of his sufferings; Father Charles Bourgeois left for Moscow on May 16 (he was eventually expelled from the USSR); and Administrator Father Henry Werling was forcibly removed to Central Asia on the Assumption, August 15—leaving a single priest, the last Capuchin, Father Kraus, for the entire SSR.[10]

Saints Peter and Paul in Tallinn was served by Fathers Sosnovskis (1946–1947), Grishans (1947–1952), and Michael Krumpans (1952–1987). Saint Mary's Church in Tartu was served by the indomitable Father Kraus (from 1945 to 1964) (and by the Capuchin Father Pavlosvskis, from 1964 to 1977; after 1977 Father Krumpans would have to say Mass at both churches as a result of the government campaign to weaken the Church.)[11] None of the other parishes was ever reopened in Soviet times. Valga church was closed and escaped destruction due to the resistance of a small group of parishioners.

Latvian SSR

The Latvian Catholic Church had been reorganized by the Vatican after Latvia became independent in 1918. The archdiocese of Riga had been restored, with a priest from Petrograd as bishop. Eventually, the archdiocese was formed into a metropolitan province, under Archbishop Anthony

Saint Mary's Church, Tartu, Estonia. Courtesy of Father Vello Salo.

Springovics (destined to be the last bishop in Latvia after 1944). Three bish-ops were removed by the *Wehrmacht* in its retreat, including the confessor Boleslas Sloskans, whose family was massacred by the Soviets as punishment. Eleven priests were killed or removed under the Nazis.

The elderly Bishop Springovics ordained two bishops as auxiliaries in

1947. Auxiliary Bishop Kazimirs Dulbinskis was jailed in 1949 and impeded from serving as a bishop throughout most of the Soviet era. Auxiliary Bishop Peteris Strods was named to care for the Liepaja diocese (he became the new bishop for the entire country in 1958). Bishop Springovics was ordered to tell the forest brothers to surrender, but he refused.

In 1945, twelve priests were deported to the east; in 1946, one priest died in prison; in 1947, Dean Stan Trojanovskis was shot;[12] in 1953, the seminary rector, Father Henriks Trops, was arrested during the last Stalinist persecutions. Forcibly injected in the legs with an unknown drug that permanently crippled him, Father Trops was removed in 1953 to a prison camp in Kazakhstan, where he was one of ten Catholic priests among 5,000 inmates. (Allowed to come home in 1956, he could not function as a priest until 1957, and from 1958 to 1979 could serve only in a small and remote parish so as to keep his influence restricted.)[13] After his expulsion from Riga in 1953, Bishop Springovics took refuge at Aglona until his death in 1958.[14]

Throughout Soviet rule, the shrine of Our Lady at Aglona continued to provide solace for Latvian Catholics. Despite restrictions, and even police barricades, the pilgrimages continued, with an annual attendance of more than 60,000 faithful. The rector of the shrine was the priest Julijans Vaivods, who had studied at the seminary in Saint Petersburg before 1914. He remained at his post, and his eloquent preaching there drew crowds of thousands from 1945 until his arrest in 1958 for passing out religious literature.[15]

The pilgrimages also continued at Kraslava. (Infuriated that farm workers continued to go, and that the crowds included young people, the government would forbid priests to come to Aglona in 1959.) Only the exiled Bishop Strods and the new resident priest, Father Peter Jakovels, were allowed to hear confessions; they had to give general absolution because there were so many believers who wished to confess. After the Assumption pilgrimage in 1959, Father Jakovels was arrested and removed for installing loudspeakers so the pilgrims could hear the Mass and sermon, and the Latvian deacon Michevich was expelled from the Riga seminary as a punishment.[16]

Latvia lost 50 priests in the Stalinist era, and 43 were exiled—a full one-third of the clergy. Preaching was forbidden, religious rites restricted, and the remaining priests subjected to almost round-the-clock surveillance.[17] The religious orders of men and women were not allowed to be reconstituted, although the nineteen surviving nuns were still at their post in a hospital in the early 1950s. Five Sisters were removed to Siberia, they were shot or died of starvation there; in 1948, the remaining fourteen Sisters were allowed back to

Aglona Basilica, Riga. Courtesy of the Riga Curial Office.

their hospital, now a Soviet State hospital, as cleaning women. They were permitted to live in the ruins of the convent, which had been shelled, but not to make any repairs. (Only five Sisters would survive until 1989, when Latvia became independent. Although never allowed to wear a habit again, not one would give up her vocation, a testimony to the hardiness of the believers who came under Communist rule.) [18]

Lithuanian SSR

Under the Nazi occupation, Lithuania lost 21 priests to execution, another 39 were jailed, and 253 priests fled to the West with their flocks. Forcible removals from Lithuania commenced immediately after the war, the first being in August 1945. Others followed, on February 16, 1946; December 19, 1947; May 22, 1948 (in which 100,000 people were removed); March 24–27, 1949; and June 7, 1949.

Reduction of the Hierarchy

In 1944, the Germans had forcibly evacuated Archbishop Joseph Skvireckas and his auxiliary Bishop Vincent Brizgys, both of Kaunas. At the end of the war, Archbishop Jałbrzykowski of Vilnius was expelled from the USSR. Apostolic Administrator Archbishop Reinys, who succeeded him, was sent in 1945 to the Vladimir prison in Soviet Russia, where he died in 1953. Bishop Vincent Borisevicius of Telsiai was arrested in 1946 and executed in 1947 (his body was thought to be found in 1995 in a mass grave in a railway yard). Bishop Teofil Matulionis, who had served as administrator of the Archdiocese of Mogilev and been exiled to Lithuania in 1936, was arrested in 1946 and also sent to the Vladimir prison. Only the bishop of Vilkaviskis remained at liberty, and he died in 1947. The Lithuanian Catholic Church was leaderless. [19]

Church Closings

Unbelievably high taxes were placed on Latin Catholic churches in Lithuania. When the money simply could not be raised, the churches were shut down or secularized. In Kaunas (Kovno), the Vytautas church was converted into a granary, the Jesuit church into a warehouse for the furniture of those forcibly removed. When the Marian Fathers' church was closed, the girls who tore down the paper sealing the church were sent to Siberia for six years, along with other teenagers who were passing by and witnessed this bold act. By 1949, Kaunas had only two churches for a mostly Catholic population of 120,000. In Vilnius (Vilna), Saint Stanislaus's Church became a Russian dance hall, despite the presence of the graves of the saints. Indeed, dance halls and recreation centers were set up on top of many cemeteries.[20] By 1955, there were only 580 churches and chapels, roughly half the independence total of 1,047. Only the Kaunas seminary was spared; in imitation of the tsarist rules, entry was limited by a state quota and state standards.[21]

In 1947, the consecrated life was banned in Lithuania, the various houses of religious orders confiscated, and the Sisters, priests, and Brothers dispersed to their family homes or removed to Siberia or Central Asia. All the religious superiors were imprisoned.[22]

Fate of the Priests

In 1945–1946, practically all of the priests still in Lithuania were summoned for interrogation by the NKVD. A spirited attempt was made to create a schismatic Living or National Catholic Church, to compel the priests to spy on their parishioners, and to file reports with the police. In this first assault, Lithuania lost 180 priests to deportation to Siberia or the Arctic north, and 100 priests to prison. Bishop Matulionis (Kaisiadorys), Bishop Pranas Ramanauskas (Telsiai), and Archbishop Reinis (Vilnius) were forcibly removed. On January 3, 1947, Archbishop Vincentas Borisevicius was executed.[23]

In 1944, the Franciscan guardian at Kretinga's shrine of Saint Anthony of Padua had been publicly tortured and exiled; like all other religious orders in the Lithuanian SSR, the Franciscans were forcibly disbanded.[24] Provincial of the Society of Jesus Benediktas Andruska was arrested, along with 10 other Jesuits—this from an order whose Lithuanian province had only 77 members in 1941.[25]

Writing to Pope Pius XII in 1948, the Lithuanian underground reported that of 1,646 Latin Catholic priests serving in Lithuania in 1940, there were only 400 at liberty to work. Of the 1,202 churches and chapels, only half (600) were still functioning. There were no religious orders of men or women and only one seminary open.[26] The seminary was restricted to 25 students, who had to be approved by the government delegate for religious affairs. Each diocese had its own such delegate, directed by Moscow, who in turn appointed other atheists at local levels to control the Church.[27]

From 1946 to 1948, a second assault on the Lithuanian clergy resulted in the arrest and removal of deans, energetic pastors, and noted priests, a total of 350 (35 percent of the remaining priests). These clerics would serve Catholic prisoners and exiles scattered across the Gulag.[28]

Kaliningrad Oblast

Though mostly Lutheran, East Prussia had a strong Catholic minority, with the dioceses of the Kaliningrad oblast having numerous parishes counting 350 priests and 600,000 faithful (nearly 25 percent of East Prussians) before the war. The flat landscape of East Prussia was marked by the steeples of its Gothic-style Catholic churches.

Apart from the three Catholic parishes of Kaliningrad (Königsberg), the oblast capital, there were churches in the towns of Tilsit and Insterburg and in numerous villages, such as Cranz, Tapiau, Heiligenbeil, and Heinrichswalde.[29] By 1947, however, the capital's three parishes were all closed: Saint Adalbert's lost its bell tower and part of the main church and became an office building; the domed Church of the Holy Family became a music hall, with its organ used to accompany concerts; Saint Joseph's became a sports hall. The Insterburg church was converted into an army arsenal. Elsewhere, churches were crudely secularized: used as chicken runs or cow stalls. The majority of both Catholic and Protestant churches, however, met the fate of the Neuhausen and Peterswalde churches: they were left to slowly fall in on themselves and collapse.

In Peterswalde, Mass was celebrated until 1948, when the last priest "left the country." Latin Catholicism was completely extinguished in the oblast until the late 1950s, when Catholic settlers came in from other parts of the USSR.

The Belorussian SSR

Soviet Belorussia suffered grievous losses in the mass removals of 1939–1941 and in the fighting during World War II. As soon as they had returned, the Soviets had again pursued their twin goals for the BSSR—to make it completely atheist and completely Russified. Neither goal was achieved, but it was not for lack of trying. Mass removals, sending youths to the "Virgin Lands," collectivization, and widespread poverty meant that the Belorussian SSR would not reach its 1939 population again until 1971.

Even as priests were being removed, all seminaries, monasteries, and convents were closed, and their students, Brothers, and Sisters arrested or sent into secular life. There was no official Catholic publishing at all: no prayer books, calendars, or catechisms. The hierarchy was suppressed: there were no bishops in Mogilev or Minsk, the Pinsk diocese was left vacant, and the auxiliary bishop of Vilnius (Vilna), Archbishop Mechyslav Reinis, forcibly removed to the east. The only source of Church administration was from Poland, where apostolic administrators were named to continue the vacant dioceses.

Perhaps most difficult of all for the Latin Catholics of Soviet Belorussia to bear was the ban on seminaries in 1944, which guaranteed that the Church would not survive. A secret seminary was founded only in 1970, apparently on orders from Rome, and this produced several secretly trained and ordained priests. Clandestine religious orders of women also carried on in secret, and Sisters formed a network working across the BSSR in hospitals and schools and as pastoral assistants in the surviving churches.[30]

Publication in Belorussian had ceased by 1938; under the restored Soviet regime in the enlarged BSSR after 1945, publication was almost exclusively in Russian, which promoted Sovietization.[31] Having no legal status in 1940–1944 under the Nazis, and not sponsored by the USSR, Belorussian became more and more the language of the peasants; Latin Catholic services were conducted in Polish, and Orthodox services in Russian.[32] The BSSR grew steadily more Russified; Russian became the native language of more and more of its city dwellers (by 1970 nearly 26 percent would consider Russian their native language).[33]

Boundary Changes, "Repatriation," and Losses

After the annexation of eastern Polish territory to the BSSR in 1939, Moscow had transferred the Vilna (Vilnius) district to the then-independent Republic of Lithuania, resulting in a loss of 422,000 Catholics from Soviet Belorussia. The first postwar reduction of the Belorussian Catholic Church took place on July 16, 1945, when the Białystok region, with its Catholic population of 478,000, was returned to Poland.[34]

In 1944, the Communist Polish Committee had agreed with Moscow to repatriate ethnic Belorussians, Poles, Ukrainians, and Lithuanians in the border provinces, and to establish new borders over which these people would be moved.[35] In 1945–1947, repatriation to Poland was offered to Latin Catholics living in the western BSSR (who, the Soviets assumed, were necessarily Poles). Although a successful drive at first, with ethnic Belorussians who were Latin Catholic also taking the opportunity to leave, as Poland became progressively more Sovietized, more and more Belorussian Catholics declined to leave: of nearly 741,000 registered to leave, fewer than half actually did (others estimate that as many as 500,000 Latin Catholics went to Poland by 1947).[36] Among the émigrés to Poland through 1947 were some 300 priests, Sisters, and monks, many of whom were pressured to leave the BSSR.[37] Whereas Poland was supposed to repatriate all ethnic Belorussians of the Białystok region to the USSR, only 30,000 were actually repatriated, most under duress.[38]

The ethnic Polish population remained strong in Grodno (now Hrodna), Lida, Oszmiany, Brasław, and Głebokie. Lay believers did not want to leave, and many priests resisted the pressures. That Polish partisans were still active in the western BSSR in these postwar years, putting up posters pleading with the people not to leave, also encouraged ethnic Poles to stay in their towns and villages. A Polish Jesuit, Father Wacław Sek petitioned to remain in the BSSR, fully knowing what risks he ran. Father Stanisław Ryzko, and Canon Jan Wasilewski of Pinsk diocese, discussed whether they should go west of the Bug river, to the new Polish state. Even though both knew that prison or death awaited them, and that whole villages of ethnic Poles were leaving, they agreed to remain behind to serve parishes left priestless.[39]

But all in the BSSR faced dangers. Farmers who aided the partisans were arrested: 38 of the 40 men at Radun were taken away by the police for allowing the Polish partisans to harvest rye. Collectivization was resisted. Young men were being drafted into the Red Army. Pressure was put on the traditional leaders of the ethnic Polish Latin Catholics, their priests, to emigrate to Poland or face exile to Siberia. Some went into hiding with their parishioners during the worst time, 1945–1948: Father Stanisław Bohatkiewicz was hidden in a wood pile, then in a concealed room in a barn, where he could say Mass, and finally in an old air raid shelter, where he ministered to the faithful for an entire year without emerging. In Grauzyszki and Gudohaje, believers successfully hid their priests under similar conditions. Father Bohatkiewicz later said: "These people had authentic faith and the necessity to use it. For the Faith, the Church, and their priest, they were taking their chances to defend their "treasures of the soul."[40]

Diocesan priests, priests and Brothers of religious orders, Sisters, and tens of thousands of lay believers were arrested for a vast variety of "reasons" and sent to Siberia or Central Asia. Of the priests who were caught and arrested, twelve died in prison camps and two immediately after release because they were so sick.[41]

Persecution and Changes

Much of the network of churches painstakingly restored during the Nazi occupation was attacked. When the Soviets liberated the BSSR in 1944, there were 349 churches and 86 filial chapels in the western BSSR, with 380 priests to serve 342 parishes. Archbishop Romuald Jałbrzykowski and Bishop Casimir Bukraba, both of whom were expelled from the USSR in 1945, had ordered their parish priests to remain at their posts.[42] Also, they successfully named vicars general to administer their territories: initially all of the deaneries were organized under several priests, but their number was gradually whittled down to only two: Father Hernyk Humnicki, at Bielsk Podlaski (who went to Poland in the late 1940s) and Canon Jan Wasiliewski of the Pinsk cathedral. For the priests, these vicars became the sole Church authority, and because they were not bishops, they were not expelled by the Soviets. These priests had the right to nominate pastors and deans in the parishes of the BSSR.[43]

Repression of the clergy and parishioners, begun during the war years with arrests in the autumn of 1944 in the eastern BSSR, escalated in 1945. The NKVD moved, first, against priests known to have ministered to Polish partisans of the *Armia Krajowej* (AK) and to partisans who had emerged from the woods with the expulsion of the Nazis; second, against priests who had served both in parishes and in the AK as chaplains; and third, against priests who had been arrested in 1939–1941 but freed by the Germans ("the Soviets forget nothing")—these were returned to the Gulag to complete their terms. Thus Father Kazimierz Swiatek from Pruzany, arrested and interned in a labor camp in December 1940 because of his strong anti-Communist positions in preaching, and freed by the Germans in 1941, was rearrested by the Soviets in and sent back to the Gulag. Vicar General Father Wasilewski of Pinsk, arrested in August 1945, was sentenced in 1947 to 10 years' exile (he died shortly thereafter from his sufferings). Father Albin Horba, imprisoned in Grodno in 1945, reported from his cell that the mood in the western BSSR was "glorious" because the ordinary people firmly believed that their region would soon be returned to Republic of Poland.[44] This belief proved groundless.

In 1947–1948, all convents and monasteries in the BSSR were closed. Many of the priests from the religious orders, including Capuchins, Carmelites, Jesuits, Salesians, Marians, and Piarists went to work in priestless parishes; Sisters, in disguise, preserved their religious community life in the cities of Grodno and Pinsk or moved out to assist priests in parishes.[45] The provincial of the Sisters of the Holy Family of Nazareth in Poland offered her Sisters repatriation. Some did go back (the conditions in the BSSR were certainly frightening enough), but others stayed at Nowogródek and Grodno. These Sisters spent fifty years in lay clothing and secular jobs, but continued to work with children, teenagers, and adults, encouraging believers in their Faith during persecutions.[46] Sister Margaret, the sole survivor of the Nowogródek Massacre, spent nine years living in a closet behind the sacristy cabinets of the Fara church, where she taught children and conducted prayer services at the church when there was no priest available. She was able to assist Father Antonowicz, who fought strenuously to keep churches and chapels open, with the aid of the Catholic believers (and who would become the oldest living priest in Soviet Belorussia).[47] Similar stories could be told about the Pallotine, Bernardine, and other Sisters who stayed in the BSSR.

The steady loss of priests and churches (detailed below by diocese) led to the rise of lay ministry in the BSSR. Sacristans, sextons, organists, catechists, and other lay believers took on leadership roles in the parishes. They would work to bring in a priest from another working parish or, failing that, would themselves lead prayer services in the churches. These lay people made great sacrifices to keep the churches open: sometimes they succeeded, though the church lost all public utilities; sometimes they lost, and the building was secularized or pulled down. (When priests began to return after 1954 and had to take care of several parishes at a time, these same lay believers kept things going to ensure the survival of parish life as the priests traveled from place to place.)[48]

Destruction of the Churches

Although the old churches that had survived Bolsheviks and Nazis alike were still standing—Holy Mother of God (1822) in Gomel; Holy Cross and Saint Casimir's (1604) in Lepel; Saint Joseph's (1819) in Orsha; Holy Rosary (1804) in Polotsk; Holy Trinity (1792) in Rosica; Holy Spirit (1669) in Ulla; and Saint Barbara's (1783) in Vitsyebsk—none could be used for services. Saint Joseph's in Orsha had been converted to an ammunition depot; the cathedral of Mogilev (1765) into a government archive. Catholic beliefs survived, but there were no public Masses.[49]

The churches in Dawigródek (now David-Gorodok), Lunno, Hancewicze, Drohiczyn, Bezdziez, Janow, Telechany, Łachwa, and Miklaszewicze were all closed. Saint Charles's Church in Pinsk had its doors torn off, everything removed, and the interior filled with wheat. The church in Widez became home to a football club, with parties held on Communist holidays. The forced neglect or deliberate misuse of church buildings for all kinds of purposes led to their deterioration and, for many, ruin.[50]

Archdiocese of Mogilev

Tadeusz Poleski writes that the "return of the Red Army in 1944 put an end to the hopes of Catholics [in the eastern part of the archdiocese] for the reconstruction of a normal pastoral structure."[51] Here there was never a relaxation of anti-Catholic activity by the Communists, and not a single parish survived. Even so, while the Reds were focused on defeating the Axis, Latin Catholic priests took advantage of what became known as "the time of peace" to head east for ministry. Father Bolesław Sperski ministered in Mogilev and Orsha from September 1944 until his arrest in May 1945. A number of priests being "repatriated" to Poland from the Gulag, among them, Father Adam Puczkar-Chielewski, passed through the archdiocese of Mogilev and offered sporadic ministry. Their visits were short, however, and parish life could not be resumed.[52] The priests in Polotsk, arrested and imprisoned in 1944–1945, were forcibly repatriated to Poland in 1948. The Jesuit Father Antoni Zabek from Orsha managed to return after Stalin's death, only to be expelled to Poland.[53]

Minsk Diocese

Religious life here survived the war, often with priests from farther west. In the city of Minsk, on June 29, 1944, Father Wiktor Szutowicz took over Saint Mary's, and Father Antoni Botysowicz took over Saints Simon and Helen's, where he introduced (whether under government pressure or on his own initiative, no one knows) Polish in the vernacular services.[54] Catholic services had continued at Minsk after 1945, as reported by Italian prisoners of war who had been among the worshipers as late as after 1947.[55] The churches in the city were crowded, and the press complained repeatedly about young people attending Mass.[56] However, Minsk diocese was also destined to be purged of churches and priests in the renewed campaign against religion. The church at Kalvariya was turned into a stonemason's workshop (and would remain closed until 1981). Over time, the churches in Kojdanow (Dzherzhinsk), Uzda, Zaslavl', and Timkovichi were all closed.

The church of Saints Simon and Helen was closed in 1947 (priests had worked there in 1945, but would not do so again until 1956 and then only until 1960). Two priests continued to work in the cities of Borisov and Slutsk until 1957, when they, too, were removed and the churches closed; the Borisov church fell into ruins. As in the archdiocese of Mogilev, there were still old churches standing, at Bobruysk (1903), Kopyl (1859), Lelczyce (1909), Lohosk (1793), Mozyrz (1654), Swietlogorsk (1813), and Zamość (1649), although, again, none was used for Mass. The diocese's other churches did not survive.[57]

Pinsk Diocese

Having suffered heavy losses in the war, this diocese was to suffer still more. In 1944, Father Casimir Swiatek was again arrested at Pruzana for "anti-Soviet activities." When he was returned to the Gulag, the Soviets made sure he could not escape, sending him to the frozen north.[58] From August 1948 to January 1950, nine priests were removed from Pinsk diocese, which had already lost 101 priests during the war.

During the postwar repatriations, some of the diocese's remaining priests emigrated to Poland. In a sweeping assault on the Latin Catholic Church from 1946 to 1948, Minsk oblast lost all but one parish (in Nieswiez); Brest oblast lost most of its parishes. The priests in Brest and Polotsk were arrested, although those who had been arrested during the war years were eventually repatriated to Poland.[59]

(After 1954, survivors from the 25 priests sent to Siberia would begin to return, and 12 parishes with 17 churches would be restored to active religious life. As elsewhere in the USSR, the return of priests would mean a religious revival. The vicars general would again be able to administer Confirmation; in 1956–1957, large crowds of believers would receive the sacrament.)

Of the 140 documented churches of the Pinsk diocese, 46 were secularized into warehouses, clubs, and museums, 15 were given to the Orthodox, 33 were destroyed outright by the Soviets, another 10 were destroyed during the war, 19 were left to fall to ruin. Only 17 survived as still working Latin Catholic churches (and of those, only 12 had a resident priest in 1985).[60] Thus Saints Peter and Paul's in Lahisyn was spared, but had no priest from 1945 until 1956. The Pinsk cathedral had no priest from the arrest of Father Stanisław Ryzko in 1945 until Father Swiatek took over the parish in 1955. Nowa Mysz kept its church open, but there was no priest from 1945 until 1978; Saint Joseph's in Lahowicze had no priest from 1949 until 1990. The Fara church at Nowogrodek, where the Holy Family Sisters had been martyred, stayed open, but lost its priest in 1948.[61] (In 1958–1962, 20 churches would be closed in Grodno province, and 8 in Brest. By 1965, there would be 111 left open, but not all had the Mass available.)[62]

Archdiocese of Vilnius

In the northwest, the huge part of the archdiocese that was annexed to the BSSR in 1945 had 136 chapels and 53 monastic and nonparochial churches serving 238 parishes and nearly 900,000 Catholics. Of these, only 37 parishes survived the persecutions with resident priests; those priests visited 28 parishes, with nine parishes kept open by the laity having no contact with a priest at all.[63] Thus Saint Francis Xavier's in Grodno (1584) had no priest from 1958 to 1988; Saint Ann's in Mosarz none from 1961 to 1989; and Holy Mother of God in Porzecze (1906) none from 1963 to 1990. Father Albin Horba of Grodno was arrested in 1945, as were the remaining priests in Grodno's several churches and all the priests in Brest in 1947. (Church closings, most notably of Holy Trinity in Hermaniszki, continued right into the 1970s.) Nearly all the archdiocese's Lithuanian Catholic churches (serving some 30,000 faithful) were secularized, and only Polish could be used in the ones that survived—the use of Lithuanian was forbidden by the State.[64]

Łomża Diocese

In 1947, four priests from the Belorussian part of this diocese were removed to Siberia.[65] Of the diocese's seven parishes here, two were closed down in the 1940s (Balla Koscielna and Perstun), and a third was closed but reopened after Stalin's death (Teolin). The Church of Our Lady in Adamowicze and the Church of Our Lord in Sylwanowce remained open throughout the postwar period under the care of their 1945 pastors. The church in Labno remained open (and would go only two years without a priest, 1982–1984). The church in Holynka lost its priest in 1947, but the congregation was able to pray there regularly until a new priest finally came (in 1984).[66]

Fates of the Priests

Conditions for the BSSR's *"kszendy"* (as Latin Catholic priests, especially Polish priests, were called in Russian) were definitely not good. Many had been removed and sent to prison or labor camps for terms of from 10 to 25 years. Adam Hlebowicz reports that 70 percent of the Latin Catholic priests in the BSSR were arrested and imprisoned, and 10 percent died in prison or labor camps. Many priests were hidden by their parishioners in barns, haystacks, even under piles of logs.[67]

Some surviving priests chose to move to Poland, with the encouragement of the Soviet authorities; others chose to remain in Siberia and Central Asia, and to minister to believers there. Still others died of old age, mourning that there was no one to succeed them in their parishes. One very old priest worried that there would not even be anyone to left to bury him when the time came.

On the other hand, there the vicars general provided at least some organization (there was no contact with Poland until 1957), rule on marriage cases, appoint and transfer the dwindling number of priests, and ordain new priests. Ordinations did take place, to the furor of the Soviet authorities, and the Council on Religious Affairs was forced to deal with the vicars general and their successors because the parish clergy would do nothing without their permission.[68] At the same time, the press complained that Latin Catholic priests were treated with great respect, and that baptisms were celebrated by grandparents in the areas deprived of priests.

In 1949–1951, nearly 80 percent of the Catholic clergy were jailed on charges of anti-Soviet activity or Polish nationalism, for sending state secrets to foreign powers (by communicating with the bishops in Poland or with the Holy See) or for owning Polish books published before 1939. Where priests arrested in 1945–1947 had been sentenced to 10 years in prison or the labor camps, those arrested now faced sentences of 25 years, confiscation of all possessions, and deprivation of all civil rights. In 1951, the purge began to ease, and sentences were again lowered to 10 years in prison or the labor camps.

Propaganda Against the Latin Catholic Church

The antireligious campaign began early in the BSSR. Anti-Catholic propaganda dominated Belorussian atheist work. The Belorussian-language broadcasts from Radio Vatican were jammed throughout the Stalinist period, with the Vatican reportedly accused of fomenting a new world war and of being in league with American militarism. Pope Pius XII was reported as being in the company of "damned pirates and gangsters" in 1951; Janka Bryl was awarded the Stalin Prize (before 1953) for her book calling the Catholic Church a "nest of snakes."[69]

That Catholic belief endured was clearly reflected in the anti-Catholic propaganda itself. Publications complained in 1954 that Catholic children still went to Mass, and that Catholic students in Grodno actually took the Party's religious policy to mean that they could receive the sacraments.

When the bodies of the eleven Sisters of Nowogródek were exhumed in

September 1945, the sight of the corpse of Sister Kanuta had astonished all the witnesses. She was half bent over, kneeling above the rest of her Sisters. A witness said she looked like a mother mourning her loss.

Ukrainian SSR

Although organized Latin Catholicism had been extinguished here by 1937, despite the mass removals of the largely Catholic national minorities, there were still Catholic believers in the Soviet Ukraine, perhaps as many as 150,000 who still nominally considered themselves members of the Church. Five years after the 1939 expansion of Ukraine's borders eastward into Galicia and Ruthenia (Transcarpathia) brought in millions of Catholics of three rites, however, the Latin Catholics suffered a major loss in the repatriation of ethnic Poles to Poland: a population of 1.5 million faithful in western Ukraine dropped by as much as one-half.

Emigration to Poland was neither voluntary nor complete. Only about 10 percent of the urban ethnic Polish population in the newly annexed lands left, and the majority of ethnic Poles in districts adjoining the new Polish-Soviet border remained. Nevertheless, thousands of Poles left Volhynia, where the civil war between ethnic Ukrainians and Poles and the Ugrainska Povstanska Armiia (UPA) and Armia Krajnowej (AK) forces, egged on by the Reds, reached a bloody peak.[71]

The height of emigration was in 1944–1948, with people fleeing Communism. With the establishment of the Communist People's Republic of Poland, emigration dropped. It would only pick up with survivors of the Stalinist camps who chose to go to Poland after 1953. Hlebowicz reports that of the nearly 780,000 people who left Soviet Ukraine for Poland (and who were overwhelmingly Latin Catholic), 2,493 were diocesan priests, priests of religious orders, Sisters, and monks.[72]

The core community of old Latin Catholics (Ukrainianized Poles) continued to exist in central and eastern Ukraine, as did the *Latynnyky,* who considered themselves to be Poles up until the war, and who eventually came to see themselves as Ukrainian Latin Catholics.[73] The border regions of Galicia continued to be home to many Latin Catholics. Further, after the 1946 suppression of the Greek Catholic Church in Galicia, many Ukrainian Catholics began attending Mass in the ethnic Polish Latin Rite parishes to avoid contact with the Orthodox.

Repression of the Clergy

In July 1944, Bishop Adolph Szelazek of Lutsk nominated apostolic administrators for the old Soviet territory in Zhitomir and Kamenets-Podolski dioceses. An indomitable figure in interwar Poland, the bishop proved to be so under both Nazis and Bolsheviks as well. Kamenets-Podolski came under Father Josef Kuczynski and Zhitomir under Father Bronisław Drzepecki. These two men went east with other priests to the churches that had been reopened in the Axis occupation zones at Human, Kiev, Kharkov, Dnepropetrovsk (Dnipropetrovs'k), as well as the see cities themselves.[74] Two priests were still serving in central and eastern Ukraine for the Latin Catholics in Kiev, Kharkov, Dnepropetrovsk, and Human. In 1945, the NKVD arrested Bishop Szelazek, the administrators of Zhitomir and Kamenets, and several other clerics, including Father Wladislaus Bukowinski. All parish priests and missionaries were also arrested, and sentenced to terms of from 5 to 10 years in the labor camps; it was the news of such arrests that drove so many members of the clergy and religious orders to leave for Poland.

Arrested as well were diocesan priests and priests of religious orders who had served as chaplains to the *Armia Krajowej* (AK; Home Army). They were caught in the repression against the Polish partisans who continued to fight the Soviets after 1944–1945. These priests included a Franciscan from Lwów, the vicar of Volodomyr-Volynski, and forest brethren chaplains who had spent the whole Nazi occupation with the AK troops.[75]

By 1948, all of the diocesan curias, archives, and seminaries in Soviet Ukraine were either closed or removed to Poland; monastic life was drawing to a close. Yet the Faith would endure.

Fate of the Parishes

With the massive exodus from the UkSSR in 1945–1947, the State could claim that many churches would have to be closed because there were no longer Catholic believers in the villages.[76] In 1944, the archdiocese of Lwów had 400 parishes, with 32 churches in Lwów itself; the Lutsk diocese had 140 parishes; the part of the Przemyśl diocese that came under Soviet rule had 75 parishes. Closings occurred in three successive waves: in 1945–1948; in the 1950s; and again under Khrushchev. (By 1961, the number of diocesan churches was reduced to 25; in 1980, the total for all of Soviet Ukraine was 30, including the 20 churches in Zakarpatskaya oblast, the former Czechoslovak province of Ruthenia).

With the western Ukrainian Latin Catholic dioceses all vacant, administrators from Poland tried to keep contact with the dwindling number of priests. Eastern Ukraine's few remaining communities were technically under the archdiocese of Riga. Nothing was left of the different attempts to organize Catholic life before the war.

Despite the handicaps, ethnic Polish Catholics in Ukraine remained courageous and stubborn, with many vocations to secret communities of Sisters and many attempts by young men to enter the seminary in Riga (often thwarted by the police). As a sign of national identification, Polish was used in sermons and hymns, even though many people no longer spoke the language.

Lutsk Diocese

Bishop Szelazek, who had said he would never leave his diocese as long as one Catholic remained in its territory, was arrested and removed. The church in Rovno was converted into a gymnastics hall in 1945; Saints Peter and Paul Cathedral was converted into a museum of atheism in 1947 (although the rector, Father Jan Rutkowski, would continue to celebrate Mass at the cemetery chapel until that, too, was closed in 1955).

(Diocesan parishes would survive until Khrushchev's 1961 persecution of Latin Catholics in Ostrog and Korzec. In the entire diocese, only the Church of Saint Stanislaus in Krzemieniec would remained open. It would be served by a succession of only three priests between 1945 and 1990.)

Archdiocese of Lwów

The Latin Catholic archbishop, Eugenius Baziak, allowed priests to leave for Poland if their parishioners did, but if the people stayed, the priest had to also.[77] When these priests were threatened with arrest by the Communists or their churches were closed, the priests were to go underground. Because of this attitude, the archbishop was "invited" to nighttime interrogations with the NKVD. The Polish collaborator Stanisław Grabski, who had joined the National Home Council in 1944, came to encourage the archbishop to emigrate. He did so, but only because of the Soviet suppression of the Greek Catholic Church. The last Pontifical High Mass was sung in the cathedral at Easter in 1946, and he left Lwów on April 26.[78] With him went with the seminarians, the archdiocesan archives, and the curia.

In 1945–1950, the cloisters and monasteries were all closed, the last one being the Bernardine monastery in Samborze. Capuchins, Franciscans, Bernardines, Jesuits, Redemptorists, and all the religious orders of Sisters lost their houses. Although many priests of the religious orders emigrated to Poland under the continuing pressures, others served as pastors in the dwindling number of parishes. Many of the priests arrested were sentenced to 25 years in the Gulag.

Although the fifteenth-century Cathedral of Saint Mary Magdalene in Lwów was never closed, and the Church of Saint Anthony was also spared, in 1946, Saint Elizabeth's Church was closed. Its young priest, who began the Litany of the Sacred Heart of Jesus after the last Mass in the church, broke down in tears at the phrase "Heart of Jesus, full of love and every good." The parishioners wept with him, and took flower petals from the altar as souvenirs.[79] One of the very tall steeples of this Gothic church is missing a cross. The Communists ordered Saint Elizabeth's crosses removed as an affront to atheism. No one would come and do the deed, however. Finally, a prisoner agreed to do so, and was suspended from a helicopter to chop the cross off at its base. As it fell, the prisoner became entangled in the arms of the cross and was hurled to his death on the street below. After that, the Communists gave up on tearing down crosses.[80] Throughout Soviet rule, flowers were left at the door of the church as it crumbled into ruin. Eventually, all twenty-nine other churches in the city were taken over by the State. The Dominican Friars' church became the new museum of atheism, with the altar being replaced by a giant globe; Saint John's a hospital; and Saint Nicholas's a book depository. Other churches served as warehouses and stores, or were simply wrecked.

In 1947–1948, all the other parishes in sixteen of the archdiocese's deaneries were closed, even though there were still believing Catholics present in the towns and villages. In the others, only one or two parishes were spared, and most of these were closed in 1953 (or 1961). The Brzezanach Church was converted into a sports hall; the Halicz church into a theater. Some churches were given to the Russian Orthodox for use. The Tarnopol church was dynamited, and the Gniewan church became a distillery for vodka. Only three parishes remained open with priests in residence throughout this era: Borszczow, Haluszczynce, and Zloclow. Two parishes, briefly deprived of priests, were kept open by the laity: Szczerzec (no priest in 1954) and Stryj (no priest from 1953 to 1956).

Underground and semi-clandestine priests along with their lay helpers were arrested in the repression of 1948–1952. Thus the priests from Kamenets Podolski were taken along with a laywoman, Julia Bojarska, who had been their coworker and a provider of food to the imprisoned, and who was sentenced to 5 years in a labor camp as a spy of the Vatican. But others continued Bojarska's good work; many of the prisoners survived through the packages received by the priests and laity in the Gulag.

Odessa. With the arrest of the two missionaries, Saint Peter's Church had lost its priests; 8,000 parishioners had been left without pastoral care.[81] Allowed to stay open under a lay committee throughout the Great Terror (but with no Masses), the church was confiscated after the war. In 1947, Father Butrowicz was allowed to take up the pastorate in Odessa; the church was returned to Catholic use (and would not be closed again). On the other hand, Assumption Cathedral, closed with the reoccupation of the city by the Soviets, remained secularized and became a sports hall.[82]

Zakarpatskaya Oblast. Almost totally cut off from the rest of the USSR, this border oblast had 41 Latin Catholic parishes in 1944.[83] Among its faithful were as many as 80,000 ethnic Hungarians and an unknown number from the other national minorities, chiefly Slovaks and Carpathian Germans who had not been evacuated. Because of the border changes, they were under the administration of the Greek Catholic bishop of Mukachevo, confirmed by a letter from the papal nuncio to Hungary in 1944 urging the appointment of a new Greek Catholic bishop (who would become Bishop Theodore Romzha).

The Latin Catholic Church in Trans-Carpathia was hard hit by a Soviet persecution of ethnic Germans and Hungarians. Launched in October 1944, this practice was supposedly directed at men of fighting age, from ages 18 to 50 or 55, who were to do compulsory labor inside the province out of an alleged fear that they would join the Hungarian Army or support the departed Nazis. Boys as young as 16 were taken, and in November 1944, entire families from German and Hungarian villages and districts were rounded up. Ultimately, about 40,000 people—mostly Hungarians and Germans but also including Gypsies, Romanians, and Slovaks—were removed from their homes in 1944–1945, and sent either to the local concentration camps at Szolyva and Tuvan, or further into the USSR for labor in the Gulag or rebuilding ruined cities. About 12,000 people died in the camps; most of the survivors returned after 1946, but some of the German villagers were kept in Siberia until 1960.

A total of 18 Latin priests were arrested. The dean of Berehovo, Father Ferenc Pasztor, and the crippled priest Sando Haklik, dean of Kisrat, both died in Siberia, and two priests returned home completely crippled from their sufferings. Of the other 14 priests, Fathers Josef Csati (Mukachevo), Erno Tindira (from Bardhaus), and Josef Troth (from Seredne) survived their imprisonment but were not allowed to return to their parishes for a number of years. Ultimately, 21 of the 41 parishes were permanently closed by the government, and ordinations of local men to the priesthood were totally forbidden.

As elsewhere in the western Soviet Union, closed churches were secularized or allowed to collapse in on themselves. The ethnic German parish church outside Mukachevo was turned into an electrical workshop; in Palanka Munkatsch, Red Army troops desecrated the ethnic German Latin Catholic church, destroyed the tower cross, bells, four altars, and organ, and burned the trees around the building. Secularized Latin Catholic churches were converted into libraries, apartment houses, a cinema, and a paint studio. Stained-glass windows were torn out and replaced with ordinary glass or bricks. Even so, one émigré Carpathian German estimated that 80 percent of those who stayed behind in 1944 remained faithful to their religious beliefs.[84]

The Faith Goes On

Even though many Latin Catholic priests in the Ukrainian SSR had been arrested in 1948 as "Vatican spies" and sentenced to 25 years in the Gulag, and even though dioceses had been completely purged of priests, in 1953, the few surviving priests prayed their breviary and lay believers continued to trust in the Mother of God.[85] Among priests exiled to Kazakhstan, Father Władysław Bukowinski of Lutsk Cathedral parish served as missionary to the Latin Catholic exiles of Central Asia, as did Fathers Bronisław Drzepecki and Josef Kuczynski, who also remained there after their prison terms ended.

At Mosciska, organized religious life survived among the Redemptorists Fathers until 1948, with their normal schedule continuing uninterrupted; at Sambor, among the Bernardines, until 1950. The Sisters of the various religious orders organized clandestine lives, meeting in evenings for prayers and devotions, according to their various rules. (Secret communities of Jesuit, Capuchin, and Franciscan priests would survive until 1991.)

A priest hiding in Bar in 1953 decribed worship in the Latin Catholic communities of Ukraine. As in priestless communities throughout the Soviet Union, the priestly vestments were laid on the altar, and a lay leader (in Ukraine, the sacristan of the parish; in the Catholic diaspora, often women) would lead the people in prayer and also take up a collection to keep the building open. Servers would ring the bells at the traditional times, as the congregation recited the Mass prayers in Latin, with litanies in Polish to the Blessed Virgin. At the *Sanctus,* the crowd would fall silent and unite themselves with the churches "far away where Jesus is adored in the signs of bread and wine."[86]

Russian SFR

Moscow

Conditions at Saint Louis des Français remained tenuous: when Father Bourgeois arrived at the parish, he was bluntly told that he could no longer celebrate the Byzantine Rite—that "one Eastern ceremony in the church . . . would be enough to have it closed."[87] The parish retained a strong French identity, though its native parishioners were all ethnic Russians, Poles, or Balts. Indeed, this identity saved it: the faithful regularly sang French hymns and kept up French devotions and practices; the historical loyalty of Moscow's French residents to the ruling regime persisted, even under severe testing. The parishioners had all been interrogated or arrested; and some had been sent to prison; yet the parish continued to have daily Masses in the early morning for workers, and High Mass every Sunday for the Soviet faithful. Moreover, there was a Sunday Mass with an English sermon and another with a French sermon for diplomats and tourists. The faith of the Saint Louis parish is typified by the story of one woman parishioner, who, overcome by a devastating depression while in prison, overcame it by repeating, "Not my will but Thine," and thus found relief.[88]

In 1945, Father George Laberge came to Moscow to relieve the long-suffering Father Braun. Also an American Assumptionist, Father Laberge continued the practice of traveling into the countryside to bring the sacraments to the Soviet faithful, as had been guaranteed by the Roosevelt-Litvinov Agreement of 1933. In 1947, Father Jean Thomas, a French Assumptionist, arrived to help Father Laberge. When, however, Father Laberge traveled to America in 1949, the Soviets canceled his visa, leaving Father Thomas alone in Moscow.

In 1950, the government expelled Father Thomas and installed a Latvian priest at Saint Louis; the new chaplain for the foreigners, Father Brassard, became the apostolic administrator. Despite his title, Father Brassard restricted his ministry to the foreign colony so as not to give the Soviets a pretext for expelling him also. This was successful, and he ministered quietly at an apartment leased by the French government until 1953.[89]

The Communists did not make life easy for his successor, Father Georges Bissonnette, whose Russian Catholic housekeeper was removed when she attended Mass.[90] Father Bissonnette was very active among the foreign Catholics and other Christians living in Moscow, but had little contact with the Soviet Catholic Church and its members. He did receive ex-prisoners from

North Korea, including priests and nuns, in 1953, who had suffered terribly under abominable conditions. When, in May 1954, the heroic Assumptionist missionary Father Jean Nicolas was released after 9 years' imprisonment in Kazakhstan and at Vorkuta, Father Bissonette was able to go to Confession for the first time since his assignment.

As for Saint Louis Church, Mass continued to be celebrated by priests sent from Riga. Sunday attendance averaged 1,000 believers, enormous given the devastation suffered by the Moscow Latin Catholic community. Foreign Catholics continued to attend Mass at Saint Louis, as a sign of solidarity. In 1954, some 400 children received Confirmation from the archbishop of Riga and were given a strong sermon on how to hold to their religion in the face of atheism. The parishioners' contact with the foreigners' chaplain was limited, however, to receiving holy cards and the calendar, and to giving occasional Mass stipends.[91]

Leningrad

Although Notre Dame was closed with the expulsion of the last French priest, the church was finally reopened after 1945 with a Soviet priest. Remaining French property, it came under the Archdiocese of Riga's jurisdiction, along with most of the rest of the USSR. The parish returned to a normal life in the late 1940s, with two priests assigned to it. The large congregation consisted of ethnic Armenians, Latvians, Lithuanians, and Poles, and ultimately the parish required four Masses on Sundays to accommodate the crowds.[92] Saint Catherine's Church was given over to the Leningrad Philharmonic, with plans to build a concert hall inside. The church had not been repaired during the siege, and like all Soviet "restoration" work, progress was extremely slow. (It was still being "renovated" in 1984.)[93]

These were the only two churches left to serve all of European Soviet Russia, and throughout this era, they were the only legal Catholic churches in the entire Russian SFR.

Siberia

This was where the great majority of Latin Catholics in the Russian FSR lived. They came under three categories in the last part of the Stalin Era:

1. "Free" residents of the original Siberian cities, towns, and villages. Descendants of the original Siberian Catholic population or of ethnic Poles exiled from the UkSSR who had survived their terms but were not allowed to go

home, these Catholics had virtually no contact with a priest until access to the prisons was granted after 1953, except for the rare priest released after serving his sentence.

2. Inmates of labor camps and prisons. Citizens of the former Baltic States or Soviet citizens who had been arrested and sent to the Gulag, these Catholics had the greatest access to the sacraments.

3. Special settlement exiles. Survivors of the mass removals of Russia Germans and ethnic Poles, these Catholics had no clergy among them after the wartime repatriation of the Anders Army.

In categories 1 and 3, among the Soviet citizens, elderly women passed on the Catholic faith, using the methods taught them by the last of the priests of the pre-1939 Soviet Union. These women administered Baptism on a truly monumental scale. (In Novosibirsk in the early 1990s, Father Alexander Kahn, SJ, would declare that his grandmother had baptized more babies than he ever would in his life as a legal priest.) Basic prayers were taught, in particular the Rosary and Creed; holy pictures were installed in the Dear Lord's Corner; well-worn bibles, missals, and hymnals were carefully handed on, or songs were written down by hand. In many communities, valid Latin Rite marriages were celebrated with two witnesses, especially among the Russia Germans.

Latin Catholics among Polish citizens sent to Siberia kept up their Catholic practices and prayers, and veneration of sacred images, especially of Our Lady of Czestochowa.) The loss of priests, though, was keenly felt. There was no Mass, no possibility of Confirmation, Confession, Anointing, or consecration of the vast cemeteries. Nor was there organized instruction, and some errors inevitably crept in. Yet the Faith endured. (Exiled Polish citizens would not be allowed to leave Siberia until repatriation to Communist Poland began after 1955. The overwhelming majority returned home, or to the newly created western provinces of Poland if their homes had been in the USSR.)

In category 2, Latin Catholic labor camp inmates were able to organize "parishes" among the ethnic Polish, Lithuanian, and German prisoners and exiles (as described in detail in chapter 17).

Moldavian SSR

The Polish-Armenian-German parishes of the newly enlarged SSR suffered heavy losses: every single church was closed in the Stalinist persecutions, and the church in the capital, Kishinev, was secularized. Only the cemetery chapel in Kishinev remained open for Catholic use;[94] the faithful had to gather outside in all weather while an occasional priest celebrated Mass inside. This was how conditions would remain for many years, with the Moldavian Catholics suffering great persecution for remaining loyal to their Church.

Georgian SSR

The Church of Saints Peter and Paul in Tbilisi remained open except for brief periods. Caucasus Germans remember a priest known to them as "Father Emmanuel," who was Father Wardidze, one of the twelve survivors of the pre-1939 clergy sent to the Gulag. He performed a delicate balancing act, following Soviet law as closely as possibly while celebrating the Mass and sacraments. German Catholics being forcibly removed in 1941 went to him for Confession and Anointing before leaving Tbilisi. (Although Saints Peter and Paul's appears on the lists of open Latin Catholic churches, it was very nearly closed down in the 1960s.) The Assumption Church, closed in 1937, was not reopened, and eventually underwent renovation for use as a concert hall. The priest in the 1950s was an ethnic Georgian, and the parishioners were ethnic Georgians, Armenians, Poles, and Germans, as well as Assyrian-Chaldeans from the tiny parish that disappeared in the late 1930s. Several of the faithful of this isolated Church attended the seminary in Riga, and several were ordained to the priesthood, although they did not always come home to serve. The Akhaltsike church had survived the Great Terror, as had twelve parishes nearby. But because the town and parishes were in a closed border zone with highly restricted travel, they received practically no pastoral care.[95] Ultimately, between 1955 and the 1960s, one church was restored at Shvilis, in the Akhaltsike district.

Central Asian SSRs

Hundreds of thousands of Ukrainian Poles, Russia Germans, Polish citizens, and Balts lived here. The Ukrainian Poles were concentrated in Kazakhstan, to which so many had been sent in 1936 when the border oblasts were cleared. The Russia Germans were dispersed throughout the SSRs, as were the Balts, especially the Lithuanians.

Organized public Catholic religious life was absolutely forbidden. Believers followed the practices of the Catholics in Siberia, however, so that the Faith would be preserved. (After 1955, virtually all the Polish citizens in the Central Asian SSRs left for Communist Poland because they were not allowed to return to their old homes in western Ukraine and Belorussia.

The Russian Orthodox Patriarchate
and the Latin Catholic Church

The Moscow Patriarchate, with the encouragement of the Soviet government, published anti-Catholic articles in its journal (and, as we shall see in chapter 32, it also cooperated in the mass destruction of Eastern Catholicism in the western Soviet Union). Regarding the Latin Catholic Church, the worst excess of Orthodox-Soviet cooperation came with the Orthodox Congress of 1948, which celebrated the 500th anniversary of the Patriarchate's autocephaly. Patriarchs and delegates came from all of the Orthodox Churches, both in Communist and in free countries. This congress issued the following statements on the Latin Catholic Church:

1. The Vatican is a political machine, not a religious institution;

2. The papacy instigated the Italian-German "crusade" of 1941 against the USSR;

3. the Vatican is a reactionary organization and a supporter of Anglo-American imperialism;

4. the Vatican stifled Slavic national aspirations through the Church unions and oppression of Poland.

The nadir of this diatribe came with the declaration that the Catholic religion had been corrupted because of its belief in the

> *Filioque* and Immaculate Conception, but, above all, because of papal authority and papal infallibility, a doctrine which is totally anti-Christian. . . . [T]he Roman Church has erected an enormous block to the unity of the universal Church of Christ . . . these dogmas are purely human invention, not found in Holy Scripture, not in Holy Tradition, nor in patristic literature, nor likewise in Church history. . . . [U]p to our day the Papacy by bloody war and all sorts of violence has attempted to convert the Orthodox to Catholicism. [The Vatican] was one of the kindlers of the two imperialist wars and at present takes an active part in kindling a new war.[96]

Throughout the Stalin Era, vicious anti-Catholic lies and slander were a staple of the Patriarchate's journal, and the Holy See and the Latin Catholic religion became the source of all that was wrong in the world.

Such cooperation with the Soviets gained the Russian Orthodox Church nothing, however. Orthodoxy faced continual problems among the former Greek Catholics in the Ukrainian and Belorussian SSRs, a continual shortage of churches, and a concentration of religious life in the western areas. The

Russian FSR never had enough parishes, and there were still vast areas without a single Orthodox church. Working Orthodox churches declined from a peak of 14,421 in 1949 to only 13,422 in 1954. Registrations had been cut back in 1948, and no new parishes were registered after 1949 except in the Transcarpathian oblast, where the parishes of the Greek Catholic Church, then being destroyed there, were incorporated into the Moscow Patriarchate.

Worse, 400 Orthodox parishes were "de-registered" in 1950. Orthodox churches were torn down and secularized, as before. The Orthodox lost 7 percent of their parishes throughout the USSR, and 8 percent of those in the RFSFR. Sixteen monastic houses were closed, and new restrictions placed on public services.[94] But worse still was yet to come.

Nevertheless, the recurring purges and persecutions under Khrushchev and his successors would not break believers' spirits. Father Bissonnette recorded a story told him by a member of the French Embassy staff about her daily commute. When her bus on this particular day passed a former church that had been turned into a cinema, an old Russian woman blessed herself when she saw the old icon still enshrined in the wall. At that point the young soldier sitting across from her began laughing and asked, "Why do you do that, *babushka?* Do you believe that old picture will help your rheumatism?" The old woman did not answer, and the soldier, thinking he had the support of the other travelers, went on loudly: "I suppose you believe in the devil, too, and blame him every time something goes wrong. Poor devil, he has a heavy load to carry. Have you ever seen the devil?" Turning to the soldier, the old woman answered, *"Seychas, ya yego vizhu"* (I see him right now.) The soldier got off at the next stop, and the passengers almost cheered.[98]

CHAPTER 32

The War to Destroy the Eastern Catholic Churches, 1945–1953

> I fear we shall fall under the yoke of the Bolsheviks.
> —Metropolitan Sheptytsky, 1943

> [A]postate priest Kostelnyk: Martyrdom suits only the dark Middle Ages. We are now living in modern times.

> Canon Alexander Chira: And eternal life, dear Doctor? It also suits only the dark Middle Ages?
> —personal diary of Bishop Alexander Chira, 1947

With the expansion of the USSR, millions of Eastern Catholics came under its control. Stalin had revived the martyred Russian Orthodox Church during the war, and patriarch and dictator had achieved an uncomfortable, but viable, partnership. To many critics, the Moscow Patriarchate now became a department of the Soviet system.

Stalin adopted many goals of the tsars, and one of those goals was eliminating the Greek Catholics, a goal that harmonized with the spread of Orthodoxy and age-old dreams of the Patriarchate. The cooperation of the Moscow patriarchal clergy in the persecution of their fellow Christians exceeded anything achieved under the tsars. Indeed, so blatant was this cooperation that Pope Pius XII was led to mourn "the vile dependency shown by certain representatives of the religion called 'Orthodox' on a concept of life whose ultimate goal is the elimination of all religion" in his 1947 New Year's address.[1]

In his April 1945 letter to the members of the "Uniate Church," Patriarch Alexei wrote:

> I beseech you to remember your ancestors, to turn away from Rome towards your Mother, the Orthodox Church, who awaits you with open arms; so that

we all, sons of Great Russia and Glacial Russia [Ukraine] feel ourselves to be truly brothers in Jesus Christ, and may advance in the bosom of the Orthodox Church towards eternal salvation. . . . I say unto you, break with Rome which has led you into darkness and spiritual degradation![2]

Opinions have varied over the years as to whether the Eastern Catholic Churches could have been saved. Certainly, the connection of the Eastern Catholics with Rome and their close resemblance to the Orthodox Churches was a major factor in their destruction: Stalin could not tolerate Churches that presented Orthodox with an acceptable alternative.

In addition, the Eastern Catholics were doomed by international politics. Pius XII was openly anti-Communist after the war, especially in the face of growing Soviet repression. The Vatican was appalled by the Yalta and Potsdam decisions consigning half of Europe to Soviet control, and Moscow saw Rome as being clearly on the side of the United States in the Cold War. As we shall see, Rome's condemnations of Communism always brought on more troubles in the USSR. Stalin's fear of a Ukrainian revival was directly linked to the anti-Soviet partisan forces active in the western UkSSR after 1944; indeed, the Greek Catholic Church was ordered to get the partisans to surrender under the terms of a Soviet amnesty. As we shall also see, Stalinist paranoia about foreign contacts would doom Bishop Romzha in 1947.[3]

Perhaps the destruction, purges, and persecutions could have been delayed by a more quiescent attitude from Pius XII, perhaps not. In the long run, it is highly unlikely that any public structure of an Eastern Catholic Church in union with Rome could have survived in the USSR.

The Armenian Catholic Church

Archdiocese of Lvov

In this archdiocese, which embraced Galicia and northern Bukovina (territories annexed in part or whole to the Ukrainian SSR in 1939–1940), the Armenian priests who resided in Lvov (L'viv) were first arrested in 1944, based on the collaboration of the one priest who had assisted the formation of the foreign legion under the Nazis. This priest's behavior was also used as grounds for charging the Armenian apostolic administrator, Monsignor Dionysius Kajetanowicz, with having allowed such behavior and with having authorized one of his priests to do so—a charge that was obviously false.

On May 8, 1945, the Soviets arrested the administrator, along with the canons of the cathedral—Fathers Victor Kvapinsky, Kazymyr Romoskano, and Stanislav Dobryta—and all the city priests.[4] The eight Armenian Catholic priests in the countryside were dispersed and prevented from working as priests; the Armenian Benedictine Nuns arrested and scattered, and their convent confiscated; the Armenian Catholic school and bank both suppressed, and the precious library and museum looted. The eight priests at liberty, and a large part of the archdiocese's population in Galicia applied as Poles for repatriation to Poland.[5]

While in prison, the administrator was offered the position of Armenian Apostolic archbishop if he would break with Rome. When he refused, he was sentenced to 10 years in the infamous Solovetski prison camp. (He would die on November 18, 1954, at Abiez, above the Arctic Circle.)[6]

When Father Pietro Alagiagian came through Lvov on his repatriation trip to Italy, he visited the cathedral complex where he had once worked. He was stunned to discover the streets were now paved with the tombstones of the Armenian nobility and clergy. At the chancery, an old man told him that all of the ethnic Armenian, Polish, and Ukrainian families who had been sheltered there had been forcibly removed. The cathedral was closed, and access to the library collection barred by a locked gate.[7] The heart had been torn out of this ancient center of Armenian cultural and religious life.

The Armenian Catholic Church of northern Bukovina had been repressed in 1946; its church and chapels closed. As in Galicia, most Armenian Catholics here considered themselves Poles; indeed, they were often referred to as "Armeno-Poles." Only for their liturgy did they use Armenian: in daily speech, they used Polish; in church, they sang Polish hymns. As a result, when ethnic Poles were repatriated from northern Bukovina, most Armenians left as well in 1945–1946.[8] The pastor in Czernowitz (Chenivtsi), the 1939 nominee for the archbishopric, Monsignor Andreas Lukasiewicz, was also able to come to Poland: he settled with Armenian refugees in Krakow. He had removed all of the historic registers of the Armenian Catholic community, which are now with the archives of the archdiocese of Posen.[9] A few Armenian Catholic families remained behind, after 1946, and practiced their Faith in secret.[10]

Poland

The Armenian Catholics in Poland were joined by the Armenian Catholics who had fled from Bessarabia, and a number of Armenian Catholics who had crossed the frontier with the Red Army. Thus, after the war, a new community of nearly 8,000 believers was reconstituted in central Poland and its "new territories" taken from Germany.[11] Leadership among these scattered people was held by the vicar general, Father Kazimierz Filipiak, who had emigrated from the USSR in 1946 and been resettled in the former German city of Oppeln. Denied jurisdiction by the Polish Roman Catholic hierarchy, Father Filipiak faithfully ministered to the Armenian Catholic community on his own (he would be named vicar general for Armenian Catholics in Poland in 1986—forty years after his arrival in the country).[12] Anti-Eastern Catholic Polish chauvinism caused great heartaches to Armenian and Ukrainian Catholics living in Poland after 1945.

The Administration of Tbilisi

In 1945, one Armenian Catholic parish was reported to have been restored in Leninakan (Alexandropol), Soviet Armenia, a traditional center of Armenian Catholic life[13]—but not for long. Under Soviet rule, the Armenian Catholics were treated worse than the Armenian Apostolic Church, both because of their tie with Rome and because they were suspected of supporting the anti-Communist Dashnak movement. In the early 1950s, approximately 10,000 lived in the border zone, concentrated at Akhaltsike and Alkhalek, with another 20,000 elsewhere in Soviet Georgia and Armenia.[14] The Armenian Catholics of the last church in Tbilisi and those in Soviet Georgia's border zone with Turkey had a reputation for being dedicated to their Catholic religion, "even when isolated." (A few priests who survived the Stalinist horrors would return home after 1954.)[15]

The Chaldean Catholic Church

Although the Chaldean parish of Syagut was never restored after the arrest and final exile of its priest in the Great Terror, Chaldean Catholics, noted for being Aramaic-speakers, still existed and remained faithful to the Catholic religion, even in the absence of any Church structure. They were principally found in Tbilisi, at the Latin Catholic parish, and in the border zone communities of Soviet Georgia.

The Greek Catholic Church in Soviet Ukraine and Belorussia

The Metropolinate of L'viv

The Soviet suppression of the Greek Catholic Church after World War II directly parallels the tsarist suppressions of 1839 and 1875.[16] Moreover, the parallels to the past ironically include the death of the Church's leader at absolutely the worst possible time.

The return of the Soviets in August 1944 was marked by general panic. Thousands of Greek Catholics joined the exodus west, including some 300 priests and many lay leaders. On November 1, 1944, the great leader of the Ukrainian Catholics, Metropolitan Andrew Sheptytsky, died in L'viv. Despite his having been old and ill, there were persistent rumors that the metropolitan had in fact been poisoned by the Soviets, the fate awaiting Bishop Romzha in 1947.

When permission was granted for a public funeral, Byzantine, Latin, and Armenian Catholic Requiems were held in L'viv at Saint George's Cathedral. The Metropolitan's funeral procession was an enormous event: the streets were packed with mourners, both Polish and Ukrainian, and even the Red Army paid its respects to the Metropolitan's remains before their burial in the cathedral crypt. When Bishop Josef Slipyj became the new Metropolitan by right of succession, and was recognized as such, there was hope that perhaps, after all, Moscow would allow the Greek Catholic Church to survive.

Slipyj himself was told that the policies of 1939–1941 would not be repeated and not to fear repression. Indeed, he was told that the Metropolinate of L'viv would be able to exercise its authority in Poland. A Church delegation went to Moscow in December 1944 with a contribution of 100,000 rubles for the Red Army and was assured there would be no persecution. Although some believed that Stalin decided not to antagonize the Americans at Yalta by launching overt persecution the Vatican remained unconvinced.[17]

The Campaign to "Convert" the Greek Catholic Church. The 1943 "concordat" between the Kremlin and the Moscow Patriarchate had given new life to Russian Orthodoxy. The Greek Catholics were strongly suspected of supporting Ukrainian nationalism, ties with Rome were undesirable, and the Church needed to be suppressed in order to accomplish the rapid Sovietization of the country.

On March 2, 1945, as the war raged on in Europe, Stalin and Molotov ordered the head of the Council of Affairs of the Russian Orthodox Church, Colonel Georgii Karpov, to submit a memorandum on the relations of the Pa-

Saint George's Cathedral, L'viv (Lvov). Courtesy of the author.

triarchate and the Vatican and how the Patriarchate could be used to fight Catholicism. Karpov's memorandum, approved on March 16, called for the unification of the Greek Catholic and Russian Orthodox Churches; support of an "Old Catholic Church" to fight the Latin Catholics; and support of Russian Orthodox activity overseas. Among the specific means proposed by Karpov to liquidate the Greek Catholic Church was the establishment of an

Orthodox eparchy in Lwów (L'viv), issuing an invitation from the Patriarchate to the Greek Catholic Church to "reunite" with Moscow (despite there having never been such a union), and the formation of an initiative group from among the Greek Catholic priests. All of this was duly implemented in 1945–1946 against the Metropolia of L'viv.

With the Yalta Agreement, rejuvenation of the Russian Orthodox Church and the Armenian Apostolic Church, and Soviet expansion to the west, there was growing need to regulate the non-Orthodox. The Council of Religious Affairs (CRA), created by Stalin in 1929 to monitor the Churches and to coordinate Soviet anti-religious policies, would play only a minor role in destroying the Greek Catholic Church, however (indeed, Ukraine's CRA commissioner was stunned when the Ukrainian bishops were arrested in 1945).[18] Instead, the attacks on the Church would be coordinated by the NKVD and the Ministry of State Security (MGB).

Moscow had opted to suppress the Greek Catholic Church through a supposedly legal means, namely, the convocation of a Church synod, hoping that such would ease the conscience of the West. A massive overt persecution was deemed unwise in light of the extension of Soviet rule into Central Europe. Thus began the campaign to "convert" the Greek Catholic Church to Russian Orthodoxy, with the full cooperation of the Moscow Patriarchate.

(After the Greek Catholics' great shrine at Zarvanitsya to Our Lady was destroyed in 1944, the stream where the miraculous icon was said to have been found in 1240 filled up with dirt. It would remain so until 1991, when the Greek Catholic Church found itself for the first time in an independent Ukraine.)

In 1944 a delegation was sent by Metropolitan Slipyj to Moscow to congratulate the new Orthodox Patriarch, Alexis, to inform Stalin that the Greek Catholic Church was willing to cooperate with the Soviets, and to convey the Church's donation of 100,000 rubles to the Red Army. Its leader was Father Gabriel Kostelnyk, who was destined to betray his Church. They met with Alexis, and were invited to Orthodox services, which the hegumen of the Studite monks (and brother to the deceased metropolitan), Father Klement Sheptytsky, refused to attend. Nevertheless, the Greek Catholic Church was asked to cooperate in the suppression of the UPA units. An attempt at arranging this failed because the partisans did not trust the Bolsheviks.[19]

Overt Persecution Resumes. The "Uniate" priests were ordered to attend anti-Catholic meetings, and the bishops were prevented from communicating with the clergy. Anti-Catholic propaganda resumed in April of 1945 (setting the tone for the next forty-four years). Metropolitan Slipyj was condemned as a collaborator of the Nazis, and an enemy of the Ukrainian people. The Russian Orthodox Synod, which had elected Alexis, roundly condemned the Holy See, and called for the reunion of the "Uniates" in the USSR, and indeed probably laid the plans for the "reunion." [20]

On April 11, 1945, the entire Ukrainian Greek Catholic hierarchy was arrested and imprisoned (in June 1946, the Ukrainian Catholic bishops of Poland would be deported to the USSR, where they would be imprisoned as well). At the end of the month, Patriarch Alexis asked the Greek Catholics to submit to reunion and break with Rome. Suddenly, on May 28, an "Action Group" was announced by some of the Ukrainian clergy, under the leadership of Father Kostelnyk. Partly hoping to save his son (who, he had been told was a prisoner of the Soviets), partly out of anti-Latin Catholic feelings, partly out of conviction, Kostelnyk led the destruction of his own Church with the assistance of two other apostate priests, Antoni Pelvetsky and Mykhailo Melnyk. A Russian Orthodox priest was named the bishop for western Ukraine. This Action Group, aided by the newly appointed Orthodox Bishop Makarius (who had only one parish in the city of L'viv), petitioned on May 28, 1945, for reunion with Russian Orthodoxy.

Shortly after 300 Greek Catholic priests sent a letter of protest to Moscow, in September 1945, some 500 were arrested and removed, as were Greek Catholic seminary teachers, monks, and nuns. Some priests yielded under torture, were released, and later tried in vain to retract their support of Orthodoxy. Others were begged to sign by their parishioners, so as to guarantee that their churches would remain open and that Greek Catholic clergy would serve them instead of Russian Orthodox missionaries.

The State pursued its overt persecution, confiscating Church property and assets, and suppressing all Greek Catholic religious communities with the exception of the Sisters of Saint Vincent de Paul, who were still nominally a Latin Catholic order and whose mother superior held Belgian citizenship. These Sisters, forbidden to openly practice the Byzantine rite, nevertheless remained faithful to the shattered Church throughout the time of suppression and managed to hold secret services in their government-recognized chapel with secret Greek Catholic priests. On March 1, 1946, the bishops were all sentenced to prison, and exile, and the Church was decapitated.

The "Synod of Lvov." There had been complaints about Russian Orthodox passivity regarding the suppression of the Greek Catholics.[21] It is believed that Stalin himself ordered the synod, and it is known that NKVD agents organized it. At the time it was held, on March 8–10, 1946, in Saint George's Cathedral, there were still 2,500 Greek Catholic parishes in the Metropolinate of

Christmas in Ukraine

Ukrainian Greek Catholics praying in cemetery, a scene commonly depicted throughout most of the former Soviet Union for more than seventy years. Aid to the Church in Need Christmas card for 1997. Courtesy of the author.

L'viv, with several million faithful.[22] A "vote" was taken to leave the Catholic Church and "reunite" with the "Mother Church" of Moscow—characterized by some as the "self-liquidation of the Ukrainian Greek Catholic Church" and the "end of the Union of Brest-Litovsk."

There were no Greek Catholic bishops present; rather, the delegates were astounded to discover that their confreres, Fathers Melnyk and Pelvetsky, had been secretly ordained Russian Orthodox bishops and, along with Kostelnyk (who was by now an Orthodox priest), were to lead the discussions. The two new bishops were named to the newly created Russian Orthodox sees of Drogobych and Stanislav.

The pro-Orthodox action group had handpicked the delegates to the synod, and there was no chance to resist. Telegrams were sent to Stalin, the Patriarch, and the faithful to announce this "joyful" occasion. By then, some 1,600 Greek Catholic priests were in prison or exile in Siberia and Asia. The number would reach over 2,000 before Stalin died.

In Germany, the Red Army arrested the Exarch Monsignor Petro Verhun in the ruins of Berlin. He was forcibly removed to Siberia along with hundreds of the Ukrainian Catholics living in Berlin.[23]

Fate of the Bishops. All the Ukrainian Catholic hierarchs were imprisoned or shipped off to the Gulag for various terms. Bishop Hrihorii Khomyshyn died in a Kiev prison on January 17, 1947; Bishop Josaphat Kotsylovsky in Siberia in November of that year. Bishop Niketa Budka died in a Karaganda prison in 1949; Bishop Hrihori Lakota in the infamous Vorkuta prison camp in November 1950. (Father Klement Sheptytsky of the Studites was sent to the Vladimir prison where he would die in 1958.) Exarch Verhun from Berlin survived the Gulag, but was never freed from exile (he would die in Krasnoyarsk oblast on February 7, 1957).[24]

Other Casualties. The apostate priest Kostelnyk was shot in 1948, supposedly by UPA partisans, but it is also equally possible—and indeed highly probable—that his usefulness to the Soviets had ended, and he was killed by the NKVD to create an "Orthodox martyr." (It is worth noting that Kostelnyk's wife and all his descendants remained in the Greek Catholic Church down to our time.) Both Bishops Melnyk and Pelvetsky died under mysterious circumstances, very likely killed by the NKVD because they could not be trusted to stay silent about what had happened in the suppressions.[25]

Father Volodmyr Sterniuk, the future metropolitan of L'viv, was arrested in 1947 and subjected to protracted torture. He was not allowed to sleep for the first two weeks, and for the next three months he could only sleep on weekends. "They tried to force me to say things I didn't want to say, convince of my own insignificance, that I was nothing." Convicted of crimes against the State at a Moscow trial held in absentia Father Sterniuk was sentenced to 5 years in exile and prison. Upon his release, he would work secretly as a priest, and later as a bishop while holding different jobs.[26]

Fate of the Religious Communities. No Greek Catholic religious community in Soviet Ukraine accepted the action group or forcible incorporation into Russian Orthodoxy. As a result, between 1946 and 1950, all the Ukrainian Catholic monasteries, convents, sketes, and their churches and related institutions were suppressed. A number were given over to Russian Orthodoxy, and even those were closed later. The rest were secularized.

There were numerous communities of sisters and nuns in Soviet Ukraine in 1939 (see table 7). Some of these were quite large, others were very small. All were affected by the 1946 "Synod of Lvov." For the Sister Servants, Sister Andrea became provincial (serving in that capacity until her death in 1967). Some 300 Sisters remained in Galicia, while others successfully escaped abroad in the exodus of 1944. Their provincial house was confiscated in 1949. The Sisters refused to convert to Orthodoxy, and so were disbanded. Some 30 of them were sent to Siberia, and those who were left behind took up work as nurses, seamstresses, laundry workers, and collective farm workers. They were

Father Stefan Bendas as prisoner in Karaganda camp. Pencil
drawing. Courtesy of his son, Father Daniel Bendas.

often subjected to ridicule, foul language, and scant wages; their communal
apartments were continually searched.[27]

Only one community was spared: the Sisters of Charity of Saint Vincent
de Paul. Because the superior was a Belgian countess and the community had
never been formally transferred from the Latin rite to the Byzantine Rite, the
Sisters were able to reestablish community in a house in L'viv (both convents
and their hospital were confiscated). Allowed to wear their habits only at their
profession, the Sisters worked in the city hospitals, obtaining secret priests for
sick patients and relying on secret Redemptorist monks to celebrate the Greek

Table 7

Religious Orders of Women Before World War II in Galicia

Order	Members	Houses
Saint Josaphat	64	2
Myrrh Bearers	94	4
Holy Family	33	4
Sister Servants	71	7
Saint Basil	307	17
Saint Vincent	80	3
Studite	71	7

Source: Blazhejovskyj, 143–7.

Catholic Liturgy in secret. Though these unofficial chaplains were later arrested, and the Sisters interrogated and subjected to repeated searches and merciless harassment, their community survived and even grew.[28]

In 1950, eight Basilian nuns were forcibly removed to a prison camp in Khabarovsk oblast in the Soviet Far East, where they conducted catechism classes and prayer services among themselves, the prisoners, and the "free" population. In 1953, their prayers for a priest were answered. The severely weakened Father Macarius Rozumijka arrived in a nearby prison camp. He celebrated Christmas services and Holy Supper on January 6, 1953 (Christmas Eve, old style), and the Sisters successfully carried the Eucharist back to their camp.[29]

Like the Greek Catholic women's religious communities, the men's communities all resisted conversion to Orthodoxy (see table 8). A few Basilian houses held out as Greek Catholic enclaves until 1950. Basilian monasteries were generally confiscated in 1946 and the monks were either arrested or dispersed into secular life (while retaining their religious vocation).

The Greek Catholic Enclave in Chernovtsy Oblast. On the return of the Red Army in 1944, Administrator Mykhailo Simovych had been sent to Siberia, which became his burial ground.[30] In April 1946, the State declared that the Greek Catholic Church of northern Bukovina (now the Chernovtsy oblast of the UkSSR) no longer existed and that the Greek Catholics had returned to the "womb of their Mother Church," namely, Russian Orthodoxy.[31] The Chernovtsy (Czernowitz) church was then turned over to the Russian Orthodox Church (it would serve as such until its renovation in 1987).[32] All of the Greek

Table 8

Religious Orders of Men before World War II in Galicia

Order	Members	Houses
Redemptorists	119	6
Studites	225	10
Basilians	373	18

Source: Blazhejovskyj, 143–7; see also 120 n. 21.

Catholic churches of the nine northern parishes became—at least temporarily—Russian Orthodox. Some were eventually destroyed or given over to secular uses.

The "Neo-Uniate" Parishes and Missions. Following the Russian Synodal Rite imposed on Greek Catholics in 1839 and 1870, the "Neo-Uniates" of former eastern Poland, when they were reunited with Rome again in the interwar period, had specified that they would retain that rite and its calendar. They did not want the services of the Galician Catholic Church (though some authors contradict this). All of the "Neo-Uniate" parishes in the UkSSR (as elsewhere in the Soviet Union) were suppressed, either by being closed completely or given over to the Russian Orthodox.

The Eparchy of Mukachevo

> Of this sure: that we will never abandon our faith nor betray our Church.
> —Bishop Theodore Romzha

The Greek Catholic Eparchy of Mukachevo dates from the Middle Ages, with its bishops residing on Chernecha Hora, the Mountain of Monks above Mukachevo, until their move in 1761 to Assumption Church in the town itself, and later to Uzhgorod. The heart of the eparchy, however, remained at Saint Nicholas's Monastery on the mountain. A major focal point of prayer was the Miraculous Icon of the Mother of God, painted in 1453. This was the site of an annual pilgrimage in August, in honor of the Dormition of the Virgin, a pilgrimage that would figure strongly in the history of the struggle for the Greek Catholic Church.

The principal territory of the eparchy was contained in what had now become known as "Carpatho-Ukraine." The province was split in 1938 with the cities of Mukachevo and Uzhgorod going to Hungary, and the remainder becoming an autonomous province of what was left of Czechoslovakia. A Greek Catholic priest, Monsignor Augustyn Voloshyn, became prime minister of the province. In 1939, Czechoslovakia was completely dissolved: Slovakia declared its independence, and the Czech lands became a German protectorate. "Carpatho-Ukraine" proclaimed independence, Hungary promptly invaded, and the Carpatho-Ukrainian government was forced to flee from its capital, Chust, and seek refuge in Yugoslavia. Members of the government eventually settled in Prague, where Monsignor Voloshyn taught at the Ukrainian University and officiated at Saint Clement's Church. Arrested by the Czechs in 1945 as Nazi collaborators, Voloshyn and his remaining ministers were deported to the USSR. Voloshyn was tortured at Lefortovo Prison and died there on July 11, 1945. The presence of some Greek Catholic support for the independence of the province and the Church's alleged connections with Nazi Germany provided grist for Soviet propaganda mills.[33]

The Red Army liberated Uzhgorod at the end of October 1944. Trouble began immediately for the Church.

First Signs. Bishop Theodore George Romzha was invited to speak at the celebrations to welcome the Red Army in the city theater, across from the Latin Catholic parish church. He was given a prepared speech, in which he was supposed to ask President Benes of the Republic of Czechoslovakia, to recognize the "voluntary unification" of Transcarpathia (as Ruthenia was now called) with the Ukrainian SSR. Bishop Romzha refused to do so, but the "request" was included in the official printed copies of the speech, to the complete dismay of the crowd.

In November 1944, Greek Catholic churches were confiscated and turned over to Russian Orthodox use. Greek Catholic liturgical books were piled up and burned in Tsehelnya, Ploskiv, and Radvantski. To the 15 parishes forcibly converted to Orthodoxy, another 29 parishes were added in December. The hegumen of the small but religiously important monastery of Our Lady of Boronyavo was arrested in 1944 and sent to Siberia.

Colonel Tiulpanov of the political section of the Red Army took up quarters in the neighborhood of the Episcopal Palace, and became a frequent caller on Bishop Romzha. In January 1945, Bishop Romzha and Canon Alexander Chira were sent to meet with General Petrov at Michalovce, ostensibly to thank him for the liberation. Instead, the meeting turned into a session on the bishop's views of the papal primacy, with the general making both threats and promises to him. Canon Chira finally brought it all to end by quoting the Soviets' own propaganda regarding the need for a mutual decision by the Czechoslovak and Soviet governments.[34]

Although General Petrov had promised Bishop Romzha and Canon Chira that the Red Army would treat them with "grateful cooperation," pressures on the Greek Catholic Church began to build. In July 1945, Red soldiers confiscated the seminary in Uzhgorod Castle and moved its contents into the eparchy's two boarding schools. The press trumpeted that the castle was no longer a "cradle of dark criminal reactionaries" and that it would become a national museum.[35] This was the first ecclesiastical building to be lost to the eparchy.

In the autumn of 1945, an enthusiastic young priest, Father Stephen Danielovich, was singled out for persecution; forbidden to minister and forcibly removed from his parish of Imshad', Volove County, he was imprisoned and later sent to Siberia.

First Martyr. Although the eparchy was spared during the church closings elsewhere in Ukraine in 1946, the parish of Imshad' once again became a focal point of Soviet persecution. In the village of Negrovc'i, the local Orthodox parish cooperated with the Soviet police in instigating trouble with the Greek Catholic majority. After a nighttime removal of all their icons and liturgical items, the Orthodox church suddenly burned down. The Catholics were accused of arson, and the case went to trial. In one of the last free trials in the region, the Catholics were vindicated. But in the winter of 1946, the young pastor, Father Peter Legeza, was lured out on a sick call, and brutally murdered. Although this shocked even the Orthodox, once again they cooperated with the police: they obtained a court order claiming ownership of the Greek Catholic church. The newly ordained pastor of the church, Father Victor Ivancho, refused, invoking the Soviet Constitution's article on freedom of religion to defend the church against a takeover by armed militia. The NKVD then occupied the town, and the local court gave the church over to the Orthodox. Father Ivancho and many of his parishioners were condemned for anti-Soviet agitation and for opposing legal authority, and shipped off to Siberia. The Orthodox moved in, and the surviving Greek Catholics had neither a priest nor a church.[36]

Promotion of Schism. In August 1946, Canon Chira had been arrested and taken to the headquarters of SMERSH, the Soviet counterintelligence organ (disbanded by Khrushchev in 1958). He had been subjected to intense interrogation, and especially questioned regarding his loyalty to the Holy See and finally had been told to spy on Bishop Romzha and his contacts with Rome. Despite his firm refusal to do so, SMERSH had released him, with orders to report on August 10. This he had done, to find the offices abandoned. Later summoned to the National Council (founded in 1944 and suppressed in

1945), in yet another attempt to induce him to join Russian Orthodoxy, Canon Chira had declared that he would remain loyal to the Greek Catholic Church, to the Pope in Rome as Head of the Church, and that neither torture nor treasure would "make me abandon my Catholic faith and my Church." Furious, the head of the council had screamed at the canon that because of canon's personal popularity in the region and the Church: "Your place is in the Orthodox Church, and you can be sure that I do not accept your declaration under any condition!"

Resistance and Reunions. At the Dormition Pilgrimage held August 1946, an astounding 50,000 pilgrims came: more than twice the usual number. The authorities were stunned. But when they imposed a 20,000-ruble permit fee for Bishop Romzha to preach, the pilgrims raised every last kopeck from their own pockets. His sermon was electrifying, and at the last blessing priests and people were moved to tears. The pilgrims carried the message home with them, and the eparchy experienced both an internal renewal and a wave of petitions from Orthodox parishes wishing to be reunited with the Greek Catholic Church, which they had left twenty years before.[37]

Despite the confiscation of provisions and revenue, Greek Catholic seminary education continued, with 32 men ordained to the priesthood in the years 1945–1947. On several occasions, however, seminarians had to block the doors to stop armed soldiers from taking over, and one of the seminary's two buildings was lost in the spring of 1947. Bishop Romzha sent a secret emissary to Moscow to obtain official permission to keep the seminary alive. Although the initial response seemed favorable, emissary was forced to flee for his life, finally reaching America.[38] The noose was slowly closing in on the eparchy, its bishop, and its future.

Persecution: 1947. On October 26, 1946, the Russian Orthodox installed Bishop Nestor Sydoruk in Mukachevo as the newly established bishop of Uzhgorod-Mukachevo Russian Orthodox Eparchy.

On March 24, 1947, the principal Basilian monastery, Saint Nicholas's on Chernecha Hora, was occupied by the Soviet police and given over to the Russian Orthodox. The arrested monks were concentrated at the monastery's house in Imstychevo,[39] as were monks from the closed monasteries of Berezne, Uzhgorod, and Boronoyavo. At Chernecha Hora, the Orthodox hegumen arriving to take over the complex had the audacity to inform the arrested Basilians that they were welcome to stay on under his rule and the Orthodox Church. No one took him up on his offer.[40] Later the Greek Catholic convents of nuns were similarly claimed for the Orthodox Church, with Greek Catholic Sisters being expelled and Orthodox ones being brought in.

(In the end, however, the four convents were closed in 1956, and the Orthodox nuns all brought to Saint Nicholas's Monastery on Chernecha Hora.)[41]

In his Good Friday and Easter sermons of April 11 and 13, 1947, Bishop Romzha condemned the unjust persecution and the forces of "dark powers" at work in Transcarpathia. He also announced that the Dormition Pilgrimage would take place, but at the church in Mukachevo becasue Chernecha Hora was under Orthodox control. On July 25, the Soviet authorities decided to liquidate the eparchy and transfer the cathedral and churches over to the Moscow Patriarchate.[42] Bishop Nestor was to proclaim the "union with Orthodoxy" at the Dormition Pilgrimage, in the company of the new Orthodox prelates from Stanislav and L'viv, as well as from the Ukrainian centers of Kiev, Odessa, Lutsk, and Drogobych. Just before the Dormition Pilgrimage in 1947, the apostate priest Kostelnyk was sent to Uzhgorod to convince Canon Chira to join the Russian Church.

At the Dormition Pilgrimage in Mukachevo, first Bishop Romzha, then Canon Chira was denied permission to preach, although the services were allowed to be held. Bishop Nestor was to announce the "reunification" of the "Ruthenian Greek Catholic Church." To ensure this, the press trumpeted the "annual pilgrimage at Chernecha Horä for four weeks, and armed militiamen were assembled to direct all the pilgrims up to the mount. There were 80,000 pilgrims present, and the situation seemed to be going well, until the Greek Catholic churches in the city began to toll their bells as an alarm. When word was passed of what was planned, the pilgrims abandoned the mount, fleeing along paths well known to them, and even fording the river. The Russian Orthodox delegates were left with only a handful of pilgrims to address. A letter from Bishop Romzha was read aloud, exhorting the faithful to be willing to "achieve the glorious crown of martyrdom." It was the "most memorable pilgrimage" in the history of the little eparchy.

When Bishop Nestor did not, as planned, announce the end of the Union of Uzhgorod, his 3,000 followers and the Orthodox guests were disappointed. However, Kostelnyk did preach, dressed like a Greek Catholic priest, but giving a bitter sermon against the Vatican and Union. He did not impress the people, however, for when his car drove through Mukachevo, the crowds pelted it with tomatoes.[43] The ceremonies had been attended by Archbishop Oksiiuk Makarius from L'viv, Kostelnyk, the apostate Bishop Hrihorii Pelvetsky, and Hegumen Pimen, the future Patriarch of Moscow.[44]

Apostates and Heroes. Now a campaign of demoralization and intimidation began in earnest. Archdeacon Irenaeus Kondratovich drafted a "declaration of union" for the Transcarpathian Greek Catholic Church with Moscow,[45] and the Greek Catholic priests Stephen Kopik, Stephen Danielovich, Julius Kossey, and Peter Pohorilyak joined him. One of them, Stephen Kopik, approached Bishop Romzha with the audacious request to create an "action group" as was done in Galicia, at the same time arranging with the Latin Catholic priest Stephen Lorincz to come and absolve him on his deathbed. As it turned out, Father Lorincz heard about Kopik's death three days after his funeral on. As Bishop Chira wrote: "Man proposes, but God disposes, and in Kopik's case God disposed of the matter in His Way."

The fourth—and fifth-year Greek Catholic seminarians, meanwhile, begged to be ordained as quickly as possible, and this was done on September 14, 1947, at Holy Cross Cathedral. Among the new priests was Father Joseph Holovach (who would be ordained a secret bishop in 1983).[46] Meanwhile, it had been decided in Kiev and Moscow to kill Bishop Romzha because of his continued loyalty to Rome.

The "Accident." In October 1947, Bishop Romzha went to the rededication of a newly renovated church in Lavki, a filial church of the parish of Lochovo near Mukachevo, despite the warnings and pleas of the cathedral chapter and parish clergy.

The Liturgy was celebrated without incident on October 26, and the bishop preached a vigorous sermon on Christ the King, stating that "to die for Christ means to live forever!" Villagers reported a suspicious-looking Studebaker truck with men in uniform, later joined by a jeep with more troops. On October 27, the bishop set out, accompanied by Fathers Andrew Bereznaj and Daniel Bachinsky, and the deacons Michael Bugir and Michael Maslej, in a horse-drawn carriage, heading to the bus stop on the Uzhgorod road. The truck followed, and just outside Ivanovce, accelerated and rammed into the carriage.

One horse was killed outright, the other mortally wounded, and the bishop trapped between the wreckage of the carriage and the wheels of the truck. Although everyone survived the crash, the bishop and his party were immediately attacked by the soldiers, who beat them with iron rods. Enraged by the killing of his beloved horses, the coachman fought the attackers and was beaten until his brains came out of his ears. He died in the hospital a short time later. The bishop was beaten from head to toe, his lower jaw broken in several places, his teeth knocked out, and his head and hands slashed. Father Bachinsky was also severely beaten (under the mistaken belief that *he* was the bishop) and needed extensive surgery to his legs, ribs, and arms. The others were badly bruised and bleeding, and one of the deacons, known to be an athlete, fled into the cornfields to hide near the parish rectory, where he was later found unconscious.

Fortuitously, a local farmer in the fields heard the terrible noise, ran to the road, and raised the alarm among the people of Ivanovce. The mail truck from Mukachevo arrived, as did the local peasants, putting an end to the attempted massacre.[47] The young farmer flagged down the truck, and the victims were loaded in to be taken to Mukachevo city hospital, staffed by the Sisters of Saint Basil, but under government control.[48]

The coachman left behind a widow with five children, and Father Bachinsky was hospitalized with a fractured skull, a broken shoulder blade, broken ribs, and a spiral fracture of his right leg. The bishop had a severe head injury, with a twofold fracture of his jaw and only seven teeth left intact. His whole body was covered with black and blue bruises from the beating he suffered. The surgeons, Alexander Fedinec and Nicholas Witemberger, worked hard to save their patients, and the bishop's jaws had to be wired together and braced. He could neither eat nor, far worse, receive Holy Communion. Nevertheless, he could speak, and his prognosis for recovery was excellent. On October 31, the bishop got out of bed and embraced Father Bachinsky. Father Peter Washko of the Lavki parish came to hear the bishop's confession and, still unable to eat, the bishop worshiped the Holy Eucharist. Father Bachinsky was confessed and communicated, while the bishop watched, weeping that he could not receive His Lord and adoring the Sacrament for four hours.

By this point, Anatoli Sudoplatov reports, Khrushchev had panicked and again turned to Moscow, falsely claiming that the recovering bishop was due to receive couriers from "Germany and the Vatican." Stalin ordered Victor Abakumov of the Ministry of State Security to send a team to Uzhgorod. The head of Moscow's toxicology laboratory arrived in Uzhgorod with a vial of poison, and the plan was set in motion to kill the bishop in the hospital.

Murder of Bishop Romzha. Sister Theophila, OSBM, was the chief hospital nurse, and she and the chief surgical nurse were to care for the survivors under the direction of Dr. Alexander Fedinec. On October 29, 1947, a new nurse was introduced into the case, known only as "Odarka," through the intervention of a Doctor Bergman. Odarka was specifically brought into the case at the instance of Soviet officials who came to interrogate the bishop. Instead of nursing, she spent her time watching the visitors to the sickroom. On October 31, Doctor Bergman tried to send Sisters Irena and Innocent away from the bishop on night rounds. When they told him they were off duty and did not work the night shift, he chased them out into the women's ward. He had already approached Mother Ihnatia, the Superioress of the Basilian nuns, to have Sister Theophila removed from the night watch to "give her rest." Bishop

Monument at the site of the attack on Bishop Theodore Romzha, Ivanovce, Transcarpathian oblast. Erected in 1993. Courtesy of the author.

Romzha told Sister Theophila to leave, despite her strong misgivings. Doctor Fedinec had already been removed from the scene.

Father Bachinsky heard the bishop begin to moan as the doctor and "nurse" left the room. He rang the nursing bell, which summoned Sister Theophilia, who had hidden nearby. She tried to give the bishop water, but he choked. Downstairs, the telephone rang; it was a government official wanting to know whether the bishop was already dead. Suddenly, just after midnight on November 1, Doctor Bergman ordered the nuns keeping watch in the sick room to leave. When they hurried back less than ten minutes later, they heard the bishop moan, "Oh, Jesus!" and saw his body wrench in a fierce convulsion. Despite the efforts of the staff, his heart gave out, and he died at 12:30 A.M.

Father Bachinsky told them that the bishop had been murdered by a woman who had held something up to his face, apparently the poison.[49] Doctors Fedinec and Mishkolczy concurred in this, for Bishop Romzha's nose was turning blue, and this hue was then spreading through him. The two doctors at the time determined that Bishop Romzha had been poisoned with potassium cyanide. All accounts of the murder concur that the poison was administered by the strange nurse Odarka, with the obvious collaboration of Doctor Bergman in removing the nuns. When Doctor Mishkolczy picked up the telephone to report the death of Bishop Romzha, he heard Bergman's voice saying, "The assignment was accomplished." The staff was not officially notified of the bishop's death until after dawn; Bergman allowed the Sisters to remove the bishop's body to the hospital chapel to be laid out for a wake.

On Sunday, November 2, a special commission was hastily assembled, and an "official" report published, finding that Bishop Romzha died of a cerebral hemorrhage. Although a Soviet pathologist performed the autopsy and prepared the report, and none of the doctors was allowed to examine the body and see the alleged ruptured vein, they were all forced to sign the report.[50] The Sisters were allowed to dress the bishop's body in vestments and take it to the Greek Catholic church. Later that night, when the roads were deserted, his remains were transported to Uzgorod.

The nurse Odarka—who had done the deed—was bold enough to ask to be at the funeral, and then disappeared. The Soviet press, when announcing the death of Bishop Romzha, alleged that nationalist Bandera partisans had driven the truck that rammed the carriage. Meanwhile, Sudoplatov telephoned Moscow the night of the murder, and was congratulated on the success. He was ordered to remain at Uzhgorod and trace the bishop's contacts with foreign agents. To his surprise, there were none to report, and there was no conspiracy against Soviet power. Khrushchev, however, now decided to destroy the Vatican's "terrorist nest" at Uzgorod, which meant the destruction of the eparchy.

The Soviets would not give Bishop Romzha his due, even in death. He could not be laid in state in the city, but only in the Sisters' tiny chapel at the hospital. They tried to secretly remove the body at night to Uzhgorod, so as to avoid demonstrations. However, observers in the cathedral belfry were keeping watch, and when the truck drew near, they began to ring all of the bells. The entire population turned out in tears and filling the cathedral with their lamentations.

On November 4, the day of the funeral, the Soviets shut down the rail and bus lines, and blocked highways and sidewalks alike. Even so, a large crowd attended. The bishop was laid to rest in the cathedral crypt, not up at Calvary Cemetery, which was feared by the Soviets as giving him too public a grave. Still, many Communists regretted the murder, acknowledging that "now the Uniates have a full right to say that we have made a martyr for them!"[51]

Bishop Romzha's tomb was eventually cut off from public veneration by a locked gate. However, the police did go down once, and ordered the bricklayer to open the vault so that they could remove the body. But then they changed their mind, and ordered him to reseal the vault. Bishop Romzha was at least allowed to sleep beneath his cathedral altar. Stories abounded in the region of Bishop Romzha's intercession for the people, and his memory was kept alive. His sleep was interrupted, however, by the Russian Orthodox Church, which successfully removed his body in 1949 to avoid pilgrimages.

The murder of Bishop Romzha orphaned the Eparchy of Mukachevo and the Latin Catholic parishes of the oblast as well. Bishop Romzha was their ordaining bishop,[52] too; thus Greek and Latin Catholics alike faced the bitter prospect of no more new priests and the imminent destruction of their Churches.

Orthodox and Communist Reaction. Though Russian Orthodox churchmen had clearly cooperated in the destruction of Greek Catholicism, the murder of Bishop Romzha was too much even for them. The three new Orthodox bishops in western Ukraine, Nestor of Mukachevo—who led the reunion work—Antonii Pelvetsky of Stanislav, and Mykhail Melnyk of Drogobych, who had abandoned the Greek Catholic Church, sent protest to Khrushchev in January 1948, accusing the MGB of the deed.

Moreover, the local Soviet CRA (Council of Religious Affairs) official, Vil'khovyi, complained of "gross violations" of Soviet law committed by the oblast government in the reunion work. He forwarded a complaint from 20 peasants in Kolochava-Laz, on behalf of 580 Greek Catholic parishioners over their beatings and the forcible seizure of their church for Orthodox use, even though the village already had an Orthodox parish church. Vil'khovyi wrote to Khrushchev such actions were by no means exceptional, and stated that CARC's goal was to register more loyal religious organizations and to tolerate all faiths, not to give the Russian Orthodox Church a privileged position.

Aftermath of the Murder. In June 1948, Bishop Nestor of Mukachevo was removed by the Patriarchate, and the eparchy was placed under the jurisdiction of Archbishop Makarius of L'viv who would preside over its dissolution.[53]

Father Bachinsky, released from the hospital only in early 1948, was arrested on June 21, 1949, and sentenced to 10 years in the Gulag. Because of his injuries, he was sent to a camp for disabled prisoners near Kuybyshev (Samara), RSFSR. (On his return home in broken health in 1955, the Uzgorod authorities would set him to forced labor; he would die of a heart attack in Uzgorod city hospital in 1968.) Father Bachinsky's father, Daniel Senior, having been expelled from Dubrovka parish, was arrested in 1950. (He would die of torture in prison in 1951.)

Father Berezany, secretary to Bishop Romzha, refused to convert to Orthodoxy; he went from one secular job to the next while conducting priestly works. (When his wounds opened up and he died in 1969 on the operating table at the age of 45, most people believed he was murdered.) Father Washko, who brought the Sacraments to the bishop, was arrested in 1949 and sentenced to 15 years' hard labor. (Although he would be amnestied in 1957, his health was ruined; he would die in 1981.) Sister Theophila was also arrested, and exiled to Siberia for 10 years. (Like the other surviving Sisters, on her release, she would have to take up secular work and would be forbidden to live in community or wear her habit. She lived to see the fall of Communism and visit the United States and tell the story of the martyrdom of the bishop.)

Abolition of Union of Uzhgorod. At the end of 1947, the Basilian Order was banned in Transcarpathia because of its strong Catholic sympathies. The remaining seminarians were dispersed following the occupation of the Three Holy Hierarchs Seminary after Bishop Romzha's funeral. Most moved into the bishop's palace, and were instructed by Canon Chira. To evade the censors, they also carried messages throughout the eparchy to the parishes. In February 1949, the bishop's palace was itself confiscated and secularized. This left the seminarians without a place to live or study, and so they went into secular work.

Monks were concentrated in one location. The CARC arranged for the transfer of Orthodox priests into the oblast to work with Archbishop Makarius. Anti-Uniate articles appeared regularly. Vil'khovyi refused to register the Greek Catholic parishes as requested by Administrator Nicholas Muranyi. A massive campaign was launched against the clergy, with the knowledge of Archbishop Makarius. A former Communist turned priest, Irenaeus Kondratovych, apostasized, but agree to lead a "movement" only if Muranyi and Chira were removed from the scene. The notorious Makarius, who had organized the destruction of the Ukrainian Metropolinate, became the new Orthodox bishop of Uzgorod in early 1949.

Arrest of Bishop Chira. Bishop Romzha named Monsignor Alexander Chira, his close advisor since his ordination as bishop in 1944, to be his auxiliary. Chira was secretly ordained in a private ceremony in 1945; not even his closest relatives knew of his elevation in status.

With the martyrdom of Bishop Romzha, Bishop Chira should have succeeded to the see, but instead the three remaining Canons—Bishop Chira, Father Theodore Kohutich, and Father Victor Khoma—elected Chancellor Nicholas Muranyi to serve as administrator of the eparchy. This Muranyi managed to do until February 10, 1949, when all of the Canons and most of the influential priests were arrested.

In December 1948, Administrator Muranyi, Bishop Chira, and the recently ordained Father Ivan Semedi (who would become the first Greek Catholic bishop to be allowed to serve again in the Uzhgorod cathedral in 1991) went to Kiev to secure the return of Church buildings from the State. They were strongly advised to give up the struggle for the Greek Catholic Church and to become Orthodox. Threatened with removal to the Gulag if they did not, the priests remained firm, with Muranyi declaring, "We are Greek Catholics and we will remain Greek Catholics to our last breath!"

Throughout 1948 and into 1949, a stream of Orthodox collaborators came to Bishop Chira to persuade him to join the Patriarchate. The priests Irenaeus Kondratovych, Stephen Danielovich, and Porhilyak apostasized and tried to persuade Chira to do the same. Even some faithful Catholics began to suggest this, as a way of saving his life and protecting the orphaned Church. (One friend was the wife of the public prosecutor, bringing to mind the case of Pilate's wife interceding for Jesus.) Yet Chira continued to preach at the cathedral, refusing to give up the Church and Faith.

The Purge. On February 10, 1949, leading Greek Catholic priests were arrested. The police took Chira himself at 3 A.M., after ransacking his house for six hours. On February 16, the militia stormed Holy Cross Cathedral, and Archbishop Makarius installed Kondratovych as rector. Administrator Muranyi was subjected to 54 hours of torture and forced to sign a statement of his "resignation at the request of the people." On February 20, the government announced that the cathedral was now Russian Orthodox, and the palace was secularized as part of Uzhgorod University.[54] In the week of February 23, all of the churches in the eparchy were closed, except for the chapel at Imstichevo (see below) and all of the priests imprisoned and subjected to relentless interrogation. Archbishop Makarius called this reign of terror "missionary work" conducted with "evangelical charity" (in collusion with the NKVD). For six long months, the priests were alternately threatened, cajoled, and tortured. The tribulations of Bishop Chira will stand as a typical example.

Interrogated relentlessly, Bishop Chira refused to abandon the Greek Catholic Church. (He would write in 1982 that it was only "God's grace and loyalty to the Apostolic See" that enabled him to withstand the threats and promises, so severe was the interrogation.) He was put in solitary confinement in a windowless pit, with no room to lie down or even sit, and forbidden to write to anyone concerning his confinement. One interrogator, Major Kharitonov, urged him to "settle [his] religious differences" with the metropolitan of Kiev so he could be sent home safe and sound. (Similar promises would be made to him when he was in the labor camps at Kemerovo and

Omsk.)[55] Removed to L'viv and condemned as a leader of the Catholic resistance to Communism, he was sentenced to 25 years in prison, 5 years' loss of civil rights, and lifelong exile.

On the eve of his removal to Siberia, the police discovered that he was, after all, a bishop. For this, he was charged with being a traitor to the Soviet state through his alleged chairmanship of the Christian National Party, being in collusion with a foreign power (the Vatican) and receiving secret messengers from the pope. His original sentence was confirmed in all particulars and was sent to work in the coal mines of Kazakhstan.[56]

With the exile of Chira, the entire public Greek Catholic hierarchy in western Ukraine had been removed, and everyone knew that the days of the Church were truly numbered. At the Dormition Pilgrimage, the apostates who had become bishops in their new Church joined Archbishop Makarius.

Ministry and martyrdom of an Underground Ruthenian Bishop. On December 19, 1944, Bishop Romzha had secretly ordained Father Petro Oros as a bishop, who was assigned as a parish priest to Bilky, Irshava county, after the police arrested the local pastor, Father Ivan Popovich, in 1946. Due to his popularity, the police persecuted the secret bishop, wanting him to join Orthodoxy, which he refused to do. He was prohibited in 1948 from performing religious services, and so he went underground with Fathers Ivan Horonetsky, Ivan Margitich (later a secret assistant bishop of Mukachevo), Ivan Roman, and Ivan Chenheri. They were in charge of Irshava and Vinohradiv regions. For a long time, the militia and KGB could not catch them. Vasil Rishka betrayed Fathers Margitich and Roman in 1951. As a result, Bishop Oros and Father Chenheri went to the Chenheri family home in Velikij Bichkiv, where they continued the underground work. Father Ivan Horonetsky was hiding at relatives' homes in Sasovo and Chornotisovo, Vinohradivsky region, and traveled through the forests to celebrate the sacraments. Bishop Oros then moved alone to the Irshavsky region in the villages of Borshavska valley and Vinogradiv region. Police kept interrogations going among villages of Borshavska valley and Vinogradiv region. Police kep interrogations going among villagers to betray Bishop Oros, but he did not stop his preaching or conducting marriages and baptisms.

In January 1953, the NKVD captured Bishop Oros after surrounding the Stanko family house in Bilky. He was arrested and sent to Uzhgorod for two weeks, where he was mocked by the police as they would sarcastically ask him to teach them how to pray and how to answer various theological questions. He did teach them about Christ, and was actually released. After Stalin's death, people were looking even more for Bishop Oros to lead them. In the Irshavsky regional office of the MGB, the head of the office, Hachenko, told everyone about Bishop Oros, and distributed pictures of the priest. In the summer of 1953, near the Imstichevo bridge, a militia man tried to arrest Bishop Oros who was walking with recently released Father Vasil' Yackanich. Bishop Oros was lucky to be able to disappear into the forest. The militiaman fired at him and missed, but Father Vasil was arrested and briefly jailed in Irshava.

On August 27, 1953, in the evening before Assumption (old calendar), in the village of Velikiy Komyaty, a large crowd of believers gathered at the cemetery with Bishop Oros for the Liturgy and sermons. In the afternoon of August 28, with Katherine Stanko, he walked to the train station in Ciltse, where he was going to take the train to Bilky. Someone recognized him and betrayed him, and the militiaman Povshik came right away. He questioned people, and he arrested Bishop Oros and Katherine in the evening. On the way to the village of Zariche, Bishop Oros asked the militiaman to let him go. He knelt down to pray, and Povshik shot him in the legs and head. Bishop Oros fell and whispered to Katherine that he had sixty intentions for the Divine Liturgy that needed to be given to another priest, and then he died.

Bishop Oros' body was taken to the morgue in Irshavskhy hospital, where it lay naked and exposed. After two days, the believers from Bilky and Velikiy Komyaty came to ask for the body to bury it, as should be done for a person of his position. The authorities refused and buried him in secret, in a deserted place outside the village of Kam'yanske. Some children herding cows saw the burial and went to tell the people, who headed out to rebury the body. The militia found out first, and they dug him up and moved the body under the floor of the torture chamber of the Irshava NKVD offices, where it would be hidden unil revealed by a repentant militiaman in 1992.

Resistance by the Clergy. According to a 1991 study by Bishop Semedi, of the 315 parish priests still in the Mukachevo eparchy in 1949, 140 "signed" as "converts" to Orthodoxy (although more than 70 of these rejected their signing and returned to the secret Church). The remaining 175 priests were sentenced to prison terms—or took to the woods. Of the 170 imprisoned, 93 died in the Gulag. None of the Basilian monks signed; 8 were sentenced to prison.[57]

Both canons arrested with Bishop Chira in February 1949, were sent to the Gulag. Offered an Orthodox bishop's crown by the NKVD, Canon Khoma refused, saying that even if he were offered the Patriarchate he would not join the Orthodox Church.[58] He died at Minsk in 1953, and Canon Kohutich at Koma in 1955.

Table 9

Destiny of Priests in the Mukachevo Eparchy, 1944–1950

Underground after 1949	5[a]
Died in interrogations	18
Killed in "accidents"	3[b]
Converts to Orthodoxy	32
Fled abroad	36[c]
Killed in prisons/camps	40
Exiled to Siberia, Central Asia, or Arctic	150

[a] These priests were never arrested but went into hiding in or before 1949 and ministered secretly to parishioners until their deaths. Because of the rugged terrain of the Mukachevo Eparchy and the close-knit nature of its villages, many priests who survived the Gulag would do likewise.

[b] These priests died under mysterious circumstances in Ruthenia proper, being killed in factories or in road incidents that had no witnesses.

[c] Of these priests, a very few happened to be studying abroad; others managed to cross the mountains into Czechoslovakia or Hungary in 1946–1949, and remained there or went to the West.

(For one reckoning of what became of the priests of the Mukachevo eparchy, see table 9.)

End of the Eparchy. In August 1949, the government forbade the Dormition Pilgrimage. Pilgrims who came anyway were sent to the Saint Nicholas's Monastery, to be greeted by Archbishop Makarius, who had so energetically destroyed his fellow Christians, by the apostate bishops from Galicia, Melnyk and Pelvetsky, and, through them, by the Patriarch of Moscow. The apostate Kondratovych read out a simple declaration that the Greek Catholic Church no longer existed, and that the Union of 1646 had been annulled.[59] There was no "synod," no staged assembly, simply a piece of paper that declared 303 years of unity no longer existed.

Casualties were high among Greek Catholic lay believers as well. The Rusyn population lost some 20,000, which included most of its educated members, to the "far corners" of the Gulag. This serious loss was worsened by the immigration of ethnic Russians and Eastern Ukrainians into the oblast. Large numbers of Transcarpathians, including many Greek Catholic believers and Church activists, emigrated to Czechoslovakia and Hungary (which were still non-Communist) in 1948.[60]

A final casualty was the focal point of the Dormition Pilgrimage, the icon of the Mukachevo Mother of God, which had been given by Pope Pius XI to the Monastery. It was removed by the new Orthodox, and sent to Moscow. In its place, the Patriarch sent an icon of Our Lady of Vladimir.[61] This icon—once venerated in Ukraine—is at the heart of popular Russian devotion, hence highly symbolic of the forced Russification of the local Church.

From August 1949 on, only one Greek Catholic church was allowed to perform its original function, and that was the chapel at the Imstichevo Monastery, where the Basilian monks had been interned.[62] Father John Satmarij, OSBM, was appointed hegumen of the monastery by the State, with responsibility that no monk should escape. Through his influence, 23 Brothers and students had been released from the monastery-concentration camp in 1947, and were sent back to their families, rather than to Siberia. Of the 13 monks still interned at Imstichevo, 2 broke down under the pressures of interrogation and signed the declaration to join Orthodoxy, although they resolutely refused to work as Orthodox priests; 3 were let go because of poor health; and 8 were "tried" and exiled to Siberia for their alleged crimes.

Father Satmarij was thus left all alone. He had emphasized to the police that the Basilians were concerned only with religion, and not politics. He continued to celebrate the liturgical services throughout the three years of police persecution, and celebrated Resurrection services in 1950. (The Divine Liturgy of that Easter Sunday would be the last public and legal Greek Catholic service until 1990.)

After Easter, the NKVD liquidated the monastery and expelled Father Satmarij. (He would live out his days in a tiny house, with his alcoholic sister, ministering to believers and atheists seeking solace, always defending the truth and subjected to various interrogations. Blinded by a cerebral hemorrhage on Holy Saturday, 1980, he would die and be buried at Imstichevo in October 1982.)

In the supposedly Russian Orthodox churches of western Ukraine, "Catholic" practices continued to be followed until 1950: the Rosary, Sacred Heart devotion, Saint Josaphat icons, singing of the Filioque in the Creed, Corpus Christi processions. The "Orthodoxation" campaign of Archbishop Makarius to convert the non-Orthodox never did take root, though it provided the government with the opportunity to arrest more priests and close churches. From the suppression of 1945 until 1950, the Russian Church tolerated the Ukrainians' "Latinizations" as being necessary to keep the loyalty of the people. But Archbishop Makarius launched a drive to eliminate these practices. Priests and parishioners resisted, many priests resigned because they could not keep elements of their Catholic identity, or were dismissed, and a host of churches were deregistered by the State.[63]

Although a number of the believers did ultimately choose Orthodoxy, a much larger number remained Catholic.[64] Some attended Latin Catholic parishes; some who could not trust the local Orthodox priest fully attended the services of the underground Greek Catholic Church; many fought to keep the supposedly Orthodox parishes open for the day of Greek Catholic restoration. Even so, books published in the West lamented the "fact" that within a generation, there would be no Greek Catholic Church left in Ukraine, cut off as it was from Rome and all contact with the free world.

Ironically, the former Greek Catholic churches of the western Ukrainian SSR produced the bulk of the Moscow Patriarchate's vocations and income. The supposedly Russian Orthodox Church was in many ways a Ukrainian-Carpathian-Belorussian-Baltic Church (the Russian heartland and Siberia would suffer a severe and crippling shortage of priests and churches for decades to come). The people who frequented the Orthodox churches were heavily crypto-Catholics, who fought to keep the parishes going during the persecutions. A substantial number of Catholics refused to attend any Orthodox services at all, and made use of the services of the priests in hiding, or held prayer services in supposedly sealed churches.

Ukrainian Greek Catholics in Poland,
Czechoslovakia, and Romania

The destruction of the Greek Catholic Church in Soviet Ukraine and Belorussia was thus only a prelude to its destruction in a substantial part of the Soviet Bloc nations.[65]

Poland. Communist terrorism against the Ukrainian Catholics here was directed at Greek Catholic priests and parishioners alike, who were subject to massacre and whose churches were burned in the Lemko region.[66] The fratricidal war between the Ukrainska Povstanska Armiia (UPA) and the Armia Krajowej (AK), now confused with Communist actions simply worsened an already bad situation. Ultimately, the Ukrainian Greek Catholic enclave around Przemyśl and in the Lemko territory was almost completely cleared of its native inhabitants, with forcible removals to the north and west or deportations to the USSR, and the establishment of Orthodox parishes among the few remaining Greek Catholics. All of the Greek Catholic churches were either given over to Latin Catholic or Orthodox use, secularized, or destroyed.

The "Vistula Action" in Poland against the Ukrainian minority in Galicia severely weakened the Greek Catholic Church. The Poles forced 483,000 Ukrainians into the USSR by 1948, and removed another 150,000 to the former German territories in the north and west.[67] In Poland, the Greek Catholic Church lost all existence as an organized community: only one "Neo-Uniate" parish survived[68] (see below), and two other Greek Catholic parishes in Khsanow and Komancha.

Czechoslovakia and Romania. The Greek Catholic Church would survive in Czechoslovakia only until 1950, and in Romania only until 1948.

The Belorussian Greek Catholic Church

The antireligious campaign against Greek Catholics in the BSSR was fierce and thorough. The entire Belorussian Greek Catholic Church was eliminated: the parishes in the BSSR were closed in 1945 (as were most of those in the Białystok enclave in 1947).[69] When the Marian Fathers returned home from their exile in Harbin, China, in 1948, they were all arrested; their archimandrite, Andrej Cikota, MIC, died in a concentration camp.[70]

The various monastic houses were all confiscated, and the Jesuit complex in Albertyn converted into an orphanage for victims of the war. The churches were secularized; a theater was installed in one, with guards placed to keep the children from going to religious services held in the adjacent cemetery on holy days by the Catholics and Orthodox who still remained in the area.[71]

The parish churches were promptly absorbed into Russian Orthodoxy as the Patriarchate was reestablished in the expanded BSSR. There were no "Acts of Union" or "synods." The few working churches were simply staffed by Patriarchal priests.

Intense propaganda against the Greek Catholic Church was initiated by both the Communists and the Russian Orthodox in the BSSR.[72] Indeed, the *Journal of the Moscow Patriarchate* carried venomous articles from 1946 to 1951, some engaging in personal attacks on Belorussian Greek Catholic priests. One such article falsely accused the brother of a priest of being an active anti-Soviet guerrilla. The bitterness of these attacks goes back to the old Orthodox view of Union, but now with a Stalinist twist:

> under [Church Union] Ukrainians and Belorussians would soon forget their glorious and rich culture, would no longer consider the great Russian people

as their kinsmen and older brother, defender and ally, or rely upon the latter in their struggle for liberation, and would cease to strive for state union with them.[73]

Nevertheless, as in the past, the Union remained alive in the hearts of the people, and would emerge again forty-five years later.

In 1991, the Holy Cross Cathedral in Uzhgorod was finally returned to Greek Catholic use. In the crypt, the clergy found evidence of both the barbarism of the Soviets and their fear of the power of Bishop Romzha and the martyrs. All the graves of the other bishops had been desecrated, the bodies stripped of all valuables, and then the bones dumped into a huge pile. Bishop Romzha's grave, it turned out, had indeed been emptied sometime in the 1950s, as rumor had it. His body was gone; only dust remained. Surely that was the hope of the Communists, that only dust would remain of the Greek Catholic Church. They were sorely mistaken.

Catholics and Jews in the Nazi-Occupied Soviet Territories

A human life in these days is not even worth a cigarette.
—the rescuer Oskar Schindler, 1941

Although the trauma of the extermination of the Jews in Eastern Europe would not seem to come under the title of this work, the Catholics of the territory that became the USSR again or anew after 1945 were affected and involved in that trauma, and there are still serious misconceptions concerning Catholics in the Nazi-occupied territories of the USSR and the fate of the Jews. From 1944 almost until the collapse of the Soviet Empire in 1991, the Communist press repeatedly condemned Catholics of both the Latin and the Byzantine Rites for "collaborating with the Nazis," for killing Jews, and for failing to defend Jewish lives. Countless newspaper and magazine articles and books were published condemning the Church, especially Archbishop Andrew Sheptytsky, the Ukrainians, and the Poles.

Although we must recognize that there were not enough "righteous Gentiles" involved in saving Jews in 1941–1945, for posterity and the sake of the historical record, we must also recognize the activities of those who were busy saving lives. There are more memorials at Yad Vashem to Polish rescuers than to the rescuers of any other nationality.

In 1998, the Holy See published "We Remember: A Reflection on the *Shoah*." Though criticized by some, it is the papacy's first serious reflection on the *Shoah* (Holocaust), and follows a series of dramatic Catholic apologies from Germany in 1975 to France at the Drancy concentration camp in 1997, in which the French Catholic bishops mourned that there were not enough Catholics involved in rescue work, and that "indifference won the day over indignation in the face of the persecution" (French bishops' statement). Although the "Reflection" is defensive regarding Catholic anti-Judaism and anti-Semitism, in it the Holy See and Pope John Paul II accept the need for repentance.[1] This appendix does not seek to elude that need, but rather to point out that the propaganda used against Catholicism by the USSR totally failed to record the actions of those, Catholic and non-Catholic alike, who *were* righteous.

It should also be noted that giving aid to Jews in the Nazi-occupied territories was exceptionally dangerous and difficult. Poverty quickly became the norm for everyone,

447

and food was not easily available. Many Jews had no experience of Christian culture or spoke only Yiddish and thus could not easily "pass" outside the ghettos. There was always the danger that anti-Semites or people would turn in both Jews and rescuers for the sake of German rewards. In Nazi-occupied Poland, the death penalty was extended to helpers and those connected with helpers, including relatives and coworkers and even tenants of the same apartment building. If a Jewish child was discovered in an orphanage (where many children were saved), then all of the children were to be shipped to a death camp. The finding of a single Jew in a village meant the destruction of the entire village.

As the Polish Bishops' Pastoral Letter of 1990 declared: "Many Poles rescued Jews during the last war. Hundreds if not thousands paid for that help with their own lives and the lives of those closest to them. For every Jew that was rescued there was a chain of hearts of people with good will and helping hands."[2] Thus, to rescue a Jew necessarily involved bringing other people into the rescue and placing one's family and neighbors at risk of death.

Conditions for Poles and other Slavs and the Balts were very bad, far worse than in Western Europe. There was no attempt to have "normal" life go on, as in Denmark or Occupied France. Indeed, plans were in place for the expansion of the death camps, once the Jews and Gypsies were exterminated, to exterminate all non-Jewish Slavs as well. The first death camp at Auschwitz was built to kill Poles, and hundreds of Polish Catholic priests were put to death in Dachau in Germany.

Because many rescuers died with those they were saving, it is difficut to determine who the rescuers were and what role the Catholic population played in the rescue of Jews. Moreover, rescuers as a whole were reluctant to relate their deeds, whether out of humility or for fear of postwar anti-Semitism and persecutions. Finally, as the years go by, both those saved and those who saved them are dying off, and with them their untold stories.

It is worth noting that Catholic convents and monasteries provided sanctuary to unknown numbers of Jewish children, particularly children who had a "Semitic" appearance, which put them at risk with the Nazis, or children who spoke little Polish or Lithuanian. In addition, adults were disguised as members of religious orders. Because the actual members of those orders saw hiding Jews as their duty to the Faith, they were—and are—reluctant to discuss their role as rescuers. Indeed, they are more reticent than other rescuers.[3] Although some Catholic rescuers did instruct Jews in the Faith and a few even demanded conversion, the vast majority did not. Nevertheless, many Jewish children were conditionally baptized, taught Catholic prayers, and admitted to Holy Communion to make them feel they were a true part of the community; knowledge of and participation in Catholicism provided a "cover" for them and prevented suspicions from arising.[4]

Estonia

The Jewish population of Estonia that remained after the Soviet withdrawal was devastated in the early days of the occupation. Ghettos and death camps established in Estonia were populated by Jews relocated from the Reich or from Lithuania: no Estonian Jews survived the Nazi occupation.

Latvia

Latvian Jewry numbered about 93,000 in 1939, including some refugees from Nazi-occupied countries. Although the Bolsheviks persecuted these refugees, and although some Jews were among the Latvians removed by the Soviets in 1940–1941, many were still present when the *Wehrmacht* army arrived. *Einsatzgruppe* A and Latvian collaborators were responsible for the slaughter of about 35,000 Jews in and around Riga from July 1 to December 9, 1941. Relatively few Latvians took part in these killings: although some 400 Jews died in an initial pogrom in Riga, the local people quickly came to their senses, and the Germans noted that additional pogroms "would be unthinkable." [5]

The Riga ghetto was established in the "Moscow Suburb," the poor neighborhood that was home to the Catholic parish of Saint Francis. Most Latvian Jews here were massacred: only 2,500 Jewish men were alive by the time, the first contingents of 20,000 Reich Jews arrived in Riga in December. When the Riga ghetto was dissolved in late 1943, only 800 people were left alive. [6] I have not been able to discover any information about Latvian Catholic rescuers.

Lithuania

The Jewish population of Lithuania, which numbered some 100,000 in 1938, was concentrated in the capital, Kaunas, and in predominantly Jewish towns and villages. It grew to 250,000 with the annexation of Vilnius (Vilna) and its district in 1939. Although relations between Jews and Lithuanians had generally been good, there was anti-Semitism present in the republic. [7]

Soviet appointment of Jews to government posts after the 1940 annexation had heightened local anti-Semitism, which was made still worse by the role played by highly placed Jews among the police in the mass removals of Lithuanians. The fact that 5,000 Jews were among the 40,000 Lithuanians removed made no difference.

When Nazis invaded Lithuania, fewer than 7 percent of Lithuanian Jews were able to escape by trains or trucks. In the aftermath of the Soviet retreat, Lithuanian collaborators, angry officers, displaced officials, relatives of those removed by the Soviets, and "avaricious riffraff" killed 4,000 Jews in local pogroms; many of these same people would participate in the Nazi massacres. It is sad to note that some Lithuanian Catholic priests and lay believers participated in both these massacres and the large-scale "actions" taken against Jews. A few rabidly anti-Semitic priests are said to have accompanied the Nazis to concentration camps like Treblinka and participated in still more crimes. *Einsatzkommandogruppe* 3 reported 133,346 Jews and Communists killed between July and November 1941 alone.

Jews who were still in Lithuania at the time of the Nazi occupation were trapped there. There was no local underground movement to aid the Jews in 1941: the Germans were seen by the Lithuanians as being their liberators from the Red Terror and an organized underground did not exist until much later in the war.

At the same time, there were Lithuanians who refused to condone the killings. Individuals who were shocked by the massacres included employees, coworkers, and friends of the Jews, as well as ordinary folk moved by their consciences. The archives of Yad Vashem list over 100 people from Lithuania as being among the "Righteous Gentiles," most of whom were "presumably . . . of the Catholic faith"[8] and as noted, the lists of the righteous are necessarily incomplete.

Among the employees, there are numerous accounts of Polish and Lithuanian servants who accompanied their Jewish employers into the ghettos and on the transports to the concentration camps to give them assistance.[9]

Some Lithuanian townspeople built bunkers in their urban homes to shelter Jews, mostly women, who provided nursing care, child care, or sewing for the family while they were in hiding. Antanas and Maria Macineviciene saved several people from the Kaunas ghetto; Doctor Elena Kutorgiene and her son Doctor Viktoras Kutorga obtained weapons for the same ghetto. Some Jewish children were saved by being placed in Lithuanian orphanages, through the connivance of doctors or nurses.

Under the leadership of a farmer named Striaupis four farm families in Sarneliai saved 22 Jews; two babies were born to this group of Jews during the war. There were farmers who took in Jewish children (see below), and farmers who helped provide food for Jewish families living in bunkers in the forests; there were other rural Lithuanians who guided Jews into the forests. Some peasants built bunkers for Jews in their houses or farm buildings, or helped Jews do so.

In addition, members of the non-Lithuanian minorities helped Jews, especially in 1941, when massacres were the order of the day. Ethnic Russians, Poles, and even Germans gave aid. In Vilnius, Polish Benedictine nuns hid 17 Jews in their monastery, with a Polish Girl Scout, Jadwiga Dudziec, serving as intermediary between the Jews and the nuns.[10] Mother Anna Borkowska, Superior of the Dominican Sisters of Kolonia Wilenska near Vilnius, became "a living legend in Jewish communities." She even obtained hand grenades for the Jewish Fighters' Organization in the Vilnius ghetto, instructed Aba Kowner in their proper use, and obtained other weapons for the Jews. Two of the Dominican Sisters were arrested in September 1943, and the convent was dispersed.[11] Maria Lescinskiene, an ethnic Pole, was called "the mother of the Jewish partisans from the Kovno [Kaunas] Ghetto." Two elderly Greek Catholic monks from the Vilnius monastery assisted Jews: they were arrested, the monastery closed, and the monks were never seen again.[12] Also in Vilnius, Father Andreas

Gdowski, of the Ostrabama Church, hid several Jews, even setting up a camouflaged room to be used as a synagogue.[13] The Lithuanian Sister Ona Brokaite helped transfer Jewish children to hiding places. She was caught and tortured.

Many writers state that there was no leadership from the Lithuanian Latin Catholic hierarchy: indeed, Bishop Vincentas Brizgys was said to have told Kaunas Jews who asked for help "I can only cry and pray myself; the Church cannot help you." Bishop Měislovas Reinys is cited as having turned down requests for help, on the one hand, and as having instructed monasteries to assist Jews and having refused to bless a Ukrainian battalion that had killed Jews, on the other.[14] Archbishop Romuald JaĹbrzykowski is said to have called upon the clergy and religious orders of the Vilnius archdiocese to assist Jews.[15]

Among the Lithuanian Catholic clergy who helped Jews were Father Juozas Stakauskas, who with his friend Vlad Zemaitis built a secret hiding place for 13 Jews in Vilnius; Fathers Lapys and Borevicius, who with Doctor and Missus Jasaitiene led a small group in Siaulai that saved the family of Doctor Yerushalmi. Father Borisevicius formed a group composed of a woman doctor in Siaulai, the agronomist Ibenskis, and three nurses in order to save Jews. This became especially important after Lithuanian children's homes refused to take in 221 Jewish children from the Siaulai ghetto. Another priest involved was Father Puzonas, who ran a farm for older children that provided refuge for Jewish children from Kaunas ghetto. Father Paukshtys, who lived in Vilnius near the Jesuit church, rescued about 100 Jewish children. Although he baptized between 60 and 70 of these children to be raised as Catholics, he was involved in the rescue of all Jews, including adults and children who did not want to convert. In the last weeks of the war, he hid a Jewish girl, a partisan from the ghetto, in the seminary itself, and placed other Jews with farmers. A Father Lipnianus is recorded as having preached sermons in Vilnius requesting assistance for Jews, and being killed as a result.[16]

Many Jewish children were saved from the Nazis by Lithuanian Catholics who took great risks in hiding them or raising them as their own. When surviving adult relatives returned to Lithuania after the war, there were "heartbreaking decisions for all involved": the families who had raised them deeply loved these children, and the children had no memory of the relatives who were seeking to reclaim them.[17]

In the latter part of 1943, there were greater opportunities to save the surviving Jews. Partisan networks had been formed in the forests by then, and partisans also were placing their own Jewish children in Lithuanian homes. As the war turned against Germany, more Lithuanians were emboldened to take anti-Nazi action. Other priests took an active part in helping the Jews: more priests denounced the killings publicly and others provided fake baptismal certificates for Jews seeking to hide in Lithuanian homes, although some demanded that Jews, children and adults alike, convert to Catholicism to be rescued, as at Z'emaiciu Kalvaria Monastery.

A notable Catholic rescuer was Bronius Gotatutas, an illiterate peasant who had once served at a monastery, who, with the help of an elderly lady known to us only as

"Serafiniene," developed a network among priests and homeowners in Kaunas, Siaulai, and the surrounding villages that saved as many as 50 Jews. He was eventually sent to a death camp. When asked if he was afraid of dying, he answered he was prepared to anything so that "the world would know that there were some decent people among the Lithuanians." The problem is that there were not enough people who could brave the risks of rescuing Jews or giving other assistance under the Nazi occupation.

A closing note on Lithuania and the Vilnius district: the largest number of Jews rescued were those sheltered by the peasants. Among the educated classes, chiefly in the cities, most rescuers were doctors and priests; in the towns, most were ordinary workers and domestics, with practically none from the middle classes.

Eastern Poland

Under the leadership of the Council to Aid Jews *(Żegota)*, thousands of Poles extended relief to Jews, many without thought of recompense. The martyred scholar Emmanuel Ringelblum praised the dedication of the Poles who risked their lives to save Jews under these difficult conditions.[18]

Although the council was not able to do large-scale relief work because of its chronic lack of funds, its members risked their lives, acting "with great dedication, under all conditions, until liberation" in their efforts to rescue Jews. Founded in Warsaw, the council functioned throughout Nazi-occupied Poland. I deal only with formerly Polish Belorussia and Galicia, territories reincorporated into the USSR in 1944–1945.

Western Belorussia

In Białystok, the former anti-Semite, Doctor Filipowski, gave medical assistance to Jewish fighters after the August 1943 ghetto uprising.[19] In Grodno, both the Roman Catholic dean and the local Franciscan Prior were sent to Łomża in the autumn of 1943 and shot for aiding Jews.[20] German reports from Belorussia consistently note that the population was appalled by the actions of the *Einsatzgruppen,* and that it was difficult to foment "spontaneous" actions against the Jews. Western Belorussia also offered a number of primeval forests and swamps in which many Jews took refuge; as the war tore through the provinces, Christians fled to these same swamps. Conditions there, however, were abominable: many refugees died of starvation, disease, and attacks by Axis troops.

Western Ukraine

Here, in the eastern part of Galicia annexed to the UkSSR in 1939, anger against the Jews had been stirred up by the cooperation of some Jews with the Soviets, and by the reports that Jews had occupied important positions under Soviet rule and had both denounced anti-Soviet Ukrainians to the NKVD and participated in the horrendous massacres in the prisons that accompanied the Soviet withdrawal. Both the German forces and Ukrainian collaborators promulgated these reports. Many Jews were slaughtered in pogroms in the cities and villages as a result. Greed for Jewish possessions or positions also played a role.

The violence reached a climax in 1941–1942, with the atrocities taking a terrible toll. Lvov (Lwów) fell to the Germans on June 28, 1941, and in less than three weeks some 7,000 Jews had been slain. A massacre action there in August 10–22, 1942, took another 50,000 Jewish lives. The ghetto established in September for the survivors would last only a year.

The tragedy of the situation in Galicia becomes apparent in the incident of Rabbi Ezekiel Lewin's appeal to Metropolitan Sheptytsky to use his influence to stop Ukrainian cooperation in the killings, on July 2, 1941. The metropolitan asked the rabbi to remain in the safety of the episcopal palace. The rabbi, however, chose to return to his congregation, and was seized while crossing Saint George's Square. As one writer notes, "whereas the leading Ukrainian ecclesiastical personality offered his assistance to Rabbi Lewin, other Ukrainians took part in killing him."[21] Such a dichotomy marked the entire occupation period.

In Przemyśl, a German decree of July 27, 1942 threatened the Ukrainians and Poles with death for giving any assistance to Jews during the "action" to be conducted in the county. In September 1942, the death penalty was extended to all helpers and rescuers of Jews in Galicia.

Although the threat to Jewish lives was constant, there were several specific times of mortal danger to Ukrainian Jews in Galicia. The massacres of June–July 1941 were followed by a number of "actions" carried out by the Germans and Ukrainian militia in the summer of 1942 (after the Wannsee Conference that determined the Final Solution for the Jews). Finally, in May 1943, the *"Judenrein* action" engulfed the remainder of Galician Jews.

Many Jews who escaped these massacres later fell victim to the various partisan groups operating in western Ukraine. The Ukrainian nationalist UPA, the Polish AK, "Independent" and pro-Soviet partisans all had anti-Semitic members who killed Jews.

At the same time, the AK units around Lwów did assist some of the city's Jews. Although, in the horrible clearing of the ghetto in June 1943, the AK was unable to launch a coordinated resistance (as noted by the Israeli Prosecutor in the Eichmann Trial, "organization of an armed resistance in the city was out of the question"), many escapees from the ghetto were hidden by the city's Ukrainians and Poles.[22]

At Jagielnica, in the far eastern region of Nazi-occupied Galicia, the Catholic doctor Wojciech Lachowicz saved a Jewish dentist and the entire Hungarian Jewish family of Ignacy Jospiwocz, keeping them in his house from 1941 until 1942, when they were able to leave for Hungary (which was then relatively safe for Jews). He also extended aid to local Jews.[23]

In the city of Stanislawiw (Stanislav), which was half Jewish before the war, the Zuławski family "always concealed eight to ten Jews" in their home, and displayed "unusual bravery, courage, fortitude" in hiding Polish and Czech Jews, confronting the police, finding other hiding spaces (such as a convent for one young girl), and providing an oasis for the hunted.[24] Of the 66 Jews who emerged from hiding in the city when the Soviets returned in 1944, 32 had been hidden by Staszek Jackowski, a young Polish Catholic carriage maker, who had constructed three bunkers for them in his cellar, two blocks from the local Gestapo headquarters. He was aided by his cousin and some other helpers, and was nearly caught several times.[25]

The Roman Catholic Ursuline Sisters also interceded on behalf of Jews. The convent in Kolomyja, under the direction of Mother Teresa Dettlaff, was known as a refuge for Jews during "actions" and executions. A noted coworker of Mother Teresa was Sister Hiacenta, who escorted several Jews out of the area to safer places. Mother Elzbieta Łubienska, Mother Władysława Lewicka, Sisters Celestyna, Maria Stella Trzecieska, and Ewlina, among other Lwów Ursulines, assisted Mother Teresa. Blackmailers who threatened the nuns with exposure had to be paid off with 10,000 zlotys.[26]

In Ternopil County, a Polish couple obtained a false baptismal certificate from the priest in Dunajów to save a Jewish girl, and hid her in Lwów and then in Czudziec throughout the war.[27] In Buczac, in Podolia, Father Kazimierz Słupski hid Jews in the rectory and with trusted parishioners. One Jewish woman, Rozalia Bauer, spent three years at the parish disguised as a Sister of the Family of Mary. Słupski's network saved a number of Jews by hiding them in the villages or giving aid to those in the woods.

The risk of death run by Christian rescuers came from all quarters. One group of Jews and their Polish protector were killed when betrayed by Ukrainian nationalists.[28] The fratricidal warfare that engulfed the Galician countryside swept up many such victims: the Polish colonist farmer Hajnusz and his son saved 65 Jews in the forest near Brzezany, south of Lwów, only to see 51 massacred by Ukrainian nationalists and their own farm and the local Polish colonists' village burned to the ground.[29] Alexander Sosnowski, a Polish school principal, was killed along with three Jewish women he had hidden since the beginning of the German occupation in February 1944, by another band of Ukrainian nationalists in Kałusz County.[30]

When the Axis forces came into Galicia, they were welcomed with bread and salt in recognition of freeing the people from Communism. The "liberation" was quickly marked by horrendous pogroms.[31] On the day after the liberation of L'viv, Ukrainians attacked Jews. Rabbi Lewin immediately went to see Metropolitan Sheyptytsky, who was horrified to learn that Ukrainians were involved with the Nazis in the slaughter. It took two days for the priests and monks he sent out to restrain and calm the crowds.

Passions were further inflamed with the discovery that not only had the Soviets executed hundreds of ethnic Poles, Ukrainians, and Jews in the main prison, but that, as they retreated, they had put the prison to the torch, burning as many as 2,000 prisoners alive. The Germans charged "Jewish Communists" with this crime. Some of the local Jews rounded up to remove the corpses were shot immediately. After the disbanding of the Ukrainian independent government of Bandera, the Germans resorted to a new method, creating a "Ukrainian militia," which butchered still more Jews in the "Petlura Days," ostensibly to avenge the murder of a Ukrainian nationalist years before by a Jewish boy orphaned in Petlurist pogroms of 1918.

In the winter of 1941, the Nazis opened a new death camp at Belzec, where Soviet, French, Dutch, and Belgian prisoners were starved by the hundreds; they made the camp ready for Jews, and a great roundup began. Local Catholic peasants were able to rescue some who escaped.

Many Ukrainians deplored the killings. Moderate Ukrainian political organizations had nothing to do with these slaughters. As in Nazi-occupied Lithuania, former servants and other employees of Jews, peasants, and some middle-class city dwellers came to the aid of the Jews. A group of Ukrainian and Polish foresters hid 1,700 Jews in Przemyslany district's woods.[32] Father Marko Stek served as the contact between the Saint George Cathedral complex and Ukrainian Catholic monasteries and convents that were sheltering Jews (see below).

In 1942, as ghettos were established for Jews, the looting and killings increased. When Kurt Lewin, the rabbi's eldest son, went to Saint George's to tell Metropolitan Sheptytsky of the new death camps, the archbishop wept at the news. He hid the rabbi's precious papers, and then arranged to hide the rabbi's eldest and middle sons (the rest of the family chose to return to the ghetto). Kurt Lewin was introduced to the Metropolitan's network of Studite and Basilian monks and Basilian nuns who were hiding Jewish refugees. The principal leader was the Metropolitan's brother, Hegumen Klement of the Studites (whose order had been founded as a community open to all, both poor and rich, in 1901 as part of the Greek Catholic religious renewal). That this was dangerous was borne out in 1942, when the SS invaded the Saint George complex and Saint Josaphat monastery, and two Studite priests arrested. Father Johannes Peters, a German citizen, was sent back to the Reich to be executed.

Studite monks helped some Jews escape to Romania and Hungary, when those countries were still havens. The metropolitan's network rescued many Jews, despite the risks of being caught by the Germans or betrayed by anti-Semites among their countrymen.[33] Father Tirpovitz, in Dukla, intervened to save the Jews of that town from a pogrom. Father Korduba, in Mosty, hid a Jewish woman in his rectory for eight months.[34] The priest of Peremyshlany hid Jews, only to be betrayed by the Ukrainian militia; he was killed at the Majdanek death camp.[35] As many as 240 Greek Catholic priests may have been involved in the rescue of Jews.[36]

The threat of capture or betrayal was quite real. Not only was the death penalty imposed for aiding or sheltering Jews in Nazi-occupied Poland, there were substantial rewards for turning in those who did. It is worth noting that, between October 1943 and June 1944, about 100 Ukrainians are recorded as having been formally executed in Galicia for aiding Jews. As one survivor noted, the number of Ukrainian Catholic helpers was considerably larger because only a "fraction" of Ukrainian rescuers were caught and many of these were killed on the spot, along with the Jews they were help-ing.[37] A German police secret report in October 1943 noted that the number of cases of those helping Jews in Galicia was steadily increasing, and recommended that of-fenders be immediately hanged, without any court procedures. Among those executed were a baker who sold bread to a Jew (shot with his wife and son), a Polish woman who hid her former employer (hanged), and the cattle dealer Kazimierz Jozefek, who fed and hid Jews (hanged in 1944 along with four helpers of Jews).[38]

In Lwów (L'viv), many people tried to help Jewish escapees in 1943, as noted. One thousand Poles from the city were killed at the Bełzec death camp for giving as-sistance to Jews, the only Poles to be executed in that camp.[39] A Polish housing admin-istrator, Josef Materklas, lied to the Gestapo to protect Jewish tenants by saying that they were all people of Aryan descent. His action was "by no means a noble excep-tion," although it is notable that he interceded on the behalf of complete strangers.[40]

The most noted opposition came from the strongest moral force in the region, Metropolitan Sheptytsky, the primate of the Greek Catholic Church. Like other Ukrainians, he had welcomed the Germans as liberators, and thought that they would bring an end to the violence. He quickly became disillusioned with the occupation forces and the Nazis. In February 1942, he protested to Himmler himself about the massacres of Jews. The metropolitan was especially upset by the August 1942 forced removal and killing of Jews, and he complained bitterly to the Holy See and the Ori-ental Congregation about the Germans' behavior toward the Jews and the negative ef-fect of this behavior on the Ukrainian populace. On August 24, Sheptytsky wrote to Pope Pius XII: "There is a tremendous need for blood voluntarily offered, to atone for the blood criminally shed." The Pope's response came on September 12, and the next day the Metropolitan sent out a circular to all the priests in Galicia in opposition to racial persecution.[41]

His pastoral letter of November 1942, "Thou Shalt Not Murder," threatened all involved in killing with excommunication. Although the letter does not specifically mention Jews, that it was published before the Ukrainian-Polish civil war had escalated and when the extermination of Jews was peaking in the area makes "its relevance . . . clear."[42] (One must remember that pro-Jewish statements by the Catholic Church during the war were carefully coded to prevent giving the Germans an excuse for fur-ther atrocities.)

In addition, the metropolitan arranged for the protection of Jews and Torah scrolls from the Lwów (L'viv) synagogues in the cathedral complex, and for his brother, Father Klement, head of the Studite monks, and his sister, Mother Josepha, superior of the Studite convents, to conceal 156 Jewish children. Rabbi David Kahane found sanctuary in the metropolitan's episcopal palace in 1943, as did the sons of the martyred Rabbi Lewin and others, for a total of 21 people. A number of Jews who escaped from the Lwów (L'viv) ghetto from August 1942 through May 1943 found sanctuary in his metropolitan's residence or in other Ukrainian Catholic centers. The Basilian monasteries concealed 28 Jewish men. Some 500 Greek Catholic monks and nuns were involved in the rescue of Jews: not one of them betrayed their charges.[43] It is notable that the Ukrainian Catholic network, unlike some other Christian rescue groups, did not try to convert the Jewish children they saved: indeed, the children were returned to the Jewish community after the war.

The metropolitan's pleas must have influenced peasants and workmen.[44] For just one example, Maria Rybenczuk, a married Greek Catholic woman in Kosow, Kolomiya County, concealed the entire Stadler family throughout the occupation in a hidden bunker on her farm; she fed and sheltered Jewish refugees fleeing the different "actions," making sure that the food she provided in a time of strict rationing was kosher.[45]

The most tragic part of the Jewish community's life, I think, came after the Soviet liberation. Jews who had survived in hiding began to emerge, only to be slain by the AK forces in the towns. Although Ukrainian fascists had fled to the Reich with the retreating Nazis, members of the UPA also killed Jews. That people should have successfully hidden through three bloody years of Nazi occupation and then have been slaughtered by their countrymen simply because they were Jews seems especially awful.

In 1945, Kurt Lewin returned to Lwów (now Lvov again) to find Father Stek Marko, the priest who had rescued him. He successfully convinced the Studites to let him take Father Marko with him, and so the Jewish boy rescued the Greek Catholic priest who had once rescued him.

Western Soviet Union: Pre-1939 Boundaries

Within the Nazi-occupied territories of the pre-1939 Soviet Union, organized Catholicism had ceased to exist, as we have seen. But the Nazi massacres left villagers stunned. In many cases, non-Jewish spouses refused to leave their Jewish husbands and wives, and were butchered with them. There were of course no priests or nuns left, but religious belief played a role in the revulsion felt, in the dedication of Christian spouses who willingly went to their deaths, and surely in some rescues. Sadly, I have not been able to find anything relating specifically to Catholics other than references to the horror of Russia Germans and the self-sacrifice of German spouses in the colonies in southern Ukrainian SSR when it was invaded—except for one German Catholic teacher in Odessa who tried to save Jewish students in an orphanage. She was shot.

Anti-Nazi Resistance by Reich Germans

Many German soldiers and officers were revolted by the killings, and some did act. Dating from 1941, there are memos to *Wehrmacht* superiors from field officers decrying the slaughter, and soldiers complained about the terrible conditions in letters to their families. At Białystok and Vilnius, Reich Germans actively helped Jews in the ghettos, and suffered grievously as a result.[46] Two particular Reich Germans stand out. Fritz Graebe, a Protestant from western Germany, became the "Moses of Rovno." An employee of a firm that held a contract with the railroad, he saved hundreds of Jews and Poles in the occupied Ukraine, successfully evacuating many Jews to the west in the longest train seen in Eastern Europe during the war.[47] A Sudeten Catholic, Oskar Schindler, organized a factory in Poland to shelter some 1,000 Jews and is credited with saving "more Jews at greater risk than any other person."[48]

The Silence of the Catholic Church

Although the Soviets continually accused Pope Pius XII of collaborating with the Nazis in the Jewish holocaust, the Jews themselves thanked the pope frequently during the war for his actions in Italy, Slovakia, Hungary, Bulgaria.

One of the great anxieties Pius XII had was to avoid a repetition of the 1942 disaster in the occupied Netherlands. There the Catholic bishops issued a pastoral letter denouncing the removal of Dutch and foreign Jews, while the Protestant Churches were silent. The bishops' outspokenness cost the lives of some 40,000 Dutch Catholic Jews, whom the Nazis sent to the death camps as punishment for the Catholic letter. The pope was devastated. Sister Pascalina, his housekeeper and helper, wrote that when the papers announced the action, Pius deliberately burned a papal protest being prepared against the persecution of the Jews.[49] Whether this is true or not, we do know that Pius XII himself said, "No doubt a protest would have gained me the praise and respect of the civilized world, but it would have submitted the poor Jews to an even worse persecution."[50]

Harbin and the Soviet Catholics
of Manchuria

As we have seen, millions of people fled the civil war and the hardships of Bolshevik rule, flooding into Western Europe or into the successor borderland states throughout the 1920s. However, there were smaller outflows: one, from the Caucasus to Turkey, and the other to the Far East. The Republic of China, itself torn by civil war, provided sanctuary for many Soviet citizens, albeit under sometimes harsh conditions.

Central Asians of a variety of nationalities fled east across the frontier into the Central Asian province of Sinkiang, which became home to 70,000 ethnic Russian refugees. By 1945, more than 200,000 White Russians had made their way to China, joined by an unknown number of other European refugees from the USSR. Every major Chinese city had a colony of White Russians, most living in poverty and some worse off still, with the fabled city of Shanghai being home to some 40,000. But it was in the far north, in the industrial stronghold of China, the steppes of Manchuria, that the White Russians created their great cultural and intellectual center, and it was here that Soviet Catholics found not only refuge, but also the opportunity to rebuild.

Manchuria consisted of three provinces: Heilongjiang, Jilin, and Liaoning, known collectively to Chinese as Dongbei. Homeland to the Manchus, and thus to the Ch'ing Dynasty that had ruled the Chinese Empire until 1911, Manchuria was doomed to becoming part of the great game of Asian politics in the 1930s. The Soviet Orthodox, Protestant, and Catholic refugees who created a vibrant culture became victims of that power struggle. The refugees were concentrated in Heilongjiang, the northernmost province closest to Siberia, and Harbin was their center.

As noted in chapter 3, Harbin was founded by the Russians as a center for their great railway project across Manchuria, the Chinese Eastern Railroad. In 1913, the city counted nearly 70,000 residents: Russians represented slightly more than one-half, Chinese just over one-third, and Poles, Jews, and a mix of Japanese, Koreans, Germans, Tatars, Latvians, Georgians, Estonians, and Armenians almost one-sixth of the population.[1] This exotic polyglot community was a Russian imperial colony in the Manchu homeland, and was destined to become even more polyglot in the momentous years ahead.

As was to be expected in a Russian city, there was a splendid Orthodox cathedral:

dedicated to Saint Nicholas's, built in 1899, dominated the city's skyline.[2] The railroad gave the city's Polish community a house to use as a chapel in 1901, and a lot on Bolshoi Propekt in the heart of the "New City" of Harbin, on which they built a handsome Gothic church in 1907, a church famous among the people for its magnificent altars and statues. The city boasted Muslim mosques, Jewish synagogues, Protestant churches for Baptists and Lutherans, Buddhist temples, and many ethnic associations for all the nationalities.[3]

Early Growth: 1920–1938

With the establishment of Communism in Russia, the Chinese Eastern Railway came under Soviet control, and eventually Harbin became home to a small Soviet colony. It was, however, also a center for tens of thousands of anti-Soviet refugees. The demise of White rule in eastern Siberia, the tragic fall of Vladivostok in late 1922, and the collapse of partisan movements, which (as we saw in chapter 7) sent the remnants of the Volunteer Army, other forces, and their dependents over the border into Manchuria. They were joined by a large number of anti-Bolshevik civilians, especially in the 1930s, when a wave of Russia Germans, Jews, and Siberians of different ethnic backgrounds fleeing religious persecution and forced collectivization arrived there.

The American Consulate in Harbin[4] recorded the dismal conditions both in the USSR and in Manchuria. Collectivization in and following 1930 drove people over the frontier: one American report says that "there was a veritable stampede" across the Ussuri, Argun, and Amur. Anti-Soviet uprisings in Siberia (aided by émigré military organizations based in Harbin) sent more people fleeing as the Red Army defeated them. In 1931, they came at a rate of 500 per month. Crossing the border rivers became increasingly hazardous, and yet still they came. In April 1938, there were only 1,500 Poles in Harbin; by November, this number had soared to over 5,000.

The refugees came over frozen rivers; they risked being shot by border patrols or being captured by Chinese slavers, who would force their women into prostitution or sell the refugees back to the Soviet police (reported in 1933). On the other hand, some Chinese and White Russian smugglers would lead refugees past the patrols, and then return to smuggle food to the starving back home in Siberia, especially during the famines of 1930–1933 brought on by collectivization.

Border controls on the Soviet side became steadily more efficient after 1931, but the consulate repeatedly reports Soviet citizens fleeing from the Transbaikal in 1932, from the Amur oblast in 1933, and along the whole frontier in 1934. With the Great Terror scooping up victims even in Manchuria, many Soviets rushed to renounce their citizenship from 1931 through 1934. Soviet employees of the railroad refused to go home when their contracts were up: they had heard too many stories of the horrors in the homeland. In 1935, despite all hardships and difficulties, they continued to enter Mancuria, even in the Great Terror, when the trek south seemed well worth the risk.

(Despite this, it is worth noting that the consular reports often cite refugee reports of conditions in the Soviet Union as being "impossible to believe," especially regarding the status of nonpersons, the extent of the Great Terror, and the power of the NKVD. Not even the haunted faces of these unfortunates could convince Westerners determined to hold on to their naïveté.)

Once in Manchuria, people settled in neat little farming villages along the railroad or just outside cities where they tried to re-create their old life, or they moved into the cities to find industrial work. Many lived in extreme poverty. All were subject to the banditry of the ex-Red Army men, to NKVD raids, to the expanding Chinese civil war, and to confrontations between the Chinese Republic and the Japanese Empire. Those who had founded villages in the "protected zone" of the Chinese Eastern Railroad abandoned them in 1932 for the safety of territory controlled by the Japanese Imperial Army.

Thus, despite the handsome buildings and tree-lined boulevards, life in Harbin was often perilous. Red Army deserters terrorized the farm villages around the city; there were continual epidemics of cholera, typhus, diphtheria and smallpox in Harbin as well as in other Manchurian cities. NKVD forces kidnapped Soviet refugees and Chinese citizens alike right from the towns in 1929 and took them back over the border. In 1931, the consulate records the Russia Germans as living in poverty and slavery. Some people despaired and applied for repatriation to the Soviet Union. Few were taken back, though; because Stalin feared a Japanese invasion, those applying for repatriation were suspected of being potential saboteurs. In 1936, only 68 families were allowed back to the USSR.

Through all its problems, Harbin remained very much a pre-1914 Russian city, with a high standard of living, academic institutions and a host of religious centers, a handsome, well-kept city that prospered in Manchuria's industrial and agricultural booms, as well as during and immediately after World War II.[5]

Religious Life

The Jewish population swelled to over 10,000 in the 1930s, supporting a hospital, orphanage, synagogues, and twenty newspapers and journals. The Russian Orthodox diocese also had an extensive network of churches, schools, and orphanages to serve the ethnic Russian populace, which was returning to religion in the wake of what they saw as a national disaster. There were churches, monasteries, and convents for Orthodox and Old Believers alike.

Although Catholic missionary work in Manchuria dated back to 1838,[6] it centered in the south, where an apostolic vicariate was founded at Mukden in 1924. The Soviet Catholic influx to the north would result in many changes.

Although the overwhelming majority of Russian refugees were of Orthodox origin, Harbin had a large resident Latin Catholic population. In 1926, under the influence of the local Polish clergy, Father Ivan Koronin's Orthodox parish of several thousand people entered into union with Rome. After their pastor's death, only 30 of these parishioners remained Catholic. This little community, however, formed the nucleus for Harbin's Byzantine Catholic exarchate.[7] The Jesuits who came in 1927 founded a school, orphanage, and chapel, and experienced some conversions among people disillusioned with Orthodoxy and seeking answers in their disrupted lives. The vast majority of the Russian Orthodox, however, remained loyal to their ancestral Church.

The Byzantine Catholic Apostolic Exarchate of Harbin was founded in May 1928, not just for ethnic Russians, but for "all Oriental Rite Catholics" (according to the *Annuario Pontificio*), which suggests there were non-Russian Eastern Catholic faithful living in the Harbin area. Indeed, the city had a Ukrainian Home for many years, with Greek Catholic and Orthodox members. Its first bishop, the Most Reverend Fabian Abrantovich, MIC, who had only two convert Russian priests at Harbin, was assisted by Father Diodor Kolpinsky, originally one of Exarch Feodorov's priests from Poland. Father Kolpinsky worked very hard to overcome Orthodox fears of a Latin Catholic conquest, and founded a school for the sons of Orthodox families without any missionary work among them at all. But he was persecuted by the local Poles and quarreled with the Exarch and apparently considered returning to Orthodoxy. When he died suddenly in 1932, both the Orthodox and Greek Catholics fought for the right to bury him. Bishop Fabian was recalled to Rome in 1933, and replaced by a Jesuit, Father Javorka.[8] The last exarch in Harbin was Archimandrite Nicholas, who would serve until 1950.[9]

This exarchate was well supplied with both clergy and members of religious orders: the Society of Jesus and the Marians of the Immaculate Conception had houses and schools, including a small seminary, and Byzantine Rite Ursuline nuns (headed by an English Mother Superior who adopted the Byzantine-Russian Rite), conducted a school for girls. The exarchate, which was also served by married convert Russian priests, sponsored an orphanage (badly needed given the trials of the faithful); it had its own cathedral church in Harbin and churches in Shanghai (where there were English and Russian Jesuits, a convert Russian archimandrite, and a Russian Catholic school staffed by Irish Columban nuns) and in Peiping, the former capital (now known as Beijing).[10] The exarchate's Marians had been forced out of Poland because of their work on behalf of the "Neo-Uniate" movement (see chapter 17). But the number of conversions remained small, and there was no ecumenical work such as that done by Father Kolpinsky until 1932. Manchuria had 60 Russian Orthodox parishes with 100,000 Orthodox believers, 200 priests, as well as an Orthodox university, monastery, convent, and seminary in 1939, whereas China as a whole had five Orthodox dioceses, with another 200,000 believers.[11]

In response to the increase in Harbin's Latin Catholic population, a second church, Saint Josaphat's was built in 1925 on Apteka Street for European Latin Catholics. Father Vladislav Ostrovskii pastored Saint Stanislaus's for many years; his last successor was Father Alexander Ejsmont, a refugee. Saint Josaphat's first pastor Father Anthony Leshevich, who emigrated in 1938, was succeeded by Father Pavel Khodkevich, who served until about 1950.

The Chinese and Korean Roman Catholics had a third church, in the "Chinese quarter" of Harbin on Futszyadyan Street, with French missionary priests and Franciscan Sisters. There were also outdoor Catholic shrines.[12]

The first—and thus far, the last—Catholic bishop of Vladivostok, Karol Sliwowski, had been ordained at Saint Josaphat's in Harbin. Because he had jurisdiction over the ethnic Polish parishes in Manchuria as well as over his diocese in the Maritime Provinces, his pastoral ministry became exceedingly difficult as the USSR slid into deeper persecution and the borders became ever tighter.[13] Given the inability of exercising diocesan care from Siberia and the reluctance of many Latin Catholic priests to serve under a Greek Catholic bishop, the Latin Catholics were finally placed under the apostolic delegate to China in 1931.[14]

Japanese Rule: 1934–1945

The Mukden Incident of 1931 was but a prelude to the Japanese conquest of Manchuria. Japan created the state of Manchuoko, with the last of the Ch'ings, Henry P'u Yi, as Chief Executive; in 1934, he became emperor. (By 1938, the Japan-Manchuoko Company reported that Harbin had over 660,000 inhabitants.) Manchuoko became a target of Japanese colonization. By 1940, the country had 1.3 million Imperial Japanese soldiers and more than 704,000 Japanese civilian colonists out of a population of over 42.3 million total,[15] almost twice the estimated maximum of 22 million in 1900 under Chinese imperial rule. The puppet state was granted diplomatic recognition by the Axis Powers, their allies, and fascist Spain; by Thailand (in 1941, as Japan raced across China and threatened all East Asia) and the Polish government in exile (in October 1939, so as to serve the Polish émigré community there), and by two neutrals, El Salvador (March 1934), and the Holy See (April 1934—after the accession of the new emperor—to maintain communication with the Church in Manchuria).[16]

The worsening Sino-Japanese War took its toll in the north. Many people applied to emigrate overseas. In 1940, the Polish population of Manchuria had dropped to 1,322, and Germans, Balts, and others were emigrating. Japanese rule was not peaceful for the non-Orientals or the Chinese, and many of the Soviet refugees were in a difficult position because they were stateless persons. Banks began closing in November 1940, and evacuation of American citizens was ordered. In March 1941, the last Russian villages in Manchuria were ordered abandoned by the Japanese, as being in dangerous areas. The noose was closing, and the consulate reports continually contain information about people leaving, institutions closing, the countryside becoming ever more dangerous. Nondiplomatic foreigners who had passports were being urged to leave. The Catholic missionaries, however, refused to leave their parishes, and were still at their stations when Japan attacked the United States on December 7, 1941.

Postwar Era: 1945–1949

World War II ended with Manchuria coming under Soviet occupation. The USSR had declared war on the Japanese Empire only when it was on its last legs after Hiroshima and Nagasaki, and fresh Soviet troops were rushed down into Manchuria's three provinces, which were ruthlessly plundered. Huge arms depots were turned over to the Chinese Communists, contributing to their military victory over the Nationalists in 1949.

Soviet occupation terrorized a refugee population already worn down by Japanese misrule and abuses. The same pattern of forced repatriation seen in Western Europe was followed in Manchuria, including a new generation who had never seen Soviet Russia. Much of the émigré Russian leadership was kidnapped at a meeting in 1945. There was even a special category for the Manchurian victims: *Kharbintsy,* who were sentenced to from 5 to 25 years in the Gulag or to execution. Many were taken away at night, or forced into USSR-bound trucks and trains at gunpoint (the fate that befell the Polish and Belorussian Marian Fathers and Brothers early on). By 1949, of all the Byzantine Catholic religious communities in Manchuria, only the Ursuline Sisters remained.

At the same time, many White Russians, weary of being stateless persons, believed Soviet and Western propaganda that "Uncle Joe" Stalin and his system had changed. They accepted Soviet offers to return to the Motherland with Soviet citizenship and an amnesty, only to be shot or sent to the Gulag.[17] Most anti-Communists who escaped forcible removal headed south, congregating in Shanghai. The Chinese Communists allowed many of these people to emigrate.[18] One of the most successful exoduses was arranged by a Jesuit missionary to the Russian Catholics, Father Feodor Wilcock, who personally chartered three condemned freighters to evacuate 6,500 White Russian Catholics and Orthodox to the Philippines, whence they emigrated to the United States and South America.[19]

Harbin and Manchuria in Communist China

In 1953, five years after Communist rule was established, there were still 100,000 White Russians living in Manchuria and the coastal cities. This community would slowly dwindle, as people went to the USSR or were reunited with relatives in Western countries.

Roman Catholic Masses continued to be held for the ever-dwindling refugee European population of Harbin. Father Ejsmont would leave in 1956, with the last of his European parishioners, for Australia.[20] The Byzantine Catholic exarchate was extinct by then, and the Latin Catholic Administration of Harbin contained only Chinese and Korean faithful. The last of the Orthodox Christian churches would be closed by the Red Guards during Mao's Cultural Revolution in 1966.

Epilogue

The Chinese Roman Catholics of Harbin were given the former Saint Alexis Ortho-dox church, with the new name "Church of the Virgin Mary" on Ma jia gou Shike Street in 1980, after 13 years' service as a public cafeteria. It opened with Mass in Latin, celebrated by the old bishop, Peter Wong, born in 1905. The congregation is Chinese and Korean, and a bishop is in residence. After 1980, the old Russia-German Lutheran "Kirche" was restored to Chinese Protestant worship (and is still referred to by its German name). In 1990, there were a few old "foreigners" in a special home, with a handful of Polish and Russian residents, including two American citizens de-scended from a San Francisco trading family. One Orthodox parish was reopened for Chinese Orthodox in 1984, in the church on Dazhi Street.[21]

Harbin's fascinating past lives on in the many examples of Russian architecture that survived the Maoist purges, in the thoughts of the local Christian populace, and in the memories of those who once lived there and are now scattered across the globe.

Notes

1. The Inheritance

1. My analysis of the three policies of the Russian Empire and the Soviet Union here is based on Sergei Madksudov and William Taubman, "Russian-Soviet Nationality Policy and Foreign Policy: A Historical Overview of the Linkage between Them," in *The Rise of Nations in the Soviet Union* ed. Michael Mandebaum (New York: Council on Foreign Relations, 1991); of Russification, on Hugh Seton-Watson, "Russian Nationalism in Historical Perspective," in *The Last Empire* ed. Robert Conquest (Stanford, Calif.: Hoover Institution Press, 1986); and of Catholic-State conflict under both imperial and Soviet governments, on the *Chronicle of the Catholic Church in Lithuania* (Chicago: Lithuanian Roman Catholic Federation of America, 1975); Dennis Dunn, *The Catholic Church and the Soviet Government: 1939–1949* (Boulder, Colo.: East European Quarterly, 1977); Paul Mailleux, SJ, *Exarch Leonid Feodorov: Bridgebuilder between Rome and Moscow* (New York: P. J. Kenedy, 1964); Hansjakob Stehle, *The Eastern Politics of the Vatican: 1917–1979,* trans. Sandra Smith (Athens: Ohio Univ. Press, 1981); Saulius Suziedelis, *The Sword and the Cross: A History of the Church in Lithuania* (Huntington, Ind.: Our Sunday Visitor Press, 1988); and James Zatko, *Descent into Darkness: The Destruction of the Roman Catholic Church in Russia, 1917–1923* (South Bend, Ind.: University of Notre Dame Press, 1965).

2. Lenin as quoted in Trevor Beeson, *Discretion and Valour* (Philadelphia: Fortress Press, 1982), 19.

3. Beeson, 32–33.

4. Nathaniel Davis, *A Long Walk to Church* (Boulder, Colo.: Westview Press, 1995), 6–7.

5. Nicholas Berdyaev, *The Russian Revolution* (London: Sheed and Ward, 1931), 49–71. Berdyaev's second chapter is entitled "The Religion of Communism."

6. Film review from *Sovetskaya Moldava,* quoted in *Religion in Communist Lands* 2, no. 2 (summer 1980): 158.

7. *Pravda* article, quoted in *Religion in Communist Lands* 8, no. 8 (autumn 1980): 242.

8. Rusyn was an isolated, Ukranian-related nationality in the Carpathian Mountains.

9. J. Derek Holmes, *The Papacy in the Modern World* (New York: Crossroad, 1981), 94.

2. The Silver Mosaic of the Church in Russia

1. Adrian Fortescue, "Eastern Churches," in *Catholic Encyclopedia,* ed. Charles G. Herbermann et al. (New York: Appleton, 1907–1912), vol. 5, p. 239.

2. An excellent summary of this dynamic era, which was carried on in the Russian emi-

gration, is found in Marc Raeff, *Russia Abroad: A Cultural History of the Russian Emigration: 1919–1939* (New York: Oxford University Press, 1990), 100 *passim.*

3. See James W. Cunningham, *Vanquished Hope: The Movement for Church Renewal in Russia, 1905–1906* (Crestwood, N.Y.: St. Vladimir's Seminary Press, 1981).

4. Cunningham, 281–82.

5. Ossyp Zinkewych and Andrew Sorokowski, eds., *A Thousand Years of Christianity in Ukraine: An Encyclopedic Chronology* (New York: Smoloskyp and National Committee to Commemorate Millenium of Christianity in Ukraine, 1988), 58.

6. Zinkewych and Sorokowski, 68.

7. Demetrius E. Wyochansky, OSBM, *Saint Josaphat Kuntsevych: Apostle of Church Unity* (Detroit: Basilian Fathers, 1986), 298.

8. Jan Zaprudnik, *Belarus: At a Crossroads in History* (Boulder, Colo.: Westview Press, 1993), 50.

9. Zaprudnik, 57–58.

10. Simeon, Vailhe, "Lutzk, Zhitomir and Kamenetz," in *Catholic Encyclopedia,* vol. 9, pp. 463–65.

11. Aurelio Palmieri, OSA, "Russia," in *Catholic Encyclopedia,* volume 13, p. 259.

12. Joseph Lins, "Siberia" in *Catholic Encyclopedia,* vol. 13, pp. 767–8.

13. Tadeusz Poleski, "Pastoral Work in Byelorussia," *Religion in Communist Lands* 13, no. 2 (winter 1985): 300.

14. Leon Tretjakewitsch, *Bishop Michel d'Herbigny, SJ, and Russia: A Pre-Ecumenical Approach to Christian Unity* (Würzburg: Augustinus, 1990), 47.

15. Mykolas Drunga, "Remnants of a Tradition," *Atlaidai: Lithuanian Pilgrimages,* ed. Algimantas Kezys (Chicago: Loyola Univ. Press, 1990), ii-vii.

16. Kezys, esp. 50–58.

17. Kezys, 189–90.

18. Kezys, chaps. 37 and 44. Also see Adam Weisbecker, "Catholic Consecration Festivals in the Catholic Villages on the Volga," *American Historial Society of Germans from Russia Journal* 10, no. 2 (1987): 37–39. Information on the specific villages is found in the listing of the parishes under the deaneries of the diocese in Joseph Schurr, "Die Pfarreien und ihre Kirchen, nach Dekanaten zusammengestellt," in Schnurr, ed., *Die Kirchen und das Religiöse Leben der Russland-Deutschen* (Stuttgart: Landsmannschaft der Deutschen aus Russland, 1972).

3. The Catholic Communities of Imperial Russia, Part One

1. Eastern Orthodoxy had 50,000 followers in eastern Finland (Karelia) and in Lapland. Its interesting history is well told in *Orthodoxy in Finland: Past and Present,* ed. Veikko Purmonen (Kuopio, Finland: Orthodox Clergy Association, 1981).

2. Pius Wittman, "Finland," in *Catholic Encyclopedia,* vol. 6, p. 77.

3. *Catholic Almanac, 1989* ed. Felician A. Foy, OFM (Huntington, Ind.: Our Sunday Visitor Press, 1989), 343.

4. *The Catholic Church in Finland* (Helsinki: Catholic Information Centre, 1988), 4, 10, 15, 18.

5. Karl Lorenz, ed., *Die römisch-katholische Kirche in der Sowjetunion* (Munich: Kirche in Not/Ostpriesterhilfe, 1989), 17–18.

6. Lorenz, *Römisch-katholische Kirche,* 18.

7. *Encyclopaedia Britannica* (New York: Britannica, 1926), "Livonia," vol. 16, p. 816–17.

8. *Encyclopaedia Britannica,* "Kovno," vol. 15, 791; "Courland," vol. 7, 320. Courland was only 1 percent Polish and 1 percent Lithuanian, but Catholics and Orthodox together represented 16 percent of the province's population. Courland was home to Latgalians, whose statistics were not given in the 1906 information I had access to, but who were exclusively Catholic.

9. Alexander V. Berkis, *History of the Duchy of Courland: 1561–1795* (Towson, Md.: Paul M. Harrod, 1969), 248.

10. Suziedelis, 135–38.

11. *Encyclopaedia Britannica,* "Kiev," vol. 15, 788–90.

12. Suziedelis, 142–45.

13. Alexander Cherney, *The Latvian Orthodox Church* (Welshpool, UK.: Stylite, 1985), 90.

14. Most Rev. Joseph Kessler, *Geschichte der Tiraspoler Diözese* (Dickinson, N.D.: Rev. George Aberle, 1930), 138.

15. Joseph C'amans, "Lettonia: Terra mariana," in *Maria e la Chiesa del Silenzio* (Rome: Accademia Mariana Internazionale, 1957), 60–61.

16. C'amans, 61.

17. Rev. Michael Bourdeaux, *Land of Crosses* (Devon, U.K.: Pitman Press, 1979), 207.

18. Bourdeaux, 199.

19. Suziedelis, 66.

20. Joseph Vais'nora, MIC, "La Madonna Piangente, Prettrice della Lituania," in *Maria e la Chiesa del Silenzio,* 65.

21. Lithuanian Franciscan Custody (Kennebunkport, Me.: Custody of St. Casimir, 1952).

22. Suziedelis, 149.

23. Aurelio Palmieri, OSA, "Vilna" in *Catholic Encyclopedia,* vol. 15, p. 433.

24. Stephen Guthrie, "The Belorussians: National Identity and Assimilation, 1897–1970," *Soviet Studies* 29, no. 1 (1977): 47.

25. Kessler, 170.

26. Palmieri, "Vilna," 434.

27. Zatko, 27.

28. Guthrie, 41–43.

29. Cunningham, 246.

30. Lev Haroshka, "Religion in Byelorussia Today," *Byelorussian Review* 3 (1956): 102.

31. Zaprudnik, 63.

32. Guthrie, 47. Many respondents to the 1897 census in Belorussia identified themselves as being "from here." Known as "White Russians" in common English parlance, Belorussians were widely considered part of the Great Russian nation.

33. Aliz Ambrose, "Language and Church in Byelorussia," *Religion in Communist Lands* 2, no. 1 (1990): 20.

34. *The Francis Skaryna Byelorussian Library and Museum, 1971–1981* (London: Francis Skaryna Byelorussian Library and Museum, 1981), 15.

35. Zaprudnik, 64–65.

36. Zaprudnik, 61.

37. Vitaut Kipel, "The Early Byelorussian Presence in America" in *Zapisy* (Byelorussian Institute of Arts and Sciences in the United States), vol. 17 (1983): 115–16.

38. Peter Tatarynović, "La Chiesa del silenzio nella Biancorutenia e il culto mariano," in *Maria e la Chiesa del Silenzio,* 24–25; "Our Lady of Zhyrovitsi," *Eastern Catholic Life,* Nov. 22, 1987, p. 1.

39. Karl Baedeker, *Russia: A Handbook for Travelers* (1914; reprint, New York: Arno Press and Random House, 1971), 46.

40. Baedeker, 37.

41. Bourdeaux, 198.

42. Andrew J. Shipman, "Lutzk, Zhitomir, and Kamenetz," in *Catholic Encyclopedia,* vol. 9, pp. 463–65. In 1914, Lutsk had 279,157 Catholics; Zhitomir, 220,893; Kamenets, 317,235.

43. The title of Kamenets, though, was transferred to the Greek Catholic Metropolitan See of Lemberg (Lwów) in Austria-Hungary (this latter point became important in 1918 when Metropolitan Sheptytsky attempted to provide a Greek Catholic hierarchy in Russia again).

44. Cunningham, 325.

45. *Encyclopaedia Britannica,* "Volhynia," vol. 27, p. 195; "Podolia," vol. 21, p. 875, "Kiev," vol. 15, p. 788.

46. Palmieri, "Russia," 260.

47. Cunningham, 185.

48. Cunningham, 66.

49. Baedeker, 379.

50. Titus D. Hewryk, *The Lost Architecture of Kiev* (New York: Ukrainian Museum, 1982), 57, cites Saint Alexander's as being a transferred structure, but Bohdan Bociurkiw in *The Ukrainian Greek Catholic Church and the Soviet State (1939–1950)* (Edmonton: Canadian Institute of Ukrainian Studies, 1996), n. 79, p. 19, states that Saint Alexander's was a new parish established by Metropolitan Sheptytsky, one that miraculously survived until the Great Terror.

51. Nadezhda Teodorovich, "The Roman Catholics," in *Genocide in the USSR: Studies in Group Destruction,* ed. Nikolai Deker and Andrej Lebed (New York: Scarecrow Press, 1958), 211.

52. *Catholic Encyclopedia,* "Lutzk," pp. 463–65.

53. Some 45,000 Polish and Belorussian Catholic families were exiled to "South Russia" after the 1830 Uprising; cf. Hermes Kreilkamp, OFM, *These Friars Went East* (Huntington, Ind.: St. Felix Friary, 1954), 12; Walter Kolarz, *Religion in the Soviet Union* (New York: St. Martin's Press, 1961), 180.

54. Kessler, 147–48.

55. It is interesting to note that in correspondence with Germans from the Soviet Union, I am always first addressed as "Pater": evidently, the custom still holds.

56. Kessler, 149–50.

57. Teodorovich, 211; Zatko, 87.

58. Kessler, 152–53.

59. Joseph Schnurr, "Streiflichter aus der Geschichte der Tiraspoler Diözese," in Schnurr, *Kirchen,* 1972 ed., 10.

60. Kessler, 150–51.

61. Kessler, 187.

62. See listings in Schnurr, "Pfarreien," 1972 ed., 61–63; and also Kessler, 138.

63. The Richelieu Steps were to appear in the Communist-era movie "Potemkin" in one of the most important scenes in Russian film history.

64. Cf. Schnurr, "Streiflichter," 1972 ed.; Teodorovich, 211.

65. Schnurr, "Pfarreien," 1972 ed., 103.

66. Schnurr, "Pfarreien," 1972 ed., 105.

67. Schnurr, "Pfarreien," 1972 ed., 103.

68. Schnurr, *Die Kirchen und das Religiöse Leben . . . ,* 1980 ed., 298–99; Baedeker, 435. Masses and later prayer services were held in the graveyard, apparently until the Great Terror.

69. Robert G. Roberson, *The Eastern Christian Churches: A Brief Survey* (Rome: Pontifical Oriental Institute, 1988), 15.

70. Donald Attwater, *The Dissident Eastern Churches* (Milwaukee: Bruce, 1965), 150–51.

71. Roberson, 37.

72. Attwater, *Dissident,* 151–52.

73. Kreilkamp, 8–11; Kolarz, 179–80. Forbidden to practice their faith in the Russian Empire, many Byzantine Catholic Georgians fled to the Ottoman Empire, where they were permitted both to worship and to use vernacular Georgian in their services.

74. Donald Attwater, *The Catholic Eastern Churches* (Milwaukee: Bruce, 1935), 131.

75. Roberson, 37.

76. The Akhaltsike parish was granted permission by Rome in the 1740s to offer prayers in classical Georgian in place of Latin.

77. Schnurr, "Pfarreien," 1972 ed., 150–51; Baedeker, 456.

78. Joseph Schnurr, "Verzeichnis der Priester, die auf dem Boden der Tiraspoler Diöcese wirkten," in Schnurr, 1972 ed., 200–201; Schnurr, "Pfarreien," 1972 ed., 151.

79. Manfred Klaube, *Die Deutschen Dörfer in der westsibirischen Kulunda-Steppe: Entwicklung-Strukturen-Probleme* (Marburg: Elwert, 1991), 21–24.

80. These were Nova Romanovka (40 percent Catholic), Trockaja (33 percent) and Dobrovolskaja (45 percent): Klaube, *Deutschen Dörfer,* 96.

81. Kessler, 183–84.

82. Kessler, 158.

83. Schnurr, "Streiflichter," 1972 ed., 15–16, 119; Kessler, 192–94.

84. Translations from Western Armenian done by H.K., 1996. List of 172 churches and prayer houses from interview with H.K., 1996.

85. *Almanac of the Apostolic Administration of the Armenian Catholic Church in the Russian Empire, 1915* (Tbilisi: 1916; cited as *Almanac*), 67.

86. *Catholic Encyclopedia,* "Tiraspol," vol. 14, p. 739.

87. *Almanac,* 62.

88. Kessler, 140.

89. Charles Frazee, *Catholics and Sultans* (New York: Cambridge Univ. Press, 1983), 105.

90. *Almanac,* 77, 97.

91. Frazee, 188.

92. *Almanac,* 75–76.

93. Interview with H.K., 1996.

94. *Almanac,* 94.

95. Lorenz, *Kirche,* 17.

96. Ronald Wixman, *The Peoples of the USSR: An Ethnographic Handbook* (London: Macmillan Reference Books, 1984), 14.

4. The Catholic Communities of Imperial Russia, Part Two

1. All information on Moscow, Saint Petersburg, Siberia, and the northern and Asian parishes is taken from Joseph Lins, "Saint Petersburg," in *Catholic Encyclopedia,* vol. 13, 375–76; Lins, "Siberia," vol. 13, 767–68; Andrew J. Shipman, "Moscow" in *Catholic Encyclopedia,* vol. 10, 596, unless otherwise specified.

2. Palmieri, "Russia," 259.

3. Capt. Francis McCullagh, *The Bolshevik Persecution of Christianity* (New York: Dutton, 1924), 179–80.

4. McCullagh, 179–80.

5. McCullagh, 179.

6. Locations of the Catholic churches in Saint Petersburg are detailed in Baedeker on pp. 104 (Saint Catherine's), 124 (Saint Stanislaus's), 128 (Assumption), and by consulting its maps and its chapters on the capital and suburbs.

7. We will meet Father O'Rourke again in independent Latvia.

8. McCullagh, 372–73; Martha Edith Almedingen, *The Catholic Church in Russia Today* (New York: Kenedy, 1923), 30.

9. Mailleux, *Exarch Feodorov,* 98; Baedeker, 124–28; McCullagh 373; Almedingen, 30–31.

10. Antoine Wenger, *Rome et Moscou* (Paris: Desclée de Brouwer, 1987), chaps. 1–2; *Catholic Encyclopedia,* "Sisters of St. Joseph," vol. 5, 516.

11. The Theological Academy, transferred to the Republic of Poland after the Communist persecutions began, is the mother of the Catholic University of Lublin, the only such school to survive under Communist rule in all of Eastern Europe.

12. Lorenz, *Römisch-katholische Kirche,* 18.

13. Andrew J. Shipman, "Moscow," *Catholic Encyclopedia,* 591–96.

14. McCullagh lists the filial church, a chapel, as being under the patronage of the Immaculate Conception and newly built before World War I, yet Almedingen gives its name as "All Saints." Attempts in 1991 to gain the restoration of the church list it as under the title "Immaculate Conception."

15. Joan of Arc was canonized in 1920, Therese in 1925, and Bernadette in 1933.

16. Charles Bourgeois, *A Priest in Russia and the Baltic* (Dublin: Clonmore and Reynolds, 1958), 97–99.

17. Kolarz, 179.

18. McCullagh, 129.

19. Father Werczynski also worked in the Roman Rite. A secret Jesuit from Poland, he received 500 converts into the Catholic Church from 1906 to 1911. Cf. Tretjakewitsch, 40–1 n. 28.

20. Ambrosius K. Eszer, OP, "Ekaterina sienskaja und die Gemeinschaft der Schwestern des III. Ordens vom Heiligen Dominikus zu Moskaü," *Archivum Fratrum Praedicatorum* 40 (1970): 288–90. Eszer calls the Polish Jesuit "Wernicki," but contemporary accounts render his surname "Werczynski," which is the form used in this work.

21. McCullagh, 374.

22. Lorenz, *Römisch-katholische Kirche,* 18.

23. Frieda Schlau, "The German Settlements in the Belovezh Parish in Chernigov Province," *American Historical Society of Germans from Russia Journal* 12, no. 2 (1989): 18.

24. Kessler, 160.

25. Zatko, 23–24.

26. Tatarynović, "La Chiesa," 25–26.

27. Joseph Ledit, *Archbishop John Baptist Cieplak* (Montreal: Palm, 1963), 24–27.

28. Ingeborg Fleischhauer and Benjamin Pinkus, *The Soviet Germans: Past and Present* (London: Hurst, 1986), 22.

29. Bitautas Saulius, OFM. "Ein Expose über die Kirche in Siberien," Koenigstein Archives, 1990.

30. Some Poles did become Russian Orthodox, and a minority have remained Orthodox to this day. An Orthodox church in the Gothic style was built by Polish converts at Procop'yevsk, completed in 1858. This church was burned by Soviet forces in 1920; see *Letters from Siberia,* no. 11 (June 15, 1994); and Kolarz, 493.

31. Ledit, 20–21; also see histories of Siberian towns and Siberian expansion in *Columbia Lippincott Gazetteer of the World* (New York: Columbia University Press, 1970) for the rapidity of change in the affected cities and towns.

32. Teodorovich, 211; Lins, "Siberia," 767–68; *American Historical Society of Germans from Russia Journal* (spring 1983): *Vladivostok Sunrise* 6:5; 17:10–11; Bitaultas Saulius, 4–5.

33. Ledit, 19–20.

34. All Siberian locations except Novonikolaevsk are from Baedeker, 527–38. The Novonikolaevsk location is from Saulius, 5–6.

35. Catholic statistics are from Joseph Lins, "Mohileff," *Catholic Encyclopedia,* vol. 10, 429; city populations are from Baedeker, .

36. *Vladivostok Sunrise,* no. 3 (1992): 1–2.

37. Francis Domanski, SJ, *The Great Apostle of Russia: the Servant of God Archbishop John Baptist Cieplak* (Mundelein, Ill.: Saint Mary of the Lake Univ., 1953), 11.

38. Both Bishops Cieplak and Lozinski have been declared "Venerable" by the Church, and are candidates for beatification.

39. Information on Bishop Cieplak's 1909 tour is taken from Ledit, 20–23, unless otherwise cited.

40. *The Poles in the Far East* (in Polish; Harbin, China: 1928), 175–79. Found in the State Archive in Tomsk, Russia; author unknown. This information was retrieved by Father Myron Effing, CJD, *Vladivostok Sunrise,* no. 3, 1–2.

41. *Catholic Encyclopedia,* "Siberia," vol. 13, p. 768.

42. Fleischhauer and Pinkus, 22.

43. Samuel Hugh Moffett, *History of Christianity in Asia* (San Francisco: Harper, 1992), vol. 1, 428–30.

44. Bishop Jan Pavel Lenga, MIC, speech of June 10, 1995, at Colorado Springs Conference.

45. Roman Dzwonkowski, SAC, *Kościół katolicki w ZSSR, 1917–1939: Zarys historii* (Lublin: Catholic University of Lublin, 1997), 46.

46. Ledit, 27.

47. Lins, "Mohileff," 429.

48. David Dunford, *Catholic Encyclopedia,* "Dean" vol. 4, pp. 659–60.

49. Simon Karlinsky, "Memoirs of Harbin," *Slavic Review* 48, no. 2 (1989): 284.

50. Karlinsky, 285.

51. Olga Bakich, "A Russian City in China: Harbin Before 1917," *Canadian Slavonic Papers* 28, no. 2: 142–43.

52. Photographs of the variety of religious buildings in Harbin, including Russian Orthodox, Old Believer, Muslim, Armenian Apostolic, Lutheran, Buddhist, Jewish, Confucian, and Catholic, can be found in *Politekhnik,* no. 10 (1979), an annual journal published by alumni of the Harbin Polytechnical Institute in Sydney, Australia. Thanks are due to Professor Simon Karlinsky for directing me to this valuable source. Church information is taken from p. 140 and from correspondence with Boris Mirkin, editor of the *Bulletin* of the Association of Former Residents of China in Tel Aviv, Israel.

53. Ivan Muzyczka, "Sheptyts'kyi in the Russian Empire," in *Morality and Reality: The Life and Times of Andrei Sheptyts'kyi,* ed. Paul Robert Magocsi (Edmonton: Canadian Institute of Ukrainian Studies, Univ. of Alberta, 1989), 314–15.

54. Ledit, 33–35.

55. Ledit, 316.

56. Tretjakewitsch, 47.

57. Old Belief is descended from the schism *(rasko)* of 1650 over liturgical reform introduced by Patriarch Nikon. It is divided into several groups, and still commands a large following in Russia and elsewhere. Metropolitan Sheptytsky, in his study of Old Belief, discovered that the Greek Catholics, also unaffected by the Nikonian Reform, had retained West Slavic practices similar to Old Belief. He had a good rapport with Old Believers in Austria-Hungary, and there was a Catholic chapel at his palace complex that followed the Old Ritual for a small community.

58. Mailleux, *Exarch Feodorov,* 61.

59. Information on the Russian Greek Catholics is taken from Mailleux, *Exarch Feodorov,* 85 ff., unless otherwise noted.

60. *Orientalium dignitas* decreed that the Latin and Eastern Catholic Churches were of "equal dignity" and forbade Orthodox converts to be received into the Latin Catholic rite. Latin Catholic missionaries in Africa, Asia, and the Middle East routinely ignored this, saying it applied only in Europe. At the same time, Latin Catholic clergy in Europe said it only applied outside the continent. In short, most Latin Catholic prelates and priests simply ignored its conditions, well into the late twentieth century.

61. Tretjakewitsch, 47.

62. Mailleux, *Exarch Feodorov,* 91–92.

63. Tretjakewitsch, 49–50.

64. Zinkewych and Sorokowski, 185.

65. Wasyl Lencyk, *The Eastern Catholic Church and Czar Nicholas I* (New York: Pontifical Oriental Institute, 1966), 123–24.

66. Kreilkamp, 12.

67. See Lencyk, *The Eastern Catholic Church and Czar.*

68. Zinkewych and Sorokowski, 186–88.

69. One of the more despicable of these machinations occurred in 1838. Having refused to sign the proposed "Synodal Act of Unification," Metropolitan Bulhak died in Saint Petersburg while being pressured to convert. Tsar Nicholas I announced that Bulhak had intended to

convert, and ordered that the Catholic metropolitan be buried in the Alexander Nevsky Monastery with the Orthodox metropolitans of Moscow. See Zinkewych and Sorokowski, 187.

70. Lencyk, 120ff.; Davies, vol. 2, *God's Playground,* 210–11

71. Cunningham, 28.

72. George Fedoriw, *History of the Church in Ukraine,* trans. Petro Krawchuk (St. Catherine's, Ont.: St. Sophia Religious Association, 1983), 203–4.

73. Fedoriw, 200–204; Fr. Nicholas L. Chirovsky, *An Introduction to Ukrainian History* (New York: Philosophical Library, 1987), vol. 3, pp. 54–56.

74. Davies, vol. 2, *Playground,* 210–11.

75. Cunningham, 28–29.

76. Constantine Simon, SJ, "Jesuits and Belorussians: On the Fringe of Civilization or at the Cultural Crossroads?" *Diakonia* 28, no. 3: 207.

77. *Catholic Encyclopedia,* "Minsk," 333–34; "Mohileff," vol. 10, pp. 429; Attwater, *Catholic,* 80; Zatko, 25.

78. *Catholic Encyclopedia,* "Russia," vol. 11, p. 259; Fedoriw, 204.

79. Cunningham, 301, 325.

80. See W. Bruce Lincoln, *In War's Dark Shadow* (New York: Dial Press, 1983), 390–95.

81. Kessler, 161; 181–82.

82. Kessler, 147.

83. Kessler, 185.

84. Kessler, 182.

85. See James Long, *From Privileged to Dispossessed: The Volga Germans, 1860–1917* (Lincoln: Univ. of Nebraska Press, 1988), chaps. 8–9.

86. Russians were despised by the Muslim natives of the conquered Caucasus region, and so the imperial government sent in Polish and Lithuanian troops (who were of course Catholics) to keep the peace after the conquest was completed in the late 1800s.

87. *Lithuanian Franciscan Friars* (Kennebunkport, Me.: Custody of Saint Casimir, 1952).

88. Ledit, 44.

89. Lorenz, *Römisch-katholische Kirche,* 17.

90. Palmieri, *Catholic Encyclopedia,* vol. 13, "Russia," 259.

91. Tretjakewitsch, 40–41 n. 28.

5. World War I

1. Warren H. Carroll, *1917: Red Banners and White Mantle* (Front Royal, Va.: Christendom, 1984), 26–27.

2. Rev. George Maloney, SJ, *Our Lady of the Kremlin* (Saint Louis: Queen's Work, 1956), 21–22.

3. Carroll, 63–64.

4. Mailleux, *Exarch Feodorov,* 96–99.

5. Forced to flee to Poland to escape execution by the Communists in 1918, Archbishop Alexis was astounded to be graciously received by his ex-prisoner at the palace in Lemberg (Lwów).

6. Wim Rood, *Rom und Moskau: Der heilige Stuhl und Russland beziehungsweise die Sowjetunion von der Oktoberrevolution 1917 bis zum 1. Dezember 1989* (Altenbirge: Oros, 1993), 37.

7. Countess Ledochowska was noted for her holiness and energetic work. She was the sister of the Jesuits' Superior General Wlodomierz Ledochowski. Foundress of the Grey Ursulines, she had been deported to Sweden in 1914 because of her Austro-Hungarian citizenship. She died in 1939 and was beatified in 1983.

8. Although "a thorough Pole in both sentiment and outlook," Bishop von der Ropp sought to keep the catholic ideal alive in the Church and was equal in his treatment of all the nationalities and both rites. Zatko, 44.

9. Rood, 34–36.

10. Rood, 44–48.

11. Muzyczka, 319–21.

12. Cyril Korolevsky, *Metropolitan Andrew, 1865–1944,* trans. and ed. Serge Keleher (L'viv: Stauropegion, 1993), 261–68.

13. Korolevsky, 189.

14. Bociurkiw, *Church,* 19 n. 79.

15. Mailleux, *Exarch Feodorov,* 100.

16. Mailleux, *Exarch Feodorov,* 104–5.

17. Korolevsky, 283 n.

18. Mailleux, *Exarch Feodorov,* 103–4

19. See Serge Keleher, *Passion and Resurrection: The Greek Catholic Church in Soviet Ukraine, 1939–1989* (L'viv: Stauropegion, 1993), 198–206.

20. Mailleux, *Exarch Feodorov,* 110.

21. Ledit, 52.

22. Ledit, 48.

23. Zatko, 51–52.

24. *Vladivostok Sunrise,* no. 3: 2.

25. Sergei Filatov, "Religion, Power, and Nationhood in Sovereign Bashkortostan," *Religion, State and Society* 25, no. 3 (1998): 270.

26. Ledit, 47.

27. Zatko, 45 ff.

28. Zatko, 48–52.

29. *Catholic Encyclopedia,* "Minsk," vol. 10, p. 333.

30. Zatko, 52

31. Baedeker, 250.

32. Dunn, *Church,* 14; Zatko, 45.

33. Rood, 34.

34. Zatko, 55.

35. Zatko, 40–41.

36. Rood, 42.

37. The chronology of Fatima and events of the Great War are taken from Carroll, 70–111, unless otherwise cited.

38. The Committee for Public Safety (Socialist Revolutionary and Constitutional Democrats) led the only organized opposition in Moscow, and surrendered the city to the Bolsheviks on November 4, 1917.

6. "And the Flood Swept Them All Away," November 1917–Winter 1918

1. See E. H. Carr, *The Russian Revolution from Lenin to Stalin* (New York: Free Press, 1979), chaps. 2–3; Evan Mawdsley, *The Russian Civil War* (Boston: Allen and Unwin, 1987), chap. 1, esp. pp. 12–14.

2. Michael Polsky, *The New Martyrs of Russia* (Montreal: Brotherhood of St. John of Pochaev, 1972), 43–44.

3. Zatko, 66–68; Pospielovsky, *Church,* vol. 1, pp. 20–22.

4. Felix Corley, *Religion in the Soviet Union: An Archival Reader* (London: Macmillan, 1996), 13.

5. Zatko, 51. The January 1920 issue was the last to be published after the paper was first suppressed by the Bolsheviks in June 1918, and before it was permanently closed down in 1923.

6. Zatko, 69.

7. Stehle, 16.

8. Zatko, 67–68.

9. Zatko, 73, quoting the Mogilev *Chronicle* of January 1920.

10. Filatov, "Bashkortostan," 270.

11. McCullagh, 126.

12. Stehle, 11–12 (contrary to Stehle's comment, the May 1918 procession was not the first and only Corpus Christi procession under Soviet rule: sporadic processions were held until the early 1920s); Mailleux, *Exarch Feodorov,* 112.

13. Zatko, 69.

14. Zatko, 68.

15. Zatko, 64.

16. Dunn, *Church,* 31; Zatko, 69–72.

17. Zatko, 50–51.

18. Stehle, 20; see also U.S. Library of Congress, "Revelations from the Russian Archives," *America Online,* July 8, 1992).

19. Polsky, 81–84.

20. Corley, *Religion,* 14.

21. Stehle, 19.

8. The Russo-Polish War: Red Star versus White Eagle

1. Norman Davies, *White Eagle, Red Star: The Polish-Soviet War 1919–1920* (London: Orbis, 1986), 27.

2. Zatko, 92

3. Zatko, 97.

4. Davies, *White Eagle* 123–5; Zatko, 96–97.

5. Davies, 97.

6. Rev. Henry Rope, *Benedict XV: The Pope of Peace* (London: Catholic Book Club, 1940), 244–45.

7. Rope, 248.

8. See Davies, *White Eagle,* 199–207.

9. Rope, 249.

10. Kessler, 270.

11. Zatko, 82–83.

12. Almedingen, 35–37.

13. Almedingen, 79–81.

14. Walter H. Peters, *The Life of Benedict XV* (Milwaukee: Bruce, 1959), 247–9.

15. Zatko, 87.

16. Kessler, chap. 59; Zatko, 88.

17. Biographical references to priests are taken from Schnurr, "Verzeichnis," *Die Kirchen . . . ,* 1972 ed.

18. Joseph S. Height, *Paradise on the Steppe* (Bismarck: North Dakota Historical Society of Germans from Russia, 1980), 327.

19. The 6,000 Saratov Catholics were left orphaned and the cathedral was threatened with permanent closure, until the fortuitous arrival of Father Adam Desch, recently released from jail. Catholic services at Saint Clement's would continue for some years to come. Kessler, 254.

20. Kessler, 254–5.

21. Kessler, 271.

22. Zatko, 80.

23. Almedingen, 86. The resistance by parishioners was used by the Soviets in the Cieplak show trial of 1923 as proof that Catholic priests were "exciting the people to rebellion" against Soviet power.

24. Almedingen, 89.

25. Almedingen, 89–90; Zatko, 79. It seems that both authors are referring to the same incident.

26. Kessler, 271.

27. Zatko, 75–76.

28. Stehle, 395 n. 26.

29. Zatko, 77 ff.

30. Zatko, 80–83.

31. Mikhail Heller and Aleksandr Nekrich, *Utopia in Power,* trans. Phyllis B. Carlos (New York: Summit Books, 1986), 112–14.

32. See Ewald Ammende, *Human Life in Russia* (London: Allen and Unwin, 1936), 136–37.

33. A detailed history of the Armenians' struggle for independence, their repeated massacre and flight, their fight against superior forces, and their ultimate abandonment by the West and conquest by the Bolsheviks can be found in Richard Hovannisian's *Remembrance and Denial: The Case of the Armenian Genocide* (Detroit: Wayne Univ. Press, 1998).

34. Zatko, 56.

35. C. J. Peters, "The Georgian Orthodox Church," *Eastern Christianity and Politics in the Twentieth Century,* ed. Pedro Ramet (Durham, N.C.: Duke Univ. Press, 1988), 289–90.

36. Attwater, *Catholic,* 132; personal correspondence with Rev. Edmund Idranyi, 1988; Roberson, 37.

37. Personal correspondence with Rev. Edmund Idranyi, 1988.

38. *Ecumenical News International,* Nov. 16, 1997; Catholic news report in *Hong Kong Sunday Examiner,* Dec. 7, 1997.

39. Lorenz, *Römisch-katholische Kirche,* 138. Deanery listing is from Kessler, which in turn is based on Schnurr, *Die Kirchen.* 1972 ed.

40. Lorenz, *Römisch-katholische Kirche,* 79.

41. Paul Mailleux, SJ, "Catholics in the Soviet Union," in *Aspects of Religion in the Soviet Union, 1917–67,* ed. Richard N. Marshall, Jr. (Chicago: Univ. of Chicago Press, 1971), 376–77; Lorenz, *Römisch-katolische Kirche,* 20.

42. Peter Alagiagian, SJ, *My Prisons in Soviet Paradise* trans. Mary Heney, SCIM (Gardenvale, Quebec: Harpell's Press, 1969), viii.

43. Carr, 229.

44. Schnurr, *Die Kirchen,* 1972 ed., 31; Height, 235. Although Bishop Kessler never returned to his homeland again, he continued to raise money for the Russia Germans for famine relief, and wrote his history of the diocese while living at a convent at Zinnowitz. The *Klemensblatt* continued to be published in Germany for some years, receiving letters from the Catholics living along the Volga and Black Sea. Bishop Kessler died in 1933, and was buried in Bavaria alongside the body of Bishop Zottman, who had also died away from home.

45. Zatko, 97.

46. Zatko, 88–90.

9. The Golgotha of Siberia and the Far East, 1918–1922

1. One can question the judgment of Rome in nominating de Guebriant, a citizen of an Allied Power that had intervened on the side of the Whites in the civil war—surely not a move that would be welcomed either by nationalists or by Bolsheviks.

2. Zatko, 76.

3. Albert Galter, *Red Book of the Persecuted Church* (Westminster, Md.: Newman Press, 1957), 40.

4. McCullagh, 106–7.

5. W. H. Peters, 247–48.

6. Russell E. Snow, *The Bolsheviks in Siberia: 1917–18* (London: Univ. Press, 1977), 214–229.

7. Canfield F. Smith, *Vladivostok under Red and White Rule* (Seattle: Univ. of Washington Press, 1975), esp. 158–65.

8. See Dzwonkowski, 49.

9. Teodorovich, 211.

10. Zatko, 56.

11. *Vladivostok Sunrise,* nos. 2, 3; Galter, 40.

12. Dzwonkowski, 46.

13. *Annuario Pontificio, 1930,* 67; *Vladivostok Sunrise,* no. 15 (1996), 3.

14. Communication with Brother Daniel Maurer, CJD, 1994.

15. Kolarz, 198; Teodorovich, 211.

16. *Poles in Far East, Vladivostok Sunrise,* no. 3, 1–2.

17. Communications with Father Myron Effing, 1996–1997.

18. Lenga speech, 1995.

10. Survival—But What Next? 1920–1922

1. The participants in the Kronshtadt rebellion were finally exonerated in January 1994 with a decree of rehabilitation by President Boris Yeltsin and with the commissioning of a monument to their memory. The decree made clear that Lenin was intimately involved in the implementation of terror in Russia after 1917.

2. Robert Conquest, *Harvest of Sorrow: Soviet Collectivization and the Terror Famine* (New York: Oxford Univ. Press, 1986), 53–54.

3. Beeson, 36–37.

4. Zatko, 80.

5. Kessler, chap. 61.

6. Zatko, 88–89.

7. Biographical reference to priests are from Schnurr, "Verzeichnis," *Die Kirchen,* 1972 ed., and from Kessler, 255–61.

11. The Surprising Interlude: Germany, the Vatican, and the Bolsheviks

1. Indeed, diplomatic relations between the Holy See and the Soviet Union were not to be achieved until the Vatican's declaration of March 15, 1990, sixty-seven years after the breaking of formal diplomatic contacts *(New York Times,* Mar. 16, 1990). Even so, this was a situation of "pre-diplomatic relations" with the representatives holding the "personal status" of ambassadors: even with all the momentous events of 1989–1990, the Vatican was being traditionally cautious.

2. Information in this subsection is from Stehle, chaps. 2–3, and from Dunn, *Church,* 36.

3. Although part of the Weimar Republic, Bavaria and Prussia maintained separate concordats and diplomatic relations with the Holy See. Bavaria had an envoy at Rome; Prussia, an ambassador.

12. As Soon as Grass Began to Grow, It Was Eaten

1. Heller and Nekrich, 117.

2. Heller and Nekrich, 136–37.

3. Stehle, 397 n. 48.

4. Stehle, 398 n. 16.

5. Kessler, 277.

6. Alexander Vvedensky's Judas-like behavior weakened his own Church. His betrayal of Metropolitan Benjamin was especially painful: Benjamin had appointed him his chaplain and had treated him "with the greatest kindness." See McCullagh, 49–51.

7. Pospielovsky, *Church,* vol. 1, 97–8; McCullagh, 49–52.

8. Heller and Nekrich, 137.

9. Zatko, 121.

10. *Vladivostok Sunrise,* 1–2.

11. *Vladivostok Sunrise,* 1–2; McCullagh, 111.

12. Kessler, 277.

13. Kessler, 273.

14. McCullagh, 141.

15. Zatko, 172.

16. Almedingen, 33–34.

17. Zatko, 171, 183.

18. Rope, 283–84.

19. See W. H. Peters, 180–81.

20. Stehle, 43.

21. Natalia Petrova, *Twice Born in Russia* (New York: Morrow, 1930), 170–71, 177–79. Stehle, 399–400 n. 43, reports that Petrova was really Princess Maria Volkonskaya, who later married the German journalist Paul Scheffer and was thus able to leave Russia with her surviving child.

22. McCullagh, 303ff.

23. Stehle, 42–43.

24. Petrova, 172–73.

25. Stehle, 110.

26. Stehle, 44–45; Zatko, 113–15.

27. Stehle, 44.

28. Stehle, 61–66.

29. Stehle, 66.

30. Almedingen, 128–30.

13. The Passion Bearers of the Russian Catholic Exarchate

1. Bozidar Vidov, *Right Reverend Leontius Leonid Federov: Eparch of the Catholic Church of the Eastern Rite in Russia, 1917–1935,* trans. Hrvoje S. Beg (Woodstock, Ontario: Studite Fathers, 1992), 30.

2. Mailleux, *Exarch Feodorov,* 121; Korolevsky, 294.

3. Archidale A. King, *The Rites of Eastern Christendom* (Rome: Tipografia Poliglotta, 1948), vol. 2, 84.

4. Zatko, 59–60.

5. Korolevsky, 292–93.

6. Mary Grace Swift, OSU. "Moscow's Catherine of Siena," *America,* July 26, 1986, p. 30.

7. Feodor Wilcock, SJ, *Leonid Feodorov and the Catholic Russians* (New York: Russian Center, 1954), 16.

8. Korolevsky, 312–13.

9. Zatko, 180.

10. Mailleux, *Exarch Feodorov,* 159.

11. Korolevsky, 317–18n.

12. Zatko, 179.

13. Mailleux, *Exarch Feodorov,* 146.

14. Korolevsky, 296.

15. Korolevsky, 298.

16. Mailleux, *Exarch Feodorov,* 151.

17. Mailleux, *Exarch Feodorov,* 152–53.

18. Mailleux, *Exarch Feodorov,* 164–66.

19. Mailleux, *Exarch Feodorov,* 183.

20. Mailleux, *Exarch Feodorov,* 186–87.

21. Korolevsky, 313–14.

22. Korolevsky, 314–15. Emphasis in her own hand.

23. Wenger, 292.

24. Mailleux, *Exarch Feodorov,* 222.

25. Swift, 32.

26. Zatko, 181.

27. Mailleux, "Catholics," 368–69.

28. Zatko, 182.

29. Mailleux, *Exarch Feodorov,* chap. 16.

30. Unless noted otherwise, all information in this subsection is from Mailleux, *Exarch Feodorov,* 205–12.

31. Korolevsky, 302.

32. Vidov, 39.

33. Korolevsky, 302.

34. Wenger, 370.

35. Wenger, 288–89.

36. Vidov, 40.

37. Wenger, 290.

38. Vidov, 41.

39. Korolevsky, 304.

40. All information in this subsection is taken from Vidov, 43–47; Mailleux, *Exarch Feodorov,* 212–20.

41. Wilcock, 16.

42. Korolevsky, 318–19.

43. Korolevsky, 317n.

44. Wilcock, 15.

45. Korolevsky, 318n.

46. Jonathan Luxmoore, *The Tablet,* Jan. 4–10, 1998.

47. Tretjakewitsch, 181, 254–55.

48. Wilcock, 17.

49. Korolevsky, 308.

50. Wenger, 305.

14. "Icicles Formed Fantastic Gargoyles above the Altars": 1922–1923

1. Galter, 45.

2. See Dzwonkowski, 48–51, 73; V. Stanley Vardys, *The Catholic Church, Dissent, and Nationality in Soviet Lithuania* (Boulder, Colo.: East European Quarterly, 1978), 68; Zatko and Lorenz also cite statistics in their works. Dzwonkowski's are probably the most complete.

3. Almedingen, 28–30. On Kolpino Church, see McCullagh, 109.

4. Kessler, 269.

5. Anthony Rhodes, *The Power of Rome in the Twentieth Century: The Vatican in the Age of Dictators, 1922–1945* (Toronto: Hodder and Stoughton, 1973), 137.

6. All information in this subsection is from Almedingen, chaps. 4 and 7, unless otherwise noted.

7. McCullagh, 164.

8. Zatko, 123–5.

9. Rhodes, *Dictators,* 137.

10. Heller and Nekrich, 148–50.

11. Zatko, 119.

12. Almedingen, 29.

13. McCullagh, 165–67.

14. Zatko, 125.

15. Zatko, 126–27.

16. McCullagh, 373.

17. Mailleux, *Exarch Feodorov,* 164.

18. McCullagh, 311.

19. McCullag, 179.

20. Zatko, 127n.

21. Mailleux, *Exarch Feodorov,* 165.

22. Zatko, 128–30.

23. Zatko, 131; see also Monsignor Budkiewicz's report in Zatko, 189–203; McCullagh, 309.

24. Zatko, 131.

25. McCullagh, 387. At the same time, McCullagh comments, all remaining non-Soviet Protestant clergy decided to emigrate out of Soviet Russia. The only foreign clergy to remain were the Catholics; see McCullagh, 388.

26. McCullagh, 132–34.

27. McCullagh, 217–18.

28. McCullagh, 251.

29. Indeed, ten years later at a suburban train yard, the Lutheran Finns of Ingermannland were being removed from the Leningrad area. When, however, they and those remaining behind broke into a chorus of "A Mighty Fortress Is Our God," the Red Army did open fire, and scores died in a bloody massacre.

30. McCullagh, 114; Mailleux, *Exarch Feodorov,* 167.

15. The Cieplak Trial and Disruption of the Church

1. Ledit, 83–84.

2. All information about the Cieplak trial is taken from McCullagh, 170–78, and Zatko, 140–55, unless otherwise noted. It bears repeating that McCullagh was a direct observer, whereas Zatko drew on contemporary accounts such as McCullagh's, Soviet newspapers, and the writings of Father Rutkowski after his exile.

3. Mailleux, *Exarch Feodorov,* 168, describes Galkin as an ex-priest.

4. Kolarz, 198.

5. McCullagh, 143; 172.

6. McCullagh, 187.

7. McCullagh, 201–2.

8. McCullagh, 221.

9. See McCullagh, 238–41, 247.

10. McCullagh, 274–75.

11. *New York Times,* Mar. 27, 1923.

12. *New York Times,* Mar. 31, 1923.

13. *New York Times,* Apr. 4, 1923.

14. Ledit, 102–4.

15. Zatko, 174–75; Ledit, 114–5.

16. Zatko, 171–73.

17. See Mailleux, *Exarch Feodorov,* 111, 186, 221.

16. Catholics in the Gulag

1. To readers who doubt what follows, I recommend you peruse Solzhenitsyn's classic account, *The Gulag Archipelago* (New York: Harper and Row, 1973), from which much of this material comes. From the 1930s on, other accounts of the prison camps by émigrés, escapees, and deported Soviet citizens were published in the West, yet there were Westerners who denied all the barbarism and suffering these authors described until the Soviet Union itself collapsed and exposed its own shame. And there are probably still some who deny the enormity of its crimes.

2. Haruki Wada, "Koreans in the Soviet Far East, 1917–1937," and Hidesuke Kimura, "Korean Minorities in Soviet Central Asia and Kazakhstan," in *Koreans in the Soviet Union,* ed. Dae-Sook Suh (Honolulu: Univ. of Hawaii Center for Korean Studies, 1987), 51, 88–91, respectively.

3. *America,* Mar. 8, 1996.

4. Adam Hochschild, *The Unquiet Ghost: Russians Remember Stalin* (New York: Penguin Press, 1994), 126.

5. See Collen Combes. "Arctic Paradise," *Russian Life,* July, 1996, pp. 22–26; George Martin, "The Resurrection of Solovetsky," *Catholic Near East,* Jan.-Feb. 1998, 7–11.

6. Gary Wescott, "The Road of Bones," *Radio Liberty Report on the Soviet Union,* Mar. 1997, 19.

7. Hochschild, 202–3.

8. From a pamphlet published by the Archdiocese of Riga in 1995.

9. C. DeClercq, *Les églises unies d'orient* (Paris: Bloud et Gay, 1934), 97.

10. Bukowinski, "Memoirs of a Priest from Kazakhstan," Keston College, n.d., 10.

11. See Raphael Rupert, *A Hidden World: Nine Years of Confinement in Communist Prisons and Camps* (New York: World, 1963), 104–113, regarding medicine, which includes accounts of how medical students, veterinarians, or even foreigners with first-aid knowledge became recognized as full doctors.

12. Miracles of Mary, no. 2, trans. Timothy pp. 24–26.

13. Rupert, 146.

14. Johannes Steinhoff, et al., eds., *Voices from the Third Reich: An Oral History* (Washington: Regnery-Gateway, 1989), 164–66.

15. Steinhoff, 519.

16. Alagiagian, 105–6.

17. It is now finally accepted that the USSR also imprisoned thousands of innocent foreigners, Catholic and non-Catholic alike, in its prison camp system. Among these, according to the written accounts of Gulag survivors, were British and other Allied citizens (including American citizens); Allied POWs from all over the world; White Russians born in France and Belgium; Axis and neutral diplomats and other civilians, including the famous Swedish rescuer of Jews, Raoul Wallenberg; and great numbers both of Balkan and Czechoslovak nationals and of young people kidnapped, as forced labor "war reparations," from the new "progressive democracies" of Central Europe.

Italians, Spaniards, Yugoslavs, French, Belgians, German civilians, and Poles were generally sentenced to twenty-five years in special regime camps. Most who survived were released in 1955–1956—but not all. In the 1970s "era of stagnation," foreigners were again sent to the camps, usually on charges of "distributing anti-Soviet literature." Al Shifrin, "Foreign Nationals in Soviet Concentration Camps," *Ukrainian Review,* spring 1979, p. 59.

18. Rupert, 146; Bukowinski, 16, 27, 56.

19. Rupert, 147.

20. Georges Bissonnette, AA, *Moscow Was My Parish* (New York: McGraw-Hill, 1956), 165–66.

21. "Uncertain Freedom," *Frontier,* Jan.-Feb., 1990, pp. 13–14.

22. Rupert, 149–50.

23. *Miracles* 16–17.

24. Donald Nicholl, *Triumphs of the Spirit in Russia* (London: Darton, Longman and Todd, 1997), 221–22.

25. Rupert, 147–48.

26. Basil Boysak, *The Fate of the Holy Union in Carpatho-Ukraine* (Toronto: 1963), 226.

27. "Uncertain," 24.

17. The New Economic Policy, 1921–1928

1. Heller and Nekrich, 167.

2. Nicholas Brianchaninov, *The Russian Church,* trans. Warren B. Welles (London: Burns, Oates, and Washbourne, 1930), 177.

3. Carroll, 129–30.

4. Heller and Nekrich, 166.

5. Davis, 8–9; the title *Land Without Sunday* was given to a popular book published in Austria in the 1930s about the USSR.

6. Brianchaninov, 168.

7. Dzwonkowski, 323.

8. Fleischhauer and Pinkus, 51–52.

9. Brianchaninov, 179.

10. Heller and Nekrich, 166.

11. Zatko, 172.

12. Wenger, 495–97.

13. Ivan Lubachko. *Belorussia under Soviet Rule: 1917–1957* (Lexington: Univ. of Kentucky Press, 1972), 64–67.

14. Galter, 40.

15. Galter, 40; Schnurr, "Pfarreien," *Die Kirchen,* 1972 ed., 156.

16. Alagiagian, viii.

17. In the first religious service in the Kremlin since early 1918, the Divine Liturgy was celebrated in Assumption Cathedral in October 1989, for the 400th anniversary of the founding of the Russian Patriarchate. A number of Kremlin churches, including the oldest one and the famous chapel of the Iberian Mother of God at the Kremlin Gates, have not survived Soviet construction projects.

18. Schnurr, "Streiflichter," *Die Kirchen,* 1972 ed., 13–16.

19. Schnurr, "Streiflichter," *Die Kirchen,* 1972 ed., 14.

20. This trend toward increased religious belief and activity was noted (and deplored) by the Communists themselves, and led to the strict regulations of the 1929 constitution.

21. Fleischhauer and Pinkus, 52.

22. Kolarz, 201.

23. Schnurr, "Streiflichter," *Die Kirchen,* 1972 ed., 18.

24. Information on German ordinations in this subsection is taken from Schnurr, 1980 ed., 372–75 "Geistliche," *Die Kirchen,* 1972 ed., 206–9; Dzwonkowski, 142–46.

25. Dzwonkowski, 142–46.

26. Letter dated Apr. 30, 1930, from the Polish Foreign Ministry to the Primate of Poland, on the dispersal of the Franciscan Sisters of Leningrad, as quoted in Dzwonkowski, 200–201.

27. Schnurr, *Die Kirchen,* 1980 ed., 72–73, 115–16, 119.

28. Alagiagian, 34.

29. Almedingen, 110.

30. Almedingen, 110.

31. Jan Librach, *The Rise of the Soviet Empire: A Study of Soviet Foreign Policy,* rev. ed. (New York: Praeger, 1965), 44.

32. Henry Löber, "First-Hand Account of the Flight from Russia by a Group of Volga Germans in 1922," 1948.

33. John Toews, "Flight Across the Amur into China", *American Historical Society of Germans from Russia Journal* 2, no. 1: 7.

34. Nekrich and Heller, 112–14.

35. Attwater, *Catholic,* 131.

36. Roberson, 37.

37. Michael Tarchnisvili, SIC, "Das Christentum in Georgien," 1936, reprinted in *Der Christliche Osten* 49 (1994), nos. 3–4: 216. Father Tarchnisvili was a member of the Georgian Society of the Immaculate Conception, which is now extinct.

38. Teodorovich, 211.

39. Baedeker, 456.

40. Kolarz, 165.

41. Wenger, 304–6.

42. Kolarz, 479.

43. *Our Sunday Visitor,* June 26, 1994.

44. Schnurr, "Verzeichnis," *Die Kirchen,* 1972 ed., 207.

45. Pinsk was where Blessed Andrew Bobola had been buried.

46. A major irony of this period concerns the Polish government's campaign against the Eastern Orthodox minorities. When Orthodox churches in Poland were closed or turned over

to Catholic use—despite the protests of the Greek Catholic hierarchy in Poland—the USSR had the audacity to protest to Warsaw.

47. Zaprudnik, 86–88.

18. Secret Agent and Secret Hierarchy

1. Tretjakewitsch, 140–142.

2. Stehle, 82.

3. Tretjakewitsch, 142.

4. Wenger, 257.

5. Tretjakewitsch, 143, remarks: "This was perhaps indicative that Pius XI, not without a touch of humor, saw his Jesuit entering Russia as a sort of Trojan horse."

6. Stehle, 86–89, Dunn, 36.

7. John Pfeffer, *In Memoriam: Alexander Frison, Bishop and Martyr* (n.p., n.d.), unpaginated.

8. Wenger, 107–12, 121–22.

9. Wenger, 257.

10. Wenger, 94–96.

11. Kolarz, 201.

12. Stehle, 68.

13. Kolarz, 201; Galter, 49–50.

14. As quoted in Kolarz, 202.

15. Dunn, *Church,* 37.

16. Pfeiffer, *In Memoriam,* unpaginated.

17. Wenger, 258.

18. Stehle, 100–102.

19. Rhodes, *Dictators,* 135.

20. Rhodes, *Dictators,* 109–10; Stehle, 104–5

21. Wenger, 271–72.

22. Wenger, 273.

23. Wenger, 273–74.

24. Wenger, 366.

25. Tretjakewitsch, 145.

26. The sufferings of Bishop Sloskans did not end in Latvia, however. He was forcibly removed by the Germans in 1944; he died an exile in Belgium in 1981.

27. *Mirror,* no. 5 (1981): 1–2.

28. Rhodes, *Dictators,* 139–40.

29. See Kolarz, 199–200, Galter, 49–50.

30. List information taken from *Annuario Pontificio,* 1930

19. The Destruction of Rural Life and the Great Change, 1929–1936

1. Information on the years 1926–1928 and the beginning of collectivization is taken from Heller and Nekrich, chaps. 4–5, unless otherwise cited.

2. Merle Farnsod, *Smolensk under Soviet Rule* (Cambridge, Mass.: Harvard Univ. Press, 1956), 448–52.

3. Farnsod, 308–9.

4. Beeson, 38–39; Davis, 8.

5. William C. Fletcher, *The Russian Orthodox Church Underground: 1917–1970* (New York: Oxford Univ. Press), 97–98.

6. This would change only after the Sixteenth Party Congress, in 1929, when many churches were ordered returned because of "excesses" on the part of the agitators, although a church could still be closed if (1) another was located within three to seven kilometers (roughly two to four and a half miles); (2) the church's taxes were not paid; or (3) the overwhelming majority of residents near the church "petitioned" that it be closed. Farnsod, 435–36.

7. Fletcher, 80.

8. Fletcher, 81.

9. Davis, 10.

10. See Hewryk, which details the incredible destruction unleashed on Kiev.

11. Lubachko, 103 *passim.*

12. Nathaniel Davis, 7–10.

13. Gerd Stricker, "Die Kirchen der Russland deutschen," in *Der Kirchenkampf im deutschen Osten und in den deutschsprachigen Kirchen Osteuropas,* ed. Peter Maser (Göttingen: Vandenhoek and Ruprecht, 1993), 197.

14. Edward Walsh, SJ, "The Church in Contemporary Russia," in *The Catholic Church in Contemporary Europe, 1919–1931,* ed. Peter Guilday (New York: Kenedy, 1932), 265.

15. *Tablet* (London), Dec. 23/30, 1995.

16. Ammende, 146–48.

17. *Hong Kong Sunday Examiner,* Dec. 7, 1997.

18. Kolarz, 203.

19. Height, 351.

20. *Hong Kong Sunday Examiner,* Dec. 7, 1997.

21. Luxmoore, *The Tablet,* Jan. 4–10, 1998.

22. Dzwonkowski, 323.

23. Wenger, 299.

24. Korolevsky, 303.

25. Luxmoore, *The Tablet,* Jan. 4–10, 1998.

26. Height, 354–55.

27. Wenger, 362.

28. Schnurr, *Die Kirchen,* 1980 ed., 109.

29. Diplomatic notice sent to Warsaw by Kiev's Polish Consulate, printed in Dzwonkowski, 250.

30. See Schnurr, "Pfarreien," *Die Kirchen,* 1972 ed., 64–75.

31. Teodorovich, 215.

32. Kolarz, 479.

33. Mailleux, *Catholics,* 377.

34. Kolarz, 165.

35. Mailleux, *Catholics,* 378.

36. Karl August Fischer, "The Germans in the Caucasus, Particularly in Transcaucasia," *American Historical Society of Germans from Russia Journal* 9, no. 1 (spring 1986): 11.

37. Dunn, *Church,* 40.

38. Dunn, *Church,* 43.

39. Holmes, 95.

40. Alexis U. Floridi, *Moscow and the Vatican* (Ann Arbor, Mich.: Ardis, 1986), 11.

41. Floridi, 15.

42. Dunn, *Church,* 40.

43. Fletcher, *Underground,* 101.

44. Bissonnette, 6–7.

45. Dunn, *Church,* 41.

46. Dunn, *Church,* 41.

47. Walsh, 291–92.

48. Luxmoore, *The Tablet,* Jan. 4–10, 1998.

20. The Great Terror and the Annihilation of the Church, December 1934–September 1, 1939

1. Robert Conquest, *The Great Terror: A Reassessment* (New York: Oxford Univ. Press, 1990), 127–28.

2. Ammende, 147–48.

3. Fleischhauer and Pinkus, 71.

4. Fleischhauer and Pinkus, 63.

5. Wenger, 538.

6. Dzwonkowski, 170–71.

7. Alexander Weissberg, *The Accused,* trans. Edward Fitzgerald (New York: Simon and Schuster, 1951), 517–18.

8. Fitzpatrick, 359 n. 103.

9. The entire list of Catholic priests slaughtered at Sandomorch is given in Dzwonkowski, 235–36.

10. *Hong Kong Sunday Examiner,* Dec. 7, 1997; *Ecumenical News Service,* Nov. 16, 1997.

11. Stehle, 180.

12. Dunn, *Church,* 42.

13. Dunn, *Church,* 43.

14. Wenger, 274–79.

15. Wenger, 545.

16. Wenger, 373.

17. Wenger, 549; 552.

18. Wenger, 551.

19. Wenger, 559–60.

20. Anatol Levitin-Krasnov as cited in Nicholl, 219.

21. Wenger, 537–38.

22. Wenger, 480–81.

23. Wenger, 539–41.

24. Dzwonkowski, 258–262.

25. Adam Hlebowicz, *Kościół w niewoli: Kościół rzymskokatolicki na Białorusi i Ukraine po II wojnie światowej* (Warsaw: Glos, 1991), 128.

26. Wenger, 496.

27. Hlebowicz, 130.

28. Timasheff, 80.

29. The story was that, to placate Stalin's eye doctor, who pleaded that an Orthodox church be allowed to function for the believers in Odessa, one church was indeed spared. Every priest who celebrated in the church, however, was ultimately arrested (although the parish would survive until the German occupation in 1941).

30. John Phillipps, *The Tragedy of the Soviet Germans: A Story of Survival* (N.p., 1983), 99–100.

31. Wenger, 546.

32. Wenger, 545.

33. The account of the Karlsruhe show trial is from an eyewitness in Phillipps, 98; additional information on Father Greiner and Monsignor Krushchinsky is from Schnurr, "Verzeichnis," *Die Kirchen,* 1972 ed., 181 and 183–84, respectively. Whereas Phillipps puts the trial in 1934, Schnurr has the defendants being tried in 1935, as the Terror began to take root. Schnurr lists Father Köhler as having been arrested in 1934, although he was definitely put on trial with the others at Landau.

34. Height, 350.

35. Phillipps, 98.

36. Phillipps, 64.

37. Stricker, 197.

38. Felix Corley, "Believers' Responses to the 1937 and 1939 Soviet Censuses," *Religion, State and Society* 22, no. 4 (1994): 405–6.

39. Corley, "Responses," 406–7.

40. Wenger, 538–39.

41. Davis, 407–8, tables 1 and 3.

42. Davis, 408.

43. Kolarz, 204.

44. Conquest, *Terror,* 285.

45. Height, 358–59.

46. Hlebowicz, 93–95.

47. *Vladivostok Sunrise,* no. 7 (1994): 4.

48. *Vladivostok Sunrise,* no. 8 (1994): 3.

49. Dmitri Spilarski was reconciled to the Faith in 1991, when Catholic missionaries returned.

50. *Vladivostok Sunrise,* no. 7 (1994): 4.

51. *Vladivostok Sunrise,* no. 11 (1994): 4.

52. Kimura, esp. 88–90.

53. According to a report by Yasuo Mishima in Kimura, 90–91.

54. Stehle, 191.

55. Korolevsky, 505.

56. Mailleux, *Exarch Feodorov,* 221.

57. Wenter, 333.

58. Ambrosius K. Eszer, OP, "Ekaterina Sienskaja (Anna I) Abrikosova und die Geimschaft der Schwestern des III. Ordens vom Heiligen Dominikus zu Moskau," *Archivum fratrum Praedicatorum* (vol. 40, 1970), 347–51; Swift, 31–32.

59. Eszer, 357–59; 366–67; Swift, 32.

60. Wenger, 481–83.

61. Weissberg, 353.

62. Wada, 51.

63. The same pattern and destination were used in 1940–1944 with the forced relocation of Polish citizens, Balts, Soviet Germans, Tatars, and several Caucasus Turkic peoples.

64. Weissberg, 353.

65. Rev. Robert J. Fox, *Rediscovering Fatima* (Huntington, Ind.: Our Sunday Visitor, 1982), 112.

66. *Tablet* (London), Dec. 23/30, 1995.

67. Dzwonkowski, 237.

68. Rhodes, *Dictators,* 246–47.

21. The Crucifixion of Poland

1. Contrary to legend, the Polish cavalry did not charge the German tanks but rather tried to fight its way out of encirclements. Cavalry was important to the fighting in Eastern Europe throughout the war, and all the armies relied on horsepower at least to some extent.

2. See Davies, *God's Playground* vol. 2, chap. 19, "Niepodległość: Twenty Years of Independence" which details the turbulent history of the Republic of Poland, and esp. pp. 404–11, which deal with the minority issue. See also Neal Ascherson, *The Struggles for Poland* (New York: Random House, 1987), 77–81, for information on the plight of the minorities, the "Jewish Question," and the Polish right wing's mistakes.

3. See Andrej Chojnowski, "The Controversy over Former Uniate property in Poland," *Nationalities Papers* 16, no. 2: 177–90.

4. Korolevsky, 245–46, 247–48.

5. See Volodymyr Kubijovych, *Ethnic Groups of the South-Western Ukraine (Halycyna-Galicia) [January 1,] 1939* (Munich: Shevchenko Gesellschaft der Wissenschaften, 1983). Even in a cursory reading of Kubijovych's notes on pages 127–36, one repeatedly encounters phrases about forced conversions to Latin Catholicism and pressures to become Polish.

6. Rev. Krikor Petrowicz, *La Chiesa Armena in Polonia e nei paesi limitrofi:* [Part 3,] *1686–1954* (Rome: Collegio Armeno, 1988), 377–78.

7. Irena Grudzinska-Gross and Jan Tomasz Gross, eds., *War Through Children's Eyes: The Soviet Occupation of Poland and the Deportations, 1939–1941* (Stanford, Calif.: Hoover Institution Press, 1981), 8.

8. Grudzinska-Gross and Gross, 8. An excellent summary of the conditions in occupied Poland can be found in the introduction to Grudzinska-Gross and Gross, 1–28. A similar account, focusing on Lwów, is found in George Leski, *Poland's Secret Envoy* (New York: Bicentennial, 1988), 13–23. Information in this subsection is from these two works, unless otherwise noted.

9. Similar accounts of the obvious disparity between the Soviet standard of living and that of the countries "liberated" by the Red Army appear in virtually every book and article on the Soviet occupation by eyewitnesses and neutral scholars alike.

10. Related to author by Ukrainian Catholic émigré, January 1989.

11. Walter Ciszek, SJ, and Daniel Flaherty, SJ, *With God in Russia: My 23 Years as a Priest in Soviet Prisons and Labor Camps in Siberia* (Garden City, N.Y.: Doubleday, 1966), 30–33.

12. Dunn, *Church,* 51–55.

13. Dunn, *Church,* 69.

14. Poleski, 306.

15. Poleski, 305.

16. Poleski, 61.

17. Vincent A. Lapomarda, SJ, *The Jesuits and the Third Reich* (Lewiston, N.Y.: Edwin Mellen Press, 1989), 116.

18. Poleski, 305.

19. Cardinal Kazimir Swiatek, speech of June 10, 1995, Colorado Springs Conference.

20. Walter Ciszek, SJ, and Daniel Flaherty, SJ, *He Leadeth Me: An Extraordinary Testament of Faith* (Garden City, N.Y.: Doubleday, 1973), 22–23; Ciszek and Flaherty, *With God,* 30–31; Lapomarda, 118.

21. "Galicia" here refers only to the eastern part of the historic province, which constituted most of southern Poland, and which was annexed by the Soviet Union in 1939 and made part of the Ukrainian SSR.

22. Table of final statistics for the entire eastern province of Galicia on January 1, 1939, with percentages rounded off to the nearest percent. Kubijovych, 113; for explanation of his figuring, see xxii–xxiii.

23. See Manfred Klaube, *Deutschböhmische Siedlungen im Karpatenraum* (Marburg/Lahn: J. G. Herder Institut, 1984), 57–76. which gives information on the creation of many zones of German settlement of Galicia, while focusing on those who migrated from Bohemia, 57–76.

24. Kubijovych, 130–31.

25. Kubijovych, xxiii, gives the ethnic statistics cited here. Klaube, *Deutschböhmische Siedlungen,* 57, however, gives a total German population of about 135,000 for Galicia and Bukovina in 1939. If Bukovina had about 80,000 ethnic Germans in 1940, that would mean that Galicia had 55,000 Germans in 1939, a number larger than the non-Polish and non-Ukrainian minorities given by Kubijovych. Further, Paul Robert Magocsi, *Galicia: A Historical Survey and Bibliographic Guide* (Buffalo, N.Y.: Canadian Institute of Ukrainian Studies, 1983), 249, estimates the whole German population of Galicia as somewhat under 50,000 in the 1930s. Thus Kubijovych's minority statistics may be off by a few thousand people. Regardless of the actual total, ethnic Germans clearly did not represent a significant portion of the eastern Galician/western Ukrainian population, although their removal did have a significant impact on the Latin Catholic Church in Galicia.

26. Kubijovych, 128.

27. Dunn, *Church,* 52.

28. Dunn, *Church,* 76.

29. Lapomarda, 116–18.

30. Not all *Volksdeutsche* chose to accept repatriation to the German "homeland": there were always those who chose to remain behind because of their ties to non-German relatives, or who simply could not bear the thought of leaving their homes, regardless of the risks they ran under Soviet rule. At the same time, among the evacuees to the Third Reich, there were peo-

ple who had tenuous or absolutely no claims to a German ethnic identity, but who wanted to escape those same risks.

31. Klaube, *Deutschböhmische Siedlungen,* 103; Kubijovych, 85.

32. Kubijovych, xxiii.

33. See John-Paul Himka, *The Greek Catholic Church and Ukrainian Society in Austrian Galicia* (Cambridge: Ukrainian Studies Fund, Harvard University, 1986), chaps. 1–3.

34. Fedoriw, 224.

35. Attwater, 84–85.

36. A. A. King, 60, 63.

37. A. A. King, 66.

38. See Victor J. Pospishil, Victor "Sheptyts'kyi and Liturgical Reform," 201–21, in *Morality and Reality: The Life and Times of Andrei Sheptyts'kyi,* ed. Paul Robert Magocsi (Edmonton: Canadian Institute of Ukrainian Studies, Univ. of Alberta, 1989).

39. *Studite Monks Move Onward* (Toronto: Basilian Press, 1985), 22.

40. Ryszard Torzecki, "Der griechisch-katholische Ritus der katholische Kirche auf dem Gebiet der Republik Polen während des 2. Weltkrieges," in *Miscellanea Historiae Ecclesiaticae,* vol. 9, *Congrès de Varsovie, 25 juin–1ᵉʳ juillet 1978,* section 4, *Les églises chrétiennes dans l'Europe dominée par le IIIᵉ Reich,* 321.

41. Bohdan Bociurkiw, "Sheptyts'kyi and the Ukrainian Greek Catholic Church under the Soviet Occupation of 1939–41," in Magocsi, *Morality,* 101–2.

42. Information in this subsection on the Ukrainian Greek Catholic Church is taken from Dunn, *Church,* 74–77, unless otherwise noted.

43. Bociurkiw, "Sheptyts'kyi," 102–3.

44. *Studite Monks,* 22, 24.

45. *Studite Monks,* 24.

46. Andrew Turchyn, "The Ukrainian Catholic Church During World War II," *Ukrainian Quarterly* 51, nos. 1–2 (1985): 65.

47. Bociurkiw, "Sheptyts'kyi," 114–15.

48. Bociurkiw, "Sheptyts'kyi," 104–5.

49. Knapp-Kwasigorch, "75 Jahre Seelsorge im byzantinisch-slawischen Ritus in Berlin," *Der Christliche Osten* 39, no. 1 (1984): 29–30.

50. Dunn, *Church,* 68–69.

51. Bociurkiw, "Sheptyts'kyi," 108–9.

52. The results of the synods can be found in Korolevsky, 450–51.

53. Korolevsky, 452.

54. Korolevsky, 55, 64.

55. Bociurkiw, "Sheptyts'kyi," 106–7.

56. Bociurkiw, "Sheptyts'kyi," 105–6.

57. Information on the "Neo-Uniate" Church is taken from Edmund Przekop, "Die Neo-Union in Polen in den Jahren 1923–39," *Ostkirchliche Studieren* 32 (March 1983): 3–20, unless otherwise noted. English quotations are my translations.

58. Msgr. Alexander Nadson, "Bishop Ceslaus Sipovich, 1914–1981," *Journal of Byelorussian Studies* 5, no. 1 (1981): 7.

59. Nadson, 6.

60. *Bezbozhnik* editorial, April 1923, as quoted in McCullagh, 200.

61. Rhodes, *Dictators,* 155–56.

62. A. A. King, 87. That the use of the Russian Synodal Rite was demanded by the parishioners is rejected by Serge Keleher, "Orthodox and Greek-Catholics in Eastern Poland," *Religion, State and Society* 23, no. 4 (1995): 368, on the basis that the villagers' ancestors had been martyred and persecuted for the Greek Catholic Church and its Latinized rituals.

63. C. Simon, 208–10.

64. Korolevsky, 321–22; Fedoriw, 224.

65. Tatarynović, "Biancorutenia," 24.

66. Keleher, "Orthodox," 368.

67. One could question the wisdom of assigning a religious order with the title of a specifically Latin Catholic devotion to work among Byzantine Christians.

68. See Nadson, 5–13.

69. Through the occupation of western Poland and the annexation of Suwalki to East Prussia in 1939, at least ten "Neo-Uniate" parishes came under German rule, either in Siedlce diocese (as many as 15,000 faithful) or in Suwalki (10,000 faithful). Zygmunt Sułowski, "Statistique religieuse de la Pologne, 1939–1945: Migrations et pertes," in *Miscellanea Historiae Ecclesiaticae,* vol. 9, p. 418. Based on a figure of 40,000 "Neo-Uniates" in 1939, and Sułowski's estimate of a Greek Catholic population of 17,000 in the 1941 *Reichskommisariat Ostland,* which covered territory north of Galicia, including the Vilnius parishes, and 2,000 more in the Białystok region that was annexed to the Third Reich in 1941, 15,000 "Neo-Uniates" would be living in the 1939 Siedlce diocese.

70. Dunn, *Church,* 51–52.

71. See listing from Siedlce diocesan archives in Przekop, "Neo-Union," 15.

72. Przekop, "Neo-Union," 61–63.

73. Ciszek and Flaherty, *With God,* 33–34.

74. Kolarz, 226.

75. Lapomarda, 168–69.

76. After the revision of the Soviet-Polish boundaries after the war, only one "Neo-Uniate" parish survived, that of Saint Nikita at Kostomloty in Poland, under a remnant of the Marian Fathers.

77. Edmund Przekop, "350 Jahre der Union der polnischen Armenier mit der katholischen Kirche," *Der Christliche Osten* 35 (1980), nos. 3–4; 84.

78. Krikor Petrowicz, "The Armenians of Poland," *Eternal Flame* 3–4: 23.

79. Statistica con cenni storici della Gerarchia e dei Fedeli di Rito Orientale (Rome: Tipografia Poliglotta Vaticana, 1932), 388.

80. DeClercq, 97.

81. Magocsi, *Galicia,* 244; Simeon Vailhe, "Lemberg", *Catholic Encyclopedia,* vol. 9, 146.

82. Vailhe, "Lemberg," 144–46.

83. Petrovic, "Armenians," 3–4: 23.

84. Magocsi, *Galicia,* 245.

85. Vailhe, "Lemberg," 144–46.

86. Ernst-Christian Suttner, "Zur Geschichte kleinerer religiös-ethnischer Gruppen in Österreich-Ungarn und in den Nachfolgestaaten," *Ostkirliche Studieren* 38 (September 1989), 107.

87. Donald Attwater, *Living Languages in Catholic Worship* (Westminster, Md.: Newman Press, 1957), 22.

88. Przekop, "350 Jahre," 84.

89. DeClercq, 97.

90. Lorenz, *Römisch-katholische Kirche,* 140; Petrowicz, *Chiesa,* 378–79. Lorenz reports 27 priests, whereas Petrowicz cites a 1947 report of the Oriental Congregation, saying there were 16 priests.

91. *Statistica,* 86.

92. Kubijovych, 26, 130, 134. Armenian populations are listed in notes for the following counties: Horodenka, Kołomyja, Kosów, Sniatyn, and Stanislav. In the city of Stanislav, the number of Armenians was declining due to extensive Polonization or due to a growing population shift in favor of the Roman Catholics. There were 2000 "others" in the city; the Armenian population is not given separately. See p. 134 n. 12.

93. Kubijovych, 134.

94. Petrowicz, "Armenians," vol. 2 (no. 5–8): 18.

95. A. A. King, 553.

96. Anna Bouyanovskaya, ed., *Lvov: A Guide* (Moscow: Raduga, 1987), 121–23.

97. Petrowicz, *Chiesa,* 380.

98. *Statistica,* 388.

99. Przekop, "350 Jahre," 131 n. 17.

100. Sophie A. Welisch, *Bukovina Villages, Towns, Cities and Their Germans* (Ellis, Kans.: Bukovina Society of the Americas, 1990), 18: Welisch's listing of Gurahamora as having an Armenian Catholic church is in error. Correspondence with Father Norbert Gaschler, July, 1, 1991, which included a listing of Armenian Catholic parishes in Czernowitz from the *Bukowiner Haus Kalender für das Jahr 1911* (Czernowitz, 1911), 81.

101. Rev. Kazimierz Dola, "Life and Times of Archbishop Josyf Teofil Teodorowicz," *Armenian Review* 39, no. 4 (winter 1986): 73–82.

102. Petrowicz, *Chiesa,* 377–78.

103. Petrowicz, *Chiesa,* 379.

104. Davies, *Playground,* 448.

105. Davies, *Playground,* vol. 2, 287.

106. Lenga.

107. Jozef Gula, "Catholic Poles in the USSR During the Second World War," *Religion, State and Society* 22, no. 1 (1994): 18–19.

108. Grudzinska-Gross and Gross, xxii–xxiii. They report that 880,000 civilians were forcibly removed, although the Polish Army estimated that civilians removed from the eastern provinces totaled 1.15 million, or between 7 and 8 percent of the population. Grudzinska-Gross and Gross's figures are also used in *The Times Atlas of the Second World War,* ed. John Keegan (New York: Harper and Row, 1989), 207.

109. Kubijovych, xxiii.

22. The Great Patriotic War

1. Because the USSR was a "nation of nations," the dead were not all Russians. In Belorussia, scores of villages were burned to the ground and their inhabitants slaughtered.

Ukraine alone almost lost 5.5 million, many of them Jews and ethnic Poles. Half the Polish citizens forcibly removed by the Soviets died. The Russian war dead were estimated at fewer than 1.8 million. The low total is explained by the the preponderance of non-Russian nationalities in the Axis occupation zones. Norman Davies, "Not Twenty Million, Not Russians, Not War Dead," *Independent,* no. 380, December 29, 1987.

2. Davis, 14–15.

3. Office of Strategic Services, "The Status of Religion in the USSR," Mar. 14, 1944, secret report, declassified July 1950, from archives of Hoover Institution, Stanford University, 44–45.

4. Davis, 18–20.

5. OSS, 47.

6. OSS, 49.

7. OSS, 50–52.

8. OSS, 53.

9. Mark R. Elliott, *The Pawns of Yalta: Soviet Refugees and America's Role in their Repatriation* (Urbana: Univ. of Illinois Press, 1982), 125.

10. OSS, 42–44.

11. OSS, 27.

12. OSS, 28.

13. All information in this subsection on Catholic life in the Polish army gathering centers is from Gula.

14. Davies, *Playground,* vol. 2, 484–87.

15. Hanna Czuma, "Polish Priest Won't Forget Comrades of Youth," *Catholic Register* (Toronto), Mar. 17, 1990. The priest is Father Zdzislaw Peszkowski, a Pole who went to England after the war and who eventually was ordained a priest in the United States. A replica of Our Lady of Kozielsk hangs in a Polish chapel in London today.

16. Davies, *Playground,* 451–52; Rudolph Chelminski, "Katyn: Anatomy of a Massacre," *Reader's Digest,* May 1990, pp. 69–79.

17. "Polish Burial Site Identified," *New York Times,* June 20, 1990; CNN reports, June 17, 1990.

18. On the fiftieth anniversary of the Katyn Massacre, in 1990, the *Moscow News* weekly published research by historian Natalya Lebedeva. Drawing from the national archives, Lebedeva proved that the massacre was a "well-thought-through and carefully planned operation," and listed Soviet officials and policemen by name. They had murdered the Polish officers partly out of Stalinist revenge for the humiliating defeat of the Red Army in 1920, partly to use the emptied military camps for Baltic internees, but chiefly to carry out Stalin's plan to decapitate postwar Poland. Even so, the Kremlin did not formally accept responsibility for the deed. Apologies to the long-suffering survivors of the victims came slowly from Stalin's heirs and co-workers, and full responsibility was only accepted under the Yeltsin government. "Moscow Paper Lays Katyn Deaths to Soviets," *New York Times,* Mar. 23, 1990.

19. Gula, 33.

20. Dunn, *Church,* 80–81.

21. Dunn, *Church,* 88, 134–35.

22. OSS, 28.

23. OSS, 28.

24. Dunn, *Church,* 88, 134–35.

25. Bourgeois, 102–4.

26. Wenger, 542.

27. Bourgeois, 134–37.

28. Wenger, 553–54.

29. OSS, 31–32.

30. OSS, 32–33.

31. Vera Tolz, "New Information about the Deporation of Ethnic Groups under Stalin," *Radio Liberty Report on the Soviet Union* 3, no. 17(1991): 18–9. According to archives recently released under glasnost, Stalin knew that most of those forcibly removed were innocent of collaboration with the Nazi occupiers, but in his paranoia he had them removed anyway. The archives also show that Beria and his NKVD were involved in the whole process. Standard charges of collaboration were leveled against the Crimean Tatars, Bulgars, and Armenians, though the Crimean Greeks were removed because they had dared to engage in private trade. Tolz, 19.

32. Information in this subsection on the destruction of the German colonies and the Volga German ASSR is taken from Ingeborg Fleischhauer, "Operation Barbarossa and the Deportation," in Fleischhauer and Pinkus, 66–92, unless otherwise noted.

33. Fleischhauer, 69–70.

34. NKVD documents prove that the police agents could substantiate only two cases of spying, three of preparing terrorist acts, and four of sabotage; there was simply no evidence to justify removing, let alone executing, so many people. Tolz, 18.

35. Refugees resettled in Volga German villages found houses abandoned "in extreme haste, the tables still laid with half-eaten meals. Bellowing cattle, untended for hours or days, completed the spectacle of hasty abandonment of hereditary homesteads." Fleischhauer, 79–81.

36. Gertrud Braun, "The Deportation of the Volga Germans," *American Historical Society of Germans from Russia Journal* work paper 10 (December 1972), pp. 22–24.

37. Braun, 23.

38. Information in this subsection on the forcible removals of Crimean Germans is taken from Theodor Eisenbraun, "The Deportation of the Crimean Germans, 1941," *American Historical Society of Germans from Russia Journal* work paper 10 (December 1972), pp. 13–21.

39. Information in this subsection on the forcible removals of Russia Germans from the South Caucasus is taken from Frau K., "The Deportation of the Germans from South Caucasus," *American Historical Society of Germans from Russia Journal* work paper 10 (December 1972), pp. 25–27.

40. Fleischhauer, 77.

41. Tolz, 19

42. Nikolai Tolstoy, *Stalin's Secret War* (New York: Holt, Rinehart, Winston, 1981), 218.

43. Albert Kalme, *Total Terror: An Expose of Genocide in the Baltics* (New York: Appleton-Croft, 1951), 62–63, 72; Tolstoy, 244–47.

44. Tolstoy, 220.

45. Dunn, *Church,* 79–80.

46. Holmes, 136.

47. Rhodes, *Dictators,* 307–8.

48. Rhodes, *Dictators,* 256–60.

49. Graham, 63; Rhodes, *Dictators,* 262–63.

50. Dunn, *Church,* 90–91.

23. The Baltic States, Bukovina, and Bessarabia, 1940–1941

1. Tolstoy, 143, 148–49.

2. Princess Marie Vassilchikov, *Berlin Diaries, 1940–1945* (New York: Knopf, 1987), 42–43.

3. Information in this subsection on the Estonian Catholic Church is from Bourgeois, esp. 41–57, unless otherwise noted.

4. Tretjakewitsch, 270–71.

5. Dunn, *Church,* 65.

6. Stehle, 203, strongly contends that the Vatican did not give Archbishop von Proffitlich adequate direction and characterizes the Pope's reply as being "like the Delphic oracle," whereas Dunn, 69, asserts that the Vatican clearly told the archbishop he was free to choose whichever citizenship he judged more appropriate.

7. Rood, 318.

8. Information on the mass removal of Estonians in June 1941 is taken from Evald Laasi, "For Filling in a Few Blank Spots," *Sirp ja Vasar* (Tallin), Nov. 27, 1987, pp. 3–4, trans. Hilja Kuuk. Published in *Sirp ja Vasar* was one of the first Baltic periodicals to speak out on the Stalinist atrocities in Estonia in 1941 and 1945–1949; also R. J. Rummel, *Lethal Politics* (New Brunswick, N.J.: Transaction Publishers, 1996), 143.

9. Alexander Veinbergs, "Lutheran and Other Denominations in the Baltic Republics," in Marshall, 406.

10. Veinbergs, 406.

11. Galter, 54.

12. Arthur Vöbus, *The Martyrs of Estonia* (Stockholm: Etse, 1984), 54.

13. The 1942 figure was given by Bishop Anton Springovics of Latvia in a letter to Cardinal Luigi Maglione, cited in Dunn, *Church,* 79.

14. Dunn, *Church,* 41.

15. Lapomarda, 159 ff.

16. Rood, 318.

17. Cherney, 55.

18. Lorenz, *Römische-katholische Kirche,* 70.

19. On the urban churches of Latvia, see Baedeker, 58, 62; on its rural churches, see Lorenz, *Römisch-katholische Kirche,* 18.

20. Galter, 56–57; Lorenz, 69–70.

21. Galter, 58–59.

22. Galter, 60.

23. Lapomarda, 158.

24. Galter, 60.

25. Dunn, *Church,* 77–78.

26. Information in this subsection taken from Suziedelis, 184–86, unless otherwise noted.

27. Dunn, *Church,* 78–80.

28. Lapomarda, 154.

29. Kolarz, 207.

30. Vincentas Brizgys, *Religious Conditions in Lithuania under Russian Occupation* (Chicago: Lithuanian Catholic Press, 1968), 15.

31. Dunn, *Church,* 79.

32. Cited in Dunn, *Church,* 78–79.

33. Anthony Read and David Fisher, *The Deadly Embrace: Hitler, Stalin, and the Nazi-Soviet Pact* (New York: Norton, 1988), 471–73.

34. Nicholas Dima, *Bessarabia and Bukovina: The Soviet-Romanian Territorial Dispute* (Boulder, Colo.: East European Monographs, 1982), 30.

35. Dima, 15–18.

36. A. A. King, 32.

37. Dima, 76, table 4.

38. Duncan Gardiner, *German Towns in Slovakia and Upper Hungary* Rev. ed. (Lakewood, Ohio: Family Historian, 1993), 9.

39. Dima, 43–46.

40. Correspondence with Alex Hein of the Landsmannschaft der Bessarabiendeutschen, June 6, 1991.

41. Josef Erker, *Das Schicksal unserer Volksgruppe* (Stuttgart: Landsmannschaft des Bessarabiendeutschen, 1980), 151–152.

42. Sophie Welisch, "The Bukovina Germans in the Inter-War Period," *East European Quarterly* 14, no. 4 (1980): 423–25; Irma Bornemann and Sophie A. Welisch, *The Bukovina Germans* (Ellis, Kans.: Bukovina Society of the Americas, 1990), 1; Dima 35.

43. Attwater, *Dissident,* 113.

44. *Bukowiner Haus Kalender,* 81.

45. Rev. Norbert Gaschler, unpublished notes for "Die Kirchenbücher der Bukowina," 44.

46. Dmytro Blazhejovskyj, *Byzantine Kyivan Rite Metropolitanates, Eparchies and Exarchates: Nomenclature and Statistics* (Rome: Ukrainian Catholic Univ. Press, 1980), 58. Fedoriw, 211; *Bukowina Haus Kalender,* 80–81. The Maramoros diocese did not keep separate statistics for the Ukrainian vicariate's 17 Bukovina communities and the 21 Transcarpathian parishes in Czechoslovakia. There were 389 missions in this vicariate, and only 36 priests. With at least 21 priests serving in Bukovina, southern Trans-Carpathia had only 15 priests.

47. Although Zinkewych and Sorokowski, 239, lists Monsignor Simovych as "Mykhailo," the Bukowina religious statistics printed at Czernowitz, and provided me by Father Norbert Gaschler, list the monsignor as "Appolon."

48. Rev. Norbert Gaschler, "Nachrichten aus der alten Heimat," *Der Südostdeutsche,* June 15, 1991.

49. *Bukowiner Haus Kalender,* 79–81.

50. Norbert Gaschler, "Die Organisation der römisch-katholischen Kirche in der Bukowina," in *Kaindl-Archiv Heft 5: Mitteilungen der Raimund Friedrich Kainkl Gesellschaft* (Stuttgart and Munich: Friedrich Kaindl Gesellschaft, 1986), 47.

51. Correspondence with Father Norbert Gaschler, July 1, 1991. At the *Gymnasium* in

Radautz (Rădăuți) from 1928 to 1930, Father Gaschler worshipped in the Latin Catholic parish, where he saw the special sanctuary for the Byzantine Rite. When he returned to Radautz in 1939, a separate church had been built.

52. Gaschler, "Organisation," 45–47, 50–52.

53. *Bukowiner Haus Kalender,* 80.

54. Gaschler, "Organisation," 52–54.

55. Gaschler, "Organisation," 54.

56. Gaschler, "Organisation," 47.

57. Dunn, *Church,* 67.

58. Bornemann and Welisch, 17.

59. Welisch, "Bukovina Germans," 423–24, 433–34.

60. Gaschler, "Organisation," 55–56.

61. Correspondence with Father Norbert Gaschler, July 1, 1991.

62. Monsignor Reitmaier, like other *Volksdeutsche* "repatriated" into the "Greater Reich," did not find peace and security. In the Soviet invasion of Upper Silesia, he was at the town of Carlsruhe when it fell to the Red Army. He successfully blocked the entrance to the nuns' cloister with his own body to protect the Sisters inside from rape. (He remained in Carlsruhe, dying there in 1952.)

63. Gaschler, "Organisation," 56.

64. Lapomarda, 181–82.

65. Gaschler, "Organisation," 56.

66. Dima, 32.

67. Dima, 43–44.

68. Dima, 44.

69. Dunn, *Church,* 70.

70. See Dunn, *Church,* 72–73.

71. All reports received by the Holy See when communications were restored after the Nazi invasion corroborate this "restraint" on the part of the Soviets. Dunn, *Church,* 72–4.

24. Catholic Life in the Nazi-Occupied Baltic States

1. Dunn, *Church,* 92.

2. Galter, 61.

3. Wenger, 293.

4. Czeław Gil, OCD, "The Polish Province of the Discalced Carmelites during the Second World War," in *Miscellanea Historiae Ecclesiasticae,* vol. 9, 375–76.

5. OSS, 26.

6. Suziedelis, 189–91.

25. Catholic Revival in the Nazi-Occupied Soviet Union

1. This chapter draws chiefly on the accounts of three priests, namely that of Father Bernard Häring, now a noted theologian, then a medic and Redemptorist who accompanied the *Wehrmacht* from 1941 to 1945; that of Father Nikolaus Pieger, a Reich German diocesan priest who had worked with *Volksdeutsche* students in the 1930s, who had been to Soviet Russia once,

and who was invited by the German Embassy in Romania to follow the invaders as part of the temporary administration established by Bishop Glaser in southern Ukraine; and that of "Father George," an anonymous Slovak priest who accompanied the partisans in 1944–1945.

2. Father Häring's book, *Embattled Witness,* was at first reviled by many pro-Soviet Westerners when it was published in 1949, despite its foreword by Bishop Fulton J. Sheen, but Häring's descriptions of secret religious practices inside the USSR were verified in later years by a variety of sources.

3. Bernard Häring, *Embattled Witness: Memories of a Time of War* (1949; reprint, New York: Seabury Press, 1976), 78.

4. Häring, 25–28.

5. Gretta Palmer, as told to by Father George, *God's Underground* (New York: Appleton-Century-Crofts, 1949), 62–63.

6. Häring, 78.

7. Häring, 2.

8. Harvey Fireside, *Icon and Swastika* (Cambridge, Mass.: Harvard Univ. Press, 1971), 119.

26. Revival in Belorussia

1. Zaprudnik, 97–98.

2. *Times Atlas,* 93, 204.

3. Fireside, 128.

4. Fireside, 105, 128.

5. Fireside, 105, 128.

6. Poleski, 304–5.

7. Lapomarda, 175 n. 6.

8. Gil, 376.

9. Nicholas P. Vakar, *Belorussia: The Making of a Nation* (Cambridge, Mass.: Harvard Univ. Press, 1956), 189.

10. Poleski, 305.

11. Lapomarda, 175 n. 6.

12. Luxmoore, Jan. 4–10, 1998.

13. *Christian Orient* 14, no. 3, 158.

14. Lorenz, *Römisch-katholische Kirche,* 18.

15. Poleski, 304.

16. Fireside, 119.

17. Reports reaching Poland in the 1980s suggest that a large number of Catholic churches were functioning and were well attended in 1941–1944, Poleski, 301.

18. Häring, 79–80.

19. Fireside, 139.

20. Fireside, 139–40.

21. Lapomarda, 174 n. 6. Accounts differ as to Exarch Niemanciewicz's fate: some say he died from typhus, though most recent accounts concur he was shot; see Stehle, 220; C. Simon, 210.

27. Revival in Ukraine

1. Schnurr, "Verzeichnis", *Die Kirchen,* 1972 ed., 204.

2. Schnurr, "Verzeichnis," *Die Kirchen,* 1972 ed., 203.

3. Information in this subchapter on the Tiraspol priests is from Schnurr, "Verzeichnis." It is not known what the legal status of Fathers Schneider and Schönberger was, but it can be safely assumed that they could not serve as priests. Phillips, 98, reports that young people went to Father Greiner for these sacraments.

4. See 1942 photo in Schnurr, *Die Kirchen,* 64.

5. All information in this subsection on the mission in Transnistria is from Rev. Nikolaus Pieger, "Die religiösen Verhältnisse in der Südukraine (Transnistrien)," in Schnurr, *Die Kirchen,* 1972 ed., unless otherwise noted.

6. Height, 374–75.

7. Schnurr, "Verzeichnis," *Die Kirchen,* 1972 ed., 157.

8. Schmitz, 30–31.

9. Schmitz, 31–32.

10. Schnurr, "Verzeichnis," *Die Kirchen,* 1972 ed., 210.

11. Kolarz, 215.

12. Hlebowicz, 127.

13. Height, 362–65.

14. Information in this and the next subsection on the parishes of Zhitomir and Kamenets dioceses is from Hlebowicz, 127–37.

15. Zinkewych and Sorokowski, 241–42.

16. Stehle, "Sheptyts'kyi and the German Regime," in Magocsi, *Morality,* 130.

28. The Flight to the West

1. Christopher Duffy, *Red Storm on the Reich: The Soviet March on Germany, 1945* (New York: Atheneum, 1991), 193, 273–74.

2. *Times Atlas,* 532–33.

3. An excellent, and moving, account of the experience of Reich and ethnic Germans in the north during the last months of the war and the mass deportations that followed can be found in Hans von Lehndorff, *East Prussian Diary: A Journal of Faith* (London, Wolff, 1963).

4. *Times Atlas,* 512–14.

5. Guy Sajer, *The Forgotten Soldier* (New York: Harper and Row, 1971), 415–422.

6. Sajer, 439.

7. Duffy, 100–2, 250. At Posen, the Nazi commander was executing his soldiers who tried to surrender to the Soviets. When, however, he realized that he and they had been abandoned by Himmler and Hitler, he gave some of his troops permission to escape to the west.

8. Marjorie Knittel, *The Last Bridge: As Told by Eva Ziebart Reuer* (Aberdeen, S.D.: North Plains Press, 1984), 132–34.

9. Botting, 108–9; Visvaldis Mangolis, *Latvia in the Wars of the Twentieth Century* (Princeton Junction, N.J.: Cognition Books, 1983), 134–7, 150–52.

10. Mangolis, 156–57.

11. Earl F. Ziemke, *From Stalingrad to Berlin: The German Defeat in the East* (Washington, D.C.: U.S. Army Center of Military History, 1968), 172.

12. Elliott, 176.

13. Klaube, *Deutschböhmische Siedlungen,* 150.

14. Gaschler, "Organisation," 57.

15. Elliott, 172.

16. Theodor Schieder, *Documents on the Expulsion of the Germans from Eastern-Central Europe,* vol. 1, *The Expulsion of the German Population from the Territories East of the Oder-Neisse Line: Selection and Translation from Dokumentation der Vertreigung der Deutschen aus Ost-Mitteleuropa* (Bonn: Federal Ministry for Expellees, Refugees, and War Victims, 1958), 100.

29. Catholicism and Soviet Expansion into Europe

1. Rhodes, *Dictators,* 267–68.

2. Rhodes, *Dictators,* 259.

3. Anthony Rhodes, *The Power of Rome in the Twentieth Century: The Vatican in the Age of the Cold War, 1945–1980* (Norwich, U.K.: Michael Russell, 1992), 6–10.

4. Robert King, 27–30.

5. Gardiner, 18.

6. Paikert, 230.

7. Gaschler, "Organisation," 58.

8. Gaschler, Correspondence with Rev. Norbert, July 1, 1991.

9. Gaschler, "Kirchenbücher," 44–46.

10. Lapomarda, 184 n. 9.

11. Gaschler, "Nachrichten."

12. Cherney, 99–102.

13. Cherney, 109–19.

14. Cherney, 93.

15. A. A. King, 75; 87–88.

16. Athanasius Pekar, OSBM, *History of the Church in Carpathian Rus'* (Fairview, N.J.: Carpatho-Rusyn Research Center, 1992), 136ff.

17. Pekar, *History,* 145; Walter Warzeski, *Byzantine Rite Rusins in Carpatho-Ruthenia and America* (Pittsburgh: Byzantine Seminary Press, 1971), 168–71.

18. Robert King, n. 153.

30. Drawing in the Great Net of Stalin, 1945

1. Information in this subsection is from Tolstoy, 295–327; see also Elliott, chap. 5.

2. Davies, "Not Twenty Million."

3. Paikert, 12ff.

4. Vassilchikov, 245.

5. The fate of Wallenberg has never been satisfactorily explained by the Soviets. In 1957, they told Sweden that he had died in the Lubyanka back in 1947. There have been a host of sightings of this tragic hero, the most recent being claimed by Iosyp Terelya, who claimed he

saw Wallenberg at the Vladimir Prison in 1970; and the Ukrainian Catholic Church strove to keep track of him ever since. According to that Church, Wallenberg was transferred to a surgical suite at Vladimir Prison in January 1985. Sweden does not consider the case of Wallenberg closed as of 1999. See "Claim to Have Seen Wallenberg," *Tablet,* Jan., 1988, 43; John Bierman, *Righteous Gentile: The Story of Raoul Wallenberg, Missing Hero of the Holocaust* (New York: Viking Press, 1981); Harvey Rosenfeld, *Raoul Wallenberg, Angel of Rescue: Heroism and Torment in the Gulag* (Buffalo, N.Y.: Prometheus Books, 1982).

6. Schnurr, "Verzeichnis," *Die Kirchen,* 1972 ed., 209.

7. Schnurr, "Verzeichnis," *Die Kirchen,* 1972 ed., 210.

8. Lino Gussoni and Aristede Brunello, *The Silent Church: Facts and Documents Concerning Religious Persecution Behind the Iron Curtain* (New York, Veritas, 1954), 16.

31. The War to Destroy the Latin Catholic Church, 1945–1953

1. Davis, 27–29.

2. Heller and Neckrich, 463–65.

3. Dunn, *Church,* 114–15.

4. Dunn, *Church,* 129; 135–36.

5. Lev Haroska, "Soviet Policy Towards Religion after 1942," *Belorussian Review* 2 (1956): 23; Vardys, *Soviet Lithuania,* 78–79.

6. Vardys, *Soviet Lithuania,* 79.

7. Rein Taagepera, "Soviet Collectivization of Estonian Agriculture: The Deportee Phase," *Soviet Studies* 32, no. 3 (1980): 394–96.

8. *Catholics in Soviet-Occupied Lithuania,* 15, 26–28.

9. Vardys, *Soviet Lithuania,* 70–72.

10. Galter, 54–55; some of Galter's information is corrected by Father Velo Salo of Estonia, July-Aug. 1997.

11. Correspondence with Salo, June-Aug. 1997.

12. Kalme, 284.

13. *Our Sunday Visitor,* "Latvia Growing Stronger, but Struggles Remain," Sept. 12, 1993.

14. Pedro Ramet, ed., *Catholicism and Politics in Communist Societies* (Durham, N.C.: Duke Univ. Press, 1990), 54.

15. *Religion in Communist Lands,* "New Cardinals in Eastern Europe," vol. 11, no. 2 (1983): 206–7.

16. Kolarz, 211–12; *Aglonas Bazilika,* 43.

17. Galter, 62.

18. Father Werenfried van Straaten, O. Praem, *Where God Weeps* (San Francisco: Ignatius Press, 1989), 189.

19. Brizgys, 13–14.

20. Kalme, 257–59.

21. *Soviet-Occupied Lithuania,* 28.

22. Vardys, *Soviet Lithuania,* 77.

23. Brizgys, 18–19.

24. *Lithuanian Franciscan Friars,* op. cit.

25. *Tablet,* Mar. 16, 1991, 335.

26. Kalme, 183.

27. Brizgys, 19.

28. Vardys, *Soviet Lithuania,* 77.

29. Information on the Catholic parishes is drawn from April and May 1992 reports on Kaliningrad by Richard Blum for Aid to the Church in Need, unless otherwise noted.

30. George Schöpflin, ed., *The Soviet Union and Eastern Europe* (New York: Facts on File, 1988), 588.

31. Roman Szporluk, "West Ukraine and West Belorussia: Historical Tradition, Social Communication and Linguistic Assimilation," *Soviet Studies* 31, no. 1 (1979): 77.

32. Szporluk, 79–80.

33. By contrast, official toleration of Ukrainian in the western UkSSR hindered Russification and Sovietization there. Though widely adopted in the cities of eastern and central Ukraine, Russian failed to gain a stronghold in the cities of western Ukraine, where fewer than 3 percent of urban residents considered it their native language by 1970. Indeed, Ukrainian nationalism in the western oblasts of the UkSSR would present a problem for the Soviets until the end of the Soviet Union. Szporluk, 89ff.

34. The balance of this section on the BSSR is based on information from Haroska, 111–14, unless otherwise noted.

35. Hlebowicz, 13.

36. Simon Kabysh, "The Belorussians," in Deker and Lebed, 86–87; Haroska, "Belorussia," 111.

37. Hlebowicz, 13.

38. Zaprudnik, 102.

39. Hlebowicz, 14.

40. Hlebowicz, 14–15.

41. Hlebowicz, 18ff.

42. Marite Sapiets, ed., "The Catholic Church in Byelorussia," *Religion in Communist Lands* 10, no. 2: 180. The number of church buildings is taken from Poleski.

43. Hlebowicz, 10.

44. Hlebowicz, 11–12.

45. Hlebowicz, 16–17.

46. Report of the provincial of the Sisters of the Holy Family in Poland, 1992.

47. Report of mother general, of the Sisters of the Holy Family in Poland, 1990.

48. Hlebowicz, 23.

49. Hlebowicz, 93–94.

50. Hlebowicz, 18ff.

51. Poleski, 301.

52. Hlebowicz, 11.

53. Hlebowicz, 16; 63.

54. Hlebowicz, 10.

55. Haroska, "Byelorussia," 112.

56. Haroska, "Byelorussia," 112.

57. Poleski, 303–5; Hlebowicz, 94–95.

58. Swiatek.

59. Hlebowicz, 16.

60. Poleski, table 2, 313.

61. Hlebowicz, 89–91.

62. A. Drujski, *Religious Life in Byelorussia* (Chicago: n.p., n.d.), 4 n. 7.

63. Poleski, 306.

64. Roman Solchanykk and Ivan Hvat, "The Catholic Church in the Soviet Union," in Ramet, *Catholicism,* 62.

65. Hlebowicz, 13.

66. Poleski, 306; Hlebowicz, 68–69.

67. Hlebowicz, 152.

68. Sapiets, 180–81.

69. Haroska, "Soviet Policy," 24.

70. Maria Starzynska, *Eleven Prie-Dieux* (Rome: Pontifical Univ. Gregorian, 1992), 52.

71. Hlebowicz, 98–99.

72. Hlebowicz, 98.

73. Vasyl Markus, "Religion and Nationalism in Ukraine," in *Religion and Nationalism in Soviet and East European Politics,* ed. Pedro Ramet (Durham, N.C.: Duke Univ. Press, 1984), 139.

74. Hlebowicz, 97–98.

75. Hlebowicz, 98–99.

76. Information in this subsection is taken from Markus, "Religion and Nationalism," 139–44.

77. All information in this subsection is from Hlebowicz, 100–103.

78. Archbishop Baziak became the apostolic administrator of Krakow, following the great Sapieha, and was arrested in the Polish persecution of the Roman Catholic Church in the 1950s.

79. Hlebowicz, 101.

80. Related by residents to Brian Lenius, January 1995.

81. Hlebowicz, 100.

82. Hlebowicz, 127.

83. Information on the Latin Catholics of the Zakarpatskaya oblast is hard to come by. This is drawn from *Keston News Service,* Sept. 24, 1987; Markus, "Religion and Nationalism," 68; Lorenz, *Römisch-katholische Kirche,* 29; correspondence with *Volksdeutsche* sources in Germany; correspondence with Orsolya Molnar of the Latin Catholic Apostolic Administration of Zakarpattiya.

84. Correspondence with Emil Czipf of the Karpatendeutschenlandsmannschaft, Jan. 1991.

85. Hlebowicz, 102–3.

86. Hlebowicz, 103.

87. Bourgeois, 97.

88. Bourgeois, 102–3.

89. Bissonette, 7–9.

90. Bissonnette, 15.

91. Bissonnette, 260–61.

92. Kolarz, 214.

93. Correspondence, Dominican Vicariate of Saint Michael, Kiev, Dec. 1999.

94. Lorenz, *Römisch-katolische Kirche,* 78.

95. Kolarz, 215, Lorenz, *Römisch-katolische Kirche,* 31, 80.

96. Dunn, *Church,* 138 ff.

97. Davis, 27–29.

98. Bissonnette, 264–65.

32. The War to Destroy the Eastern Catholic Churches, 1945–1953

1. Rhodes, *Cold War,* 22.

2. Rhodes, *Cold War,* 21.

3. See Serhii Plokhy, "The Soviet Liquidation of the Greco-Catholic Church." *Logos* 35 (1994), 59–76.

4. Zinkewych and Sorokowski, 243.

5. Petrowicz, *Chiesa,* 378–81.

6. Petrowicz, *Chiesa,* 378–79.

7. Alagiagian, 166–68.

8. Gaschler, unpublished notes for *Bukowina under Austria: 1775–1918.* 42.

9. Norbert Gaschler, "Die Kirchenbücher der Bukowina," in *Kaindl-Archiv,* vol. 2 (1979), pp. 39.

10. Gaschler, notes for *Bukowina,* 44.

11. Petrowicz, *Chiesa,* 378–81.

12. *Hong Kong Sunday Examiner,* Dec. 7, 1977

13. Lev Haroska, "Soviet Policy," *Belorussian Review* 2 (1956): 26.

14. Kolarz, 90, 165, 214; Teodorovich, 215.

15. Mailleux, "Catholics," 377–78; Kolarz, 165–66.

16. Information in this subsection on Greek Catholics in the Metropolinate of L'viv is taken from Fedoriw, 237–38; Zinkewych and Sorokowski, 242; Dunn, *Church,* 108–10; and Korolevsky, 476.

17. Plokhy, 72–73.

18. Plokhy, 62–63.

19. Keleher, *Passion,* 40–41.

20. Dunn, *Church,* 115.

21. Note that the title of the "synod" uses the Russian form of the city's name, not the Ukrainian form.

22. Davis, 22.

23. The Ukrainian and Russian Catholic Church of Berlin managed to survive, though just barely. By 1960, refugees would boost the membership to nearly 30,000 faithful. The Liturgies were celebrated sporadically in the western sectors of the city by a Russian Catholic priest, Father Vladimir Dlusski, and by a German Jesuit authorized to minister in both Latin and Byzantine Rites. However, Soviet oppression had terrorized the people and many were reluctant to identify themselves as Greek Catholics. After the erection of the Berlin Wall, this would change. Organized parish life would resume after 1963, and the community was able to purchase a house and set up a church in Kreuzberg. See Knapp-Kwasigroch.

24. Knapp-Kwasigorch, 29–30.

25. Keleher, *Passion,* 50.

26. *Eastern Catholic Life,* "Archbishop Remembers," June 9, 1991.

27. Blazejovsky, 143–47.

28. Slawuta, 25–27.

29. Keleher, *Passion,* 63–64.

30. Slawuta, 26–27.

31. Blazejovsky, 143–47; Gaschler, "Kirchenbücher," 39.

32. Gaschler, "Kirchenbücher," 39.

33. Haroska, "Byelorussia," 112–13.

34. D. E. Mikhnevich, cited in Haroska, 113.

35. Keleher, "Orthodox," 369–71.

36. See chapter 29; see also Peter G. Sercho, *Diplomacy of Double Morality* (New York: Carpathian Research Center, 1971), esp. his chronology on pp. 494–96, and note on 386.

37. Bishop Alexander Chira, "Personal Diary of Bishop Alexander Chira," *Byzantine Catholic World,* Oct. 27-Nov. 10, 1991.

38. Chira.

39. Athanasius Pekar, OSBM, *You Shall Be Witnesses to Me* (Pittsburgh: Byzantine Seminary Press, 1989), 11–14.

40. Pekar, *Witnesses,* 22–23.

41. Pekar, *Witnesses,* 16–19.

42. Zinkewych and Sorokowski, 245.

43. Pekar, *Witnesses,* 23–24.

44. Pekar, *Witnesses,* 39; ECL, Feb. 16, 1992, article by Fr. Athanasius Pekar, OSBM, on forcible reunion.

45. This secret declaration was not published until June 26, 1990, when the archives were opened by the Transcarpathian Regional Soviet to right this wrong and restore churches to the Greek Catholics.

46. Zinkewych and Sorokowski, 245; *Byzantine Catholic World,* "Diary of Chira"; Pekar, *Witnesses,* 25–27.

47. In 1961, when the military court sentenced a Captain Indio to 10 years in prison for the murder of his wife, the accused cried out, "You sentence me to ten years since I killed my unfaithful wife. But when I was told to kill Bishop Romzha, you rewarded me with 10,000 rubles!" Needless to say, the captain was promptly hauled away.

48. Pekar, *Witnesses,* 32–33; Sr. Theophila, OSBM, "Testimony of an Eyewitness: The Last Days of Bishop Theodore G. Romzha." When Sister Theophila was quite elderly, and wanting to keep the record of the martyrdom correct, she recorded her recollections in November 1989, passing them out secretly to Monsignor Pekar. First published in the USSR in November 1990, these recollections were then published in an English translation in *Byzantine Catholic World* and *Eastern Catholic Life* in May and June 1991.

49. Earlier accounts were that the bishop was injected in the arm with a poison, as stated in Pekar, *Witnesses,* 35 and these conflicted with near-simultaneous reports that the poison was in a cloth held to the face; Pekar himself accepted the latter theory in 1997.

50. Chira; Keleher, *Passion,* 57.

51. Chira.

52. Letter of Bishop Nicholas Dudash of Hajdudorog, Hungary, quoted in Pekar, *Witnesses,* 29.

53. Bociurkiw and Strong, *Church,* 222–23.

54. Keleher, *Passion,* 59–69.

55. Chira.

56. Pekar, *Witnesses,* 89.

57. Bociurkiw and Strong, *Church,* 227.

58. Pekar, *Witnesses,* 58, 66.

59. Keleher, *Passion,* 59–60.

60. Pekar, *Witnesses,* 39.

61. Pekar, *Witnesses,* 78–84.

62. Davis, 28.

63. See Davis, chapters on Ukraine.

64. Their having chosen Orthodoxy is evidenced by the continued presence in 1995 of both Russian Orthodox and Ukrainian Autocephalous Orthodox parishes in western Ukraine.

65. The Greek Catholic Church in Bulgaria was spared destruction, though it was severely restricted regarding ordinations, parish life, and its religious communities, its bishop and many of its priests were imprisoned. Although the Greek Catholic Church in Hungary survived, with two eparchies, it lost virtually all of its monks and nuns and all its institutions beyond parishes. In Yugoslavia, the widely scattered and diverse Greek Catholics also experienced Communist oppression, but were not suppressed; in Albania, all religion was fiercely persecuted, being banned altogether in 1967.

66. Information on Ukrainian Greek Catholics in Soviet Bloc countries is taken from Iwanusiw, Oleh Wolodymyr, *Church in Ruins: The Demise of the Ukrainian Churches in the Eparchy of Peremyshyl* (St. Catherines, Ont., 1987), 14–16.

67. See Paul Robert Magocsi, *A Historical Atlas of Central Europe* (Buffalo, N.Y.: Univ. of Washington Press, 1993), map on p. 164, 165.

68. One parish of the "Neo-Uniates" has survived in Poland, the Church of Saint Nikita, in southern Białystok province; ten were forced into Latin rite and three joined Orthodoxy.

69. Mikola Volaciz, "The Population of Western Belorussia and Its Resettlement in Poland and the USSR," *Belorussian Review* 3 (1956): 15.

70. C. Simon, 211.

71. Poleski, 305.

72. Haroska, "Belorussia," 111.

73. Haroska, "Belorussia," 111.

Appendix A: Catholics and Jews in the Nazi-Occupied Soviet Territories

1. Avery Dulles, "The Church and the Shoah," *America,* Apr. 4, 1998, 3–4.

2. John M. Grondelski, "Auschwitz Revisited . . . The Polish Bishops on Christian-Jewish Relations," *America,* Apr. 27, 1991, 470.

3. Władysław Bartoszewski and Zofia Lewin, *Righteous among Nations: How Poles Helped the Jews, 1939–1945* (London: Earlscourt, 1969), 330–1.

4. After the war, "converted" Jews were seldom expected to continue in the Catholic religion, although many Jewish children who had been babies or toddlers at the time of rescue did not recognize their returning relatives in 1945–1946 and did not want to return to Judaism.

5. Nuremberg report by Franz Stahlecker, as cited in Sarah Neshamit, "Rescue in Lithua-

nia During the Nazi Occupation," in Yisrael Gutman and Efraim Zuroff, *Rescue Attempts During the Holocaust* (Jerusalem: Yad Vashem, 1977), 295 n. 12.

6. Cf. Gertrude Schneider, *Journey into Terror: The Story of the Riga Ghetto* (New York: Ark House, 1979), chaps. 1–12.

7. Information in the subsection on Lithuania is taken from Neshamit, unless otherwise noted.

8. Letter from Doctor Mordecai Paldiel, Director of Department for the Righteous, Yad Vashem (Holocaust Martyrs' and Heroes' Remembrance Authority) Aug. 26, 1990.

9. For an interesting account by the son of a Polish bricklayer who rescued the family of his Jewish former landlord, see "Bronek," in Bartoszewski and Lewin, 325ff. Accounts of servants accompanying Jewish employers are scattered throughout the book.

10. Philip Friedman, *Roads to Extinction: Essays on the Holocaust* (New York: Jewish Publication Society of America and Conference on Jewish Social Studies, 1980), 414.

11. Bartoszewski and Lewin, 516–17.

12. See Friedman, 417.

13. Bartoszewski and Lewin, 14.

14. Friedman, 416. Because of these conflicting reports, Bishop Rainis has a mixed reputation in Holocaust literature.

15. Bartoszewski and Lewin, 517.

16. Friedman, 417.

17. William Mishell, *Kaddish for Kovno: Life and Death in a Lithuanian Ghetto* (Chicago: Chicago Review Press, 1988), 361.

18. Joseph Kermish, "The Activities of żegota," in Gutman and Zuroff, 395.

19. Bartoszewski and Lewin, 17.

20. Bartoszewski and Lewin, 15

21. Stephen Redlich, "Sheptyts'kyi and the Jews" in Magocsi, *Morality,* 156. Information on the metropolitan is taken from this essay unless otherwise noted.

22. Bartoszewski and Lewin, 101ff.

23. Bartoszewski and Lewin, 209.

24. Bartoszewski and Lewin, 209–10.

25. The amazing story of rescuer Staszek is recounted by one of the survivors, Ruth Gruber, in Bartoszewski and Lewin, 428–32.

26. For Sister Maria Stella's account of the nuns' work, see Bartoszewski and Lewin, 352–60.

27. For the account given by the husband of the rescued girl, see Bartoszewski and Lewin, 405–6.

28. Bartoszewski and Lewin, 338–40.

29. For the account of this tragedy related by Mojszez Kin, who lost all of his immediate family, see Bartoszewski and Lewin, 437–40.

30. Bartoszewski and Lewin, 599.

31. The next four paragraphs are based on Kurt I. Lewin, *Journey Through Illusions* (Santa Barbara, Calif.: Fithian Press, 1994), unless otherwise noted. Kurt's father, Rabbi Lewin, was shot on the first day the Nazis occupied Lwów (Lviv).

32. Friedman, 190.

33. Redlich, 156.

34. Friedman, 208 n. 80.

35. Lewin, 109.

36. Turchyn, 66.

37. Friedman, 190.

38. Bartoszewski and Lewin, 602.

39. Bartoszewski and Lewin, 101–2.

40. Bartoszewski and Lewin, 217–18.

41. Pinchas Lapide, *Three Popes and the Jews* (New York: Hawthorn Books, 1967), 185–86.

42. Friedman, 191. See also Redlich, 161 n. 52.

43. Lapide, 186.

44. Lapide, 186.

45. Interviews with Maria Rybenczuk, 1994–1995, in Albuquerque, N.M. Her response was typical of many rescuers: "They were shooting people just becausse they were Jews. How could I not do something?"

46. Friedman, 448–49.

47. The fascinating tale of Fritz Graebe is related in Douglas K. Huneke, *The Moses of Rovno* (New York: Dodd, Mead, 1985).

48. Buried in the Latin Catholic cemetery in Jerusalem, Schindler, one of "the Church's least observant sons," remains an enigma; see Thomas Keneally, *Schindler's List* (New York: Simon and Schuster, 1982) and Dennis Hackett's review of the television documentary "Schindler," in *Tablet*, June 30, 1990.

49. Rhodes, *Cold War*, 225–26.

50. Dulles, 4.

Appendix B: Harbin and the Soviet Catholics of Manchuria

1. Bakich, 142–48.

2. Bakich, 135.

3. *Harbin Politekhnik Almanak*, no. 10 (1979), 140; Bakich, 143.

4. Stanford University Archives, "Political Reports from the United States Consulate at Harbin," Reels 2151, 3849, 3991 covering 1930–1941. The consulate was closed in December 1941, after the attack on Pearl Harbor. No specific citations are given in the endnotes from these copious reels. Dates are given in the text. All information on the refugee situation and the pre-war period is from these reels unless otherwise noted.

5. Karlinsky, 285.

6. *Guide to Catholic Church in China*, 126.

7. Tretjakewitsch, 168, 254.

8. Tretjakewitsch, 254–55.

9. Attwater, *Catholic* (1965 ed.), 120.

10. Attwater, *Catholic* (1935 ed.), 127–28; Feodor Wilcock, SJ, "Reminiscences," "To Our Friends," 16 (Summer 1974), no pp.

11. Roberson, 70.

12. Correspondence with Boris Mirkin, Nov. 7 and Dec. 3, 1989; *Harbin Almanak*, p. 140.

13. Correspondence with Father Myron Effing of Vladivostok, 1995; see also various issues of *Vladivostok Sunrise* 15 (1996) and discussions of Vladivostok diocese in chapters 4 and 9 of the main text for details.

14. Tretjakewitsch, 255.

15. *Orient Yearbook 1942* (Tokyo: Asia Statistics Co., 1942), p. 507; 510–12.

16. *Orient Yearbook,* 537.

17. George Ginsburgs, "Citizenship Questions in Postwar Sino-Soviet Relations," *Chronicle of Human Rights in USSR,* Apr.-June 1977, pp. 67–75. 67–9.

18. Ginsburgs, 69.

19. Wilcock, "Reminiscences."

20. *Harbin Almanak.*

21. *Harbin Almanak,* 143–44; *Guide to Catholic Church in China,* 97; correspondence with Moana McGlaughlin-Tregaskis, Mar. 5, 1990.

Bibliography

Unpublished Sources

Bendas, Rev. Daniel. Bendas Archives of the Ruthenian Greek-Catholic Church, Vinogradov, Ukraine.

Domanski, Francis, SJ. *The Great Apostle of Russia: the Servant of God Archbishop John Baptist Cieplak*. Saint Mary of the Lake University, Mundelein, Ill. 1953.

Gaschler, Rev. Norbert. Notes for *Bukowina under Austria: 1775–1918*.

⸻. Unpublished notes for "Die Kirchenbücher der Bukowina."

Kappes, Fr. Alois. Letter of Jul. 26, 1931, to parishioners in Josefstal. Provided by Lawrence A. Weigel.

Lenga, Bishop Jan Pavel, MIC. Speech of June 10, 1995, at Colorado Springs Conference on Aid to the Church in Russia, Siberia, and Kazakhstan.

Löber, Henry. "First-Hand Account of the Flight from Russia by a Group of Volga Germans in 1922." 1948. Provided by American Historical Society of Germans from Russia.

Office of Strategic Services, "The status of Religion in the USSR," Mar. 14, 1944. [Secret report declassified July 1950]; from archives of Hoover Institution, Stanford University.

Personal correspondence with: Most Rev. Josef Werth, SJ (apostolic administrator of Novosibirsk); Very Rev. Myron Effing, CDJ (Russian Far East); Rev. Brian Eyman (Byzantine Catholic Eparchy of Parma); Rev. Edmund Idranyi (Byzantine Catholic Eparchy of Van Nuys); Rev. Athanasius Pekar, OSBM (Ukrainian House of Studies, Washington, D.C.); Rev. Vello Salo (Estonia); Rev. John Kenrick and Rev. Krzysztof Broszkowski, OP, Dominican Vicariate of Saint Michael, Kiev (Ukraine); Dr. Sophie Senyk (Pontifical Oriental Institute, Rome); Phillip Simko; Felix Corley; Armenian Sisters of the Immaculate Conception; Sisters of Saint Basil the Great; Rev. Sergius Golovanov (Russian Orthodox in Communion with the Holy See, Siberia); Anita Kalnins (Archdiocese of Riga); Orsolya Molanar (Latin Administration of Zakarpattia); Boris Mirkin (Association of Former Residents of China in Israel).

Personal interviews with Armenian and Ukrainian Catholics who requested not to be identified.

Stadnyk, Methodios. "Nec Plus, Nec Minus, Nec Aliter: A Brief History of the Russian Byzantine Catholic Church and the Russian Catholics," Saint Michael Church Internet Site.

Sulius, Bitautis, OFM. "Ein Expose über die Kirche in Sibierien," 1990. Archives in Königstein, Germany, of Kirche in Not/Ostpriesterhilfe.

Swiatek, Cardinal Kazimir. Speech of June 10, 1995, at Colorado Springs Conference on Aid to the Church in Russia, Siberia, and Kazakhstan.

U.S. Library of Congress. "Revelations from the Russian Archives." *America Online,* July 8, 1992.

Books

Aberle, Msgr. George P. *From the Steppes to the Prairies.* 9th ed. Bismarck, N.D.: Tumbleweed Press, 1981.

Academy of Sciences of the Ukrainian Soviet Socialist Republic. *Soviet Ukraine.* Kiev, n.d.

Aglonas Bazilika Latvia: Katolu Dzeive, Rezekne, 1993.

Alagiagian, Peter, SJ. *My Prisons in Soviet Paradise.* Translated by Mary Heney, SCIM. Gardenvale, Quebec: Harpell's Press Co-operative, 1969.

Alexeev, Wassilij, and Theofanis G. Stavrou, *The Great Revival: The Russian Church under German Occupation* Minneapolis: Burgess, 1976.

Almanac of the Apostolic Administration of the Armenian Catholic Church in the Russian Empire, 1915. Tbilisi, 1916.

Almedingen, Martha Edith. *The Catholic Church in Russia Today.* New York: P. J. Kenedy and Sons, 1923.

Ammende, Ewald. *Human Life in Russia.* London: Allen and Unwin, 1936.

Armstrong, John A. *Ukrainian Nationalism.* New York: Columbia Univ. Press, 1963.

Ascherson, Neal. *The Struggles for Poland.* New York: Random House, 1987.

Attwater, Donald. *The Catholic Eastern Churches.* Milwaukee: Bruce, 1937 and 1965.

———. *The Dissident Eastern Churches.* Milwaukee: Bruce, 1937 and 1965 editions.

———. *Living Languages in Catholic Worship.* Westminster, Md.: Newman Press, 1957.

Bachatlowsky, Stephen J., CSSR, and George Perejda, CSSR, trans. *Vasyl' Vsevolody Velychkovsky: Redemptorist, Bishop-Confessor of the Faith.* Yorktown, Saskatchewan: Redeemer's Voice Press, 1991.

Baedeker, Karl. *Russia: A Handbook for Travelers.* 1914. New York: Arno Press and Random House, 1971.

Balic, Carlo, OFM, ed. *Maria e la Chiesa del Silenzio.* Rome: Accademia Mariana Internazionale, 1957.

Bardach, Janusz, and Kathleen Gleeson. *Man Is Wolf to Man: Surviving the Gulag.* Los Angeles: Univ. of California Press, 1998.

Bartoszewski, Władysław, and Zofia Lewin, eds. *Righteous Among Nations: How Poles Helped the Jews, 1939–1945.* London: Earlscourt, 1969.

Beeson, Trevor. *Discretion and Valour.* Philadelphia: Fortress Press, 1982.

Bennigsen, Georgii Pavlovich. ed. *Religion in Russia: A Collection of Essays.* London: Burns, Oates, and Washbourne, 1939.

Berdyaev, Nicholas. *The Russian Revolution.* London: Sheed and Ward, 1931.

Berkis, Alexander V. *History of the Duchy of Courland 1561–1795.* Towson, Md.: Harrod, 1969.

Bethell, Nicholas, et al. *Russia Besieged.* Alexandria, Va.: Time-Life Books, 1977.

Bierman, John. *Righteous Gentile: The Story of Raoul Wallenberg, Missing Hero of the Holocaust.* New York: Viking Press, 1981.

Bilaniuk, Petro. *Christianity in Eastern Europe and Ancient Rus' from Pentecost to St. Volodomyr (988).* Studies in Eastern Christianity, vol. 3. Toronto: Ukrainian Free Univ., 1983.

Biskup et al. *The Uniate Church: Forcible Establishment, National Failure.* Kiev: Politvidav, 1983.

Bissonnette, Georges, AA. *Moscow Was My Parish.* New York: McGraw-Hill, 1956.

Blazhejovskyj, Dmytro. *Byzantine Kyivan Rite Metropolitanates, Eparchies, and Exarchates: Nomenclature and Statistics.* Rome: Ukrainian Catholic Univ. Press, 1980.

Bociurkiw, Bohdan. "Religion and Nationalism in Contemporary Ukraine." In *Nationalism in the USSR and Eastern Europe in the Era of Brezhnev and Kosygin,* edited by George Simmonds. Detroit: Univ. of Detroit, 1977.

———. "Sheptyts'kyi and the Ukrainian Greek Catholic Church under the Soviet Occupation of 1939–41." In *Morality and Reality: The Life and Times of Andrei Sheptyts'kyi,* edited by Paul Robert Magocsi. Edmonton: Univ. of Alberta, Canadian Institute of Ukrainian Studies, 1989.

———. "The Suppression of the Ukrainian Greek Catholic Church in Postwar Soviet Union and Poland." In *Religion and Nationalism in Eastern Europe and the Soviet Union,* edited by Dennis Dunn. Boulder, Colo.: Westview Press, 1977.

———. *The Ukrainian Greek Catholic Church and the Soviet State, 1939–1950.* Edmonton: Canadian Institute of Ukrainian Studies, 1996.

Bociurkiw, Bohdan, and John W. Strong. *Religion and Atheism in USSR and Eastern Europe.* New York: Macmillan, 1975.

Bornemann, Irma, and Sophie A. Welisch. *The Bukovina Germans.* Ellis, Kans.: Bukovina Society of the Americas, 1990.

Botting, Douglas. *From the Ruins of the Reich: Germany 1945–1949.* New York: Crown, 1985.

Bourdeaux, Rev. Michael. *Land of Crosses.* Devon, U.K.: Pitman Press, 1979

Bourgeois, Charles. *A Priest in Russia and the Baltic.* Dublin: Clonmore and Reynolds, 1958.

Bouyanovskaya, Anna, ed. *Lvov: A Guide.* Moscow: Raduga, 1987.

Boysak, Basil. *The Fate of the Holy Union in Carpatho-Ukraine.* Toronto: n.p., 1963.

Brianchaninov, Nicholas. *The Russian Church*. Translated by Warren B. Welles. London: Burns, Oates, and Washbourne, 1930.

Brizgys, Vincentas. *Religious Conditions in Lithuania under Soviet Russian Occupation*. Chicago: Lithuanian Catholic Press, 1968.

Bukowiner Haus Kalender für das Jahr 1911. Czernowitz, Austria-Hungary, 1911.

Bukowinski, Władysław. *Memoirs from Kazakhstan*. Keston, Kent, U.K.: Keston College, n.d.

Camans, Joseph. "Lettonia: Terra mariana." In *Marie e la Chiesa del Silenzio*, 57–61.

Carr, E. H. *The Russian Revolution: From Lenin to Stalin*. New York: Free Press, 1979.

Carroll, Warren H. *1917: Red Banners and White Mantle*. Front Royal, Va.: Christendom, 1984.

Catholic Almanac. Edited by Felician A. Foy, OFM. Huntington, Ind.: Our Sunday Visitor Publishing, annual editions.

Catholic Church in Finland, The. Helsinki: Catholic Information Centre, 1988.

Catholic Encyclopedia. Edited by Charles G. Hebermann et al. New York: Appleton, 1907–12.

Chabonnier, Father Jean. *Guide to the Catholic Church in China, 1997*. Singapore: China Catholic Communication, 1997.

Charny, Israel W., ed. *Genocide: A Critical Bibliographical Review*. London: Mansell, 1988.

Cherney, Alexander. *The Latvian Orthodox Church*. Welshpool, U.K.: Stylite, 1985.

Chirovsky, Fr. Nicholas L. *An Introduction to Ukrainian History*. Vol. 3. New York: Philosophical Library, 1987.

Chronicle of the Catholic Church in Lithuania. Translated and published by the Lithuanian Roman Catholic Federation of America. 1975.

Cioroch, Salomia, OSBM. *Poglad na istoru ta vikhovnu dyalnict, Monaxin Vasilyanok*. Rome: Biblotheca Scientificarum et Popularium Operum Monarcum Basilianarum, 1964.

Ciszek, Walter, SJ, and Daniel Flaherty, SJ. *He Leadeth Me: An Extraordinary Testament of Faith*. Garden City, N.Y.: Doubleday, 1973.

———. *With God in Russia: My 23 Years as a Priest in Soviet Prisons and Labor Camps in Siberia*. Garden City, N.Y.: Doubleday, 1966.

Condon, Richard W. *The Winter War: Russia Against Finland*. New York: Ballantine Books, 1972.

Conquest, Robert. *The Great Terror: A Reassessment*. New York: Oxford Press, 1990.

———. *Harvest of Sorrow: Soviet Collectivization and the Terror Famine*. New York: Oxford Univ. Press, 1986.

———. *Kolyma: The Arctic Death Camps*. New York: Viking Press, 1978.

———. *The Nation Killers: Soviet Deportation of Nationalities*. New York: Macmillan, 1970.

———, ed. *The Last Empire*. Stanford, Calif.: Hoover Institution Press, 1986.

Corley, Felix. *Armenia and Karabakh*. London: Catholic Truth Society, 1992.

———. *Religion in the Soviet Union: An Archival Reader*. London: Macmillan, 1996.

Cunningham, James W. *A Vanquished Hope: The Movement for Church Renewal in Russia, 1905–1906.* Crestwood, N.Y.: St. Vladimir's Seminary Press, 1981.

Dae-Sook Suh, ed. *Koreans in the Soviet Union.* Honolulu: Univ. of Hawaii Center for Korean Studies, 1987.

Dallin, Alexander. *German Rule in Russia, 1941–1945: A Study of Occupation Policies.* New York: Octagon, 1980.

Davies, Norman. *God's Playground: A History of Poland,* 2 vols. New York: Columbia Univ. Press, 1985; *White Eagle Red Star: The Polish-Soviet War, 1919–20* (London: Orbis, 1983).

———. *Heart of Europe: A Short History of Poland.* Oxford: Clarendon Press, 1985.

Davis, Nathaniel. *A Long Walk to Church.* Boulder, Colo.: Westview Press, 1995.

DeClercq, C. *Les églises unies d'orient.* Paris: Bloud et Gay, 1934.

Deker, Nikolai, and Andrej Lebed, eds. *Genocide in the USSR: Studies in Group Destruction.* New York: Scarecrow Press, 1958.

Dima, Nicholas. *Bessarabia and Bukovina: The Soviet-Romanian Territorial Dispute.* Boulder, Colo.: East European Monographs, 1982.

Drunga, Mykolas. "Remnants of a Traditions." In *Atlaidai: Lithuanian Pilgrimages,* edited by Agimantas Kezys. Chicago: Loyola Univ. Press, 1990.

Drujski, A. [pseudonym]. *Religious Life in Byelorussia.* Chicago: n.p., n.d.

Duffy, Christopher. *Red Storm on the Reich: The Soviet March on Germany, 1945.* New York: Atheneum, 1991.

Dunford, David. "Dean." In *Catholic Encyclopedia,* vol. 4, 659–660.

Dunn, Dennis. *The Catholic Church and the Soviet Government: 1939–1949.* Boulder, Colo.: East European Quarterly, 1977.

———, ed. *Religion and Nationalism in Eastern Europe and the Soviet Union.* Boulder Colo.: Rienner, 1986.

———, ed. *Religion and Modernization in the Soviet Union.* Boulder, Colo.: Westview Press, 1977.

Dzwonkowski, Roman, SAC. *Kościół katolicki w ZSSR, 1917–1939, Zarys: historii.* Lublin: Catholic Univ. of Lublin, 1997.

Efimova, Miroslava I., and E. N. Chernolutskaya. *The Vladivostok Catholic Church under the Pressure of the Soviet Policy Against Religion, 1920s-middle 1930s.* Vladivostok: Samizdat, 1999.

Elliott, Mark R. *The Pawns of Yalta: Soviet Refugees and America's Role in Their Repatriation.* Urbana: Univ. of Illinois Press, 1982.

Ellis, Jane. *The Russian Orthodox Church: A Contemporary History.* Bloomington: Indiana Univ. Press, 1986.

Encyclopaedia Britannica. New York: Britannica, 1926.

Erker, Josef. *Das Schicksal unserer Volksgruppe.* Stuttgart: Landsmannschaft der Bessarabiendeutschen, 1980.

Fedoriw, George. *History of Church in Ukraine,* Translated by Petro Krawchuk. St. Catherine's, Ont.: St. Sophia Religious Assoc. 1983.

Fireside, Harvey. *Icon and Swastika.* Cambridge, Mass.: Harvard Univ. Press, 1971.

Fitzpatrick, Sheila. *Stalin's Peasants.* New York: Oxford Univ. Press, 1994.

Fleischhauer, Ingeborg, and Benjamin Pinkus. *The Soviet Germans: Past and Present.* London: C. Hurst, 1986.

Fletcher, William C. *The Russian Orthodox Church Underground: 1917–1970.* New York: Oxford Univ. Press, 1970.

Floridi, Alexis U., SJ. *Moscow and the Vatican.* Ann Arbor, Mich.: Ardis, 1986.

Fox, Rev. Robert J. *Rediscovering Fatima.* Huntington, Ind.: Our Sunday Visitor Press, 1982.

The Francis Skaryna Byelorussian Library and Museum, 1971–1981. London: Francis Skaryna Byelorussian Library and Museum, 1981.

Frazee, Charles. *Catholics and Sultans.* New York: Cambridge Univ. Press, 1983.

Friedman, Philip. *Roads to Extinction: Essays on the Holocaust.* New York: Jewish Publication Society of America and Conference on Jewish Social Studies, 1980.

Gallagher, Louis, SJ, and Paul Donovan, SJ. *The Life of Saint Andrew Bobola, of the Society of Jesus, Martyr.* Boston: Humphries, 1939.

Galter, Albert. *Red Book of the Persecuted Church.* Westminster, Md.: Newman Press, 1957.

Gardiner, Duncan. *German Towns in Slovakia and Upper Hungary.* Rev. ed. Lakewood, Ohio: Family Historian, 1993.

Garstein, Oskar. *Rome and the Counter-Reformation in Scandinavia.* Vol. 2. Oslo: Universitetsforlaget, 1980.

Gaschler, Norbert. "Die Kirchenbücher der Bukowina." In *Kaindl-Archiv,* vol. 2 (1979), 25–56.

———. "Die Organisation der römisch-katholischen Kirche in der Bukowina." In *Kaindl-Archiv,* vol. 5 (1986), 34–62.

Getter, Marek. "Die Behörden des Generalgouvernements und die Orthodoxe Kirche." *Miscellanea Historiae Ecclesiasticae. Vol. 9, Congrès de Varsovie, 25 Juin–1er Juillet 1978. Section 4, Les églises chrétiennes dans l'Europe dominée par le IIIe Reich.*

Gil, Czesław, OCD. "The Polish Province of the Discalced Carmelites During the Second World War," *Miscellanea Historiae Ecclesiasticae, Vol. 9, Congrès de Varsovie 25 Juin–1er Juillet 1978,* Section 4, *Les églises Chrétiennes dans l'Europe dominée par le IIIe Reich.*

Girmius, Kestutis K. "Nationalism and Catholic Church in Lithuania." In *Religion and Nationalism in Soviet and East European Politics,* edited by Pedro Ramet. Durham, N.C.: Duke Univ. Press, 1984.

Glowinsky, Eugen. "Western Ukraine." In *Genocide in the USSR: Studies in Group Destruction,* edited by Nikolai Deker and Andrej Lebed, 147–154. New York: Scarecrow, 1958.

Golovanov, Rev. Sergius. *Katolicheskaya tserkov I Rossiya.* Omsk, Samizdat, Region, 1998.

Graham, Robert A., SJ, ed. *Pius XII and the Holocaust: A Reader.* Milwaukee: Catholic League for Civil and Religious Rights, 1988.

Grudzinska-Gross, Irena, and Jan Tomasz Gross, eds. *War Through Children's Eyes: The Soviet Occupation of Poland and the Deportations, 1939–1941.* Stanford, Calif.: Hoover Institution Press, 1981.

Guilday, Peter, ed. *The Catholic Church in Contemporary Europe, 1919–1931,* New York: Kenedy, 1932.

Gulovich, Stephen. *Windows Westward: Rome, Russia, Reunion.* New York: McMullen, 1947.

Gussoni, Lino, and Aristede Brunello. *The Silent Church: Facts and Documents Concerning Religious Persecution Behind the Iron Curtain.* New York: Veritas, 1954.

Gutman, Yisrael, and Efraim Zuroff, eds. *Rescue Attempts During the Holocaust.* Jerusalem: Yad Vashem, 1977.

Häring, Bernard. *Embattled Witness: Memories of a Time of War.* 1949. Reprint, New York: Seabury Press, 1976.

Height, Joseph S. *Paradise on the Steppe.* Bismarck: North Dakota Historical Society of Germans from Russia, 1980.

Heller, Mikhail, and Aleksandr Nekrich. *Utopia in Power.* Translated by Phyllis B. Carlos. New York: Summit Books, 1986.

Herling, Gustav. *A World Apart: The Journal of a Gulag Survivor.* New York: Arbor House, 1986.

Hewryk, Titus D. *The Lost Architecture of Kiev.* New York: Ukrainian Museum, 1982.

Himka, John-Paul. *The Greek Catholic Church and Ukrainian Society in Austrian Galicia.* Cambridge: Harvard Univ. Ukrainian Studies Fund, 1983.

Hlebowicz, Adam. *Kościół w niewoli: Kościół rzymskokatolicki na Białorusi i Ukraine po II wojnie światowej.* Warsaw: Glos, 1991.

Hochschild, Adam. *The Unquiet Ghost: Russians Remember Stalin.* New York: Penguin Press, 1994.

Holmes, J. Derek. *The Papacy in the Modern World.* New York: Crossroad, 1981.

Horak, Stepan M., ed. *Guide to the Study of the Soviet Nationalities.* Littleton: Libraries Unlimited. 1982.

Horodenko, I. *On the Thorny Path: Martyrology of the Ukrainian Catholic Church in Pictures.* Regensburg: Association of the Ukrainian Graduates of the Metropolitan Andrej Sheptytsky Seminary of Munich and the League of Political Prisoners, Regensburg Chapter, 1948.

Hovannisian, Richard G. *The Republic of Armenia.* Vol. 4, Between Crescent and Sickle: Partition and Sovietization Berkley: Univ. of California Press, 1996.

———. *Remembrance and Denial: The Case of the Armenian Genocide.* Detroit: Wayne State Univ. Press, 1998.

Huneke, Douglas K. *The Moses of Rovno.* New York: Dodd, Mead, 1985.

Ilyin, Olga. *White Road.* New York: Holt, 1984.

Iwanusiw, Oleh Wolodymir. *Church in Ruins: The Demise of Ukrainian Churches in the Eparchy of Peremyshy.* St. Catherines, Ont., 1987.

Just, Sister Mary. *Rome and Russia: A Tragedy of Errors.* Westminster, Md.: Newman Press, 1954.

Kabysh, Simon. "The Belorussians." In *Genocide in the USSR: Studies in Group Destruction,* edited by Nikolai Deker and Andrej Lebed, 77–88. New York: Scarecrow Press, 1958.

Kalme, Albert. *Total Terror: An Expose of Genocide in the Baltics.* New York: Appleton-Century-Crofts, 1951.

Keegan, John. *The Second World War.* New York: Viking, 1990.

———, ed. *The Times Atlas of the Second World War.* New York: Harper & Row, 1989.

Keleher, Serge. *Passion and Resurrection: The Greek Catholic Church in Soviet Ukraine, 1939–1989.* L'viv: Stauropegion, 1993.

Keneally, Thomas. *Schindler's List.* New York: Simon and Schuster, 1982.

Kermish, Joseph. "The Activities of żegota." In *Rescue Attempts During the Holocaust.* Jerusalem: Yad Vashem, 1977.

Kern, Albert. *Homeland Book of the Bessarabian Germans.* Translated by Ilona Richey. Fargo: North Dakota State Univ., 1998.

Kessler, Most Rev. Joseph. *Geschichte der Tiraspoler Diözese.* Dickinson, N.D.: Rev. George Aberle, 1930.

Kezys, Algimantas, ed. *Atlaidai: Lithuanian Pilgrimages.* Chicago: Loyola Univ. Press, 1990.

"Kiev" *EB* 15:790–91.

Kimura, Hidesuke. "Korean Minorities in Soviet Central Asia and Kazakhstan." In *Koreans in the Soviet Union,* edited by Dae-Sook Suh. Honolulu: Univ. of Hawaii Center for Korean Studies, 1987.

King, Archidale A. *The Rites of Eastern Christendom.* Vol. 2. Rome: Tipografia Poliglotta, 1948.

King, Robert R. *Minorities under Communism: Nationalities as a Source of Tension among Balkan Communist States.* Cambridge: Harvard Univ. Press, 1973.

Kipel, Vitaut. "The Early Byelorussian Presence in America," *Zapisy* 17 (1983): 113–31.

Klaube, Manfred. *Deutschböhmische Siedlungen im Karpatenraum.* Marburg and Lahn: J. G. Herder Institut, 1984.

———. *Die Deutschen Dörfer in der westsibirischen Kulunda-Steppe: Entwicklung-Strukturen-Probleme.* Marburg: Elwert, 1991.

Kloberdanz, Timothy and Rosalinda. *Thunder on the Steppe: Volga German Folklife in a Changing Russia.* Lincoln, Neb.: American Historical Society of Germans from Russia Journal, 1993.

Knittel, Marjorie. *The Last Bridge: As Told by Eva Ziebart Reuer.* Aberdeen, S.D.: North Plains Press, 1984.

Kolarz, Walter. *Religion in the Soviet Union.* New York: St. Martin's Press, 1961.

Komjathy, Anthony, and Rebecca Stockwell. *German Minorities and the Third Reich.* New York: Holmes and Meier, 1980.

Korolevsky, Cyril. *Metropolitan Andrew, 1865–1944.* Translated by Serge Keleher. L'viv: Strauropegion, 1993.

"Kovno," *EB* 15:791.

Kozlov, Viktor. *The Peoples of the Soviet Union.* Bloomington: Indiana Univ. Press, 1988.

Kreilkamp, Hermes, OFM Cap. *These Friars Went East.* Huntington, Ind.: St. Felix's Friary, 1954.

Kubijovych, Volodymyr. *Ethnic Groups of the South-Western Ukraine (Halyc'yna-Galicia) [January 1,] 1939* Munich: Shevchenko Gesellschaft der Wissenschaften, 1983.

Küng, Andres. *A Dream of Freedom.* New York: Boreas, 1980.

Lane, Christel. *Christian Religions in the Soviet Union: A Sociological Study.* London: George Allen and Unwin, 1978.

Lapide, Pinchas. *Three Popes and the Jews.* New York: Hawthorn Books, 1967.

Lapomarda, Vincent, SJ. *The Jesuits and the Third Reich.* Lewiston, N.Y.: Edwin Mellen Press, 1989.

Ledit, Joseph. *Archbishop John Baptist Cieplak.* Montreal: Palm, 1963.

Lehndorff, Hans von. *East Prussian Diary: A Journal of Faith.* London, Wolff, 1963.

Lencyk, Wasyl. *The Eastern Catholic Church and Czar Nicholas I.* New York: Pontifical Oriental Institute, 1966.

Lerski, George. *Poland's Secret Envoy.* New York: Bicentennial Publications, 1988.

Lewin, Kurt I. *A Journey Through Illusions.* Santa Barbara, Calif.: Fithian Press, 1994.

Librach, Jan. *The Rise of the Soviet Empire: A Study of Soviet Foreign Policy.* Rev. ed. New York: Praeger, 1965.

Lieven, Anatol. *The Baltic Revolution.* New Haven: Yale Univ. Press, 1993.

Lincoln, W. Bruce. *In War's Dark Shadow.* New York: Dial Press, 1983.

Lins, Joseph, "Artvin." In *Catholic Encyclopedia,* vol. 1, 765.

———. "Minsk." In *Catholic Encyclopedia,* vol. 10, 333.

———. "Mohileff" In *Catholic Encyclopedia,* vol. 10, 428–29.

———. "Moscow" In *Catholic Encyclopedia,* vol. 10, 591–96.

———. "Saint Petersburg" In *Catholic Encyclopedia,* vol. 13, 374–76.

———. "Siberia" In *Catholic Encyclopedia,* vol. 13, 767–69.

———. "Tiraspol" In *Catholic Encyclopedia,* vol. 14, 738–39.

Lithuanian Franciscan Custody. Kennebunkport, Maine: Custody of Saint Casimir, 1952.

"Livonia," *EB,* vol. 16, 816–817.

Long, James W. *A Russia-German Bibliography.* Santa Barbara, Calif.: Clio Books, 1978.

———. *From Privileged to Dispossessed: The Volga Germans, 1860–1917.* Lincoln: Univ. of Nebraska Press, 1988.

Lorenz, Karl, ed. *Die römisch-katholische Kirche in der Sowjetunion.* Munich: Kirche in Not/Ostpriesterhilfe, 1989.

———. *Die ukrainische katholische Kirche.* Munich: Kirche in Not/Ostpriesterhilfe, 1989.

Lubachko, Ivan. *Belorussia under Soviet Rule: 1917–1957.* Lexington: Univ. of Kentucky Press, 1972.

Mace, James E. "Genocide in the USSR." In *Genocide: A Critical Bibliographical Review,* edited by Israel W. Charny. London: Mansell, 1988.

Madey, Johnannes. *Kirche zwischen Ost und West: Beiträge zur Geschichte der ukrainischen und weissrussischen Kirche.* Munich: Ukrainian Free Univ. Press, 1969.

Madksudov, Sergei, and William Taubman. "Russian-Soviet Nationality Policy and Foreign Policy: A Historical Overview of the Linkage Between Them." In *The Rise of Nations in the Soviet Union,* edited by Michael Mandelbaum. New York: Council on Foreign Relations, 1991.

Magocsi, Paul Robert. "The Language Question among the Subcarpathian Rusyns." In *Aspects of Slavic Language Questions,* vol. 2, edited by Riccardo Pichio and Harvey Goldblatt. New Haven: Yale Concilium on International and Area Studies, 1984.

———. *Galicia: A Historical Survey and Bibliographic Guide.* Buffalo, N.Y.: Canadian Institute of Ukrainian Studies, 1983.

———. *The Shaping of a National Identity: Subcarpathian Rus', 1848–1948.* Cambridge, Mass.: Harvard Univ. Press, 1978.

———. *Ukraine: A Historical Atlas.* Buffalo, N.Y.: Univ. of Toronto Press, 1985.

———. ed. *Morality and Reality: The Life and Times of Andrei Sheptyts'kyi.* Edmonton: Canadian Institute of Ukrainian Studies, Univ. of Alberta, 1989.

Mailleux, Paul, SJ. "Catholics in the Soviet Union." In *Aspects of Religion in the Soviet Union, 1917–67,* edited by Richard N. Marshall, Jr. Chicago: Univ. of Chicago Press, 1971.

———. "The Catholic Church in Russia and the Exarch Feodorov." In *Religion in Russia: A Collection of Essays,* edited by Georgii Pavlovich Bennigsen. London: Burns, Oates, and Washbourne, 1939.

———. *Exarch Leonid Feodorov: Bridgebuilder Between Rome and Moscow.* New York: Kenedy, 1964.

Maloney, Rev. George, SJ. *Our Lady of the Kremlin.* Saint Louis: Queen's Work, 1956.

Mandelbaum, Michael, ed. *The Rise of Nations in the Soviet Union.* New York: Council on Foreign Relations, 1991.

Mangolis, Visvaldis. *Latvia in the Wars of the Twentieth Century.* Princeton Junction, N.J.: Cognition Books, 1983.

Maria e la chiesa del Silenzio. Rome: Accademia Mariana Internazionale, 1957.

Markus, Vasyl. "Religion and Nationalism in Ukraine." In *Religion and Nationalism in Soviet and East European Politics,* edited by Pedro Ramet. Durham, N.C.: Duke Univ. Press, 1984.

————. "Religion and Nationality: The Uniates of Ukraine." In *Religion and Atheism in USSR and Eastern Europe,* edited by Bohdan Bociurkiw and John W. Strong. New York: Macmillan, 1975.

————. "The Religious Situation of Ukrainians in Poland and Poles in Ukraine." In *Poland and Ukraine: Past and Present,* edited by Peter Potichnyj. Toronto: Canadian Institute of Ukrainian Studies, 1980.

Marshall, Richard N., Jr., ed. *Aspects of Religion in the Soviet Union, 1917–67.* Chicago: Univ. of Chicago Press, 1971.

Mastro, Joseph P. *USSR: Calendar of Events.* Gulf Breeze, Fla.: Academic International Press, 1988.

Mawdsley, Evan. *The Russian Civil War.* Boston: Allen and Unwin, 1987.

McCullagh, Capt. Francis. *The Bolshevik Persecution of Christianity.* New York: Dutton, 1924.

Milosz, CzesŁaw. *The Captive Mind.* Translated by Jane Zielonko. New York: Knopf, 1953.

Miracles of Mary, no. 2. Translated by Timothy. Tindal-Robertson. Chuleigh, U.K.: Augustine, 1988.

Miscellanea Historiae Ecclesiasticae. Vol. 9: Congrès de Varsovie, 25 juin–1ᵉʳ juillet 1978. Section 4: *Les églises chrétiennes dans l'Europe dominée par le IIIᵉ Reich.* Brussels: Editions Nauwelaerts, 1984.

Mishell, William. *Kaddish for Kovno: Life and Death in a Lithuanian Ghetto.* Chicago: Chicago Review Press, 1988.

Moffett, Samuel Hugh. *History of Christianity in Asia.* Volume 1. San Francisco: Harper, 1992.

Muzyczka, Ivan. "Sheptyts'kyi in the Russian Empire." In *Morality and Reality: The Life and Times of Andrei Sheptyts'kyi,* edited by Robert Magocsi. Edmonton: Univ. of Alberta, Canadian Institute of Ukrainian Studies, 1989.

Mulligan, Timothy. *The Politics of Illusion and Empire: German Occupation Policy in the Soviet Union, 1942–1943.* New York: Praeger, 1988.

Neshamit, Sarah, "Rescue in Lithuania During the Nazi Occupation." In *Rescue Attempts During the Holocaust,* edited by Yisrael Gutman and Efraim Zuroff. Jerusalem: Yad Vashem, 1977.

Nicholl, Donald. *Triumphs of the Spirit in Russia.* London: Darton, Longman and Todd, 1997.

O'Connor, Michael. *Pius XII: Greatness Dishonoured.* Dublin: Laetare Press, 1980.

Orient Yearbook 1942, The. Tokyo: Asian Statistics Co., 1942.

Paikert, G. C. *The German Exodus.* The Hague: Martinus Nijhoff, 1962.

Palmer, Gretta. As told to by Father George. *God's Underground.* New York: Appleton-Century-Crofts, 1949.

Palmieri, Aurelio, OSA. "Russia." In *Catholic Encyclopedia,* vol. 13, 321–325.

Pekar, Athanasius, OSBM. *Bishop Alexander Chira: Prisoner of Christ.* Pittsburgh, Byzantine Seminary Press, 1988.

————. *History of the Church in Carpathian Rus'*. Fairview, N.J.: Carpatho-Rusyn Research Center, 1992.

————. *You Shall Be Witnesses to Me*. Pittsburgh: Byzantine Seminary Press, 1989.

Pelikan, Jaroslav. *Confessor Between East and West: A Portrait of Ukrainian Cardinal Josyf Slipyj*. Grand Rapids, Mich.: Eerdmans, 1990.

Peris, Daniel. *Storming the Heavens: The Soviet League of the Militant Godless*. Ithaca, New York: Cornell Univ. Press, 1998.

Peters, Walter H. *The Life of Benedict XV*. Milwaukee: Bruce, 1959.

Petrova, Natalia [Princess Maria Volkonskaya]. *Twice Born in Russia*. New York: William Morrow, 1930.

Petrowicz, Krikor. *La Chiesa Armena in Polonia e nei paesi limitrofi. [Part 3]: 1686–1954*. Rome: Collegio Armeno, 1988.

Pfeiffer, John E. *In Memoriam: Alexander Frison, Bishop and Martyr*. N.p., n.d.

Phillips, John. *The Tragedy of the Soviet Germans: A Story of Survival*. N.p., 1983.

Picchio, Riccardo and Harvey Goldblatt, eds. *Aspects of the Slavic Language Question*. Vol 2. New Haven: Yale Concilium on International and Area Studies, 1984.

Pieger, Rev. Nikolaus. "Die religiösen Verhältnisse in der Südukraine (Transnistrien)." In *Die Kirchen und das Religiöse Leben der Russlanddeutschen*. Stuttgart: Landsmannschaft der Deutschen aus Russland, 1972.

Polsky, Michael. *The New Martyrs of Russia*. Montreal: Brotherhood of Saint Job of Pochaev, 1972.

Portisch, Hugo, Henry Fox, and Ewal Osers, trans. *I Saw Siberia*. London: George C. Hurrap, 1972.

Pospielovsky, Dmitrii. *The Russian Church under the Soviet Regime, 1917–82*. Crestwood, New York: St. Vladimir Seminary Press, 1984.

————. *Soviet Anti-Religious Campaigns and Persecutions*. New York: St. Martin's Press, 1988.

Pospishil, Victor J. "Shyeptytsk'kyi and Liturgical Reform." In *Morality and Reality: The Life and Times of Andrei Sheptyts'kyi*, edited by Paul Robert Magocsi. Edmonton: Univ. of Alberta, Institute of Ukrainian Studies, 1989.

Potichnyj, Peter, ed. *Poland and Ukraine: Past and Present*. Toronto: Canadian Institute of Ukrainian Studies, 1980.

Proudfoot, Malcolm J. *European Refugees: 1939–52: A Study in Forced Population Movement*. Evanston, Ill.: Northwestern Univ. Press, 1956.

Pugevicius, Casimir, ed. and trans. *Catholics in Soviet-Occupied Lithuania*. Brooklyn: Aid to the Church in Need, 1981.

Pumonen, Veikko. *Orthodoxy in Finland: Past and Present*. Kuopio, Finland: Orthodox Clergy Association, 1981.

Rader, John S., and Kateryna Fedoryka. *The Pope and the Holocaust*. Alexandria, S.D.: Family Apostolate, 1994.

Ramet, Pedro. *Catholicism and Politics in Communist Societies*. Durham, N.C.: Duke Univ. Press, 1990.

————. *Eastern Christianity and Politics in the Twentieth Century.* Durham, N.C.: Duke Univ. Press, 1988.

————. *Religion and Nationalism in Soviet and East European Politics.* Durham, N.C.: Duke Press Policy Studies, 1984.

————. *Religion and Nationalism in Soviet and East European Politics, Revised Edition.* Durham, N.C.: Duke Univ. Press, 1989.

Rauch, Georg von. *The Baltic States: The Years of Independence: Estonia, Latvia, Lithuania, 1917–1940.* London: C. Hurst, 1974.

Read, Anthony, and David Fisher. *The Deadly Embrace: Hitler, Stalin, and the Nazi-Soviet Pact, 1939–1941.* New York: Norton, 1988.

Redlick, Stephen. "Sheptys'kyi and the Jews." In *Morality and Reality: The Life and Times of Andrei Sheptyts'kyi,* edited by Paul Robert Magocsi. Edmondton: Canadian Institute of Ukrainian Studies, Univ. of Alberta, 1989.

Remeikis. T. *Opposition to Soviet Rule in Lithuania, 1945–80.* Chicago: Institute of Lithuanian Studies Press, 1980.

Rhodes, Anthony. *The Power of Rome in the Twentieth Century: The Vatican in the Age of Liberal Democracies, 1870–1922.* New York: Franklin Watts, 1983.

————. *The Power of Rome in the Twentieth Century: The Vatican in the Age of the Dictators, 1922–1945.* Toronto: Hodder and Stoughton, 1973.

————. *The Power of Rome in the Twentieth Century: The Vatican in the Age of the Cold War, 1945–1980.* Norwich, U.K.: Michael Russell, 1992.

Rings, Werner. *Life with the Enemy: Collaboration and Resistance in Hitler's Europe: 1939–1945.* Translated by J. Maxwell Brownjohn. N.Y.; Doubleday, 1982

Roberson, Ronald G., CSP. *The Eastern Christian Churches: A Brief Survey.* Rome: Pontifical Oriental Institute, 1988.

Rood, Wim. *Rom und Moskau: Der heilige Stuhl und Russland beziehungsweise die Sowjetunion von der Oktoberrevolution 1917 bis zum 1. Dezember 1989.* Altenberge: Oros, 1993.

Rope, Rev. Henry. *Benedict XV: The Pope of Peace.* London: Catholic Book Club, 1940.

Rosenfeld, Harvey. *Raoul Wallenberg, Angel of Rescue: Heroism and Torment in the Gulag.* Buffalo, N.Y.: Prometheus Books, 1982.

Rummel, R. J. *Lethal Politics: Soviet Genocide and Mass Murder Since 1917.* New Brunswick, N.J.: Transaction, 1996.

Rupert, Raphael. *A Hidden World: Nine Years of Confinement in Communist Prisons and Camps.* New York: World, 1963.

Sabol, Sebastiana, OSBM. *Ukrita fiyalka-cestra Vasiliya glbovitska, ChCVV.* Prešov, Slovakia: Slovatskke pedagogichne vidavnitsvo v Bratislavi; Viddil yrkrainskoi Literaturi, 1992.

Sadunaite, Nijole. *Radiance in the Gulag.* Translated by Rev. Casimir Pugevicius and Marian Skabeikis. Manassas, Va.: Trinity Communications, 1987.

Sajer, Guy. *The Forgotten Soldier.* New York: Harper and Row, 1971.

Schieder, Theodor. *Documents on the Expulsion of the Germans from Eastern-Central Europe. Vol. 1, The Expulsion of the German Population from the Territories East of the Oder-*

Neisse Line: Selection and Translation from Dokumentation der Vertreigung der Deutschen aus Ost-Mitteleuropa. Bonn: Federal Ministry for Expellees, Refugees, and War Victims, 1958.

Schneider, Gertrude. *Journey into Terror: The Story of the Riga Ghetto.* New York: Ark House, 1979.

Schnurr, Joseph, ed. *Die Kirchen und das religiöse Leben der Russlanddeutschen.* . . . Stuttgart: Landsmannschaft der Deutschen aus Russland, 1972.

———. *Die Kirchen und das Religiöse Leben der Russlanddeutschen.* . . . Revised Edition. Stuttgart: Selbstverlag Joseph Schnurr, 1980.

———. "Die Pfarreien und ihre Kirchen, nach Dekanaten zusammengestellt." In *Die Kirchen und das Religiöse Leben der Russlanddeutschen.* . . . Stuttgart: Landsmannschaft der Deutschen aus Russland, 1972.

———. "Streiflichter aus der Geschichte der Tiraspoler Diözese." In *Die Kirchen und das Religiöse Leben der Russlanddeutschen.* . . . Stuttgart: Landsmannschaft der Deutschen aus Russland, 1972.

———. "Verzeichnis der Priester, die auf dem Boden der Tiraspoler Diözese wirkten." In *Die Kirchen.* . . . Stuttgart: Landsmannschaft der Deutschen aus Russland, 1972.

Schöpflin, George, ed. *The Soviet Union and Eastern Europe.* New York: Facts on File, 1988.

Sercho, Peter G. *Diplomacy of Double Morality.* New York: Carpathian Research Center, 1971.

Setian, Bishop Nerses. *Armenian Nation and Armenian Catholic Church,* Los Angeles: Armenian Exarchate, 1994.

Seton-Watson, Hugh. "Russian Nationalism in Historical Perspective." In *The Last Empire,* edited by Robert Conquest. Stanford, Calif.: Hoover Institute Press, 1986.

Shipman, Andrew J. "Lutzk, Zhitomir, and Kamenetz." In *Catholic Encyclopedia,* vol. 9, 463–65.

———. "Moscow." In *Catholic Encyclopedia,* vol. 10, 591–96.

Shulte, Theodore J. *German Army and Nazi Policies in Occupied Russia.* New York: St. Martin's Press, 1989.

Simis, Konstantin. *USSR: The Corrupt Society.* Translated by Jacquleine Edwards and Mitchell Schneider. New York: Simon and Schuster, 1982.

Simmonds, George, ed. *Nationalism in the USSR and Eastern Europe in the Era of Brezhnev and Kosygin.* Detroit: Univ. of Detroit, 1977.

Simon, Gerhard. *Church, State, and Opposition in the USSR.* Translated by Kathleen Matchett. London: C. Hurst, 1974.

———. "The Catholic Church and the Communist State in the Soviet Union and Eastern Europe." In *Religion and Atheism in USSR and Eastern Europe,* edited by Bohdan Bociurkiw and John W. Strong. New York: Macmillan, 1975.

————. ed. *Die Deutschen im Russichen Reich und im Sowjetstaat.* Cologne: Markus, 1987.

Slawuta, Sister Dominica, SSMI, and Sister Victoria Hunchak, SSMI. *Glory to You, O God: Sisters Servants of Mary Immaculate, the First Hundred Years.* Rome: Sisters Servants of Mary Immaculate, 1992.

Smith, Canfield F. *Vladivostok under Red and White Rule.* Seattle: Univ. of Washington Press, 1975.

Snow, Russell E. *The Bolsheviks in Siberia: 1917–18.* London: University Press, 1977.

Solchanyk, Roman, and Ivan Hvat. "The Catholic Church in the Soviet Union." In *Catholicism and Politics in Communist Societies,* edited by Pedro Ramet. Durham, N.C.: Duke Univ. Press, 1990.

Starzynska, Maria. *Eleven Prie-Dieux.* Translated by Sr. M. Roselita Bradley, CSFN, and Sr. M. Frances Sikorski, CSFN. Rome: Pontifical Gregorian University, 1992.

Statistica con cenni storici della Gerarchia e dei Fedeli di Rito Orientale. Rome: Tipografia Poliglotta Vaticana, 1932.

Stehle, Hansjakob. *The Eastern Politics of the Vatican: 1917–1979.* Translated by Sandra Smith. Athens: Ohio Univ. Press, 1981.

————. "Shpetyts'kyi and the German Regime." In *Morality and Reality: The Life and Times of Andrei Sheptyts'kyi,* edited by Paul Robert Magosci. Edmonton: Univ. of Alberta, Canadian Institute of Ukrainian Studies, 1989.

Steigerwald, Jacob. *Tracing Romania's Heterogeneous German Minority from its Origins to the Diaspora.* Winona, Minn.: Translation and Interpretation Service, 1985.

Steinhoff, Johannes et al, eds. *Voices from the Third Reich: An Oral History.* Washington, D.C.: Regnery-Gateway, 1989.

Strahkovsky, Leonid. "The Church in Contemporary Poland." In *The Catholic Church in Contemporary Europe, 1919–1931,* edited by Peter Guiday. New York: Kenedy, 1932.

Stricker, Gerd. "Die Kirchen der Russlanddeutschen." In *Der Kirchenkampf im deutschen Osten und in den deutschsprachigen Kirchen Osteuropas,* edited by Peter Maser. Göttingen: Vandenhoeck and Ruprecht, 1993.

Studite Monks Move Onward. Toronto: Basilian Press, 1985.

Subtelny, Orest. *Ukraine: A History.* Buffalo, N.Y.: Univ. of Toronto Press, 1988.

Suh, Dae-Sook, ed. *Koreans in the Soviet Union.* Honolulu: Univ. of Hawaii Center for Korean Studies, 1987.

Sułowski, Zygmunt. "Statistique religeuse de la Pologne, 1939–1945: Migration et pertes." In *Miscellanea Historiae Ecclesiasticae.* Vol. 9, *Congrès de Varsovie, 25 juin–1er juillet 1987.* Section 4, *Les églises chrétiennes dans l'Europe dominée par le IIIᵉ Reich.* Brussels: Editions Nauwelaerts, 1984.

Suttner, Rev. Dr. Ernst Christian. *Die katholische Kirche in der Sowjetunion.* Wurzburg: Christliche Osten, 1992.

Suziedelis, Saulius. *The Sword and the Cross: A History of the Church in Lithuania.* Huntington, Ind.: Our Sunday Visitor Press, 1988.

Swidnicki, Rev. Josef. *Vospominaniya Uznika.* Omsk: Samizdat, 1998.

Szewciw, Fr. Ivan. *Millenium of Christianity in Ukraine,* 2d ed. Melbourne: Millenium Committee of the Ukrainian Catholic Council in Australia, 1987.

Tatarynović, Peter. "La Chiesa del silenzio nella Biancorutenia e il culto mariano." In *Maria e la Chiesa del Silenzio.* Rome: Accademia Mariana Internationale, 1957.

Teodorovich, Nadezhda. "The Roman Catholics." 211–16. In *Genocide in the USSR: Studies in Group Destruction,* edited by Nikolai Deker and Andrej Lebed. New York: Scarecrow Press, 1958.

Terelya, Iosyp. *For My Name's Sake: Selections from the Writings of Iosyp Terelya.* Keston, U.K.: Keston College, 1986.

Tolstoy, Nikolai. *Stalin's Secret War.* New York: Holt, Rinehart, Winston, 1981.

Torzecki, Ryszard. "Der griechisch-katholische Ritus der katholischen Kirche auf dem Gebiet der Republik Polen während des 2. Weltkrieges." In *Miscellanea Historiae Ecclesiasticae.* Vol. 9, *Congrès de Varsovie, 25 juin–1er juillet 1978.* Section 4, *Les églises chrétiennes dans l'Europe dominée par le IIIe Reich.* Brussels: Editions Nauwelaerts, 1984.

Tretjakewitsch, Leon. *Bishop Michel d'Herbigny, SJ, and Russia: A Pre-Ecumenical Approach to Christian Unity.* Würzburg: Augustinus, 1990.

Trimakas, Kestutis, SJ, trans. *Mary Save Us.* Putnam, Conn.: Immaculata Press, 1963.

Twining, David T. *Guide to the Republics of the FSU,* Westport, Conn.: Greenwood Press, 1993.

Vailhe, Simeon. "Lemberg." In *Catholic Enclycopedia,* vol. 9, 144–46.

Vais'nora, Joseph, MIC. "La Madonna Piangente, Prettrice della Lituania." In *Maria e la Chiesa del Silenzio.* Rome: Accademia Mariana Internationale, 1957.

Vakar, Nicholas P. *Belorussia: the Making of a Nation.* Cambridge, Mass.: Harvard Univ. Press, 1956.

van Stratten, Fr. Werenfried O. Praem. *Where God Weeps.* San Francisco: Ignatius Press, 1989.

Vardys, V. Stanley. *The Catholic Church, Dissent, and Nationality in Soviet Lithuania.* Boulder, Colo.: *East European Quarterly,* 1978.

———. "Latin Catholicism and Modernization." In *Religion and Modernization in the Soviet Union,* edited by Dennis J. Dunn. Boulder, Colo.: Rienner, 1986.

Vassiltchikov, Marie. *Berlin Diaries, 1940–1945.* New York: Knopf, 1987.

Veinbergs, Alexander. "Lutheran and Other Denominations in the Baltic Republics." In *Aspects of Religion in the Soviet Union, 1917–67,* edited by Richard H. Marshall, Jr. Univ. of Chicago Press, 1971.

Vello, Fr Salo. *Population Losses in Estonia, June 1940-August 1941.* Vol. 1. Scarborough, Ont.: Maarjamaa, 1989.

Vidov, Bozidar, *Right Reverend Leontius Leonid Feodorov: Eparch of the Catholic Church of the Eastern Rite in Russia, 1917–1935.* Translated by Hrvoje S. Beg. Woodstock, Ont.: Studite Fathers, 1992.

Wada, Haruki, "Koreans in the Soviet Far East, 1917–1937," in *Koreans in the Soviet Union*. Honolulu: Univ. of Hawaii Center for Korean Studies, 1987.

Ware, Bishop Kallistos [Timothy]. *The Orthodox Church: New Edition*. London: Penguin, 1993.

Walsh, Edward, SJ. "The Church in Contemporary Russia." In *The Catholic Church in Contemporary Europe, 1919–1931,* edited by Peter Guilday. New York: Kenedy, 1932.

Warczak, Jan. *The Glory of Nazareth*. Chicago: Stanek Press, 1960.

Warzeski, Walter. *Byzantine Rite Rusins in Carpatho-Ruthenia and America*. Pittsburgh: Byzantine Seminary Press, 1971.

Weissberg, Alexander. *The Accused*. Translated by Edward Fitzgerald. New York: Simon and Schuster, 1951.

Welisch, Sophie A. *Bukovina Villages, Towns, Cities and Their Germans*. Ellis, Kans.: Bukovina Society of the Americas, 1990.

Wenger, Antoine. *Rome et Moscou, 1988–1950*. Paris: Desclée de Brouwer, 1987.

Wilcock, Feodor, SJ. *Leonid Feodorov and the Catholic Russians*. New York: Russian Center, 1954.

Wittman, Pius. "Finland." In *Catholic Encyclopedia*, vol. 6.

Wixman, Ronald. *The Peoples of the USSR: An Ethnographic Handbook*. London: Macmillan Reference Books, 1984.

Woodruff, Douglas. *Church and State*. New York: Hawthorn Books, 1961.

Wysochansky, Demetrius E., OSBM. *Saint Josaphat Kuntsevych: Apostle of Church Unity*. Detroit: Basilian Fathers, 1987.

Zaprudnik, Jan. *Belarus: At a Crossroads in History*. Boulder, Colo.: Westview Press, 1993.

Zatko, James. *Descent into Darkness: The Destruction of the Roman Catholic Church in Russia, 1917–1923*. South Bend, Ind.: Univ. of Notre Dame Press, 1965.

Zawodny, J. *Death in the Forest: The Katyn Forest Massacre*. South Bend, Ind.: Univ. of Notre Dame Press, 1962.

Ziemke, Earl F. *From Stalingrad to Berlin: The German Defeat in the East*. Washington, D.C.: U.S. Army Center of Military History, 1968.

Ziemke, Earl F. et al. *The Soviet Juggernaut*. Alexandria, Va.: Time-Life Books, 1980.

Zinkewych, Ossyp, and Andrew Sorokowski, eds. *A Thousand Years of Christianity in Ukraine: An Encyclopedic Chronology*. New York: Smoloskyp and National Committee to Commemorate Millenium of Christianity in Ukraine, 1988.

Journal Articles

Adler, Erwin. "Lenin's Views on Religion." *Studies on the Soviet Union* 10, no. 10 (1970): 61–68.

Albert, Gerhard. "Katholiken zwischen Ural und Wladiwostok." *Herder Korrespondenz* 10 (1990): 478–81.

Ambrose, Aliz. "Language and Church in Belroussia." *Religion in Communist Lands* 2, no. 1 (1990): 18–24.

Armstrong, John. "Ukrainians in World War II: Points and Views." *Nationalities Papers* 10, no. 1: 3–9.

Billington, James. "Christianity in the USSR." *Theology Today.* 37 (1980): 199–209.

Bakich, Olga. "A Russian City in China: Harbin Before 1917." *Canadian Slavonic Papers* 28, no. 2 (June 1986): 129–48.

Bociurkiw, Bohdan. "Uniate Church in the Soviet Ukraine: A Case Study in Soviet Church Policy." *Canadian Slavonic Papers,* July 1967, pp. 89–113.

Bourdeaux, Michael. "Christians under Gorbachev." *Tablet,* Dec. 12, 1987, pp. 1344–45.

————. "Pilgrimage to Siberia: One Man's Impressions of Its Christians and Their Churches." *Christianity Today* 23, Sept 7, 1979, 22–24.

Braun, Gertrud. "The Deportation of the Volga Germans." *American Historical Society of Germans from Russia Journal* Work Paper 10 (Dec. 1972): 22–24.

Bungs, Dzintra. "Are the Latvians Dying Out?" *Radio Liberty Report on the Soviet Union* 3, no. 16 (1991): 16–19.

Carmel of Finland. "Second Letter from Finland, October 1989." *Carmelite Digest* 5, no. 3 (1990): 50–55.

Chelminski, Rudolph. "Katyn: Anatomy of a Massacre." *Reader's Digest,* May 1990, pp. 69–79.

Chojnowski, Andrej. "The Controversy over Former Uniate Property in Poland." *Nationalities Papers* 16, no. 2: 177–90.

Cobejová, Eva. Patricia Krafcik, trans. "Who Betrayed Subcarpathian Rus'? Who Will Help the Transcarpthian Ukraine?" *Carpatho-Rusyn American* 14, no. 2: 4–6.

Corley, Felix. "Believers' Responses to the 1937 and 1939 Soviet Censuses." *Religion, State and Society* 22, no. 4 (1994): 403–18.

Czuma, Hanna. "Polish Priest Won't Forget Comrades of Youth." *Catholic Register (Toronto),* Mar. 17, 1990.

Davies, Norman. "Not 20 Million, Not Russians, Not War Dead." *Independent,* no. 380, Dec. 29, 1987.

Dmytryshyn, Basil "Ukrainians in World War II: Points and Views." Edited by Stephan Horak et al. *Nationalities Papers* 10, no. 1: 9–14.

Dola, Rev. Kazimierz. "The Life and Times of Archbishop Josef Teofil Teodorowicz." *Armenian Review* 39, no. 4: 73–82.

Dunn, Dennis. "Pre-World War II Relations Between Stalin and the Catholic Church." *Journal of Church and State* 15, no. 2: 193–204.

Dyd, Michael. "The Situation of the Ukrainian Catholic Church in the Soviet Union." *Christian Orient,* nos. 1–2 (March-June 1986): 82–90.

Economist. "The Byelorussia Mystery." Mar. 19, 1987, pp. 2–3.

Eisenbraun, Theodor. "The Deportation of the Crimean Germans, 1941." *American Historical Society of Germans from Russia Journal* work paper 10 (Dec. 1972): 13–24.

Ellman, Michael. "A Note on the Number of 1933 Famine Victims." *Soviet Studies* 43, no. 2 (1991): 375–79.

Eszer, Ambrosius K., OP. "Ekaterina sienskaja und die Gemeinschaft der Schwestern des III. Ordens vom Heiligen Dominikus zu Moskau." *Archivum Fratrum Praedicatorum* 40 (1970): 277–373.

Feisst, Sebastian. "Die Lage der katholische Kirche in Russland." *Clemens-Blatt,* May 1924, pp. 72–73.

Filatov, Sergei. "Religion, Power, and Nationhood in Sovereign Bashkortostan." *Religion, State and Society* 25, no. 3 (1997): 267–80.

———. "Tatarstan: At the Crossroads of Islam and Orthodoxy." *Religion, State and Society* 26, nos. 3–4 (1998): 265–78.

Fischer, Karl August, "The Germans in the Caucasus, Particularly in Transcaucasia" *American Historical Society of Germans from Russia Journal* 9, no. 1 (Spring 1986): 1–12.

Gardner, Johann von. "Attraction of Church Ritual among Soviet Youth." *Studies on the Soviet Union* 6, no. 1 (1966): 57–61.

Gaschler, Norbert. "Nachrichten aus der alten Heimat." *Der Südostdeutsche,* June 15, 1991.

Gasior, Kristopher. "Poles in the Soviet Union." *Radio Liberty Report on the Soviet Union* 2, no. 52 (1990): 10–17.

Giesinger, Adam. "Villages in Which Our Forefathers Lived: German Villages in the Slavgorod Region in Siberia." *American Historical Society of Germans from Russia Journal* 6, no. 1 (1983): 39–42.

Ginsburgs, George. "Citizenship Questions in Postwar Sino-Soviet Relations." *Chronicle of Human Rights in USSR,* Apr.-June 1977, pp. 67–75.

Grondelski, John M. "Auschwitz Revisited . . . The Polish Bishops on Christian-Jewish Relations." *America,* Apr. 27, 1991, pp. 469–71.

Gula, Jozef. "Catholic Poles in the USSR During the Second World War." *Religion, State and Society* 22, no. 1 (1994): 9–64.

Guthrie, Stephen. "The Belorussians: National Identity and Assimilation, 1897–1970." *Soviet Studies* 29, nos. 1–2 (1977): Part I, 37–61, Part II, 270–83.

Haroshka, Lev. "Soviet Policy Towards Religion after 1942." *Byelorussian Review* 2 (1956): 5–36.

———. "Religion in Byelorussia Today." *Byelorussian Review* 3 (1956): 102–19.

Himka, John-Paul. "The Greek Catholic Church and Nation-building, 1772–1918" *Harvard Ukrainian Studies* 8, nos. 3–4: 426–52.

———. "Priests and Peasants: The Greek Catholic Pastors and the Ukrainian National Movement in Austria, 1867–1900." *Canadian Slavonic Papers* 221, no. 1: 1–14.

Horak, Stepan, et al. "Ukrainians in World War II: Views and Points." *Nationalities Papers* 10, no. 1: 1–39.

K. Frau. "The Deportation of the Germans from South Caucasus." *American Historical Society of Germany from Russia Journal* work paper no. 10 (Dec. 1972): 25–27.

Karklins, Rasma. "A Note on 'Nationality' and 'Native Tongue' as Census Categories in 1979." *Soviet Studies* 32, no. 3 (1980): 415–22.

Karlinsky, Simon. "Memoirs of Harbin." *Slavic Review* 48, no. 2 (1989): 284–88.

Kauffman, Ivan. "Christianity in the Soviet Union." *Catholic Near East,* Jan. 1990, 12–15.

Keleher, Serge. "Trapped Between Two Churches: Orthodox and Greek Catholics in Eastern Poland." *Religion, State and Society* 23, no. 4 (1995): 365–72.

Kinsella, David, and Rein Taagepera. "Religious Incident Statistics for Soviet Lithuanian Schools." *Journal of Baltic Studies* 15, no. 1 (1984): 27–47.

Kloberdanz, Rosalinda A. "Last Glimpses of Home: A Trip to the Former Volga German Villages, 1983." *American Historical Society of Germans from Russia Journal* 7, no. 3 (1984): 1–8.

Knapp-Kwasigorch. "75 Jahre Seelsorge im byzantinisch-slawischen Ritus in Berlin." *Der Christliche Osten* 39, no. 1 (1984): 29–30.

Kojevnikov, Alyona. "Religious Renaissance in the Russian Orthodox Church: Fact or Fiction?" *Journal of Church and State* 28, no. 3 (1986): 459–73.

Kokhanovsky, M. "Examination of a Priest in the Bolshevik Prisons." *Ukrainian Quarterly* 10, no. 2 (1954): 166–76.

Kralewski, W. "Zu Lage der Katholische Kirche in der UdSSR." *Der Christliche Osten* 43, no. 6 (1988): 266–71.

Laasi, Evald. "For Filling in a Few Blank Spots." *Sirp ja Vasar,* Nov. 27, 1987, pp. 3–4.

Lemiski, Karen. "Polish Political Activism in the USSR." *Radio Liberty* 2, no. 36 (1990): 13–18.

Lorenz, Andreas. "Among the Germans in the Soviet Republic of Kazakhstan" *American Historical Society of Germans from Russia Journal* 6, no. 1 (1983): 9–12.

Loya, Fr. Thomas J. "A Lay Religious Leader's Suffering Teaches Faith over Fear." *Horizons,* Nov. 8, 1987.

Martovych, O. "Ukrainian Insurgent Army." *Ukrainian Review* 30, no. 2 (1982): 3–26; no. 3, 3–28; no. 4, 54–72.

Melvin, Katie Michelson. "Escape From Russia." *American Historical Society of Germans from Russia Journal* 10, no. 2 (1987): 1–7.

Milosz, Czeslaw. "A Poet's Poland." *New York Times Magazine,* Jan. 14, 1990, pp. 22–27.

Moss, James. "The Latvian Catholic Church." *Religion in Communist-Dominated Areas* 22, nos. 4–6 (1983): pp. 76–77.

Nadson, Msgr. Alexander. "Bishop Ceslaus Sipovich, 1914–1981." *Journal of Byelorussian Studies* 5, no. 1 (1981): 5–13.

Nakus, Victor. "National Opposition in Lithuania." *Religion in Communist-Dominated Areas* 23, nos. 4–6 (1984).

Nove, Alec. "How Many Victims in the 1930s?" *Soviet Studies* 42, no. 2 (Apr. 1990): 369–73.

Pankhurst, Jerry. "Soviet Society and Soviet Religion" *Journal of Church and State* 28, no. 3 (1986): 409–22.

Paskevich, Helen, SSMI. "The Gift of Faith: One Thousand Years Young." *Sisters Today* 59 (Nov. 1987): 131–33.

Pawalkis, Rev. Victor. "The Catholic Church in the Baltic States and the Holy See, 1939–45." *Baltic Review* 38 (1971): 54–63.

Petrowicz, Krikor. "The Armenians of Poland." *The Eternal Flame,* vol. 1–2, (1983–84).

Pfeiffer, John E. "A Historical Sketch of the Diocese of Tiraspol." *American Historical Society of Germans from Russia Journal* Work Paper number 7 (Dec. 1971): 23–26.

———. "I Went to Russia." *American Historical Society of Germans from Russia Journal* work paper no. 10 (Dec. 1972): 29–40.

Picarda, Guy de. "The Byelorussian Church." Privately supplied reprint from Chrysostom Society. London: N.d., unpaginated.

———. "Byelorussian Episcopate." *Tablet,* Aug. 12, 1989.

Plokhy, Serhii. "Soviet Liquidation of the Greco-Catholic Church," *Logos* 35 (1994), 59–76.

Poleski, Tadeusz. "Pastoral Work in Byelorussia." *Religion in Communist Lands* 13, no. 3 (Winter 1985): 298–313.

"Poles in the Far East." *Vladivostok Sunrise* 3 (1928): 175–79.

Politekhnik Almanak Harbin, "Katolicheskie Khrami-Kostelyi," no. 10 (1979): 140.

Prinz, A. "The Kolkhozy in the USSR: 1918–1939." *American Historical Society of Germans from Russia Journal* 10, no. 2 (1987): 39–45.

Przepkop, Edmund. "Die Neo-Union in Polen in den Jahren 1923–39." *Ostkirchliche Studien* 32 (Mar. 1983): 3–20.

———. "350 Jahre der Union der polnischen Armenier mit der katholischen Kirche." *Der Christliche Osten* 35 (1980), nos. 3–4: 81–84.

Religion in Communist-Dominated Areas. "Catholic News from USSR." Jan.-Mar. 1972.

———. "Appeals from Lithuania." Apr.-June 1972.

———. "Before the Court of History." July-Sept. 1973.

———. "Chronicle: A Report on the Catholic Church in Lithuania and Various Republics of the USSR." Vol. 17, nos. 1–3 (1978): 14–20.

"Soviet Vatican Watchers Concerned." Nos. 1–3, 1982.

Reddaway, Peter. "Religious Rights in the USSR." *Chronicle of Human Rights in the USSR,* Apr.-June 1977, pp. 60–67.

"Review of Religion in Soviet Russia, 1917–42." in *China Mission,* Mar. 1949, pp. 254–61.

Rich, Vera. "Catholic Episcopate Restored." *Tablet,* Aug. 5, 1989.

———. "Revival of Catholic Byzantine Rites." *Tablet,* Aug. 18, 1990.

———. "The Mass Returns to Minsk." *Tablet,* Mar. 24, 1990.

Rittersporn, Gabor. "Believers in the USSR: Some Data and Trends" *Telos* 61 (Fall 1984): 144–52.

Samizdat Bulletin. Center For Democracy, P.O. Box 6128, San Mateo, Calif. 94403.

Sapiets, Marite, ed. "The Catholic Church in Belorussia." *Religion in Communist Lands* 10, no. 2: 178–87.

Schlau, Frieda. "The German Settlements in the Belovezh Parish in Chernigov Province" *American Historical Society of Germans from Russia Journal* 12, no. 2 (1989): 7–17.

Schmitz, Helen Dauenhauer. "Memories." *American Historical Society of Germans from Russia Journal* 16, no. 4 (Winter 1993), 25–38.

Senyk, Sr. Sophia. "Ukrainian Catholic Episcopal Sees in the *Annuario Pontifico.*" *Jurist* 46, no. 2 (1986): 632–41.

———. "Religion in the USSR: Laws, Policy, and Propaganda." *Reflections* (Center for Religion and Human Rights) 24, no. 1 (Winter 1985): 19–29; no. 2 (Spring 1985): 47–54.

———. "Under the Guise of Piety." *Reflections* (Center for Religion and Human Rights) 23, nos. 10–12 (1984): 170–72.

Shifrin, Al. "Foreign Nationals in Soviet Concentration Camps." *Ukrainian Review* 26 (Spring 1978): 58–63.

Sikorska, Grazyna. "Come and See Our Church." *Frontier,* July-Aug. 1989, pp. 2–3.

Simon, Constantine, SJ. "How Russians See Us: Jesuit-Russian Relations Then and Now." *Religion, State, and Society* 23, no. 4 (1995): 343–58.

———. "Jesuits and Belorussians: On the Fringe of Civilization or at the Cultural Crossroads" *Diakonia,* 28, 3, pp. 2.

Slipyj, Cardinal Josef. "Church of the Martyrs: A Report on the Ukrainian Catholic Church after 35 Years of Persecution." *Forum: A Ukrainian Review* 55 (Summer 1983): 13.

Stojko, Woloymyr. "The Ukrainian Catholic Church in the Catacombs." *Ukrainian Quarterly* 43, nos. 1–2 (1985): 7–22.

Strohm, Carl Gustav. "After Chernobyl." *Frontier,* Mar.-Apr. 1989, 8–9.

Stumpp, Dr. Karl. "In the Wake of the German Army on the Eastern Front, August 1941 to May 1942." *American Historical Society of Germans from Russia Journal* 7, no. 3 (Fall 1984): 33–38.

Suttner, Ernst-Christian. "Zur Geschichte kleinerer religiös-ethnischer Gruppen in Österreich-Ungarn und in den Nachfolgestaaten." *Ostkirchliche Studien* 38 (Sept. 1989): 105–35.

Szporluk, Roman. "West Ukraine and West Belorussia: Historical Tradition, Social Communication and Linguistic Assimilation." *Soviet Studies* 31, no. 1 (1979): 76–98.

Taagepera, Rein. "Soviet Collectivization of Estonian Agriculture: The Deportee Phase." *Soviet Studies* 32, no. 3 (1980): 379–97.

Tablet (London) "Baltic Nationalist Protests." Sept. 19, 1987.

————. "Call for Atheism in Moldavia." Sept. 19, 1987.

————. "Catholic Seminary Opens in Belorussia." Sept. 22, 1990.

————. "Catholics in Ukraine Speak Out." Aug. 22, 1987.

————. "Report." Jan. 4–10, 1998.

Tarchnishivili, Michael, SIC. "Das Christentum in Georgien" 1936, reprinted in *Der Christliche Osten,* 49, nos. 3–4 (1994): 216–17.

Ter-Oranian, Lev. "Polish Armenians Form Cultural Society" *Armenian Review* 34, no. 4 (1981): 136.

Thurston, Robert W. "The Soviet Family During the Great Terror," *Soviet Studies* 43, no. 3 (1991): 553–74.

Toews, John B. "Flight Across the Amur into China" *AHSGR* 2, no. 1 (1979): 7–10.

Tolz, Vera. "New Information about the Deportation of Ethnic Groups Under Stalin." *Radio Liberty Report on the Soviet Union* 3, no. 17 (1991): 16–20.

Turchyn, Andrew. "The Ukrainian Catholic Church During World War II" *Ukrainian Quarterly* 51, nos. 1–2 (1985): 57–67.

"Uncertain Freedom" *Frontier,* Jan.-Feb. 1990, 13–14.

United States Department of State. Bureau of Public Affairs. "Soviet Repression of Ukrainian Catholic Church." *Ukrainian Quarterly* 43, nos. 3–4 (1987): 187–99.

————. "Ukrainian Catholics in Poland." *Christian Orient* no. 6, (March 1985), pp. 47–48.

Volacic, Mikola. "The Population of Western Belorussia and Its Resettlement in Poland and the USSR" *Belorussian Review* 3 (1956): 5–30.

Weisbecker, Adam. "Catholic Consecration Festivals in the Catholic Villages on the Volga." *American Historical Society of Germans from Russia Journal* 10, no. 2 (1987): 37–39.

Welsch, Roger, trans. "The Homeless: The Tragedy of the Volga German Farmers." *American Historical Society of Germans from Russa Journal* 2, no. 1 (1979): 15–17.

Welisch, Sophie A. "Faith of Our Fathers: Ethos and Popular Religious Practices among the German Catholics of Bukovina in the Early Twentieth Century." *American Historical Society of Germans from Russia Journal* 11, no. 2 (1988): 21–28.

————. "The Bukovina Germans in the Inter-War Period." *East European Quarterly* 14, no. 4 (1980): 423–37.

Wheatcroft, S. G. "More Light on the Scale of Repression and Excess Mortality in the Soviet Union in the 1930s." *Soviet Studies* 42, no. 2 (Apr. 1990): 355–67.

Wilcock, Feodor, SJ. "Reminiscences," *To Our Friends,* no. 76 (Summer 1974).

Wynot, Edward D., Jr. "World of Delusions and Illusions: The National Minorities of Poland During World War II." *Nationalities Papers* 7, no. 2: 177–96.

Zawerucha, Ihor. "The Situation of Roman Catholics in Belorussia." *Radio Liberty Report on the Soviet Union* 2, no. 19: 19–20.

Index

Italic page number denotes illustration.